NEW YORK CITY

Editorial Director   Cynthia Clayton Ochterbeck

THE GREEN GUIDE NEW YORK CITY

Editor	Gwen Cannon
Principal Writer	Shea Dean
Production Coordinator	Natasha G. George
Cartography	Peter Wrenn
Photo Editor	Lydia Strong
Researcher	Sean Cannon
Layout & Design	Alison Rayner and John Higginbottom
Cover Design	Laurent Muller and Ute Weber

Contact Us: The Green Guide
Michelin Maps and Guides
One Parkway South
Greenville, SC 29615
USA
www.michelintravel.com
michelin.guides@us.michelin.com

Michelin Maps and Guides
Hannay House
39 Clarendon Road
Watford, Herts WD17 1JA
UK
☎ 01923 205240
www.ViaMichelin.com
travelpubsales@uk.michelin.com

Special Sales: For information regarding bulk sales,
customized editions and premium sales,
please contact our Customer Service
Departments:
USA   1-800-432-6277
UK   01923 205240
Canada 1-800-361-8236

Note to the Reader
While every effort is made to ensure that all information printed in this guide is correct and up-to-date, Michelin Apa Publications Ltd. accepts no liability for any direct, indirect or consequential losses howsoever caused so far as such can be excluded by law.

One Team…
A Commitment to Quality

There's just one reason our team is dedicated to producing quality travel publications—you, our reader.

Throughout our guides we offer **practical information**, **touring tips** and **suggestions** for finding the best places for a break.

Michelin driving tours help you hit the highlights and quickly absorb the best of the region. Our descriptive **walking tours** make you your own guide, armed with directions, maps and expert information.

We scout out the attractions, classify them with **star ratings**, and describe in detail what you will find when you visit them.

Michelin maps featured throughout the guide offer vibrant, detailed and easy-to-follow outlines of everything from close-up museum plans to international maps.

Places to stay and eat are always a big part of travel, so we research **hotels and restaurants** that we think convey the essence of the destination and arrange them by geographic area and price. We walk you through the best shopping districts and point you towards the host of entertainment and recreation possibilities available.

We **test**, **retest**, **check and recheck** to make sure that our guidebooks are truly just that: a personalized guide to help you make the most of your visit. And if you still want a speaking guide, we list local tour guides who will lead you on all the boat, bus, guided, historical, culinary, and other tours you shouldn't miss.

In short, we remove the guesswork involved with travel. After all, we want you to enjoy exploring with Michelin as much as we do.

The Michelin Green Guide Team

PLANNING YOUR TRIP

WELCOME TO NEW YORK CITY

Brigitta L. House – MICHELIN

SYMBOLS

☒	**Tourist Information**
⏱	**Hours of Operation**
⏰	**Periods of Closure**
☺	**A Bit of Advice**
☻	**Details to Consider**
☞	**Entry Fees**
Kids	**Especially for Children**
☜	**Tours**
♿	**Wheelchair Accessible**

CONTENTS

DISCOVERING
NEW YORK CITY

YOUR STAY IN
NEW YORK CITY

Peter Wrenn/MICHELIN

HOW TO USE THIS GUIDE

Orientation

To help you grasp the "lay of the land" quickly and easily, so you'll feel confident and comfortable finding your way around the city, we offer the following tools in this guide:

- Detailed table of contents for an overview of what you'll find in the guide, and how the guide is organized.
- Map of Manhattan at the front of the guide, with the color-coded neighborhoods for easy reference.
- Detailed maps for neighborhoods and walking tours.
- Subway map of Manhattan on the inside back cover, showing the metro lines by color.
- Manhattan attractions are described by neighborhoods, which are organized from south to north within Downtown (Battery Park to 34th Street), Midtown (34th Street to 59th Street) and Uptown (north of 59th Street). The other boroughs' attractions are described within each borough as Principal Sights.

Practicalities

At the front of the guide, you'll see a section called "Planning Your Trip" that contains information about planning your trip, the best time to go, different ways of getting to the region and getting around, and basic facts and tips for making the most of your visit. You'll find driving and themed tours, and suggestions for outdoor fun. There's also a calendar of popular annual events. Information on shopping, sightseeing, kids' activities and sports and recreational opportunities is included as well.

WHERE TO STAY

We've made a selection of hotels and arranged them within the neighborhoods by price category to fit all budgets (*see the Legend on the cover flap for an explanation of the price categories*). For the most part, we've selected accommodations based on their unique quality, their New York City feel, as it were. So, unless the individual hotel embodies local ambience, it's rare that we include chain properties, which typically have their own imprint. If you want a more comprehensive selection of accommodations, see the red-cover **Michelin Guide New York City**.

WHERE TO EAT

We thought you'd like to know the popular eating spots in New York City. So we selected restaurants that capture the New York City experience—those that have a unique flavor and local atmosphere. We're not rating the quality of the food per se. As we did with the hotels, we selected restaurants and categorized them by price to appeal to all wallets (*see the Legend on the cover flap for an explanation of the price categories*). If you want a more comprehensive selection of dining recommendations, see the red-cover **Michelin Guide New York City**.

Attractions

Principal Sights are arranged by neighborhood within each borough. Within the neighborhood, attractions are divided into local Sights or Walking Tours. Contact information, admission charges and hours of operation are given for the majority of attractions. Unless otherwise noted, admission prices shown are for a single adult only. Discounts for children, seniors, students, teachers, etc. may be available; be sure to ask. If no admission charge is shown, entrance to the attraction is free.

If you're pressed for time, we recommend you visit the three- and two-star sights first: the stars are your guide.

STAR RATINGS

Michelin has used stars as a rating tool for more than 100 years:

★★★	Highly recommended
★★	Recommended
★	Interesting

SYMBOLS IN THE TEXT

Besides the stars, other symbols in the text indicate sights that are closed to the public ⚷; on-site eating facilities ✕; also see ☾; breakfast included in the nightly rate ⌕; on-site parking 🅿; spa facilities Spa; camping facilities △; swimming pool ⤢; and beaches ⌂.

See the box appearing on the Contents page and the Legend on the cover flap for other symbols used in the text.

See the Maps explanation below for symbols appearing on the maps.

Throughout the guide you will find peach-coloured text boxes or sidebars containing anecdotal or background information. Green-coloured boxes contain information to help you save time or money

Maps

All maps in this guide are oriented north, unless otherwise indicated by a directional arrow. See the map Legend at the back of the guide for an explanation of other map symbols. A complete list of the maps found in the guide appears at the back of this book.

Addresses, phone numbers, opening hours and prices published in this guide are accurate at press time. We welcome corrections and suggestions that may assist us in preparing the next edition. Please send your comments to:

Michelin Maps and Guides
Hannay House
39 Clarendon Road
Watford, Herts WD17 1JA
UK
travelpubsales@uk.michelin.com
www.michelin.co.uk

Michelin Maps and Guides
Editorial Department
P.O. Box 19001
Greenville, SC 29602-9001
USA
michelin.guides@us.michelin.com
www.michelintravel.com

Grand Central Terminal
©iStockphoto.com/Jeremy Edwards

WHEN AND WHERE TO GO

Carriage Ride in Central Park

When to Go

New York's four distinct seasons each lend a particular character to the city. The mild months of April, May, September and October are especially pleasant. Hotels are heavily booked during these times and advance reservations are recommended.

Spring – A brief and generally unpredictable season, spring brings New Yorkers out of doors to enjoy the mild temperatures (42° to 62°F). From late March through May, sunny days may give way to rain or to snow showers (not uncommon in April).

Summer – The weather can be unpleasantly muggy in the summer and many New Yorkers head out of town, leaving the city calmer and less crowded. Daytime temperatures can reach into the 90s, especially in July and August. The many shady green parks throughout the city, alive with free summer events, provide a welcome respite from the heat.

Fall – Warm temperatures (47° to 68°F), crisp, clear days and the brilliant colors of the trees (especially the reds and oranges of the maples) make this a favored time to visit New York. Fall also heralds the opening of the city's renowned cultural season.

Winter – Although winds blowing in off the Hudson and East rivers can cause bitterly cold days, New York's winters are usually not too severe. Temperatures hover around 32°F, and the days are short but often clear and bright. Sudden heavy snowfalls and frequent snow accumulation can cause chaos in the city. The holiday season in New York is festive, indoors and out, with seasonal performances and decorations.

New York City Temperature Chart *(recorded at Central Park)*			
	average high	average low	precipitation
January	38°F (3°C)	26°F (-3°C)	3.9in (9.9cm)
April	61°F (16°C)	44°F (7°C)	3.9in (9.9cm)
July	85°F (29°C)	70°F (20°C)	4.5in (11.4cm)
October	66°F (19°C)	50°F (10°C)	4.5in (11.4cm)

Suggested Two-Day Itinerary

FIRST DAY

Getting Acquainted with New York

Morning	Double decker bus or Circle Line boat tour
Lunch	Grand Central Terminal★★★
Afternoon	Fifth Avenue★★★, Rockefeller Center★★★, Metropolitan Museum of Art★★★
Evening	Broadway★★ – Times Square★★ or Lincoln Center★★

SECOND DAY

The Best of Manhattan

Morning	Ferry to Statue of Liberty★★★, Financial District★★
Lunch	In Chinatown★★
Afternoon	SoHo★ shopping or Chelsea★★ galleries
Evening	Dine in TriBeCa★, jazz in Greenwich Village★★

Suggested Four-Day Itinerary

FIRST DAY

From Rockefeller Center to Broadway

Morning	Rockefeller Center★★★, Museum of Modern Art★★★
Lunch	In Midtown
Afternoon	Circle Line boat tour
Evening	Dine in Theater District★, see a Broadway show

SECOND DAY

From the Empire State Building to Lincoln Center

Morning	Empire State Building★★★, stroll along Fifth Avenue★★★ in Midtown, Central Park★★★
Lunch	Picnic in Central Park *(numerous food markets are located in Upper West Side)*
Afternoon	American Museum of Natural History★★★
Evening	Dine on the Upper West Side, Lincoln Center★★ performance

THIRD DAY

From the Statue of Liberty to SoHo and Greenwich Village

Morning	Statue of Liberty★★★ and Ellis Island★★
Lunch	Stone Street Historic District in the Financial District★★
Afternoon	Civic Center★, Brooklyn Bridge★★★, Chinatown★★, Little Italy★
Evening	Dine in TriBeCa★, jazz in Greenwich Village★★

FOURTH DAY

From the United Nations to Uptown

Morning	UN Headquarters★★★, Grand Central Terminal★★★, East Midtown★★
Lunch	In Midtown or the Upper East Side
Afternoon	Metropolitan Museum of Art★★★ or Guggenheim Museum★★
Evening	Dine on the Upper East Side, cabaret at The Carlyle

KNOW BEFORE YOU GO

Useful Websites

www.nycvisit.com
Official city tourism organization's website is packed with up-to-date information on New York City events, hotels, restaurants, shopping, etc.

www.nytimes.com
This online version of the *New York Times* has a New York City travel guide that includes articles focusing on city life, as well as information on news, hotels, restaurants, events and shows.

http://newyork.citysearch.com
Allows users to access a directory of services and find specific nightclubs, spas, hotels, restaurants, and more. Also movies, events and shopping.

http://nymag.com
An online version of *New York Magazine* filled with articles on the city's movers and shakers as well as news, events, fashion and shopping.

www.ny.com
Information on trip planning, music, shopping, entertainment, sports, real estate, transportation. Includes a map of the city and weather forecasts.

www.in-newyork.com
This website of *IN-New York* magazine features art and collectibles, Broadway shows, museums, shopping, musical events and a neighborhood guide. A monthly feature spotlights topics such as Broadway's backstage.

Visitor Information

To obtain maps and information on points of interest, accommodations and seasonal events contact the following agencies. NYC & Company, the city's official marketing and tourism organization, also publishes the annually updated *Official NYC Guide*, which is available free of charge.

NYC & Company
☎212-484-1200 or 800-692-8474
810 Seventh Avenue,
New York NY 10019
www.nycvisit.com

New York State Division of Tourism
☎518-474-4116 or 800-225-5697
1 Commerce Plaza,
Albany NY 12245
www.iloveny.com

Four free publications, *City Guide Magazine* (www.cityguidemagazine. com), *IN-New York Magazine* (www.in-newyorkmag.com), *Where New York* and the *Official City Guide*, offer information on events, attractions, shopping and dining. They are available at hotels and visitor information kiosks. The **Official NYC Guide** is available free of charge from New York City & Company *(☎212-397-8222 or 800-692-8474; www.nycvisit.com).*
Volunteer New Yorkers take out-of-towners on two- to four-hour visits of city neighborhoods as part of a unique free service called **Big Apple Greeter**. Particular emphasis is placed on matching interests and language requirements of visitors and

---

NYC Online

In addition to the websites shown above, the following sites provide a wealth of information about the Big Apple.

http://gonyc.about.com
www.citidex.com
www.downtownny.com

www.nyc.gov
www.cityguidemagazine.com
www.newyorkcityfood.com

volunteers *(advance reservations required; ☏212-669-8159; www.bigapplegreeter.org).*

Consider purchasing a **CityPass** ticket booklet *(✆$65; ☏888-330-5008; www.citypass.com)* that includes discounted admission to six major sights in New York (Guggenheim Museum; Empire State Building Observatory; Museum of Modern Art; American Museum of Natural History; Metropolitan Museum of Art; and Circle Line sightseeing cruises) and allows you to skip most ticket lines. Buy your CityPass online or at any of the participating attractions.

Local Tourism Offices

NYC & Company Official Visitor Information Center
810 Seventh Ave., between W. 52nd & W. 53rd Sts. ☏212-484-1200. www.nycvisit.com ⏲Open year-round Mon-Fri 8:30am-6pm,weekends & holidays 9am-5pm.

Chinatown Visitor Information Kiosk
At the triangle of Canal, Walker & Baxter Sts. ⏲Open year-round Sun-Fri 10am-6pm, Sat 10am-7pm.

NYC Heritage Tourism Center
Southern tip of City Hall Park on the Broadway sidewalk at Park Row. ⏲Open year-round Mon-Fri 9am-6pm, weekends & holidays 10am-5pm.

Harlem Visitor Information Kiosk
163 W. 125th St., just east of Seventh Ave. ⏲Open year-round Mon-Fri 9am-6pm, weekends & holidays 10am-6pm.

Times Square Information Center
1560 Broadway between W. 46th & W. 47th Sts. ☏212-768-1560. www.timessquarenyc.org. ⏲Open year-round daily 8am-8pm. ⏲Closed Jan 1 & Dec 25.

International Visitors

Visitors from outside the US can obtain information from the multilingual staff at NYC & Company *(☏212-484-1200; www.nycvisit.com)*, or from the US embassy in their country.

EMBASSIES AND CONSULATES

In New York international visitors can contact the consulate of their country of residence. *⌖See chart on the next page.*

ENTRY REQUIREMENTS

Travelers entering the United States under the **Visa Waiver Program** (VWP) must present a machine-readable passport to enter the US without a visa; otherwise a US visa is required. Starting October 26, 2005, required entry documents must include biometric identifiers (fingerscans). Visa Waiver Program requirements can be found on the official Visa Services website: *http://travel.state.gov.*
Citizens of countries participating in the VWP are permitted to enter the US for general business or tourist purposes for a maximum of 90 days without needing a visa. For a list of countries participating in the VWP, contact the US consulate in your country of residence. Citizens of nonparticipating countries must have a visitor's visa. Upon entry, nonresident foreign visitors must present a valid passport and round-trip transportation ticket. Effective January 2007, all US citizens (including infants and children) need a **valid passport** to re-enter the US from Bermuda, Canada, Mexico, Central and South America, and the Caribbean (excluding Puerto Rico and the US Virgin Islands). This policy also applies to foreign nationals of Canada, Bermuda and Mexico. Travelers to and from Canada must present a valid passport to enter the US. Naturalized Canadian citizens should also carry their citizenship papers. Inoculations are generally not required, but check with the US embassy or consulate before departing.

FOREIGN CONSULATES			
Country	Address	Web site	☎
Australia	150 E. 42nd St.	www.australianyc.org	212-351-6500
Belgium	1065 Ave. of the Americas.	www.diplomatie.be/newyork	212-586-5110
Canada	1251 Ave. of the Americas	www.canada-ny.org	212-596-1628
China	520 Twelfth Ave.	www.nyconsulate.prchina.org	212-244-9456
France	934 Fifth Ave.	www.consulfrance-newyork.org	212-606-3600
India	3 E. 64th St.	www.indiaserver.com/cginy.consulate.html	212-774-0600
Italy	690 Park Ave.	www.consnewyork.esteri.it.org	212-737-9100
Mexico	27 E. 39th St.	www.consulmexny.org	212-217-6400
Netherlands	1 Rockefeller Plaza	www.cgny.org	877-388-2443
Spain	150 E. 58th St.	www.maec.es/consulados/nuevayork	212-355-4080
Switzerland	633 Third Ave.	www.swissemb.org	212-599-5700
United Kingdom	845 Third Ave.	www.britainusa.com/ny	212-745-0200

CUSTOMS REGULATIONS

All articles brought into the US must be declared at the time of entry. **Exempt** from customs regulations: personal effects; one liter (33.8 fl oz) of alcoholic beverages (providing visitor is at least 21 years old); either 200 cigarettes, 50 cigars or 2 kilograms of smoking tobacco; and gifts (to persons in the US) that do not exceed $100 in value. **Prohibited items** include plant material; firearms and ammunition (if not intended for sporting purposes); meat or poultry products. For other prohibited items, exemptions and information, contact the US embassy or consulate before departing, or the US Customs Service (☎877-227-5511; www.customs.treas.gov).

HEALTH

The US does not have a national health program. Before departing, visitors from abroad should check with their health care insurance to determine if their medical insurance covers doctors' visits, medication and hospitalization in the US. Prescription drugs should be properly identified, and accompanied by a copy of the prescription.

Accessibility &

In this guide wheelchair access is indicated in admission information accompanying sight descriptions with a &symbol. Most public buildings, attractions, churches, hotels and restaurants provide wheelchair access. All New York City Transit buses and some subway lines are wheelchair-accessible. *For information, contact MTA Customer Assistance: ☎718-596-8585 or www.mta.nyc.ny.us*. Discounted fares are available. NYC Transit operates a shared-ride, door-to-door service for people with disabilities who are unable to use public transport; for information about eligibility, call ☎718-596-8585. *Access for All* provides a wealth of information about many sights and entertainment venues in New York *(available from Hospital Audiences, Inc., 548 Broadway, 3rd floor, New York, NY 10012; ☜$5; ☎212-575-7676; www.hospitalaudiences.org).*

GETTING THERE

By Plane

New York City is served by three airports, two in the borough of Queens and one in New Jersey. They are all run by the Port Authority of New York and New Jersey. In all three airports, ground transportation and information booths are located on the baggage-claim level. Plan to arrive at the airport at least two hours before flight departure time for domestic flights and three hours ahead for international flights. Due to increased security measures, it takes longer to get through airline security checkpoints. Carry-on restrictions vary somewhat, so be sure to check with your airline well in advance of your flight.

JOHN F. KENNEDY INTERNATIONAL AIRPORT (JFK)

in Queens, 15mi southeast of Midtown Manhattan (allow 1hr driving time). ☎718-244-4444 *or* 800-247-7433. *www.panynj.gov.*
Most international flights arrive and depart from Kennedy. Airport information counters are located in all terminals. Departing passengers should allow themselves the maximum amount of time recommended by their airline. Restaurants with sit-down service are located in all terminals. Most modes of transportation depart outside each terminal *(opposite)*. A 24hr full-service medical clinic is located in Cargo Area C.

LAGUARDIA AIRPORT (LGA)

In Queens, 8mi northeast of Midtown Manhattan (allow 30min driving time). ☎718-533-3400 *or* 800-247-7433. *www. panynj.gov.*
LaGuardia is serviced by most domestic and North American air carriers. The airport information counter is located between concourses C and D on the departure level. Restaurants with sit-down service are located in the USAir and Delta terminals *(free shuttle service*

available). Most modes of transportation depart outside each terminal (opposite).

NEWARK LIBERTY INTERNATIONAL AIRPORT (EWR)

In Newark, New Jersey, 16mi southwest of Midtown Manhattan (allow 45min driving time). ☎973-961-6000 *or* 800-397-4636. *www.panynj.gov.*
Many travelers find this airport easier to navigate; flights include both international and domestic air carriers. The airport information counter is located on the lower level of Terminal B. Restaurants with sit-down service are located on the concourse level of all terminals. Intra-airport monorail stations are available at each terminal. Most modes of ground transportation depart outside each terminal *(see below).*

Airport Ground Transportation

It's advisable to accept rides only from authorized ground-transportation agents; contact ground-transportation information counters for agent listing. For additional information on transportation to and from John F. Kennedy, LaGuardia and Newark airports, contact the Port Authority of New York & New Jersey *(☎212-435-7000 or 800-247-7433; www.panynj.gov).*

BY BUS

The **Port Authority Bus Terminal** *(W. 42nd St. & Eighth Ave.;* ☎212-564-8484), the city's main bus terminal, is used by long-distance and commuter services. From here buses to the area's three major airports leave regularly. Airline ticket counters are located on the main floor of the building. Some travelers may find long-distance bus travel uncomfortable due to the lack of sleeping accommodations, but in general, fares are lower than other forms of public transportation. **Greyhound** *(advance reservations suggested; ☎800-231-2222; www. greyhound.com)* provides access to New York City at a leisurely pace; its Discovery Pass allows unlimited travel for 7, 15, 30 or 60 days. **Peter Pan** *(☎800-343-9999; www.peterpanbus. com)* offers service throughout the Northeastern portion of the US.

TAXIS

Taxi service is available outside each terminal. Only yellow taxi cabs with roof medallions showing the taxi number are authorized by the New York City Taxi & Limousine Commission to pick up passengers on the street. Passengers at Kennedy and LaGuardia airports should wait in line and allow a uniformed dispatcher to hail the next available cab. Fares to Manhattan: from JFK, $45 flat rate

😊 A Bit of Advice 😊

Always note the medallion number (on the roof of the taxi) and driver's six-digit license number (inside on the passenger-driver partition) of the taxi you ride in, in case there's a problem or you mistakenly leave a belonging in the cab. Dial 311 to complain or report lost property.

to any point in Manhattan *(tolls not included)*; from LGA, $24–$28 *(average metered rate plus tolls)*; from EWR, $69–$75 *(average metered rate plus tolls)* plus a $15 surcharge. A 50¢ surcharge is added to all metered fares nightly 8pm–6am; and a $1.00 peak-time surcharge weekdays 4pm–8pm. www.nyc.gov/html/tlc.

RAIL SERVICE

Air Train Newark is an airport rail service *(operates daily 5am–midnight; fare depends on your destination; ☎888-397-4636; www. airtrainnewark.com)* that provides a rail connection from Newark airport to Amtrak *(see Trains, below)*, **New Jersey Transit** *(☎800-622-5000; www. njtransit.com)* and **PATH** (**Port**

Authority Trans-Hudson) existing rail systems. The **Air Train JFK** light-rail system *(☎877-535-2478; www.panynj. com/airtrain)* links JFK's eight terminals to PATH subway and bus lines *(☎800-234-7284; www.panynj.gov/path)* to New York City and Long Island.

SHUTTLES & LIMOUSINES

Super Shuttle offers interairport service as well as service to and from Manhattan by van *(shared ride)* 24hrs daily *(👓$16–$21; ☎212-258-3826; www.supershuttle.com)*. **New York Airport Service** express bus runs between Kennedy and LaGuardia airports and Grand Central Railroad Terminal *(free transfer to Midtown hotels)*, and between Penn Station and Port Authority Bus Terminal daily *call or go online for schedules and fares; ☎212-875-8200; www.nyairportservice. com)*. **Olympia Trails Airport Express Bus** *(call or go online for schedules and fares: ☎877-863-9275; www.coachusa. com)* runs from Newark to Pennsylvania Railroad Station, Grand Central Terminal and Port Authority Bus Terminal. **Carey Limousine** *(reservations required; ☎202-895-1200 or 800-336-0646; www.ecarey.com)* offers chauffeur-driven cars at fixed rates between Manhattan and Kennedy: *($127–$160)*, LaGuardia *($107–$140)* and Newark *($127–$160)* airports *(rates are approximate and do not include tolls)*. Other chauffeur-driven car services are available at the airport transportation counter via self-service telephones.

RENTAL CARS

Most major rental-car agencies run free shuttle buses from the airport terminals to their parking lots. *👜See listing of companies in Getting Around.*

PUBLIC TRANSPORTATION

👜See Getting Around.
From Kennedy: 🚇MTA A train from Howard Beach station *(free shuttle service from airport)*. From LaGuardia: 🚇MTA M60 bus.

By Train

AMTRAK

☎*800-872-7245, accessible in North America only; outside North America, contact your local travel agent; www.amtrak.com.*
Reserve Amtrack rail service well in advance to ensure availability and the best fares. Overnight trains offer sleeping accommodations. Daily service to Manhattan's **Pennsylvania Railroad Station** *(Seventh Ave. & W. 32nd St.)* is provided on the *Adirondack* (from Montreal), the *Maple Leaf* (from Toronto), the *Silver Service* (from Miami), the *Lake Shore Limited* (from Chicago), and the *Crescent* (from New Orleans). The *Metroliner* high-speed, all-reserved rail shuttle connects Washington DC and New York City in three hours. Travelers from Canada should inquire with their local travel agents about Amtrak/VIARail connections. **North America Rail Pass** permits unlimited travel in the US and Canada within 30 days. **USA RailPass** *(not available to US or Canadian citizens or legal residents)* offers unlimited travel within Amtrak-designated regions at discounted rates; 15- and 30-day passes are available.

LOCAL SERVICE

Rail service into Manhattan's **Grand Central Railroad Terminal** *(E. 42nd St. & Park Ave.)* is provided by **Metro-North** *(☎212-532-4900 or 800-638-7646; www.mta.nyc.ny.us/mnr)*, which runs between Manhattan and New Haven, CT and Poughkeepsie, NY. Both the **Long Island Railroad** *(☎718-217-5477; www.mta.nyc.ny.us/lirr)* and **New Jersey Transit** *(☎800-772-2222; www.njtransit.com)* operate out of Pennsylvania Railroad Station. **PATH (Port Authority Trans-Hudson)** rail lines *(☎800-234-7284; www.panynj.gov/path)* connect Manhattan with many cities in New Jersey.

By Car

✆*See Access Roads map page 35.*
Vsitors bearing valid driver's licenses issued by their country of residence are not required to obtain an International Driver's License to drive in the US. Drivers must carry vehicle registration and/or rental contract, and proof of automobile insurance at all times. Rental cars in the US are usually equipped with automatic transmission, and rental rates tend to be less expensive than overseas. **Gasoline** is sold by the gallon *(1 gallon = 3.8 liters)* and is cheaper than in other countries. Most self-service gas stations do not offer car repair, although many sell standard maintenance items. Road regulations in the US require that vehicles be driven on the right side of the road. Distances are posted in miles *(1 mile = 1.6 kilometers)*.

GETTING AROUND

Lay of the Land

Manhattan's streets are laid out in a grid pattern. Streets run east-west and avenues run north-south. Fifth Avenue is the dividing line between east and west addresses. Though Avenue of the Americas is the official name, New Yorkers rarely use it, preferring the original Sixth Avenue instead. Generally, even-numbered streets are eastbound; odd-numbered streets are westbound. In lower Manhattan (below 14th St.) most streets have names rather than numbers. North of Houston (HOW-stun) Street (with the exception of Greenwich Village), blocks are generally short and wide. To locate a particular address, consult the Manhattan Address Locator in the Yellow Pages of the telephone directory.

Subway Entrance 72nd Street

Public Transportation

The **Metropolitan Transportation Authority** (MTA) oversees an extensive network of buses, subway and commuter trains throughout the area. MTA New York City Transit runs the city bus and subway lines. Contact the agencies and companies listed under Local Service (in the *Getting There* section) for route information and schedules to Long Island and upstate New York, New Jersey and Connecticut.

The **Travel Information Center** (☎718-330-1234; www.mta.nyc.ny.us) provides route and fare information for subway and bus lines. System maps and timetables are available *(free)* on buses and at all subway stations, visitor information centers, and most hotels. In this guide, subway and bus stops are indicated with the **MTA** symbol.

> ### 😊 A Bit of Advice 😊
> Downtown refers to the area south of 34th Street. Midtown stretches from 34th Street to 59th Street. Above 59th Street is referred to as Uptown. Uptown and downtown also refer to direction: if you're at 14th Street and your destination is 50th Street, you'll be traveling uptown to get to Midtown. If you're headed the other way, you'll be traveling downtown to get downtown.

SUBWAY

Map inside back cover. The subway is the most efficient way to navigate the city. Subway entrances are indicated on street level by a staircase descending (in some cases, ascending) to the station. Large globes also mark the stations: a green globe indicates that you can buy tokens or MetroCards; stations with a red globe have no token booths – you must have the fare available to enter. Virtually all lines run 24hrs/day every 2–5 minutes during rush hours, every 5–12 minutes during the day, and every 20 minutes between midnight and 5am. The cost is $2 per ride, no matter how far you're traveling. Purchasing a **MetroCard** saves you money on multiple rides *(see Fares, opposite)*. Platform signs indicate which trains stop at the station (Uptown trains are northbound; Downtown trains are southbound). Signs on the side of each train list the route number or letter. Local trains stop at every station; express trains do not. Conductors announce each stop. Because of ongoing track work, trains may be rerouted, especially late at night *(midnight–5am);* changes are usually posted in stations near the turnstiles – read them carefully. 😊When riding the subway late at night, avoid isolated areas ("off-peak waiting areas" are provided in stations), and ride in the car carrying the train's conductor (located in the fourth car of the train).

BUSES

New York City Transit buses generally operate daily 5:30am–2am. Some routes on major corridors run 24hrs/day. Weekend hours may be reduced on some lines. During week-days, most buses run every 5-15min; frequency varies at other times. Pick-up points are recognizable by tall, round signs bearing the bus emblem and route number. Route maps are displayed at most bus stops and shelters. Stops are made at posted locations, two to three blocks apart. Stops may be made at other locations along regular routes upon request between 10pm and 5am. If you are unsure about the route, verify your desired stop with the driver. Route numbers are displayed on the front and sides (sometimes back) of each bus. Local bus routes are indicated by a letter prefix indicating the borough in which that line largely operates (for example M7):

M = Manhattan   B = Brooklyn
Bx = Bronx   Q = Queens
S = Staten Island

All buses are equipped with wheelchair lifts and related features.

FARES

All system fares are $2 one way *(exact fare is required for buses; $1 bills, pennies and half dollars are not accepted)*, with the exception of express bus fare, which is $5. The MetroCard automated fare card can be used on both systems and includes a free transfer for each fare, between subway and bus or bus to bus within 2hrs of paying the initial fare. MetroCard may be used to pay for up to 4 persons at a time. Up to 3 children *(under 44 inches tall)* may ride free when accompanied by an adult. Tokens are also accepted by subway or buses.

MetroCard offers several discount passes: 1 day (Fun Pass, ☜$7), 7 days (☜$24) and 30 days (☜$76). Reduced fares are available for senior citizens and persons with qualifying disabilities *(information: ☎718-596-8585)*. MetroCards can be purchased (or value added) at subway stations and retail

outlets. Discount passes are available only from authorized merchants, the Times Square Visitor Center, transit museum stores (Grand Central Terminal and downtown Brooklyn), and vending machines that are located in many stations.

Bus and subway travel information is available 24hrs (☎718-330-1234). Information can be obtained in 140 languages by calling ☎718-330-4847. Maps and schedules are also available online: *www.mta.nyc.ny.us*.

By Taxi

Only yellow taxi cabs with roof medallions showing the taxi number are authorized by the City of New York to pick up passengers on the street. All yellow medallion cabs are metered and share the same rate schedule (using other cabs may risk your personal safety): $2.50 upon entry, 40¢ each additional 1/5 mile. 20¢/minute is charged while the cab is stopped or in slow traffic. A 50¢ surcharge is added between 8pm and 6am, and $1.00 surcharge weekdays between 4pm and 8pm. There are no extra fees for

New York Taxis

additional riders, although taxis are able to accept only 4 passengers. In addition to the metered rates, passengers are responsible for toll fees, and drivers are usually tipped 15%–20%. You can hail a taxi from the street in most areas in Manhattan; a taxi is available when its rooftop white number is lit. Taxi stands are located at most hotels, transportation terminals and entertainment centers (in other areas call for service). For more information, access the city's Taxi & Limousine Commission on-line at *www.nyc.gov/html/tlc*.

New York Water Taxi (*☎212-742-1969, ext. 0; www.nywatertaxi.com*) is another way to get around while avoiding city traffic. Water taxi pick-up and drop-off points are as follows: Paulus Hook Terminal in Jersey City to Pier 11 in Manhattan; East 34th St. in Manhattan or Hunters Point in Queens to Pier 11 in Manhattan; Hunters Point in Queens to E. 34th St. in Manhattan; Brooklyn Army Terminal in Bay Ridge, Brooklyn to Pier 11 in Manhattan; Fulton Ferry Landing in Brooklyn to Pier 11 in Manhattan (*check the website for exact fares and schedules and for additional routes*). When you purchase a water taxi ticket, you have options: one-way, one stop (*$3–$6*); one-way, multiple stops (*$10*); all-day pass, unlimited stops (*$20; valid the day of purchase and the day after*).

By Car

A car is not necessary to visit Manhattan: public transportation is efficient and many sights can be reached easily on foot. Keep in mind that roads are usually congested, public parking lots expensive and street parking extremely difficult to find. **Rush hours**, the peak

transit times for business commuters, occur weekdays between 7am–9am and 4:30pm–6pm. It's best to avoid driving during these times. No commercial traffic may enter the city via the Holland Tunnel; only commercial traffic exiting the city can use it. Also, there are significant restrictions on vehicular traffic below Canal Street; if you're visiting downtown neighborhoods, use public transportation if possible.

RENTAL CARS

Major car-rental companies have offices in Manhattan, in the outer boroughs, and at the three New York City area airports. Most agencies will only rent to persons at least 25 years old, although some will rent to younger drivers for a daily surcharge. A major credit card and valid driver's license are required (some agencies also require proof of insurance). Most rental companies offer seasonal discounts and accept membership privileges. The average daily weekday rate for a compact car, with unlimited mileage, ranges from $65–$107. Weekly rates (*5 days*) for a compact car begin around $230. Note that rental cars are taxed 13.62% (*not included in the advertised rate*).
Many limousine and executive car-service companies offer transport within the city and to the boroughs

Alamo	☎800-462-5266 www.alamo.com
Avis	☎800-331-1212 www.avis.com
Budget	☎800-527-0700 www.budget.com
Dollar	☎866-434-2226 www.dollar.com
Enterprise	☎800-264-6350 www.enterprise.com
Hertz	☎800-654-3131 www.hertz.com
National	☎800-227-7368 www.nationalcar.com
Thrifty	☎800-847-4389 www.thrifty.com

and will customize an itinerary for a day to suit any visitor's needs. For a specific listing of companies, consult the *Official NYC Guide* (🔆*see Visitor Information in Know Before You Go*).

ROAD REGULATIONS

The maximum speed limit on major expressways is 65mph in rural areas and 55mph in and around cities. **Speed limits** in the city range from 25mph in residential areas to 30mph on major streets. Use of **seat belts** is mandatory for driver and passengers in the front seat of the car, and children under 16 years old in the back seat. Child safety seats are required for children under 4 years (seats are available from most rental-car agencies). In New York City, unless otherwise posted, drivers are not permitted to turn right on a red traffic light. The majority of streets in Manhattan are one-way (traffic flows in one direction only). In New York it is illegal to drive with a mobile phone in your hand; you must connect your phone to a hands-free device.

PARKING

If you are successful in finding street parking, pay close attention to signs indicating restrictions. Parking is prohibited during posted street-cleaning times. Parking in some residential areas is by permit only (restricted to area residents). Vehicles are systematically towed for violations. If you believe your car has been towed, dial 311 (the city government's information line), or ☎212-639-9675 if you are outside the city, to find out. The **Manhattan Tow Pound** is located at Pier 76 *(W. 38th St. at 12th Ave.; ☎212-971-0771 or 212-971-0772; www.nyc.gov)*. For parking violations, call the city's government's information line (🅿 dial 311). Spaces identified with ♿ are reserved for people with disabilities only. Anyone parking in these spaces without proper identification is subject to a heavy fine. Privately operated parking garages are abundant throughout the city; rates range from ⬭ $6–$15/hr.

WHAT TO SEE AND DO

Sightseeing

TOURS

If you have little time at your disposal, we recommend the two- or four-day itineraries described at the front of Planning Your Trip. You can also choose from a wide variety of guided tours offered in the city. Here's a selection:

City Tours
Double Decker and Trolley Tours – These tours of Manhattan aboard double-decker buses and trolleys allow visitors to board at any of over 50 stops located at major attractions in Lower and Upper Manhattan, each lasting about 2-3hrs. Tours run every 30min year-round daily (except Jan 1 & Dec 25) 8am-6pm in Lower Manhattan, and 8:30am-5pm in

Uptown; $49 both loop ($44 online). The same ticket allows free reboarding for 2 consecutive days. A 3-day ticket *($112)* includes the Statue of Liberty cruise and admission to the South Street Seaport Museum. *Tickets sold at Gray Line Visitors Center, Eighth Ave. between W. 47th & W. 48th Sts.* **Gray Line** ☎212-445-0848 or 800-669-0051; *www.newyorksightseeing.com.*
Helicopter Tours – Offering a panoramic view of Manhattan, these unforgettable flights last a brief 2-17 minutes. Tours depart year-round from 9am, weather permitting, in Midtown from heliport at Twelfth Ave. & W. 30th St *(additional $40 per person fee applies at this location; last flight 8:45pm; no reservations necessary)*; Downtown from heliport at Pier 6 *(last flight 6pm; reservations required)*; and Jersey City from Paulus Hook Pier *(last flight 6:30pm; reservations required)*.

Allison Simpson/MICHELIN

$30-$186 per person plus $2.50 security fee). Contact Liberty Helicopters ☎212-967-6464; *www.libertyhelicopters.com.*

Neighborhood Tours

The following organizations offer a number of different walking tours through New York's distinct neighborhoods, exploring the city's diverse history and architecture:

Adventure on a Shoestring – ☎ 212-265-2663. About 25 tours year-round weekends. Any tour ☞ $5.

Big Onion Walking Tours – ☎212-439-1090. *www.bigonion.com.* Year-round daily 2hr tours of historic districts and ethnic neighborhoods. ☞$15. *Ġ See schedule online.*

Foods of New York Tours, Inc – ☎212-209-3370. *www.foodsofny.com.* Year-round daily 3hr tours of Greenwich Village and Chelsea/ Meatpacking District. Call or check online for schedule. ☞$40.

Grand Tour of Midtown – ☎212-883-2420. *www.grandcentralpartnership.org.* Year-round Fri 12:30pm. The 90min tour departs from Whitney Museum's Sculpture Court, Park Ave. & E. 42nd St.

Harlem Spirituals, Inc. *(Ġ see Harlem)* – ☎212-391-0900 or 800-660-2166. *www.harlemspirituals.com.*

Municipal Art Society – ☎212-439-1049. *www.mas.org.* Two-hour themed or architectural walking tours. Also private tours *(by appointment:☎212-935-3960).* For details, call or go online. ☞$15.

New York Like a Native – ☎718-393-7537. *www.nylikeanative.com.* Offers a variety of Brooklyn tours of varying duration year-round. Call or check the website for schedule. ☞$15-$36.

NYC Discovery Tours – ☎212-465-3331. *www.ny.com/sights/tours/NYCDiscovery.* Themed tours of the city year-round, such as historic taverns at Christmas. ☞$13. For details, call or go online.

Rent a New Yorker Tours – ☎212-982-9445. *www.rentanewyorker.com.* Half a dozen 2hr neighborhood tours, including Coney Island (☞$20). Call for schedule & reservations. ☞$10.

SCENIC CRUISES AND FERRIES

Tours of New York Harbor with panoramic views of the Statue of Liberty and the city's skyline are offered by the following boat lines:

Circle Line – Full Island Cruise *(3hrs; ☞$29);* **Harbor Lights Cruise** *(2hrs; ☞$24);* **Seaport Liberty Cruise** *(1hr15min; ☞$19).* **Beast Speedboat Rides** *(30 min; ☞$18; ☞ no cruises until May 2008)). An additional $1 per passenger charge for fuel applies.* All cruises depart from Pier 83, W. 42nd St. Call or go online for schedule. ✗Ġ🅿 ☎212-563-3200. *www.circleline42.com.*

NY Waterway – Harbor Cruise & **Twilight Cruise** departs year-round daily from Pier 78, W. 39th St.; 1hr 30min. ☞$23. Call or go online for

schedule. ⚔️ ♿ ☎*800-533-3779.
www.nywaterway.com.*
Spirit Cruises – Depart year-round
daily from Pier 61, W. 23rd St. Lunch
cruises 2hrs; ☏$44 *(Jan-Mar $36).*
Dinner cruises 2hrs 30min; ☏$79-$90
(Jan-Mar $72). Gospel lunch, jazz &
dance cruises offered. ♿ 🅿*(fee)* ☎*866-
483-3866. www.spiritcruises.com.*
Bateaux New York – European-style
glass-enclosed boats depart year-
round daily from Pier 61, W. 23rd St.
Lunch cruises *(2hr; $45)* & dinner
cruises with entertainment *(3hr;
$145.22).* No jeans or sneakers. Call or
go online for schedules. ☎*866-817-
3463. www.spiritofnewyork.com.*
Staten Island Ferry –
👣*See Staten Island.*
World Yacht Cruises –
👣*See sidebar above.*

ENTERTAINMENT TOURS

The following tours give visitors a
behind-the-scenes look at some of the
city's renowned entertainment venues:
Radio City Grand Tour and **NBC
Studio Tour** (👣*see Rockefeller Center);*
Lincoln Center Tour (👣*see Lincoln
Center);* **Carnegie Hall Tour** (👣*see
Carnegie Hall);* **Madison Square
Garden Tour** (🚶*tours every half
hours daily 11am-3pm and depart from
the box office: Seventh Ave. at 33rd St.;
☏$17;* ☎*212-465-5800;
www.thegarden.com).*

TELEVISION SHOWS

Tickets for shows in New York City
are free, but are often hard to come
by since some shows have waiting lists
over a year long. Check the specific
show below for the procedure for
getting tickets.

Late Show with David Letterman –
*Ed Sullivan Theater, 1697 Broadway, NY,
NY 10019.* ☎*212-247-6497. www.cbs.com.*
For stand-by tickets to the *Late Show,*
call the above number at 11am on the
day of the show. Phones will be answered
as long as tickets are available.
Live with Regis and Kelly – For
advance tickets, send a postcard to
Live with Regis and Kelly Tickets,
Ansonia Station, PO Box 230-777, NY,
NY 10023-077 (there is a 12month wait);
or try for same-day tickets at the corner
of W. 67th St. & Columbus Ave. at 7am.
www.bventertainment.go.com.
NBC Studio Show Tickets – For
stand-by tickets to *Late Night with
Conan O'Brien (stand-by time 9am)* or
Saturday Night Live (stand-by time 9am),
arrive at the W. 49th St. entrance of
30 Rockefeller Plaza (under the NBC
Studios marquee) before the time
shown above on the day of taping. NBC
no longer accepts ticket requests by
mail. ☎*212-664-3056. www.nbc.com.*

No Tickets?

Several TV shows in New York City use
the background audiences that gather
outside the plate-glass windows of the
studio. If you are not able to acquire
tickets to be real-life audience members,
you can still appear on television. Just
arrive early outside one of these
studios:
The Early Show – *767 Fifth Ave.at
E.58th St. Mon-Fri 8am-8:30am.* ☎*212-
975-4061. www.showbiz.cbsnews.com.*
Good Morning America – *Times
Square at W. 44th St. & Broadway; Mon-
Fri 7am-9am.* ☎*212-580-5176. www.
abcnews.com.*
The Today Show – *30 Rockefeller
Plaza, between Fifth & Sixth Aves.;
Mon-Fri 7am-10am.* ☎*212-664-3056.
www.nbc.com.*

World Yacht Dinner Cruises

Spectacular views of the Manhattan skyline complement dinner and dancing
aboard World Yacht. Three-hour cruises take place each evening from May through
December *(April Thu-Mon only).* Depart from Pier 81, W. 41st St. at the Hudson River.
$89.88 Sun–Thu; $99.91 Fri & Sat; $61.85 Sun brunch. ☎*212-630-8100. www.world-
yacht.com.* Jackets required for evening cruises; no jeans, shorts or sneakers.

Activities for Children Kids

🖕 *See also Kids in New York City in Your Stay in the City at the back of this guide.* In this guide, sights of particular interest to children are indicated with a Kids symbol. Some attractions offer discount fees for children. *New York Family*, a free monthly magazine, includes articles of interest to parents as well as an extensive calendar of family-oriented events, and is available at major attractions and libraries throughout the area *(☎914-381-7474)*. Most attractions in New York offer discounted, if not free, admission to visitors under 18 years of age. In addition, many hotels make family discount packages available and some restaurants provide a children's menu.

Calendar of Events

Listed below is a selection of New York's many popular annual events; some dates may vary each year. For more information about events in New York City consult the periodicals listed on page 30 or contact the NYC & Company, the city's official tourism marketing organization*(☎ 212-484-1222 or 800-692-8474; www.nycvisit.com)*.

JANUARY–FEBRUARY

Jan
New York National Boat Show
Jacob K. Javits Center
www.newyorkboatshow.com
☎212-984-7000

mid–late Jan
Winter Antiques Show
7th Regiment Armory,
67th St. & Park Ave.
www.winterantiquesshow.com
☎718-292-7392

late Jan–Feb
Chinese New Year Celebrations
Chinatown
www.explorechinatown.com

early Feb
Empire State Building Run-Up
350 Fifth Ave.
www.nyrrc.org   ☎212-860-4455

all Feb
Black History Month
various locations

mid-Feb
Westminster Dog Show
Madison Square Garden
www.westminsterkennelclub.org
☎212-465-6741

MARCH–APRIL

early Mar
Art Expo New York
Jacob K. Javits Center
www.artexpos.com
☎888-608-5300

Mar 17
St. Patrick's Day Parade
Fifth Ave. from 44th to 86th Sts.
www.saintpatricksdayparade.com

Mar–Apr
Macy's Spring Flower Show
Macy's   ☎212-494-4495

Mar–Jun
Biennial Exhibit
Whitney Museum of American Art
☎212-570-3676

late Mar–Apr
NY International Auto Show
Jacob K. Javits Center
www.autoshowny.com
☎718-746-5300
**Ringling Bros. and
    Barnum & Bailey Circus**
Madison Square Garden
www.barnumandbailey.com

Easter Sunday
Easter Sunday Parade
Fifth Ave. between 49th & 57th Sts.

late Apr
Cherry Blossom Festival
Brooklyn Botanic Garden
www.bbg.org
☎718-623-7200

MAY–JUNE

early May
TriBeCa Film Festival
www.tribecafilmfestival.org
☏212-941-2400

May–mid-Jun
Spring Flower Exhibition
NY Botanical Garden, Bronx
www.nybg.org
☏718-817-8700

mid-May
**Ninth Avenue International
    Food Festival**
Ninth Ave. from 37th to 57th Sts.
☏212-581-7217

late May–early Jun & early Sept
**Washington Square Out-
    door Art Exhibit**
Greenwich Village
www.washingtonsquareout
doorartexhibit.org
☏212-982-6255

early Jun
National Puerto Rican Day Parade
Fifth Ave. from 44th to 86th Sts.
www.nationalpuertoricanday
parade.org
☏718-401-0404
Roses, Roses, Roses
NY Botanical Garden, Bronx
www.nybg.org   ☏718-817-8700
Museum Mile Festival
www.museummilefestival.org
☏212-606-2296

Jun–Jul
Metropolitan Opera Parks Concerts
various locations
☏212-362-6000
**NY Philharmonic
    Summer Parks Concerts**
various locations
☏212-875-5709
Midsummer-Night Swing
Josie Robertson Plaza,
Lincoln Center
www.lincolncenter.org
☏212-875-5766

Jun–Aug
SummerStage in Central Park
Rumsey Playfield
www.summerstage.org
☏212-360-2777
**Street Performers
    and Evening Concerts**
South Street Seaport
www.southstreetseaport.com
☏212-732-7678

mid–late Jun
JVC Jazz Festival New York
Carnegie Hall, Lincoln Center
and other venues
www.festivalproductions.net

late Jun
**Lesbian and Gay Pride Week
    Celebrations**
various locations
www.nycpride.org
☏212-807-7433
Mermaid Parade
Coney Island
www.coneyislandusa.com/
mermaid.sthml
☏718-372-5159

JULY–AUGUST

Jul
Lincoln Center Festival
Alice Tully Hall
www.lincolncenter.org
☏212-875-5050
NYC Tap Festival
citywide
www.atdf.org
☏646-230-9564

July 4
Macy's Fireworks Celebration
East River from 23rd to 42nd Sts.
☏212-494-4495

Aug
Lincoln Center Out-of-Doors
outdoor plazas
www.lincolncenter.org
☏212-721-6500
Mostly Mozart Festival
Lincoln Center
www.lincolncenter.org
☏212-721-6500

Harlem Jazz & Music Festival
Harlem
www.harlemdiscover.com

SEPTEMBER–OCTOBER

Labor Day
**West Indian-American Day
Carnival Parade**
Eastern Pkwy. from Utica Ave. to
Grand Army Plaza, Brooklyn
www.wiadca.org ☎718-467-1797

early Sept
US Open Tennis Tournament
USTA National Tennis Center,
Flushing
www.usta.com
☎718-760-6200

mid-Sept
Feast of San Gennaro
Mulberry St., Little Italy
www.sangennaro.org
☎212-768-9320
Race for Mayor's Cup
New York Harbor
www.nymayorscup.com
☎212-748-8738

late Sept–Oct
New York Film Festival
Lincoln Center
www.filmlinc.com
☎212-875-5050

Oct
Bonsai Festival
NY Botanical Garden, Bronx
www.nybg.org ☎718-817-8700

mid-Oct
Columbus Day Parade
Fifth Ave. from 44th to 72nd Sts.
www.columbuscitizensfd.org
☎212-249-9923

late Oct–early Jan
Big Apple Circus
Damrosch Park, Lincoln Center
http://theshow.bigapplecircus.org
☎800-899-2775

Oct 31
Halloween Parade
Greenwich Village
www.halloween-nyc.com

NOVEMBER–DECEMBER

early Nov
New York City Marathon
Verrazano-Narrows Bridge
to Central Park
www.nyrrc.org ☎212-423-2249

Nov–Dec
**The Rockettes –
Christmas Spectacular**
Radio City Music Hall
www.radiocity.com
☎212-307-1000
**Thanksgiving Day
Macy's Thanksgiving Day Parade**
Central Park West to Herald Square
☎212-494-4495

late Nov–Dec
The Chorus Tree
South Street Seaport

The 4th of July Fireworks Over Brooklyn Bridge

©iStockphoto.com/Michal Besser.

www.southstreetseaport.com
☎212-732-7678

late Nov–early Jan
The Nutcracker NY
State Theater, Lincoln Center
www.lincolncenter.org
☎212-870-5570

Christmas Tree and 18C
Neapolitan Baroque Crèche
Metropolitan Museum of Art
www.metmuseum.org
☎212-535-7710

early Dec
Lighting of the Giant
Chanukah Menorah
Grand Army Plaza, Brooklyn;
Fifth Ave. at 59th St.
Christmas Tree Lighting Ceremony
Rockefeller Center
www.rockefellercenter.com
☎212-632-3975

Dec 31
New Year's Eve Ball Drop
Times Square
www.timessquarenyc.org

Films: New York in the Movies

King Kong (1933) .... Merrian C. Cooper	Moonstruck (1987) .... Norman Jewison
Miracle on 34th Street (1947).................... George Seaton	Bright Lights, Big City (1988)............................... James Bridges
On the Town (1949) .... S. Donen, G. Kelly	Do the Right Thing (1989) .... Spike Lee
On the Waterfront (1954) .... Elia Kazan	When Harry Met Sally (1989) .... Rob Reiner
West Side Story (1961).......................... R. Wise, J. Robbins	Crimes and Misdemeanors (1989)................................ Woody Allen
Breakfast at Tiffany's (1961) .... Blake Edwards	New York Stories (1989) .... F.F. Coppola, W. Allen, M. Scorsese
Funny Girl (1968) .... Williams Wyler	Goodfellas (1990).................. Martin Scorsese
Midnight Cowboy (1968) .... John Schlesinger	Jungle Fever (1991)........................... Spike Lee
Rosemary's Baby (1968) ...... Roman Polanski	The Fisher King (1991)................. Terry Gilliam
The French Connection (1971) .... William Friedkin	The Wedding Banquet (1993).. Ang Lee
The Godfather (1972).... Francis Ford Coppola	City Hall (1995).......................... Harold Becker
Taxi Driver (1976)................... Martin Scorsese	Smoke (1995)....................... Wayne Wang
Saturday Night Fever (1977)................................ John Badham	The Mirror Has Two Faces (1996)....................... Barbra Streisand
Manhattan (1979) .... Woody Allen	As Good as It Gets (1997) ..... James L. Brooks
Arthur (1981) .... Steve Gordon	Men in Black (1997) .... Barry Sonnenfeld
Ragtime (1981)........................... Milos Forman	You've Got Mail (1998)................ Nora Ephron
The Cotton Club (1984)...... Francis F. Coppola	The Siege (1998) .... Edward Zwick
Ghostbusters (1984)................... Ivan Reitman	Pollock (2000) .... Ed Harris
Broadway Danny Rose (1985).. Woody Allen	Gangs of New York (2002) .. Martin Scorsese
Desperately Seeking Susan (1985)............................ Susan Seidelman	Day after Tomorrow (2004) .... Roland Emmerich
After Hours (1985).............................. Martin Scorsese	Batman Begins (2005) .... Christopher Nolan
Hannah and Her Sisters (1986)............................... Woody Allen	The Interpreter (2005) .... Sydney Pollack
Wall Street (1987)...................... Oliver Stone	Fantastic Four: Rise of the Silver Surfer (2007)...................................... Tim Story

BASIC INFORMATION

Business Hours

Most businesses operate Monday to Friday 9am–5pm. Banking institutions are generally open 9am–3:30pm; some offer Saturday service (9am–noon). Most retail stores and specialty shops are open Monday to Saturday 10am–6pm (Thursday til 9pm), Sunday noon–6pm. Small, neighborhood convenience stores usually stay open past 10pm. Some stores on the Lower East Side and in the Diamond District (47th St.) close on Friday afternoon and all day Saturday for the Jewish Sabbath; stores keep normal hours on Sunday.

Communications

TELEPHONE

Local calls from pay phones cost 50¢ for unlimited use (calls from Manhattan to the outer boroughs and vice versa are local but require dialing 1 and the area code). For long-distance calls, it is best to purchase a pre-paid phone card, which is available in most newsstands or drugstores.

Area Codes

Manhattan	212, 646, 917
Bronx, Brooklyn, Queens, Staten Island	347, 718, 917
Hudson River Valley	914, 845
Long Island	516, 631

Instructions for using **public telephones** are listed on or near the telephone. Some public telephones accept credit cards, and all will accept long-distance calling cards. For **long-distance calls** in the US and Canada, dial 1 + area code + number. To place an **international call**, dial 011 + country code + area code + number. A list of country codes can be found in the front of the Yellow Pages. To place a collect call (person receiving call pays charges), dial 0 + area code + number and tell the operator you are calling collect. If it is an international call, ask for the overseas operator. The cost for a local call from a pay phone is generally 50¢ (any combination of nickels, dimes and quarters is accepted). Most telephone numbers in this guide that start with **800**, **877** or **888** are toll-free (no charge) in the US and may not be accessible outside of North America. Dial **1** before dialing a toll-free number. The charge for numbers preceded by 900 can range from 50¢ to $15 per minute. Most hotels add a surcharge for local and long-distance calls. For further information, dial **0** for operator assistance.

Important Numbers	☎
Emergency Police/Ambulance/Fire (24hrs)	**911**
Police (non-emergency, Mon–Fri 9am–6pm)	311 or 646-610-5000
Doctors (24hrs)	Hotel Docs 800-468-3537
Medical House Calls	917-885-9409
NY Hotel Urgent Medical Services	212-737-1212
Dental Emergencies: NYU College of Dentistry (weekdays) NYU College of Dentistry (weekends) Jan Linhart D.D.S., P.C. (24hrs)	212-998-9458 212-998-9828 212-682-5180
24hr Pharmacies	
CVS (4 locations in Manhattan Duane Reade, 224 W. 57th St. Rite Aid (6 locations in Manhattan) Poison Control Center (24hrs)	800-746-7287 212-541-9708 800-748-3243 212-764-7667

You can send a **telegram** or money, or have money telegraphed to you, via the Western Union system (☎ 800-325-6000; www.westernunion.com).

Electricity

Voltage in the US is 110 volts AC, 60 Hz. Foreign-made appliances may need AC adapters (available at specialty travel and electronics stores) and North American flat-blade plugs.

Emergencies

In all major US cities you can telephone the police, ambulance or fire service by dialing **911**. Another way to report an emergency is to dial 0 for the operator. ♨ See chart on opposite page for important telephone numbers.

Liquor Law

The legal minimum age for purchase and consumption of alcoholic beverages is 21. Proof of age may be required. Most bars in New York City stay open until 4am. You can buy wine and liquor at liquor stores Monday to Saturday. Grocery and convenience stores sell beer anytime except Sunday 3am–noon.

Mail

The main post office (421 Eighth Ave. at W. 33rd St.; ☎800-275-8777) is open 24hrs/day. Branch offices are located in all five boroughs; for locations and phone numbers, check the phone directory under US Government. The chart on page 31 contains a selection of post offices in Manhattan.
Some sample rates for first-class mail: letter 41¢ (1oz), postcard 26¢; overseas letter 90¢ (1oz), postcard 90¢. Letters and small packages can be mailed from most hotels. Stamps and packing material may be purchased at many convenience stores, drugstores and post offices. Businesses offering postal and express shipping services are located throughout the city (see Yellow Pages under Mailing Services).
For additional information, contact the US Postal Customer Assistance Center (☎ 800-275-8777; www.usps.com).

Money

The American dollar is divided into 100 cents. A penny = 1 cent; a nickel = 5 cents; a dime = 10 cents; a quarter = 25 cents.

CREDIT CARDS AND TRAVELER'S CHECKS

Rental-car agencies and many hotels require credit cards. **American Express Travel** is located at 111 Broadway, (☎ 212-693-1100). Most banks will cash brand-name traveler's checks and give cash advances on major credit cards with proper identification: American Express, ☎ 800-528-4800; Visa, ☎ 800-336-8472; MasterCard/Eurocard, ☎ 800-307-7309; Diners Club, ☎ 800-234-6377.

CURRENCY EXCHANGE

Currency exchange offices can be found at Kennedy, LaGuardia and Newark Liberty airports. **Chase Manhattan Bank** (☎ 212-935-9935) offers foreign currency exchange in all of their 500 New York City branches. Private companies that offer currency exchange include: **Travelex** (1590 Broadway, ☎ 212-265-6063; www. travelex.com). Banks charge a small fee for this service; private companies generally charge higher fees.
Most banks are members of the network of Automated Teller Machines (**ATMs**) allowing visitors from around the world to withdraw cash using bank cards and major credit cards. ATMs can usually be found in banks, airports, grocery stores and shopping malls. Networks (Cirrus, Honor, Plus) serviced by the ATM are indicated on the machine. To inquire about ATM service, locations and transaction fees, contact your local bank, Cirrus (☎ 800-424-7787) or Plus (☎ 800-843-7587). **Traveler's checks** are accepted in banks, most

☺ A Bit of Advice ☺

SAFETY TIPS

- ☺ The best way to explore New York City is on foot. Visitors are encouraged to use common sense, stay alert and avoid deserted streets and park areas after dark.
- ☺ Avoid carrying large sums of money, and don't let strangers see how much money you are carrying.
- ☺ Hold purses and knapsacks firmly, carry your wallet in your front pocket, and avoid wearing expensive jewelry.
- ☺ Stay awake when riding on public transportation, and keep packages close to you. MTA vehicles are equipped with devices that enable riders to notify personnel of emergencies. Exercise caution in the subway after 11pm. Ride in the conductor's car (usually in the middle of the train) if you are alone.
- ☺ Always park your car in a well-lit area. Close windows, lock doors and place valuables in the trunk.

stores, restaurants and hotels. American Express Travel is located at 111 Broadway, (☎ 212-693-1100). To report a lost or stolen credit card: American Express (☎ 800-528-4800); Diners Club (☎ 800-234-6377); MasterCard (☎ 800-307-7309 or the issuing bank); Visa (☎ 800-336-8472).

TAXES

Prices displayed or quoted in the US do not generally include **sales tax** (8.375% in New York City). Sales tax is added at the time of purchase and is not reimbursable (it can sometimes be avoided if purchased items are shipped to another country by the seller). Clothes and shoes valued at $110 and over are subject to the 4.375% state sales tax. In New York City, clothing and footwear purchases under $100 are tax-free. The city levies a 13.375% hotel occupancy tax per night for rooms costing $40 or more, plus $3.50 per room per night. Since hotel rates do not reflect taxes, travelers should be aware of these added charges. An 18.375% parking garage tax is charged in New York City. Clothing and footwear purchases under $100 are tax-free. Tax percentages in areas beyond the city limits may vary.

Newspapers and Magazines

The city's leading newspaper is the *New York Times (www.nytimes.com)*; check the Sunday Arts & Leisure and the Friday Weekend sections for entertainment information. Other dailies are the *Daily News (www.nydailynews.com)*, the *New York Post (www.nypost.com)* and *Newsday (www.newsday.com)*. The business-oriented *Wall Street Journal (www.wsj.com)* is published Monday through Saturday. New York also supports numerous daily and weekly foreign-language papers, ranging from *El Diario* to *Sing Tao*.

Several weekly publications provide listings of museum exhibits, art galleries, films, concerts, restaurants, readings and special events. In magazine format, the *New Yorker (www.newyorker.com)* and *Time Out New York (www.timeoutny.com)* can be purchased at newsstands. In newsprint, *L magazine (www.thelmagazine.com)* and the *Village Voice (www.villagevoice.com)*, both free, can be found in curbside newsracks and in some bookstores. The *Official NYC Guide (www.nycvisit.com)* and *NYC Arts*, free at city visitor centers, contains seasonal listings. *HX* and *Next* cater to the gay community, and are available free at downtown cafes and bookstores.

Public Holidays

Most banks and government offices in the New York City area are closed on the following legal holidays (many retail stores and restaurants remain open on days indicated with *):

New Year's Day	January 1
Martin Luther King Jr. Day*	3rd Monday in January
Presidents' Day*	3rd Monday in February
Memorial Day*	Last Monday in May
Independence Day*	July 4
Labor Day*	1st Monday in September
Columbus Day*	2nd Monday in October
Veterans Day*	November 11
Thanksgiving Day	4th Thursday in November
Christmas Day	December 25

Smoking

Smoking is prohibited throughout the state of New York in bars, restaurants, clubs and workplaces.

Tipping

In the US it is customary to give a tip (a small gift of money) for services received from waiters/waitresses, porters, hotel maids and taxi drivers.

In restaurants it is customary to tip the server 15-20% of the bill (an easy way to calculate is to double the sales tax). Taxi drivers are generally tipped 15% of the fare, hotel bellhops $1 per bag ($2 in luxury hotels), hotel doormen $1 per taxi and hotel maids $2 per day.

Telephones

♿ See Communications.

Temperature and Measurement

In the US temperatures are measured in degrees Fahrenheit and measurements are expressed according to the US Customary System of weights and measures.

Time

New York City is located in the Eastern Standard Time (EST) zone, 5hrs behind Greenwich Mean Time. Daylight Saving Time is observed from the 2nd Sunday in March (clocks are advanced 1hr) to the 1st Sunday in November.

Selected NYC Post Offices			
Post Office Station Name	**Street Address**	**Telephone number**	**Section of town**
Canal Street Station	350 Canal St.	(800) 275-8777	Downtown
Chinatown	6 Doyers St.	(800) 275-8777	Downtown
Cooper Station	93 Fourth Ave.	(800) 275-8777	Downtown
New York	421 Eighth Ave.	(800) 275-8777	Downtown
Old Chelsea Station	217 W. 18th St.	(800) 275-8777	Downtown
Patchin	70 W. 10th St.	(800) 275-8777	Downtown
Prince Station	124 Greene St.	(800) 275-8777	Downtown
Wall Street Station	73 Pine St.	(800) 275-8777	Downtown
Rockefeller Center	610 Fifth Ave.	(800) 275-8777	Midtown
Columbia University	534 W. 112th St.	(800) 275-8777	Uptown
Columbus Circle	27 W. 60th St.	(800) 275-8777	Uptown
Gracie	229 E. 85th St.	(800) 275-8777	Uptown
Lenox Hill Station	217 E. 70th St.	(800) 275-8777	Uptown
Planetarium	127 W. 83rd St.	(800) 275-8777	Uptown

View of Midtown
Brigitta L. House - MICHELIN

THE CITY OF NEW YORK

By far the most populous city in the US, New York is a world unto itself by virtue of its size, the density and diversity of its population, its dynamic economic activity and its vibrant cultural life.

Location

Situated on the East Coast of the US at 40° north latitude and 74° west longitude, New York City is bordered by the Hudson River, Long Island Sound and the Atlantic Ocean. The city occupies the western end of Long Island, all of two smaller islands (Manhattan and Staten Island) and a piece of the mainland to the north, adjacent to the Hudson River. The islands provide protection for one of the largest and safest harbors in the world, ideal for oceangoing vessels. Access to the ocean is through the Narrows, a passage between Staten Island and Long Island. More than 578mi of coastline, including some 14mi of beaches, rim the city.

In addition to its major islands, New York City also encompasses several small islands, notably Liberty Island, home of the Statue of Liberty; Ellis Island, once the nation's leading immigration center; Riker's Island (located north of LaGuardia Airport), site of a large municipal prison; Governor's Island, a former US Coast Guard site; and Roosevelt Island, once home to public health institutions and now a middle-income residential location.

The total area of the five boroughs *(below)* that make up New York City is about 320sq mi; the longest distance between its boundaries, from the northeast to the southwest, is about 35mi. New York City's height above sea level varies from 5ft (Battery Park, at the southern tip of Manhattan) to 400ft (Washington Heights, in northern Manhattan). Its climate is continental *(for information about seasonal climates, ☾ see Planning Your Trip).*

New York and Adjacent States

Access Roads

Conduit Ave.	1
Cross County Pkwy.	2
Fort Hamilton Pkwy.	3
Korean War Veterans Pkwy.	4
Nassau Expwy.	5
New England Thruway	6
Prospect Expwy.	7
West St.	8
Whitestone Expwy.	9

The Five Boroughs

New York City as it exists today was created in 1898 when, under state charter, the city was expanded from its original confines of Manhattan to incorporate Brooklyn (Kings County), Queens (Queens County), the Bronx (Bronx County) and Staten Island (Richmond County). The counties correspond to the original colonial administrative divisions, and the names still designate judicial districts. The five boroughs are not developed to the same extent: a few open spaces exist on the fringes of Brooklyn and Queens, and despite the construction of many new dwellings in the last decades, Staten Island is still somewhat countrified. Brooklyn, situated on the southwest tip of Long Island, is today the most populous of the five boroughs. Queens, to the northeast of Brooklyn, is the largest and fastest growing. The heavily developed Bronx, the only borough that is part of the mainland, forms the gateway from the city to the affluent suburbs in the north. Although it remains the least populated borough, Staten Island has been growing since the completion of the Verrazano-Narrows Bridge from Brooklyn in 1964. Manhattan, the smallest of the boroughs with an area of

22.7sq mi, constitutes the heart of the city. With a population of 1,611,581, it is the most densely populated county in the US. This tongue-shaped island is the center for much of New York's cultural, financial and retail activity. Although the consolidation of the five boroughs took place over a century ago, residents of the so-called outer boroughs traveling to Manhattan still say they are "going to the city."

Metropolitan Area

The city's vast metropolitan area, home to about 21,199,865 residents, encompasses 22 counties and planning regions extending more than 7,000sq mi. Seven of these counties are in New York State, nine in New Jersey and six in Connecticut. In addition to New York City, the area includes Newark, New Jersey (pop. 281,402) and 10 other cities with more than 100,000 people. Organizations responsible for operating regional transportation facilities are the Port Authority of New York and New Jersey, which oversees the 17-county area in those two states, and the Triborough Bridge and Tunnel Authority.

The State of New York

The city gave its name to the state (the 11th of the original 13 states of the Union), which by virtue of its economic expansion and political influence became known as the "Empire State." New York State extends from east of the Hudson River to the Great Lakes and Niagara Falls, and borders Canada on the north. The state is divided into counties, and its capital is Albany (New York City was the capital from 1784 to 1797).

HISTORY

FROM NIEUW AMSTERDAM TO NEW YORK

Before the arrival of Europeans, Algonquian- and Iroquoian-speaking Indians inhabited the island of Manhattan. The Algonquin tribe is credited for naming the island Manhattan, meaning "island of the hills." Following Henry Hudson's exploratory journey, the Dutch East India Company founded the colony of New Netherland on the site of present-day New York City in 1614. In 1625 the company established the trading post of Nieuw Amsterdam. Unlike other American colonies, New York was not founded by a religious group, but for purely commercial purposes, and it became the private property of the Dutch West India Company. This fact, combined with the difficulty of attracting immigrants from a generally content Dutch populace, gave New York a cosmopolitan makeup from the very start, attracting French Huguenots and non-Dutch immigrants from Holland. A fort and roundout batteries were constructed at the southern tip of Manhattan Island, controlling the entrance to the Hudson River. A city grew up to the south of a defensive wall, while farms and estates, called *bouweries*, were established farther north on Manhattan Island, as well as in Brooklyn, Queens, Staten Island and the Bronx. Initially ruled by a director-general, the town attained some form of self-government in 1653. The British, already established in New England to the north, took control of the colony in the late 17C, accepting the surrender of Director-General Peter Stuyvesant in 1664.

1524 – **Giovanni da Verrazano**, an Italian explorer in the service of the French king François I, is the first European to land on Manhattan.

1609 – **Henry Hudson** sails up the river (now bearing his name) in his ship, the Half Moon, while on a voyage for the Dutch East India Company.

1614 – The name New Netherland, given to the newly founded Dutch colony, designates the area around present-day New York City. The territory north of New York is called New England.

1625 – The first permanent European settlement is established on Manhattan. The trading post is named **Nieuw Amsterdam** and includes a fort and 30 houses.

1626 – **Peter Minuit** of the Dutch West India Company buys Manhattan from the Algonquin Indians in exchange for trinkets valued at 60 guilders, the equivalent of $24.

1647 – **Peter Stuyvesant** (1592-1672) is appointed director-general of New Netherland, serving until 1664.

1653 – The city of Nieuw Amsterdam receives a charter and municipal rule. Stuyvesant erects a protective wall along present-day Wall Street.

1664 – As a repercussion of the English and Dutch trading rivalries in Europe, the English take Nieuw Amsterdam without a struggle and rename it **New York** after the Duke of York, brother of the English king Charles II.

BRITISH RULE

New York blossomed as an important trading post in the colonies of North America, second only to Boston in the trade of furs and farm products. By 1700 the tip of Manhattan claimed some 4,000 residents and had grown north beyond the Dutch palisade fortifications at Wall Street. The city began its passionate embrace of journalism with the creation of several newspapers. Columbia University and the city's first library were founded. Dutch language and culture began to wane in the century following Stuyvesant's surrender, although numerous Dutch families remained important in local society, government and business. New York's pivotal role as a commercial port for the American colonies placed the city in the center of the taxation controversies leading up to the American Revolution. The city was one of the first targets of the British Army, which occupied New York throughout the War for Independence.

1667 – The Treaty of Breda, ending the second Anglo-Dutch war, confirms English control over the province of New Netherland. The city of New York passes under the English system of municipal government, and English replaces Dutch as the official language.

1673 – The Dutch retake New York without a fight and rename it New Orange.

1674 – By the Treaty of Westminster in 1674, the province of New Netherland becomes permanently English.

1720 – With 7,000 inhabitants, New York is the third-largest city in the colonies.

1725 – The city's first newspaper, the *New-York Gazette*, is founded by William Bradford.

1733 – **John Peter Zenger** founds the *New York Weekly Journal*, in which he attacks the governor. A year later Zenger is imprisoned for slander. His acquittal marks the beginning of a free press.

1754 – The city's first college, **King's College**, now Columbia University, opens. The New York Society Library is founded.

1763 – Marking the end of the French and Indian War, or **Seven Years' War** (1756-63), the Treaty of Paris confirms English control of the North American continent.

1765 – The Stamp Act Congress meets in New York, and representatives from nine colonies denounce the English colonial policy of taxation without representation.

1766 – Repeal of the Stamp Act. A statue is erected to **William Pitt**, the British statesman who did most to obtain the repeal.

1767 – Parliament passes the Townshend Acts, a series of four acts that increase taxation and threaten the already established traditions of colonial self-government. The repeal three years later coincides with the Boston Massacre.

1776 – The **Declaration of Independence** (July 4) is adopted and New Yorkers pull down the statue of George III at Bowling Green. On November 17, Fort Washington (*p 221*) in northern Manhattan falls and the British occupy all of present-day New York City until 1783.

1783 – The **Treaty of Paris** (September 3) ends the American Revolution and England recognizes the independence of the 13 colonies. The last British troops evacuate New York, and George Washington returns to the city in triumph before bidding farewell to his troops at Fraunces Tavern on December 4.

EMPIRE CITY

After briefly serving as US capital, New York established the commercial links and financial institutions that led the new nation into the Industrial Age. As the population of New York exploded beyond all predictions – despite outbreaks of yellow fever and cholera – the island of Manhattan grew northward along the gridiron plan established in the early 19C. Broadway, a poplar-lined residential boulevard in 1790, became a commercial thoroughfare by 1820. Following the opening of the Erie Canal in 1825, the city handled more trade than all other US ports combined and became a leading shipbuilding center. The population doubled in the 1820s as immigrants arrived by the thousands from Germany, Ireland and Scandinavia.

1784 – New York City becomes the capital of New York State and a year later is named US capital under the Articles of Confederation.

1789 – **George Washington**, elected first president, takes the oath of office at Federal Hall.

1790 – The first official census counts 33,000 people in Manhattan. The federal capital moves to Philadelphia.

1792 – The forerunner to the New York Stock Exchange is founded.

1804 – Vice President Aaron Burr mortally wounds political rival Alexander Hamilton in a duel on the Hudson River.

1812 – **War of 1812**: the US declares war on Britain and the Port of New York suffers from the ensuing blockade until the war ends in 1814. Present City Hall opens.

1820 – New York is the most populous city in the nation with 123,705 inhabitants. Growth also brings disease, including a severe yellow fever epidemic in 1822.

1825 – Opening of the **Erie Canal**. New York becomes the gateway to the Great Lakes and the West as 500 new mercantile businesses open.

1832 – Cholera epidemic kills 4,000 citizens.

1835 – The Great Fire destroys an extensive area in the business district.

1845 – Another fire levels 300 buildings in lower Manhattan. The first telegraph line connects the city to Philadelphia. The first baseball club, the New York Knickerbockers, is organized.

GROWTH AND GREENING

Large waves of immigration from Europe and the Americas spurred commercial and industrial growth which led to a doubling of the city's population every 20 years, exceeding a million people by 1875. Shantytowns developed on vacant land to the north of the growing city, while

Eno Collection. New York Public Library

View of New York (c. 1850)

aging neighborhoods became slums, including the infamous "Five Points" district north of City Hall. The massive immigrant population fed a political machine based at Tammany Hall that established new heights of public graft and corruption in the 1860s and 70s by bilking taxpayers of tens of millions of dollars – more than $9 million during construction of the "Tweed Courthouse" alone. The adjacent city of Brooklyn blossomed with residences and factories. Following the success of America's first World's Fair here in 1853, New York established itself as the cultural capital of America with the creation of Central Park, the American Museum of Natural History and the Metropolitan Museum of Art.

1849 – Astor Place Riot: 31 die and 150 are wounded in a theater riot protesting British actor William Macready.

1851 – The *New York Times* is published for the first time.

1853 – The World's Fair opens at the Crystal Palace. Modeled on London's Great Exhibition of 1851, the fair is an early showplace for iron and glass architecture and the technological advances of the Industrial Revolution.

1857 – Construction of **Central Park** begins in the wake of a depression brought on by financial panic; the park is officially completed in 1876.

1860 – New York City counts 813,660 inhabitants, as immigration from Ireland, Germany and other European countries continues. Brooklyn counts 279,000 residents, double the number it had 10 years earlier.

1863 – The city is rocked by the Draft Riots. Opposition by the poor to the rich man's practice of hiring a substitute to fight the Civil War spreads to encompass general discontent and racism, leaving 1,200 dead and 8,000 injured.

1865 – The Civil War ends. After President Abraham Lincoln is assassinated, his body lies in state at New York's City Hall.

1868 – Opening of **the El**, the first elevated railway in lower Manhattan.

1869 – On September 24, financier Jay Gould, who had tried to corner the gold market with his associate James Fisk, sells out and brings about the financial panic known as "Black Friday." The American Museum of Natural History is founded in Central Park's Arsenal.

1871 – The *New York Times* finally exposes Boss Tweed's Tammany Hall ring of corrupt city officials. Tweed goes to prison, where he dies in 1878.

1872 – The **Metropolitan Museum of Art** opens, moving to its present location in 1880.

A CITY OF IMMIGRANTS

Wall Street became the center of banking, finance and insurance in the US, and by the second decade of the 20C it began occupying its key position in the world economy. Immigration not only continued but increased dramatically as the 19C waned, bringing new groups from Southern and Eastern Europe. New York became home to the largest Jewish community in the world as millions fled Russian persecution. Italian immigrants created Little Italy next to Chinatown, established in the 1870s but stunted by the Chinese Exclusion Act of 1882. Beginning in the late 1880s, **Jacob Riis** took his camera to New York's dark streets to expose the social ills of the tenement districts, ushering in the Progressive Era. Tammany Hall is exposed by an 1894 investigation, led by New York native **Theodore Roosevelt**, of police corruption, thus launching a political career that would take him to the presidency. William Randolph Hearst's purchase of the *New York Journal* in 1895 and subsequent circulation battle with Joseph Pulitzer's *New York World* instigated the era of yellow journalism – largely responsible for the Spanish-American War.

1880-84 – Some two million people arrive in New York City during a period of rapid immigration. Tenements and sweatshops proliferate, exploiting the new residents.

1882 – Electricity is first offered for general use by Thomas Edison's plant in lower Manhattan.

1886 – Inauguration of the **Statue of Liberty**.

1889 – The first telephone exchange opens on Nassau Street two years after Alexander Graham Bell demonstrated his invention in New York.

1891 – Carnegie Hall opens with Tchaikovsky's American conducting debut.

1892 – The ongoing rush of immigration leads to the completion of the Ellis Island facility – more than 12 million persons will be processed here by the mid-1920s.

1898 – **Greater New York City** is created, comprising five boroughs: Manhattan, the Bronx, Brooklyn, Queens and Staten Island. With a population of more than three million, New York is the world's largest city.

1902 – One of the city's first skyscrapers, the **Flatiron Building**, is completed.

1904 – The first underground subway line opens.

CULTURE AND CRASH

New York served as the major US transshipment point for Allied matériel during World War I. Immigration began to slow following exclusionary legislation in the 1920s, but the city's population still increased from 4.8 million in 1910 to almost 7 million in 1930. Prohibition began in 1920, doubling the number of illegal liquor outlets in the city to 32,000 and providing the backdrop for bootlegging gangs and underworld influence in politics and government. **Greenwich Village** became an intellectual and artistic bohemia and the Algonquin Hotel's Round Table hosted the likes of the witty writers of the new *New Yorker* magazine. The Harlem Renaissance in African-American arts and letters introduced writers like Zora Neale Hurston and Langston Hughes, and jazz legends like Duke Ellington and Cab Calloway. A host of new theaters along 42nd Street perfected the Broadway musical with tunes written in Tin Pan Alley. The Armory Show and the Ashcan school promoted modern art in America in the 1910s, and the following decades saw the founding of the **Museum of Modern Art**, the Whitney Museum of American Art and the Solomon R. Guggenheim Museum. The gaiety of the Roaring 20s came to an end with the Wall Street stock market crash on Black Tuesday, October 29, 1929, signaling the onset of the Great Depression.

1908 – First celebration of New Year's Eve at Times Square.

1911 – The Triangle Shirtwaist Company fire kills 145 sweatshop employees.

1913 – The **Armory Show** introduces modern art to America.

1920 – **On September 16**, a bombing on Wall Street takes 38 lives.

1925 – The *New Yorker* magazine is founded. Alain Locke's anthology *The New Negro: An Interpretation* marks the heyday of the Harlem Renaissance.

1929 – Stock market crash (financial panic of October) signals the start of the Great Depression.

1931 – The Empire State Building is completed after almost two years of work.

1932 – Mayor Jimmy Walker resigns from office in another Tammany Hall scandal.

BUST AND BOOM

The Great Depression prompted the closing of manufacturing plants in the city – thousands of homeless people slept in subway tunnels and waited in bread lines. Construction of the **Rockefeller Center** and two World's Fairs buoyed New York as reform mayor Fiorello La Guardia – "the Little Flower" – led the city through the trials of the Depression, arresting gangsters like "Lucky" Luciano and supervising huge public works projects. The first US public housing project – First Houses – was built in 1935 and followed by a dozen more in the next decade.

World War II made New York the busiest port in the world and solidified its international position in industry, commerce and finance. The United Nations established its headquarters in Manhattan following the war as the city began building again. The 1950s brought new immigrants, with large numbers arriving from Puerto Rico and Asia. A haven for refugee intelligentsia from Europe, New York made its bid for international cultural capital in the 1950s and 60s, welcoming painters Piet Mondrian, Jacques Lipchitz, Fernand Léger and others, while fostering a new generation of avant-garde artists such as Jackson Pollock, Willem de Kooning, Louise Nevelson and Andy Warhol. Off Broadway theaters enlivened the cultural scene and New York became a center for film and television.

1934 – **Fiorello H. La Guardia** becomes mayor of New York City, serving until 1945.

1935 – Harlem Riot exposes the effects of the Depression on African Americans.

1939-40 – World's Fair at Flushing Meadow attracts more than 44 million visitors to preview postwar advances in domestic technology.

1945 – **United Nations** charter is drafted in San Francisco, and the organization announces it will locate in New York City.

1959 – Construction of Lincoln Center begins.

TERRORIST STRIKES

Racial and labor tensions beset the city in the 1960s, and in 1975 the city government defaulted into bankruptcy. The setbacks only stimulated New Yorker pluck, though, and by 1981, the city's budget was balanced. Despite the 1987 stock market crash, by the late 1980s an upswing in the world economy led to a massive expansion on Wall Street that continued straight through the Bull Market of the late 1990s. Presaged by a truck-bomb explosion at the World Trade Center in 1993, the attack on the World Trade Center on September 11, 2001, signaled the end of the stock market boom and brought the city into the international spotlight as residents banded together to mourn the dead.

1964 – The longest suspension bridge in the US, the Verrazano-Narrows Bridge opens between Brooklyn and Staten Island. The **Harlem Uprising** is the first major manifestation of Northern black unrest in the Civil Rights era.

1964-65 – **World's Fair** held on the same site as the 1939-40 fair features the 140ft-tall Unisphere model of the earth.

1965 – Malcolm X is assassinated at the Audubon Ballroom in Harlem.

1973 – The **World Trade Center** opens in Manhattan.

1977 – Ed Koch becomes mayor.

1980 – John Lennon is assassinated in front of his New York City residence, the Dakota.

1989 – New York City's first African-American mayor, **David Dinkins**, is elected.

1993 – Terrorist bomb rocks the World Trade Center, injuring hundreds. **Rudy Giuliani** is elected mayor.

1996 – New York endures its worst blizzard in a century.

1999 – Two million people fill Times Square for a 24-hour-long New Year's Eve celebration to welcome the new millennium.

2000 – Yankees win Subway Series against Mets.

2001 – On the morning of September 11th, in the worst terrorist attack in US history, hijackers crash two passenger planes into the Twin Towers, destroying the entire World Trade Center and resulting in the loss of 2,979 lives.

STANDING TALL

In the wake of September 11, 2001, New Yorkers banded together with resolve. Cleanup was completed on schedule, but design, safety, and cost issues held up new construction at the site for five years. Forced out of office by term limits, Rudy Giuliani ceded the mayor's office to billionaire **Mike Bloomberg**, who put the city on stable financial footing and passed a raft of legislation in an effort to make New Yorkers healthier.

2002 – Billionaire financial-data baron Mike Bloomberg is sworn in as mayor. Cleanup crews remove 1.5 million tons of debris from the World Trade Center site.

2003 – A cascading power outage leaves New York City in the dark for 29 hours beginning at 4pm on Thursday, August 14. The New York legislature enacts a law banning smoking in virtually all bars, clubs, and restaurants statewide.

2004 – Marking its 75th anniversary, the Museum of Modern Art reopens its Midtown location after two and a half years of renovation and expansion. Bloomberg is elected to a second term and bans trans fats from city restaurants.

2005 – For 16 days in February, Central Park is transformed by artists Christo and Jeanne-Claude's *The Gates* – 7,500 orange-fabric panels mounted on poles placed over walkways throughout the park. The installation attracts hundreds of thousands of visitors.

2006 – Work begins on the Freedom Tower, a 1,776ft skyscraper on the former World Trade Center site. The city welcomes a record 43.8 million visitors, up from 33.1 million in 1998, and ends the fiscal year with a $6 billion surplus.

2007 – Mayor Bloomberg drops out of the Republican Party and declares himself an independent. In October he announces a plan to plant 650,000 trees in the city by 2017, more than five times the number planted in the preceding decade.

ART AND CULTURE

Architecture

A stunning showcase for contemporary architecture, New York is first and foremost a city of skyscrapers. Yet beyond the skyline's perennially changing profile of steel and glass lies an architectural landscape remarkably rich in history and variety; indeed, the city leads the nation in preservation, encompassing thousands of buildings and historic districts that illustrate its development. From the elegant and elemental New York City brownstone to the dramatic ziggurat towers of the Roaring 20s, architecture is both stage and player in the drama of New York City.

FROM COMMERCIAL COLONY TO DEMOCRATIC REPUBLIC

Engineer Cryn Fredericksz laid out the fort and town of Nieuw Amsterdam in 1625. The earliest views of the colony depict narrow, irregular streets (still seen in lower Manhattan) and quaint homes sporting sloping gambrel roofs and columned porches (see illustration below). The English takeover of Manhattan in 1664 brought the Georgian style, whose symmetrical, solid facades typified the next phase of development, pushing north of Wall Street by 1700. Building in New York City halted during the British occupation, but renewed as the young Republic came into its own from 1790 to 1820, adopting a modified Roman Classical architecture known as the **Federal style**. The style defined not only grand public edifices and mansions, but also commercial warehouses and shops that were fast replacing their Dutch antecedents (as seen at South Street Seaport). In the 1830s Americans turned to ancient **Greek architecture** as a symbol of the new nation. Public buildings and homes across the nation displayed Greek temple entrances in a new, confident show of democracy. Upper-class residential communities north of Houston Street saw the erection of "the Row" at Washington Square North (1831, Town & Davis) and Colonnade Row on Lafayette Street (1831, Seth Greer), wherein dwelt Delanos, Astors and Vanderbilts. The Federal Hall National Memorial, with its Doric temple facade of Westchester County marble, is a landmark example of the style.

MANHATTAN MARCHES NORTH

As New York rebounded from the Revolutionary War and grew in prosperity, it expanded to the north. City Engineer John Randel released the Randel Plan in 1811, which laid out a grid of streets from Houston Street all the way north to 155th Street and divided the city into narrow east-west blocks with 100ft-deep lots. The plan was criticized for ignoring the island's topography and extending so far north. The scale would prove prescient, but Manhattan's hills and outcroppings were methodically flattened over time. Throughout the 19C, new residential areas were erected and then replaced with shops, hotels, restaurants and offices 10 or 20 years later. A serious fire in 1835 leveled 700 buildings in lower Manhattan, and another in 1845 consumed 300 structures, accelerating the process of building and rebuilding. New development reached Houston Street in 1820, 14th Street by 1840, 23rd Street by 1850 and 42nd Street by 1860. The improvement of public transportation from horse-drawn omnibuses in the 1830s to street railroads in the 1850s helped make the growth possible. Slums grew along with the city, as "rear buildings" and **tenements** proliferated in the 1840s and 50s and shantytowns filled the vacant lands in Central Park and upper Manhattan.

R. Corbel/ MICHELIN

Dutch Colonial House

Broadway became the barometer of Manhattan's urban and architectural development. By the 1830s hotels on Broadway had pushed residential uses into Washington Square and Greenwich Village. Union Square became a fashionable address by mid-century. In 1862 George William Curtis lamented Broadway's changes in *Harper's* magazine: "It was a street of three-story redbrick houses. Now it is a highway of stone and iron, and marble buildings." The Randel Plan had not provided for open space, and existing private parks like the Elgin Botanic Garden and St. John's soon became lucrative building sites. The development of Central Park in mid-century created much-needed open space and enhanced the prospect of real estate development around it.

MID-CENTURY ECLECTICISM

Gothic Revival architecture, inspired by John Ruskin in England and suited especially to churches, was popular in the US from 1840 on. Richard Upjohn's landmark Trinity Church, built in 1846, epitomized the style and the **Romantic movement** that fostered it, with its dark, dramatic central spire and atmospheric cemetery. Withers and Vaux used the style for the Jefferson Market Library in 1874 and the first Metropolitan Museum of Art building in 1880. Peter B. Wight's National Academy of Design (1865, demolished) at East 23rd Street and Park Avenue was an important example of "Ruskinian" Gothic, as is the surviving National Arts Club (1884, Calvert Vaux) at 15 Gramercy Park South.

By mid-century the vertical, rectangular facades of the Italianate style proved ideal for the narrow lots of the booming city. Easily adapted to row houses, storefronts or warehouses, this decorative style first appeared with the 1846 A.T. Stewart's department store (280 Broadway). Italianate became the preferred style for row houses, as witnessed in the brownstones of Brooklyn Heights, Gramercy Park and Harlem. Anglo-Italianate row houses, with lower entrance stairs and narrow facades, filled the streets of Chelsea.

The **Italianate style** was the basis for cast-iron commercial loft buildings constructed throughout lower Manhattan in the 1850s. The new "fireproof" material was easily detailed with ornamental flourishes, and the rhythm of round-arched window arcades separated by attached columns could be repeated on multiple floors as buildings grew taller in an era of skyrocketing land values. The facades were often marbleized or painted like stone to reassure a public distrustful of the new glass-and-iron architecture. By 1872 there were almost three miles of cast-iron facades in lower Manhattan, including the elegant **E.V. Haughwout Building**.

Baron Haussmann's redesign of Paris in the 1850s and 1860s spawned a brief but intense affection for Parisian **Second Empire** architecture. Distinguished by the double-pitched mansard roof, the style befitted the extravagance of the Gilded Age and coincided with the 1870s development of the "Ladies Mile" along Fifth Avenue and Broadway from 10th Street to Madison Square. Former row houses sprouted mansard roofs punctuated by elaborate dormer windows as they were converted to retail uses, while new shops and department stores were designed in the style.

BADLANDS AND BEYOND – MANHATTAN FILLS UP

By 1875 New York counted a million residents, and its neighboring boroughs were growing as well. The new elevated railroads built from 1868 on connected downtown with once-distant areas around Central Park, leading to their rapid development.

R. Corbel / MICHELIN

Haughwout Building

Brownstones

In *A Backward Glance*, Edith Wharton, who was born in a brownstone in 1862, decried "this little low-studded rectangular New York, cursed with its universal chocolate-colored coating of the most hideous stone ever quarried." Despite such claims, the brownstone has become the quintessential symbol of the New York neighborhood, a legacy of various speculative booms of the 19C, when row after rhythmic row of identical town houses appeared along the city's long residential blocks. Characterized by high stoops, elegant cornices and large plate-glass windows, the four- and

R. Corbel / MICHELIN

five-story buildings adopted many popular architectural stylings; initially the Italianate style (with heavy cornice and brackets) predominated, giving way to Renaissance Revival, Romanesque and Queen Anne designs. Builders first used cheap brown sandstone in the 1820s and 1830s as a substitute for limestone or marble. Over time, the term "brownstone" came to refer to the entire category of 19C town houses – be they faced with stone or brick.

Originally built to house a single family in grand style, the edifices were subdivided into apartments as neighborhoods declined, and rapidly came to symbolize inner-city decay. In recent years, however, brownstones have become fashionable as preservation enthusiasts reconvert many into single-family homes, restoring their original function and cachet. Found in Greenwich Village, Murray Hill, Gramercy Park, Harlem, and the Upper East and West sides of Manhattan, brownstones are also the dominant architectural feature in many parts of Brooklyn, including Park Slope and Brooklyn Heights.

The Sixth Avenue El began operating in 1877, followed by the Third Avenue El in 1878, offering service all the way to 129th Street. Within two years elevated lines opened on Second and Ninth avenues. The year 1883 saw the completion of the Brooklyn Bridge, a dazzling display of structural supremacy that ushered in the era of **skyscrapers**. Elevated railways transformed the city's streetscapes, as did telegraph, telephone and electric lines, causing the city to require that such lines be buried after 1884.

As immigration expanded in the late 19C, slums grew as well, presenting new challenges for architecture and city planning. New York passed its first tenement law in 1867, with a much stricter version following in 1879. In 1880 the Improved Dwellings Assn. built a model tenement on First Avenue north of 71st Street designed by Vaux and Radford, but design did not solve social ills. Urban reform efforts in the 1890s demolished some slums to make way for Columbus and Seward parks.

The continuing growth of Manhattan led to the first **apartment buildings**, beginning with Richard Morris Hunt's 1869 Stuyvesant (demolished) on East 18th Street. Old Fifth Avenue mansions were razed for retail landmarks such as Tiffany & Co., and the entertainment district at Union Square was replaced in the 1880s by the "Rialto" along Broadway from Madison Square to 42nd Street. The Upper West Side grew less rapidly than the Upper East Side, even though Riverside Drive had been laid out in 1865. Upper-class apartment housing designed for Singer sewing-machine magnate Edward S. Clark was derided for being so far uptown it might as well be in the Dakotas. The assessment proved flawed, as buildings sprouted up along the Ninth Avenue El line, but the name stuck to Clark's Dakota Apartments (1884, Henry J. Hardenbergh), a triumph of Victorian eclecticism. By the end of the century, the last farms and fields in northern Manhattan had been developed.

ARCHITECTURE FOR AN INDUSTRIAL AGE

Homes erected in the 1880s sported late Victorian styles, including the **Queen Anne**, with its picturesque, asymmetrical compositions; the **Romanesque Revival**, with its rusticated sense of repose and strength; and the **Beaux-Arts**, with its connotations of continental sophistication and elegance.

West End Avenue and Park Slope in Brooklyn included elegant examples of Queen Anne town houses and mansions, as did several apartment buildings on Gramercy Square. Romanesque Revival architecture came into national vogue with the career of Henry Hobson Richardson, who lived on Staten Island. The semicircular arches and heavy masonry of the style defined the City of Brooklyn Fire Headquarters (1892, Frank Freeman) and religious buildings such as the Eldridge Street Synagogue (1887, Herter Bros.), with its Moorish and Gothic elements.

Woolworth Building

R. Corbel / MICHELIN

The **Richardsonian Romanesque** style found robust expression in the DeVinne Press Building (1885, Babb, Cook & Willard) at 399 Lafayette Street.

The success of the Chicago World's Columbian Exposition of 1893 created a rage for Neoclassical architecture, and the New York firm of McKim, Mead and White was among its best practitioners, designing grand public edifices as embodied in the US Custom House (1907) at Bowling Green, and retail establishments like the original Tiffany's (1906) at 409 Fifth Avenue. The architects' work at Columbia University and New York University in the 1890s epitomized Beaux-Arts planning and design, and their incomparable Pennsylvania Railroad Station (demolished) of 1910 was modeled on the ancient Baths of Caracalla in Rome.

Richard Morris Hunt designed the Neoclassical facade of the Metropolitan Museum of Art between 1895 and 1902. Several apartment buildings on Broadway, such as the richly encrusted Ansonia Hotel (1904) and the Apthorp (1908), adopted elegant Beaux-Arts ornaments. The style was well suited to a mercantile capital like New York City and characterized the new residential areas on the Upper East and West sides. Grand Central Terminal (1913, Warren & Wetmore) and the New York Public Library (1911, Carrère and Hastings) are considered the height of Beaux-Arts design in New York City.

The early 20C was a period of historical revival in architecture, as the Beaux-Arts style was joined by Dutch Colonial, **Georgian, Tudor** and Gothic Revival. A wealth of terra-cotta ornament made the various mimicries all the more effective. Eclectic revivals reached their height in vaudeville movie palaces like the Apollo (1914, George Keister) and the many theaters on Broadway.

SKYSCRAPERS AND SETBACKS

Rapid growth in Manhattan helped pave the way for the skyscraper. James Bogardus erected the first **cast-iron building** at Washington and Murray streets (reconstructed) in 1848, and Elisha Graves Otis installed the first safety elevator in E.V. Haughwout's building in 1857, an innovation that made taller buildings practical. Iron beams – a predecessor to the skeletal steel frames of skyscrapers – were used for the Cooper Union of 1859. The first true skyscraper – supported entirely by a steel frame – appeared in Chicago in 1884. Chicago school architect Louis Sullivan designed the Bayard-Condict Building in 1894, but New York preferred a more eclectic design approach, from the 1899 Neoclassical Park Row Building by R.H. Robertson to Daniel H. Burnham's epochal Flatiron Building of 1902. The tradition of enveloping new architecture in historical forms reached its literal height in Cass Gilbert's stunning Gothic Revival **Woolworth Building** of 1913, which at 792ft remained the world's tallest building for a generation.

In 1916 New York City passed the nation's first zoning law to ensure adequate light and air into the canyonlike streets of the metropolis. Zoning required buildings to set their facades back from the street as they grew higher, and soon towers shaped like ancient ziggurats dotted the Manhattan skyline. This form, combined with new technologies and the streamlined aesthetics of modern art, led to the Art Deco skyscraper, which achieved its greatest expressions in New York. By the late 1920s vertical stone panels with expressionistic ornament and recessed windows marked the emergence of **Art Deco** architecture in landmarks like the Chrysler Building, with its zigzag steel conical crown, and the expressive General Electric Building, with its complex brick and terra-cotta skin. The **Empire State Building** is a muscular example of Art Deco refinement; it was the tallest building on earth for more than 40 years.

BUILDING UP AND OUT

By the 1930s development could no longer march north in Manhattan to vacant land – areas had to be found where structures could be demolished and rebuilt, or built higher. The Financial District at the southern end of the island and Fifth Avenue near 42nd Street became high-rise office districts, and high-rise residential buildings appeared near Central Park. Park commissioner and city construction coordinator **Robert Moses** began a rapid park expansion program under Mayor **Fiorello La Guardia** in 1934, increasing park space by a third in two years and planning the 1939 World's Fair at Flushing Meadow. La Guardia and Moses brought New York City into the automobile age with the construction of the Triborough Bridge; they approved the submergence of the last of the old elevated railways and oversaw construction of Laguardia Airport, the largest Works Progress Administration project in the country.

The Great Depression put a halt to most development for 20 years, but Rockefeller Center was built throughout the 1930s, proving that New York would continue to be the commercial capital of the world.

POSTWAR PROSPERITY AND PRESERVATION

Real estate awoke from its Depression-induced slumber in the late 1940s and New York began to build skyscrapers in the new **International style**, which eschewed ornament and setbacks for a boxlike slab set in an open plaza. Appropriately, one of these skyscrapers was the United Nations Headquarters, designed in 1947 by an international committee. The 1952 Lever House by **Skidmore, Owings & Merrill** introduced both the slab-plaza form and the new technology of the glass curtain wall, which soon achieved its clearest expression in the 1956 **Seagram Building** by **Ludwig Mies van der Rohe**. The style defined 1960s prosperity in buildings like the Marine Midland Bank (1967, Skidmore, Owings & Merrill).

Fulfilling its growing role as a world cultural mecca, Manhattan played host to innovative designs like Frank Lloyd Wright's spiraling study in white concrete, the Solomon R. Guggenheim Museum, a landmark of **Modernism**. The Whitney Museum of American Art (1966, Marcel Breuer) employed concrete in the very different vocabulary of a menacing **Brutalist** overhang, while the sensuous curves of Eero Saarinen's 1962 TWA Terminal at John F. Kennedy Airport were an international sensation.

Robert Moses continued to rebuild the city under a succession of mayors, creating a ring of expressways around the city, demolishing "slum" areas in urban

Lever House

R. Corbel / MICHELIN

where lights and signs are the rule, features numerous examples of this architectural playfulness. Office buildings in the area have been growing more playful, too, as seen in the collage of styles and geometries that make up Fox and Fowle's Condé Nast Building (1999) and Reuters Building (2001). Sir Norman Foster's 42-story, accordion-like Hearst Tower (2006) combines post-Modern style with "green" building principles: 90 percent of the steel used in construction was recycled, the roof collects and distributes rainwater to area trees and the glass-paneled walls let in natural light while blocking solar radiation.

renewal efforts and constructing tunnels and bridges that were later blamed for inducing blight. The continued rebuilding finally provoked public outcry against the demolition of Penn Station in 1962. Although the station was destroyed, the city passed one of the nation's strongest landmarks laws in 1965. Grand Central Terminal's attempt to demolish its landmark building led to the 1978 Supreme Court case upholding landmarks laws throughout the US.

MODERNISM AND BEYOND

Modernism reached its Manhattan apogee with the twin towers of the World Trade Center (1973), encompassing an unprecedented 10 million square feet of office space. **Post-Modernism** arrived with the dramatic roofline of the 1978 Citicorp (now Citigroup) Center (Hugh Stubbins & Assocs.) and **Philip Johnson**'s 1984 AT&T Headquarters (now Sony Plaza), with its famous Chippendale top. Other notable post-Modern building features include the mirrorglass facades of the Jacob Javits Convention Center (1986, I.M. Pei & Partners) and the varied roof designs of Cesar Pelli's several World Financial Center buildings (1985-88).

The late 1990s have ushered in an era of **Entertainment Architecture**, an eclectic post-Modernism that revels in layered facades, dramatic lighting and signage that seems to explode from the traditional wall plane. Not surprisingly, Times Square,

Architectural Glossary

DUTCH COLONIAL (1620–1700)

Colonial architectural styles were imitations of their European contemporaries, modified slightly in deference to materials and climate. Dutch architecture during the 17C and 18C was characterized by tall, narrow buildings with steppedgable rooflines, familiar from the streets and grachten (canals) of Amsterdam and other port cities, where homes were taxed on their frontage. Farm (bouwerie) estates took their cues from the Dutch countryside, with sloping gambrel roofs and columned porches, as seen in the surviving Dyckman House in Manhattan and Wyckoff House in Brooklyn.

GEORGIAN (1720–1790)

English Colonial architecture adopted the Renaissance interpretations of Classical architecture popular in the England of George I and George II, which emphasized symmetry and decorum. Frame, brick, and stone houses featured hipped or sloping roofs with the gable end on the side, symmetrical window openings and a prominent central entrance, often ornamented with sidelights and a transom. The Van Cortlandt House is a good example. In larger public buildings, the style adopted more of the columns and pediments of its Classical ancestors, as seen in St. Paul's Chapel.

FEDERAL (1780–1830)

Federal is the term used to describe the more robust and Roman interpretation of Georgian architecture adopted by the newly freed colonies at the end of the 18C. These buildings saw a more liberal use of Classical columns and pediments, especially on entrance doorways, which often sported fanlights, and an occasional balustrade rimming the roofline. New York's City Hall of 1811 represents a lovely example of the style.

GREEK REVIVAL (1820–1850)

The dramatic expansion of American democracy across the continent led to an architecture based on the pedimented, symmetrical orders of Classical Greek temples. Large public buildings often sported a lantern or cupola, with a two-story colonnaded facade. Vernacular versions included a low attic story; shallow roof; Doric, Ionic or Corinthian columns; and a pediment over the entrance. The Federal Hall National Memorial on Wall Street is a textbook Greek temple.

GOTHIC REVIVAL (1840–1880)

Popular in England from the beginning of the 19C, the picturesque, asymmetrical forms of Gothic Revival facades often included towers, battlements and pointed-arch windows and gables. Linked to the Romantic movement, the style laid the basis for later picturesque movements like the Queen Anne. Smaller homes had intricately detailed bargeboards at the eaves and vertical siding, while larger homes and commercial buildings might include battlements, spires and gargoyles. Derived principally from medieval European cathedrals, the style was used for churches to great effect, as seen in Richard Upjohn's Trinity Church.

ITALIANATE (1840–1880)

By mid-century, the Italianate style – with its heavy cornices and large brackets, decorated window lintels and convenient, rectangular massing – became the American standard for homes and commercial buildings. Based on more orna-

St. Paul's Chapel

Allison M. Simpson - MICHELIN

mental Renaissance forms than its staid Georgian cousin, the style featured tall, narrow windows with rounded arches often including incised or relief ornament, and high-stooped entrances accentuating the vertical rhythm of the style. Lower stoops typified the Anglo-Italianate style, adapted to Manhattan's narrow building lots. Executed in frame, brick and stone, the style is the basis for both New York brownstones and the typical cast-iron commercial facades, seen clearly in the E.V. Haughwout Building in lower Manhattan. More elaborate homes adopted the Italian-villa variant, with a Classical cupola, rusticated corner quoins, pediments and paired or arcaded windows.

SECOND EMPIRE (1860–1880)

Inspired by Baron Haussmann's redesign of Paris in the 1850s, this grandiose style is characterized by a short, steeply-pitched mansard roof pierced by dormer windows. Generally symmetrical facades include quoined corners, projecting bays, windows flanked by pilasters, balustrades and an abundance of Classical decoration. Often mansard roofs were added to Italianate buildings in a close approximation of the style. Good examples include the former Arnold Constable and Lord & Taylor stores on Broadway.

ROMANESQUE REVIVAL (1860–1900)

Suggestive of medieval castles, the round arches, deeply inset window and door openings, and rough stone finishes of the Romanesque style inspired architects attempting to create a sense of permanence in the rapidly changing landscape of industrial America. The style was refined by Boston architect H.H. Richardson and helped define American architecture. The original City of Brooklyn Firehouse on Jay Street and the American Museum of Natural History are excellent examples of the style.

QUEEN ANNE (1880–1905)

This style is the one most commonly identified as "Victorian," with its asymmetrical composition, exuberant ornamentation and picturesque design marked by conical towers, projecting bays and elaborately decorated dormers and gables. The style is seen primarily in residential architecture like the Henderson Place Historic District.

CHICAGO SCHOOL (1885–1905)

The new structural technology of the steel frame allowed for the development of the first skyscrapers in Chicago in the 1880s. The design of these buildings celebrated their engineering and purpose, summed up by Louis Sullivan's phrase "Form follows function" and expressed in a gridlike facade of brick or terra-cotta, pierced by large panes of glass. The earliest skyscrapers adopted elements of Queen Anne and Romanesque design, and by the late 1890s incorporated the Beaux-Arts as well. Sullivan's 12-story Bayard-Condict Building (1899) on Bleecker Street bears the architect's characteristic foliate ornamentation.

NEOCLASSICAL OR BEAUX-ARTS (1890–1920)

As architecture became an established profession in the 19C, a study of Classical orders at Paris' famous École des Beaux-Arts became de rigueur. At the same time, the success of Chicago's 1893 World's Columbian Exposition popularized the monumental forms of the Roman republic. Unlike the simpler Greek Revival style, Beaux-Arts architecture is more ornamental and sumptuous. Arched and arcaded windows, balustrades at every level, grand staircases, applied columns, deco-

Flatiron Building, detail

rative swags, garlands and even statuary embellish the edifices. The New York Public Library (1911), Grand Central Terminal (1913) and US Custom House (1907) at Bowling Green are premier examples of the style. Daniel Burnham's 1902 Flatiron Building made the style popular for skyscrapers.

ECLECTIC REVIVALS (1900–1925)

The plasticity of terra-cotta and the search for appropriate forms to herald the dawn of the American empire made a wide range of historical styles achievable and popular in the first three decades of the 20C. The Beaux-Arts evolved into Georgian Revival and Renaissance Revival styles used for clubs, town houses, hotels and apartment buildings. Gothic Revival distinguished schools like Hunter College and came to be called Collegiate Gothic. Colonial Revival was the preferred suburban house style, and Moorish, Tudor, Egyptian and Chinese designs encrusted numerous buildings, especially theaters. The increasing eclecticism of skyscraper design literally reached a new height with Cass Gilbert's Gothic-inspired Woolworth Building.

ART DECO/MODERNE (1925–1940)

Rejecting the historical ornament applied to commercial buildings in the 1910s, Art Deco first appeared as a style of decoration during the 1925 Exposition Internationale des Arts Décoratifs et Industriels Modernes in Paris. New York's 1916 zoning law, which called for skyscrapers to "step back" to provide light and air to the street, helped define the architectural aspects of Art Deco, which utilized setbacks, recessed windows and spandrels, and continuous piers to emphasize verticality. Designed in smooth stone or shiny terra-cotta surfaces, edifices featured highly stylized decorative and sculptural elements in low relief with a pronounced muscularity and abstraction. The Chrysler Building, Empire State Building and Rockefeller Center are landmark examples.

©Peter Wrenn/MICHELIN

Sculpture for Living building

INTERNATIONAL STYLE (1930–1970)

Applied ornament was abandoned altogether for sleek, sculptural lines in buildings, furniture and other designed objects, summarized by Mies van der Rohe's dictum "Less is more." Concrete, glass and steel were celebrated in buildings with box-like massing set in open plazas. Exterior walls of glass and steel derived their design from proportion and materials alone, allowing the structures to express their function. The Lever House by Skidmore, Owings & Merrill (1952) and the Seagram Building by Mies van der Rohe (1958) are famous early International-style high rises.

POST-MODERN (1975–PRESENT)

This style is recognizable by its cavalier application of historical references and materials to modern steel-frame buildings. Surfaces of stone and mirrored glass are generally more colorful and modulated than their rigid and severe International-style predecessors, and elements of Classical architecture reappear on a grand scale. The AT&T Headquarters (1984, Johnson & Burgee)—now Sony Plaza—introduced post-Modernism to the nation with its whimsical "Chippendale" roofline, which resembles the top of a colonial cupboard. Philip Johnson and John Burgee's elliptical pink tower at 995 Third Avenue (1986)—the so-called Lipstick Building—captures the playfulness of post-Modernism.

The newest trend is to blend post-Modern design with "green" building principles. Sir Norman Foster's 42-story accordion-like Hearst Tower (2006) does that marvelously, using recycled steel, natural light and energy-efficient heating and cooling systems without sacrificing aesthetic appeal.

Visual Arts

Preoccupied with settling their new nation, colonial New Yorkers had little time to spend painting or sculpting for other than the most practical reasons. The art of portraiture, though popular, was more a craft, practiced by itinerants and painters who had other livelihoods. In the decorative and household arts, ethnic custom and functionality reigned. Because of such practicality, New York became a center of cabinet- and silver making long before its fairly recent ascent as a hub of the visual arts. Silversmith Cornelius Kierstede and furniture maker Duncan Phyfe stand out among early New York's finest artisans.

HUDSON RIVER SCHOOL

The painters of the first distinctly American school of painting (1825-75) took their main inspiration from the dramatic scenery of the Hudson River Valley north of New York City. Artists **Thomas Cole** (1801-48), Asher B. Durand, Albert Bierstadt and Frederic E. Church embraced a romantic vision of nature and art, and imbued epic portrayals of America's grandiose landscapes with moral and transcendental meaning. These painters were among the many artists who swelled the ranks of the new art academies established in the city during the period, including the National Academy of Design (1825) and the Art Students League (1875).

EMERGENCE OF MODERN ART

Founded in 1908, the artistic group "The Eight" sought to rebel against the conservatism of the New York academic establishment. Dubbed the **Ashcan school** in derisive reference to its bald urban realism, "The Eight" (particularly its most prominent members Robert Henri, George Luks and John Sloan) produced vivid, sympathetic portrayals of the rough edges of urban life, which inspired a rich tradition of 20C American Realism (George Bellows and Edward Hopper) and found parallels in Jacob Riis' and Lewis W. Hine's docu-

New York Historical Society

Catskill Creek (1845) by Thomas Cole

mentary photographs of the immigrant population.

Photographer Alfred Stieglitz exhibited avant-garde European art in his Little Galleries of the Photo Secession from 1905 to 1917. Also known as "291," Stieglitz' gallery served as a launching pad for New York's first Modernist painters Arthur Dove, John Marin and Georgia O'Keeffe. The watershed event in the history of modern art in America was New York's 1913 **Armory Show**, or International Exhibition of Modern Art, which displayed more than 1,300 objects – including works by European post-Impressionists, Fauvists and Cubists – and introduced the most recent European art to a largely unprepared and bewildered American public. Marcel Duchamp's Cubist-inspired *Nude Descending a Staircase* provoked particular controversy. Despite the hostile public response, the exhibit attracted important collectors and can be credited with encouraging the tradition of patronage, which culminated in the founding of the Museum of Modern Art in 1929, the Whitney Museum of American Art in 1931 and the Guggenheim Foundation in 1937. After World War I, aspects of abstraction were explored by Stuart Davis, Patrick Henry Bruce and Charles Sheeler. The Great Depression brought an insular mood and public programs that fostered the social realism of Reginald Marsh and the mural painting of Thomas Hart Benton.

THE BALANCE SHIFTS

Prior to the 1930s many American artists traveled abroad to study and observe the latest developments in experimental art. However, as war fermented and the Great Depression lingered in Europe, foreign artists fled to New York. The arrival of Frenchmen Fernand Léger and André Masson, Spaniard Joan Miró, and Germans Josef Albers and Max Ernst brought an unprecedented opportunity for direct contact with Surrealist and Abstract art. In the decade after World War II, a true American avant-garde flowered, and New York emerged as a cultural mecca and world leader in the production and promotion of modern art. This period of fertile artistic activity culminated in the first radical American artistic movement, **Abstract Expressionism** (1946–late 1950s). Also known as the New York school, the Abstract Expressionists were divided among Action or Gesture painters (Jackson Pollock, Willem de Kooning, Franz Kline, Robert Motherwell and Clyfford Still), who emphasized the use of thick, sweeping brush strokes or dripped paint in the spontaneous, intuitive act of painting; and Color Field painters (Mark Rothko, Barnett Newman), who employed equally large but color-saturated canvases to envelop the spectator in meditative calm. As the Abstract Expressionists received international recognition, postwar American affluence prompted collecting and gallery activity. New York gradually came to the fore, replacing Paris as the epicenter of the art world. The late 1950s saw new artistic developments inspired by Abstract Expressionists: the brilliantly colored canvases of Stain Painting (Helen Frankenthaler), the simplified color fields of Hard Edge Painting (Al Held, Kenneth Noland) and the dramatic, shaped canvases of Frank Stella. In the 1960s, artists Roy Lichtenstein, Robert Rauschenberg, Andy Warhol and Claes Oldenburg debunked the high-art notions of Abstract Expressionism and irreverently employed comic-strip subjects and billboard painting techniques in the production of **Pop Art**. Also emerging in reaction to Abstract Expressionism, 1960s **Minimalist** sculptors (Donald Judd, Carl Andre) used non-referential, geometric industrial forms to produce works of immediate and bold impact. The 1970s witnessed **Conceptual art**, whose adherents – environmental sculptors and performance artists – proposed ideas rather than the collectible object as the essence of art, and the revival of Realism (Chuck Close, Alex Katz and George Segal).

A CHANGING SCENE

The richly pluralistic artistic atmosphere of the 1980s and 90s embraced the post-Modern movements of neo-Expressionism (Julian Schnabel, David Salle), Graffiti art (Keith Haring, Jean-Michel Basquiat) and neo-Conceptualism (Barbara Kruger,

Jenny Holzer), along with long-standing traditions of representation and painterly abstraction. In recent years, subjects anatomical, political and environmental have inspired artists on the leading edge – among them Damien Hirst and the "young British artists" who invaded New York in the Brooklyn Museum's "Sensation" show in 1999. Contemporary art can be viewed today in the galleries of SoHo, the East and the West villages, West Chelsea and TriBeCa, as well as in New York's many museums.

Outdoor Sculpture

Manhattan's plazas, courtyards and open spaces have long been used as showcases for the city's monumental sculpture. In fact, some of the world's greatest sculptors have been called upon to adorn the city's public places with their works of art. As you visit Manhattan, be on the lookout for the works listed below, which represent only a selection of 20C outdoor sculpture gracing New York City's streetscapes.

Downtown		
The Red Cube (1967)	Isamu Noguchi	Plaza in front of Marine Midland Bank
Group of Four Trees (1972)	Jean Dubuffet	Plaza in front of Chase Manhattan Bank
Untitled (1973)	Yu Yu Yang	Plaza in front of Wall Street Plaza
American Merchant Mariner Memorial (1991)	Marisol	Battery Park
Shadows and Flags (1977)	Louise Nevelson	Louise Nevelson Plaza, intersection of Maiden Lane, William & Liberty Sts.
Gay Liberation (1980)	George Segal	Christopher Park, at Christopher St. & Sheridan Square
Alamo (1967)	Bernard Rosenthal	Astor Place, Lafayette & W. 8th Sts.

Midtown		
Eye of Fashion (1976)	Robert M. Cronbach	Fashion Institute of Technology Plaza, at W. 27th St. & Seventh Ave.
The Garment Worker (1984)	Judith Weller	Plaza at 555 Seventh Ave., at W. 39th St
Prometheus (1934)	Paul Manship	Lower Plaza, Rockefeller Center
Atlas (1937)	Lee Lawrie	In front of International Building, Rockefeller Center
News (1940)	Isamu Noguchi	Associated Press Building, Rockefeller Center
Lapstrake (1987)	Jésus Bautista Moroles	Plaza in front of 31 W. 52nd St.
Looking Toward the Avenue (1989)	Jim Dine	Crédit Lyonnias Building plaza, Sixth Ave. between 52nd & 53rd Sts.
Virgin Mother (2005)	Damien Hirst	Lever House Courtyard, 390 Park Ave, between 52nd & 53rd
Peace Form One (1980)	Daniel Larue Johnson	Ralph J. Bunche Park, United Nations
No. 9 (1974)	Ivan Chermayeff	9 W. 57th St.
Moonbird	Joan Miró	58th St. plaza of 9 W. 57th St

Uptown		
Reclining Figure (1965)	Henry Moore	Plaza Pool, Lincoln Center
Romeo and Juliet (1977)	Milton Hebald	Central Park, near entrance to Delacorte Theater at W. 81st St.
Night Presence IV (1972)	Louise Nevelson	Park Ave. & 92nd St.

Literature

In the rich literary life of contemporary America, New York is no doubt the most vital force. Indeed, the Naked City is home to many notable figures in fiction and journalism, from Walt Whitman to Norman Mailer, each celebrating the city's enduring vibrancy.

EARLY LITERATI

Two kinds of writers have left an indelible mark on New York's literary scene: those who were born here and those who came here as to a cultural mecca, adopting the city as their own with an almost religious fervor. The first of the latter group was probably "Common Sense" author and patriot Thomas Paine, who spent his last years in Greenwich Village at the dawn of the 19C. New York City typified the confidence and spunk of the young Republic at the time, although literary themes remained pastoral rather than urban. One of America's first literary giants was New York City-born **Washington Irving** (1783-1859). In his 1807 satirical essay collection Salmagundi, he referred to New York City as Gotham – the 13C English village where the inhabitants acted like madmen to prevent King John from residing there. Irving also wrote the parodic *A History of New York from the Beginning of the World to the End of the Dutch Dynasty* (1809) under the name Diedrich Knickerbocker, translated as "baker of marbles." He achieved lasting fame in America with *Rip Van Winkle* (1819) and *The Legend of Sleepy Hollow* (1820).

Best known for his work *The Last of the Mohicans*, contemporary **James Fenimore Cooper** (1789-1851) lived in the city in the 1820s and wrote *The Pioneers* and *The Pilot* here, finding adventure not in the city but at sea and in the wilds of the frontier.

Herman Melville (1819-91) was born and lived most of his life in New York, writing his great seafaring saga *Moby-Dick* here and continuing the literary tradition of the early 19C that focused on wilderness and adventure. Melville also set pieces in and around the city, including "Bartleby the Scrivener," an early perspective on the commercial metropolis. **Clement Clarke Moore** (1779-1863) resided south of 23rd Street in Chelsea, where he wrote the famous poem "A Visit from St. Nicholas," that defined the modern image of Santa Claus.

LATE 19TH-CENTURY NEW YORK

By the mid-1800s, Americans had grown aware of their distinct national character, defined in part by the frontier but also by the energy generated through booming economic and technological growth.

The Red Cube by Isamu Noguchi

©Shea Dean

The Industrial Revolution brought about a transformation in the circumstances of life, changing forever the importance of the city, culture and morality. The new morality of the modern world was epitomized by one of America's greatest poets, **Walt Whitman** (1819-92). Born in New York City, Whitman worked as reporter and editor for the *Brooklyn Eagle* in the 1840s, developing his forceful physical style and pathbreaking sensuality in the bustling metropolis. Shortly after the first edition of *Leaves of Grass* in 1855, he served as editor for the *Brooklyn Times* and continued to capture the lusty spirit of his city in works like the classic *Crossing Brooklyn Ferry*.

Henry James (1843-1916) reversed the traditional role of writers coming to New York seeking fame. Born in the city, he set several novels and stories in New York, including *Washington Square* (1880), but spent most of his literary career as an expatriate in London, where he published his most famous work, *The Turn of the Screw*, in 1898. He returned to write *The American Scene* in 1907 but died a British subject in 1916. New York native **Edith Wharton** (1862-1937) berated and celebrated the Gilded Age of her hometown in novels like *The Age of Innocence*, which won the Pulitzer prize. The great romantic Gothicist **Edgar Allan Poe** (1809-49) lived in the Bronx in the 1840s as well as in Greenwich Village and wrote several of his poems and stories here, including "The Raven," first published in the *New York Evening Mirror* in 1845. A former *New York Tribune* reporter, **Stephen Crane**

(1871-1900), helped bring the American novel into the big city with *New York City Sketches* and *Maggie: A Girl of the Streets* (1893), gaining his greatest fame with *The Red Badge of Courage* (1894). **Mark Twain** (Samuel Clemens, 1835-1910) reported on the city for several Western newspapers, residing in the Village during his sojourns here. **William Dean Howells** (1837-1920), the "dean of American letters," came to New York in 1889 to serve as a *Harper's* magazine editor. By the late 19C, the city had become the literary capital of the US, surpassing Boston and Philadelphia. The lure was so strong that English poet laureate John Masefield scrubbed floors in a saloon to support his New York address in the 1890s.

BOHEMIAN ENCLAVE

By the 1910s, Greenwich Village had become the country's bohemia, attracting avant-garde writers, artists and thespians, including playwright **Eugene O'Neill** (1888-1953), poet **Edna St. Vincent Millay** (1892-1950), author **Theodore Dreiser** (1871-1945) and poet **Edwin Arlington Robinson** (1869-1935). O'Neill based *The Iceman Cometh* and his 1921 Pulitzer prize-winning *Anna Christie* on his 1916 forays in the Village, while Millay used the neighborhood as the setting for *Second April* and *Renascence*. The radical aspects of Village life included the socialist magazines *Seven Arts* and *The Masses*, the latter involving revolutionaries Max Eastman, Art Young, John Reed and Floyd Dell. Poet **Marianne Moore** (1887-1972) arrived in the city in 1921, becoming editor of the *Dial* in 1925 and living out her life in Brooklyn. She was followed in 1923 by North Carolina transplant **Thomas Wolfe** (1900-38), who wrote *Look Homeward, Angel* in 1929 and *You Can't Go Home Again* (published 1940). F. Scott Fitzgerald (1896-1940) brought his party to town on more than one occasion as the city cemented its cultural position in the late 1920s.

As the Village continued its ferment, the midtown Algonquin Hotel became host to the Thanatopsis, Literary Inside Straight and **Round Table** clubs. The latter group became an institution, led by drama critic and raconteur Alexander Woolcott, col-

Washington Irving

Historic Hudson Valley

umnist Franklin P. Adams, and three figures associated with The **New Yorker** magazine: editor Harold Ross, author Dorothy Parker and humorist **Robert Benchley**. Established in 1925, the *New Yorker* elevated the standard of American discourse to a new, articulate and sophisticated level. For three generations its writing and criticism have attracted a nationwide audience, and its list of contributors includes many of the greatest 20C American writers, including essayists E.B. White and Edmund Wilson; novelists J.D. Salinger, Saul Bellow, John O'Hara and John Updike; film critic Pauline Kael; humorists James Thurber and Calvin Trillin; and musicologist Whitney Baillett.

AFRICAN-AMERICAN LETTERS

The concentration of African Americans in Manhattan's Harlem neighborhood after the turn of the century created an atmosphere of independence and cultural pride that fostered the 1920s awakening known as the Harlem Renaissance. Even earlier, pioneering poet and author **Paul Laurence Dunbar** (1872-1906), living in the African-American bohemia of the Tenderloin, had celebrated the black spirit in his 1902 *Sport of the Gods*. **W.E.B. DuBois**' *The Souls of Black Folk* (1903) brought recognition to the problem of the "color line"; he formed the NAACP in New York with poet James Weldon Johnson and others in 1909.

But it was the rapid growth and sometime prosperity of Harlem after 1910 that nurtured the greatest flowering of African-American arts and literature in the 1920s. **Alain Locke**'s 1925 *The New Negro: An Interpretation* summarized the attitude and expectations of a community that found, in New York City, the support and freedom to express itself. **Langston Hughes** (1902-67) captured the streets of Harlem in *The Weary Blues* (1926) and recognized that Harlem was no longer simply a place but a symbol of African-American identity. Other important poets included Countee Cullen (1903-46), with *One Way to Heaven* (1932), and James Weldon Johnson (1871-1938), who released *The Book of American Negro Poetry* in 1922. Novelists included Jean Toomer (1894-1967), author of *Cane* (1923); West

> *"There is no place like [New York], no place with an atom of its glory, pride, and exultancy. It lays its hand upon a man's bowels; he grows drunk with ecstasy; he grows young and full of glory, he feels that he can never die."*
>
> **Thomas Wolfe**
> from *Death to Morning* (1935)

Indian native Claude McKay (1890-1948), who wrote *Home to Harlem* (1928); and **Zora Neale Hurston** (1891-60), whose landmark *Their Eyes Were Watching God* was published in 1937, when the stark realities of the Great Depression and racism had eclipsed the optimism of the Harlem Renaissance.

COMING OUT OF THE DEPRESSION

The Great Depression marked a respite in New York's literary history as the city's urban atmosphere provided the backdrop for Ellery Queen mysteries and for sophisticated sleuths Nick and Nora Charles in Dashiell Hammett's *The Thin Man*. New York-born **Henry Miller** (1891-1980) went bumming around Paris in the 1930s, where he wrote the pathbreaking *Tropic of Cancer* before returning to the city in 1940 and then relocating to the West Coast. New Yorker **John Dos Passos** (1896-1970) served up his critique of the nation in the novels *USA* and *Manhattan Transfer*. *Day of the Locust* author **Nathanael West** (1903-40) was born Nathan Weinstein in New York City before moving on to Hollywood. Others continued to make the pilgrimage to New York, including Spanish poet and playwright Federico García Lorca (*Poet in New York*) and Russian poet Vladimir Mayakovsky (*Brooklyn Bridge*).

POSTWAR PENMANSHIP

New York emerged from World War II more powerful, attractive and determined than ever as it sought to become the world's cultural capital. **Norman Mailer**'s hard-bitten, macho New York style rocked the world in 1948 with his sensational novel *The Naked and the Dead*. He continues to serve as a literary native son for the increasingly cosmopolitan metropolis. Playwright **Arthur Miller** (1915-2005) wrote the epochal *Death of a Salesman* in 1949. The 1950s saw the great Welsh poet **Dylan Thomas** (1914-53) succumb to the lure of New York City and an excess of drink at the White Horse Tavern.

In the 1950s and 60s, New York evolved into the cultural capital of the Jet Age, as writers, artists and aesthetes gathered in Greenwich Village's Cedar Tavern, fostering the spontaneity and experimentation of New York-school poets like Frank O'Hara and Barbara Guest and beats like **Allen Ginsberg** (1926-97), Jack Kerouac and Gregory Corso. The period marked a resurgence of African-American literature in New York, with poet **Amiri Baraka** (LeRoi Jones) and author **James Baldwin**, whose important novels *Go Tell It on the Mountain* (1952) and *Another Country* (1962) are set in the city. Langston Hughes achieved new levels of poetry and commentary with *Shakespeare in Harlem* (1942) and *Montage of a Dream Deferred* (1951), while **Ralph Ellison** (1914-94) fired an early civil rights salvo in 1952's *Invisible Man*.

A LIVING TRADITION

During a 1963 newspaper strike, editors Robert E. Silver and Barbara Epstein founded one of the most important literary publications of the 20C, the *New York Review of Books*, now a biweekly that is indispensable to the serious and amateur critic alike. New York City is often the centerpiece for American comedies and slice-of-life dramas, as exemplified by comic playwrights **Neil Simon** and **Wendy Wasserstein**, and film directors **Woody Allen** and **Spike Lee**. The Black Arts movement of the 1960s brought **Nikki Giovanni**, **Maya Angelou** and **Gil Scott-Heron** to a growing audience that had become national in scope by the 1980s. **E.L. Doctorow** captured modern Gotham in a series of tragic and violent novels, including *Ragtime* (1978) and *Billy Bathgate* (1989). The moral vacuity of the 1980s provided the setting for **Tom Wolfe**'s searing *Bonfire of the Vanities* (1987), while Oscar Hijuelos' Pulitzer prize-winning *The Mambo Kings Play Songs of Love* (1989) captured the rhythms of the city's Cuban community. In *Underworld* (1997), Don DeLillo weaves the Bronx of the 1950s and 1990s into a complex tapestry of the postwar era. Other leading New York authors include Gore Vidal, Paul Auster and the late Susan Sontag, The Nuyorican Poets Café in Alphabet City, propelled by its weekly poetry slams, has in recent years become a mecca for an exuberant, multicultural spokenword movement. The city continues to draw literary pilgrims from across America and the globe, seeking critical approval, publishing opportunities and the manifold inspiration presented by the city's ongoing human drama.

Spectator Sports

Since the 1920s New York's teams and its athletes have played in the limelight of the world's media capital. First there was **Babe Ruth** (1895-1948), who came to the city in 1920 as a great ballplayer and in a few years became an immortal. The Babe's Yankees are, of course, the prime symbol of the city's dominance, but are only one of a total of nine professional sports teams in the four major sports—baseball, basketball, football and hockey.

BASEBALL

The very first baseball games were played in Manhattan in the 1840s by players such as Alexander Joy Cartwright who formalized the layout of the diamond and the rules of the game. In October 1845, he and

Arthur Miller (1967)

Hulton Archive - Getty Images

others organized themselves as the New York Knickerbockers, the game's first team. The city entered the big leagues for good with the formation of the New York Giants in 1883, and by 1924 the team had won 10 pennants in 20 years under manager John McGraw. The Polo Grounds, their horseshoe-shaped home in upper Manhattan (shared with the Yankees until Babe Ruth's popularity led McGraw to evict them), was the site of one of baseball's enduring moments: "the Catch," made by **Willie Mays**, running full speed, back turned to the plate, in the 1954 World Series. The Giants' nemesis, the Brooklyn Dodgers, lost when they were bad and lost in heartbreaking fashion when they were good. No matter. Brooklynites flocked to Ebbets Field to root for "dem bums." In 1947 **Jackie Robinson** (1919-72) broke baseball's color line, heralding the Civil Rights movement. Robinson, Duke Snider and the Boys of Summer were the class of the league in the 1950s. Noted for their succession of strong arms (Tom Seaver, Jerry Koosman, Dwight Gooden) at pitcher-friendly Shea Stadium (◉ see Queens), the expansion Mets are loved less for their dominance than for their underdog spirit. The Yankees (who were, like Babe Ruth, born in Baltimore) moved to New York in 1903, their third season. In 100 years the team has won 39 American League pennants and 26 World Series.

The team's pantheon of sluggers—the Babe, **Lou Gehrig, Joe DiMaggio, Mickey Mantle, Yogi Berra, Reggie Jackson**—have all achieved a fame that transcends the game. With the 1996 arrival of manager Joe Torre and short-stop Derek Jeter, the latest Yankees dynasty won six pennants and four World Series between 1996 and 2003. In 2005, 2006 and 2007 the team made it to the playoffs, only to lose in the first round.

FOOTBALL

New Yorkers didn't catch football fever, until 1925, when Tim Mara started the Giants in the fledgling NFL. That year, 70,000 filled the Polo Grounds to see the team take on Red Grange and the Chicago Bears. Season tickets to "Big Blue" games, at Yankee Stadium, and since 1976 at Giants Stadium in the Meadowlands, have been handed down through the generations. The team's loss in the 2001 Super Bowl to the Baltimore Ravens evoked memories of the 1958 Championship Game, "the Greatest Football Game Ever Played," a seesaw battle it lost in overtime to the Baltimore Colts. The underdog Jets' 1969 Super Bowl victory over, once again, the Colts, "guaranteed" by flamboyant quarterback "Broadway" **Joe Namath**, legitimized the upstart AFL and paved the way for the leagues' eventual merger.

The Subway Series

From 1947 to 1956, coinciding with the city's postwar golden era, the Yankees played seven (and won six) Subway Series (World Series matches involving only NYC teams) against the Dodgers and Giants. In 1951 no fan was left out: Giant Bobby Thomson's "shot heard round the world" off Dodger Ralph Branca decided a three-game play-off for the pennant. Then, in the World Series, with Brooklyn fans' approval, the Yankees beat the Giants. The Dodgers' 1955 victory over the Yanks marked Brooklyn's brightest moment, a mood captured by the Daily News' front page: a drawing of an ecstatic hobo under the headline "Who's a Bum?" The Yankees won the 1956 rematch, and a year later, the Giants and Dodgers moved west, prompting, fans presume, the city's decline. New York's recent resurgence seemed to augur the Subway Series' return. And in 2000 it came to be. The Mets assumed the Dodgers' role of outer-borough underdog, and fans hoped for miracles. Fiery Mets manager Bobby Valentine, son-in-law of Ralph Branca, faced off against his stoic counterpart, onetime Mets manager Joe Torre, a Brooklyn kid who saw Don Larsen's perfect game against the Dodgers in the 1956 Series. The city turned inward. A base hit or clean stop cheered on the Grand Concourse was met with stony silence in Astoria and Benson-hurst. And vice versa. The old days had returned to New York. Predictably, the Yankees won in five games.

BASKETBALL

New York basketball is first and foremost a street game. Only blizzards interrupt half-court games of "21." Not surprisingly, New York has sent a stream of flashy point guards to the pros, from Bob Cousy to Stephon Marbury. Atop the city's hoops world sits the Knicks, an original NBA franchise whose legendary early-1970s squad, led by Willis Reed, Walt "Clyde" Frazier, and "Dollar" **Bill Bradley**, twice won championships. After a period of decline, the team rebounded with the hiring of Pat Riley as coach in 1991; fans flocked to Madison Square Garden to cheer (and boo) center Pat Ewing and the intimidating, defense-oriented Knicks. Born with the ABA in 1967, the Nets, featuring the gravity-defying **"Dr. J," Julius Erving**, enjoyed early success and a few ABA titles. The team entered the NBA in 1976, then moved to New Jersey, where they remained on the periphery of the city's sports consciousness until 2002, when they rocketed to the NBA finals as the Knicks team disintegrated. The Nets returned to the NBA finals in 2003, losing to the San Antonio Spurs.

HOCKEY

One of the NHL's "original six" teams, the Rangers, and the team's intensely loyal fans, had suffered through a 54-year drought between championships when **Mark Messier**, exiled from Edmonton, led the squad to a Stanley Cup in 1994. The Islanders, an expansion team formed in 1972, quickly assembled a nucleus of eventual Hall of Famers (**Bryan Trottier, Mike Bossy, Denis Potvin**) whose graceful play won four straight Stanley Cups in the early 1980s and helped transform the game's roughhouse image. The Islanders made it to the play-offs in 2007, but the New Jersey Devils, who arrived from Colorado in 1982, are generally regarded as the area's best team. Their tenacious defense, spearheaded by goalie **Martin Brodeur**, has brought them three Stanley Cups—in 1995, 2000, and 2003—and a sizable following.

BOXING

John L. Sullivan (1858-1918) fought at the first Madison Square Garden, located in, yes, Madison Square, in 1883. In subsequent years and incarnations, the Garden became the country's boxing mecca. The current Garden was the site of the famous 1971 Ali-Frazier fight. Yankee Stadium also hosted key bouts, including **Joe Louis'** (1914-81) victory over German Max Schmeling, before 70,000 fans. The ascendance of Las Vegas and Atlantic City as boxing locales spelled the end of the city's preeminence.

OTHER

The **Belmont Stakes**, the third leg of thoroughbred racing's Triple Crown, is held at Belmont Park, on Long Island. The National Tennis Center in Flushing Meadows hosts the US Open, a grand-slam event. Lifelong New Yorker **John McEnroe**, famous for his big mouth, short fuse and quirky, brilliant play, won the tournament four times, to the delight of local fans. Brazilian soccer legend Pélé, playing for the Cosmos, electrified New York in the mid-1970s, though local enthusiasm, and the league itself, petered out a few years later. The famed **New York City Marathon**, held the first Sunday in November, draws some 30,000 runners and more than 2 million spectators.

THE CITY TODAY

The New York area has the largest concentration of people, income, finance, industry and transportation of any urban area in the US. New York streets have long been synonymous with some of the city's key industries: Wall Street with finance, Broadway with entertainment, Madison Avenue with advertising and Seventh Avenue with fashion. Today some 8 million people live in New York City, twice as many as in any other American city.

The Economy

New York's $450 billion economy would rank 17th among the nations of the world. The powerful economy provides more than 3.7 million people, and local real estate is worth more than $800 billion. The city is home to the headquarters of 44 Fortune 500 companies.

SHIPPING

New York's sheltered, ice-free harbor and 750mi of shoreline are easily accessible to the Atlantic. The port is the nation's third largest, although the advent of containership technology has forced most active piers from crowded Manhattan to roomier sites in Brooklyn, Staten Island and New Jersey, where the world's largest container terminal is at Port Newark/Elizabeth. More than 60 shipping lines serve the port. In 2004 the harbor handled $110 billion worth of cargo.

The Port Authority of New York and New Jersey manages the harbor's general cargo and containership terminals; six tunnels and bridges connecting the city with New Jersey; the region's major bus terminal on West 42nd Street; the Port Authority TransHudson (PATH) rapid-transit rail system; three major airports; and a heliport. The Port Authority built and owned the World Trade Center; it retains ownership of the site and is playing an important role in determining its future.

FINANCE

The city is home to two of the country's three largest commercial banks, owned by financial services titans Citigroup and J.P. Morgan Chase, which have combined commercial banking assets of two trillion dollars. In mid-2004, J.P. Morgan Chase merged with Bank One Corporation, boosting the company to No. 2 behind

Inside the New York Stock Exchange

Courtesy NYSE

The Fifth Avenue Street Sign

Citigroup. Citigroup comprises Citibank, insurance giant Travelers and brokerage house Salomon Smith Barney. All major financial institutions, domestic and foreign, maintain a presence in New York; among them are 219 foreign banks, including 20 of the top 25 foreign branches of international banks. More than 85 percent of US-based stock trades are conducted here, notably on Wall Street's New York Stock Exchange, the largest stock exchange in the world by dollar volume. The 2,764 companies listed by the NYSE had a combined value of $25 trillion in December 2006.

TRANSPORTATION

New York is the only US city accessible by three major airports (John F. Kennedy, LaGuardia and Newark Liberty), which annually handle more than 100 million passengers. Travelers also arrive via a rail and bus network that brings in a million people daily, mostly commuters. The streets of New York are served by 12,778 taxicabs and 6,202 buses. The subway system, stretching from Coney Island to the North Bronx, with some 468 stations, serves 4.9 million passengers a day. The free Staten Island Ferry takes more than 100 trips a day, conveying 65,000 passengers.

MEDIA

New York also reaches out to the world through communications. The city is home to four major television networks (ABC, NBC, CBS and Fox) and numerous cable channels (MTV, HBO, Biography). Its film industry is the largest in the US after Hollywood, employing 100,000 New Yorkers and generating $5 billion for the city's economy each year.

The city is also the nation's print capital. Home to Time/Life, Hearst and Condé Nast among other Midtown magazine empires, New York churns out some 350 consumer magazines. Major publishing houses McGraw-Hill and Random House also have headquarters in the area. Four of the ten largest newspapers in the United States are based in New York: the *New York Times, Post* and *Daily News,* and the *Wall Street Journal.* Madison Avenue still the nation's advertising capital.

HIGH-TECH

The city's high-tech industry is growing rapidly: telecom and cable companies, together with Internet service providers and publishers, constituted a $23 billion industry in 2003 and employed 43,000 city residents. In a move that augurs well for the future of the new-media sector, in 2006 Google chose New York's Chelsea neighborhood for its largest engineering complex outside of company headquarters in Mountain View, California. Five hundred people are employed at the new facility.

MANUFACTURING

Manufacturing's share of the economy has long been declining – from 900,000 jobs in 1950 to 233,000 today; first-generation immigrants account for 64 percent of these workers. Still, New York's highly diverse industrial sector base comprises more than 10,000 establishments, many relying on a reservoir of specialized labor skills. Food processing is a $5 billion industry that employs 19,000 residents. Apparel manufacturing, employing about 60,000 people, brings about $3 billion to the city annually.

TOURISM AND CULTURE

Visitors to New York are drawn by the city's glamour, fine dining and shopping, and cultural attractions. In 2006, New York welcomed nearly 36 million visitors, who spent more than $24 billion. Internationally, Great Britain sends the most visitors to the city, followed by Canada and Germany.

Theater attendance reached more than 10 million during the 2001-2002 season. Fine art in New York is both an attraction to visitors and an industry in itself. Some 500 art galleries can be found in the city; more than 300 of these are in Chelsea, with smaller clusters of galleries in SoHo and TriBeCa, as well as in Williamsburg and DUMBO (District Under the Manhattan Bridge Overpass) in Brooklyn. One hundred and sixty museums make their home in New York.

Population

A Cosmopolitan Mix

In the 19C and at the beginning of the 20C, recent immigrants, referred to as "hyphenated citizens" (such as Irish-Americans, Italian-Americans, German-Americans and so on), were often denied social status by the "aristocracy" of British and Dutch origin. However, the pyramid of New York society was unable to withstand the forces of change, and today these multicultural strands, together with the more recent waves of immigrants, make up the very fabric of New York's population; indeed 36 percent of the city's population is foreign-born.

THE IRISH

Nearly half a million New Yorkers are of Irish descent, many emigrating to the city during the Irish potato famine in 1846. From the beginning the Irish were drawn to public affairs and city government. Carrying on the religious tradition of their homeland, they have contributed significantly to the influence of the Roman Catholic Church in the US. Irish-Americans are famous for their exuberant celebration of St. Patrick's Day, March 17, to honor their patron saint.

Italian family en route to Ellis Island (c.1905) photograph by Lewis W. Hine

Lewis W. Hine Collection, New York Public Library

ITALIANS

New York's 700,000 Italians make up the second-largest ethnic group in the city. Large-scale immigration, mainly of laborers and peasants from southern Italy and Sicily, started only after 1870. Many Italian immigrants started out in the building industry, where they worked under the heavy hands of padroni (construction bosses); however, over the years, hard work and enterprise often combined to establish small family businesses, especially in restaurants, contracting and trucking. Italian's convivial spirit and love of great food can still be found in Manhattan's Little Italy and on Arthur Avenue in the Bronx.

GERMANS

More than 250,000 New Yorkers claim German ancestry. More than six million Germans arrived in New York between the failed 1848-49 revolution in Germany and World War I. Many settled mostly around Tompkins Square in the East Village, later moving farther uptown. Most Germans rapidly assimilated into New York society, but some German atmosphere can still be found in Yorkville on the Upper East Side.

CHINESE AND SOUTH ASIANS

Coming to the US in the mid-19C to work on railway lines and in mines, Chinese immigrants hailed mainly from Canton. The most recent newcomers, primarily from Hong Kong, Shanghai and Taiwan,

63

have swelled their numbers to more than 360,000, with the greatest concentration living in steadily expanding Chinatowns in Manhattan and Flushing, Queens. In addition, there are approximately 275,000 immigrants from India (226,587), Pakistan (34,310), Bangladesh (18,825), and Sri Lanka (1,094) living in New York.

EASTERN EUROPEANS

Before World War I, the massive waves of immigrants from the old Russian empire were not made up of Russians, but mostly of members of various minority nationalities – Ukrainians, Poles, Lithuanians and others. LThe 1917 Revolution brought only a trickle of so-called White Russians to New York as compared to the large numbers who immigrated to European capitals. Many Ukrainians and Russians, however, were among the displaced persons who settled in New York in the wake of World War II. The former Soviet Union has been a major source of new immigrants to New York; their numbers have increased from 81,000 in 1990 to some 230,000 in 1999. The city's Romanian community is the largest in North America, numbering about 160,000.

JEWS

New York City's population of 972,000 Jews is the largest Jewish population outside of Israel though only half of what it was in 1957, when one-fourth of New Yorkers were Jewish. The decline is mainly attributed to the dispersion of the population to the suburbs but has been tempered by the influx in the 1990s of Jewish immigrants from the former Soviet Union. Sephardic Jews, originally from Spain and Portugal, had come to New York in the 17C, mostly via Holland and Latin America, though today most New York Jews are of Ashkenazi descent. Manhattan's Lower East Side was the first home for 1.5 million Jews who entered America between 1880 and 1910; a great number also settled in Brooklyn communities.

AFRICAN AMERICANS

New York has more African Americans than any other US city, totaling about 1.6 million. Initial black migration came from the American South. In the past two decades, migration from the Caribbean has resulted in a new Caribbean community in upper Manhattan and Brooklyn. The black community has produced distinguished writers, playwrights and performers, and the influence of "rhythm and blues" and jazz has greatly impacted the American musical scene. During recent decades many blacks have availed themselves of educational and economic opportunities offered in New York, though the disparity between black and white New Yorkers in almost all indices – education, income, heath and infant mortality – is still striking and, to many, shameful.

LATINOS

New York City's Puerto Rican population once numbered over a million; now at 800,000, it is still the largest outside of Puerto Rico. All told, the Latino population, including Puerto Ricans, Dominicans, Mexicans, Cubans, Colombians and Ecuadorians, forms more than one-fourth of the city's population, numbering more than 2.1 million in 2000. The major concentration of the Puerto Rican population is in the Bronx, but the heart of New York's Puerto Rican community is East Harlem, better known as El Barrio. Mindful of their culture, Latinos have emerged as a vital community, lending a distinctive flavor to the city.

		POPULATION FROM 1626 TO 2005
1626	200	The first boatload of settlers brought by the Dutch to Nieuw Amsterdam consists primarily of French Huguenots.
1656	1,000	The first immigrants are followed by English, Scots, Germans and Scandinavians.
1800	60,000	Half of New York's population is of English origin.
1850s	630,000	Germans, Irish and Scandinavians arrive in large numbers.
1880	1,911,700	Eastern Europeans and Southern Italians immigrate in great waves; this influx continues until 1924.
1900	3,437,200	This figure includes residents of the five boroughs, which were incorporated in 1898.
1920	5,620,000	After World War I, black migration increases both from the American South and from the West Indies.
1924		Immigration laws limit foreign immigration.
1930	6,930,500	City grows, but growth rate declines.
1950	7,892,000	After World War II many Puerto Ricans settle in New York, topping a million in 1957.
1960	7,782,000	From 1950 to 1960, the city loses more than 100,000 residents to the suburbs.
1970	7,896,000	Out-migration of New York's population from the city to the suburbs continues but is offset by immigration.
1980	7,071,639	Hard times in the 1970s cause many to flee the city.
1990	7,322,600	New York's foreign-born population of two million persons reflects the great influx of immigrants from Asia, Latin America and the Caribbean since 1965.
1995	7,312,000	Population declines slightly.
1999	7,428,162	Newcomers from the former Soviet Union, China, South Asia and Central and South America arrive at a rate of 100,000 a year in the 1990s, offsetting other population losses.
2000	8,008,278	In the new millennium, the city's population tops 8 million.
2003	8,019,033	New York City's Jewish population dips below a million for first time in a century
2005	8,213,839	Population reaches new high and is expected to reach 9.4 million by 2025.

View of Central Park
©Photo Disc

MANHATTAN: DOWNTOWN

MANHATTAN'S AREA: 22.7 SQUARE MILES
MANHATTAN'S POPULATION: 1,537,195

Manhattan is the heart of New York City. The smallest of the city's five boroughs, it's a tongue-shaped island bordered by the Hudson River on the west and the Harlem and East rivers on the east. The island measures only 13.4 miles long—about half the distance of a marathon race—and just 2.3 miles at its widest point.

The Dutch were the first Europeans to settle here, on the southern tip, calling their new territory Nieuw Amsterdam. Blame the Dutch for the irregular street pattern found in the Financial District. Next came the British, expanding settlement northward. Credit the British for the neat grid of numbered streets throughout most of the island.

Downtown New York is New York at its most vital. So many disparate neighborhoods are crowded together, with so much to offer. At the toe of the island lies the **Financial District**, where the city was born in 1625. Today skyscrapers loom over a maze of colonial streets—most famously **Wall Street**—and ferries depart for the **Statue of Liberty** and **Ellis Island**. The World Trade Center once stood here; out of its ashes, New York will see some exciting new buildings rise in coming years.

Directly north of the financial district stands **Civic Center**, seat of city government. **TriBeCa**, to the west, is a warehouse district known for its chi-chi restaurants, design galleries and film festival, spearheaded by actor Robert De Niro. There are still a few rowdy red-sauce joints on Mulberry Street, but for the most part **Little Italy** has been

Union Square, Manhattan

engulfed by sprawling **Chinatown**, where every conceivable kind of jade statue, noodle, fish, dumpling, lantern and, on Canal Street, knock-off handbag, can be found. For the real McCoy (handbag, that is), venture north to **SoHo**, where stores from Armani to Zara have pushed out most (but not all) of the art galleries (roomier **Chelsea** is now New York's prime gallery district). The historic brownstones of **Greenwich Village**, arranged along picture-perfect streets, are a wonder to behold but home to few artists (aside from movie stars): the city's bohemia has shifted to the grittier **Lower East Side** and **East Village**, where Old World immigrants rub shoulders with heavily pierced hipsters. The **Lower East Side** has a hot nightlife scene. From **Union Square** to Madison Square, things get more sedate, especially around Gramercy Park. Midtown begins at 34th Street. Uptown is considered north of 59th Street.

STATUE OF LIBERTY★★★
ELLIS ISLAND★★ AND GOVERNORS ISLAND
MTA SUBWAY: 4 AND 5 TRAINS TO BOWLING GREEN,
R AND W TRAINS TO WHITEHALL STREET OR 1 TRAIN TO SOUTH FERRY

The Statue of Liberty is one of New York City's most popular (and free) attractions. Nothing can compare with standing in front of the colossal statue—her arm raised high with a torch in her hand and broken shackles at her feet. A visit to the Ellis Island Immigration Museum on neighboring Ellis Island should be part of your trip. Some 12 million people gained permanent entry to the US between 1892 and 1954 at this federal "processing center," now restored. East of Liberty Island, Governors Island is home to historic military installations.

🛈 **Information:** National Park Service. ☎212-363-3200. www.nps.gov/stli.

▶ **Orient Yourself:** Accessible only by ferry. All ferries make a circuit that includes Liberty Island and Ellis Island. Ferries *(⊜$11.50 round-trip)* leave every 25min Jun–Aug 8:30am–4:30pm *(rest of the year every 45min 9am–3:30pm)* from **Battery Park** at the southern tip of Manhattan; the ferry ride takes about 15min. Buy advance ferry tickets online or same-day tickets at the ticket office inside Castle Clinton National Monument at Battery Park; advance tickets may be picked up at the Will Call window. Ferries are boarded on a first-come, first-served basis. **Statue Cruises** ☎877-523-9849. www.statuecruises.com. Ferries leave every 45 minutes in summer 8:30am–4:30pm from **Liberty State Park** in New Jersey *(PATH subway to Hoboken; then take the Light Rail to Liberty State Park; open year-round daily 6am–8pm; ☎201-435-9499 ferries, ☎201-915-3440 park; www.state.nj.us/dep/parksandforests)*. No ferry service Dec 25.

🕐 **Organizing Your Time:** Allow a full day for a visit of these islands.

A Bit of History

Birth of a Notion – The friendship between France and the US dates back to the American Revolution. In 1865 French law professor Édouard-René de Laboulaye came up with the idea to present the

Statue of Liberty

National Park Service

American people with a memorial commemorating this friendship. Six years later, the committee he formed to make the idea a reality selected Alsatian sculptor **Frédéric-Auguste Bartholdi** (1834-1904), who then traveled to America to study and promote the project.

In 1869 Bartholdi had attended the opening ceremonies of the Suez Canal in hopes of getting a commission for a huge statue-lighthouse at the entrance to the new canal. Unsuccessful in nabbing the contract, he turned his energy to creating a similar monument in the US.

When he entered New York Harbor, he was overwhelmed by the grandeur of the scene before him, and its significance as the main gateway to the New World. Then and there he knew that de Laboulaye's monument would be a figure of Liberty, and that one of the tiny harbor islands in this breathtaking setting would be an ideal site for it.

To raise funds and coordinate matters regarding the statue, a Franco-American union was established, with de Laboulaye as president. The project was to be a joint effort—the French would underwrite the statue itself, and the Americans, the pedestal.

Liberty on the Rise – As work on the statue progressed, the cost of construction almost doubled. To reach their goal, the French launched a massive fund drive, and by 1884 Liberty Enlightening the World was complete. At a ceremony held July 4, 1884, in Paris, the statue was presented to the ambassador of the US as a gift from the people of France. Following the festivities, Liberty was dismantled and packed in 220 crates, in preparation for the ocean voyage to her permanent home across the Atlantic.

In the meantime little progress had been made in the US in raising funds for the pedestal. Benefit balls, theatrical and sporting events, even a poetry contest were held, and in 1884 Liberty's arm, complete with torch, was exhibited in Madison Square. By 1885 the statue was ready for shipment to the US, but funds were still lacking. Due largely to the fund-raising campaign of **Joseph Pulitzer** (1847-1911), the publisher of the *New York World*, donations were forthcoming. In front-page editorials, he criticized the rich for not providing funds, and encouraged all Americans to contribute as the masses of French people had. He promised to publish in his newspaper the name of every donor, no matter how small the gift. With this, the drive rapidly assumed a new impetus, and contributions began to pour in.

The Dedication – In May 1885 the French ship *Isère*, carrying its precious cargo, set sail from Rouen and about a month later dropped anchor in New York harbor. Bartholdi traveled once more to New York to confer with the engineers and the architect chosen to design the pedestal, **Richard Morris Hunt**, one of the leading American architects of the day. Hunt's final design blended in character and scale to form an integrated unit with the statue. October 28, 1886 – the day the festivities took place – was declared an official holiday in New York City. US president **Grover Cleveland** presided over the unveiling on Bedloe's Island (renamed Liberty Island in 1956). Dignitaries huddled at the foot of the statue while speech after speech was made. When the statue was unveiled, foghorns bellowed and a 21-gun salute sounded from nearby bat-

😊 **A Bit of Advice** 😊

Buy ferry tickets by phone or online at least two days (up to 60 days) in advance. There is a $1.75 surcharge per ticket, but in buying advance tickets you not only avoid long lines but receive a "time stamp" reserving your place on one of the National Park Service tours (👣 *see* VISIT) of the statue. If you have statue tour reservations, get to the boat 2hrs before your scheduled tour time.

Statue of Liberty (close-up)

©iStockphoto.com/Tom Hall

fered degradation in the salty air) and to re-landscape the grounds in time for Liberty's centennial bash. Following the attacks of September 11, 2001, the statue was closed to visitors for three years. The pedestal and observation deck were reopened in late 2004, but the crown remains off limits. The torch has not been accessible since 1916.

Visit

🕐 *There is no entrance fee to the park grounds, which are open year-round daily 8:30am–5:15pm.* 🕐 *Closed Dec 25. National Park Service ☎212-363-3200. www.nps. gov/stli.*

Timed passes are needed for the 🚶‍♀️guided tours, the only way to enter the monument. A limited number of timed passes are available at the ferry ticket office on a first-come, first-served basis. It's best to reserve in advance by calling the ferry company at ☎877-523-9849, or online at www.statuecruises.com.

Ferry Crossing

The *(15min)* ferry crossing offers great **views**★★★ of the lower Manhattan skyline gradually receding into the background, and of the majestic and massive Statue of Liberty standing at the eastern end of the island, above the 11-point-star-shaped Fort Wood (1808-11). To your left, you'll see Governors Island, which can be toured in the summer.

teries. Liberty's crown was illuminated simultaneously, symbolizing prophetically the beacon of hope she would be to the millions who would flock to these shores.

Modern Liberty – For the most part Lady Liberty appears as she did at her dedication. In 1956 Congress approved plans to expand the base of the statue to make room for a museum; the American Museum of Immigration was dedicated in 1972. Between 1984 and 1986 individuals and corporations donated $150 million to repair the statue (the exterior had suf-

---

Lady Liberty's Stats

Lady Liberty contains 125 tons of steel. The verdigrised sheets of copper that form her skin are a mere 3/32-inch thick, but all told they weigh 31 tons. Her concrete foundation weighs 27,000 tons. There are 25 windows in her crown, symbolizing the gemstones found on earth. The seven points of the crown signify liberty radiating to the seven continents and the seven seas. The tablet (23-1/2ft long, 2ft thick) in her left hand represents the Declaration of Independence and is printed with the year of its proclamation in Roman numerals: july iv mdcclxxvi.

Other mind-boggling measurements:

Height from head to toe – 111ft
Height from tip of torch to her toes – 151ft
Height from the tip of torch to the water – 395ft
Right hand – 16-1/2ft long
Index finger – 8ft long

Right arm – 42ft long
Nose – 4ft long
Eyes – each 2 1/2ft wide
Head – 17ft tall, 10ft wide
Waist – 35ft across

How Bartholdi Built It

Frédéric-Auguste Bartholdi began work on the sculpture in 1874. He first made a clay figure 4ft high, and then three successively larger working models in plaster, which were corrected and refined before final dimensions were achieved. Turning his attention to the framework that would support the statue, Bartholdi called upon the skill and knowledge of the inventive French engineer **Gustave Eiffel** (1832-1923), who was later to build the Eiffel Tower. Employing construction techniques similar to the ones used for the skyscrapers of the 1880s, Eiffel created an intricate iron and steel skeletal frame to which 300 copper plates (each 3/32in thick) forming the skin of Liberty were applied.

Liberty Island

Ranger-guided tours of the island's grounds are offered free of charge at regularly scheduled times through the day (staff permitting). Program listings are posted at the island's Administration/Information building. Audio tours in English, Italian, French, German, Spanish and Japanese may be rented from the island's food and gift concessionaire (☜$6).

Originally known as Bedloe's Island, after Isaac Bedloe, a French-born merchant whose family owned it until 1732, the island was chosen as a site, along with Governors Island and Ellis Island, for a land battery in 1800. Begun in 1806, construction of Fort Wood was finished five years later; its zigzagging walls formed an 11-point star. For years the fort lay abandoned; in 1877 its site was chosen as the future home of the Statue of Liberty. You can still see the fortifications.

Bordering the walkway near the Statue of Liberty's pedestal are six slender sculptures by Phillip Ratner of key figures in the history of the statue: de Laboulaye, Bartholdi, Eiffel, Hunt, Pulitzer, and Lazarus.

Inside the Monument

Visitors may enter the monument by guided tour only. There are two tours to choose from. The Promenade Tour (☜1hr) includes the lobby, where the original torch is located, and the Statue of Liberty Exhibit. The Observatory Tour (☜90min) incorporates all the elements of the Promenade Tour, then proceeds to the observatory atop the pedestal, 10 stories above ground level. Here, visitors can wander the deck outside and peer up into the statue's copper interior. Located on the second floor in the pedestal, the **Statue of Liberty Exhibit** traces the history and symbolism of the Statue of Liberty through museum objects, photographs, prints, videos and oral histories. In addition to historical artifacts and descriptive text, full scale replicas of the Statue's face and foot are also on display.

The **Torch Exhibit** includes the original 1886 torch and much altered flame in the lobby. On the second floor balcony overlooking this torch is a display on the history of the torch and flame, explaining the various alterations through diagrams, photographs, drawings and cartoons.

Observation Deck

At the top of the pedestal, the four-sided **observation deck** provides spectacular **views**★★★ of the New York Harbor, lower Manhattan and the Financial District, the Verrazano-Narrows Bridge and New Jersey.

ELLIS ISLAND ★★

Ellis Island is situated about halfway between lower Manhattan and the Statue of Liberty in New York Harbor. Its grandly refurbished processing center stands as a testament to what it means to start life over in a new land. Between 1892 and 1954 Ellis Island received more than 12 million immigrants, one of the greatest mass migrations in history. Today more 100 million Americans, some 30 percent of the country's population, can trace their ancestry in the US to one of the men, women, or children who passed from a steamship to a ferry to the inspection lines in the great Registry Room at Ellis Island.

- **Information:** National Park Service. ☎212-363-3200. www.ellisisland.com or www.nps.gov/elis.
- ▶ **Orient Yourself:** Ellis Island is accessible by ferry only. Ferries (*$11.50 round-trip*) leave every 25min from Battery Park in Manhattan and every 45min from Liberty State Park in New Jersey daily 8:30am–4:30pm *(last ferry leaves Ellis Island at 5:45pm)*. All ferries make a circuit that includes both Liberty Island and Ellis Island.
- ◷ **Organizing Your Time:** Visit Ellis Island after visiting the Statue of Liberty.

A Bit of History

The Island – During the 1700s, the island was irreverently known as Gibbet Island, thanks to the fact that state criminals were executed here by means of hanging them from a "gibbet," or gallows tree. Samuel Ellis bought the land in 1785, and his heirs sold it to the state of New York in 1808. Like Governors Island and Bedloe's (now Liberty) Island, it held a fort to defend the harbor. In 1890 the island was chosen as a site for a federal immigrant processing center.

America's Great Immigrant Gateway – Inaugurated in 1892, Ellis Island quickly became the main port of entry for newcomers to America, replacing the old Immigrant Landing Station at Castle Garden, now known as **Castle Clinton,** which had operated from 1855 to 1890. From 1900 to 1924, an average of 5,000 new arrivals were processed daily, the

Ellis Island Immigration Museum

National Park Service

majority in less than eight hours (only 2 percent of hopefuls were denied entry and shipped back to their country of origin, mainly for health reasons). Once cleared, immigrants took a ferry to the Battery in Manhattan. One third of them settled in or near New York City; the rest traveled on to other parts of the country, often to meet relatives.

The Complex – The wooden buildings first used to house the immigration center were destroyed by fire in 1897, only five years after opening. A fireproof replacement, designed in the Beaux-Arts style by the local firm of Boring and Tilton, opened in December 1900. Despite its massive proportions, that building quickly proved too small, prompting the addition of wings and a third floor, as well as the expansion of the island, with landfill, from three acres to 27.5 acres. Thirty-three additional buildings were ultimately constructed. Most remain standing, but shuttered. Restrictive laws and quotas passed in the 1920s diminished Ellis Island's importance as a reception site, and by 1953 the facility was deemed too expensive to keep open – the island's staff numbered 250 to oversee a population of about 230 detained immigrants. In 1954 the last detainee, a seaman who had overstayed his shore leave, was ferried back to the mainland, and the doors were closed. Shortly afterward, the government tried to sell the site as surplus federal property, but no bid was judged high enough.

Decades of Neglect – For 10 years Ellis Island stood vacant, subject to vandals and looters who made off with anything they could carry, from doorknobs to filing cabinets. The building's Beaux-Arts copper ornamentation deteriorated. Snow swirled through broken windows, roofs leaked, and weeds sprang up in corridors. Upon seeing the island's dilapidated state, Stewart Udall, Secretary of the Interior for President Lyndon Johnson, urged President Johnson to place the island in the permanent care of the National Park Service. Johnson complied, and Ellis Island became part of the Statue of Liberty National Monument in 1965.

A New Beginning – Restoration of the Main Building began in earnest in the 1980s. Often compared to the refurbishment of the Palace of Versailles in France, the project took eight years to complete, at a cost of $156 million. The building reopened its doors in September 1990 as the Ellis Island Immigration Museum.

Ellis Island Immigration Museum★★

Free ranger-guided tours (45min) of the museum are offered throughout the day; the schedule is posted at the information desk located in the first-floor baggage room. Recorded audio tours of the museum are available in English, French, German, Spanish, Italian and Japanese; headsets (☜$6) can be rented at the concession stand: ☎212-344-0996. ⏱Open year-

An Island Divided

Who owns Ellis Island: New York or New Jersey? The answer, according to the Supreme Court, is both. Blame it on the landfill. In 1834 the two states agreed to give New York the three-acre island and New Jersey the waters around it, but as the tide of immigration increased in the early 20C, so did the island itself: by 1936 Ellis Island measured 27.5 acres and held more than 30 buildings. For half a century New York assumed that it owned the whole thing. Then New Jersey sued, claiming that Ellis Island's landfill was actually in the waters that it owned. In 1998 the High Court agreed, granting New Jersey 24.2 acres of as-yet-undeveloped Ellis Island landfill and New York the original 3.3 acres, which hold the museum and the ferry slip. Predictably, both states declared victory.

Manifest Destiny

Think you might have a relative who passed through Ellis Island? Check and see at the museum's **American Family Immigration History Center** or online at www.ellisisland.org. Developed and administered by the Statue of Liberty–Ellis Island Foundation, the center provides easy access to the ships' passenger manifest records of the 12 million people who entered America through the Port of New York and Ellis Island between 1892 and 1954. The database is searchable by immigrant name, but it is helpful if you also know the approximate age at arrival and date of arrival, as well as the port of departure. If you do get a "hit," you will be provided with the following information: immigrant's given name and surname, ethnicity, last residence (town and country), date of arrival, age at arrival, gender, marital status, ship of travel, port of departure, and line number on the manifest. Visitors can also obtain a reproduction of the original ship's manifest as well as a picture of the ship of passage. For further information call ☎ 212- 561-4500.

round daily 9:30am–5:15pm. ◐ Closed Dec. 25. ☎212-363-3200. www.ellisisland.com or www.nps.gov/elis.

Crowned by four copper-domed towers, the former processing center (1900) has been restored to reflect its appearance from 1918 to 1924, the years of peak immigration. Five thousand artifacts spread throughout the museum's 30 galleries, along with recordings, films, and live performances, tell the story of the building's role in the Great Migration to America.

First Floor

Visitors enter the baggage room, where immigrants were separated, sometimes forever, from their precious belongings. The old railroad office, to the north, houses the "**Peopling of America**" exhibit, which uses statistical displays to chronicle the history of immigration and ethnicity in the US from the 17C to the present. Highlights include a 6ft globe that traces worldwide migration patterns since the 18C; and the "Word Tree," which explains the origin of many American words. A poignant 30min film titled Island of Hope/Island of Tears portrays the human face of migration; it is screened in the two theaters located in the eastern wing (⌖pick up free tickets to the film at the Information Desk as soon as you enter the museum; shows fill up quickly). The western wing houses the **American Family Immigration History Center**, where visitors can research their family heritage via a computerized database (⌖see sidebar).

Second Floor

The sweeping two-story **Registry Room/Great Hall**★★ was the site of the initial inspection of immigrants, who awaited their fate while queuing behind metal pens. The hall that once accommodated thousands has been left empty, save for a few scattered benches, to serve as a grand, quiet memorial. The pride of the 17,300sq ft hall is its impressive vaulted ceiling. After a fire, the ceiling was rebuilt in 1917 by Spaniard Rafael Guastavino and his son with interlocking tiles; only 17 of the 28,000 tiles had to be replaced during restoration.

Third Floor

The highlight of this floor, "Treasures from Home," presents objects donated by immigrants and their families, from a teddy bear to an elaborate wedding gown. In "**Silent Voices**," large photographs taken before the restoration evoke the eerie feeling of an abandoned place, while furnishings recall the daily routine of processing, registering and caring for immigrants. Another exhibit, tracing 300 years of the island's history, displays five detailed models showing the evolving site plans of the island between 1897 and 1940.

Along the north wall of the mezzanine, a narrow **dorm room** has been furnished to reflect the cramped living conditions experienced by some of the detainees.

Live Performances

Regularly scheduled theater pieces are performed at the museum. Currently being staged May–Oct only is "**Liberty Dance**" (⊜$3), dramatizing aspects of Ellis Island history. Recent shows have included "Irving Berlin's America," "Bela Lugosi and the Legend of Dracula," and "The Titanic: A Survivor's Story." Show times are posted at the Information Desk, where tickets (⊜$3) may be purchased.

Grounds

Facing Manhattan, the **American Immigrant Wall of Honor** serves as a memorial to the nation's immigrant heritage. The 652.5ft-long, double-sided, semicircular wall contains the names of more than 600,000 individuals and families whose descendants have honored them by donating to the Ellis Island restoration project *(for more information on how to add a name, call* ☎*212-561-4500).* The terrace offers breathtaking **views**★★ of the Manhattan skyline.

Additional Sight

Governors Island

Accessible by ferry (⬤*see Visit).* ☎*212-825-3045. www.nps.gov/gois.*
Known in Dutch times as Nutten's Island, because of the many nut trees that grew here, the 150-acre island affords spectacular views of Manhattan and Brooklyn. It is the site of two pre-1800 structures: the

Governor's House and **Fort Jay**. Another fort, **Castle Williams**, was built on the island at the beginning of the 19C, at the same time as **Castle Clinton**. For two centuries the island was a military reservation, most recently home to the Coast Guard. Then, in 2001, the two forts were designated national monuments. In early 2003 the federal government sold the island back to the state of New York for $1. Since then, there has been talk about building a resort, a college campus, a golf course, an environmental center, and an arts complex on Governors Island. Commissioned by the island's Preservation and Education Corporation, five designs have recently been proposed but a winner has yet to be decided.

Visit

🦉🎫*The island is open Jun–Labor Day for guided tours (90min) Wed–Fri 10am & 1pm; free tickets are distributed at 9am for the 10am tour & noon for the 1pm tour.* ⊙*The island is open weekends 10am–5pm (last return ferry).* ⊙*The island is closed Mon & Tue. Free ferries (10min one-way) depart from the Battery Maritime Building (10 South St.) near the East River Wed–Fri 10am & 1pm, weekends hourly on the hr 10am–3pm.* In 2007 the island was opened for guided walking tours by a National Park Service ranger during the summer season only. The tour schedule is subject to change, however, so be sure to call or check the website before planning a visit.

FINANCIAL DISTRICT★★

MTA SUBWAY: 4, 5 TRAINS TO FULTON ST.

MAP P 80

Widely considered the financial center of the world, the southern tip of Manhattan isn't as buttoned-up as you might expect. Its U-shaped waterfront, lined with parks, draws hordes of visitors to view New York Harbor and catch ferries to Staten Island or the Statue of Liberty. Cradled within are the narrow streets laid out by New York's first Dutch settlers in the 17C. Nearly all of those original structures were destroyed, but developers left largely intact the curvy street plan when they built their gargantuan office towers. Two of those 'scrapers were the World Trade Center towers. People you'll see in the Financial District may have witnessed the events of September 11, 2001, firsthand. But fears that the neighborhood would always be marred by that day turned out to be unfounded: several of the district's attractions, including a number of museums, have undergone renovations and more improvements are in the works.

- 🛈 **Information:** ♿ *See A Bit of Advice sidebar page 82.*
- ▶ **Orient Yourself:** Use the map to locate St. Paul's first, then walk south from there on Broadway to Trinity Church before heading east on Wall Street. Detour north on William Street to tour the Federal Reserve Bank and its gold vault. Then head south to Battery Park for a relaxing stroll along the Promenade.
- 🅿 **Parking:** Don't even try. Finding a parking space here is like searching for the proverbial needle in the haystack. Free shuttle buses run along the waterfront between historic South Street Seaport and Battery Park City, stopping at Financial District attractions in between *(for more information, call ☎212-566-6700 or visit online www.downtownNY.com/DowntownConnection.)*
- 🚢 **Don't Miss:** A free ride on the Staten Island ferry.
- 🕐 **Organizing Your Time:** With the exception of Wall Street, the sights selected here are described in descending star order, rather than geographically, so you'll know which attractions to see first, especially if you are short on time. Allow at least four hours to do all the sights in the district justice.
- 🧒 **Especially for Kids:** The gold vault in the Federal Reserve Bank of New York will wow the elementary-school set and older. The bronze bull—the preeminent symbol of Wall Street—on Bowling Green, comes in a close second.

A Bit of History

New York City was born in what is now the Financial District in 1625. The Dutch West India Company's trade was flourishing, and the town of Nieuw Amsterdam quickly developed as the center of Dutch influence in the colonies. The small town was defended to the south by a fort and to the north by a wall of thick wooden planks constructed in 1653 between the Hudson and East rivers. A canal dug in the middle of Broad Street as well as a windmill attested to the town's Dutch heritage. About 1,000 persons lived here in wood and brick houses topped with Dutch gables and tile roofs. The inhabitants, though, were of varied origins; in 1642, when the

first Stadt Huys (City Hall) was built at 71 Pearl Street, no less than 18 languages were spoken in Nieuw Amsterdam. A commercial agent of the Dutch West India Company first governed the town, followed by a succession of governors, including Peter Stuyvesant. In 1664 the British took over Nieuw Amsterdam. During the 18C, colonial Georgian houses began to replace the narrow Dutch dwellings.

Sights

Federal Reserve Bank of New York★★

33 Liberty St. ♿ 🕐*Coin exhibit open year-round Mon–Fri 10am–4pm, except on* bank holidays. *Gold vault may be viewed by free guided tour (1hr) only, Mon–Fri 9:30am, 10:30am, 11:30am, 1:30pm & 2:30pm. One-month advance reservations required by email (frbnytours@ny.frb. org) or phone.* ☏*212-720-6130. www. ny.frb.org.*

One of 12 US reserve banks in the country, the New York "Fed," as it is somewhat affectionately known, occupies an entire city block. It's meant to look imposing. Indeed, it's the most heavily fortified building in the city. But behind this gruff exterior lies a surprisingly soft heart. Through its gold-vault tour, its "History of Money" exhibit and its delightful publications (including hilarious comic books), the Fed makes the world financial system seem not only logical, but surprisingly interesting.

The Federal Reserve Bank of New York was completed in 1924 and expanded in 1935. Distinguished by massive rusticated walls of Indiana limestone and Ohio sandstone, it influenced bank architecture around the country. Architect Phillip Sawyer based his design on that of several 15C Italian Renaissance palazzos that were built to house the wealthiest banking and merchant families in Florence.

Visit

The New York Fed ceded its cash-collecting and cash-disbursing functions in 1992 to a New Jersey facility, largely because the Brinks trucks were constantly getting snarled in traffic. But there's still plenty of riches here. Inside the building, 80ft below street level (50ft below sea level), lies the Federal Reserve's **gold vault★★**. The vault was actually excavated in 1921 and the building built on top of it. Today it contains about $90 billion worth of gold bullion, most belonging to foreign governments (most of the gold belonging to the US is stored in Kentucky's Fort Knox). As visitors gaze at a sparkling wall of gold bars—some rectangular, some trapezoidal, all utterly fake-looking—a tour guide details the astounding security measures taken to protect them: hidden cameras, motion detectors, combination and time locks, a revolving 90-ton "door" that lowers three-eighths of an inch into the concrete floor, forming an airtight and watertight seal. Finally, among the New York Fed's 3,000 employees are several dozen expert marksmen, who regularly hone their skills on the second-floor shooting range.

Visitors who did not reserve a space on the tour can view the excellent **"Drachmas, Doubloons and Dollars: The History of Money" exhibit★**, co-curated by the American Numismatic Society. Here, hundreds of artifacts illustrate the many forms money can take: coins, cowrie shells, salt, tokens, gold, paper money and credit cards, for example. Take special note of the 1933 gold **"double eagle,"** designed by Auguste Saint-Gau-

New York Stock Exchange

Brigitta L. House - MICHELIN

dens, and read about the fascinating history of this $20 coin. Also be sure to see the interactive, multimedia exhibit **"Fed Works: Money, Banking and the Federal Reserve System,"** an economic education in itself.

National Museum of the American Indian★★

1 Bowling Green. ♿For description, see Museums.

LOWER MANHATTAN

1/10mi
0
0   200m

WEEHAWKEN

Hotels
1 Ritz-Carlton Battery Park
2 Wall Street Inn

Restaurants
1 Full Shilling
2 Gigino at Wagner Park
3 Les Halles Downtown

Governor Rockefeller Park

River Terrace

Solaire

Esplanade

Irish Hunger Memorial

New York Mercantile Exchange

Belvedere

PATH Line Trains

North Cove

★ Winter Garden

WORLD FINANCIAL CENTER

Gateway Plaza

Esplanade

Albany

★**BATTERY**

PARK

South Cove

★★**Museum of Jewish Heritage**

CITY

★ Skyscraper Museum

Robert F. Wagner Jr. Park

Pier A

NY Korean War Veterans Memorial

★Castle Clinton NM

★★**Museum of the American Indian**

Battery Park★

East Coast Memorial

Promenade

HUDSON RIVER

Murray St.
Vesey St.
North End Ave.
West St.
River Terrace

★★**WORLD TRADE CENTER SITE**

WORLD TRADE CENTER

Liberty St.

Albany St.
Carlisle St.

Tribute

RECTOR ST.

★★**Trinity Church**

US Realty Bldg.

Rector St.
W. Thames St.
Rector Pl.

Greenwich St.

Washington St.

West St.

South End Ave.

1st Pl.
2nd Pl.
3rd Pl.
Battery Pl.
Little West St.

Bank of New York Building

★Cunard Bldg.

NY Stock Exchange

Morgan Guaranty Trust

New St.
Broad St.

★**Bowling Green**

BOWLING GREEN

US Custom House

STONE STREET HISTORIC DISTRICT

Stone St.
S. William St.

Bridge St.
Pearl St.

Fraunces Tavern

J. Watson House

Whitehall St.
Water St.

WHITEHALL ST.

SOUTH FERRY

NY Plaza

NY Plaza

Vietnam Veterans Plaza

NYC Police Museum

CHAMBERS ST.
Warren St.
Murray St.
Barclay St.

Greenwich St.
West Broadway
Church St.
Park Pl.

PARK PL.

Washington St.

WOOLWORTH BLDG.

Vesey St.
Dey St.
Cortlandt St.
Fulton St.

★★St. Paul's Chapel★★

Ann St.
Fulton St.
John St.

One Liberty Plaza

★★**FINANCIAL DISTRICT**

BROADWAY
NASSAU

Maiden Ln.

Broadway

Liberty St.

Chamber of Commerce of the State of NY

★★**Federal Reserve Bank of NY**

Equitable Bldg.

Nassau St.

Chase Manhattan

Federal Hall★★

Platt St.
Cedar St.

Bank of New York Building

Pine St.

Deutsche Bank

Wall St.

William St.

Water St.
Front St.
South St.

Second Merchants Exchange Building

Hanover Sq.

India House

Gouverneur Ln.
Old Slip

Pine St.

Coenties Slip

FRANKLIN D. ROOSEVELT DR.

PIER 13

PIER 11

Staten Island Ferry Terminal

Battery Maritime Building

★**Staten Island Ferry**

Port Authority Downtown Heliport

EAST RIVER

Brooklyn-Battery Tunnel

Saint Paul's Chapel★★

On Broadway, between Fulton and Vesey Sts. ♿ ◷*Open year-round Mon–Sat 10am–6pm, Sun 9am–4pm.* ◷*Closed major holidays.* ☎*212-233-4164.* www.saintpaulschapel.org.

Belonging to the Trinity Church parish, this small chapel opposite the World Trade Center site is the oldest public building in continuous use in Manhattan. In the weeks following the attacks of September 11, 2001, it served as an aid station for rescue workers and a pilgrimage site for mourners. That history is recounted in the permanent exhibit "Unwavering Spirit: Hope and Healing at Ground Zero."

A Bit of History

Completed in 1766, St. Paul's Chapel resembles the Church of St.-Martin-in-the-Fields in Trafalgar Square, London. That is no coincidence: its architect, Thomas McBean, studied under James Gibbs, who designed St. Martin's. St. Paul's is constructed of native stone: Manhattan mica-schist with quoins of brownstone. In its early days, the church stood in a field outside the city proper. **George Washington** prayed here in 1789, after his inauguration as the first president of the US. *(The inauguration ceremony itself took place at the site of today's Federal Hall.)* Washington continued to worship here for the two years that New York City was the nation's capital.

Visit

The chapel stands in its own cemetery, a delightful spot full of trees and 18C tombstones, most of which are cracker-thin and illegible due to age. The **Bell of Hope** standing in front of the chapel entrance is a gift to New Yorkers from the Lord Mayor of the City of London on the first anniversary of the 9/11 attacks. It was cast in the same foundry as the Liberty Bell and Big Ben.

Inside the Georgian chapel, notice the woodwork, carving and door hinges; all were handmade under the direction of master craftsman Andrew Gautier. The ornamental design over the altar is the work of Pierre Charles L'Enfant, the French architect who designed the city of Washington, DC. Above **George Washington's pew** in the north aisle hangs an 18C oil painting of the Great Seal of the US, which was adopted in 1782.

The elegant interior is visually overwhelmed, however, with the profusion of Ground Zero paraphernalia making up the **Unwavering Spirit exhibit**. Handmade banners, letters to missing relatives, photographs and documentary oral history stations surround the pews, an evocative re-creation of how the chapel looked and felt in the emotionally wrenching days following the attacks.

Staten Island Ferry★★

Whitehall Ferry Terminal in Manhattan at southern tip of Battery Park. ♿ *See Staten Island.*

Trinity Church★★

74 Trinity Pl. (corner of Broadway at Wall St.). ♿◷*Open year-round Mon–Fri 7am–6pm (churchyard until 4pm), Sat 8am–4pm, Sun 7am–4pm;* ⟿*guided tours daily 2pm; classical music concerts Mon & Thu 1pm.* ☎*212-602-0800; www.trinitywall-street.org.*

How the Federal Reserve System Works

President Woodrow Wilson brought the Fed into being on December 23, 1913, with the signing of the Federal Reserve Act. The aim of the law was to prevent a repeat of the liquidity crises and financial panics that occurred sporadically in the US throughout the 19C. The Fed is composed of 12 regional reserve banks spread across the country and a board of governors in Washington, DC. The system's function is twofold: the banks themselves handle the flow of coin and currency to and from local banks, and the board of governors sets US monetary policy, including all-important interest rates. By raising or lowering interest rates, the chairman of the Federal Reserve tries to keep the economy from either sagging or going into overdrive and then crashing, as it did in 2000. In performing this single task, the Fed chairman may be the most influential person in America.

☺ A Bit of Advice ☺

FOR MORE INFORMATION

For information about **free concerts, exhibits and performances**, contact: the **Alliance for Downtown New York** ☎212-566-6700 www.downtownNY.com or the **Lower Manhattan Cultural Council** ☎212-219-9401.

For **brochures** and **maps**, visit the **information kiosk** at the **World Trade Center site**, near the corner of Church and Vesey streets (🕐 *daily 10am–6pm*) or the **bookstore** at **Castle Clinton**, which keeps its supply well-stocked.

Free Wall Street walking tours, sponsored by the Downtown Alliance, are held every Thursday and Saturday, rain or shine, at noon; meet on the steps of National Museum of the American Indian at One Bowling Green.
🚌 For more information, call ☎212-606-4064.

Free shuttle buses run along the waterfront between South Street Seaport and Battery Park City, with stops at attractions in between.
🚌 For more information, call ☎212-566-6700 or visit www.downtownNY.com/DowntownConnection.

To appreciate how quickly and relatively recently New York City has grown, consider the fact that Trinity Church, upon its completion in 1846, was the tallest building in Manhattan. Today its graceful Gothic spire appears quaint, framed as it is by the tunnel of Wall Street skyscrapers that extend to the East River. Yet a feeling of tranquillity continues to reign here, in the cool vaulted interior of the church and in its gated churchyard, where lie the remains of New Yorkers dating back to 1681.

A Bit of History

An Episcopal church, Trinity was founded by a charter granted by King William III in 1697. Among the influential locals who contributed to its construction was **William Kidd** (the legendary Captain Kidd) who lived nearby at Hanover Square before being hanged for piracy in London in 1701.

The first church building, completed in 1698, was devoured in the great fire of 1776. The second building's roof collapsed in 1839. The present edifice, designed by Richard Upjohn, has fared better, surviving even the September 11, 2001, attacks (just a block away) with only the loss of some of its mortar.

Visit

The building is made of red sandstone. Its spire rises 280 feet and contains 10 bells, three of which date to 1797. The elaborately wrought bronze doors were designed by **Richard Morris Hunt**, architect of the Metropolitan Museum and the pedestal of the Statue of Liberty. Inside, note the stained-glass windows behind the marble altar; they were designed by Upjohn. A small **museum** presents exhibits on Trinity Church's history and its relationship to the city (🕐 *open year-round Mon–Fri & holidays 9am–11:45am & 1pm–3:45pm, Sat 10am–3:45pm, Sun 1pm–3:45pm*).

Though seemingly frozen in time, Trinity's **cemetery** is in fact the only facility in Manhattan still taking bodies. Fortunately, you don't need a reservation to browse. It's a lovely space, with dozens of crooked and eroded tombstones shaded by 100-year-old oaks and elms. Famous internees include Alexander Hamilton and John Jacob Astor.

Wall Street★★

New York has always been a magnet for capitalists, but not even the most optimistic Dutchman could have conceived the amount of money exchanged over the years on Wall Street.

A Bit of History

Running for less than a mile between Broadway and the East River, Wall Street derives its name from the short wooden wall built along its path by the Dutch in 1653. The wall marked the northern boundary of the fledgling trading post Nieuw Amsterdam and was meant to protect the residents from Indian attack. It was never tested in battle, however; in fact, colonists considered it a handy source of firewood. In 1699 the British, who had taken over the colony in 1664, dismantled the wall for good and replaced it with a street lined with houses and administrative buildings, including the colony's second city hall, at Broad and Wall streets, site of today's Federal Hall National Memorial. (The first city hall, or Stadt Huys, was founded in a tavern on Pearl Street in 1653.)

After the Revolution, the east end of Wall Street harbored a number of coffeehouses and taverns, earning the area around Wall and Water streets the nickname "Coffeehouse Slip." The famous Tontine Coffee House, built in 1792 at that corner, served as the first home of the New York Stock Exchange.

Visit

What you'll find on Wall Street today depends entirely on when you see it and from what vantage point. On weekdays when the Exchange is open (stocks are traded between 9:30am and 4pm), it is full of frenetic bankers, traders and other office workers. During business hours, you're most likely to be allowed to step into the lobbies of some of the more historic buildings, though don't be surprised if you're refused; security all over the district has been drum-tight since 9/11 and will likely remain that way indefinitely. On weekends and holidays the street is dominated by tourists. At night it is practically deserted. Also note it's impossible to see the tops of many of Wall Street's tallest buildings from the street itself. Your best bet is to take the Circle Tour boat and let the tour guide point them out to you.

⊘Sights on Wall Street are ordered west to east by street numbers (not star order), beginning with 1 Wall Street.

Bank of New York Building

1 Wall St. Originally completed for Irving Trust Company in 1932, the 50-story white limestone tower rises 20 stories without a setback, then tapers into a graceful spire. It makes a fitting companion to neighboring Trinity Church. If you can get in, take a peek at the Art Deco lobby.

Trinity Church from Wall Street

Allison M. Simpson - MICHELIN

New York Stock Exchange

8–18 Broad St. at Wall St. Formerly one of New York's top tourist attractions (visitors were treated to a bird's-eye view of the gigantic trading floor), the stock exchange was closed to the public following the September 11, 2001, attacks. The eight-story building (1903, George B. Post), which remains surrounded by guarded barricades, resembles a Roman temple with its majestic facade of Corinthian columns, each crowned by an elaborate pediment with sculptures representing commerce. Yet the exchange itself far predates this structure. New York had an active securities market by 1790, when Alexander Hamilton, US secretary of the Treasury, first issued bonds to consolidate and refund debts incurred during the American Revolution. The small buttonwood tree (better known as a sycamore) to the left of the Broad Street entrance memorializes the legendary "buttonwood agreement." Though perhaps more fiction than fact, the story goes that in 1792 a group of 24 brokers met at the corner of Wall and Williams streets, beneath a similar tree, and founded the stock exchange. The New York Stock Exchange wasn't formally organized, however, until 1817. Despite the predictable boom and bust cycles, it grew exponentially, fueled by railroad securities, war bonds and ever-present speculators. By 1865, when it took possession of the current site, it had had 10

Stone Street Historic District

Thanks to its 1996 landmark designation, once-dingy Stone Street between Hanover Square and Coenties Slip has become one of the Financial District's most charming thoroughfares. On warm days its cobblestone expanse is festooned with umbrella tables, courtesy of eight new restaurants and pubs. On cool and rainy days, these self-same joints provide a cozy respite from the concrete jungle.

Stone Street is reputed to be New York's first paved street. Because of its proximity to the East River, it bustled with commercial activity for more than 200 years, rebounding quickly even after the 1835 fire razed 700 commercial buildings in the area. But when port activity began shifting to the west side in the early 20C, the street started a slow decline. Its recent resurrection comes courtesy of civic boosters and entrepreneurs led by Peter Poulakakos, who owns and operates the excellent **Financier** patisserie *(no. 62; ☎212-344-5600; www. financierpastries.com)* and its neighbor, **Ulysses' Bar** *(no. 58; ☎212-482-0400; www.ulyssesbarnyc.com)*, which serves up lobster every Monday night and "cobblestone brunch" on Sundays *(11am–4pm)*.

Peter Wrenn/MICHELIN

Stone Street Historic District

homes of increasing size. Today, the classical facade hides one of the most technically sophisticated financial operations on the globe, where about $67 billion worth of shares are exchanged daily.

Morgan Guaranty Trust Company

23 Wall St. at Broad St. This austere white marble building (1913, Trowbridge & Livingston) is better known for its history than its architecture. On September 16, 1920, just as the Trinity Church bells chimed noon, an anarchist ignited a wagonload of explosives outside its Wall Street facade. John Pierpont Morgan Jr., the target of the attack, was unharmed, but 33 civilians were killed and 400 were injured. Look closely at the area around the fourth window from the corner and you can still see pockmarks in the marble from the explosion.

Federal Hall National Memorial★

26 Wall St. at Broad St. ♿ ⏱*Open year-round Mon–Fri 9am–5pm.* ☎212-825-6888; www.nps.gov/feha.

Grand though it may be, this structure itself is not among the most historic in the city, but the site certainly is. It was initially occupied by New York's first official city hall, on land donated by wealthy Dutch merchant Abraham de Peyster, whose statue you can admire in nearby Hanover Square; in 1702 the city government, then British, moved in. Also used as a debtor's prison, the site later became a staging ground for the American Revolution. In October 1765 the building hosted the Stamp Act Congress to protest "taxation without representation," a slogan that ended up driving the war for independence. After ratification of the Constitution in 1788, Pierre Charles L'Enfant (who laid out Washington, DC's radial street grid) was hired to remodel the city hall for use as the nation's capitol. Though Federal Hall hosted the first congress and the swearing-in of George Washington in 1789, its time in the national limelight was short-lived. After the capitol moved to Philadelphia in 1790, the building housed city offices again, and in 1812 it was demolished and sold as salvage for $425.

Visit – The present building was designed by the firm Town and Davis and completed in 1842. It held the custom house, the US Subtreasury and various government offices before being designated a historic site in 1939 and a national memorial in 1955. The towering bronze statue of George Washington (1883, John A.Q. Ward) at the top of its wide steps is a popular place for photos. Inside the memorial, 16 marble Corinthian columns support a splendid central rotunda rimmed with balconies.

Trump Building *(A on map)*

40 Wall St. Though this 1930s building bears The Donald's signature gold imprimatur, "TRUMP," above its revolving doors, the architectural highlight, a pyramidal crown, can be seen only at a distance. Adjoining the now-lackluster lobby is Mangia (☎212-425-4040), a gourmet salad bar and sandwich maker that's justifiably popular with time-pressed Wall Streeters and sore-footed visitors.

Bank of New York Building

48 Wall St. Designed in 1927 by Benjamin Wistar Morris, who's better known for his exuberant Cunard Building at 25 Broadway, 48 Wall Street is topped by a Corinthian-columned temple and mounted bronze eagle. As with the Trump Building, it's visible only from afar, but if you step inside, Morris' original pen-and-ink architectural drawings, on display in the lobby, will give you a sense of its upper reaches. In early 2008, the **Museum of**

American Finance *(M on map)* is slated to make its new home in this building. Exhibits will focus on Wall Street's history, investing, US banking systems and the country's top entrepreneurs. A room will be devoted to Alexander Hamilton, first secretary of the Treasury.

Second Merchants Exchange Building

55 Wall St. A double colonnade of Ionic and Corinthian columns fronts this unusual structure, most recently home to the Regent Wall Street Hotel. In 1841 Isaiah Rogers designed a three-story building with a central domed trading hall to replace the original merchants exchange, which burned down in the Great Fire of 1835. When it was converted to use as the Custom House in 1907, the prolific architectural team of McKim, Mead and White added the upper tier of columns (and three more floors), doubling the building's volume. The magnificent **Great Hall**, with its 72ft coffered ceiling, is now used by the Cipriani restaurant for private functions only, unfortunately. The American Institute of Architects calls the space "unequaled in America."

Deutsche Bank

60 Wall St. With its curious pairing of reflective glass and granite pilasters, the 47-floor office tower (1988, Roche, Dinkeloo and Assocs.) is one of the tallest in the district. On the ground floor is a public space that, despite its mirrored ceiling and potted palms, feels like a slightly seedy bus station.

Nineteenth-Century Titans

The business activities and interests of the Morgans, Vanderbilts, Goulds and their descendents helped shaped New York as a financial capital. After 1860, speculation flourished. On September 24, 1869, financier **Jay Gould** (1836-92), who had tried to corner the gold market with his associate James Fisk, sold out and brought about the financial panic known as "Black Friday." **Cornelius Vanderbilt** (1794-1877), nicknamed "The Commodore" because of his interests in the shipping industry, began to extend his activities to the railroads in 1862. First the owner of small lines, he launched the famous New York-Buffalo line in 1873. At the same time, banker **J. Pierpont Morgan** (1837-1913) financed the great new industries: steel, oil and railroads. Generous, but a ruthless businessman, the founder of the famous Pierpont Morgan Library (now The Morgan Library) was succeeded by his son, John Pierpont Morgan Jr., the target of the assassination attempt in 1920 mentioned in this chapter.

World Trade Center site, 2007

World Trade Center Site★★

Bounded by Church, Liberty, West & Barclay Sts. 🅸*www.renewnyc.com and www.lowermanhattan.info.*

The world's largest commercial complex stood here from 1970 until the morning of September 11, 2001, when two hijacked planes were flown into the Twin Towers, killing 2,979 people and bringing the 110-story structures—in which 50,000 people had worked—to the ground. It was the deadliest terrorist attack in US history. Fires burned for weeks, sending acrid smoke across the city. In all, eight buildings were destroyed. Workers carted off 1.5 million tons of steel and debris until the site was cleared in May 2002, well ahead of schedule. Rebuilding the site has proved far more difficult, thanks to the vast size of the project and the number of parties (politicians, developers, victims' families, architects and the police) with strong and often conflicting visions of its future.

The Master Plan

Ultimately, the site will contain an assortment of office buildings, memorials, parks and cultural venues, arranged roughly according to a master plan created by Polish-born architect Daniel Libeskind and a revised design released by the Lower Manhattan Development Corp. mid-2005. The centerpiece of the plan is a 1,776ft-tall structure (half building, half sculpture) called the Freedom Tower, which will combine underground retail shops and above-ground office and retail space. An observation deck will sit at 1,362ft. The cornerstone for the tower was put in place in fall 2004; completion is expected in 2011.

The Memorial – The design that beat 5,000 other entries in the World Trade Center memorial design competition honors the request by some victims' families that the footprints of the towers not be built upon. "Reflecting Absence," by architects Michael Arad and Peter Walker, features a one-and-a-half-acre grove of oak trees and preserves, as multilevel reflecting pools, the two square voids where the towers once stood. Construction began in 2006 on a revised plan that scaled back the cost to $500 million. The memorial's opening is scheduled for September 11, 2009.

The Museum – In addition to the memorial, a museum complex and visitor center are planned that will relate the events of September 11. In 2006 construction began on the World Trade Center Memorial Museum, as it is now named. The projected date of completion is 2010.

The Transportation Hub – The Spanish architect Santiago Calatrava was given the green light to build a soaring $2 billion, four-level transport hub at the northeast corner of the World Trade Center site *(Church and Vesey Sts)*. The station will consist of two curved, intersecting planes of glass and steel, a design that was inspired by the image of a child opening her hand to let a bird free, Calatrava has said. Projected cost overruns have delayed the hub's completion, which is slated for late 2009.

Visiting the Site

Shortly after the debris was cleared in 2002, city officials opened a viewing platform on Church Street so that visitors could see where the World Trade Center stood, pay respects to the dead and watch the progress of rebuilding. Text and photo panels traced the history of the World Trade Center, with particularly dramatic coverage of the events of September 11, 2001. The platform and photo history are gone, but smaller photo panels and a list of the victims' names are on view near the top of the steps of the PATH station. At 120 Liberty St., the **Tribute WTC Visitor Center** *(open year-round daily Mon & Wed–Sat 10am–6pm, Tue noon–6pm, Sun noon–5pm; ☎212-393-9160; www.tributenyc.org)* has visitor information and sponsors walking tours relating to the site. Five exhibit galleries *($10 contribution suggested)* are devoted to the events of September 11. The Winter Garden provides a view of the World Trade Center site and features an exhibit charting the future of downtown Manhattan.

Battery Park★

On the southwestern tip of Manhattan, the maze of stone and steel suddenly gives way to an expanse of greenery, Battery Park. Here, strolling along the waterfront promenade, visitors can enjoy upclose views of the Statue of Liberty and the harbor islands, and catch ferries to get even closer.

A Bit of History

Battery Park gets its name from two artillery stations built by the US military

Sphere by Fritz Koenig

Brigitta L. House - MICHELIN

in anticipation of a British attack during the War of 1812. One of the structures, East Battery (Castle Williams), is located on Governors Island; the other, West Battery (Castle Clinton), was originally 300ft off-shore. Neither was ever used in combat, and in 1870 the area between Castle Clinton and the shoreline (which ran along State Street) was filled in, creating the park you see today. It contains a number of memorials and sculptures: most striking is the 15ft-diameter, 22-ton **Sphere★★** *(1 on map)* by Fritz Koenig, salvaged from the World Trade Center Plaza. Once a glimmering ball, it now resembles a battered suit of armor (located just inside Bowling Green entrance). The eternal flame was added, and lit, on September 11, 2002. A recent restoration (2005) created new paths, a fountain, gardens, lights and a carousel to the *bosque* (Spanish for grove of trees) at the southernmost tip of the park. At the north end, Pier A, the last Victorian pier shed in Manhattan, is being restored and adapted to hold a visitor center, shops and restaurants as well as to provide moorings for historic vessels.

Promenade★★

Between Pier A and Whitehall Ferry Terminal.

The waterfront path offers great views of New York Harbor. Among the points of interest that visitors can spot are the Colgate clock and, beside it, Goldman Sachs' glimmering headquarters in Jersey City; Ellis Island's Beaux-Arts processing center; the Statue of Liberty; the docks at the foot of **Brooklyn Heights**★★; the redbrick buildings on Governors Island; and the crisscrossing cables of the **Verrazano-Narrows Bridge**★★, linking Staten Island and Brooklyn.

You'll notice two prominent memorials: the **East Coast Memorial** (near the South Ferry terminal) was dedicated in 1963. Eight stark granite walls are engraved with the name, rank, and home state of 4,601 US servicemen who lost their lives in the Atlantic Ocean during World War II. A bronze Art Deco-style eagle stands at the head of the monument. The **New York Korean War Veterans Memorial** (near the West St. entrance) is a 15ft-tall granite stele (1991) containing within it the carved-out silhouette of an infantryman who represents the "universal soldier." If you look through the cutout toward the water, you can see the Statue of Liberty.

Castle Clinton
National Monument★

♿○*Open year-round daily 8:30am–5pm.*
○*Closed Dec 25.* ☎*212-www.nps.gov/cacl.*

Most people know Castle Clinton merely as the place where they go to buy tickets to the Statue of Liberty and Ellis Island; indeed, it is the main visitor center for all of the national parks in New York City, and contains an excellent array of free brochures and maps, as well as a public restroom. But the structure itself—a round fort with 8ft-thick walls pierced with gun ports —has a long and interesting history.

As noted above, it was built between 1808 and 1811 on what was then an island 300ft offshore. Known as West Battery, it was designed to protect New York during the War of 1812, but was never fired upon. In 1824, the structure was remodeled into an entertainment venue called Castle Garden. Initially the site of hot-air balloon launchings and fireworks, it hosted, after a roof was added in the 1840s, operas and performances by such superstars as Jenny Lind, "the Swedish nightingale," brought to the US by none other than circus impresario P.T. Barnum.

Between 1855 and 1892, prior to the opening of Ellis Island, the structure served as an immigrant landing depot; then, from 1898 to 1942, it was home to the New York Aquarium. Today, unfortunately, not much of this history can be seen with the naked eye; the structure has been completely gutted. But if you're like most visitors, you'll have plenty of time waiting in line for Statue of Liberty tickets to close your eyes and imagine.

Additional Sights

Bowling Green★

For the low, low price of one peppercorn per annum, gentlemen of the mid-19C

Castle Clinton National Monument

©Peter Wrenn/MICHELIN

were permitted to bowl on this egg-shaped park at the foot of Broadway. In 1776 independence-minded New Yorkers toppled a statue of King George III that stood here. Today the park is one of the Financial District's most pleasant public spaces, its fountain ringed with benches and historic plantings; the fence dates from 1771.

Museum of American Finance★

28 Broadway at Beaver St. ⊶ *The museum recently closed in anticipation of its move to the Bank of New York Building at 48 Wall Street in early 2008.* ☎212-908-4110. *www.financialhistory.org.* This small affiliate of the Smithsonian Institution occupied a street-level office suite in John D. Rockefeller's historic Standard Oil Building (1928, Carrère and Hastings). Note how gracefully the sweeping curve of its Broadway facade complements the Cunard Building across Bowling Green. Interestingly, its 480ft-high pyramidal tower is aligned with the uptown grid, not with the street below—a siting done supposedly to keep the city's skyline geometrical. Previously, Alexander Hamilton's law offices stood here.

Fraunces Tavern

54 Pearl St. ♿ ⏱*Museum open year-round Mon–Sat noon–5pm.* ⏱*Closed major holidays.* ⊗*$4.* ☎212-425-1778; *www.fraucestavernmuseum.org.*

With its tile roof and cream-colored portico, this handsome brick house gives visitors a sense of New York City as it might have appeared during the American Revolution. In 1719 Etienne de Lancey, who later gave his family name to Delancey Street, built a home here. Samuel Fraunces bought it in 1762 and turned it into a tavern. For 10 days in 1783 Fraunces Tavern served as George Washington's last residence as general, and on December 4 of that year, he bade farewell to his troops here before returning to his estate at Mount Vernon.

Visit

The authenticity of the building you see today is open to debate. In 1904 the Sons of the Revolution in the State of New York bought the structure, which by then had been significantly altered, and tried to restore it to what they believed the original might have looked like. It was opened to the public in 1907. Parts of the original walls were incorporated, but history and architecture buffs don't think that's enough to justify the museum's claim that Fraunces Tavern is the real McCoy. Today the ground floor is used as a bar/restaurant (☎212-968-1776), and the upper floors (the museum)

No Bull

Guarding the northern entrance to Bowling Green, the 3.5-ton, 16ft-long bronze statue (**2** *on map*) of a charging bull—the symbol of the stock market on the rise—may be the most photographed public artwork in the city. It may also be the most controversial. New York City artist Arturo Di Modica decided to create the

bull after the worst day in Wall Street history, so-called Black Monday (October 19, 1987), when the Dow Jones lost 22.6 percent of its value. On the night of December 15, 1989, he and his friends carried it on a flatbed truck to the New York Stock Exchange and left it there beside a 60ft tall Christmas tree. The police were called in to haul the bull away, but public outcry was such that the New York City Department of Parks and Recreation made room for it here, where it remains a "temporary" installation.

The Bull

Brigitta L. House – MICHELIN

For Architecture Buffs: Notable Buildings in the District

Spanning some 200 years, the architecture of the Financial District is some of the most noteworthy in the city. In the 19C, the Beaux-Arts and Classical Revival styles dominated. The name of the game in the 20C was skyscrapers, big skyscrapers. Some of the largest are on Water Street *(between Dover and Fulton Sts.)*, Manhattan's street of million-square-foot towers. Indeed, to fully appreciate their vastness, you need to get off the island; the Brooklyn Heights Esplanade and the Circle Line boat offer the best vantage points. But there are quite a few you can admire from the street as you make your tour of the neighborhood. Here's a sampling:

17 State Street
This sleek mirrored office tower is like an ultra-tall quarter-slice of pie. Completed in 1989, it was designed by Emery Roth & Sons. On August 1, 1819, *Moby-Dick* author **Herman Melville** was born in a house on this site. *(The archaeological exhibit at the base of the building, "New York Unearthed," run by the South Street Seaport Museum, is ○ open Mon–Fri noon–5pm, ○ closed major holidays; ☎212-748-8753.)*

Battery Maritime Building
11 South St. at the foot of Whitehall St.
The Art Nouveau ferry terminal (1909, Walker and Morris) next to the newly reno-vated Whitehall Ferry Terminal has a brightly painted cast facade, a 55,000sq ft wait-ing area, a stained-glass skylight and Guastavino tile vaults under its porch roofs. In 2006 a $60 million renovation of the building was completed. It already serves as the terminus of the ferry to **Governors Island**. Development plans include a future food market, restaurant and boutique hotel.

©Shea Dean

Chamber of Commerce of the State of New York

Chamber of Commerce of the State of New York
65 Liberty St. between Nassau St. & Broadway.
The International Commercial Bank of Chi-na occupies this wedding cake of a building (1901, James B. Baker), which sports an Ionic colonnade, a mansard roof and porthole windows.

One Chase Manhattan Plaza
On Pine St. between Nassau & William Sts.
David Rockefeller took a risk when commissioning Skidmore, Owings & Merrill to build this massive tower in Lower Manhattan for the bank he chaired. At the time of its completion in 1961 there was nothing like it, and it might have stood out like a sore thumb for decades. But the World Trade Center and other behemoths came soon after, and it melded in nicely. The building is made of glass and aluminum and rises 813ft without a setback. Jean Dubuffet's black-and-white sculpture *The Group of Four Trees*★ (**3** *on map*) (1961) enlivens the concrete plaza.

Cunard Building
25 Broadway on Bowling Green.
In the old days you could buy passage on such ocean liners as the *Queen Elizabeth* and the *Queen Mary* in the grand **lobby**★ of this Renaissance-style structure (1921, Benjamin Wistar Morris); now you can buy stamps—it's a post office. The 68ft rotunda is glorious. Note, too, how well the exterior facade complements the Stand-ard Oil Building opposite.

Equitable Building
120 Broadway between Pine & Cedar Sts.
Like the Trinity and US Realty Buildings across the street, this immense Beaux-Arts edifice (1915) comprises twin towers connected by a recessed central section. Protests over the building's bulk (it encompasses 1.2 million sq ft of office space on less than an acre, or a floor area almost 30 times as big as the site itself) gave rise to the city's first zoning resolution, passed in 1916.

India House
1 Hanover Sq. between Pearl & Stone Sts.
At the foot of the fairly new Stone Street Historic District, this 1853 Italianate brownstone fronts Hanover Square, a quiet little plaza dotted with trees.

James Watson House
7 State St. between Pearl & Water Sts.
Now the rectory of the Shrine of St. Elizabeth Ann Bayley Seton, the brick house dates from 1792, and the graceful Ionic colonnade was completed in 1806. It is the only surviving residential structure from the Federal period. Seton (1774-1821), who was born on Staten Island, was canonized as America's first saint in 1975.

James Watson House

One Liberty Plaza
Liberty St. between Church St. & Broadway.
Skidmore, Owings & Merrill designed this dark, forbidding structure (1974), a 54-storey monolith "decorated" with thick, horizontal steel beams and tinted gray windows. The bleak plaza across the street (Broadway) is brightened by sculptor Isamu Noguchi's 28ft reddish-orange cube (**4** *on map*) (1967).

Trinity (B *on map*) and US Realty Buildings
111 & 115 Broadway at Thames St.
Connected by a pedestrian walkway on the top floor, these twin limestone structures (1907) were designed in an elaborate Gothic style to harmonize with neighboring Trinity Church.

display early American decorative arts in period rooms.

New York City Police Museum
100 Old Slip (between Water St. & South St.). 🕙Open year-round Mon–Sat 10am–5pm. 🎟$5 contribution requested. ☎ 212-480-3100; www.nycpolice museum.org.
Just a stone's throw from the East River, a solid neo-Renaissance building built in 1911 for the NYPD's First Precinct house was reopened in 2002 as the home of this museum. The collection, which the police department began to assemble in the 19C, is a trove of official police equipment and artifacts. On hand are vintage firearms, such as a Prohibition-era tommy gun; and a full-size holding cell, complete with a metal bunkbed, basin and toilet. The Hall of Heroes *(third floor)* displays the shield of every New York police officer who died in the line of duty. Visitors 18 years of age and older can try out a firearms training simulator *(third floor).*

BATTERY PARK CITY★

MTA SUBWAY: 4, 5 TRAINS TO BOWLING GREEN OR
1 TRAIN TO RECTOR ST.
MAP P 80

Most visitors to this vast commercial/residential complex come to enjoy its 35 acres of parks and the 1.2mi riverfront esplanade, a flower- and art-studded path along the Hudson River. (It is part of the 5mi-long Hudson River Park, which runs from Battery Park to 59th Street.) Also in Battery Park City are the Museum of Jewish Heritage, the Skyscraper Museum, the Irish Hunger Memorial and the World Financial Center's Winter Garden.

A Bit of History

Well into the 1950s, Lower Manhattan's western shoreline was crammed with piers, wharves and ferry slips, around which longshoremen bustled to load and unload ships from all parts of the world. But in the 1960s, the advent of containership technology forced most active piers to move to roomier sites in Brooklyn, Staten Island and New Jersey. The idea to create Battery Park City was first conceived by Gov. Nelson Rockefeller in the late 1960s. Under his leadership, engineers extended Lower Manhattan with 92 acres of landfill, most of which came, conveniently, from the neighboring World Trade Center site when it was excavated for construction of the Twin Towers.

In the mid-1970s, the site was ready for development, but the city's shaky finances stalled construction. In 1979, during the administrations of Mayor Ed Koch and Gov. Hugh Carey, the original plan was scrapped in favor of a new one calling for the extension of Manhattan's street grid into the complex, as well as the public parks and esplanade. In 1982 the first tenants moved into the Gateway Plaza apartment complex. Construction and improvements have proceeded apace ever since.

Not surprisingly, all the buildings—commercial and residential alike—have as many water views as can be arranged in three dimensions. In 2004 what is touted as the world's first "green" high rise, the **Solaire**, was opened at 20 River Terrace. Designed by Cesar Pelli and Assocs., the 27-story residence has its own water treatment system, photovoltaic panels to reduce electricity use and a rooftop garden.

🚲 Biking in the City 🚲

While New York's streets remain far from bike-friendly, the city's waterfront has become tantalizingly so. In fall 2003 the Department of Parks and Recreation unveiled a 32-mile circuit that takes cyclists from the Battery up the West Side, past the George Washington Bridge almost to the northern tip of Manhattan, then down the Harlem and East rivers and back to the Battery. There are gaps that require a little street maneuvering, most notably between 125th Street and 145th Street on the West Side, and around the United Nations on the East Side—but it is a vast improvement over the days of yore. In any case, most visitors are content to bicycle up and down the West Side, which sports the smoothest paths and best views of, and around, Central Park. Battery Park City is as good a place as any to hop on. Friendly bike store **Gotham Bikes** can set you up with a pair of wheels, a helmet and a map (*112 W. Broadway between Duane & Reade Sts.;* 🕐*open year-round Mon–Sat 10am–6:30pm, Sun 10:30am–5pm;* 🚲 *rentals $30/day, including helmet;* ☎*212-732-2453; www.gothambikes.com*). Arrive early on warm weekends since bikes are available on a first-come, first-served basis only. For more information on cycling in New York, contact Transportation Alternatives: ☎*212-629-8080; www.transalt.org.*

Visit

Esplanade and Parks★★

The esplanade is anchored on its south end by pleasant **Robert F. Wagner Jr. Park**. A raised observation deck here affords sweeping **views★★** of New York Harbor. Underneath you'll find public restrooms, and **Gigino at Wagner Park**, an Italian restaurant with a large waterfront patio (20 Battery Pl.; 🔊 see Where to Eat). On the north end of the esplanade lies 7-acre **Governor Rockefeller Park**, which has a playground, basketball and volleyball courts, a grass lawn (which turns into a de facto beach in summertime) and a Greek temple pavilion.

Additional Sights

Museum of Jewish Heritage★★
36 Battery Pl. 🔊 See Museums.

Skyscraper Museum★
39 Battery Pl. 🔊 ⏱Open year-round Wed-Sun noon-6pm. 🔊$5. ☎212-968-1961; www.skyscraper.org.
High-rise construction past, present and future is the focus of this enthusiastic newcomer to New York's museum scene, a must for architecture buffs. It opened its doors on April 2, 2004, in a 38-story tower standing opposite the Museum of Jewish Heritage at the southern tip of Battery Park City.
Roger Duffy of Skidmore, Owings & Merrill visually elongated the small, bi-level space by sheathing both floors and ceiling in polished steel—an appropriate gesture for a museum that celebrates verticality. Recent exhibits have focused on Frank Lloyd Wright's skyscraper designs and Lower Manhattan's development, featuring the original 9ft-tall model of the World Trade Center. The museum's bookstore stocks a wide array of New York architecture books and guides, and its award-winning website offers "virtual tours" of Manhattan.

Irish Hunger Memorial
North End Ave. & Vesey St.
Artist Brian Tolle created this striking memorial in 2002 to commemorate the Great Hunger of 1845-52, during which

Skyscraper Museum

a million Irish died of starvation and even more went hungry. The tragedy prompted many to emigrate, and between 1847 and 1851, more than a million Irish arrived in New York City. The site re-creates a rural Irish landscape with its abandoned stone cottage, fieldstone walls, fallow potato fields and thick green flora from the north Connacht wetlands. The memorial rests 25ft above the sidewalk on a tilted limestone plinth that affords views of the Statue of Liberty and Ellis Island.

World Financial Center
The commercial heart of Battery Park City was designed by Cesar Pelli & Assocs. It consists of four towers sheathed in granite

World Financial Center

and glass, ranging in height from 33 to 51 stories. Linked by glassed-in bridges, each has a copper roof of a different geometric shape: mastaba, dome, pyramid, and stepped pyramid. Together the complex encompasses 8 million sq ft of office and retail space, including the world headquarters of American Express and Merrill Lynch. The **Winter Garden★** is the highlight. This 10-story barrel-vaulted atrium is nestled between towers 2 and 3, providing a warm indoor venue for six-teen 43ft-tall palm trees and hundreds of office workers on their lunch hours (if they can find a seat—there's a woeful lack here of benches). The Winter Garden affords great **views★** of both the water and the ongoing construction at the neighboring World Trade Center site. The space is used for free lunchtime music or dance performances about once a week (*for a schedule, call ☎212-945-2600 or visit www.worldfinancial-center.com/calendar*).

SOUTH STREET SEAPORT★★

MTA SUBWAY: A, C TRAINS TO BROADWAY-NASSAU ST.
2, 3, 4, 5, J, M OR Z TO FULTON ST.
MAP BELOW

This waterfront historic district and shopping hub ranks as New York's third-largest tourist attraction. Its cobblestone streets and wide-plank wharves are packed with sightseers, peddlers and street performers on warm days. But that's only part of the picture. Spread throughout the district are half a dozen first-rate historical sites maintained by the South Street Seaport Museum.

▶ **Orient Yourself:** The seaport consists of 12 square blocks of cobblestone streets, with shops, historic vessels and a maritime museum. Most of the outdoor restaurants and bars are on Pier 17, but **Bridge Cafe,** on Water Street (*see Where to Eat*), is also a good choice.

🅿 **Parking:** It's best to arrive by subway, but if you come by car, several paid lots lie within a six-block radius. Free shuttle buses run along the waterfront between historic South Street Seaport and Battery Park City (*for information, call ☎212-566-6700 or visit online www.downtownNY.com/DowntownConnection*).

👁 **Don't Miss:** The old-fashioned **print shop** at Bowne & Co. Stationers.

Kids **Especially for Kids:** The museum offers **activities** for children (*see sidebar*).

©Peter Wrenn/MICHELIN

South Street Seaport

Kids The Seaport – JUST for Kids Kids

Lest the next generation forgets that, yes, there used to be activity here at the seaport other than shopping and eating, the **South Street Seaport Museum** has a raft of educational family programs on weekends (🕐 *year-round weekends 1pm– 4pm*). On Saturdays kids make **arts, crafts and music** on an educational theme such as archaeology or the Chinese New Year. On Super Story Sundays, children can gather around to listen to **tales of the sea** (among other subjects); then they get to embark on a writing adventure of their own. Family programs are free with museum admission and are designed for kids four years of age and older. Toddlers are welcome to join in with an adult.

A Bit of History

Historians call the seaport district the birthplace of New York City's economy. Founded in the 1600s as a small port, it underwent a period of rapid growth in the early 19C with the rise of international maritime trade. It was boosted by the inauguration of Fulton's Brooklyn ferry service in 1814 and the establishment of Fulton Market in 1822 (the fish market moved to the Bronx in 2005). With the opening of the **Erie Canal** in 1825, goods from the Midwest poured into the harbor. South Street became known to the world as the "Street of Ships" as China clippers, trans-Atlantic packets and other boats crowded the teeming wharves. In the 1960s Manhattan lost out to more sophisticated piers in Brooklyn and New Jersey. In 1967 efforts to preserve the port's historic buildings, piers and vessels culminated in the founding of the South Street Seaport Museum. Today the seaport draws some 12 million people annually.

Visit

South Street Seaport Museum★★

♿ Kids 🕐 *Apr–Oct Tue–Sun 10am–6pm; rest of the year Fri–Sun 10am–5pm (ships noon–5pm).* 🕐 *Closed Jan 1, Thanksgiving Day & Dec 25.* ☎ *212-748-8600. www. southstreetseaportmuseum.org.*
Museum sites are scattered throughout the district, which extends from Water Street to the East River between John Street and Peck Slip. Admission to the district is free; to visit museum sites,

purchase a ticket (💳 *$8*) at the **visitor kiosk** on Pier 16 or at the Schermerhorn Row Galleries at 12 Fulton Street.

Street of Ships★

Visitors to the museum are encouraged to climb aboard and explore several of the historic vessels moored on Piers 15 and 16. The **Peking (1** *on map)* is a square-rigged, four-masted barque built in 1911 in Hamburg, Germany; informative panels within describe the history of the ship and its features. When all 32 sails were set, she presented an amazing acre of canvas to the wind. The wet lab Kids is open to kids on Sundays. The *Ambrose (2 on map)* may also be boarded. She was the first lightship to serve as a guide to vessels approaching the entrance to Ambrose Channel in New York Harbor. The **Wavertree (3** *on map)*, an 1885 square-rigger built for the jute trade between India and Europe, is open for 🚶 guided tours only.

Hotel
🏠 Best Western Seaport Hotel

Restaurants
❶ Bridge Cafe   **❷** Quartino

Shops and Galleries

Schermerhorn Row Galleries★★

12 Fulton St. between Front & South Sts.
Ship chandler and developer Peter Schermerhorn built these handsome brick structures between 1811 and 1813 during the seaport's heyday; they were used as countinghouses and warehouses. Today they hold the South Street Seaport's formidable collection of maritime art and artifacts. As part of a $21 million interior restoration completed in 2003, Schermerhorn Row was linked internally to the 1850 A.A. Low Building, which fronts John Street, to create 30,000sq ft of gallery space. On exhibit is "**Soundings: Treasures of the Collections of the South Street Seaport Museum**," which includes paintings by maritime artist James Buttersworth; prisoner-of-war ship models made from bones; scrimshaw (whalebone carvings); a print of the Titanic signed by survivors; and a collection of ivory, lacquer and silk souvenirs from the China trade. Another permanent exhibit, "**Monarchs of the Sea: Celebrating the Ocean Liner Era**," recalls the glory days of the luxury liners, through models, artifacts and plans. The museum's core permanent exhibit, "**World Port New York**," is a sweeping survey of the seaport and its economic, commercial and cultural impact on the city, region and country.

Bowne & Company Stationers

211 Water St. between Fulton & Beekman Sts. Museum ticket not required. ◷Open Fri–Tue 10am–5pm.
This charming 19C print shop, which still turns out wedding invitations and book plates on foot-powered presses, has the name and the financial support of the oldest company listed on the New York Stock Exchange. Robert Bowne founded his original stationery store on Queen Street (now Pearl Street) in 1775. Today Bowne and Co. specializes in financial printing and has seven state-of-the-art printing plants across the country and in Canada. At this creaky old throwback, you can watch (and, if you're lucky, help) one of the two printers produce a Walt Whitman book on a treadle-operated press dating from 1901.

Walter Lord and Port Life (A on map) and Melville Library Galleries (B on map)

209 and 213 Water St. between Fulton & Beekman Sts.
Temporary and permanent exhibits on waterfront and New York history are mounted in these two galleries flanking Bowne & Co. Stationers. Don't miss the massive scale model (¼in = 1ft) of the **Queen Mary**★ near the back of the Walter Lord Gallery.

Pier 17 Pavilion★

Jutting 400ft into the East River, Pier 17 is the shopping, dining and entertainment hub of South Street Seaport. The three-story glass and steel structure (1984, Benjamin Thompson & Assocs.) contains a huge indoor mall. Stroll to the end of the pier to drink in **views**★ of the Brooklyn Bridge and the East River.

Fulton Market Building

This brick and granite structure, also a Thompson & Assocs. creation (1982), is the fourth market to be built on this site. It holds a convention space as well as shops and restaurants.

Going, Going, Gone

After a run of 170 years, the **Fulton Fish Market** finally closed its doors in the summer of 2005—a year after the original departure date—and moved 12 miles uptown to **Hunts Point** in the Bronx. There, instead of selling fish on ice in the city streets, it occupies a larger, enclosed refrigerated building designed to meet today's food handling standards. It's the end not only of the ever present smell of fish here, but also of an era. For decades it was a real "New York experience" to venture to the docks at the crack of dawn and watch local chefs and grocers pick out the best catch of the day.

Harbor Cruises

Both the South Street Seaport Museum and the **Circle Line Tour Company** offer boat tours of the harbor departing from Pier 16. The museum takes visitors out on its 1885 schooner **Pioneer** for two-hour sails (*May–Sept weekends 1pm, 4pm & 7pm; Tues, Thu, Fri 7pm–9pm; 24hr advance reservations recommended; $25–$30; 212-748-8786*). The Circle Line's vessel of choice is the *Zephyr*, a high-speed catamaran, which takes passengers past the Empire State Building, the Chrysler Building, the Brooklyn Bridge and the Colgate Clock in New Jersey, and affords close views of the Statue of Liberty and the Ellis Island Immigration Museum (*Apr–Oct daily noon, 1:30pm, 3pm; 4:30pm & 6pm; call for dates of additional boat tour 7:30pm Fri & Sat; $22 advance/$24 walk-up; 866-925-4631; www.circlelinedowntown.com*).

CIVIC CENTER ★

MTA SUBWAY: R, W TRAINS TO CITY HALL OR
4, 5, 6 TRAINS TO BROOKLYN BRIDGE-CITY HALL.
MAP P 98

The thumping heart of government bureaucracy, Civic Center teems with federal, state and local employees on weekdays. You'll want to plan your visit during normal business hours to peek inside the richly ornamented Surrogates Court and the New York State Supreme Court lobbies, as well as to see the New York African Burial Ground Project at the US General Services Administration Building–all three are closed evenings and weekends. A glorious exception is the Brooklyn Bridge: its pedestrian path is open 24/7.

- **Information:** NYC & Co., the city's official tourism organization, staffs the Heritage Tourism Center at Barclay Street and Broadway, directly across from the Woolworth Building (*open Mon–Fri 9am–6pm, weekends 10am-5pm; brochures and maps are available after hours*). NYC & Co. also operates a visitor counseling service, which has multilingual operators available (*Mon–Fri 8:30am-6pm, weekends & holidays 9am-5pm; 212-484-1200. www.nycvisit.com*).
- **Organize Your Time:** Allow 3hrs to visit the area, including 30min to cross the Brooklyn Bridge on foot.

Sights

Brooklyn Bridge ★★★

The pedestrian walkway runs along the north side of the bridge. In Manhattan it begins near the south corner of the Municipal Building on Lafayette Street across from City Hall Park. In Brooklyn it begins near the High Street–Brooklyn Bridge subway stop on the A/C line. Allow 30min to cross the bridge on foot. If walking from Manhattan to Brooklyn, continue on to nearby **Brooklyn Heights ★★**.

The first bridge to link Manhattan and Brooklyn, this famed structure was one of the great engineering triumphs of the 19C and the world's longest suspension bridge for 20 years. Its graceful silhouette set against the New York City skyline has inspired many artists, writers and poets. The stroll across the bridge is one of the most dramatic walks in New York. The **view ★★** of the city and harbor through the filigree of cables is magnificent, especially as the sun sets.

Construction – In 1869 German-born John Augustus Roebling, a pioneer bridge builder responsible for the Niagara Falls and Cincinnati, Ohio suspension bridges, was commissioned to design a bridge linking Manhattan and Brooklyn. Shortly after the plans were approved, Roebling's foot was crushed while he was taking measurements for the piers. Despite an

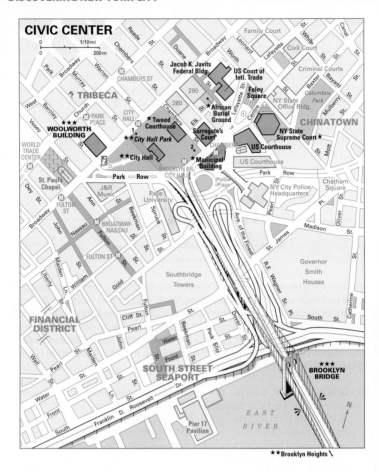

CIVIC CENTER

★★Brooklyn Heights ╲

amputation, gangrene set in and he died three weeks later. His son, Washington Roebling, carried on the work, adopting new methods in pneumatic foundations, which he had studied in Europe.

To construct the foundations, workers used caissons immersed in water and

Just the Facts

The bridge has a total length of 3,455ft with a maximum clearance above water of 133ft. The central suspended span between the two stone towers is 1,595ft long. The span is made of steel—the first time this metal was used for such a mammoth undertaking—and it is supported by four huge cables (15 ¾in thick) interconnected by a vast network of wires.

then filled with compressed air to prevent water infiltration. To adapt to the air pressure, the workmen underwent periods of gradual compression before going down to work, and decompression afterward. Despite these precautions, a few had burst eardrums or developed the "bends," which causes convulsions and can bring on partial or total paralysis. Washington Roebling himself was stricken with the bends. Confined to his sickbed, he nevertheless continued to direct the operation from his window overlooking the bridge. Finished in 1883, the bridge cost $25 million. With its intricate web of suspension cables and its majestic, pointed arches, the bridge represents an aesthetic and technical masterpiece. In 1972 the cables and piers were repainted in their original colors–beige and light brown.

Brooklyn Bridge

The walkway was rebuilt in 1983. The cables undergo regular maintenance.

History and Inspiration – The bridge immediately became the busy thoroughfare its planners had foreseen. On opening day, 150,000 people walked across it. Yet, less than a week after its inauguration by President Chester Arthur, tragedy struck. A woman fell on the stairway and her screams set off a panic killing 12 persons and injuring many more.

Fifteen years after the inauguration of the bridge, the city of Brooklyn was incorporated into New York. The bridge played a significant role in the development and growth of Brooklyn, the city's most populous borough.

Monumental and awe-inspiring, the Brooklyn Bridge has fascinated, obsessed and haunted New Yorkers. Immortalized in the works of Walt Whitman, it has also been painted on canvas by numerous artists. Colorful cubist renditions of the bridge, created in the 1920s by Joseph Stella, are among the best-known depictions of the monument.

Additional Sights

Woolworth Building★★★
233 Broadway between Park Pl. & Barclay St.; ⚬— lobby is closed to the public.
This 1913 skyscraper, the tallest in the world for 17 years, has been called a cathedral to commerce, and it's no wonder. Standing 792 feet and one inch in height, the tower is ornamented with the gargoyles, pinnacles, flying buttresses and finials more typical of ecclesiastical architecture and highly atypical of office buildings. In commissioning Cass Gilbert to design it, F.W. Woolworth, founder of the now defunct five- and ten-cent store chain, got a true masterpiece.

A Bit of History
In November 1910, plans called for the building to be only 625 feet tall, at a projected cost of $5 million. But after the caissons were sunk, Woolworth decided he wanted the structure to be the tallest in the world, which meant it had to top the 700ft Metropolitan Life Insurance Tower, completed in 1909. Gilbert happily revised his design, and the structure you see here is the result. The final cost of the building was $13.5 million, which Woolworth paid in cash.

At the opening ceremony, President Woodrow Wilson pressed a button in Washington that lit up 80,000 light bulbs in the building, an awesome spectacle at the time. In 1930 the title of world's-tallest passed to **40 Wall Street** *(now the Trump Building)*, but the Woolworth Building continues to stand out in the relatively (for New York) low-rise environment of Civic Center.

© Brigitta L. House/MICHELIN

Woolworth Building

Visit

The granite and limestone base of the building rises 27 stories without a set-back. On top of the building's mansard roof, facing Broadway, is a 27-story, terra-cotta-clad tower capped in copper. Byzantine-style mosaics and frescoes cover the three-story barrel-vaulted lobby. Among the lobby sculptures are caricatures of Gilbert clutching a model of the building and Woolworth counting his nickels.

City Hall Park★★

Bounded by Chambers & Lafayette Sts., Park Row & Broadway.

While much of the green expanse that surrounds City Hall and the Tweed Court-house is off limits to visitors, a 1999 renovation made the publicly accessible corner cupped by Park Row and Broadway a very pleasant hangout. Here wooden benches encircle a spiffy fountain, anchored by old-fashioned gas lamps. Magnolia trees and well-maintained plantings abound. The small plaza is also one of the best places to view the gilded 25ft statue *Civic Fame* on top of the Municipal Building in the distance as well as adjacent Park Row.

A Bit of History

Before the Revolutionary War, the area was a commons planted with apple trees on the northern edge of the bud-ding city. Liberty poles were erected by the Sons of Liberty, and in July 1776, the Declaration of Independence was read in the presence of Gen. George Washington, his troops and other patriots. Afterward, the crowd rushed down to **Bowling Green**★ to topple the statue of British monarch George III.

Visit

Today a statue (1893) of **Nathan Hale** (*1 on map*) (1755-76) stands in the park, with his back turned to Broadway; Frederick MacMonnies was the sculptor, and Stanford White built the base. Hale's famous last words, of course, were: "I only regret that I have but one life to lose for my country." **Horace Greeley** (*2 on map*) (1811-72), the crusading founder of the *New York Tribune*, is comfortably seated across from the Surrogates Court Building. The statue was designed by J.Q.A. Ward and completed in 1890.

City Hall★★

Visited by guided tour (1hr) only, year-round Wed noon, departing from Heritage Tourism Center (south end of City Hall Park, Broadway at Barclay St.). For a tour of City Hall and Tweed Courthouse, see Tweed Courthouse.

This is New York's second official City Hall (if you don't count the former tavern on Pearl Street that the Dutch used as a government seat). The first City Hall was opened at the corner of Wall and Broad streets in 1702, where the Federal Hall National Memorial now stands. Distinguished by a Neoclassical facade and a Georgian interior, the building you see here was completed in 1811 at a cost of about $500,000. It is the work of architects Joseph F. Mangin and John McComb Jr., who won a competition for the design and a prize of $350. To cut costs, politicians had the northern facade faced with brownstone, not marble, figuring that the city would never grow large enough for anyone to notice. By 1956 it had become clear that they had erred in their prediction, and the entire building was refaced with Alabama limestone.

The tour takes in the rotunda and the coffered dome, which evokes Rome's Pantheon; the City Council Chamber, and the Governor's Room; and a museum and reception room, with period furnishings and 19C American portraiture.

Tweed Courthouse★

Visit by guided tour (1hr 30min) only, year-round Tue 10am & Fri 2pm. Reservations required (dial 311 or ☎212-639-9675). Tour includes City Hall.

A whopping $13 million was appropriated for the construction of this courthouse between 1862 and 1870, and still the building wasn't finished! *(see sidebar on "Boss" Tweed).* After years of neglect, the Old New York County Courthouse (1872, Kellum and Little) was treated to an $85 million restoration (2001). Its grand colonnade facing Chambers Street now gleams like a fresh set of teeth. The edifice, whose style has been described as "Anglo-Italianate," contains one of the city's finest 19C interiors. Of particular interest are the iron staircases and the Gothic-style courtroom, which is now the headquarters of the city's Department of Education. The tour includes a visit to the octagonal rotunda, site of Roy Lichtenstein's sculpture entitled *Element #E* (1984).

African Burial Ground★

At the southwest corner of Duane & Elk Sts. Interpretive center at 290 Broadway. ☎212-637-2019. www.africanburial-ground.gov. *Burial ground open year-round Mon–Fri 9am–4pm; closed major holidays.*

Archaeologists happened upon this major historical site by chance in 1991. They'd been hired to do field testing in preparation for the construction of a new 34-story federal office building. Soon they discovered the first human remains from an 18C African burial ground that had been all but forgotten. Called "the Negroes Burying Ground" on maps from the period, it was a desolate five-and-a-half-acre plot outside city limits.

Until 1794, an estimated 20,000 people were buried here, stacked layer upon layer in unmarked graves, a testament to colonial New Yorkers' often-overlooked participation in the slave trade. Archaeologists ultimately unearthed more than 400 skeletal remains as well as burial artifacts from the site, and a small plot of land was set aside for a memorial, interpretive center and "new" burial ground. The site was declared a National Historic Landmark in 1993. In 2003, the remains were placed in handmade coffins from West Africa and lowered back into the ground in a ceremony of prayers, tributes, speeches, dance and song. A memorial and permanent interpretive center are to be completed late 2007.

City Hall Park

Peter Wrenn/MICHELIN

"Boss" Tweed

Though he wasn't the only corrupt political leader in New York history, "Boss" William M. Tweed (1823-78) is the most notorious. His infamy is due in no small part to the large figure he cut: a jovial man standing six feet tall and weighing nearly 300 pounds, he was popular among the immigrant groups who helped get him elected to the US House of Representatives and later, to the state senate. But it was his role in the Tammany Hall political machine that really made his reputation. From 1866 to 1871 the group who became known as the "Tweed Ring" essentially controlled all city spending–which is to say, they diverted it into their own pockets. Tweed and his crooked cronies illegally gained an estimated $30 million to $200 million in their dealings with the city. When Tweed died of pneumonia in prison, then-mayor Smith Ely refused to fly the city flag at half-staff.

Visit

Several powerful artworks are on permanent display here. Artist Roger Brown's stunning 140 sq ft **mosaic**★ shows a honeycomb of skulls buried beneath a soil-like layer of gaunt faces, topped by New York icons like the Brooklyn Bridge, the Twin Towers and the Empire State Building. Similarly striking is Barbara Chase-Riboud's bronze sculpture *Africa Rising*.

Municipal Building★

1 Centre St. at Chambers St.
Looming over the foot of Chambers Street is one of Civic Center's most striking buildings. McKim, Mead and White's first skyscraper (1914), it features a recessed central tower flanked by two protruding wings. The facade is distinguished by a monumental Neoclassical colonnade. Above the arch, Roman numerals mark the date of the founding of New Amsterdam (1626) and New York (1664). Also note the Guastavino tiles under the arcaded south wing (above the subway entrance). The gilded finial *Civic Fame*, by sculptor Adolph A. Weinman, stands at the top of the 40-story building, a barefoot female figure in a flowing dress, balancing on a copper ball. A five-pointed crown in her left hand symbolizes the five boroughs. Across the street, the **Surrogate's Court** *(31 Chambers St. at Centre St.;* ◷*open year-round Mon–Fri 9am–5pm)* is architect John Thomas's Beaux-Arts masterpiece. Composed of Maine granite, it rises seven stories, took seven years to build, and cost $7 million. The exterior is embellished with mythical figures and famous New Yorkers, and its **central hall**★ boasts marble walls and mosaic ceilings.

Foley Square

Bounded by Centre, Lafayette & Worth Sts.
This wedge-shaped plaza, named after city alderman Thomas F. Foley (1852-1925), once lay beneath a large pond, which was drained, and covered over in 1811. Houses built on the site began to sink due to inadequate drainage and poor foundations, and were abandoned. In the early 20C, the land was cleared for the New York State Supreme Court and other government offices.
A fountain, *Triumph of the Human Spirit* (2000), by Brooklyn sculptor Lorenzo Pace, stands at the southern tip of the square. The 50ft-tall black granite monument at its center was inspired by the art of Mali's Bambara tribe. The boatlike base evokes the slave trade. At the northern tip of Foley Square sits a tree-shaded park.
On the west side stands the **Jacob K. Javits Federal Building**, a 1967 high rise faced with a checkerboard pattern of white concrete and black glass. It is attached by a bridge to the glass-box **US Court of International Trade**, suspended from concrete beams.
On the east side sits the **New York State Supreme Court**★ *(60 Centre St. between Worth & Pearl Sts.;* ◷*open year-round Mon–Fri 9am–5pm).* Distinguished by monumental Corinthian colonnade, the Classical Revival structure (1927) is faced with granite on its six sides. Inside, an elaborate central rotunda is covered with 1930s murals, and a polychrome marble floor is embedded with the signs of the zodiac. Next door, the **Thurgood**

Marshall United States Courthouse *(40 Centre St.)*, designed by Cass Gilbert, was completed in 1936. It presents a curious blend of architectural elements—a square, 32-story tower capped by a pyramidal top bursts through the roof of a Classical Revival temple.

Park Row

So named because it faces City Hall Park, this stretch of road between **St. Paul's**

Chapel★★ and the foot of the Brooklyn Bridge was the center of journalism in the city: the *Times*, *Tribune*, *Herald*, *World* and *Sun* all had offices here. Today the block is occupied by the electronics emporium J&R Music. View the four-faced **brass clock** at 280 Broadway (at Chambers St.), which bears the *Sun's* motto: "The Sun: It shines for all."

CHINATOWN★★

🚇 SUBWAY: B, D TRAINS TO GRAND ST. OR©
N, Q, R, W, 6, J, M, Z TRAINS TO CANAL ST.
MAP P 104

The narrow streets at the heart of Chinatown feel utterly unlike the rest of New York City. Densely packed markets stock everything from lychee to lipstick, while storefront restaurants serve up all manner of Asian cuisine. Especially crowded on weekends, the area bursts its seams at Chinese New Year (first full moon after Jan 19), when dragons dance down the streets accompanied by banner-carrying attendants and fireworks.

ℹ️ **Information:** A staffed visitor information booth on Canal at Walker & Baxter Sts. is open year-round Sun–Fri 10am–6pm, Sat 10am–7pm. www.explorechinatown.com.

🕐 **Organize Your Time:** Allow 2hrs to visit Chinatown.

A Bit of History

Just Visiting – The first Chinese in New York came in the 1870s from the California goldfields or from jobs building the transcontinental railroad in the western US. Most were men who, unlike other immigrants, had no intention of staying: they just wished to make their fortunes and return to a comfortable life in China. By the 1880s the community numbered about 10,000. Then restrictive legislation (the Chinese Exclusion Act) was passed to stop further immigration, and growth was effectively halted. Unable to earn passage back to China, many "temporary" residents stayed. In part because single men continued to make up the majority of the population, the neighborhood took on a rough-and-tumble character in the late 19C and early 20C. Opium dens, brothels and gambling parlors sprang up, as did social clubs called tongs. While many of the tongs' activities were peaceful, turf wars

occasionally broke out. All too often they were resolved with revolvers or hatchets, the latter giving rise to the term *hatchet men*.

Lucky paper lanterns, Chinatown

Restaurants

❶ Dim Sum Go Go	❸ Oriental Garden
❷ Great N.Y. Noodletown	❹ Peking Duck House

Here to Stay – Following the 1943 repeal of the Chinese Exclusion Act, a new influx of immigrants arrived in New York from Taiwan and Hong Kong, as well as from mainland China. Garment factories, Chinese laundries, shops and restaurants appeared in the quarter, which has inexorably spread out from its dense core into neighboring Little Italy and the Lower East Side.

The present-day Asian community of New York has been estimated at 1,165,000, of which roughly three-fourths are Chinese. Today Manhattan's Chinatown now holds the largest Chinese immigrant community outside Asia. The majority of

Shopping in Chinatown

Manhattan's 195,000 Asians live in Chinatown.

Visit

The heart of Chinatown lies in the area bounded by Worth, Baxter, and Canal streets and the Bowery. **Mulberry** and **Mott** streets are lined with shops piled high with displays of bamboo plants, tea sets, silk dresses, Chinese lanterns, fans and the like. **Ten Ren Tea and Ginseng** *(75 Mott St.; ☎212-349-2286)* is a lovely spot for tea lovers: the proprietors measure out a stunning range of teas, from $125-a-pound hand-picked green oolong to more affordable jasmine tea from beautiful old canisters. Neighboring **Ten Ren's Tea Time** *(79 Mott St.; ☎212-732-7178)* serves up freshly steeped hot cups as well as sweet tapioca iced tea ("bubble tea"), which is hugely popular with young Chinese. **Maria's Bakery** *(42 Mott St.; ☎212-732-3888)* sells homemade fortune cookies by the bag, as well as other Chinese sweets.

Notable Streets

Pell, Doyers and Bayard Streets

These, the most atmospheric streets in the district, are so narrow that they are almost always in the shade. Note the red-painted brick structure on the southwest corner of Pell and the Bowery (18 Bowery). Built in 1785 by **Edward Mooney**, a butcher, this structure is reputed to be the earliest surviving row house in Manhattan. Formerly a tavern, a store, a hotel, a pool parlor, a restaurant and a social club, it is now a community bank. **Doyers Street** makes a sharp 90-degree turn in the middle: legend has it that merchants built it that way so that flying ghosts could move through it. Later it became known as "the bloody angle" for the tong wars that were fought here between 1880 and 1926.

Canal Street, between Broadway and Mulberry Street, is world-famous for being crammed full of tiny stalls selling knock-off designer goods, especially handbags and scarves. Word has it that a network of secret passages and hidden rooms connects some of the stores, allowing proprietors to hide merchandise from the

Address Book

RESTAURANTS AND CAFES

Chanoodle – *79 Mulberry St.* ☎*212-349-1495.* Peking duck is a specialty.

Dim Sum Go Go – *5 E. Broadway.* *See Where to Eat.*

Joe's Shanghai – *9 Pell St.* ☎*212-233-8888. Open daily 11am-11pm.* There's often a line out the door.

Oriental Garden – *14 Elizabeth St.* *See Where to Eat.* Fresh-from-the-tank seafood. A Chinatown favorite.

Pho Tu Do – *119 Bowery.* ☎*212-966-2666.* Vietnamese. Spring rolls, pho (soup), etc.

Tasty Dumpling – *54 Mulberry St.* ☎*212-349-0700. Open daily 9am-9pm.* Extremely cheap and fresh. Good for takeout and eating at Columbus Park across the street.

Tea & Tea – *51 Mott St.* ☎*212-766-9889.* Tapioca tea plus soups and spring rolls. Very popular.

Vegetarian Dim Sum House – *24 Pell St.* ☎*212-577-7176.* All veggie dim sum, plus a lot of vegetable dishes and imitation meat dishes.

detectives hired to nab them for copyright infringement.

Two structures on Canal Street incorporate some of the more festive elements of Chinese architecture: the red-lacquered, pagoda-roofed Hong Kong Bank Building at **No. 241 Canal Street** (*at Centre St.*), completed in 1983 (a Starbucks now occupies the ground floor); and the Mahayana Buddhist Temple at **133 Canal Street** (*between the Bowery & Chrystie Sts.*), whose entrance is flanked by gilded lions. Step inside the temple for a strong whiff of incense and to see the 10ft golden Buddha seated on a lotus; tiny fortune scrolls are available for $1.

Across the street, the **Manhattan Bridge arch** and horseshoe-shaped **colonnade** (1913, Carrère and Hastings) were spruced up by the Department of Transportation recently, after decades of neglect. A newly opened pedestrian path leads over the bridge to the hip Dumbo neighborhood (Dumbo stands for "Down Under the Manhattan Bridge Overpass") in Brooklyn.

Additional Sights

Columbus Park

Chinatown's largest park recently underwent a massive renovation. New benches, paths, picnic tables, plantings and lights were installed on the north end, which is now a great place to enjoy a takeout order from **Tasty Dumpling** across the street or to watch Chinese men play intensely competitive games of checkers. A pleasant children's playground occupies the south end, which, ironically,

used to be one of the most violent parts of the city. Known as **Five Points**, after the streets that intersected here in the early 19C—Mulberry Street, Anthony (now Worth) Street, Cross (now Park) Street, Orange (now Baxter) Street and Little Water Street (paved over)—it was a fetid, foul-smelling swampland where decaying houses, taverns, and shacks stood shakily side by side in the shadow of an immense brewery. Many of the residents were destitute Irish immigrants, whose notoriously violent gangs (the Plug Uglies, the Dead Rabbits, the Roach Guards) were featured in Martin Scorsese's 2002 film *Gangs of New York*. So infamous was the neighborhood that Charles Dickens came to write about it in 1842. What he saw appalled him (alleys knee-deep in mud; women sleeping on floors). But not until the late 1880s did conditions improve, and then only because the city leveled the whole area.

Museum of Chinese in the Americas (MoCA)

70 Mulberry St. at Bayard St., 2nd floor. Open year-round Tue–Sun noon–6pm. Closed major holidays. $2. ☎*212-619-4785. www.moca-nyc.org.*

On the second floor of a late-19C schoolhouse—now an active community

😊 A Bit of Advice 😊

When you're shopping in Chinatown, try bargaining. It might work with some vendors.

Walking Tours

Get the inside look at the neighborhood on one of the Museum of Chinese in the Americas' **Experience Chinatown** walking tours. Docents with family ties to the neighborhood will guide you around the streets, pointing out historic and personal landmarks. Tours *($12)* are held every Saturday between May and December, 1pm–2:30pm. MoCA also offers specialty tours on such topics as cuisine and religion. Call the museum for a schedule and to make a reservation (required): ☎*212-619-4785.*

center—a small warren of rooms sheds light on Chinese American history. The only permanent installation, Where Is Home?, presents military uniforms, photographs, immigration papers, and sewing machines and irons from once-prevalent Chinese laundries. Another gallery showcases temporary exhibits.

LITTLE ITALY★ – NOLITA★

MTA SUBWAY: N, Q, R, W, 6, J, M, Z TRAINS TO CANAL ST.
MAP P 108

Little Italy, which once ran from Canal Street north to Houston and from Lafayette Street east to the Bowery, may now be more aptly termed Micro Italy. There are still 700,000 Italian Americans in New York City, but the commercial heart of their onetime stronghold in Manhattan has dwindled to a corridor: Mulberry Street. Between Canal and Broome streets, this thoroughfare caters mainly to hungry tourists, though there are still some authentic delis, bakeries and gelato shops to be found. Little Italy's uber-fashionable sister, so-called Nolita (for North of Little Italy), actually sits within the neighborhood's former boundaries: four blocks long and three blocks wide, it stretches from Broome to Houston streets on Mulberry, Mott and Elizabeth streets. The moniker Nolita came courtesy of real estate developers who, in the 1990s, wanted to distinguish it from the red-sauce joints of the old neighborhood. And they did. Today Nolita is chock-a-block with trendy cafes and boutiques.

A Sidewalk Cafe in Little Italy

©iStockphoto.com/Terraxplorer

A Bit of History

Italians have played a powerful role in shaping New York even before there was a city to shape. The Italian explorer **Giovanni da Verrazano**, working under the auspices of French king François I, was the first European to set foot on the island of Manhattan, in 1524. Italians didn't cross the Great Pond en masse until the late 1800s, however. Fleeing rural poverty in southern Italy, many initially settled in the notorious **Five Points** slum, which stood on what is now a corner of Chinatown. As families got on their feet, however, they moved north to SoHo, Greenwich Village and Little Italy. Some returned to the old country, but thousands more arrived. In 1880 fewer than 20,000 Italians lived in the city. That

Address Book

BEST OF LITTLE ITALY

Alleva Dairy – *188 Grand St. at Mulberry St. Open daily 8:30am–6pm (Sun until 3pm).* ☎*212-226-7990; www.allevadairy.com.* Here's where you'll want to get your prosciutto, mozzarella and roasted-pepper sandwich, the deli's specialty. It was founded in 1892 and still has a friendly family feel.

$ Caffe Roma – *385 Broome St. at Mulberry St. Open daily 8am–midnight.* ☎*212-226-8413.* Tile floors, tin ceilings and ice-cream parlor chairs make this the most appealing of Little Italy's cafes. Sit outdoors and watch the world go by.

$ Ferrara – *195 Grand St. between Mott & Mulberry Sts. Open daily 8am–midnight.* ☎*212-226-6150; www.ferrara.com.* Tucked around the corner from the bustling main drag of Mulberry Street, Ferrara is the place for cannoli, tiramisu and Italian pastry. It's all made on-site and served up in cool, old-school ambience.

$ La Mela – *167 Mulberry St. between Broome & Grand Sts. Open daily 11am–2am (Fri–Sat until 3am).* ☎*212-431-9493; www.lamelarestaurant.com.* The food portions are fittingly humongous at this sprawling Little Italy landmark, which can seat 500 at a time now that it has two kitchens. Photos of famous and not-so-famous revelers paper the walls.

$ Lombardi's – *32 Spring St. between Mott & Mulberry Sts. Open daily 11:30am–11pm (Fri–Sat until midnight, Sun until 10pm).* ☎*212-941-7994.* Established in 1905, Lombardi's claims to be the first pizzeria in America. Its thin-crust pies are baked in coal-fired ovens and served on checkered tablecloths. Expect a wait on weekend nights.

NOLITA BONITA

Bio – *29 Prince St. between Mott & Elizabeth Sts.* ☎*212-334-3006. www.bio-nyc.com.* Fifteen up-and-coming clothing designers display their latest collections in this vast gallery space. It's often featured in fashion magazines as a breeding ground for new talent.

$$ Cafe Gitane – *242 Mott St. between Prince & Houston Sts.* ☎*212-334-9552.* This is Nolita's most popular hangout. Moroccan couscous, focaccia sandwiches, cheese plates, beer and cappuccino, all with a French accent. Open late.

McNally Robinson Booksellers – *52 Prince St. between Lafayette & Mulberry Sts. Open Mon–Sat 10am–10pm, Sun 10am–9pm.* ☎*212-274-1160. www.mcnallyrobinsonnyc.com.* Countering the trend toward national chain book-and-music stores, this bright fairly new independent professes to offer "every book you could possibly want, and not a single book more." After you've browsed a bit, order up a Japanese cherry or Moroccan mint brew in the newly remodeled **Teahouse** cafe, which also serves a variety of coffees and other beverages as well as salads, soups, sandwiches and pastries.

Otto Tootsi Plohound – *273 Lafayette St. at Prince St.* ☎ *212-431-7299.* The men's and women's shoes at this local mini-chain don't come cheap ($150–$700), but they're beautifully made (mostly in Italy) and displayed. Look for Prada and Miu-Miu as well as daring new names.

---

number rose to 220,000 by 1900, to 545,000 by 1910 and to more than a million by 1930. Women worked in the garment trade and men worked in construction, or started their own businesses as tailors, barbers, grocers or restaurateurs, bringing their native dishes into the melting pot of American cuisine.

La Cosa Nostra – Italians were no different from other immigrants, including the Irish and the Chinese, in organizing around their own interests—helping each other get jobs, for instance, and fostering their heritage. But with the onset of Prohibition in 1919, Italian social clubs gelled into unprecedented crime syndicates that together made up La Cosa Nostra. **Lucky Luciano** and **Al Capone** were two of the New York City Mafia's earliest celebrities. They pioneered bootlegging operations during Prohibition; then, after that law was repealed, they moved into illegal gambling, loan sharking, pornography, drug smuggling and labor racketeering. Internecine battles occasionally burst into the public eye, as when **"Crazy" Joey Gallo** was gunned down during his 43rd birthday dinner at the original Umberto's Clam House on Mulberry Street in 1972 (then at 129 Mulberry; the restaurant has since moved to No. 178.)

Proud Italians – Despite such lively (or deadly, as it were) characters, many local Italian Americans point out that they've

Street Cafe at Night

contributed far more to the city, particularly in the political arena, than what you'll see on the HBO series *The Sopranos* or in Francis Ford Coppola's *Godfather* trilogy. **Fiorello La Guardia**, who was born at 177 Sullivan Street in 1882, served three terms as New York City mayor (1933-45). **Mario Cuomo** of Queens was a three-term New York State governor (1982-1994). **Geraldine Ferraro**, also from Queens, became the first woman nominated by a major party (the Democrats) for national office (vice president) in 1984. Finally, **Rudolph Giuliani** of Brooklyn made his name as a mob-busting federal attorney before serving as mayor of New York from 1994 to 2002.

Visit

Little Italy

A visit to **Little Italy** basically consists of a **Mulberry Street**★ stroll. The stretch between Canal and Grand streets is a veritable restaurant row, with white-aproned waiters sweet-talking diners into choosing their linguine over all others. On weekends from May to mid-

October Mulberry Street is closed to vehicular traffic, making Little Italy one big al fresco party; the Feast of San Gennaro in mid-September is especially raucous. On summer nights a scoop of gelato, served up in a cone or cup by sidewalk vendors, tastes particularly delicious.

Nolita

Nolita is a boutique lover's paradise, a place where young designers sell funky home furnishings, one-of-a-kind necklaces, accessories and clothes from tiny storefronts. Shopkeepers tend to be friendlier here than in SoHo, making Nolita a great place to browse. The cafes are likewise ideal for people-watching. **Old St. Patrick's Church** (1815, Joseph F. Magnin), at the corner of Prince and Mulberry streets, was New York's Roman Catholic Cathedral until 1879, when it was replaced by a much larger and grander structure in what is now Midtown. If the church is open, you can step inside and view the solemn Gothic interior.

LOWER EAST SIDE★

MTA SUBWAY: F TRAIN TO DELANCEY ST. OR
B OR D TRAIN TO GRAND ST.
MAP P 110

Despite being one of New York's hippest 'hoods, the Lower East Side has, for the most part, a refreshing lack of attitude and an astounding amount of local pride. "Come one, come all" has been its message to visitors since the 1880s, when it became the quintessential American melting pot. Though today's immigrants tend to be young artists, musicians, designers and restaurateurs, history lives on in the district's one-of-a-kind tenement museum and many famous ethnic eateries.

- **Information:** Visitor Center, 261 Broome St. between Orchard and Allen Sts. ☎212-226-9010; www.lowereastsideny.com.
- **Orient Yourself:** Start at the **visitor center** at address above (⊙open daily 9am-5pm; ⊙closed major holidays). Here you'll find friendly staff to answer questions, as well as brochures, **shopping maps** of the Lower East Side (some with a discount card), citywide bus maps and information on walking tours.
- **Parking:** The Historic Orchard Street Shopping District offers three hours of **free parking** to visitors at its lot on Broome Street between Norfolk and Suffolk streets (⊙open daily year-round).

A Bit of History

The Governor's Farm – Bounded by Houston Street, the East River, East Broadway and the Bowery, Lower East Side was rural long after southern Manhattan was developed. **Peter Stuyvesant**, the last Dutch governor of Nieuw Amsterdam, bought much of the land in 1651 from the Indians. To facilitate transport between his farm, or *bouwerie*, and the urban market, he laid out a broad, straight road, now known as the Bowery. Delancey Street was named for James de Lancey, an English landowner whose farm was confiscated after the American Revolution. Free blacks cultivated the soil here until around 1800, when development encroached agriculture.

The Gateway to America – The first mass migration to the Lower East Side occurred with the arrival of Irish immigrants fleeing the Great Hunger of 1845-52. From the 1880s until World War I, millions of southern and eastern Europeans arrived via Ellis Island and were diverted to the Lower East Side, where they could meet other immigrants. The neighborhood became the most densely populated in the country. So overcrowded were some of the "railroad flats" (lots were 25ft wide and 100ft long, like railroad cars) that family members took turns sleeping. In 1890 **Jacob Riis** documented the conditions in his now-classic book on urban poverty *How the Other Half Lives: Studies among the Tenements of New York*. Eastern European Jews set down some of the strongest roots here, building nearly 500 houses of worship and schools; pub-

Lower East Side Tenement Museum

lishing Yiddish newspapers; and opening vaudeville theaters on the Bowery, otherwise known as the "poor man's Broadway." Some of the biggest names in showbiz were raised on the Lower East Side (the **Marx Brothers, Jimmy Durante, Eddie Cantor, Al Jolson, Irving Berlin** and **George Gershwin** among them). The tide of immigration was halted in the 1920s with the passage of restrictive legislation. Many Jewish families moved to the Upper West Side and after World War II, thousands of African Americans and Puerto Ricans moved in. Afterward came the Beat poets, then, after neglect in the 1970s and 80s, a new generation of artists and musicians.

Lower East Side Today – Today only 10 percent of Lower East Side residents are Jewish. The southern edge of the district is largely Chinese. Latinos still have a presence; their nickname for the quarter, "Loisaida," is still heard in some parts. But more prevalent, or at least visible, are the hordes of young Anglos who've transformed the gritty neighborhood into an urban village.

Address Book

LIVE MUSIC CLUBS IN LOWER EAST SIDE

(👣 see Nightlife in Your Stay in the City)
Arlene Grocery – 95 Stanton St.
between Ludlow & Orchard Sts.
Bowery Ballroom – 6 Delancey St.

between Bowery & Chrystie Sts.
Mercury Lounge – 217 E. Houston St.
between Ludlow & Essex Sts.
Pianos – 158 Ludlow St. at Stanton St.
TUTS – 196 Orchard St.
Rockwood Music Hall – 196 Allen St.

Visit

Orchard Street★ between Canal and Houston streets is the district's spine: to the south it is lined with bargain stores specializing in luggage, underwear and coats; farther north (around Broome Street), the trendy boutiques start. It is home to the **Lower East Side Tenement Museum**★★ (no. 90 and 97; 👣 see Museums). Orchard Street is closed to traffic on Sundays, when shopkeepers turn it into an outdoor mall.

Stanton Street and **Rivington Street** all the way east to **Clinton Street** are good places to find galleries, shops and cafes. A carnival atmosphere prevails at night in and around Ludlow Street between Houston and Delancey streets; bars, restaurants and clubs here are full to the wee hours. (👣 For live-music venues in the neighborhood, see Your Stay in the City.)

Neighborhood Tours

Walking tours 👣

The Lower East Side Business Improvement District, which runs the visitor center, sponsors a walking tour at 11am every

Sunday (Apr–Dec); meet at Katz's Deli at (Houston & Ludlow Sts.). A **cell phone walking tour** is narrated by comedian and native son **Jerry Stiller**. In addition to Stiller's narration, the 13-stop, self-paced tour provides a total of 30 minutes of historic audiotape, interviews and dramatic readings on such topics as the garment industry and Meyer Lansky, the first modern gangster, who was born and raised here (call ☎212-262-8687 for a free preview and to start the tour). The tenement museum and citywide walking tour companies, such as **Rent a New Yorker** (2 hrs; 💲$10; ☎212-982-9445; www.rentanewyorker.com) and **Big Onion Walking Tours** (2 hrs; 💲$15; ☎212-439-1090; www.bigonion.com) conduct tours of this rich neighborhood as well.

Art tours

Every Last Sunday on the Lower East Side (or ELS on the LES), neighborhood artists open their studios and galleries to the public (1pm–5pm). A free guided tour starts from the Lower East Side Visitor Information Center at 1pm. To visit galleries on your own, pick up an "art loop" map at the visitor center. For more information, go to www.elsles.org.

🎭 A Bit of Advice 🎭

DON'T FORGET THE BUS!
So mammoth is the New York City subway system that many people (locals and visitors alike) forget that there is, as well, an extensive network of buses that are not only convenient, but free with unlimited-ride metro cards (or $2 per ride for single rides, but you must have a MetroCard in advance; see Planning Your Trip). To get to and from the Lower East Side, consider taking the **M15** bus, which runs all the way up the east side of Manhattan between the **Whitehall Ferry Terminal** and **East Harlem** on 1st and 2nd avenues; from the Lower East Side, you can pick it up at the corner of Allen and Delancey streets. The **M14A** bus serves the neighborhood too, traveling along Grand and Essex streets (the latter turns into Avenue A in **East Village**), then proceeding all the way west to **Chelsea Piers** via 14th Street. Pick up a bus map at the Lower East Side Visitor Center.

A Nosher's Paradise

Though Zabar's on the Upper West Side is arguably *the* gourmet Jewish marketplace in New York, Lower East Side was the original nosher's paradise; it remains just that. (Fittingly, the Yiddish word nosh means "to eat on the sly.") Since opening in 1914, **Russ & Daughters** *(179 E. Houston St.; open Mon–Sat 9am–7pm, Sun 8am–5:30pm; ☎212-475-4880; www.russanddaughters.com)* has been winning awards for its Caspian Sea caviar and just about everything else. Come in and put together a sampler of homemade salads (Roumanian-style eggplant or whitefish and baked salmon), bagels,

©Shea Dean
Russ & Daughters

bialys, lox, roasted almonds or pistachios and homemade raspberry nut rugelach. The guys behind the counter are very friendly. For a tart accompaniment, go to **Guss' Lower East Side Pickles** *(85 Orchard St.; open Sun–Thu 9:30am–6pm; Fri 9:30am–4pm; ☎917-701-4000; www.gussworldfamouspickles.com)*, founded in 1910. Here, on the sidewalk outside a simple storefront, stand white buckets full of pickled things and, on most days, a line of people eager to sample their contents. In addition to the classic sour dills, you can get fancy olives and pickled tomatoes. To top it off, head over to the **Sweet Life** *(63 Hester St. at Ludlow St.; open Mon–Fri 10am–6:30pm, Sat 11am–5pm, Sun 10am–6pm; ☎212-598-0092)*, the Lower East Side's preeminent candy shop since 1982, which carries an awesome array of Kosher treats, including dried fruits and nuts, hand-dipped chocolates, and macaroons, as well as jelly beans, gummy bears, licorice and hard candies.

Additional Sights

Eldridge Street Synagogue★
12 Eldridge St. between Canal & Division Sts. ◷*Open year-round Sun, Tue–Thu*

Eldridge Street Synagogue
Eldridge Street Synagogue interior

11am–4pm. ◷*Closed Jewish & major holidays.*⌖*Guided tours (phone for times & prices).* ☎*212-219-0888. www.eldridgestreet.org.*

Completed in 1887, this was the first synagogue built by Eastern European Jews. In the late 1800s, as many as 1,000 people attended services here. During high holidays, police patrolled the streets on horseback to keep order. Membership began to dwindle in the 1920s. By the 1940s the sanctuary was used only for holidays and special events. It was closed in the 1950s, though the congregation continued to meet in the basement. The synagogue stood in a state of disrepair until the 1980s, when a preservation campaign was launched. The Eldridge Street Project, a nonprofit organization, is restoring the landmark into a cultural and heritage center. A Herter Brothers commission, the building displays a striking rose window set against an ornate Moorish facade. Inside, hand-stenciled walls rise to a 70ft vaulted ceiling.

Bowery Savings Bank

130 Bowery between Grand & Broome Sts.
Designed in 1895 by McKim, Mead and White, this Beaux-Arts gem is distinguished by imposing Corinthian columns and opulent detailing. The interior features an ornate, coffered vault with a large opaque skylight at its center.

Freakatorium

57 Clinton St. between Rivington & Stanton Sts. ⏱*Open year-round Wed–Sun 1pm–7pm.* 👝*$5.* ☎ *212-375-0475.*

Sword swallower and magician Johnny Fox collected carnival art for 30 years before opening his storefront museum in 1999 to display it. Also known as El Museo Loco, it harks back to P.T. Barnum's American Museum, with cabinets of curiosities, not all of which are for the faint of heart. A shrunken head, a two-headed turtle, and Sammy Davis Jr.'s glass eye are among the 1,000 objects on rotating display.

SoHo ★

MTA SUBWAY: R, W TRAINS TO PRINCE ST.
OR C, E TRAINS TO SPRING ST.
MAP P 115

The heart of Manhattan's downtown fashion scene, SoHo–short for South of Houston (pronounced HOW-stun)–is New York at its trendiest and most colorful. Visitors throng the district on weekends, making even walking down the sidewalk difficult, especially given the proliferation of sidewalk tables full of purses and jewelry, sunglasses and scarves and amateurish (or more politely speaking, "outsider") art. For more serious art appreciators, there are still some top-notch galleries here, though many in the past decade have decamped for Chelsea, where rents are (slightly) cheaper. SoHo's cast-iron architecture gives the neighborhood a look all its own.

▶ **Orient Yourself**: SoHo is bounded roughly by Sullivan, West Houston, Lafayette and Canal streets and is best experienced on foot (balance sense with style when it comes to shoes).

⏱ **Organizing Your Time:** Saturdays tend to be the most crowded, especially on warm days and during the holiday shopping season. Many galleries are closed on Sundays and Mondays.

🖾 **Don't Miss:** To learn about art exhibits and openings citywide, pick up a free New York **Gallery Guide** at any of the galleries mentioned.

Kids **Especially for Kids:** New York City Fire Museum, the real McCoy, particularly for youngsters.

A Bit of History

The site of the first free black community in Manhattan, SoHo was settled in 1644 by former slaves of the Dutch West India Company, who were granted land for farms. In the early 19C, Broadway was paved and a number of prominent citizens, including *Last of the Mohicans* author James Fenimore Cooper, moved in, bringing considerable cachet to the district. By 1825 it was the most densely populated neighborhood in Manhattan.

In the late 1850s, large stores such as Tiffany & Co. and Lord & Taylor were joined on Broadway by grand hotels. Theaters, casinos and brothels entertained visitors—and drove respectable middle-class families uptown. The exodus made room for new warehouses and factories, many built with ornamented cast-iron facades. The area thrived as a commercial center until the 1890s, when fashionable businesses began relocating to Fifth Avenue.

©iStockphoto.com/Jose Antonio Sanchez

Art Brings a New Start – By the late 1950s, the neighborhood was a slum known as "Hell's Hundred Acres," and city planners slated it for demolition to make room for an expressway. Locals fought the proposal, though, and the area soon showed new signs of life. Often in violation of building codes, painters and sculptors converted vacant warehouses into studios, galleries and living quarters. An exciting underground art scene took root and thrived until the early 1980s, when uptown galleries, boutiques and affluent professionals began to push out the very artists who'd made the neighborhood so desirable in the first place.

SoHo Today – Today, few artists can afford to live or work in Soho, and art museums haven't fared much better: the Guggenheim SoHo, the New Museum of Contemporary Art, and the Alternative Museum have all moved out. Mean-

while, the migration of galleries northward to Chelsea continues. Locally owned boutiques have been largely supplanted by international couturiers such as Chanel, Prada and Helmut Lang. Indeed, SoHo has become a mecca for fashion-obsessed celebrities. That said, several excellent galleries remain in the neighborhood, as do a number of cafes and restaurants. As for shopping, sidewalk vendors offer up some good bargains, and despite what some haughty clerks might lead you to believe, browsing in even the most expensive stores is free.

Broadway★

Overflowing with traffic, pedestrians and sidewalk vendors, this is SoHo at its most commercial. Most of the stores are bargain clothing and shoe outlets and national chains, but there are several happy exceptions: **Pearl River Mart**, once crammed into fourth-floor rooms on Canal Street, has spread out in style at no. 477 between Grand and Broome streets. The bi-level Asian emporium carries a sparkling array of slippers, silk jackets, kimonos, paper lanterns, incense, ceramics and jade figurines. At no. 504 (between Broome and Spring Sts.) stands **Bloomingdale's SoHo**, a small-scale version of the uptown department store. Opened in 2004, it has the same languid grace as the original. Finally there is **Prada** (no. 575 at Prince St.), a retail fun house designed by Dutch architect Rem Koolhaas. Inside, a cylindrical glass elevator moves silently between floors, which are joined as well by a zebrawood slide and two grand facing staircases.

Sullivan Street

Just as Little Italy has been gobbled up by Chinatown, so has the South Village, a one-time Italian stronghold, been gobbled up by SoHo. For a literal and figurative taste of what has been lost, head over to Sullivan Street. On the block between West Houston and Prince streets stands **St. Anthony of Padua Roman Catholic Church** (no. 155), dedicated in 1888. Across the street sits **Joe's Dairy** (no. 156; ☎ 212-677-8780), an old-school cheese and salami shop that specializes in fresh and smoked mozzarella. **Pepe Rosso to Go** (no. 149; ☎ 212-677-4555) actually does have two tiny tables; snag one for a delectably cheap plate of pasta and a tumbler of red wine. Nearby, **Arturo's Pizzeria** (106 W. Houston St.; ☎212-677-3820) is a rowdy dive that wins praise, even among local pizza snobs, for its coal-fired-oven pies.

SOHO

Hotel	Restaurant
🏠 Soho Grand Hotel	❶ Blue Ribbon Sushi

Broadway is also home to the two most famous buildings in the district. The 1903 **Singer Building**★ *(nos. 561-563)*, designed by Ernest Flagg, ushered in a new era of skyscraper design. Delicate wrought-iron tracery and wide expanses of recessed glass keep the 12-story building from looming heavily over the street; Kate's Paperie occupies the ground floor. Though the street-level facade of the **E.V. Haughwout Building**★ *(nos. 488-492)* now sports the garish red awnings of an office-supply chain, one need only lift one's eyes to see what all the fuss is about. This 1857 "Venetian palace," patterned with arched windows, balustrades and Corinthian columns, has the oldest cast-iron facade in the city. Built for Eder V. Haughwout, a clock and chandelier merchant, the structure also housed the first safety passenger elevator, installed by **Elisha Graves Otis**.

Other Major Streets

Broome Street★
At Broome and Greene streets, the 1873 **Gunther Building** *(nos. 469-475)* is a standout in cast-iron design. English-born architect **Calvert Vaux** designed the delicate cast-iron building at no. 448. **Gourmet Garage** *(no. 453)* has

baked goods, sandwiches and salads. You can eat them outside on benches.

Greene Street★
This narrow cobblestone gulch is flanked by the richest collection of cast-iron building facades in the district. The two that are most impressive are known as the **King and Queen of Greene Street**, designed by Isaac F. Duckworth in 1872. The "queen" (nos. 28-30) sports a mansard roof, projecting bays and ornate dormer—all hallmarks of the Second Empire style. The cream-colored "king" (nos. 72–76) has a grandiose porch supported by Corinthian columns. Farther north on Greene, at 112-114 Prince Street, you'll find a building whose facade looks like cast iron but is actually a trompe l'oeil design painted on brick by artist Richard Haas in 1975. Notable galleries on Greene Street include (from south to north) the **Artists Space Gallery** *(no. 38)*, **Arcadia Gallery** *(no. 51)* and **Pomegranate Gallery** *(no. 133)*. Notable stores on Greene Street include **Helmut Lang** *(no. 80)*, **Anna Sui** *(no. 113)* and dazzling interior-design space **Moss** *(no. 150)*.

West Broadway★
SoHo's premier corridor for fashion, art and dining is anchored on its southern end by the **SoHo Grand Hotel** *(no. 310)*, built in the 1990s. **Kenn's Broome**

Construction in Cast Iron

In the late 1700s, English designers began using cast iron to build textile mills. Iron frames were not only strong enough to hold up walls and ceilings, they were also much less bulky than brick and stone, thus allowing for more windows—crucial in the days before electricity. New York got its first cast-iron building in 1848, courtesy of ironmonger James Bogardus. It stood in TriBeCa until 1970, when the building was torn down. SoHo's cast-iron structures have fared better, in large part because, in 1973, most of the area was designated a historic district. The neighborhood contains the greatest concentration of buildings with cast-iron facades in the country. Architects in the 19C designed buildings with balustrades, cornices and columns. Then they commissioned ironmongers like Bogardus to render those facades in cast iron, which was fitted to a building. Once a mold was made, a design could be reproduced over and over again, allowing architects to mix and match elements as they saw fit. The technique flourished through the 1890s, when the development of steel framing and elevators made possible much taller commercial structures, and residential tastes turned back to brick and stone.

Street Bar (no. 363), housed in an 1825 structure, is a pleasant neighborhood pub. By contrast, the extremely swank **Downtown Cipriani** (no. 375) caters mainly to those with tans and jewels. **OK Harris Works of Art** (no. 383) pioneered SoHo's gallery district in 1969. **Franklin Bowles** (no. 431) gallery deals in contemporary art. Shoppers flock to stores like **Hilfiger** (no. 372), **Anthropologie** (no. 375), **Emporio Armani** (no. 410), **Elie Tahari** (no. 417), **Dolce & Gabbana** (no. 434) and **Coach** (no. 445).

Brigitta L. House - MICHELIN

Shops in SoHo

Wooster Street

The tranquil block between Canal and Grand streets is an example of what SoHo was like before the stores and galleries: everything has an elegant utility. The structure at nos. 28-30 dates from 1879; half of its facade (on its Grand Street side) was made of cast-iron in 1888. Between Grand and Broome are two important galleries: the nonprofit **Drawing Center** (nos. 35 and 40), which champions drawings both historical and contemporary; and **Spencer Brownstone** (no. 39), a contemporary art dealer. Around the corner, **Deitch Projects** (76 Grand St.) sponsors avant-garde, mixed-media exhibits. Local designers sell jewelry and clothes year-round on a vacant lot at the corner of Wooster and Spring streets. Big-name stores include **Costume National** (no. 108), **Barney's Co-op** (no. 116) and **BCBG Max Azria** (no. 120).

Additional Sight

New York City Fire Museum

278 Spring St. ♿ Kids ◷*Open year-round Tue–Sat 10am–5pm, Sun 10am–4pm.* ◷*Closed major holidays.* ⚏*$5.* ☎*212-691-1303. www.nycfiremuseum.org.*
Located in a 1904 firehouse, this colorful museum displays fire-related art and artifacts—from the mid-18C to the present—like buckets, pump wagons, fire sleighs, New York's first hydrant

(1818) and a sliding pole. A 6ft by 9ft memorial wall commemorates the 343 firefighters who lost their lives in the aftermath of the attack on the World Trade Center.

TriBeCa ★

MTA SUBWAY: N, Q, R, W AND 6 TRAINS TO CANAL ST.
OR 1 TRAIN TO FRANKLIN ST.
MAP P 118

An intriguing district of warehouses, loft residences, art galleries and chic restaurants, TriBeCa was named in the 1970s by a real estate agent hoping to create an identity as hip as SoHo's for the area. The acronym, which stands for Triangle Below Canal, stuck and, indeed, it's become a very trendy place. So far TriBeCa has not been commercialized nearly to the extent that SoHo has, despite being home to dozens of celebrities. For paparazzi-dodging starlets, that is precisely its appeal.

- **Information**: Tribeca Organization ☎212-966-0063; www.tribeca.org.
- ▶ **Orient Yourself**: Technically TriBeCa is not a triangle but a trapezoid. Its boundaries are (clockwise from north) **Canal Street**, **Broadway**, **Barclay Street** and the **Hudson River**. Greenwich and Hudson streets are the main thoroughfares for dining and nightlife; art and design stores are scattered throughout the district, with especially on Duane, Franklin and White streets.

A Bit of History

Once used as farmland by Dutch settlers, the area known as TriBeCa was included in a large tract granted in 1705 to Trinity Church. In the ensuing century, wealthy families built elegant residences around Hudson Square (now the Holland Tunnel traffic rotary). A produce market opened in 1813 at the western edge of the neighborhood, but the quarter remained primarily residential until the mid-19C, when the shipping and warehousing industries formerly located at the South Street Seaport moved to deepwater piers on the Hudson River. Five- and six-story "store and loft" buildings, many with cast-iron or terra-cotta facades, were built around TriBeCa to accommodate the new trade. By 1939 Washington

Street in TriBeCa

©Shea Dean

Market, as the area along Greenwich Street came to be known, had a greater volume of business than all the other markets in the city combined.

In the 1960s, urban renewal projects called for the demolition of many old buildings along the waterfront. Their replacements, (like the Borough of Manhattan Community College on West Street) are regarded as misbegotten eyesores. Luckily, enough of the old inland warehouse stock remained to attract artists pushed out of SoHo and others seeking industrial living space. The population grew from a mere 243 in 1970 to about 10,000 today. Loft apartments start at around $1 million.

Special Events – In late April and early May, about 300,000 film fans flock to screenings at the **Tribeca Film Festival** (☎212-941-2400; www.tribecafilmfestival. org). In the last weekend of the festival, TOAST, the **Tribeca Open Artist Studio Tour**, invites visitors into more than 30 working spaces of established and emerging artists. Art events are held concurrently at neighborhood galleries, art spaces and restaurants (☎212-479-7317; www.toastartwalk.com).

Visit

Major Streets

Church Street
The nonprofit **Apexart gallery** (no. 291; ☎ 212-431-5270; www.apexart.org) presents cutting-edge art and architecture exhibits.

Franklin Street
Interior design stores such as **Urban Archaeology** (no. 143) and **Interieurs** (nos. 149-51) line the block between Varick and Hudson streets. The immense proportions of some of the pieces on display suggest that many shoppers live in buildings with freight elevators. Franklin Street is also home to **Gallery Gen** (no. 158; www.gallerygen.com), which specializes in Asian fine art and design. At the edge of TriBeCa, also on Franklin Street, sits **Gigantic Art Space** (no. 59; www.giganticartspace.com), a multidisciplinary gallery.

Greenwich Street
Thanks to this street's proximity to the Borough of Manhattan Community Col-

Hotels

🏠 Cosmopolitan Hotel

Restaurants

❶ Bread Tribeca
❷ Chanterelle
❸ Next Door Nobu
❹ Odeon

"Let's Do Lunch"

Near the 1 train subway station at Franklin Street and West Broadway are popular eateries: **Pécan** *(130 Franklin St.;* ☎ *646-613-8293)*, a gourmet-sandwich-and-salad shop where aspiring screenwriters come to kvetch; and **Franklin Station Café** *(222 W. Broadway;* ☎*212-274-8525; www.franklinstationcafe.com)*, a French Malaysian bistro. **Bread Tribeca** *(301 Church St.; www.breadtribeca.com;* ☝*see Where to Eat)* is an industrial-chic, nouveau Italian restaurant; its half-sandwich and soup combo is a good value. Try **Bubby's** *(120 Hudson St. at White St.;* ☎*212-219-0666; www.bubbys.com)* for homemade meatloaf, salads made with local produce, and pies. **Yaffa's** *(353 Greenwich St. at Franklin St.;* ☎ *212-274-9403)* has a chummy vibe with its long oak bar, comfy booths and Italian and Middle Eastern pub food.

lege and the waterfront, you'll find most of TriBeCa's foot traffic here, between Chambers and Moore streets. At its southern end sits **Washington Market Park**, with flower gardens, a large children's playground and a Victorian-style gazebo. **A.L. Bazzini Co.** *(no. 339 at Jay St.; www.bazzininuts.com)* has been catering to neighborhood nut and candy lovers since 1886. Though the company moved its processing plant to the Bronx in the 1990s, its ground-floor food emporium draws a big lunchtime crowd. Bazzini pistachios, peanuts and cashews are sold in traditional tins by the register or by the pound at the deli.

Harrison Street

Just off Greenwich Street, the so-called **Harrison Street Row** *(nos. 37-41)* is a group of restored 19C Federal-style row houses dating from 1796 to 1828. Such residences used to be common in TriBeCa, but sadly no longer. These structures (some were moved here from elsewhere in the district) are now private residences.

Hudson Street

The acclaimed restaurant Chanterelle shares the ground floor of the 1884 **New York Mercantile Exchange** *(2-6 Harrison St. at Hudson St.)* with a union office. The brick and granite building once housed the offices of food brokers for the Washington Market. At no. 60 Hudson stands the **Western Union Building** *(1930, Voorhees, Gmelin & Walker)*, clad with 19 shades of brick. Its vaulted lobby ceiling also features many tons of bricks.

Walker Street

At the corner of Walker Street and Avenue of the Americas rises the **AT&T Head-** **quarters building** *(32 Ave. of the Americas)*, an ornate Art Deco tower designed by Ralph Walker in 1918. In the lobby, the original terrazzo floor and intricate wall and ceiling mosaics have been beautifully preserved. On the block between Lafayette Street and Broadway, just east of TriBeCa proper, stands **Art in General** *(no. 79;* ☎ *212-219-0473; www.artin-general.org)*, one of New York's leading nonprofit galleries since 1981.

White Street

The brick-paved stretch between Broadway and West Broadway is typically TriBeCa – many of its hulking 19C warehouses have been taken over by downtown artists. Crowned by a mansard roof, the cast-iron structure at nos. 13-17 now contains several galleries. **Let There Be Neon Gallery** *(no. 38; www.lettherebeneon. com)* features the creations of founder Rudi Stern and other American neon artists. Launched in 1996, **The Flea** *(no. 41;* ☎*212-226-2407; www.theflea.org)* has become an acclaimed space for experimental theater artists. Its two spaces host up to four performances a week. Some are fledgling works in process; others, like *The Guys*, by Anne Nelson, are topical (often political) plays with revolving casts of A-list stars such as Sigourney Weaver, Bill Murray, Susan Sarandon and Tim Robbins. The unusual bulbous building at no. 49 is the **Synagogue for the Arts**, built in 1967 to plans by William H. Breger (☉*open year-round Mon-Thu 9am-5pm, Fri 9am-2pm;* ☎*212-966-7141; www.synagogueforthearts.org)*. It features a distinctive flame-shaped, sky-lit sanctuary, an outdoor sculpture plaza, and a large gallery for events.

WEST VILLAGE★★

MTA SUBWAY: A, B, C, D, E, F AND V TRAINS
TO WEST 4TH ST.- WASHINGTON SQ. PARK
MAP OPPOSITE

New York's historic bohemia contains several distinct areas. Washington Square is surrounded by classrooms and libraries of New York University. North of the square lies the village's "Gold Coast," a genteel quarter of churches, town houses and apartment buildings, most with uniformed doormen. Picturesque Greenwich Village, reaching west from Avenue of the Americas (Sixth Avenue) is lined with Federal and Greek Revival row houses. In the northwest corner, the Meatpacking District holds chic bistros and nightclubs.

▶ **Orient Yourself:** West Village stretches from Houston (pronounced HOW-stun) Street to 14th Street and from Broadway to the Hudson River.

🕐 **Organizing Your Time:** Allow at least 4hrs to visit the West Village.

A Bit of History

A Country Village – The area once sheltered an Algonquin Indian settlement. In 1696 British colonists founded a hamlet here called Greenwich after the city in England.

After America won its independence from England, six parallel streets south of the area that became Washington Square Park (MacDougal, Sullivan, Thompson, Wooster, Greene and Mercer) were named for Revolutionary officers. The population of the village quadrupled in the early 19C when residents of "the city" (today's Financial District) came here seeking refuge from yellow fever and cholera, and then decided to stay.

Poets and Pagans – In the 1830s prominent families constructed elegant town houses on Fifth Avenue, north of Washington Square —today's Gold Coast. Meanwhile, homes on the Hudson River lost value as piers, markets, shipping offices and storage spaces proliferated there. In the late 19C, Irish, Italian and Chinese immigrants, and free blacks, came to live in the village, driving the "old money" uptown and creating an ethnically diverse bohemia.

Edgar Allan Poe (1809-49) was among the first writers to take advantage of the

Bleeker Street Sign

cheap rents and cultural diversions of the village. During the early 1900s intellectuals, social reformers, artists and radicals came in droves, making the neighborhood the nexus of the American avant-garde. **Upton Sinclair** and other political rebels organized lectures, debates and all-night dances called "Pagan Routs" at the Liberal Club on MacDougal Street. A group of painters dubbed "The Eight"—or the **Ashcan school**—challenged established academic concepts and helped organize the revolutionary 1913 Armory show. Literary salons attracted such writers as **Walt Whitman**, **Mark Twain** and **Henry James**. Dozens of small theaters took root, nurturing the talents of playwrights like **Eugene O'Neill**. In the 1940s nearly all the Abstract Expressionists, including **Robert Motherwell**, **Jackson Pollock** and **Mark Rothko**, lived here.

In the 1950s beat writers **Allen Ginsberg** and **Jack Kerouac** hung out and gave public readings in the village. In the 1960s folk musicians like **Bob Dylan** made the coffeehouses and bars on MacDougal Street their second homes. **From Stonewall to Today** – Greenwich Village's ethos of tolerance has long made it a magnet for gay men and lesbians—a fact that not all New Yorkers have appreciated. A confrontation between the police and patrons of the Stonewall Inn on Christopher Street in 1969 culminated in a riot that is widely regarded as the start of the movement for gay and lesbian rights. Christopher Street's cabaret clubs, shops and bars continue to cater to a predominantly gay clientele; farther west, on Hudson, are a couple of bars with all-women clienteles. Many of those with "alternative"

lifestyles have moved elsewhere, as Greenwich Village rents skyrocketed. Still, a creative and friendly attitude prevails here, largely unshackled to a nine-to-five schedule. Enjoying the cafes, shops, bars, parks and historic buildings is a full-time job.

Greenwich Village★★

This, the prettiest and most historic part of the West Village, is the best place in the city to get lost: the skewed layout of streets west of Avenue of the Americas (Sixth Ave.) sends the inner compass of locals spinning too. For example, West 4th and West 10th streets cross, a phenomenon unheard of in other parts of the city where the 1811 grid prevails.

Bleecker Street★★

The heart of New York University's student ghetto south of Washington Square, Bleecker Street grows increasingly upscale as it makes its way northwest toward the Meatpacking District.

Avenue of the Americas to Seventh Avenue South

More Italian than Little Italy, this one-block strip of Bleecker was called "the breadbasket of the village" in the early 20C for its profusion of bread and pastry vendors. Today it's lined with delis, bakeries, cafes and restaurants (⟲ see "A Bite of Bleecker Street" sidebar).

Magnolia Bakery

Seventh Avenue South to Bank Street

The commercial spine of Greenwich Village is especially charming north of Grove Street, where most of the structures were built between 1820 and 1855; many have shops and restaurants on their lower floors. As a sign of the area's growing cachet, New York native **Marc Jacobs** opened boutiques selling his menswear and accessories lines at no. 403 *(at Perry St.; ☎ 212-924-0026; www.marc jacobs.com)*. British handbag maker **Lulu Guinness** and Bronx-born **Ralph Lauren** (née Ralph Lifshitz) have outposts here *(at nos. 394 and 380, respectively)*. Catering to the neighborhood's sweet tooth is the charming **Magnolia Bakery** *(no. 401; ☎ 212-462-2572)*. Heavily frosted cupcakes are its specialty.

Across the street stands the **Biography Bookshop** *(no. 400; ☎212-807-8655)*, which, contrary to its name, carries books of every genre, including New York City history books and racks of half-price "remainders" (publishers' overstock).

Historic Greenwich Village★★

Bounded by (clockwise from north) Christopher St., Seventh Ave. S., St. Luke's Place and Hudson St. Within this area, the heart of Greenwich Village, crooked streets are lined with town houses and old trees.

Bedford Street★

This street holds three particularly noteworthy structures. Dating from 1873, **no. 75-1/2** measures only 9.5ft across, making it the narrowest house in the city; poet **Edna St. Vincent Millay** lived in it from 1923 to 1924. **No. 77**, built in 1799, is said to be the oldest house in the village; it was originally a freestanding Federal-style frame house with its own yard. The Greek Revival brick facade was added in 1836. At **no. 86** *(cross street: Barrow)* is **Chumley's** (☎ 212-675-4449), a former speakeasy that's now a popular bar, thanks to the fact that it has maintained its old-school look both inside (creaking wood floors, velvet curtains, black-and-white photos of pub-crawling writers such as **Lillian Hellman** and **John Dos Passos**) and out. ⟲*There's no sign:*

Address Book

A BITE (OR TWO) OF BLEECKER STREET

Murray's Cheese Shop (no. 254; ☎212-243-3289; www.murrayscheese.com) This intriguing store stocks more than 250 cheeses from countries all over the world. But that's not all. On hand are homemade bread, imported olive oil, and sausage. Murray's makes a mean pannini.

Rocco's Pastry Shop (no. 243; ☎212-242-6031; www.roccospastry.com) serves up delicious Italian ice. Relative newcomer **Amy's Bread** (no. 250; ☎212-675-7802; www.amysbread.com) is a bright, friendly corner cafe, where you can get inventive sandwiches such as roast turkey on semolina, raisin and fennel bread, as well as all manner of cakes, cookies and muffins.

look for smokers huddled on the sidewalk and ask where the door is.

Commerce Street★★

A cul-de-sac, this street feels a world apart from the hubbub of Manhattan. The group of small houses at nos. 9–17 suggests the scale of the village in the early 19C. **Washington Irving** reputedly wrote *The Legend of Sleepy Hollow* while staying at **no. 11**, the home of his sister. The **Cherry Lane Theater** occupies the old barn at no. 38. A venue for Off-Broadway productions since the 1920s, it has hosted the American premieres of plays by **Samuel Beckett**, **Edward Albee** and **Eugene Ionesco**. The "twin sisters" at **nos. 39** and **41**, dating from 1831 and 1832 respectively, had their mansard roofs added in 1873. Legend has it that they were built by a sea captain for his two daughters—one for each, because they didn't get along.

St. Luke's Place

Shaded by gingko trees and fragrant wisteria, the brick and brownstone Italianate residences at **nos. 5–16** form a stately row. They also are redolent with village literary history: poet **Marianne Moore** lived at no. 14 from 1918 to 1929; **Sherwood Anderson**, author of the interconnected stories in *Winesburg, Ohio*, lived at no. 12 in 1923. No. 16 was the home of novelist **Theodore Dreiser**.

Grove Street★

Like Bedford, Grove Street is a peaceful byway that seems miles away from feverish Manhattan. At nos. 10–12, peek through the gate of **Grove Court★**, a private cul-de-sac lined with brick-fronted, white-shuttered Federal houses of the 1850s. Known as the **West Coast,** the western edge of the village has been newly built up with celebrity-occupied glass-box apartment towers, including two by New York architect **Richard Meier**. His award-winning 16-story glass and steel towers overlooking the Hudson at 173-176 Perry Street at West Street (hence their name, Perry West) have a distinct International flavor; they are constructed around concrete cores to maximize views.

Christopher Park★

Christopher & Grove Sts. at Seventh Ave. South.

Established in 1837, this wedge-shaped park shelters a statue of Civil War Gen. Philip Sheridan and sculptures of two gay couples (1990s) by George Segal. On the north side stands the **Stonewall** (*53 Christopher St.; ☎212-463-0950*), a

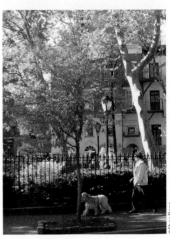

Christopher Park

popular gay bar that is situated in the original (now renovated) Stonewall Inn, site of the 1969 rebellion. The triangular **Northern Dispensary** at the east end was built in 1831 by local citizens to provide health care for the poor; it stood at the northern end of the city, hence the name. Edgar Allan Poe was treated here for a head cold in 1837. It is the only building in New York with one side on two streets *(Grove & Christopher)* and two sides on one street *(Waverly Pl.).*

Hudson Street★

This wide thoroughfare runs the length of the village from TriBeCa on its southern end all the way up to the Meatpacking District. The stretch between Christopher and Bank streets is lined with restaurants and cafes, most notably the **White Horse Tavern** *(no. 567 at 11th St; ☎212-243-9260)*. Though largely known as the place where Welsh poet **Dylan Thomas** drank himself to death, the tavern is a landmark in its own right: built in 1880, the building is one of the few wood-framed structures remaining in the city. It's also remarkably authentic: tarnished brass chandeliers, white horse figurines, a carved oak bar, outdoor picnic tables and a neighborhood crowd make it a great spot to quaff a pint.

Toy Soldier

The Forbes Collection

The "Gold Coast"★

The area from 9th and 13th streets, between University Place and Avenue of the Americas (Sixth Ave.), is sometimes trumpeted by realtors as the village's "Gold Coast." Though few locals use that term, it derives from the differences between this quarter and the one south of Washington Square. In the mid-19C, it was populated by native-born, well-to-do New Yorkers.

Today much of the neighborhood lies within the Greenwich Village historic district. Note especially the remarkably preserved streetscapes on 10th, 11th and 12th streets between Fifth Avenue and Avenue of the Americas (Sixth Ave.). Standouts on W. 10th Street include **no. 56**; dating from 1832, it's one of the oldest houses in this part of the village and retains much of its original detail, including pineapple newel posts. The playwright **Edward Albee** lived at 50 W. 10th St. On West 11th Street, note the structure with the angled steps at no. 18—no mere renovation, it replaced a brownstone that was blown up on March 6, 1970, when several members of the radical group the **Weathermen** accidentally detonated their cache of dynamite. Three people were killed; the actor **Dustin Hoffman**, who lived next door at the time, witnessed the explosion. At nos. 72-76 lies the **Second Cemetery of the Spanish and Portuguese Synagogue**. The tiny triangular patch with a few eroded headstones is the only remnant of what was a larger square plot; burials took place here from 1805 to 1829. The composer **Charles Ives** lived next door from 1908 to 1911.

The Forbes Galleries★

62 Fifth Ave. at W. 12th St. ⏱*Open year-round Tue–Wed & Fri–Sat 10am–4pm.* ⏱*Closed major holidays.* ☎*212-206-5548. www.forbesgalleries.com.*

In seven small rooms on the ground floor of the Forbes Building, home of the well-known business magazine, thousands of toys, paintings and historical objects attest to the collecting enthusiasms of three generations of the Forbes family. Due to the fact that architect Thomas Hastings died midway through the project, the grand building was jointly designed by Carrère and Hastings (New York Public Library) and Shreve and Lamb (Empire State Building); it was completed in 1925. The galleries were the repository of the largest collection of Fabergé Easter eggs in the world (9 of 50) until February 2004, when Forbes sold the eggs for more than $100 million. Many interesting collections remain here, however, among them 12,000 **toy soldiers** arranged in battle scenes; more than 500 **miniature boats**, ranging from Noah's ark to ocean liners; Abraham Lincoln's opera glasses; and the bill for Paul Revere's ride.

Jefferson Market Library★

425 Ave. of the Americas at W. 10th St. ◷*Open Mon & Wed noon–8pm, Tues 10am–6pm, Thu noon–6pm, Fri 1pm-6pm; Sat 10am–5pm.* ◷*Closed major holidays.* ☎*212-243-4334.* ⊶*May be temporarily closed due to an expected renovation.*

A profusion of pinnacles, gables, Gothic arches, turrets and traceried windows makes this redbrick building a cherished landmark. Charged with designing a courthouse, architects Frederick Clarke Withers and Calvert Vaux found inspiration in King Ludwig II's Neuschwanstein Castle in Bavaria, Germany. The completed courthouse (1877) now houses a branch of the New York Public Library. Behind it lies a formal garden managed by volunteers from the community (◷*open May–Oct afternoon only*).

Across the street from the library there are two secret little enclaves: **Patchin Place** and **Milligan Place**. On the north side of West 10th Street, between Avenue of the Americas (Sixth Ave.) and Greenwich avenues, sits Patchin Place. Theodore Dreiser and **e.e. cummings** once lived in these 1848 boardinghouses. Behind an iron gate on Avenue of the Americas (Sixth Ave.), between West 10th and West 11th streets, the houses of Milligan Place date from 1852.

Church of the Ascension

36–38 Fifth Ave. at W. 10th St. ◷*Open year-round Mon–Fri noon–1pm, Sun for services only.* ☎*212-254-8620. www. ascensionnyc.org*

Built of local brownstone, this Gothic Revival Episcopal church (1841) was designed by Richard Upjohn. Of particular interest in the soaring interior, remodeled by Stanford White in 1888, is John La Farge's superb mural of the Ascension above the altar; the stained-glass windows, some of which were also designed by La Farge (they are illuminated at night); and the box pews.

First Presbyterian Church of New York

12 W. 12th St. ◷*Open year-round Mon, Wed & Fri noon–12:30pm & Sun services.* ☎*212-675-6150; www.fpcnyc.org.*

Designed by Joseph C. Wells, this brownstone church was modeled after the Church of St. Saviour in Bath, England, with its tower inspired by that of Magdalen College, Oxford University. It was completed in 1846 for a congregation that formed in 1716. It now hosts a preschool as well as an active senior center.

New School University

66 W. 12th St. between Fifth Ave. & Ave. of the Americas. ☎*212-229-5488 (box office). www.newschool.edu.*

Originally founded in 1919, the New School for Social Research became known as the "university in exile" when intelligentsia fleeing Hitler's Germany took posts here in the 1930s. It merged with the Parsons School of Design *(66 Fifth Ave. between W. 12th & W. 13th Sts.)* in 1970 and with the Mannes College of Music in 1989. Today 7,000 students are enrolled in graduate and undergraduate programs here. Designed by Joseph Urban in 1930, the building, with its black-and-white-striped facade, is an early example of modern architecture in Manhattan. Its stunning **auditorium** is the setting for readings and literature forums, many open to the public.

Salmagundi Club

47 Fifth Ave. between E. 11th & E. 12th Sts. ◷*Open year-round daily 1pm–5pm.* ☎*212-255-7740. www.salmagundi.org.*

Built in 1852, this brownstone is the last survivor of what used to be a row of similarly grand private residences lining lower Fifth Avenue. Since 1917 it has been home to the Salmagundi Club, the oldest artists' club in the country. Famous members include John La Farge, Louis Comfort Tiffany and Stanford White. Today's members of the club take paint-

Washington Arch

the country, NYU has an undergraduate population of 40,000 and a steadily rising reputation among high school seniors. Applications to this so-called "dream school" increased by 300 percent in the 1990s, and today the acceptance rate (14 percent) is lower than that of some Ivy League schools. NYU's Tisch film school is especially prestigious, having spawned directors **Spike Lee**, **Martin Scorsese** and **Oliver Stone**.

Washington Square★

Originally a marshland and a favorite hunting ground of the colonists, the site was purchased by the city in 1788 for use as a potter's field and public gallows. (A large tree in the northwest corner of the park is the infamous Hanging Elm, said to be the oldest tree in the city.)

In 1826 the square was officially designated as the Washington Military Parade Ground, and a fashionable residential enclave grew up around it.

Today the square is a haven for skateboarders, students, street musicians, hotdog vendors, "speed chess" players (in the southwest corner of the park; hold on to your wallet) and in late May and early September, visual artists who come for the annual **Washington Square Outdoor Art Exhibit**:

Washington Arch★

Constructed in 1891 of Tuckahoe marble to a design by Stanford White, the 30ft-

ing and art appreciation classes and display their work in first-floor galleries, which are open to the public.

Washington Square★

The chunk of the village bounded by West 8th Street, Broadway, Houston Street and Avenue of the Americas (Sixth Ave.) is anchored by Washington Square. Though architecturally disparate, the area is largely defined by the presence of **New York University★ (NYU)**, founded in 1831 by Albert Gallatin, secretary of the Treasury under Thomas Jefferson. One of the largest private universities in

NYU grounds with tulips

wide, 77ft-high triumphal arch replaced a temporary wooden one commemorating the centennial of George Washington's inauguration. Gracing its north face are two sculptures of Washington – as a soldier (by Herman MacNeil) and as a civilian (by A. Sterling Calder, father of the renowned 20C sculptor Alexander Calder). On the south side, note the frieze with the American eagle, the W for Washington at the center, and the trumpet-blowing statues. The arch underwent a $3 million restoration in 2003-04, and in 2005 the city allocated $16 million to redesign the park entirely. The controversial three-year plan, which includes a perimeter fence that can be locked at night, has been challenged by several lawsuits.

Washington Square North★

Often referred to as "the Row" for its concentration of 1830s Greek Revival town houses, this is the most attractive side of the square. The oldest structure (no. 20) was built in 1828-29, widened in 1859, and had a fourth story added in 1880. Nos. 7–13 and nos. 21–26 make up the rest of the Row. **Henry James'** novel *Washington Square*, written in 1881, was set in his grandmother's house, which once stood at no. 18. Famous residents include the painter **Edward Hopper**; architect **Richard Morris Hunt**; and **John Dos Passos**, who wrote *Manhattan Transfer* while living at no. 3.

Washington Mews

This quaint alley, with its cobblestone pavement, contained stables and servants' quarters for the town houses on Washington Square North. The structures now house NYU offices. Similarly picturesque, **MacDougal Alley** *(just off MacDougal St. between Washington Sq. W. & W. 8th Sts.)* has been home to sculptor **Gertrude Vanderbilt Whitney**, whose gallery at 15½-17½ was the precursor to the **Whitney Museum of American Art**; painter **Jackson Pollock**, who stayed at no. 9 in 1949-50; and poet **Edwin Arlington Robinson**, who wrote his Pulitzer Prize-winning book *Tristram* in 1927 at no. 1.

Asch Building

29 Washington Pl. E. at Greene St. Located just a block east of Washington Square, this is the site of the worst factory fire in New York City history. The top three floors were occupied by the Triangle Shirtwaist Company when, on March 25, 1911, a blaze broke out in the eighth-floor cutting room. Fed by thousands of pounds of fabric, the fire spread rapidly, sending panicked workers (the vast majority of whom where young Jewish women and girls) to fire exits that had been locked by proprietors and fire escapes that collapsed with the weight of escapees. A total of 146 workers died, dozens by jumping to their deaths in Washington Place. The tragedy sparked protests against unsafe working conditions throughout the country, and prodded the government to enforce workplace safety standards.

Washington Square South

The farrago of buildings here ranges in style from NYU's **Elmer Bobst Library** (no. 70), a stark, red sandstone cube designed by Philip Johnson and Richard Foster in 1972, to **Judson Memorial Baptist Church**★ (no. 55), designed by Stanford White in 1893. The latter structure is clad in yellow brick, limestone and terra-cotta and adorned with elaborate Greco-Romanesque and Renaissance details. Ring the bell at 239 Thompson Street during business hours (🕐 *Open Mon–Fri 10am–6pm*) and someone might let you in to see the superb stained-glass windows by John La Farge.

Additional Sights

Bleecker Street

The four-block stretch of Bleecker Street between Avenue of the Americas (Sixth Ave.) and LaGuardia Place is an old 1960s stomping ground known for its coffeehouses, music clubs and bars. Today it's mainly thronged with college students who come for cheap food (pizza, falafel), beer, piercings and tattoos.

MacDougal Street

Vestiges of Little Italy remain on the stretch between Houston and Bleecker streets, where you'll find not one but three famous

The Highline

Running along the edge of the Hudson River between Gansevoort Street and 34th Street, this rusty elevated railroad bridge from the 1930s is slated to become Manhattan's most eagerly anticipated public park. No, it will not be torn down. The park will be built on top of the structure, 18ft to 35ft in the air, forming a 1.5mi car-free corridor of paths and gardens between the Meatpacking District and Penn Station. The space is expected to open in 2008. For more information, call ☎212-206-9922 or go online to *www.thehighline.org*.

Italian cafes – **Caffe Reggio** *(no. 119; ☎212-475-9557; www.cafereggio.com)*, **Caffe Dante** *(no. 79; ☎ 866-681-0299; www.cafe-dante.com)*, and **Le Figaro Cafe** *(184 Bleecker at MacDougal; ☎212-677-1100)*. Many say Reggio is the most authentic, but Jack Kerouac's reputed favorite was Figaro. All have sidewalk tables and serve espresso drinks, beer and wine and Italian pastries and sandwiches late into the night. **Bob Dylan** owned and occupied the brownstone at **94 MacDougal Street** for a short period in the 1960s.

Meatpacking District

A Bit of History

Bounded by West 15th, Hudson Street, Gansevoort Street and the Hudson River, the northwest corner of the West Village has blossomed into an uber-hip shopping, dining and clubbing destination. In the 1850s New York was the largest center of beef production in the country; slaughterhouses, meatpacking plants and storage facilities lined both its east and west sides. For 19 years, **Herman Melville** worked in the Meatpacking District as an outdoor customs inspector. But as refrigeration technology improved, many of the big meat companies moved their facilities to the Midwest, closer to where the cattle were. Not that New York residents minded: the industry was increasingly seen as a public health hazard, especially after **Upton Sinclair** published *The Jungle* in 1906. In the late 1940s, the slaughtering district on the east side was cleared to make way for the United Nations, and later the practice was banned from the city altogether. The Meatpacking District was a rather dangerous place until the 1990s:

after meat wholesalers would close for the day, drug dealers and prostitutes would prowl its cobblestoned streets. The booming economy, along with Mayor **Rudy Giuliani**'s effective, yet controversial, crime policy in the early 1990s, cleaned up the neighborhood, and though some meat companies remain in business, its grit is for the most part a fashion accessory.

Restaurants, Clubs and Shops

Florent *(69 Gansevoort St. between Greenwich & Washington Sts.; ☎212-989-5779; www.restaurantflorent.com)*, a 24-hour French bistro, has been here since 1985, well before there was anything remotely hip about the neighborhood. This grande dame has been joined in recent years by **Pastis** *(� Where to Eat)* and **Spice Market**, which are packed to the rafters at night; try to reserve .

As a clubbing district, the Meatpacking District seems to have some staying power. Dress to impress: the doormen can be highly selective about who gets in. A few nightspots to look into: **Lotus** *(409 W. 14th St. between Ninth Ave. & Washington St.; ☎212-243-4420)* and **PM** *(50 Gansevoort St. between Washington & Greenwich Sts., ☎212-255-6676)*. Also consider **APT** and **Cielo** *(� Nightlife)*.

That both **Stella McCartney** and **Alexander McQueen** chose to open their first boutiques on West 14th Street *(between Ninth & Tenth Aves.)* in 2002 says a lot about the sizzle of the district. Check out their clothing-as-art at nos. 429 and 417 respectively. **Jeffrey New York** *(no. 449)* is a mini-mall of ultra-expensive togs run by a former shoe buyer for Barneys. The inside of **Diane von Furstenberg**'s shop *(874 Washington Ave. at 14th St.)* resembles a glittering jewel box.

EAST VILLAGE★

MTA SUBWAY: 6 TRAIN TO ASTOR PL. OR
F, V TRAINS TO SECOND AVE.
MAP P 130

This village is the center of alternative culture in New York: rock concerts, poetry readings and Off-Off Broadway theater productions take place here nightly. It's also one of the best places in the city to shop for used books and records and vintage clothes.

▸ **Orient Yourself:** This neighborhood is bounded by 14th St., Avenue D, Houston St. and Broadway.

🕐 **Organizing Your Time:** Allow at least 2hrs to visit the East Village, and more if you like to browse in one of its several book shops.

A Bit of History

The Beginnings – In 1651 Peter Stuyvesant, the Dutch-born director-general of the New Netherland colony, purchased the land bounded by today's 17th Street, 5th Street, 4th Avenue and the East River—virtually the entire East Village—from the Indians for use as a farm. Though he lived downtown while the colony was under Dutch rule, Stuyvesant withdrew from public affairs in 1664 after surrendering to the English, and moved to his manor house on what is now Stuyvesant Street.

In Transition – Briefly in the early 1800s, the district west of Second Avenue boasted fashionable town houses; the working-class neighborhoods farther east were home to Polish, Ukrainian and German immigrants until the early 20C. In the 1950s the area's low rents attracted writers and artists such as **Jack Kerouac** and bop saxophonist **Charlie Parker** (they lived at 501 East 11th Street and 151 Avenue B, respectively). The term "East Village" was coined in the early 1960s to distinguish the neighborhood from the rest of the **Lower East Side**, of which it had previously been considered a part. The new name also linked this bohemia with the longer-lived artistic community in **Greenwich Village** across town. The glory days of the East Village were the 1980s, when rock bands like the **B-52's**, the **Talking Heads** and the **Ramones** made names

East Village

©Shea Dean

for themselves at the (former) legendary club **CBGB & OMFUG** (the acronym stands for Country, Bluegrass, Blues and Other Music for Uplifting Gourmandizers).

Today's East Village – The East Village today contains vestiges of almost all chapters of its history. Most of its side streets are lined by pretty 19C brownstones, spiffed-up tenements and lush trees; boutiques are scattered about on ground floors throughout the district. **St. Mark's Place**★ is the most densely commercial street (this is the name East 8th Street goes by between Avenue A and Third Avenue) in the East Village, drawing hordes of students and hippies with its sushi bars, jewelry and sunglass stalls, record stores (**Mondo Video** at no. 6 is a favorite) and head shops. **Second Avenue**★ is really the district's spine, though. Here you'll find an astounding variety of ethnic eateries: Italian, Russian, Korean, Thai, Jewish and Mexican among them; First Avenue at East 11th Street is home to several traditional Italian places. Sixth Street be-tween First and Second avenues is known as **Little India**★ for the many (16 and counting) festive and super-cheap Indian and Bangladeshi restaurants that line the block.

McSorley's Old Ale House (*15 E. 7th St. between Second & Third Aves.; ☎212-473-9148*), founded in 1854, is a storied dive. Celebrated in the writings of Joseph Mitchell and the paintings of John Sloan,

the pub continues to offer tastes of "Old New York" as well as two types of home-made ale: light and dark. But in general the East Village attracts a very young crowd —almost all the cafes, bars, record stores and boutiques cater to patrons in their twenties and thirties who, if they are not living on a limited budget, like to pretend they are.

Sights

Merchant's House Museum★

29 E. 4th St. between Lafayette St. & Bowery. ◐Open Thu–Mon noon–5pm. ◐Closed major holidays. ◉$8. ☛Guided tours (1hr) available on weekends. ☎212-777-1089. www.merchantshouse.org.

Constructed in 1832, this redbrick town house, with its Greek Revival doorway, has been transformed into a museum that illustrates the lifestyle of an affluent 19C family. Indeed, it is the only fully intact house museum in New York that provides a window on that period. Seabury Tredwell, a prosperous merchant, bought the structure in 1835. It remained in the family for 100 years. Today, three of its five stories are open to the public: the basement, which has a beehive oven and a gallery holding temporary exhibits (often drawn from the museum's collection of 19C costumes and textiles); the main

EAST VILLAGE

0   1/10mi
0   200m

Hotels

🛏 East Village Bed and Coffee

Restaurants

❶ Angelica Kitchen
❷ Itzocan
❸ Momofuku Ssam Bar
❹ Soba-Ya

floor, which has a spacious double parlor filled with Empire-style furnishings; and the second floor, which contains two bedrooms and a writing nook.

St. Mark's Historic District★

A small historic district centers on Stuyvesant Street, which cuts across East 9th and 10th streets between Second and Third avenues. However "crooked" it may appear, it runs in fact almost in a true east and west direction. Peter Stuyvesant laid it out that way in the 1600s. It served as the driveway to his country house, which sat roughly at the intersection of East 10th and Stuyvesant streets (the house was destroyed by fire in 1778).

St. Mark's Church-in-the-Bowery

131 E. 10th St. at Second Ave.
☎212-674-6377. www.stmarkschurch-in-the-bowery.com.

This Georgian-style Episcopal Church was built in 1799 on the site of **Peter Stuyvesant**'s 1660 family chapel. Its Greek Revival steeple (1828) and cast-iron portico (1854) are both additions. The cast-iron fence dates from 1836. The church became heavily involved in the arts starting in 1919, when the poet **Kahlil Gibran** was appointed to the St. Mark's Arts Committee. Over the years **Isadora Duncan**, **William Carlos Williams**, **W.H. Auden**, **Ben Hecht**, **Amy Lowell**, **Martha Graham** and others performed. **Sam Shepard** had his first two plays produced here in 1964. In 1978 fire devoured the building, leaving only its stone shell. The church was rebuilt in a utilitarian fashion and continues to host many poetry readings and performances (ⓒ *see East Village Book Nooks*). Seven generations of Stuyvesants, including Peter himself, who died in 1678, are buried under the building. The lovely tree-shaded **graveyard**★ out back is paved with undulating cobblestones.

Renwick Triangle

The ivy-covered town houses hugged by East 10th Street *(nos. 114-128)* and Stuyvesant Street *(nos. 23-35)* were designed in 1861 by James Renwick, architect of St. Patrick's Cathedral.

Stuyvesant Street architecture

©Shea Dean

Federal Town Houses

Two rare and well-preserved town houses from the Federal period stand on Stuyvesant Street. At **no. 21** is the **Stuyvesant-Fish House**, which was built in 1804 by Governor Stuyvesant's great-grandson Nicholas William Stuyvesant as a wedding gift for his daughter, who married one Nicholas Fish. The intent was apparently to keep an eye on the young couple: Nicholas William Stuyvesant lived at no. 44, which dates from 1795.

Tompkins Square Park★

Bounded by Aves. A & B and
E. 7th & E. 10th Sts.

Originally laid out in 1834, this 10-acre park, filled with 150-year-old elms, two dog parks, benches, flowers and fountains, is one of downtown Manhattan's most attractive public spaces. This state

Tompkins Square Park

©Shea Dean

East Village Book Nooks

Literary types love the East Village. Not only does it have a highly developed cafe culture; it has two of the finest bookstores in town. Boasting "16 miles of books" on its iconic red awning, newly expanded **Strand Book Store** *(828 Broadway at E. 12th St.; ☎212-473-1452; www.strandbooks.com)* carries thousands of used books, half-price reviewers' copies, publishers' overstock, books-on-tape, and dozens of $1-a-book racks. Unlike most used bookstores, its whole inventory is online. **St. Mark's Bookshop** *(31 Third Ave. between E. 8th & E. 9th Sts.; ☎212-260-7853; www.stmarksbookshop.com)* draws arty academics with its stock of literary theory, photography books, rare 'zines and subversive fiction. It's open – and crowded – till midnight.

Local writers strut their stuff at a number of East Village haunts as well. **KGB Bar** *(85 E. 4th St. between 2nd & 3rd Aves., 2nd floor; ☎212-505-3360; www.kgbbar.com)* usually lands at the top of the heap for its A-list fiction readers, including Rick Moody and Mary Gaitskill. **The Poetry Project** *(131 E. 10th St.; ☎212-674-0910; www.poetryproject.com)* has had an all-star lineup of readers since its inception in 1966, including Allen Ginsberg; work tends toward the experimental. The **Howl! Festival**, named for Ginsberg's most famous poem, takes place in the East Village the third week in August and is chock-a-block with literary performances and events *(☎212-673-5433; www.howlfestival.com)*. **Nuyorican Poets Cafe** *(236 E. 3rd St. between Aves. B & C; ☎212-505-8183; www.nuyorican.org)* is the place to go for streetwise poetry slams, where poetry is chanted to hip-hop beats.

of affairs is relatively recent. The park was a concert venue in the 1970s, hosting performers such as Jimi Hendrix. In the 1980s it was known as a haven for drug dealers and homeless people. Riots broke out when the city closed the park in 1990 and tore down the bandshell, but most residents supported the move. Ongoing restoration, along with rising real estate prices and plummeting crime rates, has brought back its original luster. Bars and restaurants line the west edge of the park on **Avenue A**.

Cooper Union Foundation Building

©Shea Dean

Astor Place

This two-block-long street linking Broadway and Third Avenue got its name from **John Jacob Astor**, the fur-trade and real-estate magnate who helped develop the surrounding neighborhood starting in 1825. The restored 1904 Astor Place **subway kiosk**, made of cast iron, stands on Astor Place between 4th Avenue and Lafayette Street (uptown trains only). Nearby is Bernard (Tony) Rosenthal's 1966 sculpture Alamo *(1 on map)*, a **black cube** that rotates on one corner and serves as a popular hangout for teenage skateboarders and their friends. Two interesting buildings flank the south side of Astor Place.

Cooper Union Foundation Building★

Completed in 1859, this massive brownstone is the oldest extant steel-framed structure in America. It is the headquarters of **Cooper Union for the Advancement of Science and Art**, a free educational institution founded by Peter Cooper (1791-1883), a self-made industrialist, to provide formal schooling to working-class people who otherwise couldn't afford it. Its three colleges focus on architecture, engineering and art.

Sculpture for Living

Architect Charles Gwathmey intended his undulating green-glass skyscraper (2005) to stand out from, rather than blend in with, its brick and brownstone neighbors, as would a piece of public art. He succeeded. Apartments start at $2 million.

Grace Church

802 E. Broadway at E. 10th St. ⏱ *Open Sept–Jun Tue–Fri noon–1pm. Rest of the year Wed noon–1pm.* ☎*212-254-2000. www.gracechurchnyc.org.*
James Renwick, architect of the much larger **St. Patrick's Cathedral** in Midtown, designed this Episcopal church in 1846. Its recently restored spire is an elegant example of the Gothic Revival style. In 1863 circus impresario **P.T. Barnum** arranged for the rector to marry two midgets from his company: Charles S. Stratton, better known as Tom Thumb, and Lavinia Warren. Today the church hosts classical musical concerts on a regular basis *(call ☎212-254-2000 for a recorded schedule).*

Lafayette Street

Originally called La Grange Terrace, after Revolutionary War general Marquis de Lafayette's country estate near Paris, this stretch between Astor Place and East 4th Street was home to a social elite that included "Commodore" **Cornelius Vanderbilt** and **Warren Delano** (grandfather of President **Franklin Delano Roosevelt**) in the 19C. The remnants of four magnificent Greek Revival manses constructed in 1833 stand at nos. 428-434. They're known as **Colonnade Row** for their shared Corinthian colonnade. John Jacob Astor had the monumental redbrick and brownstone building across the street (no. 425) built in 1854 to contain New York's first free library. Astor's 100,000-volume collection formed the nucleus of the New York Public Library 40 years later. The Off-Broadway **Public Theater** now occupies the building (and, it should be noted, perpetuates Astor's populist inclinations by sponsoring **Shakespeare in the Park**, a summer-long series of free plays in Central Park).

CHELSEA★★

MTA SUBWAY: 1 TRAIN TO 23RD ST. (AT SEVENTH AVE.) OR C, E TRAINS TO 23RD ST. (AT EIGHTH AVE.)
MAP P 134

Chelsea is the center of New York's art world and gay community. It's a place of rich contrasts: busy commercial avenues intersect with quiet residential side streets, and tiny neighborhood cafes abut gargantuan dance clubs. Be sure to check out the ever-evolving waterfront area, home to the mammoth Chelsea Piers recreation complex, the Hudson River Greenway and several historic ships.

▶ **Orient Yourself:** Chelsea is situated west of Avenue of the Americas (Sixth Ave.) between West 14th and 30th streets.
⏱ **Organizing Your Time:** Allow 3hrs to do Chelsea justice.

A Bit of History

London Namesake – Chelsea got its name in 1750, when British army captain Thomas Clarke bought a farm bounded by West 21st and 24th streets, Eighth Avenue and the Hudson River and named it after his London neighborhood. In 1813 the property passed to Clarke's grandson **Clement Clarke Moore** (1779-1863), an erudite scholar and literary figure who nevertheless remains best known for writing "A Visit from St. Nicholas" (also known as **The Night before Christmas**). In the 1820s Moore helped shape the development of the district by donating a large chunk of land for the building of the General Theological Seminary, where he would later teach, and by specifying that residences had to be set back from the street behind spacious front yards. Moore also set aside land for

DISCOVERING NEW YORK CITY

🙂 A Bit of Advice 🙂

The closest subway stop (C, E train to 23rd St.) will leave you two long blocks away from most ofa the galleries, but the crosstown M23 (23rd St.) bus will take you all the way through the heart of the district and on to the waterfront and Chelsea Piers.

parklike squares, giving the neighborhood a distinctly English feel, even as its population increasing hailed from Germany, Italy, Scotland and Ireland. The **Hudson River Railroad** opened along Eleventh Avenue in 1851, spawning slaughterhouses, breweries and tenements. In 1871 about 50 people were killed near the intersection of West 24th Street and Eighth Avenue during a riot between Irish Catholics and Irish Protestants. From about 1905 to 1915, several motion picture studios operated here; many visiting performers stayed at the 1884 Chelsea hotel. Hudson River

dock activity began to decline in the 1960s, opening up warehouses and industrial spaces for new uses. Slowly artists moved in, and town houses began to be refurbished.

Contemporary Chelsea – More than 200 world-class **galleries** now occupy garages and lofts on the district's western flank, offering museum-quality exhibitions alongside up-and-coming group shows. On West 20th, 21st and 22nd streets, a lovely historic district preserves Clement Clarke Moore's vision of elegant city living.

For bars, diners and cafes, check out Eighth Avenue above West 16th Street. There are two French cafes on Ninth Avenue above West 20th Street; try **La Bergamote**, a delectable French patisserie (169 Ninth Ave. at W. 20th St.; ☏212-627-9010). Farther west, at Tenth Avenue, is the **Half King**, a snazzy bar and bistro co-owned by Perfect Storm author Sebastian Junger, and thus the sponsor of many literary events *(505 W. 23rd St. at Tenth Ave.; ☎212-462-4300).*

Sights

Gallery District★★★

🕐 *Note that most galleries are closed Sun and Mon year-round; in the summer, many are open Mon–Fri only.*

Chelsea's many galleries are concentrated between West 20th and 30th streets west of Tenth Avenue. Many visitors simply wander around, drifting in and out of street-level spaces that look interesting. But to take full advantage of the district, it's essential to pick up a Gallery Guide, which contains a fold-out map locating all the galleries in the area (many of which are on upper stories of large industrial buildings). The guide also lists opening receptions, which can be a fun and festive way to drink in the scene.

Chelsea Art Museum★

556 W. 22nd St. at Eleventh Ave. 🕐*Open year-round Tue–Sat noon-6pm (Thu until 8pm).* 🕮 *$6.* ☎*212-255-0719. www.chelsea artmuseum.org.*

Housed in a three-story redbrick warehouse dating from 1850, the museum mounts a broad range of shows – from a traveling exhibition of 80 etchings by Francisco de Goya to a group show exploring the concept of the bogeyman. It is also home of the Miotte Foundation, which is dedicated to archiving and conserving the work of the French painter Jean Miotte (b.1926), an early proponent of so-called Art Informel, a school related to Abstract Expressionism that seeks to strip art of all reference to representation. In 2004 the Chelsea Art Museum's 7,000sq ft ground floor became the interim home for the **New Museum of Contemporary Art** *(☎212-219-1222; www.newmuseum.org),* which is scheduled to move to its dazzling new 60,000sq ft facility at 235 Bowery on the Lower East Side in December 2007. Expect to find cutting-edge multimedia exhibits exploring the role of art and technology in contemporary society.

Starrett-Lehigh Building★

601 W. 26th St. between Eleventh & Twelfth Aves.

Wrapped in about nine miles of glass, this 1931 factory-warehouse is a stunning example of architecture for the machine age. Freight cars were ferried across the Hudson River from New Jersey on barges, rode the elevated High Line railway into the building, and then, fully loaded, were hoisted to the upper floors by super-powered elevators. The structure was converted into offices (Martha Stewart Omnimedia and Hugo Boss are both leaseholders) and galleries in the 1990s.

Rubin Museum of Art★★

150 W. 17th St. at Seventh Ave. 🕭 *See Museums.*

Chelsea Historic District★

On West 20th, 21st and 22nd streets between Ninth and Tenth avenues stand some of Chelsea's loveliest brownstones. The well-preserved Greek Revival houses that make up **Cushman Row** *(406-418 W. 20th St.)* typify Clement Clarke Moore's vision for the neighborhood with their 10ft-deep front yards and cast-iron railings. They were built in 1840 by Moore's friend Alonzo Cushman, a merchant and banker. The pretty, green quadrangle of

©Peter Wrenn/MICHELIN

Cushman Row

General Theological Seminary stands across the street from the row, behind a high iron fence. The seminary and its grounds occupy the entire block bounded by West 20th and 21st streets and Ninth and Tenth avenues (*entrance at 175 Ninth Ave.;* ⓞ*open year-round Mon–Fri noon–3pm, Sat 11am–4pm;* ☎*212-243-5150; www.gts.edu*). Note especially the 1836 fieldstone **West Building**, one of the oldest Gothic Revival structures in New York. A half block east of the seminary sits **St. Peter's Episcopal Church** (*346 W. 20th St.*), which also dates from 1836 and is also in the Gothic Revival style. It was designed by Clement Clarke Moore for a congregation that outgrew its 1832 Greek Revival building (now the rectory). The hall east of the church was constructed as the church parish house in 1854; it's now home to the **Atlantic Theater Company** (*336 W. 20th St.;* ☎ *212-645-8015; www.atlantictheater. com*), founded in 1985 by playwright **David Mamet** and actor **William H. Macy**. The theater company presents a full schedule of Off-Broadway plays.

Additional Sights

Chelsea Piers★
Pier 62 (West Side Hwy. at W. 23rd St). ☎ *212-336-6666. www.chelseapiers.com.* There is little that this gargantuan facility, a prime example of adaptive reuse, can't offer sports enthusiasts. In 1995 four long-neglected piers were turned into a sports complex that contains an ice-skating rink, a bowling alley, a pool, batting cages, a full-service health club (New York's largest), a toddler gym, a rock climbing wall, indoor soccer and basketball courts, beach volleyball courts, a kayak launch and even a driving range at which more than 100 million golf balls have been hit. Call or consult the website for information on specific sports and activities.

Center for Jewish History
15 W. 16th St. between Fifth Ave. & Ave. of the Americas. ⓞ*Open year-round Mon–Thu 9:30am–5:30pm, Fri 9am–3pm, Sun 11am–5pm.* ⓞ*Yeshiva University Museum galleries (*🎟*$8) open Tue–Thu & Sun*

Address Book

CHELSEA GALLERIES NOT TO MISS

Paula Cooper – *534 W. 21st St. and 465 W. 23rd St.* ☎ *212-255-1105.* Long a champion of conceptual and minimalist art, Cooper has two spaces in Chelsea. The work of Zoe Leonard, Andres Serrano, Donald Judd and Sherrie Levine have shown here.

Gagosian – *555 W. 24th St. between Tenth & Eleventh Aves.* ☎ *212-741-1111. www.gagosian.com.* Larry Gagosian's 20,000sq ft gallery was inaugurated in 1999 with a stunning Richard Serra show. Other A-listers (Damien Hirst, Anselm Kiefer, Ed Ruscha) have been featured since.

Gladstone Gallery – *515 W. 24th St. between Tenth & Eleventh Aves.* ☎ *212-206-9300. www.gladstonegallery.com.* This SoHo émigré shows work by top video and conceptual artists, including Matthew Barney.

Greene Naftali – *508 W. 26th St., 8th floor.* ☎ *212-463-7770. www.greene*

naftaligallery.com. The light-drenched eighth-floor gallery showcases international conceptual art.

Lehmann Maupin – *540 W. 26th St. between Tenth & Eleventh Aves.* ☎ *212-255-2923. www.lehmannmaupin.com.* Rem Koolhaas designed this simple gallery space, where you'll find a range of work (sculpture, painting, photographs) by up-and-coming artists.

Matthew Marks – *523 W. 24th St. between Tenth & Eleventh Aves.* ☎ *212-243-0200. www.matthewmarks.com.* Arguably the most famous of Chelsea's galleries, Matthew Marks has shown work by Lucian Freud, Nan Goldin, Willem de Kooning, Jasper Johns, Weegee and others.

Wooster Projects – *418 W. 15th St. between Ninth and Tenth Aves.* ☎ *212-871-6700. www.woosterprojects.com.* This pop and contemporary art has had museum-quality exhibitions of work by Andy Warhol, Roy Lichtenstein, Frank Stella, and David Hockney, among others.

Flea Market

On weekends, scores of amateur dealers gather at **Hell's Kitchen Flea Market** near the Lincoln Tunnel *(West 39th St. between Ninth and Tenth Aves.)* to display an amazing collection of junk, antiques, and odds and ends. Joined by the Annex Market (formerly of Chelsea), the outdoor market is one of the city's largest, drawing an eclectic crowd. Try your luck and look for a silver frame or a vintage hat, but be sure to bargain and check the merchandise before paying *(☎212-243-5343; www.hellskitchenfleamarket.com).*

Vintage Flea Market Finds

©iStockphoto.com/Hedda Gjerpen

11am-5pm. ◐*Closed major holidays & Jewish holidays.* ☎ 212-294-8301. www.cjh.org.

This facility, the result of the artful merging and reconfiguration of four Chelsea brownstones, opened in 2000. Home to five organizations – the YIVO Institute for Jewish Research, the Yeshiva University Museum, the Leo Baeck Institute, the American Jewish Historical Society and the American Sephardi Federation – the center contains the largest collection of Jewish cultural and historical material outside Israel. Some 100 million archival documents, manuscripts and photos; 500,000 library volumes; and tens of thousands of artifacts, works of art and ritual objects are available to scholars and displayed on a rotating basis in the attractive central atrium and in galleries throughout the center. Also on the premises are a reading room, a kosher cafe and a theater.

Chelsea Market

75 Ninth Ave. between W. 15th & 16th Sts.

A canny example of adaptive reuse, this 1898 Nabisco factory (where, in 1912, the Oreo cookie was first made) was reopened in 1997 as an urban food market *(◐open year-round Mon–Fri 7am–9pm, weekends 10am–8pm; www.chelseamarket.com).* Interspersed with stores selling flowers, meat, cheese and other gourmet essentials are cafes and bakeries, a Thai food restaurant and several soup-and-sandwich shops that are perfect for a quick bite. Free wireless Internet access is available throughout the building.

Peter Wrenn/MICHELIN

Chelsea Piers

Garment District

Just north of Chelsea lies the Garment District, a somewhat dank, largely commercial area that runs roughly from West 30th Street to West 40th Street between Broadway and Eighth Avenue. The main drag is **Seventh Avenue**, also known as Fashion Avenue. Though very little manufacturing is done in the district, fabric and notions stores abound, especially on West 38th and 39th streets. To best appreciate the area's history, go to the **Museum at the Fashion Institute of Technology** (Seventh Ave. at W. 27th St.; ◷open year-round Tue–Fri noon–8pm, Sat 10am–5pm; closed major holidays; ☏212-217-4558; www.fitnyc.edu/museum), where student and expert work alike (Calvin Klein is an alum) is on display in several large galleries. Also in the beautification business, wholesale potted-plant and flower vendors line both sides of West 28th Street (between Sixth & Seventh Aves).

A few blocks north, between West 31st and 33rd streets, stands **Madison Square Garden** and, underneath it, **Penn Station**—a vast entertainment and retail complex that is widely regarded as the worst architectural disaster in New York history. The concrete cylinder, which seats 20,000 spectators above a cramped, airless train depot, replaced the original 1906 Penn Station, designed by McKim, Mead and White. Considered the firm's greatest local work, the cast-iron and glass structure was torn down in 1963 and replaced by the current eyesore, which hosts the New York Knicks, the Westminster Dog Show and arena rock shows (box office: ☏212-465-6741; www.thegarden.com). In 1999 plans were announced to right this historic wrong by converting the nearby **General Post Office/James A. Farley Building** (421 Eighth Ave. between W. 31st & 33rd Sts.; ☏212-967-8585)—a companion McKim, Mead and White structure completed in 1908—into a new rail hub. But to date, little progress has been made on the project, other than a new funding initiative in mid-2007.

UNION SQUARE★ – MADISON SQUARE★

MTA SUBWAY: L, N, Q, R, W, 4, 5, 6 TRAINS TO UNION SQUARE OR N, R, W TRAINS TO 23RD ST.

MAP P141

Large 19C and early-20C buildings, both brick and cast-iron, line Broadway, Fifth Avenue and Avenue of the Americas. Originally built as department stores, many of them now house national chains selling clothing or furniture. A few blocks east sits the quiet Gramercy Park neighborhood, with its lovely brownstones and big drooping trees. It centers on an idyllic private square for which you need a key to get in. In Madison Square, at the north edge of the district, you'll begin to feel the thrum of Midtown, especially on weekday afternoons, when office workers, dog-walkers and tourists alike line up for hot dogs and ice cream at the Art Deco Shake Shack and enjoy them on the outdoor terrace.

▸ **Orient Yourself:** The area that stretches from 14th to 26th streets between Third and Avenue of the Americas (Sixth Ave.) is primarily a retail district linking Downtown and Midtown.

▸ **Organizing Your Time:** Gramercy Park is great for strolling and, in its vicinity, for lunch; good cafes abound around **Irving Place**. At East 14th Street, on the south edge of the district, Union Square offers bountiful local produce and homemade foods (cheese, honey, baked goods) four days a week at its popular **farmers' market**, the city's largest.

Allison Simpson/MICHELIN

Madison Square

Sights

The sights below are arranged from south to north, not by descending stars.

Union Square★

Bounded by East 14th and East 17th streets, Union Square East (Park Avenue) and Union Square West (University Place), Union Square is a pleasant park, crisscrossed with bench- and tree-lined paths. It got its name in the early 19C because it marked the intersection (union) of two streets: Broadway and the Bowery. The park opened in 1831 and by the mid-19C, it formed the groomed and gated centerpiece of an elegant residential and entertainment district. In the late 19C **Tiffany's** jewelry store, Brentano's books, and the restaurant **Delmonico's** (now located near Wall Street) faced the square. As the city spread northward, so did the rich (into sprawling palaces on Fifth Avenue). In the early 20C Union Square became a popular place for rallies and demonstrations, thanks to the fact that several labor unions and radical publications had offices nearby. In the early 1960s **Andy Warhol** established his pop-cultural "Factory" (site of many of his movies and parties) in the ornate **Decker Building** (1893) at 33 Union Square West; it has

since been converted into condos and a wine store.

The Park Today – Three statues grace Union Square: **George Washington** (south) and **Abraham Lincoln** (north), both by Henry Kirke Brown, and the **Marquis de Lafayette** (east), by Frédéric-Auguste Bartholdi, better known as the sculptor of the Statue of Liberty. The tiered plaza on the southern end of the park still serves as a stage for protesters, who often have to share space with break-dancers and other performers. It can be quite a spectacle, a point not lost on the dozens of young people who sit on the steps on sunny days. Artists often display (and try to sell their work) near the renovated subway kiosk at the southwest corner of the park.

Union Square Greenmarket★

Farmers, bakers, flower growers, ranchers and artisanal food makers from all over New York, Pennsylvania and New Jersey bring their bounty to Union Square every Monday, Wednesday, Friday and Saturday year-round (*◎stalls open 8am-6pm, weather permitting*). Each season has its charms: in the spring come flatbed trucks full of perennials, herbs and tomato plants for rooftop gardens; in the summer, abundant produce; in the fall, apples galore, as well as hot cider and fresh doughnuts. A few

Union Square Greenmarket

farmers even show up in the winter to sell cheese, meat, pies and potatoes.

Gramercy Park★

New York City's only private park anchors this tranquil, old-fashioned neighborhood known for its lovely architecture and good cafes and restaurants. The area was laid out in 1831 by developer Samuel B. Ruggles, who drained an old marsh (the word Gramercy is a corruption of a Dutch phrase meaning "little crooked swamp") to build a new residential enclave. Patterning the area after London's residential squares, he sold more than 60 lots with the promise that owners would have exclusive access to the park at its center, between 20th and 21st streets a half-block east of Park Avenue—indeed, they still do. The city's elite built grand homes on the square beginning in the 1840s; apartment buildings catering to the middle classes went up in the 1870s. By the early 20C artists and intellectuals, including **Eugene O'Neill** and **Nathanael West**, moved in. Their presence was short-lived; the **West Village** soon beckoned, but their legacy remains in two of the city's oldest bars. O. Henry supposedly wrote his classic 1905 short story "The Gift of the Magi" in **Pete's Tavern** *(129 E. 18th St. at Irving Pl.; ☎212-473-7676)*, a cozy pub that has been in continuous operation since 1864. Dating from 1892, the **Old Town Bar** *(45 E. 18th St. between Broadway & Park Ave. South; ☎212-529-6732)* is a local favorite, with its high tin ceiling, long mahogany bar and big juicy hamburgers.

Gramercy Park★

Enclosed by an 8ft-high cast-iron fence to which only local residents have keys, Gramercy Park consists of formal gardens, paths, benches and trees dating back to Ruggles' time; in the center stands a statue (1916, Edmont Quinn) of Shakespearean actor Edwin Booth (brother of John Wilkes Booth, President Lincoln's assassin), dressed to play his favorite role, Hamlet. Around the park are several notable buildings:
Gramercy Park West★ presents a harmonious front of redbrick town houses. **Nos. 3** and **4**, designed by Alexander Jackson Davis in 1846, boast elaborate cast-iron porches, reminiscent of those found in New Orleans. No. 4, the former home of **James Harper**, mayor of New York in 1844 and one of the founders of Harper & Bros. (now HarperCollins) publishers, is flanked by a pair of iron lanterns called "mayor's lamps": the mayor could request to have such lamps installed in front of his house to facilitate locating him in case of nighttime emergencies.
Gramercy Park South is home to two distinguished private clubs. At no. 15 stands the **National Arts Club**★ *(www.nationalartsclub.org)*, which occupies the former home of **Samuel Tilden**, New York's governor from 1874 to 1876 and US presidential candidate in 1876. The mansion originally consisted of side-by-side 1840s brownstones, but in the 1870s Tilden had them overhauled and linked by **Calvert Vaux**, the co-designer of Central Park and the Metropolitan Museum of Art. The result is a stunning example of 19C architecture and design, complete with bay windows, Gothic ornamentation, Victorian furniture and exquisite stained-glass ceilings (by **John La Farge** and **Donald MacDonald**). The club, which moved into the house in 1906 and has more than 2,000 elected members in all branches of the arts, sponsors some 200 events a year here *(it is closed in July and August)*; visual artists are represented in the basement galleries *(call ☎212-475-3424 for hours)*. Next door, at no. 16, is The Players, a club for thespians founded in 1888 by Edwin Booth in what was then his home. The 1845 brownstone *(⊶closed to the public)* was renovated in the Greek Revival style by **Stanford White**.

Restaurants
1. Blue Water Grill
2. Gotham Bar and Grill
3. Tamarind
4. Union Square Cafe

Hotels
1. Carlton on Madison Ave.
2. Inn at Irving Place

Gramercy Park East – On the east side of the square are two fancy apartment buildings. Dating from 1883, no. 34 is a redbrick Queen Anne-style tower with an octagonal turret corner. The entrance to the white terra-cotta Gothic Revival building at no. 36 (1910) is flanked by two concrete knights.

Theodore Roosevelt Birthplace National Historic Site★

28 E. 20th St. ○Open year-round Tue-Sat 9am–5pm. ○Closed major holidays. ✎ Period rooms by guided tour (40min) only; on the hour 10am–4pm, except noon. ⌗$3. ☎212-260-1616. www.nps.gov/thrb. This 1920s brownstone was built to reproduce as closely as possible Teddy Roosevelt's childhood home, an 1848 brownstone that stood on the site until 1916.

A Bit of History

32nd President of the US – A driving force in US politics for 40 years, **Teddy Roosevelt** (1858-1919) was vice president of the US in 1901 when President William McKinley was assassinated by an anarchist in Buffalo, New York. Teddy succeeded to the Oval Office and won himself a second term in 1904. In 1908 he backed William Taft for the top job but, unhappy with Taft's performance, ran against his onetime friend in 1912. Taft and Roosevelt split the progressive vote, handing victory to Woodrow Wilson. But politics was only one of Roosevelt's passions: a hunter-naturalist, he gathered a large collection of wildlife specimens, which he later donated to the American Museum of Natural History and other institutions. He also gave his name to the **teddy bear** and won the Nobel Peace Prize for his mediating efforts between Russia and Japan.

His Boyhood Home – Teddy Roosevelt's parents, Theodore Sr. and Martha Bulloch, moved into the original house in 1854, and in 1858 Teddy was born. The Roosevelts were members of the city's elite; at the time, Gramercy Park was New York's most fashionable neighborhood. But by the 1870s high society began moving northward, and after a year in Europe in 1872, the Roosevelts, too, moved uptown, to a new house at 6 West 50th Street. The Gramercy Park brownstone was torn down in 1916 to make way for a commercial building, but after the former president died three years later, a citizens group raised money to purchase the site and rebuild it. Teddy's two sisters, as well as his niece **Eleanor Roosevelt** consulted with the architects on the color schemes, floor plan and other details to make the house appear as it did in 1865-1872, Teddy's formative years.

Visit

Nearly 40 percent of the furnishings are original to the house; another 20 percent belonged to other family members. Tour guides bring visitors through five period rooms, using the objects, as well as anecdotes, to describe the life and times of Teddy Roosevelt.

Madison Square★

This lovely six-acre park has been transformed in the new millennium into one of downtown's most inviting public spaces. Bounded by East 23rd and 26th streets and Madison and Fifth avenues, it was once part of a military parade ground. It was named after President **James Madison** in 1814, and in 1845 served as the playing field for the city's first baseball club, the New York Knickerbockers. From the 1850s to the 1870s the park was the center of an aristocratic neighborhood; author **Edith Wharton** was born at 14 West 23rd Street in 1862. From the 1870s to 1925 a succession of entertainment venues stood on the north end of the square, including the first two (of four) arenas called Madison Square Garden. Stanford White designed the second one in 1890 and was killed in a duel on its roof in 1906; the 8,000-seater was demolished in 1925 to make room for the New York Life Insurance Company building. Today Madison Square Garden stands 10 blocks north of Madison Square, in the Garment District.

Madison Square Park Today – Thanks to the efforts of the Madison Square Park Conservancy, the park is now a popular gathering place for people who live and work in the area. Old-fashioned benches and well-tended plantings line curving paths. In 2002 a children's playground opened on the east side of the square. The conservancy also commissions installations by prominent artists such as **Sol LeWitt**, whose *Curved Wall with Towers* (2005) grace the park. The most popular newcomer, however, is the **Shake Shack** (2004, James Wines), an ivy-covered, zinc-clad food kiosk at the park's south end that serves up ice cream sundaes, shakes and cones as well as hot dogs, wine and beer (◯ *open daily 11am–11pm)*. Surrounding the park are several landmark buildings.

Flatiron Building★★

Even if you've never been to New York City, you've likely seen this building before —it's a popular backdrop in television shows and movies. Viewed from the north side (the side that faces Madison Square Park), it looks like an iron (hence the name), the acute angle of its facade formed by Broadway and Fifth Avenue. Though it's only 6ft wide on this sharp cor-

Flatiron Building

Brigitta L. House/MICHELIN

> ## Quick Bite
>
> The coffee at **71 Irving Place Coffee and Tea Bar** (*☎212-995-5252*) was voted the best in the city by *New York Magazine,* thanks no doubt to the fact that the beans are roasted in small batches upstate. Homemade quiche, waffles, sandwiches, soups and cookies are also served in the inviting garden-level space, which is open both early (🕐 *7am on weekdays, 8am on weekends*) and late (🕐 *Sun–Wed until 11pm, Thu–Sat until midnight*).

ner, the building rises 22 stories straight up from the sidewalk. Famed Chicago architect Daniel Burnham designed the structure, which was finished in 1902. It features limestone at the bottom, then brick and terra-cotta on the upper floors. The Flatiron Building's enormous cornice makes its looming presence above the street even more pronounced.

Metropolitan Life Insurance Company Tower★
Madison Ave. between E. 23rd & E. 24th Sts.

LeBrun & Sons designed this tapered 700ft tower to resemble the campanile of St. Mark's in Venice, Italy. It was the tallest building in the world upon its completion in 1909. Today the tower is a fixture on the New York skyline, especially at night, when it looks like a glowing lantern. Note the enormous four-sided clock; its hour hand weighs 700 pounds.

New York State Supreme Court Appellate Division★
Madison Ave. at E. 25th St.

A Corinthian colonnade and about 30 figures by 16 sculptors—the most sculptors to work on a single building in the US—deck the exterior of this white marble building (1899, James Brown Lord). The marble sculptures, which weren't finished until 1901, represent allegorical figures such as Wisdom, Peace and Justice, as well as figures in legal history, such as Moses, Confucius and Justinian.

Daniel Chester French, best known for his seated Abraham Lincoln in Washington, DC, made Justice (fourth from left on 25th Street).

New York Life Insurance Company Tower★
51 Madison Ave. between E. 26th & E. 27th Sts.

Woolworth Building architect Cass Gilbert designed this 40-story Gothic Revival tower (1928), which stands on the site of Stanford White's Madison Square Garden. Its pyramidal crown also figures prominently on the skyline at night.

Museum of Sex
233 Fifth Ave. at E. 27th St. 🕐*Open daily 11am–6:30pm (Sat until 8pm).* 🕐*Closed Thanksgiving Day & Dec 25.* ⊜*$14.50* 🔞*Must be 18 years of age or older to be admitted.* ☎*212-689-6337. www.museum ofsex.com.*

Opened in 2002, the Museum of Sex is nothing if not interesting—but be forewarned: the graphic nature of its collection may come as a shock. Past exhibits, which occupy three nondescript galleries, have traced the history of the sex industry in New York City, and the origins of the pin-up girl from Victorian times. Many items on display are plucked from the museum's permanent collection, which includes erotic films and videos, magazines, books, calendars, posters, toys and other novelties.

MANHATTAN: MIDTOWN

Midtown Manhattan is the New York City you probably pictured as a kid—big and glitzy, full of fast-walking, fast-talking business people, spangled showgirls and towering skyscrapers with postcard views. But that's not all there is. You'll also find quiet side streets, pleasant parks and world-class art, if you know where to look. Stretching from 34th Street to 59th Street from the Hudson River to the East River (the entire width of Manhattan), Midtown is made up of several very distinct areas.

Fifth Avenue is New York's most elegant thoroughfare. Famous for its upscale department stores and fancy boutiques, it's also home to the **Empire State Building** *(at 34th St.)* and **St. Patrick's Cathedral** *(at 50th St.)*. Brash **Times Square**, at Broadway and 42nd Street, is just the opposite: everything here, from the peanut vendors to the taxis to the billboards, competes for a piece of your senses. As you proceed north on Broadway, you'll find yourself in the heart of the country's largest **Theater District**, where the curtain rises on up to 40 live shows every night. Be sure to catch one.

Avenue of the Americas, also known as Sixth Avenue, is the spine of **Central Midtown**, which changes from block to block. At its southern end stands **Macy's** department store, a New York institution, and famous for its Thanksgiving

Day parade. Between 40th and 42nd streets spreads picturesque **Bryant Park** (the de facto backyard of the **New York Public Library**). Between 48th and 51st streets stands **Rockefeller Center**, a masterpiece of urban planning that's also home to NBC studios and the city's most famous skating rink. Keep heading north and you'll hit the new and vastly expanded **Museum of Modern Art**.

The swatch of land east of Fifth Avenue, the area known as **East Midtown**, contains some of the city's finest office buildings, from the Art Deco **Chrysler Building** to the modernist **Lever House**, as well as the spectacular Beaux-Arts **Grand Central Terminal**.

Finally, all the way at the East River, you'll find the headquarters of the **United Nations**, where some 5,500 people from 191 countries work to create a more peaceful world.

View down Park Avenue

Brigitta L. House - MICHELIN

How Manhattan Is Divided

Downtown – south of 34th Street.
Midtown – 34th Street to 59th Street.
Uptown – north of 59th Street
East Side, West Side – Fifth Avenue marks the dividing line.

FIFTH AVENUE★★★

MTA SUBWAY: B, D, F, N, Q, R, V AND W TRAINS TO 34TH ST.–HERALD SQ.
MAP PP 148-149

New York's most prestigious thoroughfare, Fifth Avenue between 34th Street and 57th Street is studded with striking landmark skyscrapers and churches, exclusive boutiques and grand public buildings. Elaborate department-store window displays at Christmastime make this well-traveled stretch even more festive, as do some of the city's grandest parades.

▸ **Orient Yourself:** Despite the presence of such mass-market ventures as American Girl Place, the NBA Store, and NikeTown, Fifth Avenue remains quite soigné, especially as you approach 57th Street, where the most expensive boutiques, as well as a number of top-notch art galleries, are clustered. It also tends to be crowded.

🕐 **Organizing Your Time:** If you're short on time, visit Saks, Tiffany, Bergdorf Goodman, and the New York Public Library during the day; and save the Empire State Building until evening. Otherwise start at the Empire State Building and walk north. To escape the clangorous daytime activity, retreat to one of the peaceful church sanctuaries, or duck into one of the area's posh hotel bars, such as the King Cole Bar in the St. Regis or TY in the Four Seasons.

A Bit of History

Millionaires' Row – This part of Fifth Avenue has always been a magnet for the rich. In the 1860s the Irish-born department-store mogul **A.T. Stewart**, New York's wealthiest resident at the time, erected a splendid marble mansion at Fifth Avenue and 34th Street. The opposite corner—the site now occupied by the Empire State Building—was dominated by the huge brownstone of hotelier **William Astor**. The American railroad tycoon **Jay Gould** built a residence on the corner of 5th Avenue and 47th Street, while the rival **Vanderbilt** dynasty established itself around 50th Street. So great was the concentration of wealth along 5th Avenue that it became known as Millionaires' Row.

Gradually through the 1880s, however, horse-drawn buses made the avenue more accessible to the masses—and thus less desirable to the elite. After **Caroline Astor** (William's wife and the self-appointed leader of New York high society) relocated to 65th Street in 1893, the city's movers and shakers followed suit, their mansions filled by, or demolished to make room for, high-end boutiques and fancy department stores.

Sights

The sights below are arranged from south to north.

34th to 51st Street

Empire State Building★★★
350 Fifth Ave. between W. 33rd & W. 34th Sts. 🕐Observatory open year-round daily 8am–2am (last elevator up at 1:15am). 👓$16.61 (🕐see A Bit of Advice). ☎212-736-3100. www.esbnyc.com.

Strength and grace combine to make the Empire State Building the most famous skyscraper in the world and the quintessential New York landmark. Topping out at 1,454 feet, it is the city's tallest building, and one of the few you can actually experience. Go up to the tower's 86th-floor, 360-degree open-air observatory and you'll see what we mean: stomach-dropping height, jaw-dropping view.

A Bit of History
A Prestigious Site – From 1857 to 1893 the Empire State Building site was home to two mansions belonging to William and Caroline Astor. After the couple left in the 1890s, their son and nephew tore down the houses and built the jointly run Waldorf and Astoria hotels on the

Empire State Building Q&A

Who designed it?
Shreve, Lamb, & Harmon Assocs., a local architectural firm.

Where does the name come from?
From George Washington, who allegedly referred to New York as the Empire State (for its economic strength) in 1784.

How tall is it?
86 stories to the top of the tower, 102 stories to the top of the "mooring mast," 124 stories to the top of the antenna.

How many elevators are there?
73, including six freight elevators, operating at speeds from 600ft to 1,400ft per minute. It is possible to ride from the lobby to the 80th floor in 45 seconds.

How many steps?
1,860, though the 100 or so participants in the annual Empire State Building Run-Up, held in early February, climb "only" 1,576 of them. The male and female winners in 2007 were from Germany and Singapore respectively, with times of 10:25 and 13:12.

Do the colors of the lights on the tower at night have any significance?
Yes. The top 30 stories are illuminated from dusk to midnight in three tiers of color to reflect the day or the season. It's easy to guess what some colors mean (red, white and blue on July 4, green on Saint Patrick's Day), but much harder to guess others (red, yellow and green for Portuguese Independence Day, purple and white for Alzheimer's awareness). The Empire State Building's website has a complete schedule.

Is the Empire State Building ever struck by lightning?
Yes, about 100 times a year; its 22-story antenna acts as a lightning rod.

property. In October 1929, the hotels were demolished to make way for the Empire State Building. (The "new" Waldorf-Astoria Hotel opened two years later on Park Avenue, where it still stands.)

Up in a Jiffy – Building the Empire State Building was a purely speculative venture. In the 1920s New York City was experiencing a real estate boom, and former New York State governor Al Smith, along with two investors, wanted to get in on the action. Unfortunately, their timing was off: contracts were signed just weeks before Black Tuesday, the start of the Great Depression. Nonetheless, construction went forward, sometimes at a furious pace. At the peak of operations, 3,500 workers added more than a story a day to the building's steel frame. The job was completed 45 days ahead of schedule and $5 million under budget.

The Best-Laid Plans – At the opening ceremonies on May 1, 1931, Smith bragged that the building would help usher in the age of the blimp. The distinctive 16-story spire atop the building was intended to

be a dirigible "mooring mast," and the 86th floor was set aside as a ticket office and waiting room, but after one precarious trial run in 1932, the scheme was

Peter Wrenn/MICHELIN

Empire State Building

🙂 A Bit of Advice 🙂

The lines for the observatory tend to be shortest first thing in the morning. Note that even if you have a **CityPass**, you will still have to wait in line twice: first to get through the security checkpoint and then for an elevator. If you don't have a CityPass, you will have to stand in line to buy tickets as well. The only way to avoid all lines is to buy a $41.52 express pass in advance from the Empire State Building ticket office.

abandoned. In 1933 the building was scaled by a giant gorilla and his blond sweetheart in the movie *King Kong*. Then in 1945 an errant bomber plane crashed into the 79th floor, killing 14 people, including the crew (the building was structurally unharmed). A TV antenna was added to the mooring mast in 1953. At its tip is a flashing beacon that serves as a warning signal for aircraft.

Visit

To get to the **86th-floor observatory**★★★, enter the Empire State Building from Fifth Avenue. There will be a sign inside the entrance indicating the total wait time and the visibility level. The highest visibility level posted is 25 miles, and it is said that on clear days the **views**★★★ extend 80 miles, all the way to the Berkshire Mountains in Massachusetts. On overcast days the view can be less than a mile. If you decide to proceed, take the escalator to the second floor and get in line. Bags larger than an airline carry-on are not allowed, and there is no coat check, so pack lightly. Enjoy the view! A second attraction at the Empire State Building is **New York Skyride** (🕐*open year-round daily 8am–10pm;* 🕐*reduced hours Jan 1, Dec 24, 25 & 31;* 💰*$29.50, online $25.50;*

FIFTH AVENUE

Hotel
- 🏨 The Royalton

Restaurants
- ❶ Le Bernardin
- ❷ Sea Grill

particularly cherished for its Christmas windows.

New York Public Library★★★

476 Fifth Ave. between W. 40th & W. 42nd Sts. ◐Open Mon–Sat 11am–6pm (Tue & Wed until 7:30pm), Sun 1pm–5pm. ◐Closed major holidays. ☎212-340-0830. www.nypl.org.

The crown jewel of New York City's library system, this Beaux-Arts masterpiece (1911) by Carrère and Hastings contains some of the most spectacular interiors in the city, as well as one of the largest research collections in the world.

A Bit of History

In the mid-19C, when this part of Fifth Avenue was known as "Millionaires' Row," New York didn't have a single public library. Instead, there were two private libraries that were accessible to the public free of charge. One was the **Astor Library**, a reference collection opened in 1849 with funds bequeathed by **John Jacob Astor** (1763-1848), a self-taught German immigrant who at the time of his death was the wealthiest man in America. The other was the **Lenox Library**, which consisted mainly of rare books, manuscripts and Americana. Neither institution allowed patrons to check out books and by the end of the 19C, both were

☎ 212-279-9777; www.sky-ride.com), a 25min virtual-reality aerial tour of the city guided by famous actors.

Lord & Taylor

424–434 Fifth Ave. between W. 38th & W. 39th Sts. ☎212-391-3344. www.lordandtaylor.com.

New York's oldest department store—the flagship of a national chain—was founded in 1826 by Samuel Lord and George Washington Taylor as a dry-goods store in Chinatown. After a brief stint on the Lower East Side, the store expanded (in 1860) into a five-story marble building on **Ladies' Mile**. Lord & Taylor moved to its present location in 1914. The Fifth Avenue store is

©iStockphoto.com/Ben Russell

A Lion Sculpture at the Entrance of the New York Public Library

having financial difficulties. A $2.4 million bequest by former New York governor **Samuel Tilden** (1814-1886) to open a free library and reading room in the city made it possible to combine the collections and to build a grand structure to house them.

The NYPL Is Born – The New York Public Library's (NYPL) first director, a former army surgeon and librarian named Dr. John Shaw Billings, came up with the basic floor plan for the library: seven stories of stacks directly below a vast, light-filled reading room. Requests for books would be sent down to the stacks via pneumatic tubes; the books would be sent up on dumbwaiters. (Indeed, the system is so efficient that it is still used today.) Carrère and Hastings incorporated Billings' demands into their exquisite design. Shortly after the cornerstone was laid in 1901, industrialist **Andrew Carnegie**, a champion of public libraries nationwide, offered $5.2 million to establish 65 branch libraries if the city would agree to maintain them. The city agreed. Today the NYPL is the world's only research library with a circulating branch system (there are currently 85 neighborhood branches). The NYPL also has more cardholders (2.32 million) and more materials (10.5 million items in circulation; more than 50 million total) than any other public library in the nation. Holdings range from well-thumbed potboilers to a Gutenberg Bible.

Exterior

Sculptor Edward Clark Potter created the two marble lions that flank the library's grand staircase. Sometimes referred to as Patience and Fortitude, they quickly became the library's mascots; a lion's head features prominently on most NYPL publications. In warm weather, the vast front **terrace** is dotted with folding chairs and food vendors. This is but a taste, as it were, of glorious **Bryant Park**, which unfolds behind the library toward Avenue of the Americas (Sixth Ave.) and which is especially popular at lunchtime in good weather.

Interior

The library's grand white-marble lobby, **Astor Hall**, contains a staffed information desk. Pick up a floor plan and inquire about the day's events (readings, lectures, performances). Major exhibitions on historical and literary themes are held in **Gottesman Hall**, which stands directly behind Astor Hall. The richly paneled **DeWitt Wallace Periodical Room**, with its 13 murals by Richard Haas, lies at the end of the corridor to your left. This is where Wallace, the founder of Reader's Digest, spent countless hours condensing articles for his legendary magazine. Climb the main staircase (or take the elevator) to the third floor. The soaring **McGraw Rotunda** at the top of the steps is adorned with murals depicting the recorded word. It is flanked by the **Salomon Room**, a 19C picture gallery that presents small rotating exhibits, and the Bill Blass Public Catalog Room. Proceed through the catalog room to the **Rose Main Reading Room**, which is arguably the most enchanted public space in the city. Nearly two city blocks long, it has intricately carved woodwork, 51ft ceilings covered with cerulean murals, and long oak tables dotted with brass reading lamps.

Saks Fifth Avenue
611 Fifth Ave. between E. 49th & E. 50th Sts. ☎ 212-753-4000. www.saks.com.
Though now the epitome of Fifth Avenue luxe, Saks has humble roots. The original store was founded in 1902 by Andrew Saks (1847-1912), a former peddler, near Herald Square. His son Horace opened this store, Saks Fifth Avenue's flagship, in 1924. Today there are 54 Saks stores in 25 states. In December of each year, the Fifth Avenue store's holiday window displays are a popular complement to the nine-story Christmas tree across the street at **Rockefeller Center**.

Saint Patrick's Cathedral★★
On Fifth Ave. between E. 50th & E. 51st Sts. ⏰ Open year-round daily 6:30am–8:45pm. ☎ 212-753-2261. www.saint-patrickscathedral.org.
The largest Roman Catholic church in the US looks positively quaint amid the skyscrapers of Midtown today, but when the site was chosen in the 1850s, New Yorkers complained that it was too far

St. Patrick's Cathedral, sculpture of Atlas

out in the country. At the time, of course, the city's population was clustered downtown, but church officials correctly predicted the general migration northward. Native New Yorker **James Renwick** (1818-95) was chosen to design the new cathedral in large part because his design for Grace Church in the East Village, completed in 1846, was so well-received. Construction on Saint Patrick's began in 1859 and was supposed to take eight years. Instead, thanks to the intrusion of the Civil War, it took 20. The church was dedicated in 1879 but was still not complete. The 330ft spires were added in 1888. St. Patrick's is reminiscent of the cathedral of Cologne, Germany. Missing, however, are the extensive

Saks Fifth Avenue

The Tea Box at Takashimaya

693 Fifth Ave. between E. 54th & E. 55th Sts. ☎212-350-0100. www.ny-takashimaya. com. *Tea served Mon–Sat 3pm–5:45pm (extended holiday hours).* Escape Midtown's clamor in this soothing beige basement tea salon in the Takashimaya department store. Nearly 40 kinds of tea are available by the pot, and more by the ounce in loose leaf, as well as delicious pastries and green-tea ice cream. A good choice is the "East-West" tea service, which includes a pot of tea (try the sen-cha, a sweet green tea) with a tray of sandwiches (curry crab roe, salmon pressed on rice, wasabi chicken), your choice of desserts (green-tea mousse, panna cotta), sweet-potato chips, fruit and chocolates.

stone carvings (owing partially to the use of granite, a hard stone) and the flying buttresses, hallmarks of Gothic architecture.

Inside, the cathedral follows a typical cruciform plan. Three portals with intricately sculpted bronze doors open into the spacious nave, which is illuminated by stained-glass Gothic windows. A series of slender marble pillars supports the cross-ribbed vaults, which rise 110ft above the nave. Note also the graceful baldachin over the high altar, by Renwick, and the monumental organ. Located behind the apse, the Lady Chapel was added in 1906.

The cathedral hosts a series of free organ concerts and choir concerts yearly.

52nd to 57th Street

Austrian Cultural Forum

11 E. 52nd St. ⏰Open year-round *Mon–Sat 10am-6pm.* ☎212-319-5300. www.acfny.org.

This severe sliver of a building (2002, Raimund Abraham) asserts Austria's presence in the New York cultural scene. The 24-story tower presents a jagged edge to the street, its sloped, glass-wall facade marked by protruding beams and overlapping setbacks. The interior is stark but serene. Three levels of galleries

and a 90-seat theater present multimedia work by Austrian artists.

Saint Thomas Church★

1 W. 53rd St. at Fifth Ave. ⏰*Open year-round Mon–Fri 7am–6:30pm, Sat 9am–3pm, Sun 7am–6pm.* 🍽Guided tours *(1hr) Sun 12:30pm.* ☎212-757-7013. www. saintthomaschurch.org.

Topped by a single tower, this Episcopal church by Cram, Goodhue and Ferguson was completed in 1913. Gothic Revival in style, it was the fourth building to house the congregation, which was formed in 1823 in what is now SoHo. Today the church is well known for its all-male choir, which performs both at Sunday services and in concerts worldwide. The church also offers a series of organ recitals.

Exterior

A wealth of statues and delicate tracery adorns the facade on Fifth Avenue. In the center of the main portal, Saint Thomas, flanked by six of the apostles, welcomes worshipers. The remaining apostles are arrayed overhead in the tympanum. Below the sculptures, bas-reliefs depict the legend of Saint Thomas. Step to the left of the main portal to admire the narrow "Brides' Entrance," decorated with symbolically joined hands.

For Architecture Buffs

As you saunter up Fifth Avenue, take special note of these Fifth Avenue architectural gems:

Former Tiffany's store

no. 409, at E. 37th St. Tiffany & Co. occupied this Renaissance Revival corner building from 1905 (the year the structure was completed) until 1940, when the jeweler moved to its present location at 727 Fifth Avenue (at E. 57th St.). Architect Stanford

White based his design on the Palazzo Grimani in Venice.

No. 425 Fifth Avenue
Famed post-Modernist architect Michael Graves was the force behind this slender tower (2003). Faced with yellow brick and white limestone, it tapers up 55 stories.

Fred F. French Building
no. 551, at E. 45th St. The developer of the Tudor City development in East Midtown had his 1927 headquarters built with typical Art Deco pizzazz. From the polished-bronze entrance, the structure rises 38 stories in a series of massed setbacks, culminating in colorful friezes.

Former Scribner's Bookstore
no. 597, between E. 48th & E. 49th Sts. A vast wall of iron and glass lets copious light into a two-story vaulted store, once full of books. It was designed in 1913 by Ernest Flagg, architect of the Singer Building in SoHo.

Cartier
no. 651, at E. 52nd St. A century ago Fifth Avenue was lined with Renaissance Revival mansions like this one, built for banker Morton Plant in 1905. The French jeweler Cartier acquired the building and turned it into a shop in 1917.

University Club
1 W. 54th St. at Fifth Ave. Charles McKim of McKim, Mead and White designed the 1900 headquarters of this private social club in the Italian Renaissance style. Adorning the building's three-tiered granite exterior are the shields of major American universities, all carved by Daniel Chester French, creator of the Lincoln statue in Washington, DC's Lincoln Memorial.

St. Regis Hotel
2 E. 55th St. at Fifth Ave. The Beaux Arts-style St. Regis (1904) was commissioned by John Jacob Astor IV as one of the first luxury hotels in the city. Note the Maxfield Parrish mural in the swank King Cole Bar, transported here after the Knickerbocker Hotel in Times Square closed in 1921.

Trump Tower
no. 725, at E. 56th St. This flamboyant glass-sheathed tower, designed by the firm Der Scutt, is most interesting for the steep setbacks on its Fifth Avenue facade, which are lushly planted with trees and shrubs (⊶ no longer accessible to the public, unfortunately). Several levels of upscale shops surround the pink marble lobby.

Crown Building
no. 730, at W. 57th St. The chateau-like crown of this French Renaissance tower (1921, Warren & Wetmore) is richly embellished in 23-carat gold leaf. The Museum of Modern Art opened its first gallery here, on the 12th floor, in 1929. Today the building houses the headquarters of Playboy Enterprises.

©Shea Dean

9 West 57th Street★
9 W. 57th St. A twin to the Grace Building at the corner of Avenue of the Americas (Sixth Ave.) and West 42nd Street, this striking high rise of dark glass and white travertine (1974, Skidmore, Owings & Merrill) swoops up from a broad base to become a flat panel topping out at 50 stories. The chunky red "9" sculpture on 57th Street is the work of graphic designer Ivan Chermayeff.

57th Street Gallery District

Midtown anchor of the New York art world, 57th Street is home to more than 60 high-end galleries, many of which contain museum-caliber work. Pick up a **Gallery Guide** for current shows and openings. Here's a sampling of the more celebrated dealers:

Mary Boone
745 Fifth Ave., 4th floor. ☎ 212-752-2929. *www.maryboonegallery.com.*
The doyenne of the SoHo gallery scene of the 1980s puts on strong shows by young artists, often women, in her gallery above Bergdorf's. Her blockbusters show in her larger space in Chelsea.

David Findlay Jr. Fine Art
41 E. 57th St., 11th floor. ☎ 212-486-7660. *www.davidfindlayjr.com.*
Specializes in American 19C and 20C masters, American modernists from 1910 to 1950, and American contemporary art.

Marian Goodman
24 W. 57th St., 4th floor. ☎ 212-977-7160. *www.mariangoodman.com.*
Carries a slate of well-known artists, including Jeff Wall, Dan Graham, Gerhard Richter, Lawrence Wiener, William Kentridge and Thomas Struth.

Marlborough Gallery
40 W. 57th St., 2nd floor. ☎ 212-541-4900. *www.marlboroughgallery.com.*
Handles a number of important estates, such as those of James Rosati and Jacques Lipchitz, as well as the work of Fernando Botero, Red Grooms and Tom Otterness.

PaceWildenstein
32 E. 57th St., 2nd floor. ☎ 212-421-3292. *www.pacewildenstein.com.*
Represents contemporary heavy hitters like Sol LeWitt, Chuck Close and Kiki Smith. The gallery recently hosted a major retrospective of Claes Oldenburg's work.

Michael Rosenfeld
24 W. 57th St., 7th floor. ☎ 212-247-0082. *www.michaelrosenfeldart.com.*
Shows 20C American art in all media. The gallery specializes in WPA (1930s–40s) realists and modernists.

Interior
On entering the nave, note the lovely **reredos** of Dunville stone that rises to a height of 80ft above the altar. Numerous recesses shelter statues of Christ, the Virgin Mary, the apostles and other saints, carved by **Lee Lawrie**, sculptor of the monumental bronze *Atlas* at Rockefeller Center). Also of interest are the stained-glass windows in deep reds and blues, the pulpit and the sculptured organ case.

Fifth Avenue Presbyterian Church
7 W. 55th St. ◷*Open Jun–Sept Mon–Fri 9am–5pm, weekends 8am–4pm. Rest of the year Mon–Fri 9am–5pm, Sat 8am–5pm, Sun 8am–4pm.* ◷*Closed major holidays.* ☎ 212-247-0490. *www.fapc.org.*
This Gothic Revival church (1875) is one of the last churches built in brownstone in the city. The sanctuary, with a seating capacity of 1,800, is notable for its magnificent organ casing and an intricately carved ashwood pulpit.

Tiffany & Co.
727 Fifth Ave. at E. 57th St. ☎ 212-755-8000. *www.tiffany.com.*
Stop to gaze at the sparkling window displays at the legendary jewelry store, Tiffany & Co. It was founded as a stationery store by New Yorkers Charles L. Tiffany and John B. Young in 1837. Charles' son **Louis Comfort Tiffany**, the famous stained-glass artist, took over the business upon his father's death in 1902 and sold his jewelry and enamels here. The store's international reputation was sealed by Truman Capote in his novella *Breakfast at Tiffany's* and the subsequent movie with Audrey Hepburn. It remains the place for engagement rings and silver.

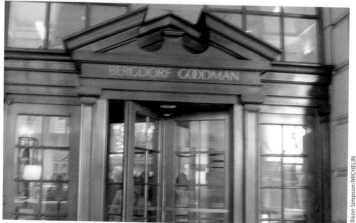

Bergdorf Goodman

Bergdorf Goodman

745 & 754 Fifth Ave. at 58th St. ☎212-753-7300. www.bergdorfgoodman.com. Considered the most elegant and understated of Fifth Avenue's department stores, Bergdorf was founded in 1894 as a tailor and furrier, gradually moving into elite women's fashion in the first part of the 20C. It acquired the present site (no. 754) in 1928, and in 1990 bumped its popular men's department across the street (to no. 745)

Like many of the other major Fifth Avenue stores, Bergdorf is noted for its eye-catching window displays.

BROADWAY★★
TIMES SQUARE★★ AND THEATER DISTRICT★
MTA SUBWAY: ANY TRAIN TO 42ND ST.–TIMES SQ,
MAP P 159

Broadway-Times Square is quintessential New York—sensory overload, in which car horns blare, sidewalks overflow with pedestrians, giant billboards glow and spin, and megastores lure shoppers not just with products but with retail "experiences." Intermingled with such global commercialism is a 100-year-old tradition of local, live entertainment. Jammed shoulder to shoulder in the Theater District are nearly 40 historic venues where you can catch everything from a Shakespeare play with a Hollywood cast to a musical performed by life-size puppets.

Information: Visitor center, Seventh Ave. between 46th and 47th Sts. ☎212-768-1560. www.timessquarenyc.org.

▶ **Orient Yourself:** Though Broadway runs the entire length of Manhattan (13.4 miles) and the Bronx (4 miles), it is the street's half mile between 40th and 50th streets that is regarded as Broadway. Times Square (which extends from Times Square proper onto the surrounding side streets) is not a square at all but rather an elongated X formed by the intersection of Seventh Avenue and Broadway.

🕓 **Organizing Your Time:** Reserve an entire evening to best experience Broadway-Times Square, unquestionably more vibrant after dark, when neon lights and glittering marquees assault the senses. Though pricey, definitely take in a play or musical in the Theater District (🕯️see Duffy Square, where **tkts** sells half-price tickets the day of the show).

Times Square★★

Throughout the 19C, Times Square was known as Longacre Square and was a center for horse trading and harness making. But when the **New York Times** decided to build a new headquarters in the trapezoidal plot formed by Broadway and Seventh Avenue between 42nd and 43rd streets, publisher Adolph Ochs asked that the name of the area be changed accordingly. The city granted his wish, and the new building, at One Times Square, was grandly christened on December 31, 1904. As part of the festivities, Ochs arranged for a brightly lit "time ball" to be lowered from atop the building precisely at midnight, a tradition that continues to this day. Roughly a million revelers converge on the square each **New Year's Eve** to count down as the ball drops, and nearly a billion more watch the spectacle on television.

A Bit of History

The Great White Way - In the first decade of the 20C, Times Square overtook the Bowery as the city's entertainment district. **Vaudeville houses** sprung up around the square, which was newly accessible via subway by 1904 and train by 1913, the year of Grand Central Terminal's completion. In 1916 a city zoning bill encouraged the construction of large electric signs in Times Square, and the "Great White Way" was officially born. The number of hotels, restaurants, dance halls and theaters steadily increased until the stock market crash of 1929, after which point legitimate theater gave way to burlesque shows in some venues and to cinema in others. The descent continued, and by the 1970s, Times Square was a shadowy world of X-rated bookstores, porn shops and prostitution. For some, the seediness had a romantic appeal– indeed, those New Yorkers wax nostalgic for the bad old days depicted in John Schelsinger's *Midnight Cowboy* (1968) and Martin Scorsese's *Taxi Driver* (1976)—but civic leaders generally saw the area as a blight on the landscape.

Attempts to clean up Times Square began as early as the 1950s, but not until the 1990s was significant progress made. Prodded by Mayor **Rudolph Giuliani**, the city and state commissioned architect **Robert A.M. Stern** and graphic artist **Tibor Kallmann** to head up a revitalization plan for West 42nd Street. Giuliani, meanwhile, used the city's powers of eminent domain to push out the sleaze factor and offered generous tax abatements to persuade giant corporations such as **Disney, MTV, Virgin Megastore** and **Condé Nast** to purchase and develop real estate in the area. The tactics worked. Now well into its third decade, the "new" Times Square bustles at every hour, a family-friendly, larger-than-life spectacle not to be missed.

Times Square

Allison Simpson/MICHELIN

Times Square Information Center

The lobby of the 1926 Embassy movie theater on the east side of Seventh Avenue, between 46th and 47th streets, has been turned into a well-organized visitor center covering sights citywide. Open year-round daily from 8am to 8pm, it contains a staffed information desk, plentiful brochures, several computer terminals with free Internet access, a US Post Office, a Broadway ticketing service, public restrooms and free newspapers known for their cultural events listings: *Village Voice* (www.villagevoice.com) and the *L Magazine* (www.thelmagazine.com). The center's website, www.timessquarenyc. org, is also chock-full of news and advice.

Times Square Information Center

Allison M. Simpson - MICHELIN

Sights

Though most of the advertising in Times Square touts products totally unrelated to the place itself (Cup of Noodles, anyone?), some retailers have linked blaring signage to actual shopping experiences. They call it "retailtainment," though the awkwardness of the word ensures that no one else will. The **ESPN Zone** (*1472 Broadway at W. 42nd St.; www.espnzone. com*) is not only a sports store but a massive arcade and sports bar with more that 200 TV screens. **Toys R Us** (*1514 Broadway at W. 44th St.; www.toysrus.com*) is both a toy store and a small amusement park, with an indoor Ferris wheel and an animatronic dinosaur. The **Virgin Megastore** (*1540 Broadway at W. 45th St.; www.virginmegamagazine.com*) merely claims to be the largest music/entertainment emporium in the world, with 70,000sq ft of space.

Sights with greater historical significance along Broadway include the following (*listed from south to north*):

Knickerbocker Hotel Building
1462–1470 Broadway at W. 42nd St. (southeast corner).
Now surrounded by shimmering skyscrapers, this Classical brick pile with the mansard roof recalls Times Square's first heyday. Financed by **John Jacob Astor**, the 556-room hotel was home to the

opera superstar **Enrico Caruso** from the time of its opening in 1907 until Caruso's death in 1921. Here, in 1912, is where an immigrant bartender named **Martini di Arma di Taggia** perfected the drink that bears his name; one of its first champions was **John D. Rockefeller**. On Armistice Day 1918, Caruso stepped out on his balcony and led the crowd of revelers in Times Square in singing the "Star-Spangled Banner," followed by the French and Italian national anthems. The hotel closed in 1921 and was converted to offices. From 1940 to 1959 the most famous tenant was **Newsweek** magazine, which was owned by John Jacob's great-great-grandson Vincent Astor until 1961. The building was converted to residential lofts in 1980 and has since undergone a $10 million renovation.

One Times Square
Bounded by W. 42nd & W. 43rd Sts., Broadway & Seventh Ave.
This 25-story building, barely visible beneath its mammoth signage (especially on the video-screen-laden north face), was the home of the *New York Times* from 1904 to 1913 and remains the centerpiece of New Year's Eve celebrations. In 1928 it became the site of the world's first **"zipper" sign**: 14,800 bulbs were arrayed in a 5ft-tall, 360ft-long ribbon that wrapped all the way around the building. By flashing bulbs on and off, messages were moved ("zipped") past

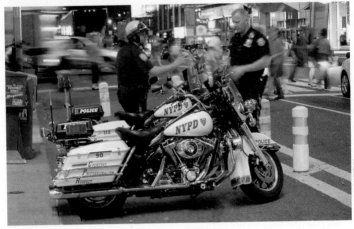

Peter Wrenn/MICHELIN

New York City Police in Times Square

stationary viewers. Today a modified version of the sign is run by **Dow Jones**; amber light-emitting diodes have replaced the old incandescent bulbs.

Condé Nast Building

4 Times Sq. (Broadway at W. 42nd St.)
Completed in 1999, this glimmering 48-story skyscraper by the firm Fox & Fowle was the first of a cluster of office buildings that now stand at the south end of the square. Its unusual crown features a jumble of elements, most prominently giant billboards with the address: 4 Times Square. The largest in the world, **NAS-DAQ**'s 120-ft-high LED (light-emitting diodes) display curves around the northwest corner of the building above a ground-floor TV studio. On upper stories are the offices of the *New Yorker, Vanity Fair, Vogue* and other Condé Nast publications *(www.condenast.com).*

Paramount Building

1501 Broadway (west side) between W. 43rd & W. 44th Sts.
This gracefully stepped building, which culminates in a clock tower topped with a (once illuminated) glass ball, held offices and the Paramount movie theater upon its completion in 1926. And what a theater it was. The lobby was modeled after the Paris Opera House, with white marble columns, balustrades and a grand staircase. Inside were red-velvet curtains, gilt ceilings, brass railings, Greek statues in wall niches and 3,600

plush seats. The theater was gutted in the 1950s, but the building got back a replica of its marquee courtesy of World Wrestling Entertainment, a recent tenant. The Hard Rock Café took over the space in 2005.

Duffy Square

The sliver of concrete bounded by Broadway, Seventh Avenue, and West 47th Street has been home to the ever popular **tkts** booth, where half-price theater tickets are sold on the day of the show. The square was named after **Francis P. Duffy** (1871-1932), the nationally revered "fighting chaplain" of New York's 69th Regiment in World War I. After the war Duffy befriended actors and playwrights as the pastor of **Holy Cross Church** *(333 W. 42nd St. between Eighth & Ninth Aves.).* Ground was broken in May 2006 for a multimillion dollar renovation of Duffy Square that will add illuminated red steps to the north end. Until the renovation's expected completion in early 2008, tkts' temporary location is in the adjacent Marriot Marquis hotel.

Brill Building

1619 Broadway between W. 49th & W. 50th Sts.
Completed in 1931, the Brill Building was the epicenter of the country's pop music industry for several decades: at its peak in 1962, the 11-story structure contained a whopping 165 music businesses: publishers, producers, agents, songwriters,

singers and musicians, everyone madly trying to come up with the next big hit. **Carole King, Paul Anka, Bobby Vee** and **Neal Sedaka** all regularly did business here. (Movie buffs will also note that the building's Art Deco brass facade and foyer featured prominently in the 1957 classic film *The Sweet Smell of Success*, starring Tony Curtis and Burt Lancaster.)

A block south, on West 48th Street between Avenue of the Americas (Sixth Ave.) and Seventh Avenue, stretches **Music Row**, where you'll find the world's largest selection of musical instruments, particularly guitars. Visiting rock musicians often come here to shop.

Theater District★

New York's historic theater district spans the blocks between West 42nd Street northward to roughly 53rd Street, fanning out on both sides of Broadway. At one time more than 80 theaters were built in the district. Some 40 remain today, still offering a wide variety of entertainment.

A Bit of History

Though theater in New York dates back to the time of the colonists, the Times Square theater district was not inaugurated until 1895, when **Oscar Hammerstein** opened the Olympia theater complex at Broadway and 45th Street. In the subsequent three decades, about 85 theaters were built between Avenue of the Americas (Sixth Ave.) and Eighth avenues in Midtown Manhattan.

Early on, many specialized in vaudeville or burlesque. Elaborate dance revues like **Florenz Ziegfeld**'s *Follies* were also tremendously popular. But in the 1920s, Broadway theaters began staging more serious fare: classic dramas (Ibsen, Shaw, Chekhov, Pirandello) as well as work by local playwrights, such as **Eugene O'Neill** and **Clifford Odets**. Rising musical talents like **George Gershwin, Cole Porter** and **Oscar Hammerstein II** (the Olympia founder's grandson) turned their attention to the stage around this time too, giving rise to a new art form: the **American musical**—still Broadway's main attraction.

Hotels
1. Broadway Inn
2. Casablanca Hotel
3. Hotel QT
4. Mayfair New York
5. Muse Hotel

Restaurants
1. Azuri Café
2. Carnegie Delicatessen
3. Firebird
4. Gallagher's
5. Marseille

New York CityPass

If you plan on doing serious sightseeing, consider buying a **New York CityPass** (☎$65; ☎888-330-5008; www.citypass.com). This handy ticket booklet gets you into the American Museum of Natural History, the Empire State Building observatory, the Guggenheim Museum, the Metropolitan Museum of Art, the Museum of Modern Art and the Circle Line sightseeing cruises at half the price you would pay for separate admissions. What's more, once you have your pass, you get to skip ticket-purchasing lines, which can be depressingly long. Buy it online or at any of the participating institutions.

Yet not all theaters in the theater district hosted live performance. Some of the grandest venues in fact were devoted to the **cinema**. The mother of them all, the **Roxy Theater** at Broadway and 50th Street, was called "the cathedral of the motion picture": it had 6,300 seats and a power plant large enough to light a city of 250,000. (Sadly, it was razed in 1961.) Live theater waned during the Depression due to its high cost, but the coup d'état for the Theater District came during World War II, when the Great White Way was darkened for two long seasons. Many venues did not reopen, or did so as second-run or adult movie houses. Not until the 1990s were they returned en masse, both architecturally and artistically, to the mainstream. Today the roughly 40 theaters here constitute the densest grouping of live-performance venues in the US.

Sights

West 42nd Street★★

Between Broadway and Eighth Ave.
Packed cheek by jowl on this bright, frenetic block are some of the most touristic attractions in Times Square, as well as some of the most historic. At no.214, the long-neglected **New Amsterdam Theater**, commissioned in 1903 by Florenz Ziegfeld and host to such stars as French legend Maurice Chevalier and Italian actress Eleonora Duse, has been restored to its Art Deco splendor by the Walt Disney Corp. The *Lion King* ran here for nearly 10 years.

Across the street stands the **New Victory Theatre** (no. 209). Originally built in 1899 by Oscar Hammerstein, it reopened as a children's performance space in December 1995 after a much-acclaimed $12 million renovation. Down the block, **Madame Tussaud's** (no. 234; ○open year-round daily 10am–8pm; ☎800-246-8872; www.nycwax.com; ☎$29) packs more than 200 wax celebrities into its nine-story, 85,000sq ft digs. Two cineplexes face off down the block: **Regal** (nos. 243-47), in Robert A. M. Stern's mall-like E-Walk Complex, and **Empire 25** (no. 234), a five-floor movie house whose 1912 facade and lobby (by architect Charles Lamb) used to stand down the block (they were lifted and moved to this more spacious locale). Behind the crisscrossed steel girders on the southwest corner of Eighth Avenue and 42nd Street stands the **Port Authority Bus Terminal**, in which you can kill time at the resident bowling alley before your bus ride.

Theater Row, a complex of five small Off-Broadway and Off-Off Broadway houses (88 to 199 seats), opened in spring 2002 at 410 West 42nd Street *(between Ninth and Tenth Aves).* Neighbors include **Playwrights Horizons** (no. 416), whose two theaters (99 and 198 seats) opened in January 2003 after a $32 million renovation, and the 499-seat **Little Shubert Theater** (no. 422), new as of November 2002.

Restaurant Row

W. 46th St. between Eighth & Ninth Aves.
Flanking both sides of this block are restaurants that cater to theatergoers with prix-fixe dinner specials and service that is timed precisely to the 8pm curtain. In other words, you can enjoy your dinner without having to constantly check your watch.

For more adventurous fare, however, you might want to explore **Ninth Avenue**; a trendy new restaurant opens here practically every week. This is the main drag

Historic Theaters

As you stroll the Theater District, take note of these particularly historic structures.

Town Hall
113-123 W. 43rd St. between Broadway & Ave. of the Americas.
Designed by McKim, Mead and White in 1921, the hall isn't fancy outside, but the acoustics have been deemed ideal by everyone from Winston Churchill to Laurie Anderson. Check online for a calendar of events: www.the-townhall-nyc.org.

Lyceum Theater
149-157 W. 45th St. between Broadway & Ave. of the Americas.
This 1903 structure boasts a grand Beaux-Arts facade and undulating marquee. It is the oldest New York theater still used for legitimate productions and was first to be landmarked.

Lunt Fontanne Theater
205 W. 46th St. between Broadway & Eighth Ave.
The palazzo-style building was designed in 1910 by Carrère and Hastings. The *Sound of Music* premiered here.

Barrymore Theater
243-251 W. 47th St. between Broadway & Eighth Ave.
The marquee of this 1928 theater is held up by stunningly ornate ironwork. *A Streetcar Named Desire* had its Broadway debut here in 1947.

Winter Garden Theater
1634 Broadway between W. 50th & W. 51st Sts.
The theater stands on the former site of the American Horse Exchange, which was built in the early 1800s by William K. Vanderbilt. The Winter Garden is now home to *Mamma Mia!*, the hit musical based on the songs of Swedish pop group ABBA.

Ed Sullivan Theater
1697 Broadway at W. 53rd St.
Comedian David Letterman films his nightly TV show here. CBS named the theater after celebrity TV host (and native New Yorker) Ed Sullivan in 1967.

Theater District: Winter Garden Theater

Brigitta L. House - MICHELIN

Back Stage Door, Theatre District

of the neighborhood called **Clinton** (by developers) or **Hell's Kitchen** (by locals).

Shubert Alley
From W. 44th to W. 45th Sts. between Broadway & Eighth Ave.

"Stagedoor Annies" line up in this pedestrian alley (one of several in the area) to get the autographs of stars going to, or coming from, performances. At intermission or after shows, many theatergoers, performers, writers and critics drop in to famous **Sardi's** restaurant, at the alley's south end *(234 W. 44th St.; ☎212-221-8440)*, for a meal or a drink. Well known for the caricatures of celebrated theatrical personalities lining the walls, Sardi's has been a fixture in the Theater District since 1921.

Additional Sights

Just four blocks west of bustling Times Square flows the wide Hudson River and alongside it, lie several points of interest. To get to the river, either walk or take the M42 bus west along 42nd Street.

The Island by Boat★★
Taking a narrated boat ride is one of the best ways to learn about the city— Manhattan is an island, after all. And on a

Circle Line Boat Tour *(departs from Pier 83, W. 42nd St. at the West Side Hwy.; ☎ 212-563-3200; www.circleline.com)*, the guides know their stuff, peppering their running historical commentary with the latest in New York gossip (which celebrities paid how many millions for their riverfront apartment, for instance). The full island tour takes three hours, and on a sunny day the time breezes by. But there are shorter tours, too. Look online or check at the ticket counter for options, schedules and prices. (The Circle Line operates boats from South Street Seaport, and to and from the Statue of Liberty as well.)

Intrepid Sea, Air & Space Museum
The USS Intrepid is in Staten Island undergoing an $8 million renovation, and is scheduled to return to Pier 86 in mid-Nov 2008. The text below reflects previous tours of the ship. After refurbishment, there will be new exhibits and access to additional ship quarters.
Pier 86, W. 46th St. at the West Side Hwy. ☎212-245-0072. www.intrepidmuseum. org.

Now a museum, the USS Intrepid aircraft carrier is a veteran of World War II and the Vietnam War; it was a NASA recovery vessel and participated in the blockade of Cuba during the 1962 Cuban Missile Crisis. Built in 1943 at a cost of $44 million, the ship was decommissioned in 1974. The main attraction is the 898ft-long, 42,000-ton carrier itself, a veritable floating city–where a member of the 3,500-man crew could get anything from a haircut to an ice cream sundae. The Hangar Deck features exhibit on navy, aviation, space and carrier technology. Intrepid Hall contains exhibits about Pearl Harbor and World War II. Visitors can also view a film titled *Air Power at Sea (17min)* and a video *(12min)* on the history of the Intrepid. Topside on the vast Flight Deck —large enough to accommodate three football games—stand aircraft such as a Lockheed A-12 Blackbird and a Concorde supersonic jet.

Admission also includes tours *(20min each)* of the fleet destroyer USS Edson and the 1958 guided missile submarine USS Growler. Simulated flights aboard

Intrepid Sea, Air & Space Museum

Destroyer USS Edson, Intrepid Sea, Air & Space Museum

an F-18 fighter jet are available at an additional cost.

Jacob K. Javits Convention Center

Eleventh Ave. between W. 34th & W. 39th Sts.☎212-216-2000. www.javitscenter. com.

I.M. Pei designed this gargantuan black-glass complex in 1986—enclosing 1.8 million square feet. The center can accommodate up to 85,000 conventioneers as well as massive exhibits. An enormous exposed-steel frame consisting of 76,000 tubes and 19,000 nodes serves as beams, walls and roof of the hall and is supported by columns rising 90ft.

CENTRAL MIDTOWN★★

MTA SUBWAY: B, D, F AND V TRAINS TO
47TH-50TH STS./ROCKEFELLER CENTER
MAP BELOW

Although Fifth Avenue officially separates the east and west sides of Manhattan, in Midtown it is Avenue of the Americas (aka Sixth Avenue) that actually feels like the dividing line. In part, that is because its neighbors are so distinct. One block west, the Theater District is a rowdy quarter of blazing marquees and chain restaurants. One block east, the department stores of Fifth Avenue are the height of gentility. Avenue of the Americas and the swath around it are more eclectic. Macy's department store ("the world's largest") anchors a frenetic shopping hub at its southern end (34th Street). The Museum of Modern Art dominates a lively museum district its at northern end (53rd Street). In between you'll find Bryant Park and, just north of it, world-famous Rockefeller Center.

▶ **Orient Yourself:** Centered on Avenue of the Americas (Sixth Ave.), Central Midtown lies a block west of Fifth Avenue. Macy's anchors the lower extremity, the Museum District the upper reaches. Rockefeller Center serves as its centerpiece.

Kids **Especially for Kids:** Ice skating at Rockefeller Center; the carousel at Bryant Park.

A Bit of History

In the colonial era, this slice of Midtown belonged to the city but was actually the country, as New York's population was concentrated well below Canal Street. Then in 1801 **David Hosack** (1769-1835), a professor of botany and medicine at **Columbia University** (and, interestingly, the surgeon in attendance at the 1804 duel between **Alexander Hamilton** and

CENTRAL MIDTOWN

Aaron Burr), purchased the land now occupied by Rockefeller Center to establish a teaching garden in which Hosack explored the medicinal properties of native plants. After 10 years, Hosack shuttered his greenhouse and sold the land to the State of New York. The state then turned it over to Columbia University with the understanding that the school would move its campus here. Instead, the university rented out parcels to farmers for $100 a year.

By the mid-19C, the area was covered with brownstone town houses, home to upper-middle-class families who couldn't afford a mansion on Fifth Avenue but were nonetheless members of high society. But upon the completion of the Sixth Avenue "El" (elevated railway) in 1878, a majority of these residents began moving farther uptown, leaving their fine houses to poorer tenants. Later, during the Prohibition era (1920–33), the district became known as the **"speakeasy belt"** for its concentration of semi-secret nightclubs. Following Prohibition's repeal, many speakeasies reopened as legitimate jazz clubs.

The construction of Rockefeller Center changed the character of the neighborhood. More than 225 buildings were demolished to make room for the orig-

21 Club

21 W. 52nd St. ☎ 212-582-7200. www.21club.com. During Prohibition New York City abounded with illegal watering holes, but none was more famous, more elegant or more ingenious than Jack and Charlie's 21, a subterranean club on West 52nd Street. Opened in 1922, it catered to New York's smart set, in particular the hard-drinking, wise-cracking members of the **Algonquin Round Table**. Jack and Charlie's had good food, good liquor and a dance floor with a full orchestra. Most importantly, it was equipped with a chute through which alcohol could be quickly disposed of in the event of a raid, as well as a secret basement wine cellar with a two-ton door and an address that actually put it next door, at no. 19. After Prohibition the speakeasy reemerged as the legendary 21 Club, a favorite haunt of **Humphrey Bogart, Richard Nixon** and, apparently, rich equestrians, who donated the 33 painted jockey statues that adorn the building's exterior. The club opened a second-floor restaurant in 2002 to rave reviews. The barroom, lined with framed cartoons by famous artists, remains a classic piece of old New York. Drop in for a drink or dinner *(jacket & tie required; reservations recommended).*

inal 12 buildings of the complex, and the residential population was dispersed to other parts of the city. But with that loss came significant gain. The center was hailed as an architectural triumph. Rockefeller's insistence that early tenants be affiliated with the television and radio industries paid off as well: other media outlets soon gravitated to the district, boosting its worldwide visibility and local cachet. The 1939 opening of the Museum of Modern Art at 11 West 53rd Street (a project championed by John D. Rockefeller Jr.'s wife, **Abby Aldrich Rockefeller**) was similarly prescient: the institution now anchors one of the city's most vital museum districts.

Cleaned up in the mid-1990s by a restoration corporation founded by the Rockefeller Brothers Fund, the Bryant Park is Midtown Manhattan's only large public green space, and a lovely one at that.

Rockefeller Center★★★

Between Fifth & Seventh Aves. and W. 47th & W. 51st Sts. ☎212-332-6868. www.rockefellercenter.com. For tours, ⚑see Things to Do in Rockefeller Center.
Located in the heart of Midtown Manhattan, this "city within a city" encompasses more than a dozen harmoniously designed skyscrapers, a formal garden, 100 works of public art, a world-famous skating rink, the headquarters of the television giant NBC and the Art Deco masterpiece Radio City Music Hall.

A Bit of History

The Center Evolves – Rockefeller Center had its start in 1926, with a proposal to build a new concert hall for the Metropolitan Opera in the heart of Midtown. Opera administrators turned to Standard Oil chairman and philanthropist **John D. Rockefeller Jr.** for help. Rockefeller was ideally suited for the job. Unlike most other New York City moguls, who had mansions on upper Fifth Avenue, "John D.," as he was known, had spent most

GE Building, Rockefeller Center

Allison Simpson/MICHELIN

of his childhood and adulthood on West 54th Street, and was eager to see the neighborhood improved. Far more important, he was one of the richest men in the world, with a fortune of about $1 billion ($10 billion in today's dollars). Rockefeller's plan was to replace the down-at-the-heels neighborhood with a new opera house and tall office buildings around a plaza. The stock-market crash of 1929 forced the opera to back out of the deal for lack of funds, but Rockefeller pushed forward with the project.

"Radio City" Is Born – Rockefeller assembled a team of architects from three firms (one of whom was Wallace K. Harrison, designer of the United Nations Headquarters and Lincoln Center) to design a city-within-a-city for the emergent radio and television industries. The architects preserved the original blueprint's central plaza; around it would be 13 Art Deco office buildings linked by underground concourses and street-level promenades.

Buoyed by Rockefeller's optimism and dollars, construction began in 1931 and continued through the Depression. The project employed 4,000 New Yorkers at a time when other developers were cautiously waiting for the economic situation to improve. Between 1947 and 1973, seven additional buildings were added to the complex (1939). Today, Rockefeller Center is generally acknowledged to be a jewel of urban design.

Rainbow Room

GE Building★★★

30 Rockefeller Plaza.

This lithe 70-story skyscraper (originally the RCA Building) is Rockefeller Center's tallest and finest structure. John D. celebrated its completion in 1933 by moving the family offices here from 26 Broadway near Bowling Green. The building is made of limestone with glass and aluminum details. Its strong vertical lines, softened with staggered setbacks in the upper stories, are considered a triumph of Art Deco design. The National Broadcasting Co. (NBC), a General Electric subsidiaries, is headquartered here.

Above the entrance to the GE Building is a bas-relief and glass screen (1933) by the sculptor **Lee Lawrie**. The figure represents Wisdom, shown grasping a drafting compass whose points are directed toward the light and sound waves carved into the cast glass below. The quotation is taken from the Bible.

Interior

Step inside the **lobby** to view the immense ceiling and wall murals by the Spanish artist **José Maria Sert**. Titled "American Progress," the murals are the second series executed on this site. The first, by Mexican muralist **Diego Rivera**, depicted a May Day workers' demonstration led by Vladimir Lenin. When Rivera refused to remove Lenin from the scene, Rockefeller destroyed the painting. (By contrast, when a fresco Rivera completed for **Henry Ford** incited similar controversy just months earlier in Detroit, Henry's son Edsel defended it, and today the painting is regarded as Rivera's most significant work in the US.)

The GE Building's **observatory**★★ contains exhibits on the history of the building as well as an open-air platform on the 70th floor with 360-degree **views** ★★★ of the city

On the 65th floor the famed **Rainbow Room** opens for drinks, dancing and great views of the sparkling city at night (⏰*Fri & Sat evenings only; reservations required; jacket & tie required;* ☎*212-632-5100; www.rainbowroom.com*).

Channel Gardens★★

This long, flower-bedecked passage was named in 1936 by a clever journalist who observed that it separated the **Maison Française** (1933) and the **British Empire Building** (1932) just as the English Channel separates France and Great Britain. The plantings change seasonally, beginning with Easter lilies on Good Friday. From the Fifth Avenue side of the gardens, take in the **view★★** of the GE Building towering over the complex; the symmetrical framing is typical of the City Beautiful movement. The **sunken plaza** lies at the heart of Rockefeller Center. Here, at the top of the steps leading to the lower plaza, is a plaque citing John D.'s personal creed. On the far side of the plaza floats Rockefeller Plaza's best-known artwork, a massive gold-leaf bronze statue of **Prometheus** *(1 on map)* (1934, Paul Manship), shown stealing fire from the gods as a gift for humankind. The floor of the plaza has been frozen into an **ice-skating rink** every winter since 1936. It is particularly festive in December, when the street-level plaza is decked with holiday decorations, including a huge Christmas tree. In warmer weather the rink holds an outdoor bar and restaurant.

Radio City Music Hall★★

(A *on map*) *1260 Ave. of the Americas.* ☎*212-247-4777. www.radiocity.com.* A treasured New York landmark, Radio City Music Hall is one of the city's most grandiose Art Deco creations and a spectacular entertainment venue.

A Bit of History

The music hall opened its doors to the public in 1932, under the direction of **Samuel "Roxy" Rothafel**, to present variety shows. To become more profitable, the hall began operating as a movie house and soon hosted great movie premieres. When the movie business became unprofitable, plans were made to tear the building down. Public outcry put an end to the plan and the building was completely renovated in 1979. Today it is famed for its musical spectaculars and for concerts by top performing artists. Visit the interior by attending a show or by taking the **Radio City Stage Door Tour** *(year-round daily 11am-3pm, every half-hour; departs from the main lobby; 1hr; $17).* All con-

Channel Gardens in Autumn

Brigitta L. House - MICHELIN

cert and tour tickets are available on a first-come, first-served basis from the box office (🕐*open year-round Mon–Sat 11:30am–6pm)* or through Ticketmaster (☎*212-307-7171; service fee applied).*

The Interior★★★

As you enter the Grand Foyer, designed by Donald Deskey, your eyes rise from the plush carpet, featuring a geometric pattern representing six musical instruments, up to the sweeping Grand Staircase and three mezzanine levels. Ezra Winter's enormous 60ft-by-40ft mural *Fountain of Youth* adorns the wall behind the staircase. Magnificent chandeliers emit a suffused light overhead. Each weighs two tons and can be lowered for cleaning by pushing a button. immense wall mirrors extend up to the sparkling ceiling, covered in gold leaf.

In the auditorium, note the curved wall-and-ceiling design and the huge proscenium arch (60ft high), the most striking feature of the 5,882-seat theater. The stage itself is equipped with complex machinery: three elevators, a three-section turntable and an orchestra elevator. The musicians in the orchestra and the two electric organs (with pipes up to 32ft high) and their organists, can be whisked away behind the walls or below the floor when necessary, without interrupting their playing. Lower level rooms form a striking Art Deco ensemble.

International Building★

630 Fifth Ave. between W. 50th & 51st Sts.

In front of the Fifth Avenue entrance of the 41-story International Building (1939) rises a spectacular two-ton bronze statue of **Atlas**★★ (1937, Lee Lawrie and René Chambellan) carrying the world as a punishment for defying Zeus.

On the building's south facade on 50th Street is an elaborate **sculptural relief** (Lee Lawrie), installed in 1935. The bottom panel portrays "the four races of mankind" in their symbolic habitats. The four outer panels at the bottom depict the old age of imperialism and the new age of republics. The relief is crowned by a sunburst and clock.

Inside, the **lobby** features columns and walls made of marble from the Greek island of Tinos; the ceiling is covered with gold leaf. Above the escalators stands a bust of **Charles Lindbergh**, a donation from the Air Mail Pioneers of America, and above the East 50th Street exit is a bronze globular clock.

Associated Press Building

(B on map) 50 Rockefeller Plaza between W. 50th & W. 51st Sts.

This 1937 building is most notable for the dynamic stainless-steel relief **panel**★★ above its entrance. Created by sculptor **Isamu Noguchi** in 1940, the panel, titled *News*, captures figures carrying tools of the journalist's trade: a camera, a notepad, a typewriter and a telephone.

Museum District★★

W. 52nd & W. 53rd Sts. between Fifth Ave. & Ave. of the Americas (Sixth Ave.). Subway: E and V trains to Fifth Ave./53rd St.

The world-famous and newly expanded Museum of Modern Art (MoMA) on West 53rd Street may be the biggest museum in Midtown, but it isn't the only museum in Midtown. It's not even the only museum on West 53rd Street. In recent years a small and evolving museum district has cropped up around it, offering excellent exhibits in more manageable settings (and for less than half the ticket price of MoMA, and with no waiting in line). The American Folk Art Museum, housed in a stunning 2001 building by Matthew Baird of the local firm Tod Williams and Billie Tsien, is particularly worth a visit: about 150 pieces from the permanent collection are always on exhibit, showing the skill and creativity of self-taught artists. The Museum of Arts & Design displays contemporary crafts with an eye toward both avant-garde materials and traditional craftsmanship. A showcase of two nationwide—and increasingly worldwide—fixtures, the Museum of Television and Radio seeks to preserve their history and contribution to American culture.

Museum of Modern Art★★★

11 W. 53rd St. See Museums.

American Folk Art Museum★★

45 W. 53rd St. See Museums.

Radio City Music Hall

Courtesy Radio City Entertainment

The Rockettes

Radio City Christmas Spectacular

. . . 5-6-7-8. Radio City Music Hall and the **Rockettes** have been intertwined liter-ally since opening night. That is not surprising: with their sparkly costumes and awesome kick-lines, this precision dance troupe may be the only group that can compete with the beauty of the theater. Born as the Missouri Rockets in St. Louis in 1925, sixteen dancers took New York by storm, wowing crowds at Radio City's inaugural concert on December 27, 1932. Expanding their ranks to 36, they per-formed four shows a day, 365 days a year, for 50 years! Today the Rockettes light up the Radio City stage at Christmastime only, with a cast of 140. If you're in town, don't miss it. This is the ultimate in New York razzle-dazzle. *Two to five perform-ances daily early Nov–late Dec.* ✆ *$40-$250.* ☎ *212-247-4777. www.radiocity.com.*

Museum of Arts & Design★

40 W. 53rd St. between Fifth & Sixth Aves. 🕐 *Open year-round daily 10am–6pm (Thu until 8pm).* 🕐 *Closed major holidays.* ✆ *$9; by donation Thu 6pm–8pm.* ☎ *212-956-3535. www.madmuseum.org.*

Few, if any, of the works on display here would seem out of place at MoMA. In fact, many artists are represented at both institutions. But the primary mission of the Museum of Arts & Design (MAD) is to show objects made from glass, ceram-ics, fiber, metal, wood and clay, or some combination thereof. Its present loca-tion is an atrium-like space with a ser-pentine staircase linking three floors of galleries (all exhibits are temporary). Be sure to check out the gift shop, stocked with unusual, design-savvy items.

In fall 2008 the museum will open in a new facility at Two Columbus Circle, a building that has been mistaken more than once for a parking garage. None-theless it was the subject of a heated dispute between the museum and an Upper West Side preservation group. The museum prevailed in 2005 and is completing an extensive renovation that will triple its exhibit space.

The Paley Center for Media

25 W. 52nd St. between Fifth & Sixth Aves. 🕐 *Open year-round Tue–Sun noon–6pm (Thu until 8pm).* 🕐 *Closed Jan 1, Jul 4, Thanksgiving Day & Dec 25.* ✆ *$10.* ☞ *Guided tours available (ask at the front desk for schedule)* ☎ *212-621-6800. www.mtr.org.*

The massive TV and radio archive of the former Museum of Television & Radio (MTR) was created by former CBS chair-man **William S. Paley** with a view toward preserving two increasingly popular but ephemeral fixtures of Amer-ican culture: radio and television. The museum was opened in 1975 and was the only one of its kind until 1996, when a sister museum built by Richard Meier

☺ Things to Do in Rockefeller Center ☺

Brigitta L. House - MICHELIN

Unlike most attractions in New York City, Rockefeller Center really sparkles in winter. If you happen to be here at that time of year, take a whirl around the sunken **skating rink** (☉*open Oct–Apr;* ☎*212-332-7654*), gawk at the six- to 10-story decorated **Christmas tree** (*early Dec–early Jan*), view the elaborate holiday window displays at adjacent Saks Fifth Avenue and other department stores, and get tickets to the Rockettes' dazzling **Christmas Spectacular** at Radio City Music Hall (☚ *see sidebar*). That said, there's plenty to do here at other times of year as well. Start your visit at the **GE Building** (*30 Rockefeller Plaza*). At the information desk in the lobby, you can pick up a self-guided **walking-tour map** of the complex and a directory of shops and get answers to your questions (the center's website, www.rockefellercenter.com, is also a good resource). Guided **art and architecture walking tours** (75min) are available daily (☞*every 2hrs on the hour, year-round Mon–Sat 11am–5pm, Sun 11am–3pm;* ☎*$12;* 🄺 *children under 6 not permitted;* ☎*212-664-3700*). Meet at the tour desk inside the **NBC Experience Store** (*W. 49th St. & Rockefeller Plaza*). **NBC Studio Tours** (☞*70min; depart from the Experience Store every 15min*) take visitors through the studios where various shows, including **NBC Nightly News** and **NBC Sports**, are taped; television technology such as the weather screen is also demonstrated (☉*year-round Mon–Thu 8:30am–4:30pm, departs every 30min; Fri & Sat 9:30am–5:30pm, departs every 15min; Sun 9:30am–4:30pm, departs every 15min;* ☉*no tours Thanksgiving Day & Dec 25;* ☎*$18.50; reservations recommended;* 🄺 *children under 6 not permitted;* ☎*212-664-7174; www.nbcuniversalstore.com*). You can attend a **live taping** of **Late Night with Conan O'Brien or Saturday Night Live**, both headquartered at the GE Building (*30 Rockefeller Center;* 🄺 *children under 16 not permitted at either show;* ☎*212-664-3056*). In both cases, your best bet is to get tickets well in advance, but there are also same-day standby tickets available in the morning for afternoon or evening tapings. To say "hi" to mom and dad on live television, show up at the corner of 49th Street and Rockefeller Plaza around 6am and sit tight for an hour. The **Today Show** is taped inside and outside the studio (*weather permitt*ing) daily from 7am to 9am. The earlier you arrive, the more likely it is you'll be in the front row. Finally, for more upscale entertainment, consider attending an auction at the world-famous fine-art auction house **Christie's** at 20 Rockefeller Plaza. Most auctions are free and open to the public. *For a schedule and information, call* ☎*212-636-2000 or go to www.christies.com.*

in Beverly Hills was inaugurated. The New York location is housed in a 17-story building (the William S. Paley Building) designed by John Burgee with Philip Johnson in 1989. In June 2007 MTR announced a name change (for both locations) to The Paley Center for Media to better convey the expanded nature of its functions. The center is broadening its focus to include all media. Likewise, it is increasing the number of its public discussions about today's media and media's impact on culture.

Visitors here may choose programs from among the 100,000-piece collection and then view them or listen to them in individual consoles.

Avenue of the Americas (Sixth Avenue)★

Subway: B, D, F, N, Q, R, V and W to 34th St.–Herald Square.

This is the spine of Central Midtown. Lined mainly with large office buildings, it has attractions of its own, most notably Macy's and Bryant Park. As you proceed north up the avenue, you'll see Rockefeller Center and the Museum District.

Macy's★

151 W. 34th St. between Broadway & Seventh Ave. ☎212-695-4400. www.macys. com.

Since 1924, Macy's has boasted that it is "the world's largest store." Ten stories tall and a city block long, this is the mother ship of department stores.

Macy's started in 1858 as a dry-goods store at the corner of 14th Street and Sixth Avenue. Founder Rowland H. Macy was the first to introduce colored bath towels, tea bags and Idaho baked potatoes. The shop moved to its present location in 1902 and opened an addition in 1931. In 2007 there were more than 800 Macy's stores in 45 states.

Macy's sponsors the annual Macy's **Thanksgiving Day Parade**, spearheaded in 1924 by company employees. Best known for its massive helium-filled balloons shaped like cartoon characters,

A Helium-Filled Balloon Ready for Macy's Thanksgiving Day Parade

the parade is attended by 2.5 million New Yorkers and watched by 44 million Americans on television.

Bryant Park★★

Sixth Ave. between W. 40th & W. 42nd Sts. www.bryantpark.org.

With its green folding chairs, pebble allées, used-book stalls, outdoor restaurants and London plane trees, this formal park behind the New York Public Library is one of the loveliest outdoor spots in the city.

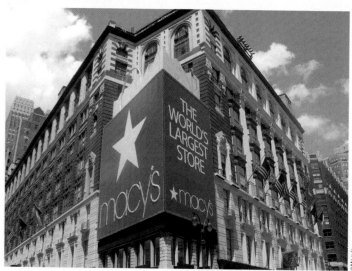

Macy's Department Store

HBO Bryant Park Summer Film Festival

On Monday nights in the summer, Bryant Park becomes a massive drive-in without the cars. At 5pm, movie lovers arrive (on foot) with blankets, lawn chairs and picnic dinners. There they soak up the atmosphere, chatting with fellow cinephiles, and wait until dark, when a free movie is projected onto a giant screen. The programming darts all over film history, with a good mix of sci-fi camp classics (like *The Fly* from 1958), Alfred Hitchcock thrillers, crowd-pleasing musicals, and blockbusters (like *Jaws*). *Schedules available at the park or online.* ☎212-512-5700. www.bryantpark.org.

A Bit of History

Built on a site once occupied by a potter's field (in 1823) and the short-lived glass-and-steel Crystal Palace (1853-58), Bryant Park was named for the poet, civic leader and firebrand newspaper editor **William Cullen Bryant** (1784-1878) in 1884. Parks Commissioner **Robert Moses** supervised a major renovation in 1934, at which time the large sunken lawn was laid out, the balustrade around the perimeter was added and the plane trees were planted. Still, the park became a haven for homeless people and drug dealers in the 1960s and 1970s, and fell into rapid decline. In the 1980s the Rockefeller Brothers Fund spearheaded a nonprofit corporation to revive the park, providing maintenance beyond what the city offered, installing food kiosks and sponsoring public events. In seven years crime dropped 92 percent and the number of park users doubled. A lavish and sensitive renovation, unveiled in 1992, made Bryant Park more beautiful than it had ever been, with new lights, entrances, plantings and other amenities.

Visit

More than 5,000 office workers come to the park for lunch on warm weekdays. Many bring their laptops: in 2002 the entire park was set up with free wireless **Internet access**. On the south side of the park there's a **Kids** small **carousel**. Among the sculptures dotting the landscaped alleys, note the 1911 bronze **statue** of William Cullen Bryant.

The skyscrapers around the park include the **American Standard Building** (1924, Raymond Hood) on the south side, made of black brick with gold terra-cotta trim. Formerly the Radiator Building, it was the subject of a painting by **Georgia O'Keeffe** done in a sharp Art Deco style in 1927 (*Radiator Building – Night, New York*). West of the park, at 1095 Sixth Avenue, rises the streamlined form of the **New York Telephone Company Building** (now Verizon), completed in 1970.

Bryant Park

©Shea Dean

But most dramatic is the building sweeping upward on the north side of the park: the **Grace Building** (1974, Skidmore, Owings and Merrill), made of travertine and tinted glass. A nearly identical building, by the same architects and built the same year, stands at **9 West 57th Street**★.

International Center of Photography

1133 Ave. of the Americas at 43rd St. ◷*Open year-round Tue–Fri 10am–6pm (Fri until 8pm), weekends 10am–6pm.* ◷*Closed major holidays.* ☞*$12.* ☎*212-857-0000. www.icp.org.*

Founded by Cornell Capa in 1974, the International Center of Photography (ICP) mounts major exhibits of work by photographers and photojournalists who engage in "concerned photography," as well as those exploring the relationship between photographic representation and politics, memory or popular culture. The Midtown gallery space was opened in 1989 as a satellite of the original museum at Fifth Avenue and 94th Street, but it became the ICP's sole exhibition area after a major renovation and expansion in 2000 and the closing of the uptown site in 2001. Today it boasts more display space than the two sites formerly did combined, as well as a cafe and a well-stocked gift shop. About 20 exhibitions are mounted per year, some of which are drawn from the museum's collection of 100,000 prints, as well as from holdings of other museums and partner facilities like the eminent George Eastman House in Rochester, New York.

Diamond and Jewelry Way

W. 47th St. between Fifth & Sixth Aves. ☎*212-302-5739. www.diamond district.org.*

Nearly 90 percent of the diamonds that enter the US make a pit stop on this 750ft-long block, the world's largest shopping district for diamonds and other precious stones, both set and loose. The diamond business in New York began in the late 19C when merchants opened stores downtown. By the 1920s the Canal Street diamond district was well established, but the diamond retailers slowly gravitated uptown along with their wealthy customers. The present district took shape in the 1940s.

Today a whopping 2,600 businesses are registered in the neighborhood, the vast majority devoted to the diamond trade. Some merchants have their own jewelry shops, but most have small booths in the district's 25 jewelry "exchanges." Each exchange contains up to 100 shops, and each of those has a specialty (pearls, wedding rings, watches, gold). You'll hear carat, cut, color and clarity discussed in Spanish, Yiddish, Armenian, Russian, Arabic. Also notice the plainclothes security guards and sophisticated security systems that protect the dealers.

CBS Building

51 W. 52nd St at Sixth Ave.

Known as the "Black Rock," this 38-story monolith is Finnish-born architect Eero Saarinen's only high-rise building; in fact, he was working on its design at the time of his death in 1961. The structure was completed in 1965. Massive Canadian black granite columns adorn the exterior (most of the weight of the building is carried by a central core), their corners pointed out for dramatic effect. The sunken plaza at the building's base is one of the most pleasant in the neighborhood.

Additional Sight

Carnegie Hall

156 W. 57th St. at Seventh Ave.

Majestic Carnegie Hall is one of the world's most prestigious concert venues, a fact that its namesake and fiscal sponsor, the steel magnate **Andrew Carnegie**, foresaw when he laid the cornerstone in 1890. Indeed, since its completion in 1891, Carnegie Hall has been graced by

---

😊 A Bit of Advice 😊

Two restaurants (☎*212-840-6500; www.bryantpark.org/amenities*) are situated on the terrace of the library: the casual outdoor **Bryant Park Cafe**, a great place for an alfresco burger and beer; and the more upscale **Bryant Park Grill**, which serves American food indoors and on its seasonal rooftop patio.

Allison Simpson/MICHELIN

Zankel Hall at Carnegie Hall

American luminaries Woodrow Wilson, Dr. Martin Luther King, Duke Ellington, Judy Garland, George Gershwin, Bob Dylan and many others both from the US and from around the world. In every language and culture, to debut at Carnegie Hall is to have "made it."

A Bit of History

The idea for Carnegie Hall came about in 1887 on an ocean liner bound from New York to London. On the ship Andrew Carnegie and his wife, Louise Whitfield, a singer, met a young conductor, **Walter Damrosh**, who had been crusading to get a world-class concert hall built in New York. Damrosh made his case to the Scottish-born millionaire, and four years later the dream was realized when Louise cemented the final stone with a silver trowel from Tiffany's. Architect and cellist William B. Tuthill designed the structure in the Italian Renaissance style, cladding its exterior with iron-spotted brick and terra cotta. So it wouldn't need support beams, Carnegie Hall's walls were made several feet thick—a major contribution to the hall's excellent acoustics.

Visit

Visit the interior by attending a concert, or taking a 1hr guided tour (⟨°⟩*Sept–Jun Mon–Fri 11:30am, 2pm & 3pm; Sat*

11:30pm & 12:30pm; Sun 12:30pm; ⟨$⟩$10). Tickets may be purchased at the box office (⟨⊙⟩*open Sept–Jun Mon–Sat 11am–6pm, Sun noon–6pm; Jul–Aug Mon–Fri 11am-6pm; ⟨⊙⟩closed major holidays). ☎ 212-247-7800. www.carnegiehall.org.*

Carnegie Hall has three performance spaces. The largest is the **Isaac Stern Auditorium**, with 2,804 seats, named after the Ukrainian-born violinist who made his debut here in 1943. The third-floor **Weill Recital Hall** (originally known as the Chamber Music Hall) seats 268 and was designed by Tuthill in the Belle Epoque style. Situated on the south side of the building and accessed from Seventh Avenue, **Zankel Hall** reopened in 2003 after a strikingly modern redesign. It seats 599.

You don't have to take a tour to visit Carnegie Hall's museum.

Rose Museum at Carnegie Hall

154 W. 57th St., 2nd Floor. ⟨⊙⟩Open Sept-Jun daily 11am–4:30pm. ⟨⊙⟩Closed major holidays.

Inaugurated in 1991, the Rose Museum chronicles Carnegie Hall's history (both the building and the performances that have taken place here) and exhibits its archival treasures, which include Benny Goodman's clarinet and Arturo Toscanini's conducting baton.

EAST MIDTOWN★★

East Midtown contains some of the city's finest 20C architecture, from the Beaux-Arts Grand Central Terminal and the Art Deco Chrysler Building to the post-Modern Sony Plaza. Betwixt and between are posh apartment buildings, historic churches and luxurious hotels, including the Waldorf-Astoria.

▸ **Orient Yourself:** East Midtown is the designation for the area roughly bounded by Madison and Third avenues between East 34th and 57th streets.

◔ **Organizing Your Time:** Allow 4hrs to do East Midtown justice, excluding visits to the museums. To enjoy the cafes, shops and the museums, reserve a full day.

A Bit of History

In the early 19C, steam-powered locomotives chugged down Park Avenue all the way to a depot on 23rd Street, bringing with them noise and dirt. Residents complained, and in 1854 an ordinance was passed banning trains south of 42nd Street. That helped pave the way for downtown development, but did nothing to improve the lot of those in East Midtown, whose tenements surrounded an open, sooty rail yard that spread from 42nd to 56th streets. (The tracks were roofed over from 56th Street to a tunnel at 96th Street.)

Underground Railroad – Railroad magnate "Commodore" **Cornelius Vanderbilt**

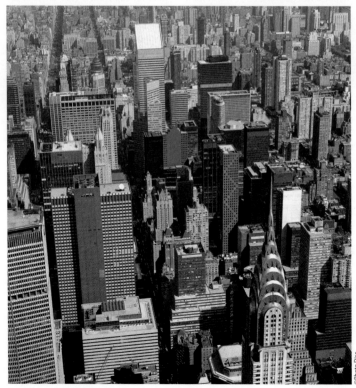

Aerial view of East Midtown

©Photo Disc

Chrysler Building

Brigitta L. House - MICHELIN

(1794-1877) opened the first Grand Central depot, a vast glass and iron shed, in 1871, on the present site of the Grand Central Terminal. Shortly thereafter, he began lowering the tracks feeding into it below street level, reducing some of the noise pollution. But it was not enough to make the area habitable; smoke was still a big problem, and in 1889 the city demanded that the railroad (now run by the Commodore's offspring) either electrify the trains or leave the city. To finance the electrification process, the Vanderbilts sunk the entire rail yard fronting the depot below ground and sold the land above it to developers, who soon lined Madison and Park avenues with exclusive apartment buildings. The Grand Central Terminal you see today was completed in 1913.

After World War II, many apartment houses along Madison, Park and Lexington avenues in Midtown were replaced by high-rise office towers: it was here that the "glass box" style of corporate architecture was pioneered. Interestingly, because the railroad tracks are so close underground, many of these skyscrapers are built on stilts.

Today the area has an eclectic mix of old and new. **Park Avenue**★★ is suited for a stroll: here, alongside the remaining apartment buildings, with uniformed

doormen, and banks, are the Waldorf-Astoria Hotel, St. Bartholomew's Church, and the Lever House. Upscale shops line **Madison Avenue**★ (especially north of 53rd Street) and **57th Street**★.

Sights

Chrysler Building★★★
405 Lexington Ave. at E. 42nd St.
This famous New York landmark pays homage to the car. Automobile magnate Walter P. Chrysler commissioned architect William Van Alen to design the tallest building in the world. Completed in 1930, it was the tallest, rising to 1,048ft (77 stories)—until the Empire State Building opened in 1931. One of the first buildings to feature exposed metal as part of its design, the Chrysler Building is topped by a distinctive spire of radiant stainless steel arches that glimmers in sunlight and glows in the nighttime illuminations. The pinnacle resembles a radiator cap from a 1930 Chrysler car. Abundant automotive decorations adorning the setbacks under the spire include silver hood ornaments, stylized racing cars and the huge radiator-cap gargoyles at the fourth level, modeled after a 1929 Chrysler. (Chrysler no longer has offices in the building.)

The **lobby**, a superb example of Art Deco, is faced with red African marble. The elevator cabs feature ornate doors and richly paneled interiors. Note also the elaborate ceiling mural by Edward Trumbull.

Grand Central Terminal★★★
Park Ave. & E. 42nd St.
Often referred to as the "gateway to the nation," this world-famous railroad terminal is a masterpiece of urban architecture. Today, more than 150,000 commuters a day pass through the terminal, which is a veritable city within a city.

A Bit of History
A Group Effort – In 1903 several prominent architectural firms were invited to submit proposals for a new train station. The winners were Reed and Stem, from St. Paul, Minnesota. Soon after the deal was made, the New York firm Warren & Wetmore submitted a different proposal.

Allegedly, because Warren was a cousin of New York Central Railroad chairman William K. Vanderbilt, the second proposal was accepted as well, and the two firms were forced to collaborate on the final design. Ten years later, when the building was inaugurated, it was hailed as a great success.

Landmark Law Tested – In the heyday of rail travel, Grand Central was hopping day and night. In 1947 more than 65 million people traveled the rails via Grand Central Terminal. In the 1950s, though, subsidized highways and parkways made driving convenient and affordable, and railroad usage plummeted. At the same time, the price of real estate in Midtown was skyrocketing. The railroad sold its office building behind the terminal in 1958 to make room for the 59-story Pan Am Building (now the MetLife Building). In 1968 the railroad wanted to demolish the terminal itself (but keep the facade) and build a 55-story tower on the site. The city's landmark commission, established in response to the destruction of Pennsylvania Station in 1967, rejected the proposal and was sued by the railroad as a result. The case went all the way to the Supreme Court, where in 1978 the city prevailed in a 6-3 decision, a true landmark ruling. Still, Grand Central was in dire need of repair. In 1990 a $425 million master plan was adopted to bring the terminal back to its 1913 splendor. Eight years later the grandly restored Grand Central was rededicated.

Clock at Grand Central Terminal

Brigitta L. House - MICHELIN

Visit

🕐 *Open year-round daily 5:30am–1:30am (shops and restaurants have reduced hours). www.grandcentralterminal.com.* To take a **self-guided tour** of the station, go to the "I LOVE NEW YORK" information window and pick up a map and directory. You can also print out a two-page walking-tour guide from the website. Free guided tours are offered Wednesdays and Fridays. The Wednesday tour is led by the **Municipal Arts Society** (☎212-935-3960): meet at the information booth in the center of the main concourse at 12:30pm. The Friday tour is led by the **Grand Central Partnership** (☎212-883-2420): meet at the corner of Park Avenue and 42nd Street in front of the Altria Building at 12:30pm.

Exterior

Cleaned and renovated in 2005, the 42nd Street granite **facade** is pierced by three massive arched windows separated by an order of double columns. Surmounting the windows are the immense 13ft clock and Jules-Félix Cou-

Grand Central Terminal: Shops to Single Out

Among the main-floor concourse shops (there are nearly 50), keep these in mind: Under the West Balcony, the **New York Transit Museum Gallery and Store** (🕐*open Mon–Fri 8am–8pm, weekends 10am–6pm;* ☎ *212-878-0106; www.mta.info/museum*), an annex of the main museum in Brooklyn Heights, mounts changing exhibits on transportation history and sells transit-related merchandise, such as wallet-size subway maps. Under the East Balcony, the **Grand Central Market** (🕐*open Mon–Fri 7am–9pm; Sat 10am–7pm; Sun 11am–6pm*) is a fresh-foods bazaar, with outposts of local gourmet companies such as Oren's Daily Roast coffee and Murray's Cheese, as well as a butcher, a fishmonger and several produce stalls.

Scandinavia House

tan's sculpture *Transportation* (1914), which incorporates the figure of Mercury (commerce) flanked by Hercules (strength) and Minerva (intellect). Below the sculpture stands a bronze statue (1869) of Cornelius Vanderbilt.

Interior
Grand Central Terminal's 12,000sq ft **Main Concourse** is one of the most spectacular spaces in the city. In the center stands a brass and onyx clock atop an information booth, a traditional New York City rendezvous point. On each end of the hall, balconies, approached by grand staircases, hold shops and restaurants. But it is the 12-story-high turquoise **vaulted ceiling**, decorated with electrified constellations of the zodiac, that makes Grand Central grand: not only is it gorgeous to look at, but its height causes sounds in the concourse to be pleasantly muffled, as they would be in a cathedral. One of the city's least-known oddities is that the zodiac was created backward in 1913; terminal representatives say it will probably never be corrected.

Beneath the Main Concourse is a sprawling **Dining Concourse** (⏱ *open Mon–Sat 11am–9pm; Sun 11am–6pm*), a food court featuring locally owned restaurants. Here you'll find the best quick bites in the area, especially on weekends, when lunch spots catering to the office crowd are closed. Try Two Boots' pizza, Pepe Rosso's pannini or Hale & Hearty's soup, and don't miss the Oyster Bar (♿ *see sidebar below*).

The Morgan Library★★
29 E. 36th St. at Fifth Ave.
♿*See Museums.*

Saint Bartholomew's Church★
109 E. 50st St. at Park Ave. ⏱*Open year-round Mon–Wed & Fri 8am–6:30pm, Thu & Sat 8am–7:30pm, Sun 8am–8:30pm.* 🎧*Art and architecture tour Sun 12:15pm.* ☎*212-378-0222. www.stbarts. org.*
Considered one of architect Bertram G. Goodhue's most successful constructions, this Episcopal church (1919) expertly blends Romanesque style with Byzantine details. Its multicolored dome and terraced garden provide a soothing contrast to a neighborhood that abounds in sharp angles, metal and glass.
The eclectic front **portal** (1903), donated by the Vanderbilts, was moved here from the original Saint Bartholomew's Church, which stood on Madison Avenue from 1872 to 1918. Its three pairs of sculptured bronze doors depict scenes from the Bible.
Immediately upon entering the **narthex**, look up: the mosaic ceiling is fantastic. In the baptistery stands the statue of a kneeling angel, the work of 19C English sculptor James Redfern. The church's Aeolian organ is the largest in the city. The church's cafe is quite popular (♿*see sidebar*).

Grand Central Oyster Bar and Restaurant

In Grand Central Terminal, lower level. ☎ *212-490-6650. www.oysterbarny.com.*
The Guastavino-tiled ceiling, so low you can practically touch it, hovers over this famed restaurant, where New Yorkers, not just travelers, come for the best selection of fresh seafood in the city. Settle in at the counter and order oysters Rockefeller and clam chowder—it's a tradition. The shellfish stews are also divine. Out of a wine list of some 400 bottles, 80 are available by the glass.

☺ A Bit of Advice ☺

Hands-down, the best place in Midtown for an outdoor meal or glass of wine on a warm day is **Café St. Bart's**. The food is great: lobster rolls, grilled fish, stone-oven pizzas—and the atmosphere is even better. Umbrella-shaded tables cover the church's historic terrace, which is elevated enough from the street to provide a soothing respite from traffic but is still very much part of the neighborhood. It offers great views of the adjoining church and nearby skyscrapers. *109 E. 50th St. at Park Ave. ○Open Apr–Oct daily for breakfast and lunch, and Mon–Sat for dinner; rest of the year Mon–Fri for breakfast and lunch.* ☎212-593-3333. www.cafestbarts.com.

Scandinavia House★

58 Park Ave. at E. 38th St. ○Open year-round Tue–Sat noon–6pm. ○Closed major holidays. ☜$3. ☎212-879-9779. www.scandinaviahouse.org.
Uncompromisingly modern, this zinc, glass and spruce structure houses the American-Scandinavian Foundation, the cultural headquarters for the five Nordic countries in the US. The building (2000, Polshek Partners) rises six stories and contains a wood-paneled theater, light-filled galleries, a glass-enclosed gift shop and the AQ Café (○open Mon–Sat 10am–5pm), a cafeteria-style restaurant run by the celebrated Restaurant Aquavit. Major exhibits on Scandinavian art and design rotate through the spacious galleries; there are also frequent film screenings, concerts, children's programs and lectures.

Sony Wonder Technology Lab★

In the Sony Plaza Bldg. 550 Madison Ave. at E. 56th St. Kids *○Open year-round Tue–Sat 10am–5pm, Sun noon–5pm. ○Closed major holidays.* ☎212-833-8100. www.sonywondertechlab.com.
Sprawling over four floors of the Sony Plaza Building, this high-tech wonderland encourages kids (eight and older) to ex-plore electronics through structured-play environments. Interactive exhibits include using digital instruments to create a song, editing a music video and assisting a doctor with an ultrasound examination. For tech-minded children it's great fun, but call in advance to make a reserva-tion, especially on weekdays, when it fills up with school groups.

Villard Houses★
(New York Palace Hotel)

451-457 Madison Ave. at E. 50th St.
In 1881 Henry Villard, a Bavarian immigrant who founded the *New York Evening Post,* hired McKim, Mead and White to design a group of six town houses: one for himself and the others for sale. The architects looked to the Palazzo della Cancelleria in Rome for inspiration, setting the brownstones in a U-shape around a central courtyard. Villard moved in with his family in 1883, but declared bankruptcy shortly afterward and had to sell the complex. It passed from private hands to the New York Archdiocese (St. Patrick's Cathedral is directly across the street) and then, in the 1970s, to Harry Helmsley, a hotel developer. Helmsley wanted to tear down the houses, but the Landmarks Preservation Commission stopped him. His solution? Build a 55-story skyscraper directly on top of the houses.

Villard Houses

New York Palace Hotel

Hotel

⭐ Roger Smith

Restaurants

① Maloney & Porcelli

② El Parador

Visit

To get a sense of the grandeur of the original homes, enter the courtyard—formerly a carriage yard—through the wrought-iron gates fronting Madison Avenue, and step inside the central mansion. Appointed in an ornate, Italian Renaissance style, this is the lobby of the luxurious **New York Palace Hotel.** On the second level, the red Verona fireplace, original to the Villard Houses, was crafted by Augustus Saint-Gaudens.

The Municipal Art Society, a local preservation group since 1893, shares the north wing of the Villard Houses with other nonprofit organizations. Here you'll find the **Urban Center Bookstore** (☎ 212-935-3595; www.urbancenter-books.org), which carries 9,000 titles on architecture, urban planning and preservation. There are free public **galleries** (🕐 open year-round Mon, Tue, Fri–Sat 10am–6pm, Wed 10am–8pm, Sun 11am–5pm) with rotating exhibits on architecture and design, and schedules of the society's **walking tours**, which are widely considered the most in-depth and engaging in the city.

Waldorf-Astoria Hotel★

301 Park Ave. between E. 49th & E. 50th Sts. ☎ 212-355-3000. www.waldorfastoria.com. This world-famous hotel (1931, Schultze and Weaver) occupies an entire city block. Distinguished by its twin chrome-capped towers rising 47 stories from an 18-story granite base, it replaced two separate hotels (the Waldorf and the Astoria) that were demolished to make way for the Empire State Building. The lush apartments in the north tower (accessible via a private entrance on 50th St.) have been occupied by such notables as Herbert Hoover, Henry Kissinger, John F. Kennedy and Cary Grant.

Lobby, Waldorf-Astoria Hotel

Courtesy Lou Hammond & Associates

Check to see which, if any, countries' flags are displayed above the entrance. According to long-standing protocol, certain dignitaries who stay at the Waldorf are entitled to see their national flags flying in front of the hotel.

The elegant main **lobby** has an eclectic mix of Art Deco ornamentation and Second Empire furnishings. Its marble floor is embellished by an intricate mosaic known as the *Wheel of Life*. The bronze clock in the east lobby was crafted in London in 1893.

Central Synagogue

652 Lexington Ave. at E. 55th St. Sanctuary tour Wed 12:45pm. ☎212-838-5122. www.centralsynagogue.org.

Distinguished by its bronze onion domes, this landmark structure was designed in 1870 by the German architect Henry Fernbach for a Reform congregation that traces its roots back to 1838. It is the oldest synagogue in continuous use in the city. The masonry exterior is dominated by two octagonal towers rising 122 feet and topped with onion domes of green copper. Following a devastating 1998 fire, the **sanctuary**★ has been fully restored, with elaborate new stenciling, woodwork and stained glass.

Whitney Museum of American Art at Altria

120 Park Ave. at E. 42nd St. ⏱ *Gallery open year-round Mon–Fri 11am–6pm (Thu until 7:30pm). Sculpture court open Mon-Sat 7:30am–9:30pm, Sun & holidays 11am-7pm.* ⏱ *Closed Jan 1, Thanksgiving Day & Dec. 25.* ☎ *917-663-2453. www.whitney.org.*

The Whitney Museum of American Art administers a 900sq ft gallery and a 5,200sq ft sculpture court on the ground floor of the Altria headquarters building, across from Grand Central Station. The quarterly shows tend to be site-specific solo exhibitions by contemporary American artists. Lunchtime gallery tours are offered (*Wed & Fri 1pm*); in the spring, check out Performance on 42nd, a series of free avant-garde music and dance concerts.

For Architecture Buffs

East Midtown contains some of New York's most distinctive high rises. Here are some of the most famous—and infamous.

Lever House

Lever House★★ – *390 Park Ave. between E. 53rd & E. 54th Sts.* When it opened in 1952, the green-glass Lever House, designed by Skidmore, Owings and Merrill, was considered avant-garde. Indeed, lit stood in sharp contrast to the stone and brick apartment buildings of Park Avenue. But the Lever House would have many international-style imitators on Park Avenue and throughout the city. Few were as elegant, though. The 21-story vertical slab of green glass and stainless steel seems to float above a two-story horizontal base. Inside is the Lever House Restaurant.

Seagram Building★★ – *375 Park Ave. between E. 52nd & E. 53rd Sts.* New York City's only creation by German-born Ludwig Mies van der Rohe (with Philip Johnson), this bronze glass and steel tower (1958) is widely regarded as one of the finest International-style skyscrapers ever made. Less than half of its "zoning envelope" was used; Mies opted instead to set the slender, 38-story tower on pillars in a vast granite plaza—a radical gesture at the time, considering the price of real estate.

53rd At Third★ – *885 Third Ave. between E. 53rd & E. 54th Sts.* It should be obvious at a glance why people call this otherwise nameless skyscraper the "lipstick building." Rising in tiers from tall columns, the elliptical tower of reddish-brown and pink stone and glass was designed by post-Modernists Philip Johnson and John Burgee and completed in 1986.

Chanin Building★ – *122 E. 42nd St. at Lexington Ave.* A prime example of the Art Deco style, this 56-story building (1929, Irwin Chanin) is wrapped with a terra-cotta frieze of floral bas-reliefs by Edward Trumbell on its bottom four floors. Inside the intricately detailed lobby, look at the door frames, convector grilles and mailboxes.

Citigroup Center★ – *153 E. 53rd St. at Lexington Ave.* This 915-ft aluminum and glass-sheathed tower (1978) is best known for its top, which slopes at a 45-degree angle and is visible in most pictures of the New York City skyline. The tower stands on four colossal pillars—each 9 stories, or 115ft high, and 22ft square—set at the center of each side, rather than at the corners of the building. Beneath these cantilevered corners, which extend 72ft from the central columns, nestles **St. Peter's Church** *(access on E. 54th St.)*, an evangelical Lutheran church that sold its land to Citicorp on the condition that a new church would be integrated within the complex.

Daily News Building★ – *Map p 177. 220 E. 42nd St. at Second Ave.* Abandoning the Gothic style popular at the time, the Daily News Building (1930) features white brick piers alternating with patterned red and black brick spandrels, giving the tower a vertical striped look and an illusion of height greater than its actual 37 stories. The lobby is famed for its huge revolving **globe** (12ft in diameter) and the clock that gives readings in 17 time zones. The floor is laid out as a giant compass indicating most of the principal cities of the world and their distance, by air, from New York City.

Fuller Building★ – *41 E. 57th St. at Madison Ave.* Art Deco from top to bottom, this black granite building (1929) is topped by a limestone tower. In the richly ornamented **lobby**, bronze elevator doors chronicle the building's construction and the mosaic floor displays other Fuller Construction Co. commissions, notably the Flatiron Building. More than 20 galleries are in the building.

General Electric Building★ – *570 Lexington Ave. at E. 51st St.* Its reddish-orange spire topped by a spiky crown, this marvelous, 51-story Art Deco creation (1931, Cross & Cross) was designed to be viewed in conjunction with its western neighbor, St. Bartholomew's Church. Decorative features include rays, flashes and lightning bolts, which are particularly appropriate to the building's principal tenant.

"Lipstick building" (foreground) and Citigroup Center

Helmsley Building★ – *230 Park Ave. at E. 46th St.* Once the headquarters of Cornelius Vanderbilt's New York Central Railroad Co., this 1929 tower is pierced by two tunnels reserved for Park Avenue motor traffic and two street-level arcades for pedestrians. The Renaissance Revival building was designed by Warren & Wetmore, the firm responsible for Grand Central Terminal's imposing exterior. Step inside the opulent lobby to admire the travertine walls and bronze detailing. Step back – way back, perhaps to 50th Street – to admire the building's gilded cupola.

LVMH Tower★ – *17-21 E. 57th St. between Fifth & Madison Aves.* Slender, multifaceted, the 23-story Louis Vuitton–Moët Hennessey building (1999, Christian de Portzamparc) looks as if it were chipped out of crystal, especially when illuminated at night. It houses retail space on the first two levels and LVMH's offices on the upper floors. The Louis Vuitton store, the world's largest, stands a few doors down, on the corner of Fifth Avenue *(1 E. 57th St.)*. Japanese architect Jun Aoki added the intriguing glass facade to the white-marble building in 2004.

Sony Plaza★ **(former AT&T headquarters)** – *550 Madison Ave. between E. 55th & E. 56th Sts.* The "lipstick building" (885 Third Ave.) isn't the only Philip Johnson–John Burgee skyscraper with a nickname. This one, completed in 1984, is called the Chippendale Building for its unusual roofline, which looks like the top of a colonial cupboard (a triangle split at the peak by a semicircular hollow). To conserve energy, only a third of the 40-story structure's pink-granite exterior is covered with windows..

590 Madison Avenue (former IBM Building) – *590 Madison Ave. at E. 56th St.* A 17ft flame-red, stabile by Alexander Calder stands sentinel at the doorway of this polished black granite, 43-story high rise (1983, Edward Larrabee Barnes). Note the imposing cut-corner overhang above its entrance, a common feature of 1980s skyscrapers. The building's greenhouse-like public **atrium**★ is one of the most pleasant in the district. Host of rotating large-scale sculpture exhibits, it has bamboo-filled planters, refreshment kiosks, and plenty of tables and chairs.

MetLife Building – *200 Park Ave. at E. 45th St.* Towering 59 stories over Grand Central Terminal, this octagonal 'scraper (1963), formerly the Pan Am Building, was conceived by a group of architects that included Walter Gropius of the Bauhaus school. Its odd shape and the fact that it blocked the formerly unobstructed view down Park Avenue raised a storm of protest, which still rumbles today.

UNITED NATIONS HEADQUARTERS★★★

MTA SUBWAY: 4, 5, 6, 7 TRAIN TO GRAND CENTRAL TERMINAL

MAP P 189, PLAN P 187

The United Nations (UN) complex in New York enjoys extraterritorial status. And it really does feel like a world unto itself. It's abuzz with diplomats from all corners of the world—some in the native dress of their home countries—when the General Assembly is in session (Sept-Dec). Even if you don't plan on taking a guided tour (the only way to gain access to the inner chambers), it's worth sending your bag through the metal detector to see the artwork and exhibits inside the General Assembly building and learn about this renowned institution.

▶ **Orient Yourself:** The UN complex is situated on 18 acres of land along the East River, between East 42nd and East 48th Streets. The General Assembly Hall and Conference Building are accessible only by guided tour. The Secretariate Building and the Library are closed to the public.

▶ **Organizing Your Time:** To avoid long lines, arrive at the UN when it opens at 9am. Be prepared for a **security screening** and a waiting period until you are called for your 1hr tour. All large parcels must be checked before entering, so go to the UN with as little as possible. The only **places to eat** are the coffee shop in the basement of the General Assembly Building and the delegates' dining room in the Conference Building *(4th floor; open for lunch by advance reservations only; ☎212-963-7625).*

A Bit of History

An Ambitious Goal – The United Nations is essentially a town hall for global affairs. Its basic structure was established in 1944 at a series of conferences held at the Dumbarton Oaks mansion in Washington, DC. The point of those meetings, which were attended by representatives from the US, the United Kingdom, China and the Soviet Union, was to create an international body more capable of maintaining world peace

View of the UN (left) and Trump World Tower (right)

Brigitta L. House • MICHELIN

than the League of Nations, the organization created by US president Woodrow Wilson after World War I.

The UN officially came into existence on October 24, 1945, when its charter—which had been signed in San Francisco on June 26 of that year—was ratified by a majority of the 51 founding members. The UN Charter's ambitious goals include fostering international cooperation to solve economic, social, cultural and humanitarian problems; resolving international disputes peacefully; and ending threats or use of force against any nation. Unlike its predecessor, the League of Nations, the United Nations has a security council that can approve the use of force against a country that is deemed to have infringed on the rights of another country.

Building the UN – The decision to build the UN headquarters in New York City was made in London by the General Assembly at its first session, on February 14, 1946, after offers for permanent sites had been received from many parts of the world. One reason New York was chosen over other US cities is that the Soviet Union threatened to boycott the organization if it was on the West Coast. In December 1946 John D. Rockefeller Jr. offered the United Nations a gift of $8.5 million to acquire the present site on the East River. At the time, this area consisted mainly of slaughterhouses and breweries. The construction program, costing more than $67 million, was financed in large part by the US government, which made available an interest-free loan of $65 million—a sum that has been entirely reimbursed.

American architect Wallace K. Harrison, who would later design Lincoln Center, oversaw a team of architects from 10 countries—including **Charles E. Le Corbusier** of France and **Oscar Niemeyer** of Brazil. They came up with a master plan of four buildings on grounds that are, at their eastern edge, cantilevered over Frankin D. Roosevelt (FDR) Drive to take advantage of the riverfront.

The 39-story Secretariat Building was inaugurated in 1950; the sloping General Assembly Building and the boxy Conference Building came next, in 1952; and the marble, glass and aluminum Dag

Hammarskjöld Memorial Library was completed in 1961. Today, five of the six main organs of the UN are housed here. The sixth—the International Court of Justice—is located at The Hague in the Netherlands.

The Grounds

Entrance on First Ave. between E. 45th & E. 46th Sts.

The United Nations flies the flags of its 191 member states on an arc of flagpoles along First Avenue. The flags are arranged north to south in English alphabetical order, from Afghanistan to Zimbabwe. (Delegations seated in the General Assembly follow the same order, although the starting point in the alphabet varies from year to year, depending on which member state is randomly selected to take the first seat.)

Two striking sculptures stand near the visitor entrance. A gift from the country of Luxembourg, **Non-Violence**★, the giant revolver with the knotted barrel, was created by the artist Carl Fredrik Reutersward in 1988. Italy donated **Sphere within a Sphere**★, by Italian sculptor Arnaldo Pomodoro, to the UN in 1996. The promenade along the north end of the General Assembly Building affords a view of the gardens (*not open to*

United Nations Headquarters
Courtesy United Nations

The UN's Top Dog

The secretary-general, the the UN's highest-ranking official, is appointed by the General Assembly on the recommendation of the Security Council for a five-year term, and is charged with carrying out the decisions made by the six organs of the UN. He or she may bring to the General Assembly any matter that appears to threaten international peace. Since 1946, eight men held this coveted and controversial title: Trygve Lie of Norway (1946-52), Dag Hammarskjöld of Sweden (1953-61), U Thant of Burma (now Myanmar) (1961-71), Kurt Waldheim of Austria (1972-81), Javier Pérez de Cuéllar of Peru (1982-91), Boutros Boutros-Ghali of Egypt (1992-96), Kofi Annan of Ghana (1997–2006) and currently Ban Ki-moon of Korea.

the public), which are dotted with outdoor sculpture. The bronze equestrian statue, *Peace* (1954, Anton Augustincic), was a gift from Yugoslavia.

The Buildings

General Assembly Building★★
Public Areas: ⏰*Open year-round daily 9am–5pm.* ⏰*Closed Jan 1, Thanksgiving Day & Dec 25.* 🚶*Other parts of the UN complex may be visited by guided tour (1hr) only, every 30min Mon–Fri 9:30am– 4:45pm, weekends 10am–4:30pm (no weekend tours Jan-Feb).* 🚶*A limited schedule may be in effect during the general debate (mid-Sept–mid-Oct).* 🧒*Children under 5 not permitted on tours. For tours in languages other than English, call* ☎*212-963-7539 after 10am on the day you would like to visit.* 💲*$13.* ☎*212-963-4475 (inquiries);* ☎*212-963-8687 (tour information). www.un.org.*

The heart of the United Nations, this long, low-lying structure, marked by a sloping roof and bowed sides, contains the vaulted Assembly Hall. The vast **lobby** is a fascinating space full of historic objects (a model of Sputnik I, a Foucault pendulum and a statue of Poseidon) as well as three rotating **art exhibits**, usually centered on international themes. On the west side of the lobby is a dramatic, 15ft-by-12ft **stained-glass window** by Marc Chagall, symbolic of humankind's struggle for peace. Unveiled in 1964 as a memorial to former UN secretary-general Dag Hammarskjöld, the window was contributed by members of the UN staff and the artist. Beside the window is a small **meditation room**, whose focal point is a massive block of iron ore dimly spotlit

from above. The **basement**, accessed by a curving staircase to the left of the entrance, contains the UN post office, which has its own postmark and stamps, as well as an old-fashioned coffee shop, a public inquiries office, a bookshop, a gift shop and public restrooms. The whole place feels frozen in time.

General Assembly Hall
🚶*Visit by guided tour only.* Decorated in blue, green, and gold, this oval hall is situated above the lobby. It is 165ft long and 115ft wide, with a ceiling that rises 75ft to an oval skylight. Some 1,321 seats on stepped platforms form an arc around the raised podium on which the president of the General Assembly, the UN secretary-general and a high-ranking UN official sit. Above the podium, the emblem of the United Nations hangs between the illuminated boards indicating members' votes. On either side are glass-enclosed booths for the interpreters who work in the six official UN languages (Arabic, Chinese, English, French, Russian and Spanish). All 1,898 seats in the hall (several hundred are reserved for the news media, for alternate delegates and for the public) are equipped with earphones that allow the listener to tune in to a translation of the proceedings in any of the six official languages. The sidewalls are decorated with **murals** by Fernand Léger of France.

The General Assembly meets every year in regular session, which starts in September. Special sessions and emergency sessions may be called at the request of the Security Council or by a majority of the member states. The Assembly may discuss any matters within the scope of the

UN Charter, except those under consideration by the Security Council.

Secretariat Building★★

☞ *Not open to the public.* This tall, thin slab of glass and marble is one of the city's most distinctive structures. Rising 39 stories without a setback, it presents broad rectangular faces of green-tinted glass to both the city and the river. In contrast, its narrow north and south facades are capped with 2,000 tons of white Vermont marble. In front of the building stands a circular marble pool that contains *Single Form* (1 *on map*), an abstract sculpture (1964) by Barbara Hepworth.

Conference Building

☞ *Visit by guided tour only.* This five-story building extends 400ft along the East River on land cantilevered over FDR Drive. As its name suggests, the structure contains a number of meeting rooms as well as darkrooms, printing presses and recording studios. Its narrow top floor contains the delegates' dining room, private dining rooms, a staff cafe and a kitchen. The three main conference rooms, each 72ft wide, 135ft long and 24ft high, contain the chambers for the Security Council, the Trusteeship Council and the Economic and Social Council.

Security Council Chamber – Donated by Norway, this chamber is decorated with gold and blue wall hangings and a mural by Norwegian artist Per Krohg symbolizing Peace and Liberty, Equality and Fraternity. The Security Council has primary responsibility for the maintenance of international peace and can be convened at any time members feel that peace is threatened. The council is made up of 15 member states: a representative from each of the five permanent member states (China, France, the Russian Federation, Great Britain, and the US) and a representative from each of 10 nonpermanent members chosen by the General Assembly for two-year terms.

Trusteeship Council – The furnishings in this room were donated by Denmark. Precious woods sheathe the walls and provide the backdrop for a large teak statue of a woman releasing a bluebird, which symbolizes Hope and Independence. The Trusteeship Council was created with the goal of helping nonautonomous colonies exercise their right to self-determination. Between 1946 and 1994, when the council formally suspended regular meetings, more than 70 former colonial territories, including all of the original 11 trust territories, exercised self-determination.

NYC Parks & Recreation

Hammarskjöld Plaza

is dedicated to the memory of the second secretary-general, Dag Hammarskjöld, killed in 1961 in a plane crash during a peacekeeping mission to the Congo. Its marble walls enclose 380,000 volumes for the use of UN delegates, Secretariat staff members and scholars. In addition, there are newspapers, reading rooms, a collection of 80,000 maps, and an auditorium.

Economic and Social Council – This room was designed by Sven Markelius of Sweden with funds contributed by Sweden. It features exposed pipes and ducts, dark-paneled walls, a dropped ceiling and a brightly lit meeting area at the center. The 54-member council coordinates the efforts and resources of various UN and affiliated organizations toward the alleviation of economic and social problems.

Garden – ⚷ *Not open to the public.* In the garden just west of the Conference Building between the Secretariat and Assembly buildings stands a pagoda sheltering a Japanese **peace bell** made of copper coins and metal donated by the children of 60 countries, as well as a **sculpture** by Henry Moore titled *Reclining Figure: Hand.*

Hammarskjöld Library

⚷ *Not open to the public.* Located on the southwest corner of the complex, the library, a gift of the Ford Foundation,

Additional Sights

Dag Hammarskjöld Plaza

E. 47th St. between First and Second Aves. www.hammarskjoldplaza.org.
This block-long promenade serves as an informal gateway to the UN. Once mainly a staging area for demonstrations, it was redesigned in the mid-1990s with help from local volunteers. Today it's the site of a woodland sanctuary known as the Katharine Hepburn Garden (Hepburn was a longtime resident of the neighborhood); a holocaust memorial wall; and a **farmers' market** (🕐*Mar–Nov, Wed*).

Japan Society

333 E. 47th St. 🕐*Open during special exhibits only, Tue–Fri 11am–6pm (Fri until 9pm), weekends 11am–5pm.* 🕐*Closed major holidays.* 💲*$12.* 👁*Docent-led tours (1hr) Tue–Sun 12:30pm.* ☎*212-832-1155 or www.japansociety.org.*
This black, low-rise building, located a short walking distance from the UN,

---

The Trump in Trump World Tower

Born in Queens in 1946, Donald Trump began perfecting the "Art of the Deal" at a young age. After graduating from Wharton, the University of Pennsylvania's prestigious school of business, he entered the world of real estate under his father's tutelage. Before long, he was on his own in Manhattan, beginning a steady acquisition of the properties and constructing the buildings that constitute his New York City empire today. Most renowned is Trump Tower, completed in 1983, which receives over 2.5 million visitors a year. The equally impressive Trump World Tower, rising high above the neighboring United Nations Headquarters, was completed in 2001. Among his many other buildings in Manhattan are Trump Place, Trump International Hotel and Tower, Trump Parc, Trump Park Avenue, Trump Plaza, Trump Palace, and 610 Park Avenue. In 2004 "The Donald"—a title bestowed by his former wife Ivana—became a television star with the instant success of his NBC business-reality show *The Apprentice.* As a result, the already famous Trump has increased his pop-culture notoriety to epic proportions. His trademark hairstyle is more recognizable than ever, as is his contribution to the American lexicon: "You're fired."

houses the headquarters of the Japan Society, a cultural and educational organization. Designed in contemporary Japanese style, the interior contains a bamboo pool, exhibit gallery, auditorium, library, language center, conference rooms and garden, all of which blend together to create a tranquil effect. The center sponsors two major art installations a year, as well as ongoing film series, lectures and peformances.

Trump World Tower

845 United Nations Plaza.
Soaring 881ft over the United Nations is **Donald Trump**'s latest contribution to the New York skyline: the world's tallest residential building. The 72-story bronze-glass box (2001, Costas Kondylis and Partners) represents a return to modernist simplicity; inside though, more is more. A deal to sell the four top-floor co-ops as a single $38 million, 20,000sq ft duplex penthouse fell through.

Undeterred, Trump raised the asking price to $56 million. Yankees shortstop Derek Jeter and Microsoft founder Bill Gates are among those who have bought more modestly priced apartments.

Tudor City

Tudor City Place at E. 42nd St.(access via stairs in Ralph J. Bunche Park at corner of First Ave. & 42nd St.).
When you step into this little oasis of Tudor Gothic apartment buildings and quaint parks, it's easy to forget you're in New York City. That was precisely developer Fred F. French's point. Around 1925 he began buying up dilapidated houses on the bluff-top site to replace them with housing affordable to the middle-class. He had the structures face inward to a pleasant central courtyard and left the riverfront facades nearly windowless. The 12 structures in Tudor City contain 3,000 apartments.

Hotels
🏨 Millennium Hotel New York UN Plaza

Restaurants
❶ Sushi Yasuda

CENTRAL PARK★★★

MTA SUBWAY N, R, W TRAINS TO FIFTH AVE.-59TH ST.
MAP P 196

Manhattan's beloved backyard, this 843-acre haven of greenery, light and air draws more than 25 million people each year. Situated in the island's geographical center, Central Park measures 2.5mi long by .5mi wide, extending from 59th to 110th streets, and Fifth Avenue to Central Park West. Framed by the silhouettes of surrounding buildings, the man-made park offers a quiet oasis in the heart of bustling Manhattan, and many opportunities for recreation.

- **Information:** For public programs, go online or call ☎212-360-1311; for sports and recreation facilities ☎212-348-4867; www.centralparknyc.org. ♿See visitor centers in the sidebar Visiting Central Park.
- **Orient Yourself:** Use the map in this chapter to get familiar with the park and for the walking tour below.
- **Especially for Kids:** ♿See the sidebar Just for Kids for a host of ideas.

A Bit of History

An Idea Takes Shape – Editor and poet **William Cullen Bryant** launched the idea of Central Park in 1844 in his newspaper, the *New York Evening Post*. Bryant and other public-minded New Yorkers urged the city to acquire a "waste land" beyond 42nd Street. Some 750 acres of rock and swamp (from 59th to 106th St.) were purchased for $5million. **Frederick Law Olmsted** (1822-1903) and **Calvert Vaux** (1824-95) won the competition for the park's design.

Years in the Making – Clearing began in 1858 with a labor force of 3,000 mostly Irish workers. After 19 years of extensive drainage, planting, road and bridge building and ingenious landscaping, the park emerged essentially as we now know it. Olmsted and Vaux blended natural and man-made elements to create a park inspired by the Romantic style highly favored in the mid-19C. Over 185 acres were set aside for lakes and ponds.

A public/private partnership between the Central Park Conservancy and the city's Parks and Recreation Department, created in 1980, oversees the park's maintenance.

Walking Tour

- *Enter Central Park South at Fifth Ave. & E. 60th St. from Grand Army Plaza. Walk north to the Wildlife Center.*

Just before the Wildlife Center, look west to see Wollman Memorial Rink, a popular spot for ice-skating in winter. To the south a crescent-shaped **pond**, surrounded by luxuriant vegetation, borders the Hallett Nature Sanctuary on a rocky outcrop.

- *Enter the Wildlife Center.*

Central Park Wildlife Center

East side between 63rd & 66th Sts. Map available at entrance. Kids ◷*Open Apr–Oct Mon–Fri 10am–5pm, weekends &*

Sunday Brunch in the Park

Edging the west side of Central Park, the famed **Tavern on the Green** restaurant is a perfect Sunday brunch spot (*at W. 67th St; ☎ 212-873-3200; www.tavernonthegreen.com; be sure to reserve in advance*). Its stained-glass windows, sand-carved mirrors and glittering crystal chandeliers brighten even the gloomiest day. Weather permitting, head for the outdoor cafe, lit by thousands of colored lights strung through the branches, and enjoy the view of the park. The site of innumerable film and television scenes, this restaurant also serves as the finish line for the New York Marathon.

Gondola on the Lake in Central Park

holidays 10am–5:30pm. Rest of the year daily 10am–4:30pm. $8 (includes admission to children's zoo). ☎212-439-6500. www.wcs.org.

This 5.5-acre zoo houses more than 450 animals in a habitat that represents three climatic regions: the tropical zone, the temperate regions and the polar circle. Kids can feed the domesticated animals in the Children's Zoo *(feed available for purchase)*. Notice the Delacorte Clock over the entrance arch, with its moving bronze animal figures.

▶ *Exit the children's zoo at the north end and walk under 65th St. Bear left at the fork, then left again to take the wide steps to cross East Dr. Enter the southern end of the Mall at the statue of Shakespeare.*

The Mall

This straight, wide path is lined with elms and sculptures of famous writers. At the north end, the Naumburg Bandshell is still used for performances. Summer evening events are staged at SummerStage at the Rumsey Playfield, east of the band shell. Lying west of the Mall,

☺ A Bit of Advice ☺

The first two digits of number plates on lampposts throughout the park indicate which cross street you are nearest.

the Sheep Meadow attracts throngs of people to its green lawn, which also offers superb views of the city skyline. To the far west of the Sheep Meadow stands Tavern on the Green *(see sidebar)*, housed in a former sheep barn (1870).

▶ *From the Mall, take the steps down to Bethesda Terrace.*

Bethesda Terrace

Considered the centerpiece of the park, this lovely sandstone plaza resembles a Spanish courtyard with its sweeping stairs and central fountain. Crowning the foun-

The Mall, Lined with Benches

☺ Visiting Central Park ☺

AREA CODE: 212

SAFETY

Central Park is patrolled by the police and park rangers in vehicles, on horseback and on skates. Direct-line emergency call boxes are located throughout the park. ☺Explore the park only in daylight hours; do not go alone, especially in the Ramble.

VISITOR INFORMATION

See **Information** at the beginning of the chapter. The park visitor centers are (call for seasonal hours): **The Dairy** (65th St.), **Belvedere Castle** (79th St.), **North Meadow Recreation Center** (97th St.) and the **Charles A. Dana Discovery Center** (Central Park North & Fifth Ave.). For additional information, contact the **Central Park Conservancy** (☎310-6600; www.centralparknyc.org).

RECREATION

The **NY Road Runners Club** ☎860-4455; www.nyrrc.org. ⚾ Baseball/softball fields are converted for ⚽ soccer/🏈 football in fall and winter (use by permit only; ☎408-0209; www.nycparks.com); 🎾**Tennis courts** are located mid-park at 94th & 96th Sts. and require a permit to use (🕐open Apr–Nov; ☎360-8133).

Ice-skating lessons and skate rentals in season at **Wollman Rink** (east side between 62nd & 63rd Sts.; 🕐Mon–Fri $9.50, weekends $12; ☎439-6900; www.wollmanskatingrink.com) and **Lasker Rink** (mid-park between 106th & 108th Sts.; 🕐$4.50; ☎917-492-3857). Loeb Boathouse rents **bicycles** (🚲Mar–Oct daily 10am–7pm; 🕐$10–$15/hr; ☎517-2233) and **rowboats** (Mar–Oct daily 10am–dusk; 🕐$9–$15/1st hr, reduced price for additional hrs); **gondola rides** are also offered on the lake (🕐May–Sept Mon–Fri 5pm–9pm; weekends 2pm–9pm; 🕐$30/30min; reservations suggested; ☎517-2233).

TOURS

Free walking tours by the **Central Park Conservancy** (for schedule, call ☎ 360-2726 or access www.centralparknyc.org). **Bike tours** (🚲daily 10am, 1pm & 4pm; $40, includes bike rental & tour guide; ☎541-8759; www.centralparkbiketour.com). **Horse-drawn-carriage rides** available at Central Park South near the Plaza Hotel and at Tavern on the Green (🐴year-round daily 24hrs/day unless temperature is below 18°F or above 89°F; 1-4 passengers; 🕐$34/per carriage for 20min, $54 for 50min; ☎246-0520; www.centralparknyc.org).

---

tain is a statue by Emma Stebbins titled *Angel of the Waters* (1868).

▶ *From the fountain, take the pathway to the left.*

The Lake

A graceful iron bridge, Bow Bridge has been the subject of many a photograph. To the west lie the **Strawberry Fields** and the International Garden of Peace honoring musician John Lennon, one of the famous Beatles. It lies steps away from the Dakota apartment building, where Lennon lived and was murdered. To the east sits the Loeb Boathouse, a popular eating spot in summer. Between the lake and Fifth Avenue, Conservatory Water attracts mariners of all ages with model sailboats.

▶ *Enter the Ramble. ☺To reduce your chances of getting lost, stay on paths on the west side of the Ramble, keeping the lake in view as much as possible.*

The Ramble

Interrupted by a meandering brook, this 38-acre wooded hill north of the lake is threaded with tree- and bush-lined paths that wind among large boulders.

▶ *You will cross two bridges before you reach West Dr. Then turn northward on West Dr.*

Swedish Cottage

This log structure, a model of a Swedish schoolhouse, was built in Central Park in 1877. It now serves as home to the **🧒Marionette Theatre**, which presents puppet shows throughout the year (🕐see *Just for Kids* for hours and prices).

In the **Shakespeare Garden**, adjacent to the cottage, flowers, herbs, trees and shrubs mentioned in the works of the Bard can be seen. Small plaques display quotes from the playwright pertinent to a garden setting.

▶ *Go up the stairs to Belvedere Castle.*

Belvedere Castle

Complete with merlons and crenels, Belvedere Castle was designed by Vaux as an imitation medieval Scottish castle (1872). Its site atop Vista Rock permits views of the northern end of the park. Just north of Belvedere Castle lie Turtle Pond and the Delacorte Theater. Beyond, the **Great Lawn** occupies the site of the Receiving Reservoir, opened in 1842 to supply the city water system. Today it is best known as the setting for performances by the Metropolitan Opera and the New York Philharmonic.

▶ *From Belvedere Castle, walk northeast toward the Metropolitan Museum of Art.*

Just before reaching the museum, note **Cleopatra's Needle**, a 77ft pink-granite obelisk (16C BC) from Heliopolis, given to the City of New York in 1880 by the Khedive Ismael Pasha. Translated hieroglyphs tell the story of Pharaoh Thutmose III.

Additional Sights

Just south of 96th Street, the 107-acre Jacqueline Kennedy Onassis Reservoir

Allison Simpson/MICHELIN

Fountain at Bethesda Terrace

is rimmed by a popular running track and a bridle path.

Conservatory Garden

Enter at E. 103rd St., opposite El Museo del Barrio.

This six-acre garden was created in 1936. The ornate wrought-iron Vanderbilt Gate (1894) was crafted in Paris for the Vanderbilt Mansion on Fifth Avenue. Opposite the entrance is the half-acre Central Garden, flanked by two crabapple allées and ending in a wisteria pergola. The South Garden, known as "The Secret Garden" after Frances Hodgson Burnett's children's classic, features 175 varieties of perennials. The French-style North Garden boasts two dazzling annual displays: 20,000 spring tulips and 5,000 chrysanthemums in fall.

Kids Just For Kids Kids

Popular destinations for children include the **Wildlife Center** (◉$3 for children ages 3-12), the Carousel (◷open Apr–Oct Mon–Fri 10am–6pm; weekends 10am–7pm; Nov–Dec daily 10am–dusk; Jan–mid-Mar weekends & holidays only 10am–dusk; ☎212-879-0244) and the **Swedish Cottage Marionette Theatre** (W. 79th St. & West Dr.; performances year-round Tue–Fri 10:30am & noon, weekends 1pm; ◉$6 adults, $5 children; reservations required; ☎212-988-9093). Educational field day kits (games and sports equipment) are available at the **North Meadow Recreation Center**, where wall climbing, challenge courses and adventure programs for youth are offered year-round (mid-park at 97th St.; ☎212-348-4867). There's ⌇ swimming at Lasker Pool (◷daily 11am–3pm & 4pm–7pm), catch-and-release ⌇ fishing at Harlem Meer (bamboo poles and bait available at the Dana Discovery Center) and storytelling at the Hans Christian Andersen statue.

Conservatory Garden, Harlem Meer, Dana Discovery Center

Jacqueline Kennedy Onassis Reservoir

Neue Galerie

★★★ THE METROPOLITAN MUSEUM OF ART

THE GREAT LAWN

Cleopatra's Needle

81 ST-MUSEUM OF NATURAL HISTORY

AMERICAN MUSEUM OF NATURAL HISTORY

Delacorte Theater

Shakespeare Garden

Swedish Cottage

Belvedere Castle

Turtle Pond

Transverse

The New-York Historical Society

San Remo

The Dakota

Strawberry Fields

The Ramble

The Lake

Bow Bridge

Loeb Boathouse

Alice in Wonderland Statue

Conservatory Water

Model Boathouse

Hans Christian Andersen Statue

Whitney Museum

Bethesda Fountain

Bethesda Terrace

Rumsey Playfield

THE FRICK COLLECTION

Naumburg Bandshell

Hotel des Artistes

THE SHEEP MEADOW

The Mall

Balto Statue

Tavern on the Green

Shakespeare Statue

Children's Zoo

Temple Emanu-El

Carousel

Heckscher Ballfields

The Dairy

Chess and Checkers House

Wildlife Center

Arsenal

Century Apartments

Heckscher Playground

Wollman Memorial Rink

Hallett Nature Sanctuary

The Pond

Trump International Hotel and Tower

Maine Monument

Columbus Statue

Time Warner Center

Columbus Circle

50 ST-COLUMBUS CIRCLE

The Plaza

Grand Army Plaza

9 W. 57th St.

CENTRAL PARK

Carnegie Hall

0   1/10 mi
0   200 m

Restaurants

1 The Boathouse

2 San Domenico NY

Harlem Meer
Central Park North at Fifth Ave.
Dutch for "lake," 11-acre Harlem Meer, sitting at the northern end of the park, is now well stocked with largemouth bass and bluegills. During the Halloween celebration, carved pumpkins, lit with candles inside, are floated on the lake as dusk falls; it's a magical scene. The Lasker Pool and Skating Rink (1964) mark the lake's west end.

Located at the north end of the Meer is **Charles A. Dana Discovery Center** Kids, which features nature exhibits.

UPPER EAST SIDE ★★
MTA SUBWAY: N, R, W TRAINS TO FIFTH AVE.–59TH ST.
MAP PP 200-201

Known primarily as an enclave for New York City's "old money," the Upper East Side is full of posh town houses and ultra-expensive shops, especially between Madison Avenue and Central Park, the catalyst to the area's settlement. But not everything here is exclusive. In the early 20C many of the Gilded Age mansions along Fifth Avenue were donated to art institutions and opened to the public. The result is Museum Mile, one of the most impressive stretches of cultural real estate anywhere.

▶ **Orient Yourself:** The Upper East Side is bounded by East 59th Street, East 96th Street, Fifth Avenue and the East River. Its heart lies east of Fifth Avenue. See the map in this chapter to orient yourself.

🕐 **Organize Your Time:** Allow a full day for the 2mi walking tour, excluding visits to the major museums (which should be seen separately), so you can enjoy morning and afternoon breaks as well as lunch along the way.

😊 **Don't Miss:** Shopping on Madison Avenue (see sidebar for select stores).

A Bit of History

The area now known as the Upper East Side was largely rural until the mid-19C. Prior to that it contained only a few scattered hamlets. In the mid-18C the village of **Yorkville** sprang up between the burgeoning town of New Amsterdam at the south tip of Manhattan and the small Dutch farming community of **New Harlem** 10 miles north. In the late 18C several prominent families built large wood-frame country manors along the East River; of these, Gracie Mansion, dating from 1799, is one of the few survivors. In 1811 Hamilton Park was established near Park Avenue and 68th Street around two English-style residential squares. But it wasn't until 1858, when 3,000 men started clearing the land for Central Park, that development of the Upper East Side started in earnest. Horsecar lines began running up Second, Third and Madison avenues to 86th Street in the years after the Civil War. Elevated trains were installed on Second and Third avenues in 1879, bringing with them German and Irish immigrants who settled into nearby brownstones and worked at newly established factories along the East River.

Looking north up Fifth Avenue

Brigitta L. House - MICHELIN

Museum Mile Festival

Once a year for the past 27 years, usually on a Tuesday night in early June (rain or shine), Fifth Avenue from East 82nd Street to East 105th Street is the site of the best block party in the city. The street is closed to traffic, and admission to all the museums within Museum Mile is free. Many venues sponsor live entertainment – from accordion and klezmer music to Weimer-era cabaret singers, from full orchestras to salsa bands – and artist-led activities like chalk drawing. Roving the streets in between are magicians, jugglers, face painters and clowns. *For more information, go online to www.museummilefestival.org.*

On Fifth Avenue, development took a different shape. The Metropolitan Museum of Art opened at 82nd Street in 1880. In the 1890s New York's high society, such as the **Astors** and the **Carnegies**, began building palatial residences overlooking Central Park. Luxury apartment buildings soon followed, especially after the railroad tracks on Park Avenue were buried in 1902. By the 1920s aging millionaires had begun donating their mansions to charity for use as cultural institutions as Gilded Age ostentation fell out of vogue. Today some of the richest New Yorkers, such as billionaire Mayor **Michael Bloomberg**, live in town houses in Upper East Side that, from the street, may not look too fancy. But, they are. Most have at least four stories and stretch farther back than you'd imagine. Apartment buildings with the requisite white-gloved doormen also remain highly desirable, as do, for a very few, residence hotels like the Pierre. Celebrities who have made their way past the old guard into the neighborhood have included **Greta Garbo**, **Katharine Hepburn**, **Jacqueline Kennedy** and **Woody Allen**.

Fifth Avenue★★★

MTA *Subway: 4, 5, 6 trains to 59th St. or N, R, W trains to Lexington Ave.–59th St.*
A hundred years ago, the strip of Fifth Avenue from East 59th Street to East 96th Street was called the **Gold Coast** for its grandiose mansions overlooking Central Park. Today's **Museum Mile** embraces the northern third of that stretch—from East 82nd Street (the Metropolitan Museum of Art) extending up to East 105th Street (El Museo del Barrio). The following walk embraces both the Gold Coast and the Museum Mile, making it a little more than two miles total.

Walking Tour

▶ *Begin this 2mi tour at the intersection of 58th St. & Fifth Ave.*

Grand Army Plaza★★
Fifth Ave. between E. 58th St. & E. 60th St.
Cut in half by Central Park South, this oval plaza marks the end of Midtown's Fifth Avenue luxury shopping district and the start of the Upper East Side's "Gold Coast." On the southern end splashes the 1915 **Pulitzer Fountain**, by Carrère and Hastings (statue of the Roman goddess Pomona by Karl Bitter). A huge gold-leaf bronze sculpture of Gen. William Tecumseh Sherman, by Augustus Saint-Gaudens (1903), stands on the north side. Nearby horse-drawn carriages are often waiting to take visitors for a ride around the south end of Central Park. Several significant buildings surround the plaza.

The Plaza★
Designed by Henry J. Hardenbergh in the French Renaissance style in 1907, the Plaza Hotel was a New York institution of status for nearly a century. Coming-out parties and charity balls drew the cream of New York society; overnight guests included the Duke and Duchess of Windsor and the Beatles. The structure itself was one of the first buildings in New York to be named a landmark, but the designation applied only to the exterior facade. So when developer Elad Properties bought the hotel in 2004 and began reconfiguring its 800 guest rooms as condominiums, the fate of the Plaza's majestic public rooms was unknown.

But today, the Oak Room is being pre-served intact, and the Grand Ballroom and Palm Court are being restored.

Paris Theatre

4 W. 58th St. at Fifth Ave. ☎212-688-3800.
Classic revivals and first-run foreign films (subtitled, not dubbed, of course) play at this charming cinema, one of the few left in Manhattan that hasn't been chopped up to house multiple screens. Its neon marquee is vintage 1960s. The interior walls are covered with blue velvet.

General Motors Building

767 Fifth Ave. between E. 58th & E. 59th Sts.
Looming over the east side of the plaza, this 50-story tower (1968) is articulated by white marble piers, alternating with black glass. In the forecourt plaza rises the stunning 32ft glass-cube of the **Apple Store** (2006), open 24/7 for product try-outs and tech help. On the ground floor sits the beloved toy store FAO Schwarz, and the CBS television studio where "The Early Show" is broadcast each weekday morning: show up outside between 8am and 8:30am and you may get on camera (*☎212-975-4061; www.cbsnews.com*).

Sherry-Netherland★

781 Fifth Ave. at E. 59th St.
The hotel/apartment building (1927) rises 38 stories from a brick base to a French Château-style tower. Above the 24th floor each apartment takes up a full floor. The small lobby has marble mosaic floors; custom-made chandeliers; and hand-painted, wood-paneled elevators.

Allison Simpson/MICHELIN

Apple Store

The sidewalk clock outside was installed when the building opened in 1927.

Hotel Pierre

2 E. 61st St. at Fifth Ave.
Opened in 1930, the luxury hotel was named after its owner, the celebrated chef Charles Pierre, who built it with a group of Wall Street backers. Most of the 700 rooms were leased annually by a wealthy clientele, either as primary residences or pieds-à-terre. Today the hotel, which is owned by the Taj hotel group, holds a mix of condominium owners, full-time renters and overnight guests. The Pierre's most famous moment: in 1972 five men in tuxedoes tied up 16 hotel workers and looted the vault, which held an estimated $11 million in cash and jewels.

810 Fifth Avenue

This elegant limestone apartment house (1926) has only one unit on each of its

Truman Capote's Black and White Ball

Among the thousands of parties held at the Plaza Hotel over the years, one stands out above all the rest: Truman Capote's Black and White Ball. Held in honor of Washington Post publisher **Katherine Graham**, the 1966 event was dubbed "the party of the century." Guests were required to dress in black and white and wear masks. **Candace Bergen**, for one, had Halston make her a fur-trimmed black strapless dress with a matching white fur mask topped with bunny ears. The elite guest list also included **Andy Warhol, Tennessee Williams, Frank Sinatra** and **Mia Farrow** (then husband and wife), **Norman Mailer** and dozens of others, as well as assorted **Rockefellers, Vanderbilts,** and **Rothschilds.** Afterward the *Breakfast at Tiffany's* author was fond of saying that he invited 500 friends (540 showed up) – and made 15,000 enemies.

13 floors. Famous former residents include William Randolph Hearst, Nelson Rockefeller, and Richard Nixon, who lived with his family on the fifth floor between 1963 and 1968.

New India House

3 E. 64th St. at Fifth Ave.

This Beaux-Arts mansion was originally built (by Warren & Westmore, architects of Grand Central Terminal) as a private residence for Mrs. Caroline Astor's daughter Carrie. It's now the headquarters of the Consulate of India and the Indian delegation to the United Nations. Note especially the copper mansard roof with its ocular windows.

Temple Emanu-El★

1 E. 65 St. at Fifth Ave. ○*Open year-round Sun–Thu 10am-4:30pm. Services Fri 5:15pm, Sat 10:30am.* ☎*212-744-1400. www.emanuelnyc.org.* Located on the site of Mrs. Astor's former mansion, this Byzantine Romanesque synagogue was completed in 1929. It is the leading Reform synagogue in New York and the largest in the world. The majestic main sanctuary, rising to 103ft, can hold 2,500 worshipers. The ceiling, the marble columns in low relief, and the great arch covered with mosaics are reminiscent of the basilicas of the Near East. The **sanctuary** harbors the Holy Ark, which contains the Torah scrolls.

The Frick Collection★★★

1 E. 70th St. at Fifth Ave.
☓*See Museums.*

7 East 72nd Street★

At Fifth Ave.

This building and its neighbor at 9 East 72nd Street were both designed as private residences. Flagg and Chambers designed no. 7, a five-story Renaissance Revival town house, for Oliver Gould and Mary Brewster Jennings in 1899. Carrère and Hastings designed the larger mansion at no. 9 for Henry T. Sloane, heir to the W. and J. Sloane home furnishing company, in 1896. The Lycée Français de New York occupied both structures from 1964 until 2001, when the mansions were sold as single-family residences. Asking prices were $15 million and $25 million, respectively. The emir of Qatar supposedly bought no. 9.

Harkness House

1 E. 75th St. at Fifth Ave.
An intricate wrought-iron fence protects this Italian-style palazzo

Hotels

1. The Carlyle
2. Hotel Wales
3. The Regency

Restaurants

1. Candle Cafe
2. Park Avenue Cafe

Jacqueline
Kennedy Onassis
Reservoir

★ National Academy
Museum

★★ Solomon R.
Guggenheim
Museum

Museum Mile

★★★
THE METROPOLITAN
MUSEUM OF ART

CARNEGIE
HILL

E. 87th St.

★ Neue
Galerie

E. 88th St.

E. 86th St.

Carl Schurz Park

Goethe-Institut

E. 85th St.

E. 84th St.

E. 83rd St.

E. 82nd St.

Islamic Cultural Center

★★★ FIFTH

CENTRAL PARK

Ukrainian Institute of America

E. 81st St.

NYU Institute
of Fine Arts

E. 80th St.

Avenue

Avenue

St.

UPPER
EAST SIDE

Issey
Miyake

E. 79th St.

Park

Alice in Wonderland
Statue

Harkness
House

980

Vera Wang
Bridal Salon

Michael Kors

The
Carlyle ★

E. 78th St.

St.

0   1/10mi
0   150m

Carolina
Herrera

Christian
Louboutin

Whitney Museum ★★

E. 77th St.

E. 76th St.

St.

77 ST

★★ Madison

Ralph Lauren

St. Jean
Baptiste

E. 75th St.

E. 74th St.

E. 73rd St.

Avenue

Third

St.

ves St. Laurent
Rive Gauche

★ Asia Society
and Museum

E. 72nd St.

E. 71st St.

E. 70th St.

Lexington

St.

St.

St.

Sotheby's

68 ST-
HUNTER COLLEGE

Third

Ave.

(1900),
built for
Edward S.
Harkness, son of
a partner of John D.
Rockefeller. Today the
building houses the Com-
monwealth Fund, a philan-
thropic organization.

New York University
Institute of Fine Arts

1 E. 78th St. at Fifth Ave.
This immense limestone town house
(1912, Horace Trumbauer) was modeled
after a Louis XV-style chateau in Bor-
deaux, France. In 1915 American Tobacco
Co. founder James B. Duke, his wife
Nanaline, their daughter, Doris, two
other relatives and 13 servants lived
here. Nanaline and Doris Duke gave the
house to New York University in 1957.

Ukrainian Institute of America

2 E. 79th St. at Fifth Ave. ○*Open year-
round Tue–Sun noon–6pm.* ☞*$5.* ☎*212-
288-8660. www.ukrainianinstitute.org.*
Architect C.P.H. Gilbert was renowned
among the rich for his opulent French

Gothic designs, of which this landmark 1897 castle is typical: it even has a (dry) moat. Financier Isaac D. Fletcher, its original owner, left the mansion, along with his art collection, to the Metropolitan Museum of Art in 1917. The Met in turn sold the house to oil tycoon Harry F. Sinclair, who later went to prison for contempt of court in the Teapot Dome scandal of the 1920s. The Ukrainian Institute of America bought the building in 1955. Step inside to view the magnificent **woodwork** and **chandeliers**; exhibits by Ukrainian artists or on Ukrainian themes are mounted on three floors.

Goethe-Institut

1014 Fifth Ave. between E. 82nd & E. 83rd Sts. ⏰*Gallery hours year-round Mon–Fri 10am–5pm, Sat noon–5pm.* ☎*212-439-8700. www.goethe.de/newyork.*
The Republic of Germany purchased this five-story limestone town house (1907, Welch, Smith & Provot) in 1960. Today it's home to the New York branch of the Goethe-Institut, one of 144 centers promoting German language and culture worldwide. Films, lectures, debates and museum-quality exhibits of German art are presented on an ongoing basis.

Neue Galerie★

1048 Fifth Ave. at E. 86th St. ♿⏰*Open year-round Thu–Mon 11am–6pm (Fri until 9pm).* ⏰*Closed major holidays.* ☞*$15.* ☎*212-628-6200. www.neuegalerie.org.*
Cosmetics mogul **Ronald Lauder** established this museum in 2001 to house his own collection of early 20C Austrian and German art and that of his friend, art dealer **Serge Sabarsky**, who died in 1996. The museum's home, a Louis XIII-style Beaux-Arts mansion built in 1914 by Carrère and Hastings, was once the residence of Mrs. Cornelius Vanderbilt III.
In the lobby, **Cafe Sabarsky** re-creates a Viennese coffeehouse of the period; taking museum fare to a higher level, it offers tortes, strudels, smooth Viennese coffee, and Austro-Viennese staples such as herring sandwiches and goulash.
The second floor is devoted to Austrian art. Works by **Gustav Klimt** (*Black Feather Hat*, 1910) and **Egon Schiele** form the heart of the collection. There are also

fine examples of decorative art and furniture by members of the Wiener Werkstaette. The third-floor houses the German collection, focusing on members of the Blaue Reiter, Neue Sachlickkeit and the Bauhaus (Wassily Kandinsky, Paul Klee, George Grosz).

Guggenheim Museum★★

1071 Fifth Ave. at E. 88th St. ♿*See Museums.*

National Academy Museum★

1083 Fifth Ave. at E. 89th St. ⏰*Open year-round Wed–Thu noon–5pm, Fri–Sun 11am–6pm.* ⏰*Closed Jan.1, Thanksgiving Day & Dec 25.* ☞*$10.* ☎*212-369-4880. www.nationalacademy.org.*
This 1902 town house contains 10,000sq ft of gallery space. Here, the museum displays rotating selections from its impressive collection of American art. American artists **Thomas Cole** (of the Hudson River School), **Samuel F. B. Morse** (who also invented the telegraph), **Rembrandt Peale** and others established the National Academy of Design in 1825. In 1940 **Archer Milton Huntington** (heir to the shipping and railroad fortune of his father, Collis P. Huntington) and his wife, the sculptor **Anna Hyatt Huntington**, deeded their bow-front town house and other properties on Fifth Avenue and East 89th Street to the academy for one dollar. A second gift in 1955 enabled the academy to build a separate school next door.
Today displays rotating selections from its 5,000-piece permanent collection, which includes work by members and former members **Winslow Homer, John Singer Sargent, Isabel Bishop, Chuck Close, Jasper Johns** and **Jim Dine**, among others. Three floors of galleries are accessed through a charming wood-paneled bookstore, which leads to a marble entrance foyer dominated by a gracefully sweeping staircase and a statue of the Greek goddess Diana by Anna Hyatt Huntington.

Cooper-Hewitt, National Design Museum★★

2 E. 91st St. at Fifth Ave. ♿*See Museums.*

Jewish Museum★

1109 Fifth Ave. at 92nd St. ◷*Open year-round Sat–Thu 11am–5:45pm (Thu until 8pm).* ☛*Guided tours (45min) available Mon–Thu; check website for times.* ◷*Closed major & Jewish holidays.* ✆*$12.* ☎*212-423-3200. www.thejewishmuseum.org.*

Founded in 1904 as part of the Jewish Theological Seminary of America *(3080 Broadway)*, this museum houses a 28,000-piece collection of Judaica that offers insight into 4,000 years of Jewish history. The French Gothic-style mansion, built in 1909 for Felix M. Warburg, a prominent Jewish banker who emigrated to the US from Germany in 1894, was donated to the seminary by his wife, Frieda, in 1947. Since 1993, it has undergone several renovations.

Large temporary shows are presented on the second floor. On the third and fourth floors is a permanent installation "Culture and Continuity: The Jewish Journey," in which 800 works from the permanent collection are arranged to examine Jewish identity from antiquity to the present. The media center *(3rd floor)* offers visitors access to the National Jewish Archive of Broadcasting.

Museum of the City of New York★★

1220 Fifth Ave. at 103rd St. ⟲*See Museums.*

El Museo del Barrio

1230 Fifth Ave. at 104th St. ◷*Open year-round Wed–Sun 11am–5pm.* ◷*Closed Jan 1, Thanksgiving Day, Dec 25.* ✆*$6* ☎*212-831-7272. www.elmuseo.org.*

Housed on the ground floor of an imposing U-shaped building, this museum and cultural center presents art from the Caribbean and Latin America.

El Museo was founded in a public-school classroom in 1969 by Puerto Rican artists and activists from *el barrio* ("the neighborhood") of East Harlem *(96th St. to 125th St., Fifth Ave. to the East River)*. Today the museum works with other institutions to create major traveling exhibitions of Latin American art. It also presents rotating selections from its permanent collection, which is especially strong in photography.

Madison Avenue★★ to Lexington Avenue

ⓂⓉⒶ *Subway: N, R, W trains to Lexington Ave.–59th St.*

East of Fifth Avenue lies the heart of the Upper East Side. Here you'll find leafy side streets lined with town houses and broad avenues, each with a different character.

Madison Avenue★★, which cuts the block between Fifth and Park (Fourth) avenues in half, is lined with elite boutiques and world-famous designer stores, as well as upscale galleries. Many are open by appointment only, but **Gagosian** *(no. 980 at E. 76th St.; ☎212-744-2313; www.gagosian.com)* and **Knoedler & Co** *(19 E. 70th St. between Fifth & Madison Aves.; ☎212-794-0550; www.knoedlergallery.com)* keep regular hours; visit either one to get a *Gallery Guide*, which pinpoints other galleries in the neighborhood. **Park Avenue** is almost entirely residential, with large apartments facing off across the elegantly manicured median strip. **Lexington Avenue**, the most congested of the three streets, is packed with shops, though none are as exclusive as those on Madison. The most famous landmark on Lexington is the Art Deco-style department store **Bloomingdale's** *(between E. 59th & E. 60th Sts.; ☎ 212-705-2000; www.bloomingdales.com)*. The 54-story **Bloomberg Tower**, by Cesar Pelli & Assocs., bloomed just one block south *(East 58th Street)* in 2005. Headquarters of Mayor Mike's media empire, it has received high marks for its graceful form and airy atrium.

Not all of the Upper East Side's treasures are on the avenues, however. As on Fifth Avenue, many former town houses have been given over to cultural institutions, consulates and clubs, some offering public access. The **China Institute Gallery** *(125 E. 65th St. between Park & Lexington Aves.;)*, located in a stately row house across from the famous French hair salon **Yves Durif**, has presented critically acclaimed shows of Chinese art in various media since 1966 *(*◷*open Mon–Sat 10am–5pm, Tue & Thu until 8pm;* ◷*closed major holidays & between exhibits: best to call ahead;* ✆*$7, free Tue & Thu after*

6pm; ☎*212-744-8181; www.chinainstitute. org).* Likewise the **Grolier Club** occupies a 1917 town house at 47 East 60th Street *(between Madison & Park Aves.).* Founded in 1884 in honor of the 16C French bibliophile Jean Grolier, it houses 90,000 volumes. The books are for scholars only, but the club regularly mounts public shows related to the book arts in the first-floor exhibit hall (◐*open year-round Sept–Jul Mon–Fri 10am–5pm;* ◐*closed major holiday;* ☎*212-838-6690; www.grolierclub.org).*

Sights

The sights below are described in descending star order.

Whitney Museum of American Art★★

945 Madison Ave. at 75th St. ◐*See Museums.*

Asia Society and Museum★

725 Park Ave. at 70th St. ◐*Open year-round Tue–Sun 11am–6pm (Fri until 9pm, except Jul 4–Labor Day).* ◐*Closed major holidays.* ◐*$10.* ◐*Guided tours Tue–Fri 12:30pm & 2pm (also Fri 6:30pm), weekends 2pm. (No 12:30pm or 6:30pm tours Jul4–Labor Day).* ☎*212-288-6400. www. asiasociety.org.*

This artfully revamped museum and cultural center is New York's leading purveyor of Asian arts and culture. The society was founded in 1956 by John D. Rockefeller III, a noted collector of Asian art. In 1960

Asia Society Museum

Interior, Asia Society and Museum

the first galleries were opened on this site, and in 1981 Edward Larrabee Barnes designed the present eight-story building in red granite and sandstone. A $30 million renovation, overseen by local architect Bartholomew Voorsanger and completed in 2001, doubled the size of the bookstore and galleries and added the glass-enclosed **Garden Café**, a popular lunch spot.

Voorsanger's sinuous white-steel **staircase** with blue-glass steps brings to mind the sun-bleached skeleton of a fish. The stairs link three levels of bamboo-floored galleries with the spacious lobby, set off from the excellent museum shop by curved shoji screens. Third-floor galleries hold rotating masterworks from the Rockefeller Collection. Other galleries contain temporary shows of predominantly contemporary art. Films, lectures and performances are presented in the basement theater *(check the website for schedule).*

Church of St. Jean Baptiste★

184 E. 76th St. at Lexington Ave. ◐*Open year-round Mon–Fri 7:30am–6:30pm, weekends 8am–6:30pm.* ☎*212-288-5082. www.sjbrcc.net.*

Completed in 1913 for a parish then largely composed of French Canadians (now it is multiethnic), this Classical Revival church has an exquisitely painted barrel-vaulted ceiling, topped by a central dome 175ft above floor level. The 50ft-high altar consists of Italian marbles and mosaics. The stained-glass windows throughout the church were crafted in Chartres, France.

The Carlyle★

35 E. 76th St. at Madison Ave. ☎*212-744-1600. www.thecarlyle.com.*

A slice of old New York, this classic Art Deco hotel was completed just before the stock-market crash in 1929. It later became a favorite of presidents Truman and Kennedy, and still today is one of the most richly atmospheric places on the Upper East Side.

On the mezzanine level, **Ursus Books and Prints** is a browser-friendly trove of popular and rare art books, as well as decorative prints from the 17C to the 19C (◐*open year-round Mon–Fri 10am–6pm,*

Sat 11am–5pm; ☎212-772-8787; www. ursusbooks.com). Tucked on the ground floor is the incomparable **Bemelmans Bar** *(☍ see sidebar page 207)*, reputedly a favorite haunt of Jackie O *(open daily noon–11:30pm; live jazz Mon–Sat nights).* Finally there is **Café Carlyle**, a 1930s-style supper club, where acts have included **Woody Allen**, **Eartha Kitt** and **Ute Lemper**. *(⯐ For entertainment schedules or to make reservations at either Café Carlyle and Bemelmans, call the hotel's main number or see the website.)*

Church of St. Vincent Ferrer

869 Lexington Ave. at 66th St. ☍Open year-round daily 7:30am–6:30pm, holidays 7:30am–3pm.
Designed by Bertram G. Goodhue in the Gothic Revival style, this church—named after the patron saint of builders—was completed in 1918 for the Dominican Order. The granite facade has a rose window and limestone trim carved by Lee Lawrie, famed for his sculpture of Atlas at Rockefeller Center. Step inside to see the altar and stained glass.

Islamic Cultural Center of New York

1711 Third Ave. at E. 96th St. Open by appointment only. ☎212-722-5234. ☍Women are requested to cover their heads with a scarf & wear long sleeves.
Completed in 1991 from designs by Skidmore, Owings & Merrill, this pink-marble center for Muslim worship is the first major mosque built in New York City. The two-story domed prayer hall, where light streams through a curtain wall of windows distinguished with Eastern motifs, is particularly stunning. Designed to serve the city's 400,000 Muslims, the mosque is flanked by a 12-story minaret, from which the faithful are called to prayer.

Seventh Regiment Armory

640 Park Ave. between E. 66th & 67th Sts. ☍Foyer is usually open to the public when there are no shows.

Madison Avenue Shopping

See map p200. Though it has stiff competition from 57th Street and Fifth Avenue—and even SoHo and Chelsea nowadays—Madison Avenue between 59th and 78th streets remains, inch for inch, the most luxurious shopping strip in the city. Here are some of the brightest stars *(for a full list, see Your Stay in the City).* Native son **Calvin Klein** anchors the southern end with a palace showcasing clothing (only his couture line, of course) and home furnishings *(no. 654 at 60th St.; ☎212-292-9000).* **Barneys** *(no. 660 at 61st St.; ☎212-826-8900; www.barneys.com)* beckons the Sex in the City crowd with nine exuberant stories of ultrachic brand names, from Manolo Blahnik to Comme des Garçons. Impeccable French accessories designer **Hermès** has its only New York store at no. 691 *(at 62nd St.; ☎212-751-3181; www. hermes.com).* **Emilio Pucci**, popularized in the 1960s by Jacqueline Kennedy Onassis, is hip again with updated versions of the same wildly patterned clothes *(24 E. 64th St. between Fifth & Madison Aves.; ☎212-752-4777; www.emiliopucci.com).* **Emanuel Ungaro** has a pink staircase to match his signature floral print dresses *(no. 792 at 67th St.; ☎212-249-4090; www.emanuelungaro.fr).* For Oscar-worthy gowns, check out **Valentino** *(no. 747 between 64th & 65th Sts.; ☎212-772-6969; www. valentino.it),* **Jean Paul Gaultier** *(no. 759 between 65th & 66th Sts.; ☎212-249-0235; www.jeanpaul-gaultier.com)* and, farther north, **Carolina Herrera** *(no. 954 at 75th St.; ☎212-249-6552; www.carolinaherrera.com).* Men gravitate toward **Giorgio Armani** for European-style suits and torso-hugging T-shirts *(no. 760; ☎212-988-9191; www.giorgioarmani.com).* Bronx-born **Ralph Lauren** (née Ralph Lifschitz) displays his timeless fashions in the opulent 1895 Gertrude Rhinelander Waldo House *(no. 867 at 72nd St.; ☎212-606-2100; www.polo.com),* replete with fresh-cut flowers and gilt-framed paintings. Farther north you'll find the super-luxe French shoe store **Christian Louboutin** *(no. 941 between 74th & 75th Sts.; ☎212-396-1884).* Japanese designer **Issey Miyake** showcases wearable art at this, his original New York location *(no. 992 at 77th St.; ☎212-439-7822; www.isseymiyake.com);* another titanium structure by Frank Gehry opened in TriBeCa in 2001.

View from Roosevelt Island Tram

Brigitta L. House/ MICHELIN

Unless there happens to be an arts or antiques show installed in the vaulted drill room, this massive redbrick fortress (1877), home to the New York National Guard, is off limits to the public. But you can still (usually) step inside and gaze at the dark-paneled foyer with ornate iron fixtures and contemplate what lies beyond. Its robust architecture became a model for urban armories nationwide. Charles W. Clinton, a veteran of the regiment and a student of architect Richard Upjohn, came up with the imposing medieval design, complete with square towers, crenellations, slits for crossbow arrows, and six-inch-thick oak doors with spiked rivets. Because such armories doubled as men's clubs, quite a bit of thought went into its interior as well, the lavish appointment, which was overseen by **Louis Comfort Tiffany**.

Kitchen Arts & Letters

1435 Lexington Ave. at E. 94th St. ☎212-876-5550. www.kitchenartsandletters. com. An intriguing little spot, Kitchen Arts & Letters only stocks books on food and wine – some 11,000 titles, in fact, ranging from traditional recipe compilations to out-of-print rarities, antique food advertisements and cooking memorabilia. Foreign language titles are available as well.

Sights along the East River

M15 Bus; 4, 5 and 6 trains to 59th St. & 86th St.

The Upper East Side may be posh, but its waterfront generally is not. There's good reason for that. In the late 18C the area was rural, an ideal site for Archibald Gracie's country manor. But by the mid-19C, the riverfront up to 86th Street was lined with factories and stables, and Second and Third avenues were overshadowed by rumbling elevated trains. Wealth, when it came to the neighborhood in the late 19C, gravitated toward Central Park. That remains largely the case, but there are a few notable exceptions to explore —especially around Gracie Mansion, the mayor of New York City's official residence. A pedestrian and bicycle path links the following sights, but because it is cut off from nearby businesses and residences by Franklin D. Roosevelt Drive, ⊜it can be quite secluded. Instead, consider taking the M15 bus (northbound on First Ave., southbound on Second Ave.) or the Lexington Avenue (4/5/6) subway.

Bridgemarket★

E. 59th St. near Queensboro Bridge.
A cathedral-like hall under the roadway to the Queensboro Bridge has been restored to its original grandeur after decades in oblivion. Until the 1930s, food vendors sold their goods in the vaulted arcade known as Bridgemarket. The city then used it for storage. The impetus to salvage Bridgemarket came when British designer Terence Conran opened **Conran's** houseware and modern design emporium in 1999 *(407 E. 59th St; ☎866-755-9079; www.conranusa.com)* An underground level holds the greater part of the shop's 22,000sq ft.
Under the soaring vaults of Bridgemarket's eastern (and higher) half is **Guastavino's** *(409 E. 59th St.; ☎212-980-2711; www. guastavinos.com)*, a chic American brasserie. The restaurant's name pays homage to Spanish architect Rafael Guastavino and his son, Rafael, who designed the space. They built the 30ft by 30ft "Catalan Vaults" completely from layers of flat rectangular tiles and mortar. Each of the 36 vaults that form the arcade's canopy is

faced with about 1,600 tiles. Their work can also be seen at the Oyster Bar in Grand Central Terminal and in the Registry Room at Ellis Island. In a return to its roots, Bridgemarket's other tenant is a Food Emporium supermarket.

Roosevelt Island

MTA *Subway: F train from Lexington Ave.-63rd St. or tramway (*🕐*departs from Second Ave. & E. 59th St. year-round Sun–Thu 6am–2am, Fri–Sat 6am–3:30am every 15min; *🚋*$2 one-way).* ☎*212-832-4555. www.rioc.com.*

Just 300 yards offshore from Manhattan, in the East River sits 2.5mi long Roosevelt Island. It's linked to Manhattan by bridge, by subway and by an aerial tramway (⏺*see A Bit of Advice*). One of the oldest farmhouses still standing in New York City resides on the island: Blackwell Farm House (1796). The 147-acre island is also home to a residential "town-in-town," built in the 1970s, which includes mixed-income housing, retail shops, schools, hospitals and parks. A waterfront promenade on both sides of the community offers views of the river and the Manhattan skyline.

Gracie Mansion★

*East End Ave. at E. 89th St. *📷📞*Visit by guided tour (1hr) only, Wed 10am, 11am, 1pm & 2pm. Reservations required.* 🚋*$7.* ☎*311 (212-639-9675 outside New York City). www.nyc.gov.*

Located in the northern section of Carl Schurz Park, this 1799 country manor is the official residence of the city's mayor. The Federal-style mansion bears the name of Archibald Gracie, a merchant who entertained many dignitaries here, including Alexander Hamilton and John Quincy Adams. After passing through several hands, the house was eventually acquired by the city in 1896, falling into

> ## 😊 A Bit of Advice 😊
>
> Although Roosevelt Island is accessible by subway, take the $4 *(round-trip)*, 4minute Roosevelt Island tram ride over the East River for great views of the city in each direction. It's an inexpensive way to get an elevated look at Manhattan and Queens. The tram parallels the Queensboro Bridge linking the two boroughs (see departure information above).

neglect until the Museum of the City of New York took it over in 1924. In 1942 it became the official home of the mayor. The current restoration features a striking marbleized entry floor and fine Federal- and Empire-style furnishings.

Carl Schurz Park

Located along East End Ave. from E. 84th to E. 90th Sts.

This appealing sliver of green, completed in 1891 and remodeled in 1938, stretches along East End Avenue, capturing East River views from the promenade. It is named for a famous 19C German immigrant who served as US senator and as secretary of the Interior under President Hayes. At the northern end stands Gracie Mansion, official residence of New York's mayor. Fronting the park across East End Avenue at East 86th Street is the Henderson Place Historic District, comprising 24 turreted houses (1881) designed in the Queen Anne style.

Sotheby's

1334 York Ave. at E. 72nd St. ☎*212-606-7070. www.sothebys.com.*

Founded in London in 1744, this famous auction house has annual sales of more than $2 billion. Here at the New York branch, auctions are held year-round, with major sales of Impressionist, mod-

Bemelmans Murals

Bemelmans Bar is named after the artist **Ludwig Bemelmans**, who in addition to creating the *Madeleine* series of children's books, painted, in 1947, all four walls of the bar with murals of his characters frolicking in Central Park. In exchange for the work, Bemelmans and his family lived free of charge at **The Carlyle** hotel for a year and a half. No wonder he wanted his headstone to read "Tell them it was wonderful." The muted colors of the paintings perfectly complement the rich leather banquettes.

ern and contemporary art in the spring and fall. But you don't have to be in the market for a Monet to view one: along with other treasures, they are displayed in the 75,000sq ft exhibition space during the four- to five-day public viewing period before the sale. Sotheby's Café on the tenth floor has sandwiches and salads—and a terrace with views (⏱open Mon–Fri for breakfast and lunch; weekends for lunch during viewings).

UPPER WEST SIDE★★

MTA SUBWAY: ANY TRAIN TO 59TH ST.–COLUMBUS CIRCLE
MAPS P 211 AND P 217

Historically the seat of the city's intelligentsia, the Upper West Side remains an enclave of performing artists and literate liberals drawn to the area's world-famous cultural venues (Lincoln Center on the south end, Columbia University on the north) and parks (Central Park to the east and Riverside Park to the west). In between are dozens of side streets lined with picturesque brownstones and trees, making the neighborhood one of New York City's most appealing.

▶ **Orient Yourself:** The Upper West Side reaches north from Columbus Circle to 125th Street between Central Park and the Hudson River. ⏳See the map in this chapter to orient yourself.

⏱ **Organizing Your Time:** Reserve a day to explore Central Park West, including the Time Warner Center, the American Museum of Natural History and neighboring sights. Allow a second day to visit Columbus University, St. John's Cathredal and Riverside Church. Take in Lincoln Center by attending a performance.

☺ **Don't Miss:** Zabar's, and the view from the Mandarin Oriental hotel's 35th-floor Lobby Lounge.

A Bit of History

The neighborhood got its start in the mid-1600s, about the time that governor Peter Stuyvesant established the village of Nieuw Haarlem around 125th Street (today's Harlem).

In the colonial era several well-to-do Englishmen, such as Col. Roger Morris (⏳see Morris-Jumel Mansion), had hilltop manor houses on bluffs overlooking the Hudson River, bringing more traffic and expansion en route. In 1844 **Edgar Allan Poe**, for instance, lived in a farmhouse (long since demolished) on West 84th

Upper West Side from Central Park

Street, just west of Amsterdam Avenue. This is the place where he wrote his famous poem "The Raven" ("…quoth the Raven, 'Nevermore' ").

As with other neighborhoods, transportation was key to the Upper West Side's urbanization. An elevated train up Ninth Avenue (today's Columbus Avenue) brought with it a wave of brownstone and tenement construction in the 1880s. But high society considered the area remote, as even its early champions acknowledged. When Singer Sewing Machine president Edward Clark hired Plaza Hotel architect Henry Hardenbergh to design an ornate apartment building at 72nd Street and Central Park West, he dubbed it **The Dakota**, after the distant Dakota Territory. Completed in 1884, it spurred a building boom of Beaux-Arts **apartment houses** catering to well-heeled professionals and celebrities. Middle-class Jewish families arrived from the congested Lower East Side in the 1930, and were soon joined by artists and intellectuals fleeing Hitler's Germany; some of these new denizens took positions at nearby Columbia University. Others pursued literature and music, both of which were nurtured in a district long known for its excellent bookstores and music schools.

In recent years the Upper West Side has attracted a raft of young professionals —initially because rents were affordable, then because the neighborhood had a lively singles scene, and now because of the proliferation of family-friendly activities.

Sights

Sights are described from south to north (not in order of star rating).

Columbus Circle

MTA *Subway: 1, A, B, C and D trains to 59th St.–Columbus Circle*
At the southwest corner of Central Park, three major arteries—Eighth Avenue, Broadway and Central Park South—all feed into one of New York's few traffic circles. This circle, Columbus Circle, is the gateway to the Upper West Side. The name comes from the 700-ton statue

Time Warner Center

©Uwe Ditz Photography/ Rubenstein Public Relations

installed at its center in 1894: explorer **Christoper Columbus** stands atop a 70ft granite column. The three prows on the column represent his famous fleet: the Nina, the Pinta and the Santa Maria. At the base is a fountain with an angel holding a globe and seasonal plantings. Another sculpture, the **Maine Monument** (1913), is located at the entrance to Central Park. This grand composition is dedicated to the 260 men who lost their lives when the battleship Maine was destroyed in Havana Harbor in 1898. Columbus Circle is surrounded by several noteworthy buildings.

Time Warner Center★

Cupping the west side of Columbus Circle with its vast semicircular facade, this huge mixed-use, twin-towered complex was inaugurated in 2004. It stands on the site of the former New York Coliseum, an unpopular structure built by the legendary parks commissioner Robert

Broadway's Beginnings

To get to Nieuw Haarlem (now Harlem) from Nieuw Amsterdam (today's Financial District), 17C travelers often followed an Indian path that ran diagonally along a ridge up Manhattan. That road—long known as the Bloomingdale Road, after Bloemendael, a flower-growing community near Haarlem—is now simply Broadway.

Moses for use as a convention center in the 1950s. When the Javits Center was opened in 1986, the coliseum's owner, the Metropolitan Transit Authority, put the site on the market. Media mogul Mort Zuckerman and others drew up a plan to raze the coliseum and replace it with a mixed-use facility that looked, on paper at least, much like the structure you see today. But the design by architect **Moishe Safdie** was savaged by the press. With Upper West Side residents prompting the backers, including Salomon Brothers, to pull out of the project, Safdie was replaced by Skidmore, Owings & Merrill's **David Childs**, whose blueprint drew less fire. The financing (some $1.7 billion) came together, and over the course of five years the coliseum was replaced by the Time Warner Center.

Two sharply angled, 80-story glass towers rise from a seven-story curved base. The idea was reputedly to echo the twin-towered design of some of the Art Deco apartment buildings on Central Park West. The interior holds 2.8 million square feet of space. Only a fraction is taken up by the world headquarters of its signature tenant, Time Warner, and the studios of its subsidiary **CNN** (☎212-275-8687; www.cnn.com). The rest has been chopped up into condos, shops, performance spaces, hotel rooms and restaurants.

Highlights of the Time Warner Center:
Jazz at Lincoln Center★ – Though still affiliated with Lincoln Center, the organization, under the guidance of **Wynton Marsalis**, stages its jazz concerts here, in three facilities on the fifth floor: the Frederick P. Rose Hall, the Allen Room, and Dizzy's Club Coca-Cola. The **box office** (◷open Mon–Sat 10am–6pm, Sun noon–6pm; ☎212-721-6500; www.jalc.org) is located outside the complex at Broadway and West 60th Street; look for the marquee. For reservations for Dizzy's Club call ☎212-258-9595.

Mandarin Oriental New York Hotel – Accessed through West 60th Street, the luxury hotel has its lobby on the 35th floor. There spreads the spectacular **Lobby Lounge★★** (◷open Sun–Thu 8am–midnight, Fri–Sat 8am–1am; ☎212-805-8876) widely regarded as the best

feature of the entire Time Warner complex.

Shops and Restaurants – Roughly 40 shops are arrayed in mall-like fashion around a four-story atrium space at the heart of the Time Warner Center. The most popular (among locals) is the gargantuan Whole Foods supermarket in the basement. Above the shops, on the fourth floor, are restaurants, including the ultra-exclusive dining spot called **Per Se**.

Trump International Hotel and Tower

Dominating the north side of Columbus Circle, this glitzy high rise contains luxury condominiums as well as 167 hotel rooms. The 52-story structure was originally designed in 1969 by Thomas E. Stanley as Gulf + Western Plaza. Donald Trump slapped his name on it in the 1990s and paid Philip Johnson and Costas Kondylis to reskin the structure in gold-tinted glass. A large hammered-steel globe sculpture was placed in front of it, a symbol of the Trump empire's international scope.

2 Columbus Circle

On the south side of Columbus Circle, a slightly bowed, almost windowless nine-story marble box—with a ground-floor arcade that resembled, according to some people, a row of lollipops—kicked up considerable debate in 2002-05. It was designed in 1964 by **Edward Durell Stone** (creator the Kennedy Center for the Performing Arts in Washington, DC) for the Huntington Hartford Gallery of Contemporary Art. After the gallery moved, 2 Columbus Circle became the headquarters of the New York City Department of Cultural Affairs.

The **Museum of Arts & Design** purchased the building in 2002 (after it had stood empty for four years) with the intention of stripping the marble off the facade and starting fresh from the I-beams, but historic preservationists raised a fuss, claiming the building was a "nationally recognized, albeit controversial, icon of the Modern Movement." A court ruling in mid-2005 gave the museum the go-ahead to make the changes; it expects to open here in fall 2008.

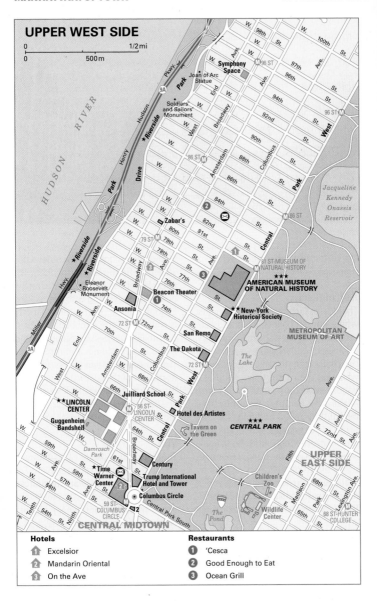

UPPER WEST SIDE

Hotels

🏠 1 Excelsior
🏠 2 Mandarin Oriental
🏠 3 On the Ave

Restaurants

1 'Cesca
2 Good Enough to Eat
3 Ocean Grill

Lincoln Center★★

MTA Subway: 1, A, B, C and D trains to 59th St.–Columbus Circle. Map above. On Broadway between W. 62nd & W. 66th Sts.
Devoted to drama, music and dance, Lincoln Center for the Performing Arts is a 16-acre complex comprising five major theater and concert buildings, a library, a band shell and two outdoor plazas *(free performances held in summer)*. It is home to 12 constituent companies, namely: the Metropolitan Opera, New York Philharmonic, New York City Ballet, New York City Opera, the Chamber Music Society of Lincoln Center, the Film Society of Lincoln Center, Jazz at Lincoln Center, the Juilliard School, Lincoln Center for the Performing Arts, Inc., Lincoln Center Theater, the New York Public Library for

Allison Simpson/MICHELIN

Lincoln Center Plaza

the Performing Arts and the School of American Ballet.

A Bit of History

The idea for such a grand cultural center, where operas, ballets, plays and concerts could take place simultaneously, originated in 1955, and two years later the city bought the necessary land in what was then a run-down neighborhood. Despite considerable controversy —the new complex prompted the demolition of 188 buildings, forcing some 1,600 residents to relocate—the project proceeded, with John D. Rockefeller III chairing the building committee. A board of architects headed by **Wallace K. Harrison**, who had helped design the United Nations and Rockefeller Center, went to work, analyzing some

60 theater designs in 20 countries. Construction finally began in 1959 with Avery Fisher Hall and continued over the next 10 years, ending with the Juilliard School. Private contributions largely accounted for the total budget (about $350 million). In 1991 the Samuel B. and David Rose Building, a multipurpose structure, was added to the complex, northwest of the Juilliard School. In all, the sleek rectangular buildings of glass and Italian travertine marble can accommodate 13,666 spectators at a time.

Visit

The best way to experience Lincoln Center, of course, is to buy tickets to an event. *For a schedule of upcoming* **performances** *and to buy tickets, call ☎212-546-2656 or access www.lincolncenter.org.* Lincoln Center also offers **tours** *(✎ 1hr; $13.50)* of its largest performance spaces: the Metropolitan Opera House, the New York State Theater and Avery Fisher Hall. A ✎**pianoforte tour** *(only for groups of 15 or more people;2hrs; ☎$16; one-month advance reservations required)* takes in a visit to the Klavierhaus, a nearby museum where pianos are restored. *For more information, access the website or call ☎212-875-5350.*

Metropolitan Opera House

✎*For backstage tours, see sidebar.* ☎212-769-7020. www.operaed.org. Distinguished by a 10-story colonnade, this opera house, which opened in 1966 with Samuel Barber's *Anthony and Cleo-*

Backstage Tours

Always wanted to know what goes on behind the scenes? Book a 90min tour of the Metropolitan Opera House, which covers areas of the opera house not included on the general tour of Lincoln Center. On the backstage tour, held on select days October through June, visitors get an overview of the process of making opera at the Met. You'll be led from the shops where artisans create, and work on, the sets, costumes and wigs; through the rehearsal spaces and dressing rooms; and finally to the vast stage and auditorium. For a schedule of available backstage tours or to buy tickets (*$15; advance reservations required*), call ☎212-769-7020 or visit www.operaed.org.

patra, forms the centerpiece of the main plaza. Designed by Wallace K. Harrison, the 3,800-seat hall was the successor to a large Italian Renaissance opera house (1883) at Broadway and 39th Street that was closed in 1966 and later demolished. The "new" Metropolitan Opera House hosts both the Metropolitan Opera and the American Ballet Theater (ABT) (not a resident company) and contains seven rehearsal halls and storage space for six opera sets. In the lobby hang large murals by Marc Chagall, *The Sources of Music* and *The Triumph of Music*. The red-carpeted double staircase is accentuated by crystal chandeliers, a gift from Austria. *For ABT tickets and information, ☎212-477-3030; www.abt.org.*

Avery Fisher Hall

Originally called Philharmonic Hall, this concert hall, designed by Max Abramovitz and set to the right of the main plaza, was renamed in 1973 in recognition of a gift from Avery Fisher, the founder of Fisher Radio. The 2,738-seat auditorium is home to the New York Philharmonic, the country's oldest orchestra, which previously played at Carnegie Hall.

New York State Theater

Designed by Philip Johnson, this theater is home to the New York City Opera and the New York City Ballet. The City Center of Music and Drama, which oversees the two companies, operates the theater, owned by the City of New York. Completed in 1964, it seats 2,713 people.

Other Venues

The Lincoln Center complex also includes the **Guggenheim Bandshell** (in Damrosch Park, behind the opera house to the south), the site of free concerts. Behind the opera house to the north is the **New York Public Library for the Performing Arts** (◐*open year-round Mon & Thu noon–8pm, Tue–Wed & Fri 11am–6pm, Sat 10am–6pm;* ◑*closed major holidays;* ♿☎*212-870-1630; www.nypl.org*). This building (1965; Skidmore, Owings & Merrill) houses a museum of the performing arts, a 200-seat auditorium and a music library whose extensive collections include original manuscripts, diaries, recordings, photographs and costumes. Founded in 1985, the not-for-profit **Lincoln Center Theater** mounts productions of new plays and classic revivals in two venues built next to the library according to plans by Eero Saarinen: the 1,050-seat **Vivian Beaumont Theater** and the 299-seat **Mitzi E. Newhouse Theater**. A footbridge leads across West 65th Street to the Juilliard Building (1968, Pietro Belluschi, Catalano and Westermann), which contains the elite **Juilliard School** for the arts and **Alice Tully Hall**, used by the Chamber Music Society of Lincoln Center.

Next door, on the plaza level of the **Rose Building** (1991), is the **Walter Reade Theater**, where the Film Society of Lincoln Center presents repertory films (both classics and new releases) throughout the year (☎*212-875-5600; www.filmlinc.com*). It's also one of the main venues for the prestigious New York Film Festival, sponsored by the film society each October.

New-York Historical Society★★

2 W. 77th St. ♿ *See Museums.*

American Museum of Natural History★★★

Central Park West between W. 77th & W. 81st Sts. ♿ *See Museums.*

Cathedral of St. John the Divine★★

MTA *Subway: Cathedral Parkway–110th St.. On Amsterdam Ave. at W. 112th St.*

Seat of the Episcopal Diocese of New York, this is reputedly the largest cathedral in the world built in the Gothic style. The massive stone edifice—begun in 1892 and still under construction—can welcome up to 3,000 worshipers at a time and is also the setting for frequent dance, music, film and drama performances, many of them free. The 13-acre area on Amsterdam Avenue between Cathedral Parkway and West 113th Street contains seven ancillary buildings and gardens.

In 1872 Horatio Potter, then bishop of New York, presented a proposal for a cathedral to the diocesan convention. Construction on this site in Morningside Heights did not begin until 1892. From the start, excavation and structural problems plagued the builders. Some 25 years into the project, the original 1888 Romanesque design by Heins and LaFarge was scrapped for a revised plan in the Gothic style by Ralph Adams Cram. The choir and sanctuary were completed in 1911, and construction of the nave began in 1916. Another century is needed to finish the cathedral.

Detail, Cathedral of St. John the Divine

Brigitta L. House - MICHELIN

Visit

🕐 *Open year-round daily 9am–6pm.* 🗣️ *Guided tours (1hr) Tue–Sat 11am & 1pm, Sun 1pm.* 💲*$6.* ☎*212-316-7540. www.stjohndivine.org. Public access may be limited in some areas.*

Two square Gothic towers (to reach 266ft when completed) flank the symmetrical west facade, where the central **Portal of Paradise** features a double set of bronze doors bearing scenes from the Old *(left doors)* and New *(right doors)* Testaments. The doors, each weighing three tons, were produced in Paris by Ferdinand Barbedienne, who also cast the Statue of Liberty. Between the doors is the carved figure of St. John the Divine surmounted by a tympanum adorned with a Christ in Glory.

The portals open into the narthex, or vestibule, where stained-glass windows from the studio of Ernest W. Lakeman represent the Creation *(on the left)* and scenes from the Old Testament *(on the right)*.

A semicircle of eight granite columns encloses the sanctuary, containing the great choir and the high altar. Niches in the marble parapet fronting the altar hold statues of notable figures, including St. Paul, Abraham Lincoln and George Washington; a stone block representing the 20C is carved with the images of Gandhi, Dr. Martin Luther King Jr., Albert Einstein and Susan B. Anthony.

The apse aisle, or ambulatory, contains seven chapels and, on the south side, displays paintings of the 16C Italian school, a glazed terra-cotta Annunciation (15C, Della Robbia school) and a 16C silk-embroidered cloth, representing the Adoration of the Magi.

The domed baptistery is decorated with niches holding figures associated with the early history of Nieuw Amsterdam, including Peter Stuyvesant, depicted with his wooden leg.

To the east of the south transept lies the small Biblical Garden, planted with flora mentioned in the Bible. The distinctive **Peace Fountain** (*1 on map*), which celebrates the triumph of good over evil, was executed by Greg Wyatt. It dominates the children's sculpture garden to the south, where animal sculptures by local youths have been cast in bronze.

Student Hangout

Since 1961 the **Hungarian Pastry Shop** *(111th St. & Amsterdam Ave.; ☎212-866-4230)* as been *the* place for Columbia University students to study, debate and hang out. The burgundy-walled interior of this bohemian, family-owned cafe is appropriately studious and smoky—you might be inspired to deconstruct Kafka over that *caffé Viennese* (☕ order it topped with whipped cream). The pastry selection includes brioches, strudel and an assortment of Eastern European standards. Outdoor tables offer a nice perspective on Morningside Park.

Columbia University★

MTA *Subway: 1 train to 116th St.–Columbia University. W. 114th to W. 120th Sts. between Amsterdam Ave. & Broadway.*

The first college in New York and the fifth oldest in the nation, Columbia is one of the country's most distinguished universities and a member of the Ivy League. Founded in 1754 by a charter from George II, King's College was first located in lower Manhattan, where the original class of eight men met in the schoolhouse of Trinity Church. Among the early students at King's College were Alexander Hamilton, aide-de-camp to General Washington

and later secretary of the Treasury; and John Jay, first chief justice of the US. After the Revolution, the school reopened in 1784 under a new name: Columbia College. In 1897 it moved to the present site after 40 years at Madison Avenue and East 49th Street. Today the coeducational university has an enrollment of some 24,000 students and an endowment of $4.3 billion.

Columbia's **main campus** occupies 36 acres in Morningside Heights. Its formal axial arrangement is typical of the turn-of-the-19C Beaux-Arts movement. Charles McKim envisioned Low Memorial Library

For Architecture Buffs: Notable Buildings

Pressed for space and for time, many New Yorkers "order in" or eat out more than they cook. Some even use their ovens as storage space. But few apartments lack kitchens altogether, as was the case with two of the Upper West Side's most famous and eye-catching buildings: the **Ansonia** *(2109 Broadway between W. 73rd & W. 74th St.)* and **Hotel des Artistes** *(1 W. 67th St. between Central Park West and Columbus Ave.)*. Like a hotel suite, apartments had parlors, dining rooms, bedrooms and bathrooms. They also had room service —residents could order food from the main kitchen and have it delivered via a dumbwaiter. Onetime home to **Arturo Toscanini, Babe Ruth** and **Igor Stravinsky**, the Ansonia *(1904, Paul E.M. Duboy)* is an exuberant Beaux-Arts wedding cake of a building, sporting a corner turret, balconies, terra-cotta ornamentation and a dormered mansard roof. **Hotel des Artistes** *(1918, George Mort Pollard)* is more subtle, but has an equally impressive roster of former tenants, among them **Isadora Duncan, Norman Rockwell** and **Noel Coward**. Given the number of artists in the neighborhood, it's hardly surprising that it contains one of the city's most beautiful theaters, the **Beacon** *(2124 Broadway at W. 74th St.; ☎212-496-7070)*. Designed by Rambusch Studio in 1929, the **interior**★★ is a marvel of ornately carved Rococo swirls and red velvet that now serves as a stunning backdrop to singer-songwriters like **Lucinda Williams** and **Norah Jones**. Finally, about those apartment buildings on Central Park West: the Gothic **Dakota**, setting for the Roman Polanski film *Rosemary's Baby*, is the most famous. Well-known residents have included **Lauren Bacall, Leonard Bernstein**—and **John Lennon**, who was shot outside the West 72nd Street entrance in 1980. Central Park's Strawberry Fields are now dedicated to him. But other apartment buildings are taller and more visible. The two that are best known both have twin towers (to provide maximal light and air): the 1931 Art Deco **Century** *(25 Central Park West between W. 62nd & W. 63rd Sts.)* and the 1930 **San Remo**, whose towers are topped by Athenian temples *(145-46 Central Park West between W. 74th & W. 75th Sts.)*.

as the focus of his 1894 design, which encompasses the area north of West 116th Street. Added in 1934, Butler Library faces Low Library across a majestic mall, while handsome limestone and brick classroom buildings define the quadrangles. The university began expanding outside the old campus in the early 20C, adding the 1926 Casa Italiana by McKim, Mead and White; and later the more contemporary Law School building and School of International and Public Affairs, all on Amsterdam Avenue. The most recent addition is the Alfred Lerner Hall at West 115th Street and Broadway.

Visit

Main entrance at W. 116th St. The **visitor center** (◔ *open year-round Mon–Fri 9am–5pm;* ◔ *closed major holidays*) is located in Low Memorial Library. ✐ Guided tours *(45min)* that access the interior of many of the buildings are available year-round (◔ *Mon–Fri 1pm*). ☎212-854-4900. *www.columbia.edu.*

Low Memorial Library★

The gift of Seth Low, president of Columbia from 1890 to 1901, this Neoclassical building, completed in 1897, was the first major structure on the campus. Designer Charles McKim modeled the library on the Roman Pantheon. Since 1934 the building has served as an administrative center and exhibit hall. Step inside to view the marble rotunda, with its 130ft dome and 16 colossal columns.

Saint Paul's Chapel, Interior

Saint Paul's Chapel★

This 1907 building, a Northern Italian Renaissance design by Isaac Phelps Stokes, features a vaulted interior with salmon-colored Guastavino tiling and chancel windows by John La Farge. The carved pulpit, choir stalls, and organ front recall those in the Church of Santa Croce in Florence, Italy. Because of the chapel's excellent acoustics, many concerts are held here.

Schapiro Center

Completed in 1992 for $62 million, this Neoclassical building was designed by Hellmuth, Obata and Kassabaum and contains state-of-the-art laboratories for research in microelectronics, video imag-

Low Memorial Library

ing and other technologies. A glass-enclosed skyway connects it to the 1927 Pupin Physics Laboratories, where the Manhattan Project, which pioneered the development of atomic energy in the US, originated.

Temple Hoyne Buell Hall

The only building remaining from the former Bloomingdale Insane Asylum, this 1878 edifice is the oldest structure on campus and now serves as a center for the study of American architecture. Frequent exhibits are mounted in the first-floor galleries. La Maison Française, the university's French cultural center, is located on the upper floor.

Outdoor Sculpture

A number of sculptures by European and American artists also distinguish the campus. Fronting Low Library is the Neoclassical bronze figure—the university's emblem—*Alma Mater (2 on map)* designed by Daniel Chester French in 1903. In front of Philosophy Hall *(east of Low Library)* is Rodin's famous bronze *The Thinker*, cast from the 1880 model in 1930. West of Low Library stands the *Great God Pan* (1899) by George Grey Barnard. Modern works include *Bellerophon Taming Pegasus (3 on map)* by Jacques Lipchitz (1967), mounted over the entrance to the Law School; and *Tightrope Walker* (1979) by Kees Verkade and *Three Way Piece: Points* (1967) by Henry Moore, both on the Amsterdam Avenue overpass.

😊 A Bit of Advice 😊

For a great **panorama** of Riverside Park, the Hudson River and the New Jersey shore, visit Riverside Church's observation deck *(call in advance for hours open)*. Take the elevator to the 20th floor, but then you'll have to climb the final 147 steps. You'll pass the chambers of the 74-bell carillon.

Riverside Park★ and Riverside Drive★

MTA *Subway: 1 train to 116th St.–Columbia University.*

Both Riverside Drive and Park take advantage of the beautiful views along the Hudson River. Frederick Law Olmsted designed them as a single entity in 1875. The curving drive, home to artists and musicians, boasts majestic elms, walkways and scenic overlooks, 19C row houses, turn-of-the-19C mansions and elegant early 20C apartment buildings. The park extends from West 72nd to West 155th streets *(recommended area: below W. 100th St.)* and contains some of the city's most important monuments such as the Soldiers' and Sailors' Monument *(W. 89th St.)* and the Firemen's Memorial *(W. 100th St.)*. The 91st Street garden, an English garden maintained by local residents, is worth seeing. Together, the park and drive are a designated New York City Historic Landmark.

Riverside Church★

On Riverside Dr. between W. 120th & W. 122nd Sts. Entrance at 91 Claremont Ave. 🕐*Open year-round daily 7am–10pm.* 🗣*Guided tours Sun 12:15pm.* ☎*212-870-6700. www.theriversidechurchny.org.* With its soaring 400ft tower—containing reputedly the largest carillon in the world—this streamlined Gothic Revival building is a dominant Upper West Side landmark. It's also an important community center offering a broad range of social services and cultural programs. It was founded before 1850 as a small Baptist congregation in the Lower East Side. John D. Rockefeller Jr. helped fund the present 1927 building of limestone, designed by Allen and Collens and Henry C. Pelton (the south wing was added in 1960).

Upper West Side Delicacies

The Upper West Side is renowned for its purveyors of specialty foods. Among the most celebrated is **Zabar's** *(2245 Broadway at W. 80th St.;* ☎*212-787-2000; www.zabars.com)*, which features a stupendous selection of unusual food from around the globe as well as a fine selection of cookware. Zabar's has come a long way since its beginnings as a Jewish deli: today the store sells more than 1,000 pounds of smoked salmon per week. The adjoining cafe may look plain, but it serves one of the best cappuccinos in town. Across the street is **H&H Bagels** *(2239 Broadway;* ☎*212-595-8003; www.hhbagels.com)*, which receives FedEx orders from around the globe and churns out more than 50,000 bagels a day. For a wonderful selection of fresh produce, stop by **Fairway Market** *(2127 Broadway between W. 74th & W. 75th Sts.;* ☎*212-595-1888; www.fairwaymarket.com)*; the supply of mushrooms alone is worth the trip. **Citarella** *(2135 Broadway at W. 75th St.;* ☎*212-874-0383; www.citarella.com)* features a variety of seafood salads for take-out as well as an outstanding range of fish. Possibly the largest, most delectable chocolate-chip cookies in Manhattan are baked by the ovenful at **Levain Bakery** *(167 W. 74th St. at Amsterdam Ave.;* ☎*212-874-6080; http://levainbakery.com)*. This cheerful basement bakery also turns out oatmeal-raisin cookies and scones, brioches and specialty sandwiches to gobble on the spot or take to go.

Zabar's

Brigitta L. House - MICHELIN

Music to Your Ears

Home to some of the country's most accomplished musicians, the Upper West Side offers a range of performances year-round. Though tickets are priced for a student budget, Columbia's **Miller Theatre** is a totally professional outfit. World-class musical performances range from Bach concertos to experimental work by living composers like Steve Reich and John Zorn, who are likely to be on hand for a Q&A *(2960 Broadway at W. 116th St.; ☎212-854-7799; www.millertheatre.com).* To hear free classical music, go to a student recital at the **Juilliard School** *(60 Lincoln Center Plaza; ☎212-769-7406; www.juilliard.edu)* or the **Manhattan School of Music** *(120 Claremont Ave. at W. 122nd St.; ☎917-493-4428; www.msmnyc.edu).* These institutions are among the country's best conservatories, so work is likely to be first-rate. Another local institution worth a visit is **Symphony Space** *(2537 Broadway at W. 95th St.; ☎212-864-1414; www.symphonyspace.org).* The programing here is extremely varied and includes the annual 12-hour Wall to Wall, a celebration of works by a specific composer (Miles Davis, Joni Mitchell and Ravel have been featured in past years) as performed by a variety of musicians; and the literary performance series, where noted Broadway and Hollywood actors read classic and new short stories.

The west portal faces Riverside Drive and evokes the sculptures at Chartres Cathedral in France. Prophets from the Old Testament are carved into the columns on the left, with New Testament figures on the right. The tympanum above features a Christ in Glory and symbols of the Four Evangelists. In the narthex two **stained-glass windows** depict the life of Christ, made in the 16C for the Cathedral of Bruges in Belgium. From the narthex, enter the nave, which is 100ft high and 215ft long, with space for 2,500 worshipers. The clerestory windows are modeled after those at Chartres, while the chancel screen is notable for 80 panels illustrating figures whose lives embodied Christian ideals: among them Luther, Milton, Lincoln and Pasteur. A passage from the narthex leads to a small, Romanesque **chapel**. If the observation desk is open (◖*see A Bit of Advice*), you'll pass the chambers of the carillon on the final 147-step climb.

General Grant
National Memorial★

On Riverside Dr. at W. 122nd St. ◷*Open year-round daily 9am–5pm (until 8:30pm Wed in Jul & Aug).* ◷*Closed Jan 1, Thanksgiving Day & Dec 25.* ☎212-666-1640. *www.*

nps.gov/gegr. ◔*Note: introductory talk on the history of the sight given on the hour*
Popularly known as Grant's Tomb, this Neoclassical monument is the final resting place of **Ulysses S. Grant** (1822-85) and his wife, Julia Dent Grant (1826-1902). Grant was commander of the Union Army during the Civil War and president of the US from 1869 to 1877. The white granite mausoleum, topped by a stepped cone, was designed in 1890 by John H. Duncan and took six years to build. The tablet above the Doric portico bears the words "Let us have peace"; the words were part of Grant's written reply to the Republican Party in 1868, in which he accepted his nomination as presidential candidate. Gold-tinted clerestory windows create a soft glow in the marble interior, which recalls Napoleon's tomb at the Invalides in Paris. A dramatic coffered dome is suspended directly over the sunken crypt, where niches contain busts of Grant's comrades-in-arms: Sherman, Sheridan, Thomas, Ord and McPherson. Two small rooms display photographs illustrating Grant's life and achievements. The free-form mosaic benches flanking the tomb outside were designed by Pedro Silva in the early 1970s as part of a community project to involve neighborhood youths with the monument.

HARLEM★

MTA SUBWAY: A, B, C, D, 2 AND 3 TRAINS TO 125TH ST.

MAP P 191

Though only a fraction of the city's African Americans live in Harlem anymore, the neighborhood continues to nurture its history as a fulcrum of African-American culture. In the 1920s and 30s, jazz greats mingled in smoky bars with writers who proclaimed their African-American identity in novels and poetry that commanded the world's attention. That period was called the Harlem Renaissance. Now another renaissance is under way as some of the famous old landmarks are being restored, museums expanded and 19C brownstones renovated by both black and white Manhattanites.

- **Information:** Harlem Visitor Information Kiosk, 163 W. 125th St., just east of Seventh Ave.
- ▶ **Orient Yourself:** Harlem lies north of Central Park, bordered by Columbia University on the west and El Barrio on the east. The majority of its attractions are found between 125th Street and 138th Street. ⚓See the map at the beginning of Uptown to orient yourself.
- 🕐 **Organizing Your Time:** Allow half a day to visit Harlem plus time to have lunch in one of its restaurants. ⚓*See Address Book.*

A Bit of History

– Established in 1658 by the Dutch governor Peter Stuyvesant in northern Manhattan, Nieuw Haarlem was mostly farmland and remained largely rural until the New York and Harlem Railroad inaugurated service along Fourth Avenue (Park Avenue) in 1837. An even bigger wave of development occurred in the latter part of the 19C with the construction of the elevated rail lines in the western part of the valley. By the early 1890s, Harlem had become one of the most fashionable residential areas in New York City, replete with fine department stores, an opera house, a symphony hall and a yacht club.

Hopes that Harlem would continue to expand foundered in the beginning of the 20C, when brownstones built by enthusiastic developers could not be filled. Despite the racism that prevailed at the time, white landlords began to rent to middle-class black families—for a price. Often, African-American real estate agents had to guarantee rent payment with their own money. By 1920 the black population of Central Harlem was estimated at about 60,000.

Harlem Renaissance – Harlem experienced its heyday in the 1920s. As bootleg liquor flowed, popular nightspots—including the original **Cotton Club** on Lenox Avenue and **Small's Paradise**—drew nightly standing-room-only crowds (some, ironically, white-only as well) with performances by jazz greats **Duke Ellington, Count Basie** and **Cab Calloway**. Harlem became the undisputed Capital of Jazz. It was also a hotbed for emerging writers and artists such as **Langston Hughes** and **Zora Neale Hurston**, who celebrated their African-American identity in original, powerful language.

The Renaissance came to an end with the Great Depression, however. Though the jazz scene remained active with the arrival of innovators such as **Charlie Parker, Miles Davis** and **John Coltrane**, older jazz artists began gravitating to Greenwich Village or touring Europe. Because jobs were scarce, middle-class blacks left too. Abandoned housing deteriorated and crime soared. By the 1960s Harlem's celebrities were distinctly political. Most famously, **Malcolm X** preached in the early 1960s at the Black Muslims' Temple of Islam (now the Masjid Malcolm Shabazz) at 116th Street and Lenox Avenue (he was assassinated in 1965 at the Audubon Ballroom on West 166th Street). Later, Harlem produced New York's only black mayor, **David Dinkins**. And after leaving office in 2000, former US president **Bill Clinton** established his office at 55 West 125th Street.

Harlem Today – Some of Harlem's landmark buildings, jazz clubs and brownstones have been lovingly restored in recent years. There are also a number of stores, restaurants and galleries. **Harlem USA**, smack dab in the center of Harlem on bustling West 125th Street and Frederick Douglass Boulevard, is the biggest complex; the glass-enclosed mall has multiple megastores and a cineplex. But there's still a ways to go, with such landmarks as the **Florence Mills Home** *(220 W. 135th St.)* and the **Renaissance Ballroom and Casino** *(2341-2359 Adam Clayton Powell Jr. Blvd. between 137th and 138th Sts.)*; recent plans call for the ballroom to be razed and replaced with condominiumns and retail and community space.

Sights

125th Street Area

Also known as Martin Luther King Jr. Boulevard, 125th Street was the site of rallies, marches and protests during the Civil Rights movement. Today it's a bustling commercial artery of discount stores and street vendors, with several Harlem landmarks and cultural centers sprinkled in between.

Try to arrive before 10am to see self-taught artist Franco Gaskin's **murals**: they're painted on the retractable metal doors that are rolled over storefront windows at night.

Then venture south to the **Mount Morris Park Historic District** *(roughly bounded by W. 119th & 124th Sts., & by Mount Morris Park West & Lenox Ave.)*, where you'll find rows of stately houses and brownstones.

125TH STREET AREA

Settepani – *196 Lenox Ave. at W. 120th St. ☎917-492-4806. www. settepani.com.* This bakery offers pastries, cappuccino and ample sidewalk seating.

Studio Museum in Harlem★

144 W. 125th St. between Lenox & Seventh Aves. **MTA** *Subway: 2 train to 125th St.* ♿ *Open year-round Wed–Fri & Sun noon–6pm, Sat 10am–6pm.* *Closed major holidays.* *$7.* *Guided tours available by appointment.* ☎*212-864-4500. www. studiomuseum.org.*

Established in 1968 to provide studio space for African-American artists, this museum has since grown into a major visual art and performance center. A rotation selection of the Studio Museum's 1,600-work permanent collection is always on view. Isaac Julien, Gwen Knight Lawrence, Julie Mehretu and Betye Saar are just a few of the artists represented. The vast majority of gallery space, however, is devoted to temporary shows in all media, ranging from folk art to watercolor to video. There's also a full calendar of jazz and tap and other types of performance.

Apollo Theater

253 W. 125th St. between Frederick Douglass & Adam Clayton Powell Jr. Blvds. *Box office open Mon–Fri 10am–6pm (Wed until 8:30pm), Sat noon–6pm.* ☎*212-531-5305.* *For backstage tours (1hr), call* ☎*212-531-5337 for schedule & reservations. www.apollotheater.com.*

Recently renovated to the tune of $12 million, the Apollo opened in 1914 as Hurtig & Seamon's New Burlesque Theatre, where black audiences were excluded. Two decades later, under a new name and management, the Apollo Theater became a mecca of black entertainment. The "Amateur Night at the Apollo" con-

Shahar Azran - Apollo Theater

Apollo Theater sign

test soon became world-famous for having given the nod to such music legends as **Ella Fitzgerald**, **Sarah Vaughan**, **James Brown** and the **Jackson Five**. After a hiatus, Amateur Night was revived in the 1980s. Held every Wednesday, it's still considered one of the most prestigious performance opportunities in the US.

Malcolm Shabazz Harlem Market

52-60 W. 116th St. between Fifth Ave. & Malcolm X Blvd. ©*Open daily 10am–8pm (9pm in summer).* ☎*212-987-8131.*

Located just down the hill from the silver-domed temple where Malcolm X (Shabazz) preached, this popular indoor-outdoor bazaar has about 80 stalls where vendors hawk everything from tube socks to African (or African-style) clothing, leather goods, masks, figurines, incense and art.

135th Street Area

Central Harlem around 135th Street became active during the Harlem Renaissance as a cultural and social center; it's now the site of a historic district of 19C row houses, several noted restaurants and churches, and an important African-American cultural archive.

Schomburg Center for Research in Black Culture★

515 Malcolm X Blvd. at W. 135th St. ©*Exhibition hall open year-round Tue–Wed noon–8pm, Thu–Fri noon–6pm, Sat 10am–6pm.* ©*Closed major holidays.* ☎*212-491-2200. www.schomburgcenter.org.*

This branch of the New York Public Library system contains one of the world's largest archives relating to black heritage and mounts temporary exhibits on African-American history.

Arthur Schomburg (1874-1938), a black Puerto Rican who was an influential cultural leader during the Harlem Renaissance of the 1920s, began the collection in an effort to discredit the contemporary belief that African Americans had no history. Today more than five million books, photographs, manuscripts, films, recordings and works of art are kept in the center, which is housed in a 1905 landmark library building designed by McKim, Mead and White (restored in 1990) and a modern 1980 annex. In the vestibule you'll find the Pietro Calvi bust of 19C actor **Ira Aldridge** in the role of Othello; and the art installation Rivers, a tribute to Langston Hughes and Arthur Schomburg. **Exhibits** such as a major photographic and audio exploration of the life of Malcolm X are located on the first floor.

A Typical Harlem Building

©iStockphoto.com/Gijs Bekenkamp

Strivers Row★

W. 138th & W. 139th Sts. between Adam Clayton Powell Jr. & Frederick Douglass Blvds.

These two blocks of Georgian and Renaissance Revival houses were developed in 1891. Developer David H. King Jr. commissioned three architects, including Stanford White, to design a residential district here for the well-to-do. What you see here—two blocks of attractive houses on quiet tree-lined streets—is the result. Also known as the St. Nicholas Historic District, the area was dubbed Strivers Row in the 1920s when it became a haven for up-and-coming black professionals. More recent strivers have brought loving attention to the homes (Stanford White's work is 203-267 W. 139th St.). On the avenues capping the rows are a couple of boutiques selling African and African-American designs and the famous restaurant and jazz club Londel's.

Abyssinian Baptist Church

132 Odell Clark Pl. (formerly W. 138th St.) Open Mon–Fri 10am–6pm; services Sun 9am & 11am. ☎212-862-7474. www. abyssinian.org.

This large 1923 Gothic Revival church is home to New York's oldest black congregation, founded in 1808. It became prominent in the 1930s under the leadership of **Adam Clayton Powell Jr.** (1908-72), the flamboyant pastor and civil rights advocate who was elected to Congress in 1944, then stripped of his congressional office for financial improprieties in 1967; he was reinstated two years later. Clippings and photos in the memorial room trace his career.

African-American Walk of Fame

W. 135th St. between Adam Clayton Powell Jr. & Frederick Douglass Blvds.; located midblock on both sides of the street.

Commissioned by the Harlem Chamber of Commerce in 1995 as part of the redesigning of the streetscape of 135th Street, the African-American Walk of Fame is a series of embedded bronze plaques crafted by New York sculptors Otto Neals and Ogundipe Fayoumi. The plaques honor people of African descent who have made significant contributions in music, science, the arts and community service. Start at 236 West 135th Street, walk west toward Frederick Douglass Boulevard, then cross the street. Plaques resume at 219 West 135th Street.

Harlem YMCA

180 & 181 W. 135th St. between Adam Clayton Powell Jr. & Malcolm X Blvds.

Literary greats **Langston Hughes, Richard Wright** and **Ralph Ellison** were only a few of the artists of the 20C to make a home at the Harlem YMCA. The building at 181 West 135th Street opened in 1919. By the late 1920s it had outgrown its new facility. A new imposing Colonial Revival building was constructed across the street and inaugurated in 1932.

Mother A.M.E. Zion

140-148 W. 137th St. between Adam Clayton Powell Jr. & Malcolm X Blvds. ☎212-234-1544.

Mother Zion, as it is affectionately called, is the oldest black church in New York state, founded in 1796 by dissatisfied congregants of the John Street Methodist Church. (A.M.E. stands for African Methodist Episcopal.) As a center of strength for the community, Mother Zion established itself wherever the African-American community would migrate: from Leonard and Church streets (now TriBeCa), to West 10th and Bleecker streets in Greenwich Village, to its final home here on West 137th Street in Harlem, where it's been since 1925. The Gothic Revival structure was designed by George W. Foster Jr., one of the first African-American architects to be registered in New York. During the 19C Mother Zion was a "freedom church"—a station on the Underground Railroad.

North of Harlem

Several interesting sights lie north of Harlem, in the hilly neighborhoods of Inwood, Hamilton Heights and Washington Heights.

Since the following attractions are far-flung and generally not conducive to a walking tour, we have listed subway information with each entry.

A Few Facts

The **George Washington Bridge** spans the Hudson River in one pure line 3,500ft long. The towers are 604ft high, and the supporting cables have a diameter of 36in. The upper level, 250ft above water, holds eight lanes; the lower level is divided into six lanes.

George Washington Bridge★★

🚇 *Subway: A train to 181st St.*
A tremendous feat of engineering, this toll bridge, which links 179th Street in Manhattan to Fort Lee in New Jersey, was, for a number of years, the longest bridge in the world and is still the only 14-lane suspension bridge. Designed by O.H. Amman (an American engineer of Swiss origin, who also conceived the Verrazano-Narrows Bridge) and architect Cass Gilbert, the bridge was opened in 1931, and cost about $59 million. In 1959 the growing volume of traffic required the construction of a lower level, opened in 1962. At the same time, an intricate system of interchanges was installed.

The best view of the George Washington Bridge may be had from the sightseeing boats (*see Sightseeing in Your Stay in the City*) that circle Manhattan, or from the Henry Hudson Parkway along the Hudson River.

Hispanic Society of America★

On Broadway between 155th & 156th Sts.
🚇 *Subway: 1 train to 157th St. or B train to 155th St.* 🕐 *Open Tue–Sat 10am–4:30pm, Sun 1pm–4pm.* 🗣*Tours (45min) are given Sat 2pm.* ☎212-926-2234. www. hispanicsociety.org.

This small but fascinating museum offers a panorama of Spanish civilization from pre-Roman times to the present and has a collection of Old Masters considered by some to be second only to those found at the Prado in Madrid.

Located opposite a bronze statue of El Cid (1927, Anna Hyatt Huntington), the two-story building is part of a cluster of cultural institutions known as **Audubon Terrace**, after naturalist James Audubon, who once had a country house on the site. Charles Pratt Huntington, nephew of railroad heir Archer M. Huntington, commissioned these Neoclassical buildings in the early 20C. Today, the American Academy of Arts and Letters, the country's most prestigious honor society for writers, artists, architects and composers, also has its headquarters here. The society exhibits public art and manuscripts twice a year (call or go online for schedule ☎212-368-5900; www.artsandletters.org).

Designed as an interior courtyard in the Renaissance style, the society's first-floor gallery presents traditional and ritual objects such as choir stalls, exquisite silverware, Paleolithic tools, Renaissance tombstones, silk brocades and altar frontals. Upon entering, notice the

Touring Harlem

Although most parts of Harlem are safe, you may want to limit your visit to daylight hours. If you plan to go to a jazz club or restaurant after dark, take a taxi or car service. Also keep in mind that major avenues have been renamed for Harlem icons. Sixth Avenue above Central Park is known as **Malcolm X Boulevard**, Seventh Avenue as **Adam Clayton Powell Jr. Boulevard**, and Eighth Avenue as **Frederick Douglass Boulevard**.

To fully grasp Harlem's significance, many visitors take **guided tours** of Harlem. Two companies to consider: **Harlem Spirituals, Inc.** (☎ 212-391-0900; www.harlem spirituals.com), which offers an evening visit of Harlem that includes soul food and jazz, a Sunday visit with a gospel and soul-food brunch, and a Wednesday-morning visit of Harlem with gospel (*all tours depart year-round from office at 690 Eighth Ave. between W. 43rd & 44th Sts.; reservations required*). The **Municipal Art Society** also conducts walking and bus tours of the neighborhood on an occasional basis, as well as private tours by appointment (☎ 212-935-3960; *recorded information* ☎ 212-439-1049; www.mas.org).

Address Book

WHERE TO EAT

Harlem has a number of excellent restaurants and cafes. Here are a few of the more established ones.

$$ The Cotton Club – *656 W. 125th St. between 12th Ave. & the West Side Hwy.* ☎ *888-640-7980. www.cottonclub-newyork.com.* A slice of old Harlem, the Cotton Club hosted some of the biggest names in jazz in the 1920s: Duke Ellington's band, Lena Horne, Josephine Baker, Cab Calloway and Louis Armstrong and many others. Today in addition to its Monday-night swing dances, the club has jazz and blues shows with a buffet dinner Thursdays through Saturdays. Be sure to make a reservation.

$ Home Sweet Harlem Cafe – *270 W. 135th St.* ☎ *212-926-9616.* Situated along the Walk of Fame, this cozy cafe serves up healthy fare like veggie burgers, smoothies and teas, as well as coffee and muffins.

$$$ Londel's Supper Club – *2620 Frederick Douglass Blvd. between W. 139th & W. 140th Sts.* ☎ *212-234-6114. www.londelsrestaurant.com.* Nestled in the Strivers Row area, this upscale Harlem restaurant has become a meeting place for local celebrities and political figures. Ask for the house specialty, Atlantic salmon in a champagne sauce, or the delicious blackened catfish. Londel's has live jazz on tap on Friday and Saturday evenings.

$$ Sylvia's Soul Food Restaurant – *Lenox Ave. between W. 126th & W. 127th Sts.* ☎ *212-996-0660. www.sylviassoulfood.com.* Sylvia Woods has delighted diners with her Southern food and hospitality since 1962, and has seen her business grow immensely as a result (regulars' waistlines have likely done the same). Order the delicious greens, candied yams and southern fried chicken, and take home some of Sylvia's famed cornbread mix or barbecue sauce. For a special treat, come for the Sunday gospel brunch *(12:30pm–4pm).*

---

two life-size portraits by 18C Spanish artist Francisco de Goya, including one of the Duchess of Alba. To the right of the gallery, the 15C Mudejar door is surrounded by colorful tiles. The Sorolla room *(far right)* features paintings by Sorolla y Bastida titled Provinces of Spain. A research library is located on the first floor.

The second-floor balustrade contains a earthenware, ceramics, metalwork, porcelain, lusterware and jewelry displayed in glass cases. Portraits by renowned artists El Greco, Morales, Ribera, Velázquez and Goya line the walls.

Morris-Jumel Mansion★

W. 160th St. & Edgecombe Ave. MTA *Subway: 1 train to W. 157th St. or C train to 163rd St.* ⏰*Open year-round Wed–Sun 10am–4pm.* ⏰*Closed major holidays.* 👝*$4.* ☎*212-923-8008. www.morrisjumel.org.*

Occupying a hilltop site with a view of the Harlem valley, this Georgian mansion is the only colonial home to survive in northern Manhattan. Today it's part of a historic district that includes 20 wood-frame row houses built in the 1880.

This mansion has an intriguing history. Col. **Roger Morris** of England built the house (originally known as Mount Morris) in 1765, but a decade later he was driven out by Patriots to England, where his Loyalist sentiments were better appreci-

---

Harlem Open Artist Studio Tour

For two days each spring, nearly 100 Harlem artists open their doors to the public, providing a window into the artistic process and a unique shopping opportunity – you can bypass dealers and retailers and purchase works directly from the artist. Both browsers and buyers are welcome. A shuttle tour service is provided. *For a schedule, event map, and other information, go to www.hoast.org.*

©Shea Dean

ated. During the Battle of Harlem Heights in 1776, the estate served as Gen. George Washington's headquarters; in 1810 it passed to **Stephen Jumel**, a wealthy French wine merchant. Jumel's wife, Eliza Bowen, was never fully accepted in New York society, and the Jumels set sail for France in 1815, where they traveled more comfortably in Napoleonic circles. Jumel died in 1832, and a year later his widow returned and married **Aaron Burr**, the third vice president of the US. After a year of marriage, the couple separated. Their divorce was granted on the day Burr died, in 1836.

While constructed of brick, the mansion features wood facades, corner quoins and a two-story Federal-style portico. The **interior** is particularly noteworthy

for the rear drawing room on the first floor, possibly the first octagonal room in the US. The front parlor contains Madame Jumel's fashionable Empire-style settee and chairs and French chandelier. On the second floor, Madame Jumel's bedroom and dressing room feature Empire furniture that once belonged to the Bonaparte family; note especially the 19C mahogany slipper chairs.

Hamilton Grange National Memorial

287 Convent Ave. at W. 142nd St. MTA *Subway: 1 or A train to 145th St.* Closed indefinitely. ☎212-283-5154. www.nps. gov/hagr.

Designed in 1801 by John McComb Jr. (architect of City Hall), this Federal-style

---

Spirituals

By the end of the 18C, spirituals, often referred to as slave songs, were becoming an integral part of the African-American worship experience and an important form of storytelling. Although the harmonies are based on Protestant hymns, the rhythms reflect ancestral African musical traditions such as the call and response, in which a primary singer's verses are echoed by a chorus. While text and harmonies are simple, emotion fills the core of every song; melodies are lined with "blue" notes (flat notes) that would later become an important part of blues and jazz compositions. Some of the best known spirituals are "Nobody Knows the Trouble I've Seen," "Go Down, Moses" and "Joshua Fit the Battle of Jericho."

clapboard house anchors a historic district that stretches between Amsterdam and St. Nicholas Avenues from West 140th to West 145th Streets.

Hamilton Grange was **Alexander Hamilton**'s country estate and his principal residence when he was killed in a duel with Aaron Burr in 1804. In 1889 the house was moved about 100 yards to its current location and altered; the rear facade now faces the street. The building was later used as a rectory for St. Luke's Church and is now owned by the National Park Service.

Historic District

The picturesque gabled row houses on Hamilton Terrace and Convent Avenue include some unusual Dutch and Flemish Revival dwellings dating from the 1880s, when the district was developed as a suburb for prosperous New Yorkers. Note St. Luke's Episcopal Church (285 Convent Ave.), designed in the Romanesque Revival style in 1892. Just south of Hamilton Heights lies City College's campus, begun in 1897. The star pupil, architecturally, is the 1907 Shepard Hall (W. 140th St between St. Nicholas Terrace & Convent Ave.), which resembles a Gothic cathedral. It is clad with Manhattan schist excavated when the subway was built.

Inwood Hill Park

MTA Subway: A train to 207th St.

It is unwise to walk in the park alone.

Set at the northwestern tip of Manhat-

Dining Room, Morris-Jumel Mansion

Courtesy Morris-Jumel Mansion

tan, this park is separated from Fort Tryon Park by a ravine dotted with apartment houses. Wooded and hilly, the terrain seems to have altered very little since the Algonquins inhabited the area. During the Revolution, British and Hessian troops were quartered here. Today the park is quite empty except Sundays when New Yorkers picnic in the park. East of the park stands **Dyckman Farmhouse Museum** (W. 204th St. & Broadway; open year-round Wed–Sat 11am–4pm, Sun noon–4pm; closed major holidays; $1; 212-304-9422; www.dyckmanfarmhouse.org), the only extant 18C Dutch Colonial farmhouse in Manhattan. Appointed with period Dutch and French furniture, and bordered by a charming herb garden and a smokehouse, the structure illustrates life in colonial America.

John James Audubon, and Lewis and Clark. An equestrian statue (1940, James Earle Fraser) featuring Roosevelt flanked by a Native American and an African American, stands sentinel at the entrance to the hall.

Second Floor – Posed with imagination, protecting its young from an allosaurus, a replica of a **barosaurus** looms over the Roosevelt rotunda. Rising to five stories (50ft), the skeleton of this Jurassic herbivore is a resin-and-foam replica of the original fossilized bones, which are too fragile to be mounted for display.

Just west of the rotunda is the spectacular **Hall of African Mammals**★ dedicated to Carl Akeley, who revolutionized museum display with his realistic dioramas in the early 20C. Highlighted by a herd of African elephants on the alert, dioramas present zebras, antelopes, gorillas, lions and gazelles in their natural surroundings. In the galleries on the third-floor level of this hall, other dioramas depict various species of monkeys, rhinoceroses, leopards and hyenas.

The **Hall of African Peoples** traces the development of complex human culture on the African continent. The **Hall of Mexico and Central America** displays an outstanding pre-Columbian collection. Of special interest are the exhibits related to the Aztec and Mayan civilizations, gold ornaments of the ancient Americas and stone and clay sculptures from central Veracruz. The **Hall of South American Peoples** exhibits Andean and Amazonian treasures, including the 2,500-year-old Paracas mantle, that are testimony to the religious beliefs and social organization of the ancient, recently extinct and existing cultures of this continent.

The **Hall of Asian Peoples**★ features a comprehensive exhibit of life from prehistoric times to the late 19C, when Western technology began to influence the traditions of the Orient.

First Floor – A seagoing Haida war canoe from the Queen Charlotte Islands in British Columbia, Canada, dominates the foyer. Carved out of one piece of cedar in 1878, the watercraft can hold more than 30 passengers. The **Hall of Northwest Coast Indians**★ presents superb totem poles, American Indian and Inuit tools and handicrafts. The newly opened **Hall of Human Origins**★ strives to place humans in the context of the natural world with displays on fossils and genomic research.

A 34-ton meteorite fragment found in Greenland, in 1895, forms the focal point of the **Hall of Meteorites**★. The hall incorporates more than 130 meteorite specimens in its investigaton of the nature and history of meteorites and their role in unlocking the history of the solar system. Among the meteorite "greatest hits" documented are the one that produced a 185mi crater in the Yucatan peninsula some 65 million years ago and is credited by some with killing off the land dinosaurs.

In the **Halls of Minerals and Gems**★★, you may feast your eyes on more than 4,000 specimens of rocks, minerals and gems, including rubies, emeralds and diamonds. Here you'll find the Star of India, the world's largest star sapphire (weight: 563 carats).

On the opposite side of the building (Central Park West), and still on the first floor, the **Hall of Biodiversity**★ bustles with an array of life-forms intended to convey the variety and interactivity of life on earth. The exhibit also communicates a strong environmental message about human impact on biodiversity worldwide. The west wall displays 1,500 specimens and models that illustrate the

Taking a Break

Take a break for a meal at one of the museum's four eateries. The **Museum Food Court** (lower level, open daily 11am–4:45pm) serves all-American barbecue specials and classic sandwiches. The new **Cafe on One** (1st floor; open daily 11am–4:45pm) has gourmet fare like beet and goat cheese salad and foccacia sandwiches. Sandwiches and salads are also available at the **Starlight Cafe** (1st floor; open daily 11am–4:45pm). A new **Juice Bar** (lower level annex, near subway entrance; open daily 11am–4:45pm) offers fresh fruit drinks as well as coffee, soda, and sweets.

©Scott Frances - American Museum of Natural History

Barosaurus skeleton

wonders of biodiversity. The heart of the exhibit, however, is the walk-through **diorama** of the Dzanga-Sangha rain forest in Africa. This lush setting includes 160 replica species and more than 500,000 carefully crafted leaves.

An immense (94ft long) model of a blue whale, suspended in a dive position, dominates the two-story **Hall of Ocean Life**★. Shimmering lights and an underwater soundscape "immerse" visitors in the whale's ocean home. Traditional dioramas – notably the two-story Andros Coral Reef – have been restored and im-proved. On the mezzanine you'll find eight high-tech exhibits that explore ocean ecosystems (such as estuaries, polar seas, the deep-sea floor).

Films on different subjects are shown in the **IMAX Theater**, a 996-seat auditorium equipped with a gigantic movie screen four stories high and 66ft wide.

Third Floor – The **Hall of Reptiles and Amphibians** features the world's largest living lizard, the 10ft Komodo dragon. The **Hall of Primates** displays animals from the same biological order as man, beginning with the tree shrew. To the west of the primates, displays on the lifestyles of the Eastern Woodlands and Plains Indians include model houses, weapons, tools and utensils. In the **Hall of North American Birds**, you'll find a variety of birds from all corners of the country, including the wild turkey, which

Benjamin Franklin wanted to designate America's national bird.

The **Hall of the Pacific Peoples**★, inspired by the work and ideas of Dr. Margaret Mead (1901-78), contains exhibits related to six cultural areas of the Pacific: Australia, Indonesia, the Philippines, Melanesia, Micronesia and Polynesia. A large display case near the center of the hall holds sacred masks, carved figures and boldly decorated shields illustrating the rich and diverse art of the peoples of the Sepik River basin.

Fourth Floor – *Begin your visit in the orientation center (☝ see green box).* Completed in 1996, the six **fossil halls**★★ on the top floor represent a visual and intellectual tour de force, but visitors should be prepared for an overwhelming experience. Curators have attempted a stunning departure from the usual presentation of this type of material by arranging the

---

☺ A Bit of Advice ☺

When you visit the Fourth Floor, be sure to stop first at the **Wallach Orientation Center**. The fossil halls are dense with information, making a preliminary visit to the orientation center essential. At the center, you'll preview the layout of the halls and learn what the key concepts are within each. You can also view a video presentation titled *The Evolution of Vertebrates* (12min).

Rose Center for Earth and Space

familiar fossil remains and interpretive exhibits along a cladogram, or "branching evolutionary tree." Such an arrangement is intended to depict evolutionary relationships among contemporaneous creatures as well as through time.

Beginning with the **Hall of Vertebrate Origins**, you can navigate along the branches of the tree, following the development of vertebrates from the earliest jawless fishes to dinosaurs and mammals. As the cladogram progresses, "advanced" features emerge (jaws, four limbs, grasping hands, and so on) to create the branching effect that furthers evolution. Specimen alcoves on either side of the main branch explore groups of related animals in detail. The museum has the largest collection of fossil vertebrates in the world, and visitors scouting out skeletal remains will not be disappointed. In the **Hall of Saurischian Dinosaurs** (distinguished by grasping hands), huge apatosaurus and Tyrannosaurus rex tower over tiny Archaeopteryx lithographica. In the **Hall of Ornithischian Dinosaurs** (whose pubis bones point backward), note the "mummy," really a fossilized imprint of a duck-billed dinosaur carcass. Discovered in 1908, the fossil is so detailed that it has even preserved the texture of the animal's skin. Together the two dinosaur halls present more than 100 specimens, 85 percent of which are real fossils. The final wing showcases "Mammals and Their Extinct Relatives," including ancient mammoths, mastodons, saber-toothed cats and giant sloths.

Rose Center for Earth and Space★★

W. 81st St., on the museum's north side. ⏰Hours are the same as the museum except the first Fri of each month, when center is open until 8:45pm. Space show every 30min 10:30am–4:30pm; first Fri of every month 10:30am–7pm. ⊜ Admission is included in museum ticket; space show tickets (without museum admission) are available in-person only ($18.50 adults, $10 children); package deals listed above. ⌕ Audio tours (75min; free with admission) are available. Advance tickets:☎212-769-5200. www.amnh.org.

Accessible via the museum *(1st and 2nd floors)*, or through its own arched entrance on West 81st Street, the center blends cutting-edge science with high-impact visuals to describe the mysteries of the cosmos.

The thrilling 30min **star show★★★**, put on inside the Hayden Sphere, is not to be missed. The most advanced of its kind, it brilliantly combines education and entertainment in an eye-popping journey to the edge of the observable universe, using 3-D maps developed with the help of NASA.

Outside the theater, a 400ft-long display, Scales of the Universe, demonstrates the enormity of space with scale models, touch screens and text panels. Dangling from the ceiling above it are models of the planets of our solar system–all except Pluto. In a controversial decision, the center has demoted the ninth planet to asteroid status. A presentation *(2min)* on the Big Bang uses lasers and SurroundSound to conjure the birth of the universe. Upon exiting, visitors descend a spiral ramp to the first-floor **Hall of Planet Earth**★, where exhibits focus on geologic and climatic features of our own planet. Down on the lower-level, the **Hall of the Universe**★, hums with up-to-the-minute video from the Hubble Telescope, models of cosmic phenomena; and artifacts including the 15-ton Willamette Meteorite.

The Cloisters★★★
MTA SUBWAY: A TRAIN TO 190TH ST.
OR BUS NO. 4 TO FORT TRYON PARK–THE CLOISTERS

Isolated on a hill in Fort Tryon Park, the Cloisters re-creates a fortified monastery. Housed in four reconstructed medieval cloisters and part of a fifth, its collections, which include sculptures, tapestries and other objects spanning over centuries, enjoy an unrivaled reputation among lovers of medieval art.

▸ **Orient Yourself:** Though it looks far on a map, the Cloisters is only about a 30min subway ride from Midtown Manhattan. From the 190th Street subway station, it's a lovely 15min walk through Fort Tryon Park to the Cloisters. You may also hop aboard the M4 bus at the traffic circle outside the subway station and take it one stop north to the museum.

🕒 **Organizing Your Time:** Plan about 2hrs to see the entire museum. We recommend purchasing the audio guide (🎧$7), which provides valuable historical commentary.

Kids **Especially for Kids:** Though the Cloisters is a bit dour for most kids, there's an enjoyable Family Tour option on the audio guide, offering medieval music and stories to go along with works in the museum.

☺ **Don't Miss:** The world-famous **Unicorn tapestries**.

A Bit of History

The Collection – The core of the collection is made up of medieval sculptures and architectural remains assembled by the American sculptor **George Grey Barnard** (1863-1938), during his frequent trips to Europe. Opened to the public in

Pontaut Chapter House

The Metropolitan Museum of Art, Cloisters Collection

THE CLOISTERS
MAIN FLOOR

West Terrace

Gothic Chapel

Pontaut Chapter House

Langon Chapel

Saint-Guilhem

ground floor

Nine Heroes Tapestries Room

Cuxa

Cloister

Unicorn Tapestries Hall

Cloister

Romanesque Hall

Fuentidueña Chapel

Boppard Room

Late Gothic Hall

Main Hall

Books and Reproductions

Campin Room

Froville Arcade

0   50 ft
0   15m

N

1914 in a brick building on Fort Washington Avenue, the collection included sections of the cloisters of Saint-Michel-de-Cuxa, Saint-Guilhem-le-Désert, Bonnefont-en-Comminges, and Trie, all from southern France.

In 1925 **John D. Rockefeller Jr.** granted a large sum to the Metropolitan Museum of Art to purchase the Barnard collection. The Rockefellers also donated more than 40 sculptures from their collection. Five years later Rockefeller presented the City of New York with an estate he owned in what is now Fort Tryon Park, stipulating that the northern part be reserved for the new Cloisters. Designed by **Charles Collens** of Boston, also responsible for Riverside Church, the complex was completed in 1938. The museum remains administratively a part of the Metropolitan Museum of Art.

The Setting – Covering 62 acres of wooded hills above the Hudson River, **Fort Tryon Park**★★ was landscaped by Frederick Law Olmsted Jr. If you're here on a temperate day, stop to visit the gorgeous **Heather Garden**★★ just south of the museum. The eponymous fort, since demolished, was the last fort to resist the British invasion of British invasion of Manhattan during the American Revolution. The fight involved the first woman soldier of the Revolution, Margaret Corbin.

Visit

🕐 Open Mar–Oct Tue–Sun 9:30am–5:15pm. Rest of the year Tue–Sun 9:30am–4:45pm. 🕐 Closed Jan 1, Thanksgiving Day & Dec 25. ⊚ $20 suggested donation. 👣 Free guided tours available Tue–Fri & Sun 3pm; garden tours Tue–Sun 1pm (May–Oct); self-guided audio tour ⊚$7. 🅿 ✕ (May–Oct). ☎212-923-3700. www.metmuseum.org.

The central structure, containing a group of cloisters, chapels and halls, is arranged around a square tower inspired by that of Saint-Michel-de-Cuxa in southern France. As you enter on the east side of the building, note the driveway paved with Belgian blocks – originally from New York streets – reminiscent of European cobblestones; a functional portcullis guards the staff parking lot.

To fully appreciate the treasures at the Cloisters, we highly recommend taking a guided tour or buying the self-guided audio tour. Following are a few highlights you should be sure not to miss.

Main Floor

👁 See floor plan.

Fuentidueña Chapel★ – This "chapel" is largely devoted to Spanish Romanesque art. Suspended from the ceiling of the apse hangs a well-preserved 12C crucifix from the Convent of Santa Clara at Astudillo in Spain.

Romanesque Hall★ – The entrance features a round-arched doorway characteristic of the Romanesque style. On the left side, the capitals are carved with graceful birds feeding on acanthus plants. The capitals on the right bear carvings of imaginary animals surmounted by a delicate acanthus motif.

Saint-Guilhem Cloister★– The covered walkway contains columns and capitals from the Benedictine abbey of Saint-Guilhem-le-Désert, near Montpellier, France. The fountain in the center of the cloister was once a Romanesque capital in the Church of Saint-Sauveur in the Auvergne region of France.

Cuxa Cloister ★★ – Although this is the museum's largest cloister, it is only one quarter the size of the original structure. The various elements came from the Benedictine monastery of Saint-Michel-de-Cuxa, near Prades, in the French Pyrenees. Abandoned during the French Revolution, the monastery was sold, but in 1913 Barnard was able to bring together about half of the original Romanesque capitals, 12 columns, 25 bases and 7 arches. Rose-colored Languedoc marble was cut from original quarries to complete the reconstruction. Both

medieval and modern plants are grown in the garden. A lovely space.

Early Gothic Hall★ – This recently renovated room contains 13C–14C French stained glass and sculpture, including an imposing painted sandstone statue of the Virgin (c.1250) that once stood in the Strasbourg Cathedral.

Nine Heroes Tapestries Room★★ – Contained within this dimly lit room are several **tapestries** (1410) that are among the oldest in existence, along with the Apocalypse tapestries in Angers, France. The theme of the Nine Heroes, very popular in the Middle Ages, includes three pagans (Hector, Alexander, Julius Caesar), three Hebrews (David, Joshua, Judas Maccabeus) and three Christians (Arthur, Charlemagne, Godfrey of Bouillon). Their feminine counterparts were the Nine Heroines.

Unicorn Tapestries Hall★★★ – The **Unicorn tapestries** are among the most exceptional of the golden age of tapestry, which flourished at the end of the 15C and the beginning of the 16C. The set of seven tapestries originally hung in the Château de Verteuil in Charente (southwestern France), the home of the well-known La Rochefoucauld family. Six of the tapestries were acquired by John D. Rockefeller Jr. in 1922; the seventh was added in 1938.

THE CLOISTERS
GROUND FLOOR

Gothic Chapel

Bonnefont

Glass
Gallery

Cloister

Trie

Cloister

Treasury

Main Floor

Postern
Gate

0   50 ft
0   15 m

New Leaf Café

1 Margaret Corbin Dr., in Fort Tryon Park. Open year-round Tue–Sat noon–3pm & 6–10pm (plus Sat 9:30–11am), Sun 11am–4pm & 5:30–9:30pm. 212-568-5323. www.nyrp.org/newleaf. Couple your visit to the Cloisters with a meal at this lovely restaurant just a short walk from the museum. Opened in 2001, it's housed in a 1930s-era stone park building that's been renovated to look both sleek and inviting, with high arched windows and rustic furniture, though a seat at one of the patio tables, surrounded by the lush foliage of Fort Tryon Park, is irresistible on a summer day. Creative fare includes pan-roasted salmon and handmade pappardelle, though the burger's always a good bet as well. All proceeds go to the upkeep of the park.

Be sure to listen to all of the audio guide commentary on these tapestries; the story they tell is fascinating.

Boppard Room★★ – The six stained-glass panels you see here were created for the Carmelite church (late 15C) in the town of Boppard, Germany. There is also an ornate Spanish alabaster altarpiece (15C) and a striking brass eagle lectern (16C) from Belgium.

Campin Room★★ – This room contains the famous **Annunciation Triptych** by 15C Flemish artist Robert Campin. The central panel represents the Annunciation. The side panels depict the donors, on the left, and on the right, St. Joseph in his workshop; notice the mousetrap on St. Joseph's workbench and the painstakingly reproduced details of the town square in the background.

Ground Floor

Gothic Chapel★★ – This structure provides a superb setting for a collection of tomb effigies and slabs. Notice the effigy of Jean d'Alluye (13C) and four monumental Catalan sarcophagi of the Counts of Urgel (14C). The tombs come from the Premonstratensian monastery of Santa Maria de Bellpuig de las Avellanas, north of Lérida in Spain. The apsidal windows are now glazed with 14C Austrian stained glass.

Bonnefont Cloister★★ – This pretty cloister, with views of the tower, the park and the Hudson River, contains elements (13-14C) of the former Cistercian abbey at Bonnefont-en-Comminges in southern France as well as an **herb garden** with 250 species of plants cultivated in the Middle Ages.

Trie Cloister – Because of its small size, this cloister induces the serenity associated with a monastery. In the summer it hosts a small outdoor cafe.

Glass Gallery – This room is named for the roundels and panels of stained glass (15-16C) representing scenes from the Old and New Testaments. Small works of art are displayed here; note especially the intricate lindenwood sculpture of a seated bishop by famed artist Tilman Riemenschneider.

Treasury – The Cloisters' collection of smaller objects of exceptionally fine quality is displayed in this recently updated gallery. The outstanding piece is a walrus-ivory cross from the 12C, the so-called Cloisters Cross, carved with great attention to detail.

Also of interest is a rosary bead of box-wood with a tiny representation of the Passion inside (16C, South Lowlands). Be sure to peer under the cloth covers over the glass cases in the anteroom, where you'll find two magnificent *Belles Heures* (Books of Hours) that once belonged to Jean, Duke of Berry, and an outstanding collection of hand-painted 15C playing cards.

The Frick Collection ★★★

One of the world's most distinguished small museums, The Frick Collection offers a unique opportunity to view an exceptional trove of Old Masters, furnishings and decorative arts in the luxurious confines of a sumptuous mansion. There are more than 1,100 works in all, ranging from the Renaissance to the 19C, most chosen by Henry Clay Frick himself.

▶ **Orient Yourself:** Museum maps are available at the admission desk at the end of the Reception Hall. Pick up your free audio tour in the Entrance Hall; packed with insightful commentary on dozens of works throughout the museum, it's an absolutely essential part of a visit. An audiovisual presentation (20min), shown in the Music Room every hour on the half-hour, describes the arc of Frick's collecting career.

🕐 **Organizing Your Time:** Plan several hours for your visit. As there is no cafe here, you may want to eat first. Ask at the admission desk for a list of nearby restaurants.

👓 **Don't Miss:** Rembrandt's arresting *Self-Portrait* (West Gallery), Ingres' beguiling *Comtesse d'Haussonville* (North Hall), Fragonard's monumental *Progress of Love* (Fragonard Room), and Bellini's masterful *St Francis in the Desert* (Living Hall).

A Bit of History

Pittsburgh coke and steel industrialist **Henry Clay Frick** (1849-1919) began collecting works of art in 1880, when he took his first trip to Europe with his friend **Andrew Mellon**, the primary benefactor of the National Gallery of Art. First concentrating on 18C English paintings, Frick later ventured into sculpture —bronzes in particular—then furniture, enamels, porcelain and Old Masters. In 1913 he commissioned **Thomas Hastings**, architect of the New York Public Library, to design this 40-room mansion for his family and his art collection with an eye toward opening it to the public after his death. Though Frick died in 1919, the opening did not take place

Fragonard Room

©The Frick Collection, New York. Photograph: Richard Bryand/ Arcaid London until 1935, four years after his wife's death.

Today the Frick Collection contains works ranging from the 14C to the 19C, many arranged in eclectic thematic ensembles, rather than by school or period, simply because Frick liked them this way. Such quirks are part of the grand institution's fusty genius.

Visit

&. ⏱Open year-round Tue–Sat 10am–6pm, Sun 11am–5pm. ⏱Closed major holidays. 🎫 $15; arrive before 1pm on Sun and pay what you wish. 🧒 Children under 10 not admitted; children 10-16 must be accompanied by an adult. 🎧 Audio tours available at no charge. ☎212-288-0700. www.frick.org.

Highlights of the collection are listed below in clockwise fashion from the entrance hall.

Anteroom★ – This room features Jan van Eyck's *Virgin and Child with Saints and Donor* (1440–41), composed in the last year of the artist's life and completed by his assistants, and El Greco's *Purification of the Temple* (c.1600), a small canvas stuffed with action and intrigue.

Dining Room★ – The spacious room includes portraits by Hogarth, Romney and Reynolds, and a masterpiece by Gainsborough, *The Mall in St. James's Park* (1783).

Fragonard Room★★★ – Eleven decorative paintings by Jean-Honoré Fragonard (1732-1806) in this recently refurbished gallery. Four of the large panels were commissioned by Madame du Barry, a mistress of Louis XV. They recount the various stages of a romantic encounter: *The Pursuit, The Meeting, The Lover Crowned* and *Love Letters*. Exquisite furnishings add to the total effect.

South Hall★ – Jean-Henri Riesener, the premier cabinetmaker during the reign of Louis XVI, designed the opulent dropfront secretary and chest of drawers seen here for Queen Marie Antoinette, possibly for her apartment in the Tuileries. Also note the two small canvases by the 17C Dutch master Vermeer; *Officer and Laughing Girl* (c.1655–60) is particularly remarkable for its radiant luminosity.

Living Hall★★ – Rich walnut paneling and elaborate plaster moldings complement the 16C masterpieces found here.

Henry Clay Frick counted two of these among his three favorites: Giovanni Bellini's *St. Francis in the Desert* (c.1480), showing the saint awestruck amid a mysteriously lit, finely rendered landscape, and Hans Holbein the Younger's searing portrait of the great humanist scholar *Sir Thomas More*, beheaded for treason in 1535.

Library – Dominated by a portrait of Henry Clay Frick over the mantel, this wood-paneled room houses an array of books, as well as English paintings from the 18C and 19C. Tucked in a corner is one of Gilbert Stuart's many portraits of George Washington, likely purchased for patriotic rather than artistic reasons.

North Hall★★ – Above the superb blue marble side table by Belanger – one of the costliest works produced under Louis XVI – hangs Ingres' renowned portrait of the *Comtesse d'Haussonville* (1845), granddaughter of the great Madame de Stael. Pictured here in her twenties, the countess is already a mother of three yet still full of smoldering sensuality and ambition. Ingres worked on the portrait for three years, after seven false starts and countless preparatory sketches. Small works by Degas and Monet hang nearby.

West Gallery★★★ – The largest gallery in the house, a vast skylit hall, contains an astonishing mix of monumental landscapes and portraits from the 16C to the 19C. Rembrandt was only 52 when he painted this heart-stopping *Self-Portrait* (1658), yet he appears far older, even ageless, with his huge hands, godlike robes and unfathomable eyes. Vermeer's luminous *Mistress and Maid* (c.1665–70) shows a domestic moment full of mysterious import, highlighted by the artist's signature golden light. The painting was Frick's last purchase.

Enamel Room★ – Several Italian Primitive and Renaissance works form an appropriate backdrop to the splendid collection of Limoges painted enamels of the 16C and 17C. The most striking painting is *St. John the Evangelist* by Piero della Francesca, the saint's jewel-encrusted robe contrasting sharply with his ashen face and bare feet.

Oval Room – Renoir's delightful *Mother and Children*, displayed at the Second Impressionist Exhibition of 1876, hangs before a well-placed bench. Take a seat and enjoy it; the audio commentary on this one is particularly witty.

East Gallery – Works in this gallery rotate more frequently than do other works in the museum. It is fairly certain, however, that the four sumptuous full-length portraits by Whistler on either end of the hall will remain on long-term display.

Garden Court – One of the most delightful parts of the museum, the court provides a cool haven in summertime thanks to its marble floor, fountain and pool, tropical plants and flowers. Originally used as a carriage court, the space was redesigned by John Russell Pope during the 1935 renovation.

Living Hall, The Frick Collection

Metropolitan Museum of Art★★★

FIFTH AVE. BETWEEN E. 80TH & E. 84TH STS.
🚇 4, 5, 6 TRAIN TO 86TH ST.
MAP P 201

Richly endowed and supported, the Metropolitan Museum of Art (informally called the Met) is the largest museum in the Western hemisphere and the pride of New York. It houses a veritable encyclopedia of the visual arts, with works on display from prehistory to the present, and draws more than five million visitors a year.

▶ **Orient Yourself:** The main entrance to the Met is on Fifth Avenue at 82nd Street. You enter the Great Hall, in the center of which is an Information Desk stuffed with literature, including a detailed floor plan and a schedule for the day's tours and events; volunteers are on hand to answer questions. There are admission booths and checkrooms on either side of the hall. The Audio Guide desk is at the rear of the hall, to the left of the Grand Staircase.

🕐 **Organizing Your Time:** Plan at least 4hrs to see the Met, more if you're a real art lover. To avoid the biggest crowds, visit on a weekday and arrive early. We highly recommend purchasing the Audio Guide (🎧$7), which provides valuable commentary on hundreds of works throughout the museum, including special exhibitions.

🧒 **Especially for Kids:** The Family Audio Guide – included in the regular Audio Guide – is a series of commentaries on artworks throughout the museum especially geared for children ages 6–12. Ask for a map of these selections at the Audio Guide desk. Programs for younger children – such as sketching and storytelling – are offered daily in the new Uris Center for Education on the Ground Floor; ask at the Information Desk for details.

☺ **Don't Miss:** The Temple of Dendur in the Egyptian Wing, the newly expanded Green and Roman galleries, and the phenomenal trove of Dutch Masters in the European Paintings galleries, and the view from the Roof Garden.

Entrance to The Met

Brigitta L. House - MICHELIN

A Bit of History

In 1866 **John Jay**, grandson of America's first chief justice of the Supreme Court, conceived the idea for a grand, European-style art museum in New York. Firebrand newspaper editor William Cullen Bryant took up the charge and enticed the culturally sophisticated Union League Club to head up just such an institution. The Met first opened in 1870 in the former Dodsworth's Dancing Academy at Fifth Avenue and 53rd Street. But already plans were in motion to build a permanent facility. Fortunately, Frederick Law Olmsted and Calvert Vaux had left room for a museum on the east side of Central Park, at 81st Street. Vaux and architect Jacob Wrey Mould designed for the site a Gothic-style, redbrick edifice that has long since been engulfed by major additions and expansions.

The Building – The Met's signature Beaux-Arts facade, designed by Richard Morris Hunt, was completed in 1902, while the north and south side wings, designed by McKim, Mead and White, were completed in 1911 and 1913 respectively. The architectural firm Roche, Dinkeloo & Assocs. designed many of the more recent additions, most notably the 1975 Robert Lehman Wing and the 1978 Sackler Wing, with its dramatic Temple of Dendur. The Petrie European Sculpture Court, a sky-lit, sun-drenched area dotted with benches, greenery and statuary, was inaugurated in 1990. A three-part renovation and expansion of the Greek and Roman Art galleries was completed in April 2007, with the opening of a 40,000sq ft Roman sculpture court and mezzanine gallery for Etruscan art. In all, the Met boasts about two million feet of exhibition space, with more being added all the time as the museum constantly reorganizes and expands to accommodate its growing collection.

The Collection – The seed of the Met's immense collection was planted in 1877 with Catherine L. Wolfe's donation of 143 paintings, representing the Dutch and Flemish schools. Ten years later railroad financier Henry Gurdon Marquand gave 37 European paintings to the museum, including Vermeer's masterpiece *Young Woman with a Water Pitcher*. Louisine

Havemeyer's collection of French Impressionists was added in 1929 and Muriel Kallis Steinberg Newman's definitive collection of American Abstract Expressionist canvases arrived in 2005. Thanks to such generous gifts, as well as a large endowment that allows the museum to purchase some of the most prized artworks in the world, the Met has built a cache of nearly three million objects, a fourth of which are on display at any given time. In addition, the Met regularly organizes blockbuster temporary shows exploring a single great artist's oeuvre. Among those who've recently received such royal treatment are David Hockney, Jasper Johns, van Gogh, and Rembrandt.

Visit

 ♿ ⏰ *Open year-round Tue–Sun 9:30am–5:30pm (Fri & Sat until 9pm). Open holiday Mondays: Columbus Day, Christmas week, Martin Luther King Jr. Day, Presidents' Day & Memorial Day.* ⏰ *Closed Jan 1, Thanksgiving Day & Dec 25.* ⏎ *Suggested donation $20 (includes same-day admission to the Cloisters.* ⏎ *Guided tours (1hr) available in 10 languages.* 🄺🄸🄳🅂 🄿 ✕ ☎212-879-5500. www.metmuseum.org.*

Egyptian Art ★★★

First floor.

The Met's 36,000-piece Egyptian art collection is one of the finest and most comprehensive outside of Egypt, a true treasure trove of priceless art and artifacts. More than half of the holdings were provided by the museum's own archaeologists, who spent 30 years in Egypt at the beginning of the 20C excavating some of the richest sites. Today almost all of the Met's exquisitely painted coffins, figurines, jewelry, stelae, and tombs are on view.

Some 69,000sq ft of gallery space is arranged chronologically from the Pre-dynastic period (c.5000-3000 BC) through 30 dynasties (c.3100-342 BC) and the eras of foreign influence to late antiquity (c.700 AD). A walk through the galleries therefore provides an illustrated history of the Ancient Egyptians. At the same time, the works stand on their own as magnificent examples of art and design. Begin your expedition in gallery 1, an orientation space that presents background information, a timeline and a wall map, along with Predynastic artifacts and sculpture, then proceed through the exhibition.

The following are highlights:

Mastaba of Perneb – Old Kingdom. While the pyramid is the best-known form of Egyptian tomb architecture, mastabas (offering chapels) like this one, which was the final resting place for a dignitary c.2450 BC, were popular among the elite. Go inside to see the elaborate hieroglyphs.

Meketre Models – Dynasty 12. This cache of models from the tomb of Meketre at Thebes – one of the richest and most complete sets ever discovered – conveys in miniature a sense of the active bustle of daily life in ancient Egypt.

Jewelry – Dynasty 12. The royal jewels of Princess Sithathoryunet are considered among the finest examples of ancient Egyptian jewelry. The stunning pectoral, a gift from her father, and the gold cowrie-shell girdle are technical and aesthetic marvels.

Statues of Hatshepsut – Dynasty 18. One of the few queens to ascend the throne, Hatshepsut was depicted by sculptors in the full regalia of her office – including, occasionally, a beard – yet still retained her feminine qualities. She built her monumental funerary temple complex at Deir al Bahri, a true ancient wonder completed around 1500 BC.

Sarcophagus of Harkhebi – Dynasty 26. This chubby basalt sarcophagus is one of the most pristine in the museum's collection, the serene facial expression and hieroglyphs seemingly untouched by time. It was found at the bottom of a 50ft-deep pit inside a limestone box.

Temple of Dendur★ – Early Roman period (c.23-10 BC). This three-room monument to the goddess Isis was among monuments rescued from submersion prior to the completion of the Aswan High Dam. A gift from Egypt, it came, piece by piece, to the U.S. in 1967 and was assembled here in 1978.

Fayum Portraits – Roman period (c. AD 160). Made of pigment mixed with hot wax (known as encaustic), these lifelike portraits were crafted as mummy masks by Greeks living in Fayum. They represent the first introduction of European-style painting techniques into Egypt.

Young Woman with a Water Jug (c.1660) by Johannes Vermeer

The Metropolitan Museum of Art, Henry G. Marquand Collection

European Paintings★★★

Second floor.

Arranged by national schools, these galleries showcase work by the European Old Masters. Religion, history, portraiture, mythology, still life and landscape fill these canvases, which together demonstrate the evolution of media and style from the early Renaissance to the Age of Reason.

The Italian Schools – As the Middle Ages waned after 1300, Europeans began to broaden their horizons beyond the Church, and the arts and sciences flourished. By the 15C, Florence teemed with artists cultivating new approaches to light, form and subject, and in 1504 three of the greatest and most fertile Renaissance minds worked in that city: Leonardo da Vinci, Michelangelo and Raphael. Other cities around Italy hatched regional styles, borne along by the creative tide of the Renaissance, but by the 16C – the high Renaissance – Venice came to dominate. There, Titian, Tintoretto and Veronese composed huge, active canvases characterized by vivid colors, large foreground figures and realistic landscape backgrounds. Their work anticipated the Baroque sense of the picture as a whole, of surface versus line, of a continuous rhythm rather than ob-jects set against a backdrop, as would later be seen in 18C Venetian master Giovanni Battista Tiepolo's luminous canvases.

Northern Europe – North of Italy, other artistic sensibilities stirred. The Catholic

European Paintings Highlights (Italian schools):

Giotto	*The Epiphany*, c.1320
Fra Filippo Lippi	*Man and Woman at a Casement*, c.1435
Sandro Botticelli	*The Last Communion of St. Jerome*, c.1491
Raphael	*The Agony in the Garden*, c.1505
Titian	*Venus and Adonis*, c.1565
Tiepolo	*A Dance in the Country*, c.1756

European Paintings Highlights (Northern Europe):

Jan van Eyck	*The Crucifixion and The Last Judgment*, c.1425
Pieter Brueghel	*The Harvesters*, 1565
Peter Paul Rubens	*Venus and Adonis*, c.1635
Rembrandt van Rijn	*Aristotle with a Bust of Homer*, 1653
Johannes Vermeer	*Young Woman with a Water Pitcher*, c.1660

Church persisted in its influence over painters of the early Netherlandish school, and their work reflects that curious Gothic mixture of the devout and the macabre. A century later Peter Paul Rubens broke the Church's spell over artistic content and expression. In Holland, 17C painters celebrated their recent independence from Spain with landscapes, portraits and scenes of everyday life. Dark and quiet, Dutch (indeed European) painting reached its apex at the hand of Rembrandt van Rijn and Johannes Vermeer.

European Sculpture and Decorative Arts★★★

First floor.

This is one of the museum's largest and broadest departments, its 50,000-piece collection spanning more than 500 years, from the Renaissance to the early 20C. The term "decorative arts" encompasses furniture, woodwork, ceramics, glass, metalwork, jewelry and textiles. These are presented alongside traditional sculpture in galleries and in meticulously re-created **period rooms★**. Italian Renaissance sculpture, French and English furniture, and French and German porcelain are the department's strong suits. **Gubbio Studiolo** – The art of intarsia is on glorious display in this studiolo (small room), which was built in the 1470s as a personal retreat for the Italian duke Federico da Montefeltro. Thousands of pieces of walnut, beech, rosewood and oak are arranged mosaic-like on the walls to create startlingly realistic images of objects related to the duke's interests, including music and books.

Jack and Belle Linsky Collection – Opened in 1984, these galleries present the private art and artifacts compiled by the Linskys over a period of 40 years. Approximately 375 works of art–paintings by early European masters, Renaissance and Baroque bronzes, European porcelains, 18C French furniture, and jewelry – are displayed in seven rooms designed to create the intimate setting of a private residence.

Petrie European Sculpture Court – One of the museum's beautiful converted courtyards, this airy space displays monumental Italian and French sculpture, including Auguste Rodin's "Burghers of Calais." Adjacent galleries in the Kravis Wing pick up the threads of European decorative arts with 19C and early 20C objects and furniture.

Greek And Roman Art★★★

First and second floors.

April 2007 marked the triumphant completion of a 40-year, $225 million plan to redesign and enlarge the museum's galleries for Ancient Greek and Roman art – one of the finest collections of its kind in the world. Prior to the redeisgn, a mere 2,000 of the Met's 17,000 artifacts were on display; today more than half are on view without crowding.

Greek Art – The grand, barrel-vaulted Jaharis Gallery, just south of the Great Hall, was inaugurated in 2005. The gallery's soaring height, skylights and new limestone walls are a fitting backdrop for large-scale sculpture from Ancient Greece, including oversize statues of a wounded Amazon and the Greek hero Protesilaos. Flanking this space are six smaller galleries presenting Greek works in roughly chronological progression from 6C BC to 4C BC.

Roman Art – At the far end of the Jaharis Gallery – past the gargantuan capital

Treasures to look for in the Greek and Roman galleries:	
Attica	Kouros: Statue of a Youth (marble), 7C BC
Attica	Grave Stele: Youth and Girl (marble), 530 BC
Attica	Red-Figured Amphora (terra cotta), 490 BC
Cyclades islands	Seated Harp Player (marble), 3C BC
Greece	Veiled and Masked Dancer (bronze), 2C BC
Rome	Hope Dionysos (marble), AD 100
Rome	Badminton Sarcophagus (marble), AD 265
Rome	Colossal Head of Constantine (marble), AD 325

and base of an ionic column from the Temple of Artemis at Sardis – lies the beautiful Leon Levy and Shelby White Court for Roman and Etruscan Art, opened in 2007. (This is actually a reinstallation: the space had been used as a sculpture court from 1913 to 1954, at which point it was replaced by a cafeteria.) The centerpiece of the sun-bathed atrium is a serene fountain surrounded by twenty Roman sculptures, almost all of which are copies of Greek originals, attesting to the Romans' intense admiration for Greek art. Two larger-than-life-size statues of Hercules – one young, one old, both from the first century AD – face off from either side of the court. Etruscan art is shown on the mezzanine around the rim of the court. The highlight here is a spectacular bronze processional chariot dating from the mid-6C BCE, with relief panels depicting the life of Achilles.

Cypriot Art – On the second floor above the Jaharis Gallery, four art galleries presenting work from Cyprus were unveiled in 2000.

19C European Paintings and Sculpture★★★

Second floor.
Recently reconfigured and expanded by 8,000sq ft, these galleries are among the most important in the museum, holding within them one of the world's greatest collections of European art from the 19C and early 20C.

Here you'll find the Museum's extensive collection of Romantic, Barbizon, Impressionist, and Post-Impressionist paintings and 19th-century European sculpture. Completed in 2007, the new arrangement includes work of the early modern era, with artists such as Bonnard, Modigliani, Matisse and Picasso shown in relation to their forebears.

Romanticism – Out of the humanitarian ideals of the Enlightenment grew two major schools of artistic thought: Neoclassicism and Romanticism. The Neo-classicists – preeminently Jacques-Louis David – turned to ancient Greece and Rome for new inspiration. Rejecting such precision, the painters of the Romantic movement reveled in a freer attitude toward brush stroke and color, relying on historic events and settings for their exoticism, drama and allegory. In a portent of Impressionism, Eugène Delacroix, master Romantic, declared, "I do not paint a sword but its sparkle."

Barbizon – The Barbizon school (c.1830–1870) – named after the village of Barbizon near Fontainebleau Forest, France, where the artists gathered – was formed in reaction to Romanticism. For these painters – the most famous of whom were Jean-Baptiste Camille Corot, Théodore Rousseau and Jean-François Millet – nature was painted not merely as a backdrop for dramatic events but as a subject in and of itself.

Impressionism – The Impressionists took this idea further, painting nature and figures alike rapidly, with quick brush strokes, to give a spontaneous "impression" of a scene. So radical did these works seem in subject, palette and technique that they were refused admission to the annual exhibitions of the conser-

---

Taking a Break

Many galleries throughout the museum are furnished with benches, ideal for contemplating a particular painting or sculpture. But for more extended relaxation periods, or to stop for a chat, consider these pleasant spots. On the first floor, the Temple of Dendur and the Charles Engelhard Court are both glass-enclosed atriums with casual seating. There's also a secluded patio on the ground floor of the Lehman Pavilion. On the second floor, the Astor Court in the Chinese galleries makes a peaceful stop. Also keep in mind that you can leave the museum, take a stroll in Central Park and come back as long as you keep your admission tag.

19C European Paintings and Sculpture Highlights:

Eugène Delacroix	*The Abduction of Rebecca*, 1846
Jean-Francois Millet	*Calling the Cows Home*, c. 1872

🍸 Address Book 🍸

EATING AND DRINKING AT THE MET

There are several food and drink options at the Met. The most casual and the least expensive is the **cafeteria** 🍴 (*ground floor, below Medieval Hall;* 🕐 *open Tue–Sun 11:30am–4:30pm, Fri–Sat until 7pm*). Here you'll find sandwiches, salads, hot entrées and desserts, with booster seats and a children's menu for kids. A more formal option is the **Petrie Court Café** (*first floor, in European Sculpture & Decorative Arts;* 🕐 *open Tue–Sun 11:30am-4:30 pm, Fri–Sat until 8:30pm*), which stands at the back of the Petrie sculpture court and overlooks Central Park; it has a full bar and a more extensive menu, including a popular daily afternoon tea and weekend brunch. You can make reservations for dinner: ☎212-570-3964. The **Roof Garden Café** (*access via first-floor elevator;* 🕐 *open May–Oct, weather permitting, Tue–Sun 10am–4:30pm, Fri-Sat until 8pm*) serves up dazzling views of Central Park along with light fare such as packaged sandwiches, chips, cookies and fruit. Beverages include espresso, soft drinks, beer, wine and sangria, plus martinis on Fri and Sat nights. You can get salads, sandwiches and desserts at the **Balcony Café**, overlooking the Great Hall (🕐 *open Tue–Sun 11am–4:30pm*); on weekend nights the space transforms into the **Balcony Bar** (🕐 *open Fri-Sat only 4:30pm–8:30pm*), where cocktails are accompanied by live classical music.

vative Paris Salon. Undaunted, the Impressionists mounted eight of their own exhibitions between 1874 and 1886, eventually gaining critical acclaim.

Post-Impressionism – Because of its very nature and the diversity of its practitioners, the Impressionist phenomenon, though short-lived, opened the floodgates of artistic interpretation. Arising both out of and in opposition to its precepts, post-Impressionism pushed the formal aspects of painting in new emotional, compositional, coloristic, symbolic and scientific directions.

American Wing★★★

First, second and third floors and mezzanine.

Spanning three centuries, the collection of American paintings, sculpture and decorative arts can be found in the northwest corner of the museum. Thanks to a major and much-needed renovation and

expansion of these rooms, this is likely to be one of the museum's most exciting departments in coming years, though visitors should expect major swaths of the wing to be closed until early 2009, including the Charles Engelhard Court. **Decorative Arts** – *Colonial and early Federal era period rooms and decorative arts galleries closed until January 2009.* The newly updated Classical Galleries (first floor) display decorative arts created between 1810 and 1845. Americans enthusiastically embraced the ancient world in this period, patterning everything from vases to sofas after Greek, Roman and Egyptian models. Gothic and Renaissance elements began creeping in shortly thereafter. An American idiom reasserted itself in the late 19C with the onset of the Arts and Crafts Movement. A handsome oak-paneled stairwell by McKim, Mead and White (1884) has been installed near the entrance to the DeeDee Wigmore Galleries, where you'll

Highlights of the American Wing:

John Singleton Copley	*Daniel Crommelin Verplanck*, 1771
Gilbert Stuart	*George Washington*, 1795
Emanuel Gottlieb Leutze	*Washington Crossing the Delaware*, 1851
Frederic Edwin Church	*The Heart of the Andes*, 1859
Thomas Eakins	*Max Schmitt in a Single Scull*, 1871
James McNeil Whistler	*Portrait of Theodore Duret*, 1883
John Singer Sargent	*Madame X*, 1884
Mary Cassatt	*Lady at the Tea Table*, 1885

Brigitta L. House - MICHELIN

Temple of Dendur

find furniture by the Herter Brothers and Stickley, in addition to several gorgeous stained-glass windows by Louis Comfort Tiffany. Late Colonial-era decorative arts, including a fine selection of tall clocks, can be found on the second floor near the Colonial-era paintings.

Painting – *Closed for renovation February 2008 until late 2010.* The museum's impressive holdings of American paintings from the 18C to the early 20C reside en masse in spacious, light-filled galleries on the mezzanine and second floors. Usually less crowded than the more centrally located European painting galleries, these are some of the most pleasant galleries in the museum, with particularly large troves of work by John Singer Sargent, James McNeill Whistler, Thomas Eakins, and Mary Cassatt on the mezzanine and John Singleton Copley, Charles Willson Peale, and John Trumbull on the second floor.

Charles Engelhard Court – *Closed for renovation until early 2009.* Sculpture, stained glass and architectural fragments occupy this glass-enclosed courtyand, which is being treated to a major redesign. Two features that will remain intact include the facade of the United States Bank (1824, Martin E. Thompson), once on Wall Street, overlooking the north side of the court, and Louis Sullivan's staircases (1883) from the Chicago Stock exchange on the south side.

Ancient Near Eastern Art★★

Second floor.

The collections of this department cover a vast region of southwestern Asia, one that today reaches from Turkey to Afghanistan and the Indus Valley, and from the Caucasus Mountains in the north to the Arabian Peninsula. The sculpture, pottery and metalwork you see here date from 8000 BC to AD 651.

The profusion of cultures that inhabited this region produced finely wrought artifacts of great beauty and sophistication. One silver piece of particular note is the silver figurine of a kneeling bull holding a vase between his hooves, a Proto-Elamite work dating from around 2900 BC. A gold Iranian cup with four bas-relief gazelles from around 1000 BC is similarly striking.

The **Sackler Gallery**★, just east of the Great Hall Balcony, has been reconstructed to mimic the proportions of an audience hall of the palace built by Assyrian king Ashurnasirpal II at Nimrud (in what is now Iraq), in the 9C BC. Two human-headed winged lions, carved meticulously from limestone, guard the doorway, and extraordinary monumental reliefs and statuary from the palace line the gallery walls.

Arms and Armor★

First floor.

This encyclopedic collection comprises more than 14,000 arms, designed mainly for display rather than for actual military use. Flanking a vast **equestrian court**★ containing parade armor from the 16C, four small western galleries present European arms – including rare pieces commissioned by various kings and rulers – while three eastern galleries focus on articles from China, Japan, India, Turkey and Iran.

Most of the works here are incredibly ornate, leagues removed from the tin-can apparel popularized by Monty Python. Sword hilts are embellished with tortoiseshell, cup hilts are encrusted with jewels and even the guns are made of gold. Late-15C helmets from Iran adopt the shape of a turban, and various sabers and their scabbards are intricately decorated with inlaid emeralds, diamonds and other precious stones.

A small gallery on the north side displays firearms from Europe and the United States, including an 1862 Colt police revival, one of the most popular firearms during the Civil War.

Arts of Africa, Oceania and the Americas★★

First floor.

Artworks from sub-Saharan Africa, the Pacific Islands, and North, Central, and South America are located in the museum's south wing, which was named in honor of Nelson Rockefeller's son, Michael, who disappeared while on an expedition to the island of New Guinea in 1961. The core of the collection encompasses approximately 3,500 works donated to the museum by Nelson Rockefeller in the late 1970s. The department now owns about 11,000 objects spanning a period of 4,000 years.

Africa – Sculpture, primarily ritualistic masks and figures carved in wood, dominates the art of Africa. A collection of monumental sculpture by the Dogon of Mali dominates one of the galleries. A terra-cotta seated figure recalls the work of Henri Matisse. Ferocious-looking Senufo helmet masks incorporate the jaws and teeth of a crocodile, the horns of an antelope and the tusks of a warthog. Note the richly detailed brass relief plaque from Nigeria (16-17C), depicting a warrior chief, warriors and attendants in full battle regalia.

Oceania – Following an extensive three-year renovation and redesign, the galleries for Oceanic art – the collective term for the more than 25,000 islands of the Pacific – reopened in November 2007. . The centerpiece of the new configuration is the spacious, sunlit gallery for Melanesian art. Highlights among the 300 works on view are a remarkable group of nine delicately carved poles, ranging up to 20ft in height, used by the Asmat people of New Guinea in ceremonies to cast death away from a community, along with the 48ft-

Gold Funerary Mask (Peru)

The Metropolitan Museum of Art, gift of Alice K. Bache

long Asmat canoe, which could hold 20 people. Also on display is a soaring, boldly colored ceiling from a ceremonial house of the Kwoma people of New Guinea, commissioned in the early 1970s.

Americas – A new gallery devoted to the art of the Native North American peoples was inaugurated in November 2007, with works arranged by region. The peoples of the Plains and the Northwest Coast Indians are particularly well represented, the former by clothing and a fascinated illustrated book known as the Maffet Ledger, the latter by colorful masks and rattles. Among the items you may see from South America are a pair of Mochica shell-and-stone-mosaic ear spools (3C-6C AD); a pendant (Colombia, 13C-16C AD) in the form of a figure wearing an elaborate headdress; and a boldly painted Sicán funerary mask (Peru, 11-9C BC). As for the arts of Mesoamerica, note especially the Mayan seated figure (6C AD), one of the few extant three-dimensional Mayan pieces in wood.

Asian Art★★

Second and third floors.

The Met's Asian art collection – the largest of its kind in the West – traces the development of Chinese, Japanese, Korean, Southeast Asian and South Asian art from the second millennium BC to the present. Ceramics, metalwork, paintings and sculptures, bronzes, jades and textiles are on display in expansive, well-appointed galleries.

China – Spanning the period from the Neolithic (early 2000 BC) through the Tang dynasty (10C AD), these galleries include jades, ceramics, bronze ritual vessels and tomb art. Just off the Great Hall Balcony, the Chinese Sculpture Court is dominated by a monumental standing boddhisatva (awakened one) from the 5C AD. In the center of the painting galleries is the tranquil glass-covered **Astor Court**★, a reproduction of a Ming dynasty courtyard and scholar's study in Soochow, China, containing traditional Chinese plantings, a moon-viewing terrace, and formal rock garden. The study, built with traditional mortise-and-tenon joining techniques, contains handsome furniture of the era.

On the third floor, several quiet rooms contain elegant Chinese decorative arts: textiles, ivory work, bamboo and box-wood items, red lacquerwork and jades.

Korea – The gallery surveying Korean art holds a collection that includes earthenware and Bronze Age pieces, scroll paintings and ceramics. Note the series of lacquered wood boxes with intricate inlay.

South and Southeast Asian Art – These 18 stunning galleries display some 1,300 works from Nepal to Burma. In the South Asian galleries, look for the ornate teakwood dome of a late-16C Jain meeting hall, carved with figures of the eight cosmic rulers and their animal and human attendants. Among the rooms devoted to Southeast Asia (Cambodia, Thailand, Vietnam and Indonesia), a sky-lit gallery of monumental Khmer sculptures from the Angkor period (8-14C AD) stands out.

Japan – The second-floor Sackler Wing galleries hold changing exhibits of Japanese paintings, sculpture, lacquer, woodblock prints, scrolls, screens and kimonos. Also on view are a shoin-style reception room modeled on a room in the Onoji temple (17C) outside Kyoto, and *Water Stone*, a sculpture by Isamu Noguchi (👁 *see the Noguchi Museum in Queens*.

Lehman Collection★★

Lehman Pavilion.

Considered one of the finest private art collections in the US, the Robert Lehman Collection was compiled by financier Philip Lehman and his son, Robert. Rather than being integrated into the museum's other departments, these works—predominantly European painting, sculpture and decorative arts from the 14C to the early 20C—are housed in a tinted-glass pavilion added to the west side of the museum in 1975. Some 3,000 works of art are displayed in 11 first-floor galleries, seven of which are appointed to resemble rooms in Robert Lehman's residence on West 54th Street, and in additional ground-floor galleries. Strengths of the collection include Italian paintings of the 14C and 15C, masterworks of the 18-19C Dutch and Spanish schools, and French Impressionist paintings of the 19C and 20C.

Lehman Collection Highlights:

Sandro Botticelli	*The Annunciation*, c.1485
Petrus Christus	*Goldsmith in His Shop, possibly St. Eligius*, 1449
El Greco	*St. Jerome as a Scholar*, c.1614
Rembrandt	*The Last Supper, after Leonardo da Vinci*, 1635
J.A.D. Ingres	*Portrait of the Princesse de Broglie*, 1853
Pierre-Auguste Renoir	*Two Young Girls at the Piano*, 1892
Balthus	*Nude Before a Mirror*, 1955

Medieval Art★★

First floor.

Tracing the development of art from the fall of Rome (4C) to the Renaissance (16C), the museum's extensive collection in medieval art comprises more than 4,000 works from the early Christian, Byzantine, Migration, Romanesque and Gothic periods. Among the treasures not to be missed are some exquisite pieces of Byzantine silver, Romanesque and Gothic metalwork, and Gothic stained glass and tapestries. Additional medieval art objects are exhibited at The Cloisters.

Byzantine Art – Secular and liturgical artworks from Constantinople, spanning the Byzantine Empire's 1000-plus-year reign, line the corridors flanking the main staircase and reclaimed space underneath and behind the stairs. The north corridor, to the right of the staircase, holds early secular art of the Byzantine Empire and works by the Franks, the Goths and other peoples at the fringes of the empire. The south corridor, dedicated to liturgical art of the Byzantine Church and middle- and late-Byzantine secular art, features among its devotional objects the Antioch Chalice, said to have been used by Christ in the Last Supper. Underneath the stairs, a crypt-like gallery features Byzantine Egyptian art under a series of low brick arches.

Medieval Tapestry Hall – Hung along the walls of this small hall is an ensemble of tapestries, dating from the 14C to the early 16C, woven principally in the workshops of Flanders (Arras, Brussels and Tournai). Dating from the late Gothic period, large panels of stained glass from Cologne, Germany and England fill two walls of the gallery.

Medieval Sculpture Hall – This large hall was built to evoke the ambience of a church, with a nave separated from the side aisles by massive columns. Stretching between two columns, a splendid wrought-iron Baroque **choir screen**★ rises almost the full height of the hall. Begun in 1668 for the Cathedral of Valladolid, in Spain, it was completed in 1764.

Medieval Treasury – In addition to portable shrines, reliquary caskets and sacramental objects, the Treasury also contains two fine sculptural groups (early 16C) of the Entombment and Pietà, from the Périgord region of France.

Modern Art★★

First and second floors, mezzanine and roof garden.

Paintings, sculptures, works on paper and decorative arts from 1900 to the present are on view in the Lila Acheson Wallace Wing, situated in the southwest corner of the building. Located on top of the wing, the **roof garden**★ offers a superb setting for contemporary sculpture while affording splendid **views** of Manhattan's midtown and uptown skylines; it also holds a cafe. The museum's collection of modern art is particularly strong in paintings of the School of Paris and in postwar art by such luminaries as Alselm Kiefer and Jasper Johns, but as space is limited, only a limited selection of works are on view. The 2005 receipt of the Muriel Kallis Steinberg Newman Collection of American Abstract Expressionist paintings – one of the most important gifts the museum has ever received – will likely prompt a reworking and expansion of the galleries here. For now, be sure to see the large-scale contemporary works on the mezzanine, including two of Chuck Close's *Lucas*, Lucian Freud's *Naked Man, Back View*, and Andy Warhol's silkscreen *Mao*.

Costume Institute ★

Ground floor.

Established in 1937, the Costume Institute collects and preserves clothing from the 16C to the present. Today, the 40,000-article collection of regional garb includes apparel from five continents, ranging from the elegant wardrobes of ancient royalty to chic fashions by the most distinguished contemporary American and French couturiers. Changing exhibits explore topics related to fashion, history and society.

Because display space here on the ground floor is limited, the institute often commandeers space upstairs for its major shows, such as a retrospective of the House of Chanel. The annual Costume Institute Gala *(in spring)* gives Hollywood starlets and fashion editors the opportunity to trot out the latest looks.

Drawings, Prints, and Photographs ★

Second floor.

The museum has a formidable collection of drawings, prints, and photographs. Drawings and prints are displayed in the Robert Wood Johnson Jr. Gallery, a long, thin hall extending from the top of the Great Staircase south toward the 19C European Paintings and Sculpture galleries, and photography can be found in the galleries that flank it.

Drawings – Some of the finest drawings in the museum's collection were gifts from railroad titan Cornelius Vanderbilt, who gave the Met 670 drawings by or attributed to European Old Masters. In 1935 the museum purchased an album of fifty sheets by Francisco Goya. Today the Met owns 11,000 drawings – some complete works, others studies for paintings – by such greats as Michelangelo, Leonardo da Vinci, and Rembrandt.

Prints – The Met's impressive cache of 1.5 million prints includes woodcuts, lithographs and other works made from engravings by some of Europe's most gifted artists: Rembrandt, Albrecht Dürer, Hogarth, Fragonard, and Toulouse-Lautrec among them.

Photographs – Opened in 2007, the sleek, high-ceilinged Joyce and Robert Menschel Hall for Modern Photography displays large-scale photographs made since 1960 to great effect; selections here change every six months. Photographs from earlier periods are shown across the hall in the Howard Gilman Galleries. In all, the museum owns about 20,000 photographic images, including large holdings of work by Alfred Stieglitz and Walker Evans.

Islamic Art ★

Second floor.

The Met's cache of Islamic art is one of the most comprehensive in the Western world. The department traces the development of Islamic art, beginning with the founding of Islam in the 7C and ending in the early 19C. Encompassing works from various geographical regions, including Mesopotamia, Persia, Morocco, Egypt, Syria and India, the collection is particularly well known for its glass- and metalwork, ceramics, miniatures and classical carpets. As part of ongoing renovations to the museum, the Islamic art galleries are being reorganized and enlarged (expected date of completion: 2009). In the meantime, small displays of Islamic art are sprinkled throughout the museum, most notably on the south side of the Great Hall balcony.

Musical Instruments ★

Second floor.

This rare, original collection is more than 4,000 strong (*the Audio Guide, contains samples of music these instruments make*). The western galleries focus on European instruments, including the oldest extant piano (1720), three Stradivarius violins, two classical guitars of Andrés Segovia, and keyboard instruments.

The eastern galleries highlight instruments from the Near and Far East, the Americas and Africa, including seldom-seen pieces such as an Indonesian sesando, a type of zither made from palm leaves, and an Indian mayuri, or bowed sitar. Most of the instruments are in working order and are used for occasional concerts.

Museum of Modern Art ★★★

One of the world's preeminent cultural institutions, the Museum of Modern Art (MoMA) offers an unparalleled overview of the modern visual arts. The rich collection includes not only painting, drawing and sculpture but also photography, decorative arts, architectural plans and models, video and the most comprehensive film archive in the US.

▶ **Orient Yourself:** The admission desk is at the right, inside the entrance; if you have a CityPass, go to the desk on the left by the coat check. All large bags must be checked (no luggage or laptops). ◀◉ Free audio tours are available past the security guards on the right. Free gallery talks convene in the second-floor atrium at 11:30am and 1:30pm daily; arrive 10min early to ensure a spot.

🕓 **Organizing Your Time:** Plan your visit for a weekday and arrive before 11am; MoMA gets uncomfortably crowded on weekends and late in the afternoon. If you choose not to take a guided tour, start with the Painting and Sculpture galleries on the fourth and fifth floors, home to most of the museum's most famous works, then pick a few other exhibits according to your interests. Don't try to see everything in one day.

Kids **Especially for Kids:** The audio tour includes Modern Kids, a delightful series of recorded commentaries to help children appreciate the museum.

👁 **Don't Miss:** Vincent van Gogh's *Starry Night* (Gallery 1), Pablo Picasso's *Desmoiselles d'Avignon* (Gallery 7), Claude Monet's *Reflections of Clouds on the Water-Lily Pond* (Gallery 9), Salvador Dali's *Persistence of Memory* (Gallery 12), Jackson Pollock's *One: Number 31* (Gallery 17).

👆 **Also See:** P.S. 1. Admission to this acclaimed contemporary art facility in Queens, a MoMA affiliate, is free if you present your MoMA ticket within 30 days of purchase.

A Bit of History

The founding of the museum dates back to 1929, when three wealthy and culturally sophisticated women – **Abby Aldrich Rockefeller, Lillie P. Bliss** and **Mary Quinn Sullivan** – led a campaign to promote the modern arts in the US. The first show, of the then little-known post-Impressionists, opened in temporary quarters that fall. Over the next decade, founding director **Alfred H. Barr Jr**. shaped the museum's philosophy, notably expanding the idea of what constitutes art. Among Barr's pioneering exhibits were shows of photography, design and architecture, none of which were acknowledged as legitimate art forms at the time. Today MoMA's holdings in all three disciplines – in addition to modern and contemporary painting and sculpture – are world-class.

The Museum of Modern Art's dramatic "new" building actually encompasses the work of several top-tier architects. The original 1939 marble and glass museum building, by **Philip Goodwin** and **Edward Durell Stone**, was one of the first examples of the International style in the US. The sculpture garden and east wing are 1964 additions by Philip Johnson. A 1979 renovation by **Cesar Pelli** more than doubled the gallery space and included the addition of the glass-faced Garden Hall and a 44-story residential tower to the west. In 2004 work was completed on the museum's most ambitious expansion and renovation to date, overseen by Japanese architect **Yoshio Taniguchi**. The redesigned building has nearly twice the capacity of the old one, including an appropriately dramatic lobby, as well as vastly improved screening rooms and food services.

Dining at MoMA

MoMA has three attractive dining facilities. Overseen by chef Danny Meyer, the force behind the celebrated Union Square Cafe *(see Where to Eat)*, they all serve food that far surpasses the usual museum fare. The **Modern** is the fanciest of the three, presenting French-American cuisine in a sleek, Bauhaus-inspired dining room overlooking the sculpture garden *(reservations recommended: ☎212-333-1220)*. Open well past museum hours due to its separate entrance on West 53rd Street, the Modern also has a more casual **Bar Room** and seasonal terrace. On the second floor of the museum, **Cafe 2** is a stylish rustic Italian diner. Patrons order from a menu posted at the entrance (panini and handmade pastas are specialties), then take a number and a seat; the food is brought to the table. In a small space overlooking the sculpture garden, **Terrace 5** serves sumptuous gourmet desserts and "savory bites" like marinated olives, smoked salmon and artisanal cheese, along with cocktails, wine and espresso drinks. Kids can order hot chocolate, chocolate milk or a rootbeer float.

Visit

🕐 *Open year-round Wed–Mon 10:30am–5:30pm (Fri until 8pm).* 🕐 *Closed Thanksgiving Day & Dec 25.* ☎ *$20 (🎟 free Fri 4pm–8pm).* 🔊 *Guided tours (1hr) daily at 11:30am and 1:30pm.* ☎ 212-708-9400. www.moma.org.

What follows is a brief overview of the museum's permanent collections, listed as you might encounter them if you worked your way through the museum from the ground up. Keep in mind that some works mentioned may not be on view, as the museum constantly rotates its collection and loans works to other institutions. In addition to the permanent displays there are usually two or three major temporary shows at MoMA. Check local listings or the museum's website for details.

Lobby

The lobby is the most stunning aspect of Taniguchi's redesign. A low, long space greets you as you enter from 53rd Street. Once you buy your ticket and check your bag, you turn right toward entrance to the galleries and are treated to a stunning view straight back through a wall of glass into the sculpture garden. Walking toward it you have a sense of release as the ceiling soars skyward. From the back right corner, you can look up into the stairwell and see two levels of delicate pedestrian walkways crossing between galleries, as well as the kelly-green *Bell-47D1 Helicopter* (1945),

by artist Arthur Young suspended above you (the best view of the helicopter is from the third floor).

Arrayed around the lobby are several works of art, most notably Rodin's larger-than-life *Monument to Balzac* (1898, cast 1954), showing the artist wrapped dramatically in the dressing gown he often wore writing.

Sculpture Garden

The sculpture garden is one of the museum's most enchanting spaces, its sleek marble patios punctuated by two rectangular pools and warmed by beech trees and seasonal plantings. Plenty of chairs make it a great place to relax in

The Abby Aldrich Rockefeller Sculpture Garden and the David and Peggy Rockefeller Building

The Museum of Modern Art · ©2005 Timothy Hursley

warm weather. The glass-walled Modern restaurant runs along the south side, while all around rise the buildings of Midtown: the International-style sky-scraper visible at the east end of the garden is Ludwig Mies van der Rohe's Seagram Building.

The sculpture in the garden rotates, though some large pieces are likely to remain in place for years at a time, the most recent addition being *Broken Obelisk* (1963–69), by Barnett Newman, a monumental steel pyramid on which an upside-down obelisk seems to balance on its point (this was formerly in the Atrium). A permanent fixture of the garden is Aristide Maillol's *The River* (1943) at the end of the far reflecting pool, originally designed in honor of a slain pacifist and cast after the artist's death.

Second Floor

Atrium – The Atrium serves as a meeting place for daily guided tours 👁🗨 of the museum. Check the sign posted here for the day's topics. While some tours broadly examine the museum's most famous works – the Highlights tours – others are a bit esoteric, with themes like "Feeling Minimalism: Exploring the Body through Minimalist Sculpture." Arrive at 11:20am or 1:20pm to ensure a spot, as the tours are limited to 25 people. The Atrium contains a rotating selection of large-scale painting and sculpture.

Prints and Illustrated Books★ – MoMA's collection of 50,000 modern prints and illustrated books is the most comprehensive collection of its kind in the world. Works range from woodcuts, etchings and lithographs to digital prints and artist reproductions, dating from the 1880s to the present. Only a tiny fraction of the works are on view at any given time, in heady exhibits put together by the museum's curators. A recent show, "Repicturing the Past/Picturing the Present," examined how artists from the late 19C to today have used historical figures or narratives in their work to address contemporary problems. The most striking piece was the young artist Kara Walker's 2005 series of 15 lithographs and screenprints based on *Harper's Pictorial History of the Civil War,* overlaid with haunting cut-paper silhouettes.

Media Gallery – This small gallery features selections from the museum's 1,200 video and media works. (Selections from the museum's archive of 20,000 **films** are shown in two state-of-the-art underground theaters; screenings cost 👁$10 per day regardless of whether you enter the rest of the museum. Consult the museum's website or local listings for advance schedule, or check at the Admission Desk or Film Desk upon arrival.)

Third Floor

Architecture and Design★★ – These delightful galleries stem from Alfred Barr's original (and confirmed) conviction that modern art should embrace the design realm. Expect to see furniture from the Arts & Crafts and Bauhaus movements, stained-glass windows by Frank Lloyd Wright, drawings and plans by Mies van der Rohe, Eames chairs and other classic works, as well as common objects that curators believe to have particularly fetching designs, such as the Bic pen and the Apple iMac computer.

Drawings★ – Thematic exhibits in these intimate galleries are drawn from MoMA's collection of more than 7,000 works in pencil, ink, charcoal, watercolor, collage and mixed media. A recent show, "Lines, Grids, Stains, Words," examined several dozen minimalist works from the 1960s to the 1990s.

Photography★★ – MoMA devotes a large section of the third floor to photography shows, thanks to the breadth and depth of its 25,000-work collection. Nearly all the great photographers in the medium's history are represented, not just with one photograph but often with whole series. Eadweard J. Muybridge's studies in animal locomotion are often on display, as are works by Alfred Stieglitz, Man Ray, Diane Arbus and Walker Evans. These are complemented with expansive single-artist retrospectives or thematic exhibitions.

Fourth Floor

Painting and Sculpture II ★★★ – Along with Painting and Sculpture I galleries on the fifth floor, these galleries form the heart of the museum, with great modern works from the 1940s and the 1960s. The galleries are organized according to a rough chronology, spanning the period from early Abstract Expressionism to Abstract and Pop Art. (The museum's contemporary works are shown in special exhibits on the second and sixth floors, and at P.S. 1.)

Works from the 1940s display a tremendous range of styles, though many share a feeling of alienation brought about by the horrors of World War II. Swiss sculptor **Alberto Giacometti**'s attenuated animal and human figures have a decidedly morbid cast, while British painter **Francis Bacon** mined the newspaper for particularly disturbing and violent images to inspire his work. **Jackson Pollock** pioneered Abstract Expresionism in 1947 by laying his canvases on the floor and splattering them with paint, creating a sinuous web of color through free, expressive movements.

The term Color Field was used in the 1950s to describe work by such painters as **Mark Rothko, Clyfford Still** and **Barnett Newman**, whose lyrical canvases explored the subtle relationships of large planes of color.

The 1960s saw both the extension of Abstract Expressionism and the repudiation of it. **Robert Rauschenberg** and **Jasper Johns** (who had studios in the same New York loft building) continued the search for expression through the innovative use of surface textures, incorporating or drawing on familiar objects and symbols such as flags and licence plates. Pop Artists also found inspiration in familiar objects—Warhol's Campbell's Soup cans being the prime example—but their playful, cartoonish style contrasted sharply with the soul-baring seriousness of Abstract Expressionism.

Fifth Floor

Painting and Sculpture I ★★★ – These galleries contain the vast majority of the museum's most famous works, including many that are widely regarded as masterpieces.

You'll see a dazzling array of styles here, representing all the major schools and artists of the early Modern period. Defining color through the interplay of reflecting light, Impressionists such as **Claude Monet** sought to create a naturalistic "impression" of their subject instead of a

Alfred H. Barr, Jr. Painting and Sculpture Galleries

The Museum of Modern Art - ©T2005 imothy Hursley

Shopping at MoMA

MoMA does a brisk business in modern-art-related items, from thick coffeetable books and tote bags to clothing. There are three main shops on West 53rd Street. Across the street from the museum stands the popular **MoMA Design Store**, which teems with funky versions of ordinary objects (silverware, stationery) as well as handmade jewelry and gifts. (If you don't want to deal with museum crowds, scoot down to SoHo, where there's another location of the MoMA Design Store at 81 Spring Street.) **MoMA Books**, on the second floor of the museum, sells books on art, architecture and design *(access by museum admission only)*.

literal rendering; Monet's late-career, 50ft-long triptych *Reflections of Clouds on the Water Lily Pond* is a perfect example, supplying "the illusion of an endless whole," according to the artist. By contrast, the post-Impressionists, including Paul Cézanne, **Vincent van Gogh** and Henri de Toulouse-Lautrec, emphasized form, rendered through simplified shapes and expressive line; van Gogh's *The Starry Night* (1889) is hands-down the most renowned painting in the museum, an evocative dreamlike landscape in which thicckly painted waves roil the sky above a sleeping town.

Pablo Picasso and Georges Braque pioneered Cubism in the early 20C,

marking a radical departure from Western art by reducing their subjects to apparently abstract geometrics; Picasso's *Les Desmoiselles D'Avignon* is one of MoMA's cherished works of this period, an eight-foot-by-seven-foot canvas showing five naked prostitutes in a brothel, their bodies flat and angular, their eyes lopsided and spooky.

Other movements covered on this floor include Fauvism (Henri Matisse), Expressionism (Wassily Kandinsky), Futurism (Umberto Boccioni), Dada (Marcel Duchamp), Surrealism (Salvador Dali) and De Stijl (Mondrian), with a few Americans (Hopper and Wyeth) thrown in for good measure.

American Folk Art Museum★★

45 W. 53RD ST. BETWEEN FIFTH AND SIXTH AVES.
🚇 E, F AND V TRAINS TO FIFTH AVE.
MAP P 149

After years of bouncing from one place to the next, this first-rate museum found a permanent home in 2001 next door to the Museum of Modern Art. Though it would seem impossible to rival its illustrious neighbor, the American Folk Art Museum presents intelligent, provocative exhibits by self-trained artists in its new space.

A Bit of History

The museum was founded in 1961 to preserve and display American folk art from 1961 to the present. Initially, it occupied various brownstones and then a ground-floor gallery near Lincoln Center before a plan for a new building finally materialized in the late 1990s. Architects Tod Williams and Billie Tsien replaced two brownstones with a seven-story struc-

ture that looks as forbidding from the outside as it is welcoming within.

Visit

♿ 🕐 *Open year-round Tue–Sun 10:30am–5:30pm (Fri until 7:30pm).* 🕐 *Closed major holidays.* 🎟 *$9 (free Fri 5:30pm–7:30pm).* ✕ ☎ *212-265-1040.* *www.folkartmuseum.org.*

The metal facade consists of tall, rectangular panels arranged like bricks. Above the entrance, one column of panels is set at a sharp angle to the rest, like a half-open door letting in a long shaft of light. Upon entering (a gift shop full of handmade crafts stands to your right), you'll feel a sense of compression, as the space narrows past the admissions desk. Then it opens into a vast atrium, around which the museum's formidable collections are arrayed, on the walls and in specially designed niches in the stairwells.

Collection – The bilevel permanent exhibit, "Folk Art Revealed," displays 150 works from the 6,000-piece permanent collection in a particularly creative way. By juxtaposing aesthetically similar works crafted as much as two centuries apart, the curators challenge viewers to consider the function of folk art and the persistence of certain themes. Patriotic symbols are a mainstay of the form, ranging from a wooden gate painted with the American flag in 1876 to a red, white and blue "freedom quilt" made by an African-American artist facing racism in the South in the 1960s.

Other folk art is utilitarian yet beautiful: the massive wooden tooth that serves as

American Folk Art Museum · August Bandal

Child-Headed Whiplash - Tail Blengins by Henry Darger

a dentist's shingle, the ship's figurehead, the Shaker cupboard. But what really captures the imagination are the wildly idiosyncratic expressions that grow out of deprivation, such as the tall sculpture made entirely from bones and the feverishly romantic storybooks by recluse Henry Darger. Other floors hold large temporary exhibits. One recent show featured nearly 100 vivid drawings by the self-taught schizophrenic artist Martin Ramirez (1895–1963), the first major examination of his work.

Cooper-Hewitt, National Design Museum★★

2 E. 91ST ST. AT FIFTH AVE.

🚇 SUBWAY: 4, 5, 6 TRAIN TO 86TH ST.

MAP P 191

Founded in 1897 by Sarah, Eleanor and Amy Hewitt (granddaughters of industrialist Peter Cooper) as part of the Cooper Union of New York, this eclectic museum explores design across continents and cultures. Visitors also get a de facto house tour, as the museum is situated in the opulent 64-room Andrew Carnegie mansion.

A Bit of History

The Complex – When it came to real estate, **Andrew Carnegie** was the boldest of the robber barons, having a luxurious Beaux-Arts mansion (1902) built on a parcel surrounded by farms and shanties far north of where his cronies resided. The move was prescient. By the time Carnegie died in 1919, Fifth Avenue

Courtesy of Cooper-Hewitt Museum

Cooper-Hewitt Museum

National Design Triennial

Following in the tradition of the famous (or infamous) Whitney Biennial, the Cooper-Hewitt now has a design triennial, featuring contemporary works in all media that the curators feel express the leading edge of design. The results are ingenious. Eighty-seven designers and firms were chosen to participate in the 2006 triennial, with works ranging from prefabricated houses to robots. Expect more surprises in December 2009.

was filled with such palaces (yet none so grand as his); Carnegie's wife Louise remained on the premises until her death in 1946. Following a major renovation, the museum opened its doors here in 1976 as the National Design Museum. It has been affiliated with the Smithsonian Institution since 1967.

The Collection – The Cooper-Hewitt owns more than 250,000 objects related to the art, craft and commerce of design. Some 24 centuries and all the world's continents are represented. The prints and drawings collection is particularly robust, with works by 15C Italian master Andrea Mantegna, Americans Frederic Church and Winslow Homer, and Italian surrealist Giorgio de Chirico. Other highlights include an assortment of 18C and 19C birdcages; 10,000 wall coverings, from embossed leather to block-printed Arts-and-Crafts wallpaper; 45 pieces of Roman-Syrian glass; and 1,000 embroidery samplers dating from the 17C to the 19C.

Visit

♿ 🕑 *Open year-round Mon–Fri 10am–5pm (Fri until 9pm), Sat 10am–6pm, Sun noon–6pm.* 🕑 *Closed Jan 1, Thanksgiving Day & Dec 25.* ⚂ *$15 (free National Design Week in mid-Oct).* ✂ ☏ *212-849-8400. www.cooperhewitt.org.*

The majority of the museum's 9,000sq ft of gallery space is devoted to major temporary exhibitions. A recent show, for example, explored the Rococo movement and its revivals. In 2007 only one small gallery—the former music room—was dedicated to displaying works from the permanent collection. But that will change in coming years as the museum embarks on a major expansion that will double exhibition space to 18,000sq ft, allowing much more of the museum's vast holdings to be seen. Expected date of completion is 2010.

Guggenheim Museum ★★

1071 FIFTH AVE. BETWEEN 88TH ST. AND 89TH ST.

MTA 4, 5, 6 TRAIN TO 86TH ST.

MAP P 201

Officially named the Solomon R. Guggenheim Museum, this spiraling concrete monument to Modernism, located on Fifth Avenue between 88th and 89th streets, is among the most original and widely recognized structures in the US. Visited more than any other building designed by Frank Lloyd Wright, it is as much a work of art as the sculptures and paintings it contains.

A Bit of History

Heir to a vast mining fortune, **Solomon R. Guggenheim** (1861-1949) and his wife, Irene Rothschild, began collecting Old Masters in the late 19C. But in the early 20C, at the urging of their artistic adviser, Hilla Rebay (an artist in her own right), they shifted their focus to non-representational, or "non-objective," works – especially those by Kandinsky, Mondrian and Moholy-Nagy. Guggenheim established a foundation to bring his collection to the public in 1937, and Rebay commissioned Frank Lloyd Wright to design a building for it in 1943, but such was the resistance to Wright's design – and Wright's reciprocal contempt for traditional New York architecture – that the project was held up for years, and Guggenheim died before construction finally began, in 1956.

"My Pantheon" – Calling it "my Pantheon," after the domed Roman monument, Wright considered the idiosyncratic building, based on a complex trigonometric spiral, his crowning achievement. From the start, however, the museum was controversial. It clashed with its surroundings, was a nightmare to construct and, with its interior ramp and sloping walls, proved a difficult place either to view or to display art. To top it all off, the smooth concrete facade began showing cracks almost as soon as it was completed in 1959.

Solomon R. Guggenheim Museum

As a result, there have been many alterations and rounds of restoration. Most recently, in 1992, a 10-story annex was added to accommodate offices and more galleries, and in 2005 twelve layers of paint were removed from the facade to reveal and repair the cracks. That work is likely to continue through 2008.

Visit

♿ 🕐 *Open year-round Fri–Wed 10am–5:45pm (Fri until 8pm).* 🕐 *Closed Dec 25.* 👓 *$15 (Fri 6pm–8pm by donation).* 👣 *Guided tours daily at 11am (highlights) and at noon and 2pm (special exhibitions).* ✖ ☎ *212-423-3500. www.guggenheim.org.*

Few public spaces in New York rival the drama of the main gallery, encircled by the famous spiraling, quarter-mile-long ramp. Depending on the current show, you can start your visit at the top or bottom; either way, it will be a journey of discovery as Wright's kaleidoscopic composition of rounded forms unfolds and changes at every level. Additional galleries are in annex galleries off the ramp and on the top three floors of the annex building.

As for the art, the museum owns some 6,000 works, but only a hundred or so are displayed at any given time. Selections from the **Thannhauser collection**★—75 Impressionist, post-Impressionist and early Modern masterpieces—are shown in the second-floor annex galleries. The earliest work in the collection is a pre-Impressionist landscape by Pissaro from around 1867. There are also canvases by Renoir, Manet, van Gogh and Toulouse-

Guggenheim Goes Global

The Guggenheim has seen the value in expanding. It has also learned the risks. After the museum opened its hugely successful Bilbao outpost in Spain, designed by Frank Gehry in 1997, other cities clamored for a Guggenheim of their own. Berlin, Venice and Las Vegas each got one; then the money dried up. In 2002 Guggenheim SoHo closed, and plans for a Gehry-designed pile on the southern tip of Manhattan were scrapped. Staff was cut in half, and talks of Edinburgh, Tokyo and Salzburg spaces ended. In May 2003 there seemed to be a break in the clouds – the mayor of Rio de Janeiro, Brazil, signed on for a waterfront Guggenheim, the first in the southern hemisphere. But almost immediately the $170 million plan was savaged for being everything from culturally imperialistic to financially risky to ugly, and by mid-2005 the project appeared doomed. In June 2005, however, the museum announced the winner of a design competition for a Guggenheim in Guadalajara, Mexico.

Lautrec, as well as still-lifes by Cézanne and small sculptures by Degas and Maillol. Picasso is especially well represented, with both early paintings (*Woman Ironing*, 1904) and late ones (*Woman with Yellow Hair*, 1931). On the third floor you're likely to see some **paintings**★ by **Wassily Kandinsky** alongside other nonobjective works from the founding collection.

The rest of the museum is given over to large-scale temporary shows, some taking up virtually the whole museum, as did a recent overview of work by photograher Richard Prince and a sweeping survey of Russian art.

Lower East Side Tenement Museum★★

97 ORCHARD ST. AT BROOME ST.
MTA SUBWAY F TRAIN TO DELANCEY ST. OR B, D TRAIN TO GRAND ST.
MAP P 110

If Ellis Island recounts chapter one of the American immigrant experience, this remarkable museum recounts chapter two—out loud and in person. Tour guides interpret several generations of immigrant life at 97 Orchard Street, a five-story tenement building (now a National Historic Landmark) in the heart of what was once the most densely populated neighborhood in the US.

▸ **Orient Yourself:** The museum may be viewed by guided tour only. Tours meet at the visitor center at 108 Orchard Street, at Delancey St. Your tour guide will walk you down the block to the actual tenement building.

🕐 **Organizing Your Time:** Tours last approximately 1hr and are limited to 15 people. Each tour is offered between 4 and 16 times per week, depending on the day and the season. Advance tickets are recommended. You may buy tickets through the museum's website or by calling ☎866-811-4111. Same-day tickets, if available, can be purchased at 108 Orchard St.

Kids **Especially for Kids:** The Confino Living History Tour is geared for children 5 and over; other tours are appropriate for children 8 and older.

♿ **Also See:** ELLIS ISLAND MUSEUM.

A Bit of History

Between 1863 and 1935, some 7,000 people lived in this single structure alone. Many worked long shifts in nearby factories and slept short ones on couches and in chairs, hoping to save enough for a bigger apartment uptown. Yet as overcrowded as the Lower East Side was at the time, there was also a powerful sense of community here, with lively markets, vaudeville theaters and social networks that helped these new Americans feel at home.

Visit

🕐 *Visitor center and gift shop (at 108 Orchard St.) open year-round Mon–Fri 11am–6pm (Mon until 5:30pm), weekends 10:45am–6pm. Tenements may be visited by 1hr guided tour only (call for hours); additional tours Jul & Aug. Tickets $17, two tours for $25. ☎ 212-431-0233. www.tenement.org.*

Getting By – This tour brings visitors into the apartments of the German-Jewish Gumpertz family in the 1870s and the Sicilian-Catholic Baldizzi family in the 1930s. In addition to describing families' lives within the building, guides talk about what kinds of social-welfare services were available to them.

Levine Kitchen at the Lower East Side Tenement Museum

Piecing it Together – During this tour visitors get to know two Jewish families affiliated with the garment industry. Visitors "meet" the Polish-born Levines in 1897 following a family birth and the Rogarshevskys in 1918 following a family death.

Confino Living History – Kids *Weekends noon, 1pm, 2pm, & 3pm.* Geared toward families with children, the tour explores the apartment once occupied by the Confinos, Sephardic Jews who emi-grated to the US from what is now Greece in the 1900s. On hand to answer questions and tell stories is a guide acting as the family's sassy teenage daughter.

Moore Family Tour – The museum's newest tour introduces visitors to a family of Irish immigrants who lost a child while living at 97 Orchard Street in 1869, and examines the health-care choices they and other immigrant families faced in the 19C.

Morgan Library and Museum★★

225 MADISON AVE. AT 36TH ST.
MTA SUBWAY: 4, 5, 6 TRAIN TO 33RD ST.
MAP P 148

A cultural treasure trove, this highly regarded institution houses an outstanding collection of rare books, manuscripts, drawings, prints, paintings, ancient seals and letters assembled by J. Pierpont Morgan (1837–1913) and augmented after his death. The recent expansion and renovation by star architect Renzo Piano gives even more reason to visit.

A Bit of History

The Collection – Son of financier Junius Spencer Morgan, **J. Pierpont Morgan** built his father's firm into the largest private bank in the USA. The House of Morgan, as it was known, bailed out the US government to head off a depression in 1895, developed the railroad system, and helped form US Steel.

Morgan began collecting seriously in 1890, eventually amassing more than 3,000 objects, including 600 medieval and Renaissance manuscripts and 1,500

Old Master drawings. The collection has since expanded with purchases and gifts, including the Pierre Matisse Gallery archives in 1998, containing letters from artists including Balthus, Chagall, Miró and others.

The Campus – In 1902 J. Pierpont Morgan commissioned the firm of **McKim, Mead and White** to build a permanent home for his collection that would be accessible to the public following his death. The Beaux-Arts main building *(33 E. 36th St.)* was completed in 1906 after several tempestuous tugs-of-war between Morgan and Charles McKim. A boxy annex on the corner of Madison Avenue and 36th Street was added by Morgan's son in 1928. These two buildings were later joined to a large brownstone building on the corner of Madison Avenue and East 37th Street – the younger Morgan's former residence. By the turn of the 20C, however, the collection had outgrown the space, and the facilities needed modernizing and upgrading. Noted for his museum work, the Italian architect Renzo Piano oversaw a three-year, $100 million redesign and expansion, linking the three buildings with glass pavilions and carving out space for a 280-seat theater underground. The new campus—with double the exhibition space as the old one—was unveiled in 2006 to critical raves.

Visit

🕐*Open Tue–Fri 10:30am–5pm (Fri until 9pm), Sat 10am–6pm & Sun 11am–6pm.* 👟 *Guided tours offered daily; call for schedule.* 🎫 *$12 (free Fri 7–9pm).* ✕ ♿ ☎ *212-685-0008. www.themorgan.org.* The most striking feature of Renzo Piano's design is the lobby, a soaring glass atrium off which the old buildings and new galleries radiate. At the rear of the lobby you'll find the casual Morgan Cafe, with the more formal Morgan Dining Room and gift shop in the brownstone to your left (south side). To the right (north) and on the second floor are the exhibtion areas.

Study and Library★★ – The opulence of Mr. Morgan's former **study** is enhanced by a painted and carved wood ceiling (16C), red damask hangings, 15-17C stained-glass windows and massive black wood furniture. Among the works of art here are Tintoretto's *Portrait of a Moor* (1570) and one of the museum's three Gutenberg bibles. Lined with three-tiered, floor-to-ceiling bookshelves, Morgan's **library** showcases the financier's passion for the written word. A 16C Flemish tapestry representing the Triumph of Avarice hangs above the marble fireplace, and the carved ceiling sports a series of lunettes and painted spandrels featuring the signs of the zodiac.

Engelhard Gallery★★ – *2nd floor.* This gallery contains rotating selections from the museum's permanent collection. Among the items you might discover here are drawings by Rembrandt, Leonardo, Degas, and Dürer; original scores by Mahler, Beethoven, Schubert, and Gilbert and Sullivan; and handwritten literary manuscripts by Dickens, Twain, Jane Austen, and Thoreau.

Morgan Stanley Galleries – Special exhibitions are mounted in these spacious galleries. One recent show, "Painted with Words," displayed the correspondence between Vincent van Gogh to his young colleague Emile Bernard.

Thaw Gallery – This tiny gallery shows off the museum's store of medieval reliquaries, manuscripts and sculptures.

Museum of the City of New York ★★

FIFTH AVE. AT 103RD ST.

MTA SUBWAY: 6 TRAIN TO 103RD ST.

MAP P 191

Founded in 1923 as America's first institution dedicated to the history of a city as well as its present and future, this museum chronicles the changing face of New York from a modest Dutch trading post to a thriving international metropolis. The museum's rich collections span three centuries of New York memorabilia, decorative arts, furnishings, silver, prints and paintings.

▸ **Orient Yourself:** A lofty rotunda, dominated by a graceful, spiraling staircase, bisects two long galleries displaying rotating exhibits. The information desk is located to the right of the entranceway and the museum shop to the left.

🕐 **Organizing Your Time:** Plan about 2hrs to see the museum.

Kids **Especially for Kids:** The Toy Gallery and model ship collections.

👍 **Also See:** NEW-YORK HISTORICAL SOCIETY.

Visit

Kids 🕐 *Open year-round Tue–Sun 10am–5pm.* 🕐 *Closed Jan 1, Thanksgiving Day & Dec 25.* 💲 *$9.* 📞 *Guided tours available.* ♿ ☎ *212-534-1672. www.mcny.org.*

Basement – The Volunteer Fire Gallery depicts the history of fire fighting through prints, texts and artifacts, including a horse-drawn double-decker Big Six model.

Second Floor – Six **period alcoves** ranging from a traditional Dutch living room (17C) to a late-19C drawing room contain appropriate furnishings and costumes reflecting the evolution of New York interiors. Highlighting the gallery, the luminous stained-glass window was crafted in Paris for the H.G. Marquand House. Examples of three centuries of **silver**, including tea services and monogrammed tankards, are displayed in the New York silver collection. Parlor furnishings found in various galleries include a cabinet-bookcase given to songstress Jenny Lind that contains seven volumes of Audubon's *Birds of America*. Other galleries present the marine history of New York through model ships, carved figureheads and paintings.

Third Floor – The Toy Gallery features playthings from the museum's collection of some 10,000 items. Arrayed thematically, the objects range from plush teddy bears to intricate mechanical banks. The exquisite **dollhouses** include the rare 1769 Ann Anthony Pavilion noted for its "shadow box" style and primitive wax figures. The Stettheimer House re-creates a 1920s New York brownstone complete with artwork by Marcel Duchamp and other avant-garde artists.

Lining the walls of the main hall, paintings of New York cityscapes provide a pictorial history of the changing urban scene from 1800 to 1900.

Fifth Floor – Two rooms from John D. Rockefeller's 1860s residence reflect the opulent tastes of the late-Victorian era. The master bedroom has heavy damask furnishings and gilt-framed paintings from Rockefeller's private collection. The American Renaissance-style dressing room contains inlaid-pearl rosewood furnishings by master woodworker George Schasty.

Museum of the City of New York

Museum of Jewish Heritage★★

36 BATTERY PL. (IN BATTERY PARK CITY).
MTA SUBWAY: 4 OR 5 TRAIN TO BOWLING GREEN.
MAP P 80

Like its eminent neighbors the Statue of Liberty and Ellis Island, this ever-evolving Jewish history museum, which titles itself "A Living Memorial to the Holocaust," celebrates freedom while remembering the stories of those who struggled to achieve it.

🕐 **Organizing Your Time:** Plan about 2–3hrs to see the museum. Consider having lunch at the Heritage Cafe, an excellent onsite kosher restaurant with harbor views.

Kids **Especially for Kids:** The museum's family guide, available at the admissions desk, contains a tour of the first floor of the museum for children ages 7 to 11. Parents should use discretion in bringing children through the "The War against the Jews" and "Ours to Fight For" exhibits, as both contain graphic material.

👁 **Also See:** THE JEWISH MUSEUM.

A Bit of History

The museum is one of the most architecturally striking in New York. Not only does it command some of the finest views of the harbor, but its design (Roche, Dinkeloo and Assocs.) is steeped in significance. The main structure's six planar facades and six-tiered roof symbolize the six points of the Star of David and recall the six million people who died in the Holocaust. This section, holding 30,000sq ft of exhibition space, opened in 1997. Expansion followed almost immediately. The 80,000sq ft Robert M. Morgenthau Wing—containing a theater, a lecture hall, more gallery space, a cafe and other features—was designed by the same architects and completed in 2003. Together the two structures form a graceful composite.

Visit

🕐 *Open year-round Sun-Thu 10am–5:45pm (Wed until 8pm), Fri 10am–5pm during daylight savings (rest of the year & on eve of Jewish holidays until 3pm).*
🕐 *Closed Thanksgiving Day & Jewish*

© Museum of Jewish Heritage

Garden of Stones, Museum of Jewish Heritage

holidays. ⏰ $10 (free Wed 4pm–8pm). ♿
✂ ☎ 646-437-4200. www.mjhnyc.org.
The main, ziggurat-shaped building holds the museum's core exhibit of 2,000 historic photographs, 800 historical and cultural artifacts and 24 original documentary films. The objects are arranged on three floors, each of which is focused on a distinct theme. Storytelling is at the heart of the museum's mission. "Jewish Life a Century Ago," on the first floor, recounts Jewish life and culture from the 1880s to the 1930s. The second floor's "War against the Jews" deals with the Holocaust. Particularly poignant are the six **Klarsfeld pillars**, columns covered with photographs of some 2,000 French citizens deported to and killed at Auschwitz. Each picture is brought to life with a short biographical sketch. **Louis Bannet's trumpet** is also on display. Nicknamed the "Dutch Louis Armstrong," the

Rotterdam native was sent to the Auschwitz-Birkenau camp but spared for his astounding musicianship; he was the personal bandleader for Dr. Josef Mengele. A massive Torah scroll ends the exhibit in the skylit galleries of the third floor, under the banner of "Jewish Renewal." Here visitors can also enjoy splendid **views**★★ of the harbor.

The galleries in the adjoining **Morgenthau Wing** hold temporary exhibits.

In 2003 the museum inaugurated English sculptor Andy Goldsworthy's permanent outdoor installation **Garden of Stones**★. To represent life emerging from lifelessness, Goldsworthy hollowed out 18 boulders, filled them with soil, and planted a single dwarf oak in each. As the trees mature in the coming decades – it will take 50 years for them to reach maturity – the trees will become part of the stone.

National Museum of the American Indian★★

1 BOWLING GREEN
MTA 4 OR 5 TRAIN TO BOWLING GREEN
MAP P 80

The Smithsonian Institution opened this small but smartly curated museum in 1994, after Congress passed an act allotting funds to foster and protect Native arts and culture. For 10 years it was the Smithsonian's only such display space; then, in September 2004, a $199 million, 250,000sq ft facility was opened on the Mall in Washington, DC to great fanfare. Still, the New York branch has plenty to recommend it.

A Bit of History

The museum's home is indeed a grand setting. The **Alexander Hamilton US Custom House**★★, overlooking Bowling Green, ranks among the finest Beaux-Arts structures in the city. Designed by Cass Gilbert and completed in 1907, the granite building rises seven stories and is embellished with 44 massive columns, each topped with the head of Mercury, the god of commerce. Daniel Chester French, sculptor of the Lincoln statue in Washington, DC's Lincoln Memorial, created the four female figures flanking the entrance: they represent the Asian, African, European and American continents.

The Man Behind the Museum – The New York branch of the National Museum of the American Indian is known as the **George Gustav Heye Center** in honor of the man who founded the collection. Heye (1874-1957), a wealthy investment banker, gathered almost a million objects from indigenous peoples throughout the Western Hemisphere, buying pretty much everything he could lay his hands on starting with a deerskin shirt in 1897. The strategy succeeded in filling first his personal museum, then this one and now much of the new museum in Washington, DC.

National Museum of the American Indian

Visit

🕐 *Open year-round daily 10am–5pm (Thur until 8pm).* 🕐 *Closed Dec 25.* ♿ ☎ *212-514-3700. www.si.edu/nmai.*
Step inside to view the soaring oval **rotunda**, encircled with murals painted by Reginald Marsh in 1936-37. The museum's galleries branch off from this central space and contain changing exhibits. One recent year-long show (2007–08) put a spotlight on the astounding craftsmanship of the Pacific Coast tribes, with more than 400 ceremonial and everyday objects on display, along with commentary on the works by contemporary native artists. The Diker Pavilion for Native Arts and Culture was inaugurated in September 2006 with a two-year-long survey of 77 works from the permanent collection. Among the most eye-catching pieces were a hand-painted set of Apache playing cards dating from 1880; a 1910 Nez Perce basketry hat; a pair of Huron mocassins, embroidered with moose hair around 1820; and a 1940 Quechua girl's dancing outfit with matching hat and cape, from Peru.

New-York Historical Society★★

2 W. 77TH ST.

🚇 B, C TRAIN TO 81ST ST. OR 1, 9 TRAIN TO 79TH ST.

MAP P211

Housed in an imposing Neoclassical building fronting Central Park, the New-York Historical Society approaches its rich trove of material with a keenly modern curatorial eye. In addition to its antique treasures, including a number of prominent Hudson River School paintings, it has amassed the world's most comprehensive collection of artifacts related to the September 11, 2001, terrorist attacks.

🏛 **Don't Miss:** The Henry Luce III Center for the Study of American Culture, an engrossing display of art and arcana, highlights of which are expounded on by prominent New Yorkers.

🏛 **Also See:** THE MUSEUM OF THE CITY OF NEW YORK.

A Bit of History

The city's oldest museum, the New-York Historical Society was chartered in 1804 with a view to preserving the history of the US, and since then has amassed a 60,000-work collection that embraces three centuries of Americana. While most exhibits usually touch on some aspect of New York and its history, some have a national scope. One of the society's most cherished holdings is its set of 435 watercolors by John James Audubon, made in preparation for the plates illustrating his classic text Birds of America (1827-38). Around 40 of these light-sensitive works are displayed each year roughly from mid-February to mid-March.

Visit

🕐 Open year-round Tue–Sat 10am–6pm (Fri until 8pm), Sun 11am–5:45pm. 🎫 $10 (free Fri 6pm–8pm). ✕ ♿ ☎ 212-873-3400. www.nyhistory.org.
First floor – The galleries on the first floor hold large temporary exhibits of art and artifacts, many of which are culled from the society's archives. In 2007, "Here Is New York: Remembering September 11" displayed photographs, audiotape, videotape and artifacts from that tragic day.

Second floor – Thomas Cole's The Course of the Empire and other works from the **Hudson River school** are hung on a rotating basis alongside smaller landscapes and portraiture by Rembrandt Peale and others.

Third floor – Located on this floor, the society's renowned library of historic prints and photographs is open to researchers only.

Fourth floor – The Henry Luce III Center for the Study of American Culture presents a mesmerizing array of nearly 40,000 objects, in what it calls a "working storage" format. Floor-to-ceiling glass cases are packed with board games, spectacles, Tiffany lamps, firefighting equipment, clocks, busts, china–you name it–all organized according to type and described in fascinating detail on the self-guided audio tour. Also on this floor is a permanent exhibit on slavery in New York.

Rubin Museum of Art★★

150 W. 17TH ST. AT 7TH AVE.
MTA 1 TRAIN TO 14TH ST.
MAP P 134

Inaugurated in October 2004, this stunning museum is the first Western institution dedicated solely to presenting and interpreting the little-known art of Bhutan, Tibet, Nepal and other parts of the Himalayas.

A Bit of History

The museum is the brainchild of businessman Donald Rubin and his wife, Shelley, who, after amassing one of the world's largest private collections of Himalayan art, decided to share it with the public. First they founded the Web site himalayanart.org, an online catalog of 25,000 works, and then they financed this lovingly curated facility in Chelsea. The space, which used to house Barney's department store, was transformed into a museum by Richard Blinder of the architectural firm Beyer Blinger Belle.

Visit

🕐 Open year-round Mon & Thu 11am–5pm, Wed 11am–7pm, Fri 11am–10pm, weekends 11am–6pm. 🕐 Closed Jan 1, Thanksgiving Day & Dec 25. 🎫 $10 (free Fri 7pm–10pm). ♿ ✕ 🎧 Guided tours (1hr) weekdays at 3pm, weekends at 1pm and 3pm. ☎ 212-620-5000. www.rmanyc.org.

Shea Dean

Rubin Museum of Art

Cool stone floors and warm, polished-wood accents make the main floor of the museum both spacious and inviting. Upper levels, reached via elevator or spiral staircase, have a hushed quality appropriate to the art on display, much of which has a spiritual component.

Some 900 paintings, sculpture, textiles and ritual objects spanning two millennia are on display. Most pieces date from the 12C to the present and were made to inspire faith, explain religious concepts or tell sacred stories, though they can be equally appreciated on the grounds of technique, imagination and individual artistry. Curators encourage both modes of appreciation, providing informative wall texts, yet letting the beauty of the work speak for itself.

Of special interest to first-time visitors is the permanent second-floor exhibit "What Is It?" – an introduction to Himalayan art. Galleries on the third and sixth floors take the viewer behind the scenes, answering questions about why and for whom the art was made. The sixth floor holds special exhibits, such as a recent display of large-scale paintings from the permanent collection.

Whitney Museum of American Art★★

945 MADISON AVE.
MTA SUBWAY: 6 TRAIN TO 77TH ST.
MAP P 200

Dedicated to the advancement of contemporary artists, this museum holds one of the world's foremost collections of 20C American art, housed in a stark granite building designed by Marcel Breuer and Hamilton Smith. Rising above a sunken sculpture garden in a series of inverted stairs, the cantilevered structure (1966) represents a striking example of the Brutalism style of architecture.

☺ **Don't Miss:** If you're lucky enough to be in the city between March and June on an even-numbered year, be sure to stop by the Whitney Biennial, a survey of the contemporary American art scene that never fails to raise eyebrows.

♿ **Also See:** The Whitney Museum of American Art at Altria, a satellite gallery and sculpture court at 120 Park Avenue at 42nd Street. Admission is free.

A Bit of History

Founded in 1931, the museum grew out of the Greenwich Village studio of sculptor and art collector **Gertrude Vanderbilt Whitney** (1875-1942). After founding the Whitney Studio Club, Whitney began acquiring works by living American artists, creating the core of today's collection of more than 10,000 works by painters such as Edward Hopper, de Kooning, Kelly, Gorky, Prendergast, Demuth and Motherwell, and sculptors such as Calder, Nevelson, Noguchi and David Smith. The museum moved to the current building, its third home, in 1966. From its inception, the museum has provided a unique venue for American artists and played a special role in the development of contemporary art. The museum's frequently changing exhibit programs have been known to explore daring, innovative and often controversial topics. The film and video department presents works by independent American film and video artists. The museum is also known for its invitational biennials, held since 1932, which attempt to offer the public a representative cross section of the current American art scene.

Visit

🕐 Open year-round Wed, Thu, Sat & Sun 11am–6pm, Fri 1pm–9pm. 🕐 Closed Jan 1, Thanksgiving Day & Dec 25. 🎫 $15 (Fri 6pm–9pm pay what you wish). ♿ ✕ 🍽 Guided tours (1hr) available. ☎ 212-570-3676 or 800-944-8639. www.whitney.org.

The **permanent collection** is displayed on a rotating basis in galleries on the fifth floor. Masterworks of American art from the first half of the 20C are continuously on view, including paintings by Hopper, Marsden Hartley, Georgia O'Keeffe, Stuart Davis and Arshile Gorky. Also featured is a selection of postwar and contemporary works by such artists as Philip Guston, Jasper Johns, Alex Katz, Lee Krasner, Jackson Pollock, Kiki Smith and Andy Warhol. Large temporary exhibits fill up the other floors.

THE BRONX

AREA: 42 SQUARE MILES

POPULATION: 1,332,650

The only New York borough located on the mainland, the Bronx typifies the contradictions of a mature urban environment. Marked by run-down apartment buildings and massive projects, the South Bronx is inhabited mainly by low-income groups – and the multibillion-dollar baseball franchise the New York Yankees. The central Bronx holds the world-famous Bronx Zoo and the New York Botanical Garden. Grand mansions and lush gardens characterize prosperous sections of the north Bronx such as Riverdale. To the east lies the largest park in New York City, Pelham Bay Park, with its popular sandy beach, Orchard Beach.

The Bronx was named after Jonas Bronck, a Swedish émigré who arrived here in 1639. In the late 1800s the borough developed around the village of Morrisania (AZ on map p 272), which now forms

the section of the Bronx centered on Third Avenue and 161st Street. The village was named after members of the Morris family, prominent during the Revolutionary period: Lewis Morris, a

©iStockphoto.com/Terraxplorer

Enid Haupt Conservatory, New York Botanical Garden

Famous Residents

Among the celebrities who have called the Bronx home are actors Tony Curtis, Anne Bancroft and Penny Marshall; athlete Lou Gehrig; writers Edgar Allan Poe, Mark Twain and Herman Wouk; statesmen John Adams, John F. Kennedy and Colin Powell; and fashion designers Calvin Klein and Ralph Lauren.

signer of the Declaration of Independence, and Gouverneur Morris, a member of the US Constitutional Convention.

As settlement of the Bronx blossomed, journalist John Mullaly led a movement to buy inexpensive land parcels and preserve them as parks. As a result, almost 25 percent of the borough today consists of parkland. In 1891 New York University opened a campus near Morris Heights; Bronx Community College later acquired the campus. Today the borough boasts some 16 colleges and universities.

The Bronx was a part of Westchester County until 1898, when it was in-corporated into New York City. In 1904 the first subway line connecting the Bronx to the island of Manhattan opened, causing significant migration to this outlying borough. Jews from Eastern and Central Europe settled here en masse, and by 1949 almost 50 percent of Bronx residents were Jewish. That figure has declined precipitously in the years since; today Hispanics make up about half of the Bronx's population. Another third are African American. The latest addition to the Bronx is the Fulton Fish Market, which moved from Lower Manhattan in 2005 to acreage near Hunts Point Cooperative Market.

Bronx Zoo★★★

Bronx River Pkwy. at Fordham Rd. MTA 2 train to West Farms Square/E. Tremont Ave. to zoo's Asian entrance or Liberty Lines BXM11 express bus, making stops along Madison Avenue, between 26th and 99th Streets.

Covering 265 acres of woodland, this popular zoo is the largest urban wildlife park in the country, exhibiting more than 4,000 creatures in settings that replicate as closely as possible the animals' natural habitats.

↑ Hudson River Museum

NEW JERSEY

Palisades Interstate Pkwy.

HUDSON RIVER

Westchester

Broadway

Riverdale Ave.

Henry Hudson Pkwy.

Van Cortland Park

★ Wave Hill 7

FIELDSTON

YONKERS

McLean Ave.

County

River Ave.

E. 241st St.

W.

Nereid Ave.

Bainbridge

WOODLAWN 5

WAKEFIELD

E. 233rd St.

Woodlawn

White Plains

WILLIAMSBRIDGE

E. 233rd St.

★ Van Cortlandt House Museum

RIVERDALE

Broadway

Mosholu

Jerome Ave.

X

Riverdale Ave.

Deegan

Henry Hudson Pkwy.

Hudson Pkwy.

8 SPUYTEN DUYVIL

W. 230th St.

Major Deegan

KINGSBRIDGE

W. Gun Hill Rd. 4

1

Gun Hill Rd.

Inwood Hill Park

MANHATTAN

Dyckman St.

Tenth Ave.

Goulden Ave.

Jerome Ave.

Lehman College

BEDFORD PARK

Valentine-Varian House 3

Plains

Boston Rd.

Allerton Ave.

1

Fort Tryon Park

9A

9

Poe Cottage ★

Webster Ave.

Fordham Univ.

Botanical Garden ★★

THE BRONX

Broadway

Drive

Harlem River Drive

6

Hall of Fame ★

Bronx Community College (CUNY)

MORRIS HEIGHTS

University Ave.

Cross

10

Bronx Ave.

FORDHAM

E. Fordham Rd.

Southern Blvd.

Bronx River Pkwy.

Bronx River

BRONX ZOO ★★★

Bronx

PELHAM PARKWAY

MORRIS PARK

VAN NEST

White Plains

E. Tremont Ave.

PARKCHESTER

Castle Hill

Y

2

HIGH BRIDGE

Jerome Ave.

Grand Concourse

Webster Ave.

TREMONT

EAST TREMONT

Third Ave.

Boston Rd.

Southern Blvd.

Crotona Park

Bronx River Expwy.

WEST FARMS

Westchester Ave.

95

Cross Expwy.

278

New Yankee Stadium (const.)

Yankee Stadium ★ 161st St.

MORRISANIA

E. 163rd St.

Sheridan Expwy.

Bruckner Expwy.

895

UNION PORT

Deegan

MELROSE

149th St.

Westchester Blvd.

Bruckner Expwy.

HUNTS POINT

Hunts Point Ave.

Bronx River

Soundview

CLASONS POINT

Soundview Ave.

Z

Lenox Ave.

Madison Ave.

Third Ave.

Willis Ave.

Grand Concourse

MOTT HAVEN

87

9

278

PORT MORRIS

EAST RIVER

Rikers Island

THE BRONX

0   1 mi
0   1 km

A   B

▶ **Orient Yourself:** When you buy your ticket, be sure to get a map. Plot out a course for the day before you begin.

◉ **Don't Miss:** The Wild Asia Monorail and Congo Gorilla Forest.

◕ **Organizing Your Time:** Lines can be long at the most popular attractions, such as the Skyfari gondola ride, the Wild Asia exhibit, Congo Gorilla Forest, and the Bug Carousel, especially on weekends and as the afternoon draws on. Plan your visit for a weekday, if possible, and aim to see these exhibits in the morning.

Kids **Especially for Kids:** The whole zoo is geared for kids, but the Bug Carousel and the Children's Zoo are particularly child-centric.

A Bit of History

The Bronx Zoo is located in Bronx Park, a vast expanse of land laid out in the late 19C on both banks of the Bronx River. Opened in 1899, it has expanded its mandate from merely presenting animals to the public to conserving them in the wild, a trend marked by the New York Zoological Society's name change to the Wildlife Conservation Society (WCS) in 1993.

Today the zoo exhibits some 2,000 mammals, 1,000 birds, and 1,000 reptiles and amphibians, in addition to more than 2,000 invertebrates, in a series of realistic exhibits that make every effort to replicate the animals' natural habitats. It is ranked among the leading zoos in

🙂 A Bit of Advice 🙂

While there are many concession stands throughout the zoo, most sell expensive and unhealthy food such as fried chicken, french fries, nachos, hot dogs, ice cream and soda. To save money and eat more healthfully we recommend that you bring your lunch. You're free to use the tables clustered around the concession stands regardless of what's on your plate.

Bronx Zoo Express

One of the easiest ways to get to the zoo is by bus. The Liberty Lines BXM11 express bus ($4; *exact change required; no MetroCards; www.libertylines.com*) runs every 20 minutes, picking up along Madison Ave. in Manhattan at 27th, 32nd, 39th, 47th, 54th, 63rd, 70th, 84th and 99th streets. The Bronx Zoo is the first stop after 99th Street.

the country for its exhibit technology and captive management techniques.

Visit

Kids &. ⏰ *Open Apr-Oct Mon–Fri 10am–5pm, weekends & holidays 10am–5:30pm. Rest of the year daily 10am–4:30pm.* ⌨ *$14 ($10 children 3–12), plus additional fees for some exhibits as indicated below; Wed by donation.* 👈 *Guided tours available; reservations required. Many exhibits close 15-30min before zoo closes.* ✗ 🅿 *$10.* ☏ *718-367-1010. www.bronxzoo.com.* The Bronx Zoo has more than 20 indoor and outdoor animal exhibits as well as a number of rides and attractions, from camel rides to the bug carousel (in lieu of carnival horses, the carousel has colorful insects for kids to ride). Here are a few of the best.

Congo Gorilla Forest★★ – ⌨ *$3*. This 6.5-acre, African rain forest habitat is the zoo's most thrilling exhibit. It provides a home to 400 animals of 55 species, including 23 lowland gorillas, one of the largest and most important breeding groups in North America. Exhibit entry fees are earmarked toward conservation programs in Africa. In addition to the gorillas, you'll find pygmy marmosets, okapi and mandrills, as well as DeBrazza's and black-and-white colobus monkeys.

Skyfari★★ – *Apr–Oct.* ⌨*$3.* Travel about the treetops from the zoo center to Wild Asia on this high-flying gondola. It's a quick and beautiful way to get across the park.

Tiger Mountain★★ – The ingenious design of this exhibit – the viewing platform is tucked within the naturalistic enclosure, behind glass – lets viewers get within several yards of gorgeous Siberian tigers. Watch these royal creatures relax by the pool, prowl the forest or play with their toys. Demonstrations at 11:30am, 1:30pm and 3:30pm daily.

Wild Asia★★ – *May–Oct.* ⌨ *$5.* Zookeepers will describe what you're seeing as you take a monorail ride (20min) through 38 acres of hilly, wooded land, home to IndoChinese tigers, gaur cattle from Thailand, red pandas, Asian rhinoceroses and Mongolian wild horses.

Children's Zoo★ – ⌨ *$3.* This zoo-within-the-zoo houses some 500 animals and features a fun prairie dog exhibit, a rope spider web and a farmyard where kids can feed domestic animals.

D. DeMello ©Wildlife Conservation Society

Siberian Tiger, Bronx Zoo

New York Botanical Garden★★

Map p271. 200th St. & Kazimiroff Blvd.
MTA *B, D or 4 train to Bedford Park Blvd., then take the Bx 26 bus east to the Mosholu Gate entrance. Or take Metro North train from Grand Central Terminal to Botanical Garden Station.* Located directly north of the zoo, this is one of the largest and oldest gardens in the country. Walking trails wind through its 250 rolling acres, past thousands of flowering trees, shrubs and plants that reach their peak in spring and early summer. A large conservatory and creative special exhibits make a visit rewarding in the fall and winter months as well.

▶ **Orient Yourself:** At the entrance you can pick up a map and learn about the day's special events.

Don't Miss: The Enid A. Haupt Conservatory, beautiful in all seasons.

Kids Especially for Kids: The **Everett Children's Adventure Garden** shows how plants live and function.

A Bit of History

The New York Botanical Garden was founded in 1891 after Columbia University botany professor Nathaniel Lord Britton and his wife, Elizabeth, visited England's Royal Botanic Gardens at Kew and decided New York should have a similar horticultural showpiece. They chose this large tract in the north Bronx and forged a public-private partnership between the city and noted philanthropists such as Andrew Carnegie, Cornelius Vanderbilt and J. Pierpont Morgan to finance the buildings and build the collections. In 1896 the New York Botanical Garden appointed Nathaniel Lord Britton its first director, and since then the garden has grown in its size and mission, both displaying a wondeful array of plants and blooms and conducting important botanical research.

Visit

♿ ⏰ *Open Apr–Oct Tue–Sun 10am–6pm. Rest of the year Tue–Sun 10am–5pm.* ⏰ *Closed Thanksgiving Day & Dec 25.*

✉ *$13 ($6 grounds only); additional fees for special exhibits; grounds admission free all day Wed & Sat 10am–noon.* 🎧 *Guided tours available.* 🍴 🅿 *$10.* ☎ *718-817-8700. www.nybg.org.*

The New York Botanical Garden has more than fifty gardens to explore, from the lovely perennial and herb gardens, to the rock garden and forest. Here are a few favorites.

Enid A. Haupt Conservatory★★ – The nation's largest Victorian glasshouse, this magical conservatory opened to the public in 1902 and is now home to "A World of Plants," a global ecotour that includes tropical rain forests, deserts, and the world's most comprehensive collection of palm trees under glass. The conservatory hosts the garden's popular seasonal flower shows, including the orchid show in March, bonsai show in October and model train show in December. Green thumbs can also get advice at the home gardening center.

Peggy Rockefeller Rose Garden★★ – Beautifully renovated in 2007, the garden dates back to 1916 and now features more than 3,000 rose plants, from antique roses to modern hybrid teas, floribundas, and shrub roses. They're in fragrant bloom each spring (beginning in late May) and fall (beginning in early September).

Everett Children's Adventure Garden★ – This garden is full of hands-on activities that allow children to learn how plants live and function.

International Plant Science Center★ – Here you can visit the library's reading room and rare book room, an exhibition gallery and the orchid rotunda. A five-story addition to the center houses a herbarium containing 7 million plant specimens, the largest such collection in the Western Hemisphere. Enjoy lunch or a snack in the Garden Cafe, bordering lush display gardens.

Around The Bronx

Map pp 272-273. Grid letters in parentheses after each attraction's name refer to map.

Yankee Stadium★ (AZ)

161st St. & River Ave. **MTA** *B, D, or 4 trains to 161st St.* **Kids** 🎧 *Tour information:*

☎ 718-579-4531. *Tour and ticket information at www.yankees.com.*

This famous baseball stadium – "the house that Ruth built" – will host its last season in 2008. Beginning in April 2009, the Bronx Bombers will play in a brand-new stadium being constructed just north of it – one with 6,000 fewer seats to make room for 60 luxury boxes, to the dismay of everyday fans.

Tours of the 1923 stadium will continue through the 2008 season and are sure to be especially poignant and popular, so book well in advance. Guides relate Yankees lore, dwelling especially on the great Babe Ruth, and lead fans through Monument Park, a series of bronze plaques behind the left-centerfield fence commemorating Yankee superstars; the club house; the press box; and a dugout. Still, nothing beats seeing a game – try to catch one if you can.

Valentine-Varian House (BX)

3266 Bainbridge Ave. at E. 208th St.
MTA *D train to 205th St., or 4 train to Mosholu Pkwy.* ○ *Visit by guided tour (30min) only, year-round Sat 10am-4pm, Sun 1pm–5pm.* ○ *Closed major holidays & Dec 25–Jan 1.* ☞ *$3.* ☎ *718-881-8900. www.bronxhistoricalsociety.org.*

This fieldstone house originally stood on the opposite side of the street, on land acquired in 1758 by Isaac Valentine. The scene of many skirmishes during the Revolution, the area was purchased in 1791 by Isaac Varian, a prosperous farmer whose son later became the 63rd mayor of New York City. Situated on its present site since 1965, the house now contains the **Museum of Bronx History**, which features changing exhibits on the history of the borough.

Poe Cottage (AY)

E. Kingsbridge Rd. & Grand Concourse.
MTA *D or 4 train to Kingsbridge Rd.* ☞ *Visit by guided tour (30min) only, year-round Sat 10am–4pm, Sun 1pm–5pm.* ○ *Closed major holidays & Dec 25–Jan 1.* ☞ *$3.* ☎ *718-881-8900. www.bronxhistoricalsociety.org.*

From 1846 to 1849 this little wooden house (1812) was the home of author **Edgar Allan Poe** (1809-49), who wrote "Annabel Lee" and other poems during his stay here. Poe moved to this cottage and away from the noise and congestion of New York City in the hope of saving his wife, Virginia Clemm, from tuberculosis; she died, however, in 1847. The author died two years later in Baltimore, while on a return trip to the cottage from Virginia. The cottage was moved across the street in 1913 and transformed into a museum in 1917. Today the restored house contains displays of memorabilia and manuscripts, and an audiovisual slide show *(20min)*.

Van Cortlandt House Museum★ (AX)

Enter Van Cortlandt Park at Broadway & 246th St. MTA *1 train to 242nd St.–Van Cortlandt Park.* ○ *Open year-round Tue–Fri 10am–3pm, weekends 11am–4pm.* ○ *Closed major holidays.* ☞ *$5 (free Wed).* ☎ *718-543-3344. www.vancortlandthouse.org.*

Built in 1748, this colonial plantation house has been admirably preserved by the city and the National Society of Colonial Dames. It is believed that George Washington used the house as headquarters before making his triumphant entry into New York City in November 1783. The manor, appointed with furnishings in the Colonial style, reflects a refinement and style of living typical of 18C and 19C New York gentry. Among the nine rooms open to the public, note the Dutch room, the kitchen, and the nursery, which contains one of America's oldest dollhouses.

Bronx Community College (AY)

University Ave. & W. 181st St. MTA *4 train to Burnside Ave.; walk 4 blocks west to University Ave., then north to campus.* ♿ ✕ Ⓟ ☞ *Free guided tours available.* ☎ *718-289-5161. www.cuny.edu/bcc.*

Founded in 1891 as the Bronx campus of New York University, the institution is now home to Bronx Community College. The 52-acre campus lines the banks of the Harlem River and boasts the **Hall of Fame for Great Americans**★ *(Hall of Fame Terrace at W. 181st St.).* Completed by Stanford White in 1900, this Beaux-Arts complex, the first American pantheon, consists of an outdoor colonnade, 630ft in length, surrounding three buildings (Gould Memorial Library, the Language

Arthur Avenue

www.arthuravenue.com. This petite stretch of red-sauce joints and pungent food markets in the Belmont community, just west of Bronx Park, is known affectionately by New Yorkers as the real Little Italy, partly because it's still an Italian-American (and not Chinese) stronghold, and partly because it's not as touristy as Manhattan's version. Start out at the **Arthur Avenue Retail Market** *(no. 2344),* which is crammed with stalls hawking everything from wheels of parmigiano reggiano to eggs and sliced veal. Some of the best stalls are **Mike's Deli** for incredible sandwiches and **Cafe al Mercato** for oven-fresh Sicilian pizza. For a meal you'll never forget, get in line at **Dominick's** *(no. 2335; ☎ 718-733-2807),* the legendary Southern Italian joint where the waiters tabulate the bills in their heads (no menu, no checks) and the crowd is always lively. For seafood antipasto of mussels, squid and lobster in a spicy tomato sauce, settle in at the slightly fancier **Mario's** *(no. 2342; ☎ 718-584-1188),* a 1919 institution made famous in Mario Puzo's book *The Godfather.*

Hall and Philosophy Hall). Bronze busts of 98 outstanding Americans in numerous fields – from Susan B. Anthony to the Wright brothers – line the niches of the colonnade.

Pelham Bay Park (CXY)

MTA *6 train to Pelham Bay Park.*

The largest park in the city offers a variety of outdoor activities including golfing, hiking, cycling, tennis, horseback riding, ball playing and fishing. Providing a welcome refuge for swimmers on hot summer days, popular Orchard Beach features one mile of sandy shore.

Bartow-Pell Mansion Museum★ (CY)

895 Shore Rd., within the park. ◑ *Open year-round Wed & weekends noon–4pm.* ◑ *Closed major holidays.* ◈ *$5.* 🅿. ☎ *718-885-1461. www.bartowpellmansionmuseum.org.*

The history of this site dates to 1654, when Thomas Pell purchased the land from the Siwanoy Indians. Robert Bartow, a descendant of Pell's, built the Neoclassical stone mansion overlooking Long Island Sound between 1836 and 1842. The elegant interior contains Greek Revival detailing, including a freestanding elliptical staircase, and furnishings in the American Empire style. The restored 1840s stone carriage house *(◑ open Apr–Nov)* serves as an interpretive center.

Wave Hill★ (AX)

W. 249th St. MTA *1 or 9 train to 231st St., then bus 7 or 10 to 252nd St; cross parkway bridge, walk 2 blocks down 252nd St., turn left onto Independence Ave. & proceed 1 block to Main Gate.* ♿ ◑ *Open mid-Apr–mid-Oct Tue–Sun 9am–5:30pm (Wed in Jul & Aug until 9pm). Rest of the year Tue–Sun 9am–4:30pm.* ◑ *Closed major holidays.* ◈ *$6 (free all day Tue, Sat 9am-noon & Dec–Feb).* ✕ 🅿. ◗◡ *Free garden tours Sun at 2:15pm.* ☎ *718-549-3200. www.wavehill.org.*

Opened to the public in 1965, this enchanting 28-acre estate comprises award-winning gardens and greenhouses, rolling meadows and lush woodlands, all overlooking the Hudson River. Built as a country home by William Lewis Morris in the 1840s, the main mansion was later owned by wealthy publisher William Appleton. Theodore Roosevelt's family occupied it in 1870 and Mark Twain leased the estate in 1901. Other celebrity residents include conductor Arturo Toscanini and George Perkins, J.P. Morgan's business partner. The building was restored in the 1960s and now serves as a visitor center.

The great asset of Wave Hill is its spectacular **site**★★ overlooking the Hudson. Some 18 acres of wonderfully landscaped gardens contain more than 3,000 species of plants and a variety of trees. Of special interest are the greenhouses, the lovely aquatic garden and fragrant herb garden. Today the garden focuses on nature appreciation and education, offering programs in landscape history, horticulture, land management and the arts.

BROOKLYN

AREA: 81 SQUARE MILES

POPULATION: 2,465,326

New York's most populous borough, Brooklyn is situated on the western tip of Long Island and extends from the East River to Coney Island and from the Narrows to Jamaica Bay. Although almost half a million Brooklynites commute to Manhattan today, the borough is far from being a bedroom community. Long a haven for writers and artists, including poet Walt Whitman, it boasts cultural institutions that rival those in Manhattan and has an attitude to match. Brooklyn is the birthplace of Arthur Miller, Barbra Streisand, and Woody Allen, among many others.

A Bit of History

A Dutch Settlement – Brooklyn was founded in 1636 by Dutch settlers, who named it *Breuckelen* ("broken land") after a small town near Utrecht. Other villages followed, spreading westward along the river, and by the late 18C regular ferry service to Manhattan was established. Brooklyn became an incorporated city with about 30,000 inhabitants in 1834, was connected to Manhattan via the Brooklyn Bridge in 1883 and was integrated into New York City in 1898.

A Mix of Neighborhoods – Brooklyn holds an impressive variety of neighborhoods, each with a distinct yet evolving look and personality. Just to name a few, there's Park Slope, a sedate enclave of brownstones bordering sylvan Prospect Park; Brooklyn Heights, home to much of Brooklyn's "old money" and the elegant harborfront promenade; Dumbo, with its dramatic bridge views and burgeoning gallery scene; Williamsburg, an extension of the East Village with its hip restaurants and shops; Brighton Beach, a thriving Russian neighborhood; and Fort

Park Slope residences

Atlantic Avenue

Map p 280. The main thoroughfare of Brooklyn's Lebanese and Middle Eastern populations has become one of New York's most popular culinary destinations. Sample delicacies like lamb kabobs and stuffed grape leaves, but try to resist snapping up little bags of every spice imaginable. Some of the avenue's highlights include **Tripoli** *(no. 156; ☎ 718-596-5800; www.tripolirestaurant.com),* a campy two-level restaurant (check out the sea mural on the main level) that serves up hummus, falafel and honeyed desserts. If you want to take something home with you, visit **Sahadi's Importing Co.** *(no. 187; ☎ 718-624-4550; www.sahadis.com)* for Lebanese pistachios, feta, spices and coffee. End your walk at the **Waterfront Ale House** *(no. 155; ☎ 718-522-3794)* for a restorative gulp of one of the 50 varieties of bottled beer.

Greene, known for its tightknit community of African-American professionals and block after block of pristine brownstones.

Brooklyn Heights★★

Map on p 280. MTA *2, 3 train to Clark St.* Heavily fortified during the Revolution, Brooklyn Heights was the site of General Washington's headquarters during the Battle of Long Island. In the mid-19C the neighborhood developed as a choice residential area, largely because of its closeness to Manhattan, and it remains an exclusive address, with brownstones and town houses representing almost every style of 19C American architecture lining its narrow, tree-shaded streets. The Heights' main commercial drag – home to most of its restaurants and shops – is **Montague Street**, though Atlantic Avenue has some good options, too.

Walking Tour

▷ *Distance: 2.8mi. Begin at Monroe Pl.*

Leaving the subway station, walk toward Monroe Place. At the corner of Clark and Henry streets stands the Hotel St. George, once the largest hotel in New York City. The building has since been converted into co-ops, luxury apartments, and dormitories for nearby Pace University.

▷ *Turn onto Monroe Place.*

At **45 Monroe Place** stands the New York State Supreme Court's Appellate Division. The Classical Revival building dates from 1938 and has two huge Doric columns flanking the entrance.

▷ *Turn left at Pierrepont St.*

The handsome 1881 Queen Anne-style brick building at no. 128 houses the **Brooklyn Historical Society**, the borough's only history museum, comprised of a few small art and history exhibits drawn from the society's extensive permanent collection *(🕐 open Wed–Sun noon–5pm; 🕐 closed Jan 1, July 4 and Dec 25; ⊛ $6; ☎ 718-222-4111; www.brooklynhistory.org).*

▷ *Backtrack on Pierrepont St. and continue to the corner of Henry St.*

82 Pierrepont Street represents a splendid example of the Richardsonian Romanesque style, with its bulky massing and its rough, unfinished masonry surfaces, rounded arches and bas-relief carving. Built in 1890 as a private residence, it was later enlarged and converted into apartments.

Turning onto Willow Street, note **nos. 155, 157** and **159**, three Federal-style houses sporting handsomely detailed entranceways. A skylight in the pavement in front of no. 157 allows daylight to filter down into a tunnel that connects no. 159 to **no. 151**, formerly a stable and now an apartment. Farther up the street, on the opposite side, **nos. 108-112** illus-

BROOKLYN HEIGHTS AND DUMBO ❶

Restaurant
❶ River Café

0   1/10mi
0   200m

trate the picturesque Queen Anne style, with their great variety of building materials and blend of elements of the Romanesque, Gothic and Renaissance styles.

▶ *Continue on Willow St. and turn right onto Orange St.*

At the corner of Hicks and Orange Street stands the 1914 parish house of the historically significant **Plymouth Church of the Pilgrims** down the block (•⊶ *visit by 15–30min guided tour only, Mon–Fri 10am–4pm & Sun noon–2pm; stop in at 75 Hicks Street and ask for assistance, or call ahead;* ☎ *718-624-4743 ; www. plymouthchurch.org).* The first Congregational Church in Brooklyn, this simple brick meetinghouse dating from 1846 served for 40 years as the pulpit for abolitionist Henry Ward Beecher and a stop on the Underground Railroad. President Lincoln worshiped here on two occasions in 1860; tour guides will point out his

pew. The church is also well known for its large stained-glass windows by Tiffany.

▶ *Backtrack to Hicks St. and continue two blocks north; turn left onto Middagh St.*

Several Federal-style clapboard houses, built in the 1820s, line the street. Among the best preserved are the double frame house at **nos. 31-33** and the charming dwelling at **no. 24**. To get to DUMBO, remain on Middagh and turn right on Columbia Heights. Otherwise, continue to the Esplanade as described below.

▶ *Take Willow St. to Cranberry St. and continue toward the East River to the Brooklyn Heights Esplanade.*

Overlooking the harbor, the esplanade offers excellent **views**★★ of the Financial District; the view is especially impressive in the early evening when the lights glimmer across the river. Behind the terrace lies a series of houses with lovely private gardens.

▶ *Walk along the esplanade; turn left onto Pierrepont St. and right onto Pierrepont Pl.*

Note the elegant brownstone mansions at **nos. 2** and **3 Pierrepont Place**.

▶ *Continue on Pierrepont Pl., which becomes Montague Terrace; turn left onto Remsen St. and right onto Hicks St.*

Off to the left is **Grace Court Alley**, a picturesque mews that was the stable alley for the fine homes on Remsen Street.

▶ *Continue along Hicks St. and turn left onto Joralemon St.*

The intersection of Hicks and Joralemon streets was the location of the country home of Philip Livingston, a signer of the Declaration of Independence. It is reported that on August 29, 1776, General Washington met at Livingston's home with his chiefs of staff to plan the evacuation of his army.

▶ *Continue east on Joralemon St. to Court St.*

The Civic Center area presents a jarring contrast to the residential section, with its monumental public buildings such as Borough Hall, the former Brooklyn City Hall and the massive Richardsonian Romanesque central post office.

▶ *Continue on Joralemon St. to Boerum Pl. and turn right.*

New York Transit Museum★

Kids *Boerum Pl. & Schermerhorn St. (*M *on map).* ♿ 🕐 *Open year-round Tue–Fri 10am–4pm, weekends noon–5pm.* 💲 *$5 ($3 children ages 3–17).* ☎ 718-694-1600. www.mta.info/mta/museum.

Located in the refurbished 1930s Court Street shuttle station, the museum tells the story of New York's labyrinthine transit system with a fascinating collection of vintage subway cars and history exhibits. The story of the New York City subway is told in text, pictures and maps along the platform. At the working signal tower (near the end of the platform), flashing lights represent trains making their way under downtown Brooklyn on the connecting track. Exhibits include **Steel, Stone and Backbone**, a look at the building of the subways, and **On the Streets**, which gives buses and trolleys their proper due. The walls of the **R-46 Gallery** are plastered with posters of films set in the subways. (♿ See also the NY Transit Museum Gallery Annex and Store in Grand Central Terminal.)

DUMBO

Map opposite. MTA *A, C Train to High Street or F Train to York Street.*

DUMBO—the acronym stands for Down Under the Manhattan Bridge Overpass —is one of the most vibrant new neighborhoods in Brooklyn, a place where moody cobblestone streets are lined with imposing warehouse buildings, many converted into loft apartments and galleries. A number of top-notch restaurants and gourmet stores have opened here in the last few years as well, and the newly renovated Brooklyn Bridge Park is a great place to rest or picnic, especially if you've just walked over the legendary span.

Tom's Luncheonette

782 Washington Ave. at Sterling Pl. ☎ *718-636-9738.*
This Brooklyn institution – it's been here for over 60 years – is the great all-time breakfast spot. It's open from 6am to 4pm Monday through Saturday. It's also a family affair with Tom, his wife and their kids all tending shop. As son Gus says, "We don't have customers, we have friends." Stop in for a cherry-lime rickey or a real egg cream after your visit to the Brooklyn Museum of Art or the Botanic Garden.

A Bit of History – DUMBO, which stretches roughly from Fulton Street to Hudson Avenue, and from Prospect Street to the East River – used to be known as Fulton Landing after Robert Fulton, who in 1814 built a pier here for the steamships he ran to Manhattan, just eight minutes away. The completion of the Brooklyn Bridge in 1883 put an end to the ferry, and the neighborhood became an industrial district with virtually no residents until the 1980s, when artists began converting its abandoned warehouses into studios. Though today it has its share of multimillion-dollar condos, DUMBO still has an adventurous spirit to it, owing partly to its protected location and partly to the passion of its residents to keep it culturally rich.

Visit – The best time to visit DUMBO is on Saturday afternoon, when the majority of its galleries and shops are open and the restaurants and parks are full of locals. The **DUMBO First Thursday Gallery Walk** – featuring open studios and gallery receptions, as well as live music, on the first Thursday of each month – is another lively option. A good place to start your visit is **111 Front Street**, where a dozen galleries occupy the second floor (the friendly Dumbo General Store cafe is on the first); for more art, check out **Powerhouse Arena** (37 Main St.), an art book publisher that also puts on photography shows. Sweet tooths flock to **Jacques Torres Chocolate** (66 Water St.) for its ethereal truffles, cookies and European-style hot chocolate, all made onsite. If you're looking for a full meal, try **Bubby's** (1 Main St.), a TriBeCa import that serves up homey staples like pie and chicken, or the upscale **River Cafe**. **Bargemusic** is the most famous entertainment option in the neighborhood, though **St. Ann's Warehouse** (38 Water St., www.stannswarehouse.org) runs a close second for its avant-garde theater performances.

Prospect Park★

Map opposite. MTA 2, 3 Train to Grand Army Plaza. ⓘ www.prospectpark.org.

Once part of an estate belonging to the Litchfield family, this 585-acre haven of woodlands and rolling hills is an outdoor oasis for Brooklynites.

A Bit of History

The land for Prospect Park was purchased by the city in piecemeal fashion in the 1850s and 1860s and landscaped by **Frederick Law Olmsted** and **Calvert Vaux**, the architects of Central Park, in 1865. Construction was completed in 1873, but it wasn't until 20 years later that work began on the ornate triumphal arch that marks its entrance at **Grand Army Plaza**. John Duncan, architect of Grant's Tomb , designed the arch, which is dedicated to the fallen Union soldiers of the Civil War, and Stanford White, architect of Washington Square Arch oversaw the placement of sculptures and bas-reliefs upon it. Cupping the southeast corner of the plaza is the main branch of the **Brooklyn Public Library**, whose Art Moderne facade was recently treated to a thorough cleaning.

Visit

Prospect Park thrums with activity year-round but is especially lively on summer weekends, when ballgames and barbecues fill up its vast grassy lawns and free outdoor concerts are held in its bandshell several evenings a week as part of the Celebrate Brooklyn! festival (see website for schedule). The park's visitor center is located in the **Audubon Center**, also home to the Songbird Cafe ✖ and many nature programs. The undulating 3.35mi loop road, **Park Drive**, is a favorite with runners, in-line skaters and cyclists; it is open to vehicular traffic only during weekday rush hours, though a **free trolley bus** ♿ traces its periphery on weekends and holidays from noon to 6pm, departing the **Wollman Ice-Skating Rink** parking lot on the hour and stopping at 15 points along the road.

Children's Corner – Kids MTA Q, S and B Trains to Prospect Park. A cluster of sights on the east side of the park is particularly appealing for children. The **Lefferts Historic House Museum** is a 1783 Dutch farmhouse whose period rooms and programs interpret daily life in Brooklyn in the 1820s (ⓞ open Apr–Nov Thu–Sun noon–5pm, Dec–Mar Sat–Sun noon–4pm; ♿; ☎ 718-789-2822). Just south of the house stands a 1912 **carousel** with 51 fancifully carved horses and other animals (🕐 operates Apr–Oct Thu–Sun & holidays noon–5pm; July–Aug until 6pm; 🎟 $1.50; ☎ 718-282-7789). To the north of the house is the nifty **Prospect Park**

Zoo★ (🕐 open Apr–Oct daily 10am–5pm, rest of the year daily 10am–4:30pm; ♿; 🎟 $6 adults, $2 children ages 3–12; ☎ 718-399-7339). Run by the distinguished Wildlife Conservation Society, it contains more than 400 animals of some 80 species, including red pandas, sea lions, kangaroos, emus, porcupines

Brooklyn Museum

and other creatures – all of which you can see at much closer range than you can at the zoo's much larger, busier and more expensive counterpart in the Bronx.

Brooklyn Botanic Garden★★

900 Washington Ave. MTA *2 or 3 train to Eastern Pkwy, or B, Q or S Train to Prospect Park.* ⏱ *Open mid-Mar–Oct Tue–Fri 8am–6pm, weekends & holidays 10am–6pm. Rest of the year Tue–Fri 8am–4:30pm, weekends 10am–4:30pm.* ⏱ *Closed Jan 1, Thanksgiving Day & Dec 25.* 💲 *$8 (free Tue, Sat 10am–noon & weekdays mid-Nov–Feb).* 🌿 *Guided tours available weekends 1pm.* 🅿 *free.* ♿ ✗ ☎ *718-623-7200. www.bbg.org.*

Located to the east of Prospect Park and to the south of the Brooklyn Museum, this outstanding botanical garden contains a great variety of vegetation, including one of the finest assemblages of roses in the country. Covering 52 acres, it invites visitors to explore its prim rows of cherry trees – site of the popular late-April Cherry Blossom Festival – and its many well-kept gardens: Shakespeare, Children's, Rose, Herb, Rock, Native Flora, Lily Pool Terrace, Japanese, Fragrance and Bluebell Wood, among others.

Built in 1988, the **Steinhardt Conservatory★** contains a Tropical Pavilion, an aquatic exhibit and the country's largest bonsai collection, as well as a gallery that hosts consistently outstanding shows of botanical illustrations and art (⏱ *open every day the garden is open*

Park Slope

Situated just west of Prospect Park, this neighborhood is one of the most desirable addresses in Brooklyn, thanks largely to the rows of handsome brownstones – two- to four-story brick townhouses covered with a distinctive sandstone paste – that line most of its wide, shaded streets. Discovered by fixer-uppers in the late 1970s, they now routinely fetch upwards of $2 million apiece – often much more. Some are single-family residences, and others are divided into apartments. The best have high stoops and rich Gothic, Italianate or Romanesque detailing. A few mansions are interspersed throughout the neighborhood. One is the Montauk Club (*northeast corner of Lincoln Pl. & 8th Ave.*), constructed in 1891 in a style reminiscent of a Venetian palace. Of particular interest are the friezes, which depict historic scenes associated with the Montauk Indians. The main commercial artery of Park Slope is Seventh Avenue. It's home to quaint boutiques and bookstores, as well as a number of good restaurants and cafes.

mid-Mar–Oct 10am–5:30pm; rest of the year 10am–4pm).

Brooklyn Museum★★

Maps p 283 and p286. 200 Eastern Pkwy. ⓂⓉⒶ *2 or 3 train to Eastern Pkwy.* ♿ 🕐 *Open year-round Wed–Fri 10am–5pm, weekends 11am–6pm (first Sat of month until 11pm).* 🕐 *Closed Jan 1, Thanksgiving Day & Dec 25.* 🎫 *$8.* 🎧 *Self-guided audio tours may be rented for $3.* 🅿 *$3 first hour, $2 each additional hour.* ✕ ☎ *718-638-5000. www.brooklynmuseum.org.*

Housed in a monumental Beaux-Arts building designed by McKim, Mead and White, the Brooklyn Museum is New York's second-largest art museum behind the Met, and well worth a visit if you happen to be in the borough. The collection contains a whopping 1.5 million works, ranging from one of the world's best troves of Egyptian antiquities to *The Dinner Party* by Judy Chicago, a hallmark of feminist art from the 1970s. A dramatic new glass entrance by Polshek Partnership Architects, unveiled in 2004, is just one of many recent improvements to this fine institution.

Visit

As you enter the museum from Eastern Parkway, take a moment to explore the Rodin sculptures arranged in the front of the lobby. At the admission desk, pick up a museum map and audio guide—the latter is well worth the $3 fee for its commentary on The Dinner Party, the "American Identities" exhibit, the Egyptian collection, and the African art galleries. These are generally regarded as the best departments in the museum, so if you're short on time, focus on them first. (The temporary shows also tend to be excellent.)

First floor – The Brooklyn Museum's collection of 5,000 works of **African art**★★ is the largest such collection in an American museum, with more than 100 cultures represented over a span of 2,500 years. Two long galleries contain a wealth of eye-catching works, including wooden statuettes, witch doctors' wands, masks and ceremonial shields, all nicely laid out and described in helpful wall texts.

The Dinner Party by Judy Chicago

Works in the **Arts of the Americas** gallery range from Pre-Columbian artifacts to magnificent totem poles from the Haida Indians of the Northwest Coast. The **Arts of the Pacific** gallery contains sculptures, musical instruments and headdresses from Papua New Guinea, New Zealand and the Solomon Islands.

Second Floor –Galleries here showcase art from China, Korea, Japan, Southeast Asia, India and the Islamic world. Of particular note is the museum's collection of **18C and 19C Persian paintings and decorative arts**★, one of the finest groupings in the Western world. The colorful carpets and mosaics reveal astounding craftsmanship. Rarely seen works on paper are rotated through the Asian and Islamic galleries, including some striking watercolors. Don't miss the ferocious *Head of a Guardian* from 13C Japan or the lovely Chinese ceramics.

Third Floor – This floor presents the museum's newly installed **Egyptian collection**★★★, one of the finest in the world. To best appreciate the display of more than 1,100 works, start in the Kervorkian Gallery of Ancient Middle Eastern art. Here you'll find impressive bas-reliefs from the palace of Assyrian king Ashur-nasir-pal II at Nimrud. This gallery opens onto an introductory gallery full of exhibits on Egyptian religion, culture and technology, stressing the theme of permanence and change. Flanking this gallery are two galleries full of artifacts, with earlier works (Old and Middle Kingdom) arrayed in the colorful room to the right and later ancient works (New Kindgdom) in the neutral-toned Rubin Gallery to the left; the latter is capped with a room displaying temple and tomb art, always some of the most fascinating ancient Egyptian works.

Selections from the museum's collection of **European paintings** are hung on the four walls surrounding the Beaux-Arts

BROOKLYN

Court, each wall addressing a theme: portraiture, landscape, narrative, and rural and urban life. Here, lesser-known works are interspersed with great ones, such as Millet's *The Shepherd Tending His Flock* (1886).

Fourth Floor – Devoted largely to the decorative arts, this floor presents a fascinating collection of **American period rooms**★ ranging from the 17C to the present. The most sumptuous is the Rockefeller smoking room from the 1880s, the sleekest is the Art Deco Wiel-Worget Study, and the simplest is the recently refurbished Jan Martense Schenck House (c.1625), moved here from the Flatlands section of Brooklyn. Also noteworthy are the tremendous Tiffany stained-glass windows outside the elevator and the Art Nouveau gates by Emile Robert down the hall.

Fifth Floor – The Brooklyn Museum has garnered international renown for its collection of **American painting**★★. Major works by almost all the heavyweights are here, from Copley, Cole, Eakins, Homer and Bierstadt to Sargent Cassatt, Chase, Durand, Saint-Gaudens and Bellows. You'll also find modern works by such well-known artists as Georgia O'Keeffe, Max Weber, Stuart Davis and Marsden Hartley.

With the creation of the Luce Center for American Art in 2001, the museum completely reorganized its display of the collection. The new installation – "American Identities" – integrates paintings with selected sculptures and decorative artworks to investigate eight themes, among them landscape, the Civil War, the modern world and daily life. The wall texts explain the juxtapositions, but it's best to have the audio guide to fully appreciate the arrangement. The Visual Storage Study Center, completed in 2004, compactly displays some 1,500 objects from the museum's American collection, organized by type and medium.

Sharing the fifth floor is the **Elizabeth A. Sackler Center for Feminist Art**★, inaugurated in March 2007. Designed to highlight women's contribution to the art world in the past 40 years, the 8,300sq ft space contains several large galleries for changing exhibits as well as the massive permanent installation of **The Dinner Party**★, constructed in 1974–79 by artist Judy Chicago and hundreds of volunteers.

The centerpiece of the work is a triangular table measuring 48ft on each side, with a total of 39 place settings for women across the ages arranged chronologically around the perihery. Each setting is hand-crafted with embroidered runners, napkins, utensils, ceramic chalices and painted china plates sculpted into feminine forms. Among those honored with a place at the table are the Primordial Goddess, Sojourner Truth, Anne Hutchinson, Eleanor of Aquitane and Georgia O'Keeffe. Heritage Panels in an adjoining gallery show Chicago and her research team's effort to build a complete women's history (or *herstory*, as they call it).

Around Brooklyn

Map pp 286–287. Grid letters in parentheses after each attraction's name refer to the map.

Coney Island★ (ABZ)

Kids MTA *D, F, Q or N trains to Stillwell Ave. (last stop). www.coneyislandusa.com.*
Located at the southern tip of Brooklyn and lapped by the Atlantic Ocean, Coney Island is the city's most famous beach, one that draws subway riders from all parts of the city not just for its plentiful sand but for its ramshackle charm.

Coney Island—the name comes from the Dutch words for "Rabbit Island"—has long been a place of honky-tonk entertainment, with seedy carnival games and a kitschy burlesque show, a rickety 1927 roller coaster (the Cyclone) and a supersize hot dog stand (Nathan's

---

Kids **Arty Facts** Kids

Every Saturday and Sunday at 11am and 2pm the Brooklyn Museum sponsors a 90min family program cleverly known as "Arty Facts." Guides introduce children ages 4–7 and their adult companions to work in a gallery, then use it as the basis as an art-making project. Meet in the main lobby; no reservations necessary.

Coney Island – The Wonderwheel

Famous). But most agree that its days are numbered: a developer bought Astroland Amusement Park in 2006 and plans to build high-rise condos, a luxury hotel and other pricey pleasures on the site. The Cyclone (a historic landmark) and some of the other attractions will remain, but the influx of money will surely change the atmosphere to some degree.

Visit

Kids Coney Island is a summertime attraction, even if you have no intention of sunning yourself on the beach. The **Cyclone**★★, the **Wonder Wheel**★★ Ferris wheel and other rides are open daily from Memorial Day to Labor Day (weekends only in spring and fall). Summer is also when the **Brooklyn Cyclones**★ minor league baseball team plays at the delightful, 7,500-seat KeySpan Park *(1904 Surf Ave., ☎718-449-8497 for information).* More than half a million spectators attend the colorful and risqué **Mermaid Parade**★★, held in late June each year; the **Nathan's Famous Fourth of July International Hot Dog Eating Contest**★ draws about 50,000 iron-stomached fans to see contestants scarf down upwards of 60 hot dogs (and buns) in 12 minutes; it's a Coney Island tradition to try at least one for yourself. **Nathan's** *(1310 Surf Ave., at Stillwell)* and

the **New York Aquarium**★★ (below) are open year-round.

New York Aquarium★★ (BZ)

W. 8th St. & Surf Ave. MTA *F or Q train to West 8th Street.* Kids ⚹ ◷ *Open Jun–Aug Mon–Fri 10am–6pm (weekends until 7pm); rest of the year closing times vary from 4:30pm to 5:30pm. Last entry 45min before close.* ◉ *$12; $8 children ages 3–12.* P *$10.* ✕. ☎ *718-265-3474. www. nyaquarium.com.*

Opened in 1896 in what is now Castle Clinton National Monument, the aquarium was reputedly the first public aquarium in the US. It has been located at the corner of the Coney Island Boardwalk and West 8th Street since 1957. As part of the Wildlife Conservation Society, the

Black-footed Penguin, New York Aquarium

aquarium is a top-of-the-line facility that aims to educate as well as entertain in its exhibits and demonstrations. It excels on both counts.

Visit

The aquarium comprises a whole complex of indoor and outdoor tanks and pools. When you enter, you'll be in the original 1957 Conservation Hall, home to the new **Glover's Reef**★ exhibit, a 165,000-gallon tank containing marine life found around that reef in the Caribbean, including moray eels and sharks. Outside the hall is the **Sea Cliffs**★ exhibit, a 300ft-long rocky coast habitat for walrus, sea otters, fur seals and penguins (be sure to check out the underground viewing platform on your way out). Ever popular **sea lion shows**★★ are held in an amphitheater just across the path.

Explore The Shore, a 20,000sq ft educational center, features 65 exhibits including a 400-gallon wave tank showing subtidal, intertidal and upper tidal zones and a salt marsh simulating the nearby Jamaica Bay wetlands, jumping with hermit crabs. Next to it is the mesmerizing and otherworldly **Alien Stingers Exhibit**★★, opened in 2002, showcasing dozens of species of sea jellies, corals and anemones from around the world.

Brooklyn Children's Museum (BX)

145 Brooklyn Ave. MTA *3 train to Kingston Ave.; cross Eastern Parkway walking north on Kingston (with traffic) to St. Mark's Ave. (6 blocks); turn left on St. Mark's and walk one block to Brooklyn Ave. Museum is on corner.* Kids ⚇ ⏱ *Open Jul–Aug Tue–Fri noon–6pm (Fri until 6:30pm), weekends*

Brooklyn Children's Museum

11am–6pm. Rest of the year Wed–Fri 1pm–6pm, weekends 11am–6pm. ⏱ *Closed major holidays.* ⚇ *$5.* ☎ *718-735-4400. www.brooklynkids.org.*

Founded in 1899 in Brower Park, this institution was one of the first museums designed especially for children, and it's undergoing an exciting expansion and renovation that will make it the most up-to-date facility of its kind in New York. Designed by renowned Uruguayan architect Rafael Viñoly, an L-shaped addition will wrap around the four-story building the museum has occupied since 1977, doubling exhibit space to 100,000sq ft. When it reopens in spring 2008 it will be the first "green" museum in Brooklyn, with a geothermal heating and cooling system, as well as solar panels for energy. All-new interactive, hands-on exhibits will cover cultural and natural history, the sciences and the performing arts. And as always, the museum will invite active participation, offer family workshops and present special performances year-round.

Brooklyn Academy of Music★ (BX)

30 Lafayette Ave. Check local newspapers for a listing of events. ⚇ 🅿 ✕ ☎ *718-636-4100. www.bam.org.*

The Brooklyn Academy of Music (BAM) is widely regarded as New York's premier venue for avant-garde performance, and a wealth of new programming in recent years ensures BAM's continued vibrancy. Founded in 1859, it is the city's oldest continually operating performing-arts center. After its original Brooklyn Heights premises burned down in 1907, it moved to its Fort Greene home. Behind its imposing brick Beaux-Arts facade lies an elegant 1,100-seat opera house that has hosted Enrico Caruso, Isadora Duncan, Arturo Toscanini, Paul Robeson and, more recently, Philip Glass, Laurie Anderson, and the Merce Cunningham Dance Company; belying its old-fashioned appearance, its technical capabilities and acoustics are first-rate. A second venue, the 900-seat Harvey Theater (formerly the Majestic), is located a block and a half away at 651 Fulton Street and is home to the Brooklyn Philharmonic Orchestra. In addition to live performances, BAM

Just the Facts

The Verrazano-Narrows Bridge has a total length of 6,690ft. The main span between the towers rises 690ft above water, allowing the largest ocean liner to pass under it, and extends 4,260ft. The main cables are 3ft in diameter. The bridge supports two levels for car traffic—six lanes each—but no sidewalk for pedestrians. Ironically, its most famous moment each year is as the starting point of the New York City Marathon (first Sun in November), when runners fill both levels of the bridge before setting off on their 26.2mi journey through the five boroughs.

has daily film screenings of classic and foreign films—part of its Cinematheque series—and new art-house fare.

Verrazano-Narrows Bridge★★ (AZ)

Toll: $4.50 per car, paid only on westbound crossing.

The spiderweb silhouette of the Verrazano-Narrows Bridge, the longest suspension bridge in the US, links Brooklyn to Staten Island above the Narrows (the entrance to New York Harbor). The bridge bears the name of Italian explorer Giovanni da Verrazano, a Florentine merchant in the service of French king François I who discovered the site of New York in 1524. At the Brooklyn entrance to the bridge stands a monument composed in part of stones from the castle of Verrazzano in Tuscany, and from the beach of Dieppe, the French port from which the pilot sailed.

The Triborough Bridge and Tunnel Authority began work on the bridge in January 1959, and on November 21, 1964, the bridge was inaugurated in the presence of Gov. Nelson Rockefeller and the bridge's engineer, O.H. Amman, who also designed the George Washington Bridge.

Shore Parkway★ (ACYZ)

This pleasant drive follows the coast from Bay Ridge all the way to Queens and John F. Kennedy Airport, affording successive views of the Verrazano-Narrows Bridge and Staten Island, the Rockaways and Jamaica Bay. On bright, sunny days, when superb views extend across the glittering water, Shore Parkway offers a refreshing respite from the bustle of Manhattan.

QUEENS

AREA: 120 SQUARE MILES
POPULATION: 2,229,379

Named after the wife of Charles II of England, Catherine of Braganza (1630-85), Queens is the largest borough of New York City. Situated on Long Island, east of Brooklyn, it extends from the East River in the north to Jamaica Bay and the Atlantic Ocean in the south. Home to both of the city's major airports—JFK and LaGuardia— it is a borough in which nearly half of its residents are foreign-born. Hispanics and Asians are the fastest-growing ethnic groups in Queens.

A Bit of History

In 1642 a Dutch settlement was founded at Maspeth, but it was not until 1645 that Queens' first permanent settlement, at Vlissingen (Flushing), was established. Clashes between English and Dutch settlers over freedom of worship marked the borough's early years. In 1662 the Dutch arrested John Bowne for allowing Quaker gatherings in his home. Bowne appealed his case, paving the way for religious freedom in the colonies.

Until the mid-19C, Queens remained a sparsely populated neighborhood of small villages and farms. As New York City blossomed, urbanization of Queens accelerated, attracting successive waves of German and Irish immigrants. By the end of the 19C, when Queens became incorporated into New York City as a borough, some 150,000 people lived here. In the 1920s Queens attracted the silent film industry, which operated some 20 studios in Astoria before relocating to sunny Hollywood. On the heels of the 1939 World's Fair, the borough developed a

Houses in Queens

Installation 15, The Noguchi Museum

reputation as a haven for sports and recreation, an image it still claims today as the home of the USTA Billie Jean King National Tennis Center and Shea Stadium (soon to be replaced by adjacent Citi Field).

The 1970s witnessed the development of an active political machine; from its ranks rose Mario Cuomo, governor of New York from 1982 to 1994. In the past decade Queens has become the city's most ethnically diverse borough, with a sizable community of Indian and Pakistani immigrants in Jackson Heights, a large Chinatown in Flushing and growing numbers of Hispanics throughout. Culturally the borough is best known for the P.S. 1 Contemporary Art Center (a MoMA affiliate), the Museum of the Moving Image and the Noguchi Museum, all in western Queens.

Around Queens

Map pp 296–297. Grid letters in parentheses after each attraction's name refer to its coordinates on the map.

The Noguchi Museum★★ (AX)
9-01 33rd Rd. at Vernon Blvd. MTA *N or W train to Broadway station in Queens; walk 10 blocks toward Manhattan; turn left on Vernon Blvd.; pass Socrates Sculpture Park*

office; walk 2 blocks to 33rd Rd. On Sun, a shuttle bus for the museum ($10 round-trip) departs from Park Ave. at 70th St. in Manhattan (in front of the Asia Society) at 12:30pm, 1:30pm, 2:30pm and 3:30pm; the trip takes 30min. ⏱ Open year-round Wed–Fri 10am–5pm, weekends 11am–6pm. ⏱ Closed Jan 1, Thanksgiving Day & Dec 25. ♿ ✕ ⬤ $10 (pay what you wish first Fri of month). ☎ 718-204-7088. www.noguchi.org.

Conflicting and harmonious relationships between nature and the man-made are a recurrent theme in the sculpture of **Isamu Noguchi** (1904-88), the renowned Japanese-American artist whose works include public spaces (Detroit's Hart Plaza), playgrounds (Atlanta's Playscapes), gardens and fountains. In addition to works in stone, terra-cotta, wood and metal, Noguchi created ethereal-looking akari light sculptures; he also designed stage sets for choreographers Martha Graham and George Balanchine.

Founded in 1985 by Noguchi himself, the museum recently underwent extensive renovations. Reopened in mid-2004, the complex consists of an outdoor sculpture garden and a two-story, 27,000sq ft building with 10 indoor galleries, an education center, a cafe and a museum shop. The ground floor displays a permanent presentation of Noguchi's works selected from his personal collection; the upper floor features rotating exhib-

The Noguchi Museum NY ©2004 · photo Elizabeth Felicella

Francis Dzikowski / Courtesy of Museum of the Moving Image. (2006)

"Behind the Screen," the core exhibition at the Museum of the Moving Image

its relating to his work. The museum shop showcases many of the artist's interior designs, including furniture and lamps.

Museum for African Art★ (AY)

36-01 43rd Ave. at 36th St. MTA *7 local train to 33rd St. Station; walk east to 36th St., then left one block to 43rd Ave.* ⊶*This exhibition space is closed; call or check the website for location and hours of traveling shows.* ☎*718-784-7700. www.africanart.org.*

Since opening as the Center for African Art in 1984, the museum has mounted dozens of major shows exploring Africa's artistic traditions and cultural heritage. And finally, after years of hopping from one neighborhood to the next, it is getting a permanent home. Governor Eliot Spitzer and other notables were on hand on September 24, 2007, for the groundbreaking ceremony at 1280 Fifth Avenue (at 110th Street) in Manhattan, where the museum will set up shop inside a new condominium tower designed by Robert A.M. Stern. Projected date of completion is late 2009. The museum is curating exhibitions in a variety of locations throughout the city in the meantime; check the website for schedule and construction updates.

Museum of the Moving Image★ (AX)

35th Ave. & 36th St. in Astoria. MTA *R or V train to Steinway St.; walk south on Steinway St. to 35th Ave; turn right and proceed 3 blocks to museum (note: V train does not run on weekends).* Kids ♿ 🕐 *Open year-round Wed & Thu 11am–5pm, Fri 11am–8pm, weekends 11am–6:30pm.* 🕐 *Closed Jul 4, Thanksgiving Day & Dec 25.* ⊜ *$10.* ✕. ☎ *718-784-0077. www.movingimage.us.*

Located on the former site of the Astoria Film Studios (built by Paramount Pictures in the 1920s), this unique museum—which is undergoing a major expansion and renovation in 2008–09—is devoted to the history, technology and the art of film, television and digital media. The 83,000-piece collection encompasses portrait and scene-still photographs, special effects materials and production equipment; costumes, props and memorabilia from the television and film industries; and clips from movies, videos and advertisements. The museum is especially fun for kids, as visitors are invited make their own short animations, experiment with sound effects, or dub their voices into a famous movie.

During construction, the museum is suspending its excellent onsite film program, but it will sponsor screenings, panel discussions and premieres at other theaters around the city. See website for schedule and ticket information.

P.S.1 Contemporary Art Center★ (AY)

22-25 Jackson Ave. at 46th Ave. MTA *7 local train to Courthouse Sq.* 🕐 *Open year-round Thu–Mon noon–6pm.* 🕐 *Closed Jan 1, Thanksgiving Day & Dec 25.* ⊜ *$5 contribution requested (free with MoMA* ticket if presented within 30 days of purchase). ✕. ☎ 718-784-2084. www.ps1.org.

Housed in a gigantic former public school building only 10min by subway from Manhattan, this MoMA affiliate is one of the city's most exciting contemporary art centers. A kind of mega-gallery, the five-story facility can hold up to 10 shows at a time, with plenty of space for large-scale work. There are also a few interesting site-specific works scattered about, by artists such as James Turrell, Richard Serra and William Kentridge-Summer's a particularly fun time to visit, as that's when the courtyard is filled by an installation by the winner of its Young Architects Program and when the popular **Warm-Up** dance party takes place (🕐 July–Aug Sat 3pm–9pm).

Jamaica Bay Wildlife Refuge (CZ)

MTA *A train to Broad Channel. From the subway station, take Noel Rd. to Cross Bay Blvd. and turn right (.8mi). A visitor center is on the left (🕐 daily 8:30am–5pm; 🕐 Jan 1, Thanksgiving Day & Dec 25). 🕐 Open year-round daily dawn–dusk.* 🅿. ☎ 718-318-4340. www.nps.gov/gate.

Located just south of JFK Airport, this peaceful wildlife refuge is a major migratory haven for birds, attracting a wide variety of waterfowl and land and shore birds. It forms part of the Gateway National Recreation Area, one of the nation's largest urban parks. A self-guided **nature trail**★ through the marshes affords pleasant views of the Manhattan skyline to the west (1.8mi; 1 1/2hrs; request free permit at the visitor center).

Farther south on Cross Bay Boulevard, beachfront communities dot the five miles of **Rockaway Beach**★ (access from MTA *A train at stations between 25th and 116th Sts.*). On sunny days, New Yorkers stroll up and down the wide boardwalk, enjoying pleasant breezes and splendid ocean views.

Flushing (CX)

MTA *7 train to Main St. Call or see websites for directions from train to sights listed below.*

Now known for its enormous East Asian population, which makes up nearly half its 142,000 residents, Flushing started in 1645 as a small Dutch settlement named Vlissingen. In 1657 the town rejected Governor Peter Stuyvesant's demand that they expel "Quakers, Papists, Jews, Turks and other heretics," thus becoming the first municipality in the US to guarantee religious freedom to all residents and visitors. At 137-15 Northern Boulevard stands the old Flushing **Town Hall**, a Romanesque Revival building (1862) that has been restored to its original appearance and now hosts art exhibits and concerts in the 342-seat theater on its first floor (🕐 open year-round Mon–Fri 9am–5pm, weekends noon–5pm; ☎718-463-7700; www.flushingtownhall.com).

Bowne House (CX A)

37-01 Bowne St. j Closed for renovation; call or check website for hours and updates. ☎718-359-0528. www.bownehouse.org.

Though they were persecuted elsewhere, Quakers, or the Society of Friends, found a home in Flushing. But

Astoria

Map p296. Though there aren't as many Greeks living in this friendly neighborhood as there were a few decades ago, Astoria is still well known throughout New York City for its Greek food. Dripping with honey and soaked in butter, the baklava at **Omonia** (32-20 Broadway; ☎ 718-274-6650) is some of the freshest you'll ever taste. A local institution, **Uncle George's** (33-19 Broadway; ☎ 718-626-0593) is a 24hr family-friendly Greek diner where you can get a huge meal—the rotisserie chicken with lemon potatoes is a specialty—with wine for well under $20. **S'Agapo** (34-21 34th Ave.; ☎ 718-626-0303), just a block from the Museum of the Moving Image, is a lovely place for a dinner of whole grilled fish or just a glass of retsina and a sampling of mezes (dips) with fresh-baked pita.

C \ *Rockaway Beach ★, Jamaica Bay Wildlife Refuge* D

not without a struggle. John Bowne, an Englishman who settled in Flushing, was arrested for allowing Quakers to hold meetings in his home but was ultimately acquitted. The oldest structure in Queens, this house (1661) was inhabited by nine successive generations of Bownes and contains a collection of 17C and 18C furniture as well as pewter, paintings and documents belonging to the Bowne family.

Kingsland Homestead (CX B)

143-35 37th Ave., Flushing. ◷ *Open year-round Tue–Sat, Sun 2:30–4:30pm.* ◷ *Closed major holidays.* ⊛ *$3.* ℗ ☎*718-939-0647. www.queenshistoricalsociety. org.*

Constructed in c.1785, this two-and-a-half-story edifice presents a mix of Dutch and English traditions; note in particular the divided front door and central chimney. The former farmhouse now serves as the headquarters of the Queens Historical Society and houses the local history museum (◷*open year-round Mon–Fri 9:30am–5pm).*

Queens Botanical Garden (CY)

43-50 Main Street, Flushing. ◷*Open Apr–Oct Tue–Fri 8am–6pm, weekends 8am–7pm; rest of the year Tue–Sun 8am–4:30pm.* ◷ *Closed major holidays.* ☎*718.886.3800. www.queensbotanical. org.* ℗*$5.*

Literally growing out of a garden planted for the 1939 World's Fair, the Queens Botanical Garden now sprawls over 39 acres, comprising a bee garden, a rose garden, a fragrance garden, woodlands, a compost garden, and oak allée, and many other discrete sections, for an engaging look at the world of plants. In October 2007 Mayor Michael Bloomberg was on hand to inaugurate the garden's new visitor center, the most environmentally friendly building in the city with its planted green roof, solar panels, geothermal heating and cooling system, and compost toilets.

Flushing Meadows Corona Park (BCXY)

www.flushingmeadowscoronapark.org. Once a swamp favored by ducks and then a sanitary landfill—F. Scott Fitzgerald famously called it a "valley of ashes" in *The Great Gatsby*— this 1,275-acre park was developed in the 1930s to accommodate New York's first World's Fair (1939). Designs for the park included the creation of **Meadow Lake**, measuring .8mi in length, and the New York City Building, which housed the United Nations General Assembly between 1946 and 1949 and now contains the **Queens Museum of Art**. A second world's fair in 1964–65 brought the **New York Hall of Science** and Queens' most distinctive work of art, the **Unisphere (D)**, a 140ft-tall steel globe encircled with atomic-age rings. That said, the park's most popular attractions are no doubt **Shea Stadium**, home of the New York Mets baseball team until 2009, when it will be replaced by Citi Field, currently under construction right next to it, and the **USTA Billie Jean King National Tennis Center**, where the US Open tournament takes place each fall.

Queens Museum of Art (CY M1)

In the New York City Building (located next to the Unisphere). Ⓜ *7 train to Willets Point/Shea Stadium; follow signs to museum.* ♿ ◷ *Open year-round Wed–Fri 10am–5pm, weekends noon–5pm.* ◷ *Closed major holidays.* ⊛ *$5 suggested donation.* ℗. ☎ *718-592-9700. www. queensmuseum.org*

Originally conceived as an arts center for the borough of Queens, the museum today features 20C and contemporary art exhibitions with a diverse global

> "Over the great bridge, with the sunlight through the girders making a constant flicker upon the moving cars, with the city rising up across the river in white heaps and sugar lumps all built with a wish out of non-olfactory money. The city seen from the Queensboro Bridge is always the city seen for the first time, in its first wild promise of all the mystery and the beauty in the world."
>
> F. Scott Fitzgerald, *The Great Gatsby* (1926)

outlook. Don't miss the highlight – a spectacular architectural model of New York City built for the 1964-65 World's Fair at a scale of 1in to 100ft and updated in 1992. Covering more than 9,335sq ft, the **Panorama of New York City**★★ contains an unbelievable 895,000 buildings in addition to parks and other features. The history of the New York City Building is recounted through photographs and other memorabilia. Another gallery in the museum presents a rotating selection of **Tiffany lamps**.

New York Hall of Science (C)

Kids ⓖ ⏱ *Open Jul–Aug Mon–Fri 9:30am–5pm, weekends 10am–6pm. Rest of the year Mon–Fri 9:30am–2pm (Fri until 5pm), weekends 10am–6pm.* ⏱ *Closed Labor Day, Thanksgiving Day & Dec 25.* ⊜ *$11 ($8 children 2–17).* ✕ 🅿 *$10.* ☎ *718-699-0005. www.nyhallsci.org.*

Though built for the 1964-65 World's Fair, this museum of science and technology has done a stand-up job of staying up to date, with 400 hands-on exhibits exploring all branches of science. Expanded in 2007, the 60,000sq ft **Science Playground** now has plenty for preschool-age children to do, like playing in sandboxes, banging on drums, and crawling through mazes. Other exhibits include "The World of Microbes," where you can look at water through a microscope and walk through the eye of a needle (enlarged, of course), and the massive new **Marvelous Molecules**★, which explores the shared chemistry of all living things.

Queens Zoo (E)

Kids ⓖ *53-51 111th Street, adjacent to Hall of Science.* ⏱ *Open Apr–Oct Mon–Fri 10am–5pm, weekends and holidays 10am–5:30pm; rest of the year daily 10am–4:30pm.* |⊜*$6 (children 3–12 $2).* ☎ *718-271-1500. www.queenszoo.org.*

The Queens Zoo, formerly the Flushing Meadows Zoo, is run by the Wildlife Conservation Society, and as befits that esteemed organization (which also runs the Bronx Zoo, the New York Aquarium and two other city zoos), it is a clean, humane place for animals and an entertaining and informative place for children and adults. Unlike the other zoos in the city, here you'll find only creatures from the Americas in naturalistic environments. From **North America** you'll find American bison, mountain lions, California sea lions *(feedings at 11:15am, 2pm and 4pm daily),* American bald eagles, Roosevelt elk and a coyote named Otis who was mysteriously discovered in and rescued from Central Park in 1999. From **South America**, you'll find spectacled bears and thick-billed parrots. There's also a **petting zoo** with domestic animals. The aviary, a geodesic dome, was designed by Buckminster Fuller and used in the 1964 World's Fair in Queens.

Louis Armstrong House Museum★ (BX)

34-56 107th St. MTA *7 train to 103rd St./Corona Plaza ; walk north on 104th St., turn right onto 37th Ave (not Dr.) & left on 107th St.* ⓖ ☞⌂ *Visit by guided tour (40min) only, year-round Tue–Fri 10am–5pm, weekends noon–5pm.* ⊜ *$8.* ⓖ *Tours begin on the hour and are limited to 8 people.* ☎ *212-478-8274. www.satchmo.net.*

Located in a residential section of Corona, Queens, not far from Shea Stadium, this two-story, redbrick house was home to jazz great Louis Armstrong from 1943 until his death in 1971. After the death of Armstrong's wife Lucille in 1983, the property came into the hands of the city. In September 2003, the house opened to the public as a museum.

The house—furnishings, personal effects and all—provides a window into the domestic life of Louis Armstrong and reveals one of America's most important musical artists as modest, fun-loving and unpretentious. An extraordinary time capsule of post-World War II decoration, the interior represents the work and taste of Lucille and her decorator—who show a predilection for beiges, creams and textured wallpapers. Though Louis was on the road up to 300 days a year, his presence can be clearly felt here. He recorded more than 1,000 hours of his home life on his ever-present reel-to-reel tape players. Snippets from the tapes are played during the tour – in the dining room, you'll hear Armstrong riff on brussels sprouts as he eats his dinner.

The museum's entrance and gift shop are built into the house's ground-level garage, as is a changing exhibit of items from the Louis Armstrong Archives, which are held at Queens College.

Queens County Farm Museum (DY)

73-50 Little Neck Pkwy. in Floral Park. Take Long Island Expwy. to Exit 32; continue south on Little Neck Pkwy. (10 blocks to museum entrance). Free parking available. MTA *E, F trains to Kew Gardens, then Q46 bus to Little Neck Pkwy.; walk north 3 blocks.* Kids &. ○ *Open year-round Mon–Fri 9am–5pm (outdoor visits only), weekends 10am–5pm (farmhouse and green-house open).* ○ *Closed major holidays.* ☎ *718-347-3276 www.queensfarm.org.* This 47-acre farm—New York City's only historical farm—provides an informative glimpse of Queens County's agrarian origins and a welcome respite from the urban sprawl. Anchoring the property is an 18C Flemish-style farmhouse with its original furniture (visit by 30min guided tour only, weekends 11am–5pm). Greenhouses brim with plants, and farm implements are on display. The museum is especially fun for children, with its petting zoo (food available in gift show), hayrides *(Apr–Oct weekends, weather permitting)*, and autumn corn maze *(Sept–Oct)*.

STATEN ISLAND

AREA: 60 SQUARE MILES

POPULATION: 443,728

Measuring about 14mi long by 8mi wide, Staten Island is still a relatively rural area, with some 2,800 acres of forest, meadow, and wetlands preserved as part of the Staten Island Greenbelt. Linked to Brooklyn by the Verrazano-Narrows Bridge and to downtown Manhattan by the delightfully free Staten Island Ferry, the borough nonetheless stands apart from the urban hubbub with its decidedly suburban feel. It's home to a large number of the city's firefighters and municipal workers.

A Bit of History

The first permanent settlement was established at Oude Dorp by Dutch and French Huguenot families in 1661. Over the next two centuries the island thrived on farming and agriculture, ferrying goods to Manhattan and New Jersey. After integration with the other boroughs in 1898, Staten Island grew considerably, attracting hardworking immigrants to its farms and factories and hard-playing society folk to its resort hotels. The boom went bust after World War I, when many

Staten Island's Alias

Dutch merchants passing through here in the early 1600s named Staten Island after the Dutch States General. But the island acquired another name: Richmond, which honors the Duke of Richmond, brother of Charles II, king of England. While you're on the island, be sure to visit Historic Richmond Town.

residents left to make their fortunes on the mainland. The borough blossomed once again when the Verrazano-Narrows

Staten Island Ferry

Cynthia Ochterbeck - MICHELIN

301

Bridge opened in 1964, bringing an influx of Manhattanites seeking to escape the bustle of New York. Today Staten Island is primarily a bedroom community, culturally and economically related more to New Jersey than to New York. But it does have a number of attractions – art, history, and nature – that merit exploration if you have the time.

Around Staten Island

Map opposite. Grid letters in parentheses after each attraction's name refer to the map. To visit the sights below, you can take buses from the ferry terminal at St. George or, in some cases, the Staten Island Rapid Transit.

Staten Island Ferry★

Kids *Ferry departs from Whitehall Terminal off Whitehall St. in lower Manhattan for the St. George Ferry Terminal on Staten Island, year-round daily every 30min (hourly midnight–6am). 25min. Free (no cars allowed on the ferry).* ♿ ✕ 🅿. *For schedule, dial 311 (outside New York City, call ☎212-NEW-YORK). www.siferry.com.* Any visit to New York should include a ride on the Staten Island Ferry. On the windy voyage, which covers 5mi and takes about 25min, the ferry skirts the Statue of Liberty, giving passengers magnificent **views**★★★ of Manhattan and the bay. The ferry that was the start of Cornelius "Commodore" Vanderbilt's fortune now runs night and day, transporting some 20 million passengers a year, many of them commuters traveling to and from work.

St. George (BY)

Facing lower Manhattan across the bay, this small town is surrounded by suburban homes and gardens. In the 1850s, in the waters near St. George, quarantine was imposed on ships arriving from overseas. St. George has been the seat of

🕮 A Bit of Advice 🕮

For the best views from the ferry outbound from Manhattan to Staten Island, sit on the right side of the boat. You'll get a fairly close view of the Statue of Liberty and Ellis Island.

the county and borough government since 1920. In 2005, the St. George terminal building officially reopened after a two-year renovation. The revamped facility sports a 40ft-tall glass viewing wall, shops and an outdoor plaza.

Staten Island Museum (BY) – Kids *75 Stuyvesant Pl. From the Staten Island ferry terminal walk 1 block west to Wall St. Turn left on Wall St. and walk 1 block to the museum, at Stuyvesant Pl.* 🕐 *Open year-round Sun & Tue–Fri noon–5pm, Sat 10am–5pm.* 🕐 *Closed Mon and major holidays.* 🎟 *$2.* ☎ *718-727-1135. www. statenislandmuseum.org.* Founded in 1881, the Staten Island Institute of Arts and Sciences, the island's oldest cultural institution, runs this museum exploring the history, art, and ecology of the island. A small exhibit explores the history of the Staten Island ferry line through photographs, ships' wheels, whistles and other artifacts as well as elaborate scale models. Another describes the Lenape Indians, "the first Staten Islanders." You can buy ferry souvenirs and nautical art in the well-stocked museum store.

Alice Austen House Museum★ (BY)(A on map)

2 Hylan Blvd. From the Staten Island ferry terminal take S51 bus to Hylan Blvd (a 15min ride), then walk one block east to water and house. ♿🕐*Open Mar–Dec Thu–Sun noon–5pm.* 🕐*Closed Jan, Feb & major holidays.* 🎟*$2.* ☎*718-816-4506 www.aliceausten.org.*
A pioneer photographer, **Alice Austen** (1866-1952) captured turn-of-the-19C life in New York City, from exclusive society gatherings to poignant scenes of immigrant life. Restored according to her photographs, this picturesque Victorian-style cottage – known as "Clear Comfort" – displays changing exhibits, including prints from her glass-plate negatives. Trimmed in gingerbread, the porch affords superb **views**★★ of the harbor and Manhattan in the distance.

Snug Harbor Cultural Center★ (BY)

1000 Richmond Terrace. From the Staten Island ferry terminal take S40 bus to Snug Harbor (about a 10min ride). 🎟 *$6 includes*

STATEN ISLAND
—Ⓜ— Staten Island Rapid Transit

0 ——— 2mi
0 ——— 2km

visitor center, Newhouse galleries, and Chinese scholar's garden. &. ⏱ Grounds open dawn-dusk daily; see hours for individual sights below. ⏱ Closed Jan 1, Thanksgiving Day & Dec 25. ◕ Guided tours available. ✗ Ⓟ. ☎ 718-448-2500. www.snug-harbor.org.

Founded in 1801 as the first maritime hospital and retired sailors' home in the US, the 83-acre park and its 28 buildings are being restored and converted to a center for the visual and performing arts. The complex also hosts a number of lovely gardens, a children's museum, and performance spaces.

Eleanor Proske Visitors' Center – &. ⏱ Open Tues–Sun 10am–5pm. ◉ $3. Snug Harbor's oldest building and a prime example of the Greek Revival architecture of the 1830s. Of special note is its restored ceiling mural, punctuated by a skylit dome.

Newhouse Center for Contemporary Art – &. ⏱ Open Tues–Sun 10am–5pm. ◉ $3. Staten Island's premier spot for contemporary art, the center mounts exhibits in 15,000sq ft of gallery space as well as creating a home for 30 artist's studios.

Noble Maritime Collection – &. ⏰ *Open Thu–Sun 1–5pm.* ⌾ *$5.* ☎ *718-447-6490. www.noblemaritime.org.* The museum examines the life and work of John A. Noble, a French-born maritime artist who established a floating house-boat studio in a "boneyard" of old boats nearby. Exhibits include examples of his writing and art, his houseboat studio, ship models, and a model dormitory room.

Staten Island Botanical Garden – &. ⏰ *Open year-round daily dawn–dusk.* ✕ 🅿. ☎ *718-273-8200. www.sibg.org.* A stroll through this lovely garden reveals a perennial garden, an herb and butterfly garden designed to attract these colorful insects, and a greenhouse sheltering orchids and other tropicals. There is an admission fee (⌾ *$5*) to the Chinese scholar's garden and the secret garden (⏰ *both open Tue–Sun 10am–5pm).*

Staten Island Children's Museum – 🧒 &. ⏰ *Open July & Aug Tue–Sun 10am–5pm; rest of the year Tue–Fri noon–5pm, weekends 10am–5pm.* ⏰ *Closed major holidays. $5.* ✕ 🅿. ☎ *718-273-2060.* Interactive exhibits, creative workshops and field trips encourage children to learn by doing. Most activities are designed for children between the ages of 2 and 10.

Staten Island Zoo (BY)

614 Broadway. From the Staten Island ferry terminal take S48 bus to Forest Ave. & Broadway. Turn left on Broadway and walk 2½ blocks. & 🧒 ⏰ *Open year-round daily 10am–4:45pm.* ⏰ *Closed Jan 1, Thanksgiving Day & Dec 25.* ⌾ *$7; children 3–14 $4, under 3 free (free Wed after 2pm).* ✕ 🅿. ☎ *718-442-3100. www.staten islandzoo.org.*

Greenbelt Nature Center - Mike Falco

Greenbelt Nature Center

Located in Barrett Park, this small zoo, is especially known for its comprehensive collection of snakes and reptiles, housed in new facilities. Other residents include leopard tortoise, mandrill, meerkat, ring-tailed lemur, red panda, and North American river otter.

Jacques Marchais Museum of Tibetan Art★ (BZ)(ʙ on map)

338 Lighthouse Ave. From the Staten Island ferry terminal take the S74 bus to Lighthouse Ave. Turn right and walk up the hill. ⏰ *Open year-round Wed–Sun 1pm–5pm.* ⏰ *Closed major holidays.* ⤙ *Guided tours available.* ⌾ *$5.* ☎ *718-987-3500 www.tibetanmuseum.org.*

Laid out on Lighthouse Hill in enchanting terraced gardens, the museum displays a rare collection of art covering the culture, religion and mythology of Tibet, Nepal, China, Mongolia and India. The museum buildings were constructed to resemble a small Buddhist mountain temple. Highlights of the collection include an authentic three-tiered Buddhist altar and a large Tibetan thangka, or scroll painting, depicting the Green Tara, goddess of universal compassion. The thangka, which was painted in the 17C, has been painstakingly restored by Tibetan artist Pema Wangyal using only traditional techniques and materials.

Staten Island Greenbelt (BY) (ᴄ on map)

Nature Center: 700 Rockland Ave. at Brielle Ave. From the Staten Island ferry terminal take the S62 bus to Bradley Avenue. Transfer to the S57 bus, which will take you to the Brielle and Rockland Ave. stop. Cross the street at the light. ⏰ *Open Apr–Oct Tue–Sun 10am–5pm, Nov–Mar Wed–Sun 11am–5pm.* 🅿. ☎ *718-351-3450. www. sigreenbelt.org.*

This 2,800-acre forest preserve is a secret gem for nature enthusiasts, with more than 30 miles of trails, including some moderately difficult ones to the summit of Todt Hill, the highest point on the Atlantic coast south of Maine. Start your visit at the Greenbelt Nature Center, which has exhibits on the ecology of the park, trail maps, and restrooms, and sponsors a variety of special programs. You can also get maps and access trails

Old Bermuda Inn Restaurant

2512 Arthur Kill Rd. (Bloomingdale Rd. & Rossville Ave.). ☎ 718-948-7600. This stately 1830 Victorian mansion-turned-restaurant has five working fireplaces, museum-quality antiques, oil portraits of old Staten Island families and even a friendly ghost (allegedly the former mistress of the house, Martha Mesereau, waiting for her husband to return from the Civil War). Though it's better known for its atmosphere than for its cuisine, the Old Bermuda Inn does turn out a moist crab cake and hosts a popular Sunday buffet brunch. Call ahead: the place is sometimes fully booked for private parties, especially on weekends.

at the High Rock Park office *(200 Nevada Ave., ☎ 718-987-3500)*, which anchors a 90-acre forest tract. An 18-hole golf course and a replica early-20C carousel round out the greenbelt's offerings.

Historic Richmond Town★ (BZ)

441 Clarke Ave. From the Staten Island ferry terminal, take the S74 bus to Richmond Rd./St. Patrick's Pl. ♿ Kids ⏱*Open Jul–Aug Wed–Sat 10am–5pm, Sun 1pm–5pm. Rest of the year Wed–Sun 1pm–5pm.* ⏱*Closed Jan 1, Easter Sunday, Thanksgiving Day & Dec 25.* ⬤$5. ✕ 🅿. ☎*718-351-1611; www.historicrichmondtown.org.* Interpreting life from the 17C to the 19C, this 25-acre living history museum is located on the site of one of the earliest settlements on Staten Island. Some 27 restored structures make up the town, including private dwellings, craft shops, a schoolhouse and municipal buildings. Staff members dressed in period costumes reenact everyday chores, and artisans occasionally demonstrate the crafts of yesteryear. You may buy tickets to the village at the visitor center, housed in the **County Courthouse**, an imposing Greek Revival structure from 1837. Highlights include the late-17C **Voorlezer House**, reputedly the oldest elementary school in the US, and the mid-18C **Guyon-Lake-Tysen House**, where domestic skills such as spinning and weaving are demonstrated seasonally.

Moravian Cemetery (BY)

This peaceful, gardenlike cemetery is affiliated with the Moravian church lo-cated at the entrance. Adorned with a columned portico, the white church was constructed in 1845 by the Vanderbilt family, one of whose ancestors belonged to the sect in the 17C. The original church, a Dutch Colonial-style structure constructed in 1763, now serves as the cemetery office.

The Moravian denomination, founded in the 15C as an evangelical communion in Bohemia (Moravia), accepted Protestantism in the 17C. Ascetic in its beliefs, the church adhered to strict observance of the teachings of the Bible.

Conference House (AZ)

7455 Hylan Blvd. From Staten Island ferry terminal take S78 bus to Craig. Ave.; walk 1 block south to Satterlee, cross street and enter park. ⏱*Open Apr–mid-Dec Fri–Sun 1pm–4pm.* ⬤$3. ☎*718-984-6046. www.theconferencehouse.org.*

Situated at the southwestern tip of Staten Island, the Conference House is named after the negotiations between the British and Americans (including John Adams and Benjamin Franklin) that took place here on September 11, 1776, in a futile attempt to end the emerging Revolutionary War. The handsome 17C fieldstone manor house has been restored and now contains a historic museum. The interior, furnished with 18C pieces, interprets the life and times of Col. Christopher Billtop, the house's original owner. The waterfront site affords fine views across the river and the bay to New Jersey.

Kykuit, Hudson River Valley
©John Hill/ Courtesy Historic Hudson Valley

HUDSON RIVER VALLEY★★★

MAP P 314

Along this famous waterway, you'll discover a storied landscape dotted with the eye-popping mansions of the Vanderbilts, Goulds and Rockefellers atop wooded bluffs above the river. You'll pass roadside fruit stands, wineries with a view and green pastures. And you'll behold the golden-hued scenes of the country's first literary and art movements – scenes that filled the canvases of Thomas Cole, Frederic Edwin Church and other painters of the Hudson River school as well as the pages of Washington Irving and James Fennimore Cooper.

- **Information:** ☎845-291-2136. www.travelhudsonvalley.org.
- **Organizing Your Time:** The best time to visit the Hudson River Valley is the fall, when Indian summer gilds the forests lining the river banks. If you plan to stay overnight, be sure to reserve a room well in advance. If you have only one day for your visit, we recommend driving north on the east bank in the morning and returning on the west bank in the afternoon.

A Bit of History

Originating high in the Adirondack mountains in upstate New York, the Hudson River flows 315mi to the sea. Navigable as far as Albany, it was linked in 1825 to the Great Lakes by the Erie Canal, once a busy waterway between Albany and Buffalo. On its journey south to New York City, the majestic Hudson flows between rocky crags and wooded peaks, still alluring despite encroaching industrial blight in some places.

Driving Tour

Distance: approximately 180mi round-trip.
Up and back, it's about 180 miles of hills, hollows and history as you tour the southern part of the Hudson River Valley. Occasionally, from Route 9 heading north, and Route 9 West, for the return, you'll be able to glimpse the river.

East Bank

- *Leave Manhattan via Henry Hudson Pkwy., which turns into the Saw Mill River Pkwy. heading north. Take Exit 9/ Executive Blvd. and continue to its end. Turn left on Broadway, then next right on Odell Ave. Follow Odell to the end and turn left on Warburton Ave. Continue south for 1.3mi.*

Hudson River Museum

511 Warburton Ave. in Yonkers. ♿
🕐 *Open year-round Wed–Sun noon–5pm (Fri until 8pm).* 🕐 *Closed major holidays.* ⌨ *$5.* ✗ 🅿. ☎ *914-963-4550. www.hrm. org.*
There's something for everyone at this combination historic house, art and history museum, and planetarium. Glenview, the late-Victorian-style stone mansion (1876), features Eastlake and Gothic Revival-style interiors, including rooms restored to show off the lifestyle of an upper-class 19C family. Paintings by Hudson River School artists Asher B. Durand, Jasper Cropsey and George Inness are part of the permanent collection. Artist Red Grooms created the fanciful bookstore space in the New Wing in 1979. Stargazers should take in a show at the **Andrus Planetarium** 🄺 (🕐 *Fri 7pm; weekends 12:30pm, 1:30pm, 2:30pm & 3:30pm;* ⌨ *$2; Fri show free).*

- *Past Yonkers, exit from Saw Mill River Pkwy. at Ashford Ave.–Dobbs Ferry. Go west on Ashford Ave., then turn right on Broadway (Rte. 9). Beyond Irvington, turn left on W. Sunnyside Lane.*

Sunnyside★

W. Sunnyside Lane, off Rte. 9 in Tarrytown. 🕐 *Visit of house by guided tour (1hr) only, Apr–Oct Wed–Mon 10am–5pm. Nov–Dec Wed–Mon 10am–4pm. Mar weekends only 10am–4pm.* 🕐 *Closed Jan–Feb, Thanks-*

Washington Irving's Sunnyside

giving Day & Dec 25. 🚫 $12. 🅿. ☎ 914-591-8763. www.hudsonvalley.org.
This wisteria-draped house on the east bank of the river was the home of author **Washington Irving** (1783-1859), chronicler of Rip van Winkle and Sleepy Hollow – now classic tales, peopled with characters of Dutch descent. A fitting introduction to "knickerbocker" country from the man who invented the term, this Dutch- and Spanish-style "snuggery," as Irving called it, was built on an existing stone cottage he purchased in 1835. Inside, you'll see family belongings and furnishings; the library is appointed largely as Irving left it. The surrounding 20-acre grounds are landscaped in the romantic style popular during the mid-19C, and provide good views of the Hudson.

▶ *Continue north on Rte. 9.*

Lyndhurst★

635 S. Broadway (Rte. 9), in Tarrytown. ⏱ *Open mid-Apr–Oct Tue–Sun 10am–5pm. Rest of the year weekends & holiday Mon 10am–4pm.* ⏱ *Closed major holidays.* 🚫 *$10.* 🚶 *Guided tours available.* 🍴 *May–Oct.* 🅿. ☎ *914-631-4481. www.lyndhurst.org.*
From a distance, this picturesque mansion looks like a baronial castle on the Rhine. The Gothic Revival-style house perches on a wooded bluff above the Hudson River. Originally a two-story villa

Stone Barns Center for Food and Agriculture

630 Bedford Road, Pocantico Hills. Open year-round Wed–Sun 10 am–5pm. Guided and audio tours of the property available. Kids programs offered. ☎914-366-6200. *www.stonebarnscenter.org.*

Set on 80 rolling acres just down the road from Union Church and Kykuit, this lively educational complex – part of the former Rockefeller estate – encompasses gardens, pasture, and woodlands, a 22,000sq ft year-round greenhouse, a restaurant, a cafe and a terrific bookstore specializing in cookbooks and gardening titles. The place gets its name from the regal Norman-style stone barns that stand at its center, built for John D. Rockefeller in the 1930s and used to house cattle through the 1970s. Today, the hay barn is used for classes on a wide range of topics, from botanical drawing to the ABCs of fennel (check the website for schedule), while the former dairy barn houses Blue Hill at Stone Barns, an award-winning gourmet restaurant featuring the farm's own Berkshire pig, broad-breasted turkey, heirloom tomatoes, exotic mushrooms and other seasonal products (reservations required: ☎914-366-9600; www.opentable.com).

Address Book

🕭 *For price ranges, see the Legend on the cover flap.*

WHERE TO STAY IN THE HUDSON RIVER VALLEY

$$$$$ Castle on the Hudson – *400 Benedict Ave., Tarrytown –* ☎ *914-631-1980 or 800-616-4487. www.castle onthehudson.com. 31 rooms.* Resembling a medieval castle, this mansion sits on a hilltop overlooking the river. Inside, stained-glass windows, Oriental rugs and period tapestries soften beamed ceilings and stone walls. Hand-carved four-poster beds draped in goose-down comforters, and custom-made chandeliers decorate the bedrooms. Dinner at **Equus** (**$$$$**), in the historic Oak Room, is sure to be a memorable experience.

$$$$ Mohonk Mountain House – *1000 Mountain Rest Rd., New Paltz –* ☎ *845-255-1000 or 800-772-6646. www.mohonk.com. 251 rooms (includes 3 daily meals).* Overlooking Lake Mohonk, this 1869 Victorian mountain lodge sprawls atop a rocky ridge within a 2,200-acre nature preserve. Guest quarters come in antique-filled rooms trimmed in dark wood, family-size suites, or luxurious tower suites complete with a fireplace. Spa facilities, golf, tennis, carriage rides and horseback riding are just some of the many recreational activities available.

$$$ Beekman Arms/Delamater Inn – *6387 Mill St. (Rte. 9), Rhinebeck –* ☎ *845-876-7077. 73 rooms. www.beekmandela-materinn.com.* Wide-planked floors and beamed ceilings recall the days when this inn – one of the oldest in the US – welcomed travelers on horseback. Today the 1766 lodging at the center of charming Rhinebeck offers 23 rooms with modern conveniences, as well as a cozy restaurant, **Traphagen** (**$$$**), serving updated comfort food like lobster pot pie and Hudson Valley duck breast. One block away, its sister property, the 1844 **Delamater Inn** comprises seven American Carpenter-syle buildings harboring 50 additional rooms, more than half with fireplaces.

$$$ Old Drovers Inn – *Old Rte. 22, Dover Plains –* ☎ *845-832-9311. www. olddroversinn.com. 4 suites.* In the 1750s, when cattle-men drove livestock down from New England to markets in New York City, this hostelry provided bed and board for wealthy drovers. Today it's a romantic bed-and-breakfast inn, with rooms outfitted with antique furniture and working fireplaces, and a fine restaurant, the **Tap Room** (**$$$**), serving savory American staples like rack of lamb and beef medallions.

WHERE TO EAT IN THE HUDSON RIVER VALLEY

Culinary Institute of America – 🕭 *See sidebar.*

$$$ Xavier's at Piermont – *506 Piermont Ave., Piermont –* ☎ *845-359-7007. www.xaviars.com. New American.* A modern ambience prevails in chef/owner Peter Xaviar Kelly's dining room, where four-course prix-fixe dinners (*$70/person; Wed–Sun*) feature the likes of Hudson Valley foie gras, slow-braised short ribs with English-pea risotto, and dry-aged New York sirloin with gingered shiitake mushrooms and truffled fries. Impressive.

$$$ Terrapin – *6426 Montgomery St., Rhinebeck –* ☎ *845-876-3330. www. terrapinrestaurant.com. New American.* This popular Hudson Valley's restaurant has a prime location at the center of Rhinebeck, in a shingle-style church building dating from 1825. Choose between the sedate, more formal restaurant or the bustling bistro – either way you'll creative cuisine: dishes like gnocchi with black truffles, salmon with artichoke sauce and creamy garlic soup.

$$$ The Red Dot – *321 Warren St., Hudson –* ☎ *518-828-3657. American.* City sophisticates and in-the-know locals flock to this friendly yet chic restaurant and bar, where you can get a gourmet burger with a cone of supercrisp fries, chicken pot pie, a salmon BLT (bacon, lettuce and tomato) and, for brunch, a terrific eggs benedict. The back garden is a lovely spot. Wed–Sun only.

Address Book

WHERE TO STAY ON LONG ISLAND

$$$$$ 1770 House – *143 Main St., East Hampton –* ☎*631-324-1770. www.1770house.com. 6 rooms. Strict cancellation policy.*

Smack in downtown Easthampton, this bed-and-breakfast inn is surprisingly swanky. Rooms have Frette linens, antiques and flat-screen televisions; some have working fireplaces. All but one room have private baths. Guests share the flower-bordered patio. If you're traveling in a group, snag the two-bedroom, two-bath carriage house with living room and butler's pantry.. A full breakfast is served daily in season (Jul–Aug) and on weekends off-season (continental breakfast on weekdays). The **1770 House Restaurant ($$$$)** wins raves for its innovative preparations and use of local products: look for pan-seared diver scallops, roasted heirloom beets and the like. For more casual fare, try the tavern downstairs.

$$$$ Ram's Head Inn – *108 Ram Island Drive, Shelter Island Heights. Closed late Nov–May.* ☎ *631-749-0811. www. shelterislandinns.com. 17 rooms.* This sprawling 1929 shingle-style inn, reached via ferry from Sag Harbor or Greenport, has the feel of a relaxed country estate, with Adirondack chairs scattered across a lawn that slopes down to sparkling Coecles Harbor. Rooms are done up in cheerful country decor; four share baths. All guests have free use of the tennis court, fitness center, sauna and private beach equipped with kayaks and sunfish; or you may just want to curl up with a book on one of the plush sofas in the sun room. The inn's **restaurant ($$$$)** draws diners from all over the area with dishes like Cedar River Run prime sirloin with arugula, crispy herb polenta and North Fork cabernet. Reservations here, as with the inn, are essential— plan a week ahead for a table, two months ahead for a room.

$$$ Ocean Resort Inn – *95 S. Emerson Ave., Montauk – Closed Nov–Mar.* ☎ *631-668-2300. www.oceanresortinn. 17 rooms.* The motel itself is nothing fancy – recently renovated rooms are clean, large, comfortable and bright, and some even have jacuzzis. But the location can't be beat. The Ocean Resort is just steps from a pristine white-sand beach with endless views over the Atlantic and a short walk from all the restaurants and shops of Montauk. There's a courtyard for picnicking and a hammock. What more could you need?

WHERE TO EAT ON LONG ISLAND

$$$ The Frisky Oyster – *27 Front St., Greenport –* ☎ *631-477-4266. thefriskyoyster.com. New American.*

This excellent little restaurant blends style and comfort with wild red-flowered wall fabrics and cozy high-backed banquettes. The changing seasonal menu, which may or may not feature oysters, offers smart renditions of bistro favorites like steak frites, as well as dishes with Asian or Italian touches, such as the grilled fig, proscuitto and wild arugula salad and the grilled grouper with shitaki fried rice and thai papaya salad. Save room for house-made desserts.

$$$ Nick and Toni's – *136 North Main St., East Hampton.* ☎*631-324-3550. nickandtonis.com. Mediterranean.* This Hamptons classic is still going strong. Walls are adorned with folk art, and the wood-burning oven is decorated with colorful mosaic tiles. The chefs draw their inspiration from local products, from the Montauk tuna that comes with white beans and pickled peppers to the Satur Farm baby beets with pomegranates, caperberries and mint. Nick and Toni also run **Rowdy Hall** *($$ 10 Main Street, East Hampton,* ☎*631-324-8555),* a family-friendly gastropub with plenty of outdoor seating in the Parrish Mews and an appropriately convivial feel: try the classic Rowdy burger, fish-and-chips or the French onion soup.

©A. Moskowitz – Courtesy Historic Hudson Valley

Philipsburg Manor

(1838, Alexander Jackson Davis) designed for a mayor of New York City, the house was enlarged for a subsequent owner in 1865. In 1880 financier and railroad tycoon Jay Gould acquired the 67-acre estate, which remained in the family until the death of Gould's daughter in 1961. Peaks, pinnacles, porches and turrets embellish the exterior, accentuating the mansion's irregular shape. Inside, ribbed and vaulted ceilings, pointed arches, stained-glass windows and imposing furnishings reinforce the Gothic mood. In the dining room, take note of the simulated marble colonnettes and leather wall coverings popular in the 19C. Walk or drive around the grounds to discover striking views of the mansion and its park-like 19C landscaping.

▶ *Continue north on Rte. 9 to Sleepy Hollow (formerly North Tarrytown).*

Philipsburg Manor★

On Rte. 9 in Sleepy Hollow. 👣🚌 *Visit of house by guided tour (1hr) only, Apr–Oct Wed–Mon 10am–5pm. Nov–Dec Wed–Mon 10am–4pm. Mar weekends only 10am–4pm.* 🕐 *Closed Jan–Feb, Thanksgiving Day, & Dec 25.* 🍴 *$12.* ✕ 🅿 ☎ *914-631-3992. www.hudsonvalley.org.*

The site conveys a sense of the manor system under which much of the Hudson River Valley was settled. At the height of its power, the influential Philips family controlled 52,000 acres of land along the river by royal charter. The family erected a stone manor by the Pocantico River to function as a business office, and a grist mill to grind the grains that tenant farmers brought as payment of their rent. Their three mills formed the basis of the successful trading network and shipping business that helped make them the richest family in the colonies. Today a working mill has been reconstructed on the site, and the house has been furnished with the help of a 1750 probate inventory. Be sure to see the barn and tenant farmhouse, which add to the ambience of the manor.

Kykuit★★

On Rte. 9 North. Tours depart from the visitor center at Philipsburg Manor. ♿ 🚌 *Visit by guided tour (1–3hrs) only, mid-May–early Nov Wed–Mon 9am–3pm (weekends until 4pm).* 🕐 *Closed mid-Nov–late Apr.* 🍴 *$15–38. Advance tickets suggested (no service charge for online purchases); see website for tour descriptions and prices.* ✕ 🅿. ☎ *914-631-9491. www.hudsonvalley.org.*

One of the last grand homes to be built in the Hudson River Valley, Kykuit (Dutch for "lookout," pronounced Kye-cut) offers a glimpse into the lives of four generations of Rockefellers. Built between 1906 and 1913 by **John D. Rockefeller Jr.** for his father, patriarch of Standard Oil, the estate sports a Beaux-Arts facade and interiors adorned in the Neoclassical style typical of English country homes.

Courtesy Historic Hudson Valley/www.hudsonvalley.org

Kukuit

Today, furnishings and room arrangements date to the residency of New York state governor **Nelson Rockefeller** and his wife, Happy, who moved into the house in 1963. By then the house brimmed with antique furniture, lovely Chinese porcelain of the Han, Tang and Ming dynasties, an assortment of china services and Nelson's burgeoning modern **art collection**★. He acquired his love of contemporary art, particularly sculpture, from his mother Abby Aldrich Rockefeller, a founder of the Museum of Modern Art in New York. His basement art galleries contain many treasures, including tapestries by Picasso.

The **gardens**★ and terraces of Kykuit, designed in the orderly, Beaux-Arts fashion by William Welles Bosworth (who also redesigned the facade), take their inspiration from Italian hilltop gardens. Nelson's careful siting of more than 70 modern sculptures around the grounds only enhances the beauty of the landscaping. Lovely **views**★ across the Hudson, particularly from the west porch, blend with gardens and art to form breathtaking vistas and painterly tableaux.

Located just north of Kykuit on Bedford Road (Rte. 448) is the lovely **Union Church of Pocantico Hills**★, a nondenominational Protestant church built on Rockefeller lands in 1921 (⟨♿⟩ ⟨🕐⟩ *open Apr–Dec Mon & Wed–Fri 11am–5pm, Sat 10am–5pm, Sun 2pm–5pm;* ⟨🕐⟩ *closed Jan–Mar,*

Lords of the Manor

In 1629, to encourage the settlement of New Netherland with private rather than company money, the Dutch West India Company granted estates, each measuring 16mi along the river, to its shareholders. Called "patroons" (patrons), these landholders agreed to send 50 tenant farmers within four years to cultivate the land. Unique in America, this feudal system worked poorly as the absentee patroons mismanaged their estates and attracted few settlers. Even so, when the English took over in 1664, they converted the patroonships into manors and continued to grant lands up and down the river to wealthy families. As freehold lands grew scarcer, more farmers began to settle as tenants on the manors of such families as the Van Rensselaers, Beekmans and Livingstons, who formed the upper crust of the valley's "nobility." Violent tenant uprisings led to a new state constitution in 1846 outlawing "feudal tenures." Soon, however, new generations of American aristocracy – Vanderbilts, Goulds and Rockefellers among them – would flock to the river's edge to build their mansions amid those of the venerable families of the Hudson Valley. Today a remarkable concentration of historic homes and properties remains the lingering legacy of this centuries-old Dutch settlement pattern.

Up to Ossining, the scenery along Route 9 is quite pretty, somewhat reminiscent of northern New England. Trees arch over the road at various points, and stone walls, made from rocks once cleared from farms, flank the route. From Ossining and Peekskill northward to Hyde Park, Route 9 is lined with fast-food restaurants, gas stations and big-box chain stores. At Peekskill, our tour leaves Route 9 temporarily for a prettier route *(see below)*.

▸ *Pass through Ossining, site of the Ossining Correctional Facility, formerly known as "Sing Sing" prison. Take the Croton Point Ave. exit. Turn right, then right again on South Riverside Ave.*

Van Cortlandt Manor★

Off Rte. 9 on S. Riverside Ave., in Croton-on-Hudson. 🚶 *Visit of house by guided tour (1hr) only, Apr–Oct Wed-Mon 10am–5pm. Nov–Dec weekends only 10am–4pm.* ⊘ *Closed Jan–Mar, Thanksgiving Day & Dec 25. $10.* 🅿 ☎ *914-271-8981. www.hudsonvalley.org.*

Legend has it that Benjamin Franklin, the Marquis de Lafayette, John Jay and other notable personalities visited this manor. Home to the Van Cortlandt family for 260 years, the house has been restored to its appearance during the tenure of Pierre Van Cortlandt, patriot and the first lieutenant-governor of New York State, who presided over 86,000 acres.

The house contains original family furnishings, paintings and pewter. Don't miss the large kitchen, with its original hearth, Dutch oven and cooking utensils. Located on the property, fields, gardens and the ferry house evoke 18C life in the Hudson Valley.

▸ *Continue on Rte. 9 North to Peekskill, then bear left onto Rte. 6/202 West; at Bear Mountain Bridge follow Rte. 9D North.*

This drive offers beautiful **views** of the river and the New Jersey Palisades as the road dips into the valley and then rises into the hills.

Boscobel Restoration★★

On Rte. 9D, 4mi north of junction with Rte. 403. 🚶 *Visit by guided tour (45min)*

Thanksgiving Day & Dec 25; 🎟 *$5.* 🅿 ☎ *914-332-6659; www.hudsonvalley.org).* It is best known for its **stained-glass windows**★, designed by Henri Matisse and Marc Chagall and commissioned by the Rockefellers. The Matisse rose window, completed two days before the artist's death, glows with shades of clear blue, bright yellow and deep green. Chagall designed the eight side panels, representing Old Testament themes, as well as the large window at the rear of the church. It is the only such assemblage created by Chagall in the US.

▸ *Return to Rte. 9 and continue northward toward Ossining.*

Antiquing in the Hudson River Valley

In the village of **Cold Spring**, two of the biggest stores here are Busy Bijou Galleries Ltd. *(50 Main St.;☎ 845-265-4337)*, which hosts about 25 dealers, and Downtown Gallery Ltd. *(40 Main St.;☎845-265-2334)*, with 30-plus dealers. Farther north, **Rhinebeck** is known for the Beekman Arms Antique Market *(24 W Market St., ☎845-876-3477)*, with 30 dealers showing their wares in an old red stable behind the Beekman Arms Hotel. Finally, at the northern tip of the valley sits **Hudson**, boasting 70 top-tier antique and design stores, plus a number of galleries and boutiques, along its main drag, Warren Street. The term "antique" here stretches well into the 20C, with sleek and stylish mid-century modern pieces juxtaposed with more traditional 19C designs *(☎800-724-1846, www.hudsonantiques.net)*.

only, Apr–Oct Wed–Mon 9:30am–5pm. Nov–Dec Wed–Mon 9:30am–4pm. ⏲ Closed Jan–Mar, Thanksgiving Day & Dec 25. ⊛ $12. 🅿. ☎ 845-265-3638. www. boscobel.org.

Set back from the road and overlooking the Hudson River, Boscobel, a handsome example of Federal domestic architecture, was begun by States Morris Dyckman (1755-1806) in 1804 and completed after his death by his wife, Elizabeth.
In the 1950s the property on which Boscobel originally stood was sold and the mansion was almost destroyed. Preservationists acquired the building and moved it piece by piece to Garrison, where it was reconstructed on grounds high above the Hudson. Rebuilt and refurbished, Boscobel opened to the public in 1961. The overall appearance is one of Federal elegance and refinement. The recessed central portion of the facade, with its slender columns and carved trim, contrasts with the otherwise unadorned exterior.

The restored interior features graceful arches, fireplaces embellished with classical motifs, delicately carved woodwork and a freestanding central staircase lit by a tall Palladian window. Furnishings include many pieces by leading New York craftsman Duncan Phyfe.

▸ *Follow Rte. 9D North to Beacon.*

Dia:Beacon★

3 Beekman St., Beacon. ♿ ⏲ *Open mid-Apr–mid-Oct Thu–Mon 11am–6pm. Rest of the year Fri–Mon 11am–4pm.* ⏲ *Closed major holidays.* ⊛ *$10.* ✖ 🅿. ☎ *845-440-0100. www.diabeacon.org.*

This 240,000sq ft gallery, housed in what used to be a Nabisco factory, is the toast of the Hudson Valley contemporary art world. In addition to showing selections from the Dia Foundation's permanent collection— which includes large-scale works by Andy Warhol, Joseph Beuys, Richard Serra, Donald Judd and others—

Van Cortlandt Manor

Courtesy Historic Hudson Valley/www.hudsonvalley.org

Dia mounts vast retrospectives of noted artists such as Agnes Martin and Robert Smithson. The bookstore and cafe are both excellent.

▶ *Follow Rte. 9D North to Rte. 9 North and continue to Poughkeepsie. Head east on Rte. 44/55, then turn right onto Raymond Ave. (Rte. 376).*

Vassar College

Raymond Ave. in Poughkeepsie. ☎ 845-437-7000. www.vassar.edu.

Vassar is one of the best-known private liberal arts colleges in the US. Founded as a women's college in 1861, it became coeducational in 1969 and now has 2,400 students, 40 percent of whom are men. The buildings reflect traditional American and European styles, as well as modern trends in architecture: notice Ferry House (Marcel Breuer) and Noyes House (Eero Saarinen), dormitories erected in 1951 and 1958, respectively. The Thompson Library houses the majority of Vassar's nearly one million print volumes.

▶ *Return to Rte. 9 and continue north to Hyde Park, where you'll find the following three sights tightly clustered.*

Home of Franklin D. Roosevelt National Historic Site★★

On Rte. 9 in Hyde Park. ✎ Visit by guided tour (1hr) only, year-round daily 9am–5pm. ♿ ⏱ Grounds (free) open dawn–dusk. ⏱ Closed Jan 1, Thanksgiving Day & Dec 25. ⌨ $14 (free children under 15). 🅿. ☎ 845-229-9115. www.nps.gov/hofr.

This vast estate—known as the "Summer White House" during FDR's presidency—is one of the most important historic sites in the Hudson Valley. It was acquired by the president's father in 1867; FDR was born here in 1882.

The mansion, Springwood, dates back to the early 19C but has since been remodeled and enlarged, and more recently, refurbished. It is unique among historic homes for the exceedingly personal experience it offers. Memorabilia of the late president (1882-1945) and his family can be found in the house, library and museum. Exhibits trace the trans-

Culinary Institute of America

1946 Campus Dr., Hyde Park. ☎ 845-471-6608. www.ciachef.edu. Reservations required.
On the premises of a former Jesuit seminary reside the five restaurants of The Culinary Institute of America (CIA). Here, 2,400 chefs-in-training gain practical experience in preparation, cooking and serving under the watchful tutelage of CIA's world-renowned faculty. Each of the restaurants offers a different – and excellent – dining experience. Here you'll find the food and atmosphere are outstanding, and the students friendly and earnest. **St. Andrew's Café** *(Mon–Fri)* serves contemporary

fare emphasizing fresh seasonal ingredients in a family-friendly setting; **American Bounty** *(Tue–Sat)* focuses on the bounty of the Hudson River Valley; the elegant **Escoffier** *(Tue–Sat)* will please the Francophile with its light take on classic French cuisine; and **Ristorante Caterina de Medici** *(Mon–Fri)* serves authentic regional Italian dishes. The casual **Apple Pie Bakery Café** *(Mon–Fri 8am–6:30pm)* offers soups, salads, sandwiches, artisanal breads and pastries (eat-in or take-out) prepared by CIA's baking and pastry arts majors. *All CIA restaurants, except the Bakery Café, are open for lunch and dinner. Dress is "country club casual" – no jeans or sneakers.*

CIA - Lorna Smith

Main Dining Room

Franklin D. Roosevelt National Historic Site

formation of a "charming New York social-ite into one of America's great statesmen." In the rose garden, a simple monument of white Vermont marble marks the final resting place of Franklin and Eleanor Roosevelt.

Eleanor Roosevelt National Historic Site★

On Rte. 9G in Hyde Park. ♿ ☞ Visit by guided tour (45min) only, May–Oct daily 9am–5pm. Rest of the year Thu–Mon 9am–4:30pm. ◷ Grounds (free) open dawn–dusk. ◷ Closed Jan 1, Thanksgiving Day & Dec 25. ☞ $8. 🅿. ☎ 845-229-9422. www.nps.gov/elro.

The Roosevelts often came to this tranquil corner of the estate on the Fall Kill for family picnics. FDR built a stone cottage on the property in 1925, and a year later **Eleanor Roosevelt** (1884-1962) and her friends opened a furniture factory nearby. After the business folded in the mid-1930s, the building was remodeled and eventually became Eleanor's beloved Val-Kill cottage. Mrs. Roosevelt considered Val-Kill her only true home, and after the president's death, she chose to spend her remaining years here working, entertaining her friends and receiving foreign dignitaries.

Vanderbilt Mansion National Historic Site★★

On Rte. 9 in Hyde Park, 2mi north of FDR National Historic Site. ♿ ☞ Visit by guided tour (45min) only, year-round daily 9am–5pm. ◷ Grounds (free) open dawn–dusk. ◷ Closed Jan 1, Thanksgiving Day & Dec 25. ☞ $8. 🅿. ☎ 845-229-9115. www.nps.gov/vama.

This sumptuous Beaux-Arts residence (1898) was designed by McKim, Mead and White for Frederick W. Vanderbilt and his wife, Louise. Remarkably preserved and luxuriously appointed, it bears witness to a bygone age of opulence. Before the Vanderbilts bought the property in the early 19C, it belonged to famed botanist Dr. David Hosack. He and other earlier owners of the estate were exceedingly interested in landscaping; as a result, the grounds represent one of the greatest intact surviving examples of the Romantic style of landscape architecture in the US. The lavish interior contains art and furniture befitting America's "nobility" and ranging from Renaissance to rococo in style. Walking trails along the river afford scenic views of the valley.

▸   *Continue north on Rte. 9 to Staatsburg.*

Staatsburgh State Historic Site★

Off Rte. 9 on Old Post Rd., in Staatsburg. ☞ Visit by guided tour (1hr) only, Apr–Oct Tue–Sat 10am–5pm, Sun noon–5pm. Rest of the year, call for hours. ☞ $5. 🅿. ☎ 845-889-8851. www.nysparks.com.

Built on land that had been in **Ruth Livingston Mills**' family since 1792, this 79-room Beaux-Arts mansion engulfs a

National Park Service, Hyde Park NY

Vanderbilt Mansion

Greek Revival home constructed in 1832. Ruth and Ogden Mills inherited the property in 1890, and hired architects McKim, Mead and White to transform the home into a "palace royale" fit for entertaining. Part English baronial hall (note the heavily wooded entryway), part French palace (the Louis XVI **dining room** rivals any in the Hudson River Valley for its scale, luster and view), the home boasted 14 bathrooms and accommodations, indoors and out, for weekend visitors. Mrs. Mills' furnishings and personal touches reflect pride in her colonial and Revolutionary War heritage as a member of the Livingston family. She considered herself heiress, as well, to Mrs. Astor as queen of American society. Take advantage of the hiking trails on the grounds, since they offer rare access to the Hudson's edge.

▶ *Continue north on Rte. 9 to Rhinebeck.*

Rhinebeck★

Founded in 1686 by Dutch settlers, Rhinebeck is perhaps the quaintest and most upscale of all the Hudson River villages, replete with antique stores, boutiques, a picturesque inn, and several tasty restaurants.

For an inexpensive breakfast or lunch, it's hard to beat **Bread Alone** (*45 E. Market St.; ☎845-876-3108; wwwbreadalone. com*), known throughout the valley for its robust breads, muffins, soups and sandwiches. On Sundays (🕐 *May–Nov 10am-2pm*), a **farmers' market** on East

Market Street (in the municipal parking lot) features fresh produce, local wines and honey, as well as gourmet foods made by local chefs.

Be sure to check out what's happening at the **Dutchess County Fair grounds** while you're in town; just north of downtown Rhinebeck on Rte. 9, the 168-acre site hosts a packed calendar of weekend events, from horse shows to arts and crafts fairs (☎ *845-876-4001; www. dutchessfair.com*). The **Old Rhinebeck Aerodrome** (Kids 🕐 *open mid-May–Oct daily 10am–5pm;* ⬤ *$10; $3 children 6–12 weekdays; $20; $5 children 6–12 weekends;* ☎ *845-752-3200; www.old-rhinebeck.org*) is known for its large collection of vintage cars, airplanes and motorbikes, as well as for its air shows (🕐*mid-Jun–mid-Oct, Sat–Sun 2pm*); rides on a 1929 biplane (⬤ *$50 per person*) offer aerial views of the Hudson Valley; call for details.

West Bank

▶ *Return to Poughkeepsie, cross the Hudson River and continue south on Rte. 9 West.*

Storm King Art Center★

Take Rte. 9 West to the Cornwall Hospital Exit, then bear left onto Rte. 107; at the intersection turn right and follow Rte. 32 North over the bridge, turning left immediately after the bridge onto Orr's Mill Rd. Kids 🕐 *Open Apr–Oct Wed–Sun 11am-5:30pm, early Nov–mid-Nov Wed–*

Sun 11am–5pm; Jun–Aug Sat grounds open until 8pm (admission fee applies). 🕐 *Closed mid-Nov–Mar.* 🎫 *$10; $7 children 5–18; under 5 free.* 🚶 *Guided tours (1hr) daily 2pm; Acoustiguide self-guided tour available ($5).* 🅿. ☎ *845-534-3115. www.stormking.org.*

This unique outdoor museum of contemporary sculpture covers 500 acres of meadow, hillsides, forest, lawns and terraces. Large-scale works by such artists as Alexander Calder (*The Arch*), Mark diSuvero, Alexander Liberman (*Iliad*), Henry Moore, Louise Nevelson, Isamu Noguchi (*Momo Taro*) and David Smith are installed on the grounds, most of them in settings that have been specially landscaped for the sculpture. Changing exhibits of paintings, graphics and smaller sculptures from the center's collection are presented in the Normandy-style museum building (1935), formerly a private residence.

West Point★★

Map p 320. 10mi southeast of Storm King Art Center on Rte. 218 South.
Overlooking the Hudson River, West Point is renowned as the site of the United States Military Academy, the oldest of the nation's service academies.

A Bit of History

Fortress West Point was established in 1778 as a series of fortifications to protect the strategically important Hudson at this most defensible location. After the Revolutionary War the grounds became a repository for trophies and captured equipment. It was not until 1802 that the US Military Academy was established by Congress, and West Point selected as its site. In the academy's first year, five officers trained and instructed the ten students; there are now more than 4,200 men and women cadets. Among its graduates West Point counts generals MacArthur (1903), Patton (1909), Eisenhower (1915) and Schwartzkopf (1956); and astronauts Borman (1950), Aldrin (1951), Collins (1952), White (1952) and Scott (1954).

Visit

The campus may be visited by guided tour (1hr) only; you need not take a tour to see the visitor center and museum. ♿ 🚶 *Tours depart about every 45min from the visitor center Apr–Oct Mon–Sat & holidays 10am–3:30pm, Sun 11am–3:30pm. Rest of the year daily 11:15am & 1:15pm (2hr tours also available; call or see website for details).* 🚶 *No tours Jan 1, Thanksgiving Day, Dec 24 & 25, on football Saturdays or during Graduation week.* 🎫 *$10.* 🅿. *West Point Tours:* ☎ *845-446-4724. www.westpointtours.com.*

In the **visitor center**, films and exhibits introduce visitors to the history and sights of West Point and the life of a cadet (🕐 *open year-round daily 9am–4:45pm;* 🕐 *closed Jan 1, Thanksgiving Day & Dec 25;* ☎ *845-938-2638; www.usma.edu*). Near the visitor center, the **museum**★★ (♿ 🕐 *open year-round daily 10:30am–*

Color Guard, West Point

©West Point

4:15pm; ⏱ *closed Jan 1, Thanksgiving Day & Dec 25.* 🅿 . ☎ *845-938-3590)* thoroughly examines the history of the military, the academy, warfare and weapons using dioramas, print materials and artifacts, including Napoleon's sword and Goering's jewel-encrusted marshal's baton. Its collection of arms, which traces the development of automatic weapons from the Civil War to the present, began with ordnance captured at the Battle of Saratoga in 1777.

Tour – Buildings that are open to the public on the private tour include the **Cadet Chapel**, an example of the "military Gothic" style, built in 1910; 18C **Fort Putnam**★ (⏱*open for Saturday football games & during Graduation week only),* partially restored in 1907 and completed in 1976; the **Battle Monument**, commemorating victims of the Civil War; and **Trophy Point**. Among the Revolutionary War relics at Trophy Point are links of the great chain that was strung across the Hudson River to prevent British ships from passing.

The Parades – These famous reviews, known for their precision of movement, are held from early September through November and from late April through May. *For schedules:* ☎ *845-938-2638 or www.usma.edu.*

▶ Continuing south, Rte. 9 West passes **Bear Mountain**, *the highest point (1,305ft) in Palisades Interstate Park.*

Stony Point Battlefield State Historic Site

Park Rd., off Rte. 9 West. ♿ ⏱ *Grounds open Apr–Oct Mon–Sat 10am–5pm, Sun noon–5pm, museum Wed–Sat 10am–4:30pm, Sun noon–4:30pm; rest of the year grounds only Mon–Fri 10am–4pm.* 🅿 *$5 on weekends.* ☎ *845-786-2521. www.nysparks.com.*

The British wrested this rocky, strategic promontory from the Americans in 1779, thereby gaining control of the entrance to the Hudson Highlands and safeguarding Kings Ferry, which connected the east and west banks at this narrow stretch of river. Anxious to retrieve it, General "Mad" Anthony Wayne mounted a surprise attack on the point in July of that year, fording the marshes below at midnight and overcoming the British in less than an hour. The battle would be the last in the north and a tremendous morale-builder for Continental troops. Now a state historic site, the rugged, windswept terrain is studded with interpretive signs that describe the fighting and with picnic spots that afford fine views over the Hudson. In the **museum**, exhibits and a 12min video offer further details of the battle. The oldest

lighthouse on the Hudson River, built in 1826 on the site of the central powder magazine, has been restored to working order with a 19C Fresnel lens (🕐 *open most weekends Apr–Oct;* 🚌 *guided tours by appointment).*

▶ *Continue the drive south on* **Palisades Interstate Parkway** *– offering superb views*★★ *of Yonkers, the Bronx and Manhattan – to the George Washington Bridge, which leads back to Manhattan.*

LONG ISLAND★★
MAP P 322-323

Long Island is the largest island linked to the continental US. Only 20 miles at its widest point, it is 118 miles long, with dramatic shoreline all along its length. Because it's so close to New York City (indeed, both Brooklyn and Queens are on Long Island), the western part of the island has become heavily suburban, with the attendant traffic and strip malls, while the eastern part is more rural and serene.

🛈 **Information:** ☎631-951-3900. www.licvb.com. ♿See p311 for a selection of hotels and restaurants on the island.

▶ **Orient Yourself:** Lying east of Manhattan, the island sweeps east-northeast from the mouth of the Hudson River into the Atlantic Ocean.

North Shore

Facing Long Island Sound, the North Shore is a place of rocky necks and steep bluffs, thick woods and picturesque coves. Gilded Age robber barons so loved the landscape that they built great estates on some of the best waterfont lots. Today several of these mansions are open to the public, offering a tantalizing glimpse into the lives of the super-rich; other attractions include history museums—including Teddy Roosevelt's former home—and stunning gardens. Farther out, the North Fork, stretching from Riverhead to Orient Point, is increasingly known for its excellent wineries, bed-and-breakfast inns, quaint towns and great restaurants.

Sands Point Preserve★
95 Middleneck Rd., Port Washington. 🕐 *Open year-round daily 10am–5pm.* 🚌 *$2 on weekends.* 🅿. ☎ *516-571-7901. www.sandspointpreserve.org.*
This former Gold Coast estate, purchased by railroad tycoon Jay Gould in 1900, features two grandiose mansions, reflecting the styles and aspirations of New York society during the Gilded Age. **Castlegould**, originally planned as stables and servants'

quarters, houses an information center and rotating exhibits. Built in 1912, the massive Tudor-style **Hempstead House** (⚭ *not open to public)* was Castlegould's main residence; it was sold by Gould to Daniel Guggenheim in 1917. The US Navy operated a naval training center here from 1946 to 1967; it's now used for special events only. The Normandy-style manor house known as **Falaise**★ gets its name from the French word for "cliff"—appropriate given its precarious seaside perch (🚌 *visit by 1hr guided tour only, late May–Oct Thu–Sun noon, 1pm, 2pm & 3pm).* The mansion was erected by Capt. Harry F. Guggenheim, son of Daniel, and now contains a wonderful collection of 16C and 17C French and Spanish artifacts. Step to the rear of the house, where you'll enjoy spectacular **views**★★ of the sound from the arcaded loggia.

Nassau County Museum of Art
M *on map. One Museum Dr., in Roslyn Harbor. Take Rte. 25A East, cross the Roslyn Viaduct and turn left on Museum Dr.* 🕐 *Open year-round Tue–Sun 11am–4:45pm.* 🕐 *Closed Dec 25 and for six weeks a year during exhibition changes; call for details.* 🚌 *$10.* 🚌 *Guided tours available Mon–Sat 2pm.* 🍴 🅿*$2 (charge*

LONG ISLAND

on weekends only). ☎ 516-484-9338. www.nassaumuseum.com.

The museum is headquartered on the grounds of a late-19C estate built for Lloyd Bryce, the paymaster-general of New York, and acquired in 1919 by Childs Frick, the son of Henry Clay Frick. Changing art exhibits covering all periods are presented in the elegant Georgian Revival mansion, which has been converted into eight galleries. The landscaped lawns, ponds and gardens encompass 145 acres, offering an ideal outdoor setting for sculpture shows. Also on the grounds is the Tee Ridder Miniatures Museum (🕑open Tue–Sun noon–4:30pm).

Old Westbury Gardens★

71 Old Westbury Rd., Old Westbury. 🕑 *Open mid-Apr–Oct Wed–Mon 10am–5pm (no entry after 4pm).* 📷 *Guided tours (45min) available on the hour and the half hour.* 🎫 *$10.* ✕ 🅿. ☎ *516-333-0048. www.oldwestburygardens.org.*

Occupying grounds formerly belonging to John S. Phipps, sportsman and finan-

cier, this 160-acre estate contains woods, meadows, lakes and formal gardens. The stately Charles II mansion has been preserved as it was during the family's occupancy in the early 20C. The interior features antique furnishings, paintings by Thomas Gainsborough and John Singer Sargent, gilded mirrors and objets d'art.

Oyster Bay

Famed as a vacation spot and for its sheltered pleasure-craft harbor, this picturesque town brims with historic landmarks, quaint shops and tree-shaded streets lined with Victorian and Colonial homes. Oyster Bay's most famous resident was **Theodore Roosevelt**, who spent 20 years at Sagamore Hill; his grave (**A** *on map*) is located in Young's Cemetery.

Planting Fields★★

Planting Fields Rd. ♿ 🕑 *Grounds open year-round daily 9am–5pm.* 🕑 *Closed Dec 25.* 🎫 *$6/car May–Oct daily; rest of the year weekends & holidays.* 🅿. ☎ *516-922-8600. www.plantingfields.com.*

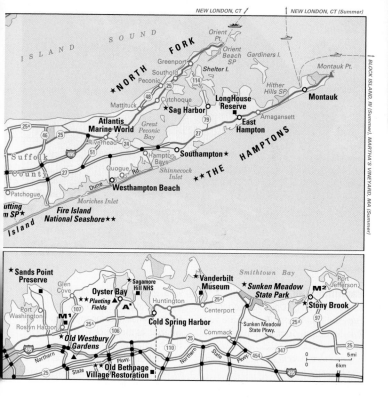

This former private estate of financier William Robertson Coe is now a state historic park. The 409 acres of planting fields contain 160 acres that have been developed as an arboretum; the remaining land has been kept as a natural habitat. The plant collections include more than 600 rhododendron and azalea species (in bloom May–June); the Synoptic Garden, comprising approximately five acres of selected ornamental shrubs for Long Island gardens; the camelia collection, the oldest and largest of its kind under glass (*blooming period: Feb–Mar*); and greenhouses filled with orchids, hibiscus, begonias and cacti. Amid these landscaped gardens and spacious lawns stands **Coe Hall**, a fine example of the Tudor Revival style (*visit by 1hr guided tour only, Apr–Sept daily noon–3:30pm;* closed Dec 25; $6.50; 516-922-9210).

Sagamore Hill National Historic Site★

Cove Neck Rd. Kids *Visit of mansion by guided tour (1hr) only, late May–Labor Day daily 9am–5pm. Rest of the year Wed–Sun 10am–4pm.* Closed major holidays. $5; children under 15 free. 516-922-4447. www.nps.gov/sahi.

Located east of the village of Oyster Bay, this gracious mansion (1885) is maintained as it was during Theodore Roosevelt's presidency (1901-09). The 23-room Queen Anne structure retains more than 90 percent of the family's original furnishings. During the guided tour, you'll hear humorous anecdotes about Teddy's life and presidential pursuits. Be sure to note the rhinoceros-foot inkstand – a trophy of his hunting days – and the bronze *Paleolithic Man* by Frederic Remington in the library. After the tour, take a seat on the wide piazza and enjoy sweeping views of the grounds. In the **Old Orchard Museum**, exhibits and a 20min biographical film trace Roosevelt's public and private life. The Georgian-style mansion was built by Theodore Roosevelt Jr. in 1938.

Sagamore Hill National Historic Site

Raynham Hall Museum

20 W. Main St. ◔ *Open Jul–Labor Day Tue–Sun noon–5pm. Rest of the year Tue–Sun 1pm–5pm.* ◔ *Closed major holidays.* ⚲ *$4.* ⚲ *Audio tour available ($1).* ☎ *516-922-6808. www.raynhamhall-museum.org.*

This old farmhouse played an important role during the American Revolution. It was the home of Samuel Townsend, whose son, Robert, was Washington's chief intelligence agent in New York City. Inside you'll see period furniture and memorabilia dating from the 1770s through the 1870s.

Cold Spring Harbor

From 1836 to 1862 the Cold Spring Harbor whaling fleet of nine ships sailed to every navigable ocean in search of whale oil and bone. The commanders of these vessels came from established whaling centers such as Sag Harbor.

Cold Spring Harbor Whaling Museum★

301 Main St. (Rte. 25A). **Kids** ⚲ ◔ *Open Memorial Day–Labor Day daily 11am–5pm; rest of the year Tue–Sun 11am–5pm.* ⚲ *$5 ($4 children 5–18).* ☎ *631-367-3418. www.cshwhalingmuseum.org.*

Dedicated to the preservation of the town's history as a whaling port, this museum features several outstanding exhibits, including a fully equipped 19C

whaleboat and a detailed diorama of Cold Spring Harbor, showing village houses, whaling company buildings and wharves as they appeared in the 1850s, the heyday of the whaling industry. Throughout the museum are examples of whalecraft: harpoons, navigational instruments and whaling-ship models. Note especially the extensive collection of scrimshaw (carvings of ivory tusks or whale bones), the whaler's folk art.

Old Bethpage Village Restoration★★

1303 Round Swamp Rd., Old Beth Page. **Kids** ◔ *Open Mar–Dec Wed–Fri 10am–4pm, weekends 10am–5pm.* ⚲ *$7.* ⚲ ☎ *516-572-8400. www.nassaucountyny.gov.*

Nestled in a 200-acre valley, Old Bethpage is an active farm community that re-creates a pre-Civil War American village. More than 55 historic buildings reflecting the architectural heritage of Long Island have been moved to the site of the former Powell Farm. Take a leisurely stroll through the village to observe the weaver making cloth, the farm wife preparing a meal and farmers working their fields. Depending on the time of year, you can also watch sheepshearing, cider making and other seasonal activities.

Vanderbilt Museum★

180 Little Neck Rd., Centerport. **Kids** ⚲ ◔ *Visit of house by guided tour (1hr) only,*

year-round Tue–Sun noon–5pm. 🕐 Closed
Jan 1, Thanksgiving Day & Dec 25. 🎟 $10.
Grounds only, $7. 🅿. ☎ 631-854-5555.
www.vanderbiltmuseum.org.

Overlooking Northport Harbor, this 43-
acre estate holds the Vanderbilt Mansion,
a marine museum and a planetarium.
The 24-room Spanish Revival mansion
belonged to William K. Vanderbilt Jr., great-
grandson of railroad tycoon Cornelius
Vanderbilt. Inside, you'll see elaborately
carved marble and woodwork and original family furnishings, as well as natural
history collections in the Habitat Wing.
Also on the grounds is the **Marine Museum**, a showcase for artifacts gathered by
William during his travels, including ship
models, arms and weaponry, and birds.
The **planetarium** presents a variety of
shows throughout the year (for admission fees & schedule: ☎ 631-854-5555).

Sunken Meadow State Park★

Sunken Meadow Pkwy at Rte. 25A, Kings
Park. ♿ 🕐 Open year-round daily dawn–
dusk. ✕ 🅿 (🎟 $8 weekends only) ☎ 631-
269-4333. www.nysparks.com.

Bordering Long Island Sound, this park
offers a wide range of recreational
activities, including golfing (27 holes),
swimming, nature trails and bike paths.
Sunken Meadow refers to the large, fine-
sand beach lining the sound.

Stony Brook★

When you visit this pleasant hamlet,
you'll think you've entered a Federal-
style village from 18C or 19C America.
It's also home to a branch of the State
University of New York.

Long Island Museum of American Art, History and Carriages★

Kids ♿ 🕐 Open year-round Wed–Sat
10am–5pm, Sun noon–5pm; closed major
holidays; 🎟 $7 ($3 children ages 6–17).
☎ 631-751-0066; www.longislandmu-
seum.org.

A Smithsonian affiliate since 2006, this
museum complex on nine acres tells the
story of Long Island. The **History
Museum**, located inside a 19C lumber
mill, has changing displays on American
life from the 18C to the 1900s. Don't miss
the an-tique wildfowl decoys and a gallery of **miniature period rooms** from
colonial times to the 1930s. The two-
story **Carriage Museum** houses an
exceptional collection of horse-drawn
carriages, some 250 of them. The show-
stopper is the c.1880 "Grace Darling"
omnibus, decorated with landscape
paintings. The paintings and drawings
of **William Sidney Mount** (1807-68), a
local landscape painter, and other 19C
and 20C artists are presented in changing exhibits in the **Art Museum**. Also on
the grounds are a blacksmith shop and
one-room schoolhouse.

North Fork★

🛈 Tourist information:
www.northfork.org.

Cold Spring Harbor Whaling Museum

Getting to and around Fire Island

You may drive to the east and west ends of the island—including Robert Moses State Park—but there are no public roads on the island itself. Most people get to the island by ferry and then explore it on foot or by **water taxi** (☎631-665-8885, www.fireislandwatertaxi.com). From Patchogue, Long Island, you can take the **Davis Park Ferry** (☎ 631-475-1665, www.davisparkferry.com) to the eastern part of the island, including beautiful Watch Hill beach. From Sayville, Long Island, you can take the **Sayville Ferry Service** (☎631-589-0810, www.sayvilleferry.com) to the central communities, including the Sunken Forest. From Bay Shore, take the **Fire Island Ferries** (☎631-665-3600, www.fireislandferries.com) to Ocean Beach. Ticket prices vary depending on route and time of day but generally cost $12–$15 per adult round-trip.

Roughly 25mi east of Stony Brook, the Long Island Expressway ends and the island splits in two, like tines of a fork. As home to the upscale resort towns of the Hamptons and miles of white-sand beaches, the South Fork has always garnered the lion's share of the tourist trade, leaving the North Fork for the locals. That is changing, however: in recent years the rural North Fork has gained a strong reputation for its award-winning **wineries** and plush bed-and-breakfast inns. Strung out along 24mi of Route 25, its 11 quaint towns boast a number of new wine bars and restaurants. Along the coastal Route 48 you'll find beaches, parks and ocean views.

At the head of the Great Peconic Bay sits Riverhead, home to **Atlantis Marine World**, an Atlantis-themed aquarium with sharks, eels, stingrays, exotic fish and a living coral reef (Kids ⑤ ⊙ open year-round daily 10am–5pm; ⊙closed Dec 25; ☜$19, $16 children 3–11; ✕ ℗ ☎ 631-208-9200 www.atlantismarineworld.com). As you proceed east on Rte. 25 the landscape takes on a rural character, with rolling farmland, vineyards and orchards on both sides.

A good place to stop for an informal breakfast or lunch is **Love Lane Kitchen** (240 Love Lane; ☎ 631-298-8989) in quaint Mattituck, where you can get homemade granola or gourmet sandwiches. A bit farther on, Cutchogue's village green sports the 1649 **Old House**, one of the oldest frame houses in the country. Also here are the 1840 Old School House and the 1890 Red Barn, both filled with period furnishings (⊙ open by 1hr guided tour only late Jun–Labor Day Sat–Mon 1pm–4pm, ☎ 631-734-7122).

Farther east, pourers at the friendly **Tasting Room** in Peconic, heart of the North Fork's winery region, will introduce you to the area's viticultural scene with tastings and flights of wines from six boutique North Fork wineries (2885 Peconic Lane, ⊙open year-round Fri–Sun 11am–6pm; ☎ 631-765-6404, www.tastingroomli.com) and give you tips about which ones to visit.

Southold is home to one of the area's best-kept secrets: the **Custer Institute Observatory,** where you can peer into the heavens through a high-powered Meade telescope at no charge every Saturday night from dusk to midnight (off Rte. 25 on Main Bayview Rd., ☎ 631-765-2626, www.custerobservatory.org).

Greenport's marina is home to the **Bounty**, the schooner built as the floating set of the 1962 film Mutiny on the Bounty and used more recently in Pirates of the Caribbean II. From Greenport you can grab the ferry to scenic **Shelter Island** (for ferry schedule call ☎631-749-0139 or visit www.northferry.com). Finally, out at the tip of the island, in Orient, is **Orient Beach State Park** (☎ 631-323-2440, http://nysparks.state.ny.us), with 45,000ft of frontage on Gardiner's Bay and a rare maritime forest with red cedar, blackjack oak trees and prickly-pear cactus. Swimming season lasts only from late June through August, but nature trails are open year-round.

South Shore

Long Island's famed beaches dot this scenic shoreline, where three long, thin barrier islands—including scenic, car-free Fire Island—front both the Atlantic Ocean and the Great South Bay. Farther east are the Hamptons resort communities, where multimillion-dollar second homes line the ocean and boutiques and restaurants cater to the tastes and pocketbooks of the wealthy. At the tip of the South Shore, laid-back Montauk sports beachside motels, a famous lighthouse, sprawling beaches and a ubiquitous bumper sticker: "Montauk: The End." Pick one up to show you've been there. Attractions below are presented west to east.

Coast Guard Lighthouse, Fire Island

©iStockphoto.com/ Kenneth C. Zirkel

Jones Beach State Park★★

Off Wantagh Pkwy., in Wantagh. ☎ 516-785-1600. www.nysparks.com.
Six and a half miles of sandy beaches are the highlight of this popular state park, with its double exposure to the ocean and bay. Other features include the massive open-air **Jones Beach Theater,** two swimming pools, sports fields, play areas, a two-mile wooden boardwalk and the **Theodore Roosevelt Nature Center** **Kids**, which has a butterfly garden and an interpretive walk on the sand dunes, among other exhibits (⏰ *open Memorial Day–Labor Day Wed–Sun 10am–4pm; rest of the year weekends 10am–4pm,* ☎516-679-7254).

Bayard Cutting Arboretum State Park★

Rte. 27A, Oakdale. ♿ ⏰ *Open Apr–Oct Tue–Sun 10am–6:30pm (last entry at 5pm), rest of the year 10am–5:30pm (last entry at 4pm).* ⏰ *Closed major holidays.* ⬤*$6/vehicle.* ✕ 🅿. ☎ 631-581-1002. www.nysparks.com.
Created in 1887 by William Cutting according to plans by **Frederick Law Olmsted**, the arboretum covers 690 acres of woodlands and planted areas. Many of the specimens in the pinetum date back to the original plantings of fir, spruce, pine and other evergreens. Rhododendrons and azaleas (*in bloom May–June*) border the walks and drives; wild-

flowers add blazes of color throughout the park.

Fire Island★

A place to relax for weary New Yorkers, this 32mi-long, car-free barrier island, varies in width from .5mi to less than 200yds and boasts more than 1,400 acres of the **Fire Island National Seashore★★** (☎ 631-289-4810, www.nps.gov/fiis). While the island has experienced a real estate boom in the past few years, it's still far more laid back than the Hamptons.

Ocean Beach is the largest and liveliest of the 17 communities on Fire Island, with a rowdy party scene on summer weekends. To soak up the sun and scene—not to mention get a great meal—grab a deck chair at **Matthew's Seafood House** (935 Bay Walk, ☎631-583-8016, matthewsseafood.com), a family-owned spot since 1974. It's your best bet for seafood in the area and just a two-minute walk from the Ocean Beach ferry terminal.

Sailors Haven, across the Great South Bay from Sayville, is home to one of the best known areas of Fire Island, the **Sunken Forest★**, a maritime woodland thick with oak and sassafras trees thought to be 200 to 300 years old. An interpretive boardwalk trail wends through its various ecosystems. There are wide sandy beaches nearby.

Old Westbury Gardens

Robert Moses State Park★ (☎ 631-669-0470. *www.nysparks.com),* on the western part of Fire Island, is a shoreline park named for Robert Moses, the former superintendent of Long Island parks. The park's dunes and sea grasses provide refuge for various waterfowl. A .75mi boardwalk leads from Parking Lot 5 to iconic **Fire Island Lighthouse**★, completed in 1858. There's a visitor center in the keeper's quarters at its base, but the real fun (for those without a fear of heights) is climbing the 156 iron steps and two ladders to the top, for spectacular panoramic **views**★★ (🕐open year round daily 9:30am–5pm May–Sept, rest of the year until 4pm; ☎ 631-661-4876, 👓 $6 adults, $4 children).

The Hamptons★★

🛈 *Tourist information:*
www.thehamptons.com.
Dominating a 35mi stretch of Long Island's South Shore, this chain of famous vacation colonies stretches from Westhampton Beach, which rims Shinnecock Bay, to Amagansett. Once a summer playground for the rich, the Hamptons continue to attract hordes of tourists to their picture-perfect town centers, packed with exclusive boutiques and first-rate restaurants.

Westhampton Beach

Once a seafaring village, Westhampton is a lively resort where New Yorkers – especially musicians, writers and artists – like to spend their weekends or take up summer residence. The annual Westhampton Beach Outdoor Art Show takes place in early August.
Take a drive along Dune Road, on the narrow barrier beach, to glimpse a variety of house styles – from brown-shingled, white-trimmed New England homes to bungalows. A 15mi-long beach extends from Moriches Inlet to Shinnecock Inlet. ⚠ *Note: sections of Dune Rd. are extremely narrow and may be impassable following a storm. In addition, it is nearly impossible to park at most Hamptons beaches during the summer, as all the permits are prepurchased by local residents. One excecption is Coopers Beach in Southampton, where you can buy a daily parking pass (🅿 $30 weekday, $35 weekend).*

Southampton★

Village maps are available from the Chamber of Commerce (76 Main St.; ♿ 🕐open Mon–Fri 10am–4pm, weekends 11am–4pm; ☎ 631-283-0402; www.southamptonchamber.com).
This famous resort town is the largest of the Hampton communities and the home of superb estates. Village streets are lined with posh boutiques and upscale restaurants. On Jobs Lane, the esteemed **Parrish Art Museum** focuses

---

The Lobster Roll

1980 Montauk Hwy., Amagansett. Closed Nov–mid-Apr. ☎631-267-3740.
www.lobsterroll.com. Seafood.

Sand dunes surround this highway shanty on Long Island, midway between Amagansett and Montauk. Regulars, including Barbra Streisand, Kathleen Turner and Alec Baldwin, have taken to calling it "lunch" thanks to a neon sign above the outdoor patio. The restaurant's famous lobster rolls, deep-fried Atlantic cod, and crab cake platter make it more than just a roadside pit stop.

on American art of the 19C and 20C, with major holdings of works by American impressionist William Merrit Chase and the 20C realist Fairfield Porter, as well as by artists who have lived or worked in the area, including Jackson Pollock, Willem de Kooning, Dan Flavin, Roy Lichtenstein, Elizabeth Peyton and Chuck Close. Changing exhibits and selections from the permanent collection are presented (25 Jobs Lane; & ○ open mid-Jun–mid-Sept Mon–Sat 11am–5pm, Fri until 9pm, Sun 1pm–5pm; rest of the year Mon, Thu–Sat 11am–5pm, Sun 1pm–5pm; closed major holidays; ☞ $7; ☎ 631-283-2118; www.parrishart.org).

East Hampton

This town's quaint charm has long attracted writers and artists; indeed, several artists are buried here, including Childe Hassam, Jackson Pollock and Stuart Davis. **Main Street**, lined on both sides by magnificent elm trees, boasts several historic structures, including **Guild Hall**, the Hamptons' preeminent cultural institution since 1931. Its busy schedule includes top-shelf art shows, staged readings, music and drama (no. 158; ☎ 631-324-0806, www.guildhall.org). At the north end of the street sits Hook Mill, an 1806 windmill. Nearby, the **LongHouse Reserve** is an extraordinary 16-acre sculpture garden with permanent works by Sol LeWitt and Yoko Ono, as well as changing exhibitions (133 Hands Creek Rd., ○ open Jun & Sept Wed and Sat 2pm–5pm, Jul–Aug Wed–Sat 2pm–5pm, ☞ $10, ☎ 631-329-3568, www.longhouse.org).

Sag Harbor★

🛈 Tourist information: ☎ 631-725-0011 or www.sagharborchamber.com.

With its docks and deep-water harbor nestled in a sheltered cove, this sea town was named port of entry for the US by George Washington. Sag Harbor's charming colonial homes and saltbox cottages preserve a nostalgic flavor of yesteryear. On Union Street, the **Whalers Presbyterian Church** (1918) is considered an outstanding example of the Egyptian Revival style of architecture. Stop by the **Custom House**, the first customhouse established in New York State, and now a museum (Main & Garden Sts.; ○ open late May–early Oct weekends 1pm–5pm; ☞ $3. 🅿. ☎ 631-692-4664). Built as a whaling captain's home, the Greek Revival **Sag Harbor Whaling and Historical Museum** on Main Street has exhibits about the town's whaling days (& ○ open mid-May–Oct Mon–Sat & holidays 10am–5pm, Sun 1pm–5pm; ☞ $5. ☎ 631-725-0770; www.sagharborwhalingmuseum.org).

A short ferry ride from Sag Harbor (as well as from Greenport on the North Fork; lies peaceful **Shelter Island**, a wonderful spot for biking and hiking – nearly one-third of the island's 8,000 acres are owned by the Nature Conservancy.

Montauk

🛈 Tourist information: www.onmontauk.com.

Named after the Montauk Indians who once inhabited the area, this town of 4,000 sits at the easternmost tip of Long Island, embracing a 10mi strip of woodlands, dramatic cliffs, dunes and white-sand beaches jutting into the ocean. Far more laid-back than the Hamptons, it's home to a number of beachfront hotels and motels, seafood restaurants and bars. While here, be sure to visit the **Montauk Point Lighthouse** in Montauk State Park; completed in 1796, it is the oldest lighthouse in the state. There's a small museum at its base, and as long as you're over 41 inches tall you can climb the 137 steps to the lookout tower for splendid views (○ open early May–early Oct daily & weekends through Dec, weather permitting; hours vary; ☞ $7, ☎ 631-668-2544, montauklighthouse.com). There are seven public beaches in Montauk; two of the most popular are **Ditch Plains Beach**, Long Island's most famous surfing beach, 2mi east of town, and **Hither Hills State Park**, 4mi west of town. **Nick's Beach** is right in the heart of the village at the end of South Edison Street.

South Street Seaport
Peter Wrenn/MICHELIN

WHERE TO STAY

To accommodate its 40 million visitors a year, New York City boasts more than 70,000 hotel rooms. The high price of real estate coupled with tremendous demand makes for what can be astronomical room rates. Visitors interested in staying in Manhattan have access to a variety of lodgings, from trendy Ian Schrager-Philippe Starck creations to the traditional elegance of The Carlyle. Budget-minded travelers will have success finding quality rooms for considerably lower rates by using the discount brokers listed below.

The properties described below were selected for their ambience, location and/or value for money. Prices reflect average cost for a standard double room (two people) in high season (not including any applicable city or state taxes). Room prices may be considerably lower in off-season, and many hotels offer discounted weekend rates. The presence of a swimming pool is indicated by the ⅃ symbol and a full-service spa by the ⟨Spa⟩ symbol.

Lodgings are organized by Manhattan neighborhoods, arranged alphabetically within Downtown, Midtown and Uptown.

$$$$$	Over $350	$$	$100-$175
$$$$	$250-$350	$	Under $100
$$$	$175-$250		

DOWNTOWN

EAST VILLAGE

$$ East Village Bed and Coffee – *110 Ave. C, between Seventh & Eighth Aves.* ☎212-533-4175. *www.bedandcoffee. com. 10 rooms.* Rooms in this funky almost-bed-and-breakfast (as the name says, there's only coffee) are bright, clean and individually decorated according to a theme: the Flight Room has maps on the wall and airplanes on the bedspread; the Zen Room has soothing colors and a Buddha statue in the corner. All the rooms share baths.

FINANCIAL DISTRICT

$$$$$ Ritz-Carlton Battery Park – *2 West St. at Battery Pl.* ⅃ ♿ ⟨Spa⟩ ☎212-344-0800 or 800-241-3333. *www.ritzcarlton.com. 298 rooms.* Spring for a harbor-view room at this monolith of a hotel towering over Battery Park, and you'll have your own telescope to view New York Harbor and its star attraction, the Statue of Liberty. Guest rooms sport rich fabrics and fine bed linens; bathrooms are awash in marble. Enjoy a cocktail at the 14th-floor Rise Bar followed by dinner at the hotel's restaurant, **2 West ($$$$)**, specializing in Prime Angus beef. The next day, tone and atone at the hotel's 2,500sq ft health club.

$$$$ Wall Street Inn – *9 S. William St. at Broad St.* ♿ ☎212-747-1500. *www.thewallstreetinn.com. 46 rooms.* Business travelers especially will find this boutique hotel, located near the New York Stock Exchange, just the ticket. Its business center and workout facility (complete with steam room and sauna) are added draws. The Jacuzzi tubs in the more spacious rooms *(seventh floor)* invite relaxation after a busy day. The hotel provides refrigerators in each room, and offers a complimentary continental breakfast.

Wall Street Inn

The Wall Street Inn

LOWER EAST SIDE

$$ Howard Johnson Express Inn –
135 E. Houston St. at Forsyth St. ♿ ☎*212-358-8844 or 800-446-4656.*
www.hojo.com. 46 rooms. Hugging
a corner on busy Houston Street, this
budget hotel, part of a national chain, is
nothing fancy, but the location is ideal
if you plan to explore the Lower East
Side, East Village and SoHo. Bedrooms
are simply and comfortably furnished.
A continental breakfast, local phone
calls, high-speed Internet access and a
newspaper are all included in the room
rate. Pets allowed.

$$$ Off Soho Suites Hotel –
11 Rivington St. between Bowery &
Chrystie Sts. ♿ ☎*212-979-9808 or 800-633-7646. www.offsoho.com. 38 rooms.*
If you'd rather not go out for meals every
day—though it'll be hard to resist in
this restaurant-laden neighborhood—
consider staying at this all-suite hotel.
It's located just two blocks south of
Houston Street within easy walking
distance of a new Whole Foods Market.
Kitchens are fully equipped, and newly
renovated rooms all have hardwood
floors and flat-screen TVs. Economy
suites share a bath, so be sure to ask for
accommodations with a private bath, if
that's your preference.

SOHO

$$$$$ SoHo Grand Hotel – *310 West*
Broadway at Grand St. 🍴 ♿ ☎*212-965-3000 or 800-965-3000.*
www.sohogrand.com. 367 rooms.
Opened in 1996, the SoHo Grand sits at
the southwest edge of the arty SoHo
neighborhood, a short walk from trendy
TriBeCa. Swathed in neutral tones, rooms
all have Bose Wave CD/radios, CD
libraries, Frette Egyptian cotton linens,
flat-screen TVs, minibars and 24-hour
room service. The swanky **Grand Bar &**
Lounge serves contemporary American
cuisine and creative cocktails. The SoHo
Grand welcomes pets, and will even
provide a goldfish for your room upon
request (and let you take it home if you
form a bond).

SOUTH STREET SEAPORT

$$$$ Best Western Seaport Inn –
33 Peck Slip at Front St. ♿ ☎*212-766-6600*
or 800-468-3569. www.seaportinn.com.
72 rooms. This hotel sits in the South
Street Seaport historic district, a
cobble-stone-paved, pedestrian-
friendly area full of bars, restaurants
and shops, and just a short walk from
the Financial District. Done up country-
style with floral prints, guest quarters
are well-maintained and comfortable.
Sixth and seventh-floor rooms have

The Scoop on New York City Hotels

Quoted rates do not include the city's substantial **hotel tax** of 13.375 percent
(for example, with a quoted room rate of $199, you will actually pay $225.62 for
that night's stay).

Rate categories below should be taken as a general guideline only. Rates can be
higher or lower depending on season, day of the week and volume of advance
reservations. Prices are generally lower on weekends and from Christmas
through March.

Guest parking is usually in a nearby garage, and will cost from $20 to $40 per
day. More expensive hotels have valet parking.

For **price-shopping**, and to find available rooms during the high season, consider using a broker like **Hotel Reservations Network** (☎ 800-715-7666; www.
hoteldiscount.com), **Quikbook** (☎ 800-789-9887; www.quikbook.com) or **Utell**
(www.utell.com).

In-room **telephone charges** can range from 50¢ to as much as $2 for local calls.
Be especially prudent when making calls using the hotel's long-distance pro-
vider. Some establishments will charge as much as four to five times the usual
rate. Even using a long-distance calling card can sometimes incur connection
fees. When checking in, be sure to ask the price for local calls and connection
fees for toll-free numbers. When in doubt, use the pay phones in the lobby.

terraces with incredible views of the East River and Brooklyn Bridge. You'll be treated to a complimentary continental breakfast in the morning and cookies each afternoon. High-speed Internet access is available at no charge.

TRIBECA

$$$ Cosmopolitan Hotel – *95 West Broadway at Chambers St.* ☎*212-566-1900 or 888-895-9400. www.cosmohotel.com. 125 rooms.* The longest continually operating hotel in New York City, dating back to 1850, the Cosmopolitan is located in the heart of TriBeCa. There are some 40 restaurants within a five-block radius, ranging from top-tier places like Chanterelle and Bouley to casual neighborhood spots like Bubby's; the Financial District, the World Trade Center site, the West Village and SoHo are all nearby as well. All the rooms come with a private bath, desk, color TV and free wireless Internet access.

UNION SQUARE/MADISON SQUARE

$$$$$ Inn at Irving Place – *56 Irving Pl. between E. 17th & E. 18th Sts., Gramercy Park.* ☎*212-533-4600 or 800-685-1447. www.innatirving.com. 12 rooms.* You won't find the name of the inn on these two 1834 brownstones; just look for the address. Within you *will* find stylish guest rooms appointed with quality 19C furnishings and named for famous New Yorkers like Washington Irving and Sarah Bernhardt who lived in the neighborhood back then. CD players and VCRs share space with iron four-poster or oak beds

and overstuffed chairs. There's also wireless Internet connection in each room. Continental breakfast is served in the cozy parlor. Afternoon tea, a real treat, is served in Lady Mendl's Victorian tea salon *(reservations required)*. Martinis and nibbles can be had in the downstairs lounge.

$$$$ The Carlton – *88 Madison Ave. at E. 29th St.* ♿ ☎*212-532-4100 or 800-542-1502. www.carltonhotelny.com. 316 rooms.* Built in the early 20C, this Beaux-Arts structure was restored, inside and out, to its former splendor in summer 2005. The lobby now has a dramatic two-story waterfall; guest rooms have been fittingly redone with luxurious Scalamandre fabrics and Frette linens, with restful colors, mahogany furnishings, and marble and granite bathrooms rounding out the decor. Amenities include in-room safes, nightly turn-down service, iPod docking stations and free wireless Internet access. Some rooms enjoy views of the Empire State Building, located a short stroll away. The top-notch hotel restaurant, **Country** ($$$$) serves French-influenced classics made with seasonal local ingredients.

GREENWICH VILLAGE

$$ Washington Square Hotel – *103 Waverly Place, at MacDougal St.* ✗ ☎*212-777-9515. www.washington-squarehotel.com. 160 rooms.* You're smack in the middle of Greenwich Village when you stay at this trim, well-maintained property, which has been family owned and run since 1973. The newly renovated deluxe rooms have Art Deco-inspired furnishings and pillow-top mattress, and while they're not fancy, they're large by New York City standards, and some even have views of the park. Friendly staff and a cozy bar off the lobby make it feel like a special place.

$$ Maritime Hotel – *363 W. 16th St. at Ninth Ave.* ✗ ☎*212-242-4300. www. themaritimehotel.com. 123 rooms.* Designed for the National Maritime Union in 1966 and meticulously renovated in 2003, the Maritime is one of the city's hippest hotels; thanks to its proximity to the shops and clubs of the Meatpacking District, it's especially popular with those in the fashion and

Inn at Irving Place – Roy Wright

Inn at Irving Place

entertainment industries. Most of the rooms face the Hudson River, and while they are quite small they have the full complement of amenities—CD/DVD players, 500-thead-count sheets, flat-screen TVs and wireless Internet access—along with sizable desks. A clutch of restaurants and bars are onsite, including chic **Matsuri $$**, serving sake black cod and 200 types of sake.

MIDTOWN

CENTRAL MIDTOWN

$$$$ City Club – *55 W. 44th St.* ⚐♿🅿 ☎*212-921-5500. www.cityclubhotel.com. 65 rooms.* Originally a gentlemen's club, the City Club now feels like an exclusive apartment building, with a discrete lobby, modern decor and attentive service. Rooms are small but luxuriously appointed with black-marble bathrooms, complimentary high-speed Internet access, supple linens and DVD players. The sleek onsite **DB Bistro Moderne** ($$$) is renowned for serving the city's most decadent hamburger: it's stuffed with black truffles and foie gras.

$$$$$ The Royalton – *44 W. 44th St.* ⚐♿🅿 ☎*212-869-4400 or 800-635-9013. www.royalton.com. 168 rooms.* In contrast to its historic exterior, dating to 1898, the inside of The Royalton is daringly modern. Recently renovated, it's the first New York product of avant-garde hotelier Ian Schrager and designer Philippe Starck. Sleek, well-appointed guest rooms are outfitted with long, plush banquettes and crisp white linens; some have fireplaces. Bathrooms offer slate- and glass-walled showers or five-foot-wide circular tubs. Drink and dine at the popular Bar Forty-Four and **Brasserie Forty-Four** ($$$).

EAST MIDTOWN

$$$$ Roger Smith – *501 Lexington Ave. at 47th St.* ⚐♿ ☎*212-755-1400. 135 rooms.* In contrast to the hushed minimalism that defines most upscale hotels, the Roger Smith basks in eccentricity: it runs its own contemporary art gallery onsite and fills the lobby with original work; rooms are individually decorated, some with iron bed frames, other with antique four-posters. Pets and children are welcome,

Hostels

Hostels are an economical alternative to high-priced Manhattan hotels; and while some can be bare-bones, others are actually nicer than budget hotels. New York hostels average $30 a night for dormitory-style accommodations and $125 a night for a private room. Amenities usually include a community living room, showers, laundry facilities, a kitchen and a dining room or restaurant. Reservations are essential during high season (summer and fall). *For further information, check out the website: www.hostels.com.*

staff is warm and friendly, and a complimentary breakfast is served.

TIMES SQUARE/THEATER DISTRICT

$$$$ Casablanca Hotel – *147 W. 43rd St. between Ave. of the Americas & Broadway.* ☎*212-869-1212. www.casablancahotel.com. 48 rooms.* Surround yourself in a Moroccan-style setting right in the middle of Manhattan. This Broadway-Times Square property opened in 1997, and has been offering respite and hospitality to its guests ever since. The recently renovated guest rooms feature comfortable furnishings, as well as high-tech amenities (there's even a telephone in the bathroom). The hotel provides a complimentary continental breakfast and use of a nearby fitness facility at no cost to you.

$$ Broadway Inn – *264 W. 46th St. at Eighth Ave.* ☎*212-997-9200 or 800-826-6300. www.broadwayinn.com. 41 rooms.* If you're a theatergoer, you'll love the location of this well-situated inn. When you exit the front door, most of Broadway's theaters are only minutes away on foot. Repeat customers from near and far rave about the friendly staff, the great location and the clean rooms, each with a private bathroom. Guests enjoy a complimentary continental breakfast in a homey, brick-walled space. Be mindful of possible drawbacks, however: the lack of elevators in this four-story building (guests must walk up the stairs) and the 24/7 noise from Times Square (ask for a room away from the street).

$$$ Hotel QT – *125 W. 45th St., between Sixth & Seventh Aves.* ♿⚐☎ *212-354-*

2323. www.hotelqt.com. 140 rooms. Celebrity hotelier Andre Balazs is the force behind this hip, contemporary property that's long on style yet easy on the pocketbook. A youthful air pervades the place, especially at the lobby-level pool with its swim-up bar and the mezzanine lounge, where DJs perform nightly. A small workout room with steam room and sauna is open to guests 24hr a day. Guest rooms are tiny but tasteful, with flat-screen TVs and bunk beds topped with Egyptian cotton sheets. Complimentary breakfast included.

$$ Mayfair New York – *242 W. 49th St. between Broadway & Eighth Ave.* ☎*212-586-0300 or 800-556-2932. www. mayfairnewyork.com. 78 rooms.* One of the few family-run hotels in Manhattan, Mayfair New York is located in the heart of Broadway theaters and Times Square nightlife. The entire building is "no smoking." Guest rooms and common areas showcase a collection of rare, historic photos from the Museum of the City of New York. Double-pane windows filter out the street noise. All accommodations come with modern conveniences including high-speed Internet connections, hair dryers and computerized wall safes. Service is extremely friendly.

$$$$$ Muse Hotel – *130 W. 46th St., between Sixth & Seventh Aves.* ☎*212-485-2400. www. themusehotel.com. 200 rooms.* This 19-story hotel recently restored its triple arched, limestone-and-brick façade and redecorated its interior with meticulous attention to detail. Halls are bright and tastefully decorated in pale-green wallpaper; rooms are contemporary yet warmly inviting, with feather beds, L'Occitane bath products, green marble bathrooms and original artwork. Twice-daily maid service, a 24hr fitness room and a daily wine hour in the lobby are added perks.

UNITED NATIONS AREA

$$$$$ Millennium Hotel New York UN Plaza – *One United Nations Plaza between First & Second Aves.* ☎*212-758-1234 or 866-866-8086. www1. millenniumhotels.com. 427 rooms.* Sitting directly across from the United Nations, the Millennium offers convenient access to the Midtown business district as well as fashionable East Side restaurants and boutiques. The hotel's spacious and elegantly appointed guest rooms start on the 28th floor and provide breathtaking views of the New York skyline and the East River. Rich tapestries dating back to the 9C adorn the lobbies, corridors and guest accommodations. The Millennium is the only Manhattan hotel to have both an indoor tennis court and a glass-enclosed swimming pool. There's also a currency exchange at the front desk, and a full-service health club and fitness center. The Ambassador Grill restaurant serves as a meeting place for many UN dignitaries.

UPTOWN

UPPER EAST SIDE

$$$$$ The Carlyle – *E. 76th St. at Madison Ave.* ☎ *212-744-1600 or 888-767-3966. www.thecarlyle. com. 123 rooms, 58 suites.* This elegant hotel has been a fixture of the Upper East Side since 1930. Its guest list includes US presidents and dignitaries from around the world. Unequaled service, comfort and fine furnishings abound at every turn. The esteemed Café Carlyle hosts cabaret performers like Eartha Kitt and Elaine Strich. Bemelmans Bar is named for the writer of the *Madeline* series, Ludwig Bemelmans, who painted the mural that graces the walls therein. Guest rooms may be small in comparison to newer properties, but they are luxuriously appointed with Louis XVI-style furnishings, plush carpets and marble baths; nearly half of the suites have baby-grand pianos. Step out your door to the shops of Madison Avenue and the greenery of Central Park.

$$$$$ The Regency – *540 Park Ave. at E. 61st St.* ☎*212-759-4100 or 800-235-6397. www.loewshotels.com. 266 rooms, 85 suites.* Recently treated to a multimillion-dollar renovation, the Regency stands just two blocks east of Central Park on tony Park Avenue. Guest quarters are spacious and luxurious, done in soft beiges with contemporary accents and complete with the latest amenities, from Frette linens to bathroom TVs. Service is the hotel's hallmark: the guest-staff ratio is one-to-one. There's a fitness center, and spa

The Regency, A Loews Hotel

Lobby of The Regency

treatments are available. Singer Michael Feinstein is often on hand to entertain in the lounge, aptly named Feinstein's at the Regency.

$$$$ Hotel Wales – *1295 Madison Ave. between E. 92nd & E. 93rd Sts.* ✗ ☎*212-876-6000. www.waleshotel.com. 46 rooms, 41 suites.* This nicely restored (2000) property, built in 1902, is situated in a pleasant residential/commercial neighborhood within walking distance of Museum Mile. Amenities include a relaxing rooftop terrace, down comforters on the beds and fresh flowers in the rooms. There's a 24hr fitness room onsite, or for $15 you can use the YMCA nearby. After your workout, head to **Sarabeth's (\$\$)**, well-known for its weekend brunch featuring homemade breads and pastries.

UPPER WEST SIDE

$$$ Excelsior Hotel – *45 W. 81st St. between Central Park West & Columbus Ave.* ☎*212-362-9200. www.excelsiorhotelny.com. 120 rooms, 80 suites.* A stone's throw from the American Museum of Natural History and Central Park, this

family-friendly hotel is decorated in a country-French motif. Rooms in the front of the hotel are brighter, while rooms in the back are quieter. There's wireless Internet throughout the hotel (for a fee), as well as an entertainment room with fitness center, surround-sound TV and library.

$$$$$ Mandarin Oriental – *80 Columbus Circle at W. 60th St.* ✗ ♿ ♨ 🧖 ☎*212-805-8800 or 866-801-8880. www.mandarinoriental.com. 251 rooms.* From its lofty perch on floors 35 to 54 of the Time Warner Center, the Mandarin Oriental boasts wide-angle views of the city, especially of Central Park. All of the soundproofed guest rooms blend Asian color schemes and 1940s-style furniture; flat-panel TVs can be found in both the bedrooms and the bathrooms, where soaking tubs sit in front of picture windows. If that isn't enough, there's a full-service spa and fitness center with an indoor lap pool on the premises. With its panoramic vistas, the Lobby Lounge is a eye-catching spot for a light bite to eat and a cocktail.

$$$$ On the Ave – *2178 Broadway at 77th St.* ♿ ☎*212-362-1100. www.ontheave.com. 260 rooms, 7 suites.* A recent renovation brought this early-20C hotel luxuriously up to date. Nightly piano music in the lobby is a soothing segueway to sleep. In your room you'll find a flat-screen plasma TV and Frette robes; on your bed Italian sheets, down comforters and, on the pillow, Belgian chocolates. Rooms on the top three floors have views of the Hudson River or Central Park; a 16th-floor balcony is dotted with Adirondack chairs for relaxing. Pets are welcome.

Bed & Breakfasts

Many B&Bs in New York are not inns but apartments whose owners rent out rooms; the best come with private baths and complimentary breakfast *($100–$200/night)*. Entire apartments are also available and can be a terrific value, especially when let by the week or month. Many properties require a two-night stay on weekends; very few allow smoking, and some may not welcome small children.

B&B Reservation Services	☎	Website
Affordable New York City	212-533-4001	www.affordablenewyorkcity.com
B&B Network of New York	212-645-8134	www.bedandbreakfastnetny.com
City Lights Bed & Breakfast	212-737-7049	www.citylightsbandb.com
City Sonnet	212-614-3034	www.citysonnet.com
Manhattan Getaways	212-956-2010	www.manhattangetaways.com

WHERE TO EAT

Rest assured that the quality and variety of New York City's cuisine equal the city's prestige as a financial and cultural center. While top restaurants command jet-set prices, the city abounds in ethnic restaurants, bistros, delis and pizza parlors that won't blow your budget.

The venues listed below are listed in descending price order alphabetically by neighborhood. They were selected for their ambience, location and/or value for money. Rates indicate the average cost of an appetizer, an entrée and dessert for one person (not including tax, gratuity or beverages). Most restaurants are open daily – except where noted – and accept major credit cards. Call for information regarding reservations and opening hours.

Additional restaurants are described throughout this guide in sidebarsthe Index provides a complete listing.

If you're a serious foodie and want to do some research on your own, visit nymag.com, New York Magazine's website, which boasts a quick search engine and hundreds of opinionated reviews. Another great site is menupages.com, which has full up-to-date menus with prices for more than six thousand New York eateries, as well as contact information and reviews.

$$$$	**Over $75**	**$$**	**$25-$50**
$$$	**$50-$75**	**$**	**Under $25**

DOWNTOWN

BATTERY PARK CITY

$$ Gigino at Wagner Park – *20 Battery Pl. at Little West St.* ☎*212-528-2228. www. gigino-trattoria.com.* **Italian.** Don't be fooled by the modest entrance underneath the brick lookout platform – Gigino has a vast back deck with expansive harbor views. And with an extensive list of reasonably priced dishes, ranging from wood-oven-fired pizzas to hearty entrées to the signature pasta, spaghetti de Padrino (made with beets, escarole, garlic and anchovy-flavored olive oil), it's sure to satisfy the appetites of every member of la famiglia. The original **Gigino**, with its warm, rustic dining room, is in nearby TriBeCa *(323 Greenwich St. between Duane & Reade Sts.;* ☎*212-431-1112).*

CHELSEA

Before or after a meal here, be sure to check out Chelsea's tony art galleries.

$$ El Cid – *322 W. 15th St. between Eighth & Ninth Aves.* ☎*212-929-9332.* **Spanish.** Family-owned and run, this unpretentious neighborhood eatery is one of the best spots in the city to get tapas (appetizer-size portions of Spanish dishes) and fresh sangria. The simple setting belies the restaurant's location in the hip-for-the-moment Meatpacking District, but El Cid was was established here long before the designer boutiques moved in. The dozen tables are jammed together and the bar is crowded, so be sure to make reservations to sample tasty tapas like white asparagus in vinaigrette, baby eels, grilled shrimp and much more.

$$ Gascogne – *158 Eighth Ave. between W. 17th & W. 18th Sts.* ☎*212-675-6564. www.gascognenyc.com.* **French.** If you're craving rustic fare from the southwest of France, make a beeline for Gascogne. Fine cassoulet (a stew of white beans, duck confit and garlic sausage), foie gras, and veal kidneys flamed with Armagnac are examples of the carefully prepared dishes here. In the summer, the delightful, shady outdoor garden is a popular place to dine.

$$ The Red Cat – *227 10th Ave. between W. 23rd & W. 24th Sts.* ☎*212-242-1122. www. theredcat.com.* **Contemporary.** A partnership between chef Jimmy Bradley and restaurateur Danny Abrams, The Red Cat combines New England-style decor – wood-paneled walls, red-and-white color scheme, with New American dishes such as grilled brook trout, pan-roasted organic chicken and sugarcane roasted pork tenderloin.

$$ Rocking Horse – *182 Eighth Ave. between W. 19th & W. 20th Sts.* ☎*212-463-9511.* **Mexican.** Mexican folk art and bright colors make a vibrant background for the Rocking Horse's authentic regional Mexican cuisine. Hangar steak, free-range chicken and grilled vegetables provide the filling for burritos, quesadillas and enchiladas at lunch, while the dinner menu selections range from chiltepe-glazed tuna to chile Ancho relleno and mustard-crusted lamb chops. Just don't eat too much, or you won't have room for the rich tres leches cake, topped with sliced bananas and banana cream. Children are welcome here, and the cafe even features a kids' menu.

CHINATOWN

$ Dim Sum Go Go – *5 E. Broadway at Chatham Sq.* ☏*212-732-0797*. **Chinese.** Don't let the Chinese take-out name throw you. This sleek restaurant is more sophisticated than many of its Chinatown counterparts. New wave dim sum is served to order, not on traditional rolling carts. Mushroom and pickled-vegetable dumplings, duck skin and crabmeat wrapped in spinach dough, or chive and shrimp dumplings in ginger-vinegar dipping sauce are but a sampling of the many choices. Those with heartier appetites will enjoy entrées such as steamed halibut on a bed of braised Chinese leeks and celery, or roast chicken with fried garlic stems.

$ Great N.Y. Noodletown – *28 Bowery at Bayard St.* ☏*212-349-0923*. **Chinese.** Oodles of noodles is what you'll find at Great N.Y. Noodletown. Served pan-fried, Cantonese-style, or Hong Kong-style in lo mein, inexpensive Chinese noodle dishes take center stage at this no-frills place – but there's also a choice of salt-baked dishes and barbecued meats. Don't wait on the server to take your check; here you have to take your own check up to the cashier to pay before you leave.

$ Oriental Garden – *14 Elizabeth St. between Bayard & Canal Sts.* ☏*212-619-0085*. **Chinese.** If you're a seafood lover, your meal will greet you at the door –

two aquariums full of fish and lobster flank the entrance. Don't like fish? No worries. There's an extensive selection of classic Chinese dishes as well. The little dining room, its walls lined with framed Chinese ideograms, is almost always packed. Just be sure to bring cash; Oriental Garden doesn't accept credit cards for bills under $60.

$ Peking Duck House – *28 Mott St. between Chatham Sq. & Pell St.* ☏*212-227-1810. www.pekingduckhousenyc.com.* **Chinese.** Food lovers flock to 28 Mott Street for the specialty of the house – the namesake Peking duck. To get it, they must come en masse, since it's prepared only for four or more diners. Topped with a ginger-accented sweet sauce, the delicacy comes with house-made pancakes, cucumbers and scallions. If you're dining solo, or as a couple, try the sea bass or the Szechuan prawns. Then, next time, gather a group of your friends and come back to sample the duck – or head for the restaurant's second location *(236 E. 53rd St. between Second & Third Aves. in East Midtown;* ☏*212-759-8260)*.

EAST VILLAGE

$$ Itzocan – *438 E. Ninth St. between Ave. A & First Ave.* ☏*212-677-5856*. **Mexican.** Set near Tompkins Square Park, tiny Itzocan is worth seeking out for fresh, well-prepared Mexican food. Burritos and quesadillas fill the menu at lunch, while at dinner the short list of entrées is more upscale (braised flank steak in chile pasilla, semolina epazote dumplings with roasted poblano peppers). Don't miss the excellent house-made guacamole, and save room for the chocolate mole cake; its rich, chocolatey flavor is kicked up with a soupçon of chile pepper. If you're visiting Museum Mile, check out Itzocan's other location in Spanish Harlem *(1575 Lexington Ave. at E. 101st St.;* ☏*212-423-0255)*.

$$ Momofuku Ssäm Bar – *207 2nd Ave. at 13th St.* ☏*212-254-3500*. **Korean.**

The Scoop on New York City Restaurants

Since April 2003, restaurants, bars and clubs in New York City have been made smoke-free by law. Although jackets may not be required, gentlemen might feel more comfortable wearing one in the more expensive establishments. Reservations are highly recommended. Gratuities are generally not included on the bill; a tip of 15 to 20 percent is considered standard.

Building on his success at nearby Momofuku Noodle Bar *(171 First Ave. at 11th St.)*, chef David Chang introduces New Yorkers to the wonders of the Korean burrito, or ssäm, at this sleekly cacophanous hotspot. In the Momofuku ssäm, a flour tortilla is stuffed with tender pork, edamame, onions, shiitake mushrooms and kimchi puree. Indeed, pork fills the menu, from the section of country hams to the juicy short ribs to the pork-bun appetizer. There are also sections devoted to local foods, particularly seasonal produce, and to dishes made with offal. FYI: *momofuku* means "little peach" in Korean.

$ Angelica Kitchen – *300 E. 12th St. between First & Second Aves.* ☎*212-228-2909*. **Vegan**. Health-conscious New Yorkers love the creative vegan fare (no meat or dairy) at this popular East Village eatery. Most of the dishes are simply prepared, letting the flavors of the vegetables (usually local and organic) speak for themselves. Many diners cobble together dinner from the wide assortment of salads, grilled vegetables, tofu and breads (the rice-dense cornbread is a meal in itself), though the most flavorful dishes are often the daily specials, which range from savory stews to tamales. If you're eating solo, take a seat at the community table, where you can read or chat with Angelica's regulars.

$ Soba-Ya – *229 E. Ninth St. between First & Second Aves.* ☎*212-533-6966*. **Japanese**. Soba-Ya's inexpensive noodle dishes and Zen-like atmosphere appeal to students from nearby New York University. On a cold day, there's nothing like a steaming bowl of soba (Japanese buckwheat noodles, made in-house) to warm you up. Noodles come in steaming bowls of hot broth complemented by your choice of additions from shrimp tempura to meat and vegetables. In warm weather, you'll probably prefer your noodles served cold, with add-on ingredients heaped on top. No matter the season, there's always a good selection of Japanese beer and sake.

FINANCIAL DISTRICT

$$ Les Halles Downtown – *15 John St. between Broadway & Nassau Sts.* ☎ *212-285-8585. www.leshalles.net*. **French**. Chef/author Anthony Bourdain (who penned the restaurant exposé *Kitchen Confidential*) opened this restaurant after the terrorist attack of September 11, 2001 – one of first new restaurants to open in the Financial District at the time. Here he serves up such palate-pleasing French dishes as steak au poivre and coq au vin. You'll find basically the same menu at his other brasserie, Les Halles on Park Avenue *(411 Park Ave., between E. 28th & 29th Sts.;* ☎*212-679-4111)*.

$ Full Shilling – *160 Pearl St. between Wall & Pine Sts.* ☎*212-422-3855. www.thefullshilling.com*. **Irish pub**. The Full Shilling serves up traditional Irish pub food, including bangers and mash, shepherd's pie and fish and chips, in a traditional Irish pub setting. (There are some allowances for American taste, from the Cajun chicken sandwich to the mozzarella sticks.) The wonder is that the place is located just steps from the power corridor of Wall Street. Something about the dim lighting, the clatter of plates, and the friendly service seems to melt away stress. A couple of (imperial) pints don't hurt either.

GREENWICH VILLAGE

$$ Pearl Oyster Bar – *18 Cornelia St. between W. 4th & Bleeker Sts.* ☎*212-691-8211. www.pearloysterbar.com*. **Seafood**. You can't get fresher fish for the price in Manhattan than at Pearl Oyster Bar. This minnow-sized, friendly eatery caters to those in the know with its two long marble counters with side-by-side seats and a small adjoining room with a smattering of bistro tables. Chef/owner Rebecca Charles' signature dish, a gargantuan lobster roll (chunks of fresh lobster moistened with mayonnaise and tucked into a toasted bun) leaves many a Maine lobster shack to shame. Be sure to check out the blackboard specials and save room for the deliciously tart blueberry crumble pie.

$ Pó – *31 Cornelia St., between Bleecker & W. 4th Sts.* ☎*212-654-2189. www.porestaurant.com*. **Italian**. Pó is the kind of neighborhood restaurant locals wish they lived around the corner from. Specializing in Tuscan fare with a well-selected, moderately priced wine list, this snug Italian trattoria makes diners feel like welcome guests at a delightful dinner party. The value for money here is hard to beat. Dinner pastas (think white bean ravioli with brown butter sauce, or linguine with fresh clams and white wine) range from $13 to $16. Chef Lee McGrath's six-course tasting menu is a great deal at only $48.

LITTLE ITALY/NOLITA

$$ Il Palazzo – *151 Mulberry St. between Grand & Hester Sts.* ☎*212-343-7000.* **Italian**. Right on Little Italy's main drag, Il Palazzo dishes up a generous selection of classics: veal saltimbocca, chicken Cacciatore, rigatoni alla vodka, linguine with clam sauce, shrimp scampi. End your meal with a glass of grappa or vintage port and then head around the corner to Ferrara *(195 Grand St.)* bakery for espresso and gelato.

$$ Nyonya – *194 Grand St. between Mott & Mulberry Sts.* ☎*212-334-3669.* **Malaysian**. As Chinatown increasingly engulfs Little Italy, it's not as odd as it might sound to come to the neighborhood for inexpensive and original Malaysian food. This fusion cuisine pairs traditional Chinese ingredients with Malay herbs and spices, resulting in dishes from seafood rice noodles to curried pork spare ribs. For dessert, try the *pulut hitam*, a sweet treat made from black rice and coconut milk.

$$ Pellegrino's – *138 Mulberry St. between Grand & Hester Sts.* ☎*212-226-3177.* **Italian**. Pelligrino's is a place that you can take the whole family. The restaurant caters to families with half-portions for children (and others with smaller appetites). Linguini alla Sinatra, the signature dish, overflows with lobster, shrimp, clams, mushrooms and pine nuts in a light red sauce. On a warm summer day, grab one of the sidewalk tables, where you can take in the Little Italy street scene.

$ Cafe Habana – *17 Prince St, at Elizabeth.* ☎*212-625-2002.* **Cuban**. Small, hip, and always crowded, this corner diner serves up some of the best skirt steak and fried plantains this side of Havana; runners-up include the grilled corn and egg burrito. For quicker service (expect a long line on weekends and at prime dinner hours) head to the take-out window next door, which has most of the same food and a mean café con leche.

LOWER EAST SIDE

$$ Schiller's Liquor Bar – *131 Rivington St. at Norfolk St.* ☎ *212-260-4555. www.*

schillersny.com. **American**. Looking for a late-night nosh? This bustling white-tiled Lower East Side mainstay, a Keith McNally property, is open until at least 1am every night, and until 3am on Friday and Saturday. The menu choices range from macaroni and cheese with bacon to moules frites to lamb curry, supplemented by set daily specials (come Monday for fried chicken, Friday for boiled lobster). The wine list is divided into three sections: cheap, decent and good; according to the restaurant, "cheap" is best.

$ 'inoteca – *98 Rivington St. at Ludlow St.* ☎*212-614-0473. www.inotecanyc.com.* **Italian**. Studiously catering to the chic young Lower East Side set, the restaurant offers a superb selection of well-priced Italian wines – some 250 in all – from every region of Italy (an enoteca is a "wine bar" in Italy). Of these, 25 wines are available by the glass. The menu emphasizes small plates and panini (stuffed with the likes of bresaola, fontina and arugula, or roasted vegetables and fresh ricotta). Laid-back little (really little) sister **'ino**, a cheaper but just as trendy alternative, can be found in Greenwich Village *(21 Bedford St., between Downing St. & Sixth Ave.;* ☎*212-989-5796).*

MEATPACKING DISTRICT

$$ The Fatty Crab – *643 Hudson St. between Gansevoort & Horatio Sts.* ☎*212-352-3590. www.fattycrab.com.* **Malaysian**. Though it's only a few years old, this diminutive restaurant feels like it's been around forever with its dark, well-worn interior, rock music and fanatical following, which keeps the place noisy and crowded at all hours. But chef Zak Pellacio takes the food seriously, having spent time in Malaysia perfecting his craft. The chili crab is excellent, with large pieces of Dungeness crab in a spicy-sweet tomato chili sauce; so is the fatty duck.

$$ Macelleria – *48 Gansevoort St. between Greenwich & Washington Sts.* ☎*212-741-2555. www.macelleriarestaurant.com.* **Italian**. Housed in a reconstructed butcher shop *(macellieria in Italian),* this engaging trattoria with its brick-walled wine cellar offers an outstanding variety of salami, homemade pastas, meat dishes and Italian wines. Start with the iceberg lettuce wedge with gorgon and peppercorn dressing, then move on to a pasta dish such as green and white tagliolini with peas and prosciutto, or garganelli with oxtail ragu. Hint for steak lovers: the prime dry-aged Porterhouse for two is the same beef that's served at Peter Luger's famed steakhouse in Brooklyn.

$$ Paradou – *8 Little W. 12th St. between Greenwich & Washington Sts. ☎212-463-8345. www.paradounyc.com.* **French**. Whitewashed walls, high ceilings, and tables fashioned out of vintage French wine crates create an airy, rustic ambience at Paradou (the name means "paradise"). While entrées such as chicken grand-mère and thick-cut pork chops recall the sunny cuisine of the Mediterranean, chocoholics will be tempted to skip the main course altogether and go right for the plate of four truffles, handmade in Provence by chocolatier Joel Durand. Thirty-two different flavors (lavender, star anise and bitter honey, etc.) capture the essence of the herbs, fruits and flowers of Southern France.

$$ Pastis – *9 Ninth Ave. at W. 12th St. ☎212-929-4844. www.pastisny.com.* **French**. Large decorative mirrors, a long zinc bar, bistro tables and walls lined with old advertisements for Pastis create an aura of France circa 1960 here. Like any good French bistro, Pastis serves three meals a day and stays open late. The menu includes all the classics (tripe grantinée, steak tartare, pissaladière), and the cocktail list features drinks made from the restaurant's namesake anise-flavored aperitif, which originated in Marseille. Stop by weekends for the popular brunch.

SOHO

$$ Blue Ribbon Sushi – *119 Sullivan St. between Prince & Spring Sts. ☎212-343-0404. www.blueribbonrestaurants.com.* **Japanese**. A downtown sushi mainstay, Blue Ribbon Sushi has a vast menu of fresh and buttery raw fish, as well as a kids' menu of assorted yakimono and maki (there's even fried chicken and catfish fingers). Thanks to its no-reservations policy, the waits at the SoHo flagship can be long. If you happen to be staying in Brooklyn, though, you can sample the same grub at the Park Slope outpost (*278 Fifth Ave. between First St. & Garfield*

Pl., ☎718-840-0408), which is equally popular but larger and less frenetic.

SOUTH STREET SEAPORT

$$ Bridge Cafe – *279 Water St. at Dover St. �&ck ☎212-227-3344. www.bridgecafe. com.citysearch.com.* **American**. Billing itself as New York's oldest drinking establishment (it's been in business since 1794), Bridge Cafe occupies a cozy 1920s building at the foot of the Brooklyn Bridge. Dishes are based on what's in season – pan-roasted lobster with heirloom apple and celery root salad, for example – and are surprisingly inexpensive, given the quality of the cuisine. Go Sunday for the Bridge Brunch, served from 11:45am to 4pm.

$$ Quartino – *21 Peck Slip at Water St. ☎212-349-4433.* **Italian**. Quartino is a welcome recent addition to the South Street Seaport restaurant scene, charming diners on first sight with its simple rustic decor and exposed brick. The all-organic menu includes a perfectly seasoned Sicilian tuna with string beans and potatoes as well as surprisingly tender whole-wheat ravioli stuffed with spinach chard and parsley. Its sister restaurant, Quartino Bottega Organica in NoHo (*11 Bleecker St. at Lafayette*), is equally inviting.

TRIBECA

$$$$ Chanterelle – *2 Harrison St. at Hudson St. ☎212-966-6960. www. chanterellenyc.com.* **French**. Set inside of the 19C Merchant Exchange Building, this New York classic (it's been here since 1979) serves contemporary French cuisine in a gorgeous Art Nouveau-style dining room, replete with fresh flowers. While the menu changes monthly, the signature grilled seafood sausage remains a staple. Before you leave, admire Chanterelle's collection of menu covers hanging in the little anteroom to the left of the reception desk. Over the years, distinguished artists such as Robert Mapplethorpe, Roy Lichtenstein and Louise Nevelson have designed covers for the restaurant.

$$$ Next Door Nobu – *105 Hudson St. at Franklin St. ☎212-334-4445. www. myriadrestaurantgroup.com.* **Japanese**. Hankering to try the mouth-watering sushi made by Japanese-born chef Nobu Matsuhisa, but you can't get in at his flagship, Nobu? Just go next door, where you'll find essentially the same food at a slightly lower price (be sure to go early to avoid a wait; Next Door Nobu doesn't accept reservations). It's all about texture here: a decor enhanced by black river stones, scorched pine tables and Indonesian market-basket light fixtures harmonizes with the sensual pleasures of clawless lobsters, sea urchins, seafood udon, and mochi ice-cream balls.

$$ Bread Tribeca – *301 Church St. at Walker St. ☎212-334-8282. www. breadtribeca.com.* **Italian**. With its vast windows and simple decor, Bread TriBeCa works well both for an early lunch and for a late dinner. Sandwiches are the specialty here, filled with the likes of Sicilian sardines, handmade mozzarella, and prosciutto di Parma stuffed between Italian ciabatta bread or crusty baguettes. Desserts like the caramelized banana tart, served with vanilla ice cream, are bound to please the most discriminating sweet tooth.

$$ Odeon – *145 West Broadway between Thomas & Duane Sts. ☎212-233-0507. www.theodeonrestaurant.com.* **American**. A TriBeCa hot spot since the early 1980s, Odeon has long been a place where the glitterati come to eat. You may still catch a glimpse of big-name entertainers and artists here, but the real draw is the refined cuisine, especially the weekday fixed-price menu at lunch. If you're interested in dining at odd hours, Odeon offers a brasserie menu of light fare daily from 4pm to 5:30pm, and from midnight until 2am every night.

UNION SQUARE/MADISON SQUARE

$$$ Gotham Bar and Grill – *12 E. 12th St. between Fifth Ave. & University Pl. ☎212-260-4020. www.gothambarandgrill.com.* **American**. Gotham Bar and Grill is consistently rated one of New York's finest restaurants, and with good reason. Executive chef Alfred Portale, who studied in France under Michel Geurard, fits the Big Apple to a tee. The pioneer of vertical food, Portale's innovative "skyscraper" presentations are a treat for the eye as well as the palate. The menu changes monthly depending on the market. If you're watching your budget, go for the $25 three-course lunch, which is served weekdays all year long.

$$$ Union Square Cafe – *21 E. 16th St. between Fifth Ave. & Union Sq. W. ☎212-243-4020.* **Italian**. Open since 1985, this popular bistro still packs in crowds every night. It's not hard to see why: the service is friendly and impeccable, the surroundings cool and comfortable, the food imaginative. Executive chef Michael Romano dishes up a selection of entrées – like creamy crab risotto, or cod with seasoned lentils – as well as daily and weekly specials (osso buco, for instance, is only served on Sunday). Don't have a reservation? Belly up to the bar for the same food in a more casual setting.

$$ Blue Water Grill – *31 Union Sq. at E. 16th St. ☎212-675-9500. www. brguestrestaurants.com.* **Seafood**. Seafood lovers will revel in the fresh fare at this lively restaurant, which overlooks Union Square. Maine lobster, Maryland crab cakes, and a selection of oysters from the raw bar keep drawing 'em in. There's also sushi and maki rolls. Jazz music enlivens the scene even more, nightly beginning at 6pm in the downstairs lounge, and on Sunday for the restaurant's popular jazz brunch.

$$ Tamarind – *41-43 E. 22nd St. between Broadway & Park Ave., Gramercy Park. ☎212-674-7400. www.tamarinde22.com.* **Indian**. There's no mistaking the setting at Tamarind – there are reminders of India everywhere. Cowbells hang in the alcoves of the gleaming-white dining room; a large, wrought-iron wall hanging from a maharaja's palace greets guests at the entrance. Bustling cooks prepare piquant regional Indian dishes in the glassed-in kitchen. And a good, balanced wine list and a staff of smiling, attentive servers add to Tamarind's appeal. For lighter, less expensive fare, go to the tea house next door.

WEST VILLAGE

$$$ Perry Street – *176 Perry St., at West St. ☎212-352-1900. www.jean-georges. com.* **Contemporary**. Marked by impeccable service, sleek surroundings and flawlessly prepared food, Perry Street may well be Jean-Georges Vongerichten's most appealing restaurant. As cool as it appears at first sight, the decor feels warm and inviting once you're deep into one of the snug chairs or banquettes. The French-inflected New American menu is focused yet inventive, particularly with seafood, and the desserts are divine. Come for the $24 three-course prix-fixe lunch; it's one of the best deals in town. And don't be surprised if you find yourself dining with celebrities: the building, a glass tower by Richard Meier, is full of multimillion-dollar condominiums owned by the likes of Nicole Kidman and Martha Stewart.

$$ Spotted Pig – *314 W. 11th St. at Greenwich St.* ☎*212-620-0393. www.thespottedpig.com.* **Gastropub**. One of the city's most popular restaurants, the Spotted Pig sports a country-cute decor that still manages to be hip, with rustic tables covered in butcher-block paper, pig paraphernalia and other bric-a-brac. Celebrities abound—Bill Clinton allegedly waited a half-hour for a table—but the food's the real star here, with young British-expat chef April Bloomfield turning out robust fare like fried calf livers and rabbit stew. Come early (before 6pm) to avoid the horrendous line; reservations are not accepted. Also be aware that vegetarian options are limited.

MIDTOWN

BROADWAY/TIMES SQUARE/ THEATER DISTRICT

$$$ Firebird – *365 W. 46th St. between Eighth & Ninth Aves. Closed Mon.* �& #x2639; ☎*212-586-0244.* **Russian**. Tsar Nicholas would no doubt feel as comfortable in these three elegantly restored town houses as he did in the Winter Palace, and would probably enjoy the cuisine as much, too – with dishes like Ukrainian borscht, poached sturgeon and chicken

Kiev, not to mention seven kinds of caviar. It's a fun place to watch the pre-theater crowd before walking over to a Broadway show. Or stay to catch the complimentary jazz at the adjacent Firebird Lounge.

$$$ Gallagher's – *228 W. 52nd St. between Broadway & Eighth Ave.* ☎*212-245-5336. www.gallaghersnysteakhouse.com.* **Steakhouse**. Billing itself as "New York City to the bone," Gallagher's steakhouse opened in 1927 next door to what is now the Neil Simon Theater. Rows of meat carcasses hanging in the meat locker are visible from the street. Inside, a wood-paneled dining room boasts checkered tablecloths, and walls lined with photographs of Broadway stars, politicians and athletes – both human and equine. What's on the menu? Beef, beef and more beef, of the finest quality and cuts.

$$ Marseille – *630 Ninth Ave. at W. 44th St.* ♿ ☎*212-333-3410. www.marseillenyc.com.* **French**. This bustling bistro within walking distance of Times Square is a terrific spot for pre- and post-theater dining. Offering French cuisine with Moroccan, Turkish and Tunisian overtones, Marseille 's menu runs the gamut from bouillabaisse to lamb tagine. The restaurant's Art Deco setting, embellished with pastel arches, handmade floor tiles and a vintage zinc bar, has a Casablanca feel. Marseille's proximity to theaters means it's busy almost constantly, but the waitstaff manages to handle the crowds with ease. Broadway headliners often drop by after performances.

☕ **Azuri Café** – *465 W. 51st St. between Ninth & Tenth Aves.* ☎*212-262-2920.* **Falafel**. Don't expect to be wined and dined at this Hell's Kitchen hole-in-the-wall. For one thing, it doesn't have a liquor license, and for another, atmosphere is pretty much nonexistent. But for fresh, savory Middle Eastern food, including some of the best falafel, tabouli and baba ghanoush you'll find in New York, Azuri can't be beat. Grab a root beer from the cooler and order one of the plates, which will give you an entrée (try the falafel or the vegetable patties) with an assortment of salads and fresh pita bread. Trust the chef; he can be surly with nit-pickers.

The Hall Company, New York

Marseille

$ Carnegie Delicatessen – *854 Seventh Ave. between W. 54th & W. 55th Sts. ☎212-757-2245. www.carnegiedeli.com.* **Jewish Kosher**. It's hard to tell whether this kosher deli is more famous for: salty service or mile-high pastrami sandwiches. At this New York institution, it's best to endure the former for the latter – split a sandwich if you want to save room for the delicious cheesecake. Be prepared to share your table here, it's all part of the fun. Film buffs will be interested to know that much of Woody Allen's 1983 flick *Broadway Danny Rose* was shot on the premises.

CENTRAL MIDTOWN

$$$$ Le Bernardin – *See Fifth Ave. map. 155 W. 51st St. between Ave. of the Americas & Seventh Ave. Closed Sun. ☎212-554-1515. www.le-bernardin.com.* **Seafood**. Expect to spend serious money at this spacious elegant restaurant, widely acclaimed as one of the city's best – it will be worth the splurge (the chef's tasting menu is $155 per person, without wine). With its coffered ceiling and white-glove service, Le Bernardin also offers a prix-fixe menu that comes almost entirely from the sea. Prepare yourself for chef Eric Ripert's delicately orchestrated dishes, which are divided into sections of "almost raw," "barely touched," and "lightly cooked" on the ala carte menu. *Jackets required.*

$$$ The Modern – *9 W. 53rd St. between Fifth & Sixth Aves. Closed Sun. ☎212-333-1220. www.themodernnyc.com.* **Contemporary**. Operated by Danny Meyer (Gramercy Tavern, Union Square Cafe), this upscale is as well known for its excllent cooking as for its unbeatable location edging the Museum of Modern Art's sculpture garden. A vast glass wall and sprays of colorful flowers add light and life to the cool space. You can order a la carte at lunch, but dinner is strictly prix-fixe ($85–138), featuring such creative fare as licorice-poached East Coast halibut on a warm salad of new onions, haricots verts and chanterelle mushrooms. The wine list offers more 900 selections.

$$$ Sea Grill – *See Fifth Ave. map. 19 W. 49th St. between Fifth Ave & Ave. of the Americas. ☎212-332-7610. www. theseagrillnyc.com.* **Seafood**. Located in

Carnegie Deli

Brigitta L. House – MICHELIN

Rockefeller Center, the Sea Grill overlooks the famous ice rink, so you can watch the skaters as you dine. There's a Spanish flair to the cuisine here; the menu includes a separate section of Spanish dishes and another listing of fish cooked "a la plancha" (on a traditional cast-iron griddle). A seafood bar and a roster of fish entrées such as grilled wild Alaskan king salmon, and roasted whole Greek daurade round out the offerings.

EAST MIDTOWN

$$$ Maloney & Porcelli – *37 East 50th St. between Madison & Park Aves. ☎212-750-2233. www.maloneyandporcelli.com.* **American**. Come here with a big appetite and a good-size wallet. Executive chef Patrick Vaccariello, who grew up in an Italian family in the Bronx, promotes the *"mangia!"* attitude with his much-ordered crackling pork shank. This hearty hunk of meat is first deep-fried, then slow-roasted to hold in the juices. It's served with jalapeno-pepper-spiked "firecracker" apple sauce. Side dishes (fresh-cut French fries, creamed spinach, whipped potatoes) come in portions big enough for two.

$$ El Parador – *325 E. 34th St. between First & Second Aves. ☎212-679-6812. www. elparadorcafe.com.* **Mexican**. Don't let the windowless facade turn you away— the upbeat ambience within far outshines your other choices in this restaurant-challenged neighborhood. Order a stiff margarita at the bar, then settle in at a table for some terrific food, from mole poblano, the traditional dish of Mexico, to bouillabaisse veracruzana, with lobster, shrimp, scallops, clams and mussels in a succulent charred tomato, jalapeno and garlic broth. If nothing strikes your fancy, follow the congenial advice on the menu and "ask for any old favorite dish you like."

UNITED NATIONS AREA

$$$$ Sushi Yasuda – *204 E. 43rd St. between Second & Third Aves.* ☎*212-972-1001. www.sushiyasuda.com.* **Japanese**. Located in a quiet corridor between Grand Central Terminal and the United Nations, Sushi Yasuda owes its popularity to namesake chef Naomichi Yasuda. His insistence on simple dishes based on the freshest products available makes it necessary to change his menu daily. Japanese eel and several selections of toro (fatty tuna) number among the specialties, and sushi servings are pre-sented in fresh Hawaiian ti leaves. As for the dining room, it's wrapped in solid bamboo planks, from the walls to the sushi bar.

UPTOWN

CENTRAL PARK

$$$ San Domenico NY – *240 Central Park South between Seventh Ave. & Broadway.* ☎*212-265-5959. www.restaurant.com/sandomenicony.* **Italian**. One of your best souvenirs from a visit to New York will be memories of dining at San Domenico. The signature dish, uovo in raviolo al burro nocciola tartufato (raviolo of soft egg yolk in truffle butter), delicately satisfies. The fillet of sea-bass poached in a fish and tomato broth reflects the importance placed on the exceptional quality of ingredients, and the remark-able wine list is sure to please the most demanding oenophile. Carrara marble, Poltrona Frau banquettes and Cassina chairs make for a discreetly elegant decor.

$$ The Boathouse – *On the lake in Central Park (E. 72nd St. & Park Dr. N.). Lunch year-round. Dinner Apr–Nov only.* ☎*212-517-2233. www.thecentralparkboathouse.com.* **Contemporary**. One of the city's best-kept secrets is hidden inside Central Park. Built in the 1950s, the Loeb Boathouse makes a romantic setting for any special occa-sion. On a sunny day, there's no better place to dine than on the lakeside veranda. During the colder months, a ski-lodge-style interior room is a cozy getaway. Dishes reflect the city's melting pot culture with everything from jumbo lump crab cakes served with cornichon and caper remoulade to pan-roasted pork tenderloin.

UPPER EAST SIDE

$$$ Park Avenue Cafe – *100 E. 63rd St. at Park Ave.* ☎*212-644-1900. www.parkavenuecafe.com.* **Contemporary**. Opened in 1992, this friendly neighborhood cafe was redone in 2004 with cheery red-and-white-striped banquettes and crimson walls. Executive chef Neil Murphy honed his cooking skills on a U.S. Navy submarine before formalizing his training at the Culinary Institute of America. His menu, which highlights the likes of crispy top Chatham cod, and tastings of farm harvest vege-tables, relies on fresh regional products. A list of more than 250 wines comple-ments the cuisine, and the restaurant offers a generous selection of wines by the glass.

$ Candle Cafe – *1307 Third Ave. between 74th & 75th Sts.* ☎*212-472-0970. www.candlecafe.com.* **Vegetarian**. This no-frills eatery specializes in vegetarian cuisine. Freshness and seasonality are prized here, and the cafe uses earth-friendly – and healthy – organic products in its dishes. Farmers market entrées include Southwestern chili made with beans and brown rice, chipotle grilled tofu, and a grilled soyburger. There's also an extensive list of smoothies, elixirs and juices to go with your meal. In 2003, sister restaurant **Candle 79** opened nearby *(154 E. 79th St.)*.

UPPER WEST SIDE

$$$ 'Cesca – *164 W. 75th St. at Amsterdam Ave.* ☎*212-787-6300. www.cescanyc.com.* **Italian**. The newest venture by Godfrey Polistina and chef Tom Valenti, 'Cesca is short for Francesca, the name of Polistina's daughter. 'Cesca's menu emphasizes Southern Italian fare such as tuna with white beans, cerignola olives and preserved lemon; swordfish with caponata; and tripe with red wine and pancetta. These selections are comple-mented by a list of daily specials. Check out 'Cesca's popular sister restaurant,

Ouest (*2315 Broadway between W. 83rd & 84th Sts.; ☎212-580-8700*), also on the Upper West Side.

$$ Good Enough to Eat – *483 Amsterdam Ave. between W. 83rd & W. 84th Sts. ☎212-496-0163. www. goodenoughtoeat.com.* **American**. A white picket fence marks the entrance to this homey little place. Taking a clue from that, you won't be surprised to find that comfort food – just like mom used to make – stars on the menu. This cute eatery, with its exposed-brick walls and folk art accents, serves up bountiful breakfasts, in addition to lunch and dinner. Supper-time brings bounteous plates of perennial favorites such as meatloaf, pumpkin pie and turkey dinner with all the trimmings.

$$ Ocean Grill – *384 Columbus Ave. between W. 78th & W. 79th Sts. ☎212-579-2300. www.brguestrestaurants.com.* **Seafood**. You'll feel as if you've just boarded an elegant ocean liner when you set foot inside the Ocean Grill's dining room, decked out with photographs of the seashore and porthole windows offering a view of the kitchen. Order a plate of oysters from the raw bar, simply grilled fish, Maine lobster or the house maki rolls. The "sunset menu" of light fare is served weekdays from 4pm to 5pm – perfect after a day at the American Museum of Natural History, which is right across the street.

BROOKLYN

$$$ River Café – *1 Water St. between Furman & Old Fulton Sts. ☎718-522-5200. www.rivercafe.com.* **Contemporary**. Set on a barge on the East River, the cafe has long – since 1977 – been renowned for its spectacular views. Be sure to ask for a table by the window, to best enjoy the vistas stretch-ing across the glittering river to Lower Manhattan. Entrées (Colorado rack of lamb, roasted hen breast, black sea bass, Icelandic cod filet) are similar for lunch and dinner; the only difference is that at dinner your only choices are the three- or six-course prix-fixe menus. To end your meal, what could be more apropos than the chocolate marquise Brooklyn Bridge?

ENTERTAINMENT

New York is famed for its entertainment, especially its nightlife. On any given evening you can attend a star-studded play or a concert, have a drink with a stupendous view, and go dancing into the early hours of the morning. Doing those three things needn't consume your whole travel budget, either. There are plenty of small concert stages and theaters, as well as out-of-the-way lounges and dance clubs with no cover charges. Below is a range of well-regarded venues to consider when making your plans. Most of the most famous performance spaces – **Carnegie Hall, Lincoln Center, the Carlyle,** and **Radio City Music Hall**, for instance – set their schedules well in advance, and allow you to buy tickets online. As Myrna Loy once said, "If you're bored in New York, it's your own fault."

Performing Arts

BROADWAY THEATER

No trip to New York is complete without taking in a play. Broadway, in fact, is the city's number-one tourist attraction, drawing more visitors than the Statue of Liberty. Broadway musicals, in particular, are surefire crowd pleasers with audiences of all ages. Aside from a handful of long-running shows – *The Lion King, The Producers, Chicago, Hairspray* and *Mamma Mia!* among them – shows change regularly. The **Broadway Line** (☎ *888-276-2392* or ☎*212-302-4111)* is an excellent source of advance information about shows, providing an easily navigable list of Broadway plays and musicals, along with times, ticket prices, and plot synopses; it also allows you to buy tickets. For online theater listings (of all New York City shows), try **TheaterMania** *(www. theatermania.com)*. TKTS, run by the Theater Development Fund, is the preeminent source for day-of-show tickets (👆 *see Sidebar below*).

OFF-BROADWAY THEATER

Many major plays are presented "Off Broadway." Though some of these theaters may be technically in the Theater District, all have fewer than 500 seats. Many have 499. Why? Because union rules are more flexible for Off-Broadway productions than for Broadway shows. So while the houses may be smaller, the overhead costs are lower (ticket prices are only marginally cheaper, unfortunately). Generally speaking, Off-Broadway shows take more risks than their Broadway counterparts and are less family-oriented; still, many Off Broadway producers want to launch a hit so big that it must move to Broadway to accommodate audiences. Here are a few highly regarded Off-Broadway theater companies.

Atlantic Theater Company
336 W. 20th St. between Eighth & Ninth Aves., Chelsea. ☎*212-645-1242.* The theater founded in 1985 by playwright **David Mamet** presents work by – who else? – David Mamet (among others).

Manhattan Theatre Club
261 W. 47th St. between Broadway & Eighth Ave., Theater District, and at City Center. ☎*212-581-1212 or 212-239-6200. www.mtc-nyc.org.* The crème de la crème of Off-Broadway theater companies, MTC stages new plays at City Center and at the recently restored 650-seat Biltmore Theatre on Broadway. Playwrights August Wilson and Athol Fugard have both have their work produced here.

New York Theater Workshop
79 E. 4th St. between Second Ave. & Bowery, East Village. ☎*212-460-5475.*

Discount Theater Tickets

TKTS is by far the most popular method of obtaining last-minute (usually same-day) discount theater tickets to Broadway and Off-Broadway shows. Tickets generally cost 25 to 50 percent less than what you'd pay in advance. The only drawback is, the choices can be limited. So if you have your heart set on seeing a specific show, it's best to order full-price tickets in advance or to check out the show's **rush ticket** policy – many smash hits now sell a handful of $20–$25 tickets just before curtain, though you may have to present a student ID, put your name in a lottery earlier in the day, wait in line or even stand during the performance. If this doesn't sound appealing, do some research and compile a list of shows you would be interested in seeing; chances are TKTS will be selling tickets to at least one of them. There are two TKTS booths to choose from: **Times Square** *(Broadway & 47th St.; tickets for evening performances sold year-round Mon–Sat 3pm–8pm, Sun 3pm–30min before performance; tickets for matinees sold Wed & Sat 10am–2pm)* and **South Street Seaport** *(corner of Front & John Sts., at the rear of 199 Water St.; open Mon–Sat 11am–6pm & Sun 11am–4pm).* Lines at the South Street Seaport location are generally much shorter, and you can buy matinee tickets here a day in advance. Purchases must be made in cash or with traveler's checks.

www.nytw.org. Jonathan Larson's hit musical *Rent* got its start here in 1996 and is still running on Broadway 10 years later. Often, though, more serious, often political fare is produced, such as plays by Tony Kushner.

Public Theater

425 Lafayette St. between Astor Pl. and E. 4th St., East Village. ☎212-260-2400. *www.publictheater.org*. The people behind the free summer Shakespeare in the Park festival has also launched such popular Broadway musicals as *Bring in da Noise, Bring in da Funk* and nurtured emerging talents including Pulitzer winner Suzan-Lori Parks.

OFF-OFF BROADWAY THEATER

This designation goes to venues with fewer than 100 seats. For the most part, these are productions done on a shoestring by playwrights whose work lies far outside the mainstream, or by actors and directors who want to "make theater" from scratch. These shows have short runs, and you can get tickets, usually for under $20 apiece, directly from the theaters. Consult the *Village Voice* for complete listings. A few venues to look for:

The Flea

41 White St. between Broadway & Church St., TriBeCa. ☎212-226-2407. *www.theflea.org*. Avant-garde work, such as that of wordsmith Mac Wellman, is presented in a space run by the husband of Sigourney Weaver.

HERE

145 Ave. of the Americas at Broome St., SoHo. ☎212-352-3101. *www.here.org*. This pleasant multi-use venue has three small stages, as well as an art gallery and a cafe. The theaters are often rented out by long-standing Off-Off Broadway companies, as well as actors trying out solo material.

PS 122

150 First Ave. at E. 9th St., East Village. ☎212-477-5288. *www.ps122.org*. A former public school, this East Village mainstay puts on a range of offbeat performances, many mixing theater with music, dance or film.

CLASSICAL MUSIC

Bargemusic

Fulton Ferry Landing, just south of the Brooklyn Bridge. Brooklyn. ☎718-624-2083 *or* 718-624-4061. *www.bargemusic.com*. Though few might have guessed that a coffee barge could be a

Times Square

proper setting for chamber music, native New Yorker Olga Bloom thought it would, and made it so. That was 20 years ago, and since then Bargemusic has been going strong, holding about 100 world-class recitals a year. It's a totally unique musical evening. To make it an all-Brooklyn night, have dinner at the nearby River Cafe (◖ *see Where to Eat*).

Carnegie Hall

156 W. 57th St. at Seventh Ave., Central Midtown. One of the world's most prestigious concert venues, the 1891 hall has three stages for classical music.

Lincoln Center

On Broadway between W. 57th & W. 62nd Sts., Upper West Side. New York's premier cultural center has 12 constituent companies, including the Metropolitan Opera, the New York Philharmonic, and the New York City Ballet.

DANCE AND PERFORMANCE

Brooklyn Academy of Music

30 Lafayette Ave. between Ashland Pl. & St. Felix St., Brooklyn. ☎718-636-4100. www.bam.org. Boasting two major performance spaces and a cinema, BAM has become Brooklyn's version of Lincoln Center. But while opera and classical music both have their place here, it's the annual **Next Wave Festival** (fall and winter) that garners the headlines, presenting a roster of established and emerging avant-garde dancers and performers.

City Center Theater

131 W. 55th St. between Ave. of the Americas & Seventh Aves., Central Midtown. ☎212-581-7907. www.citycenter.org. This ornate auditorium has been hosting first-rate dance for decades. **The American Ballet Theater** performs here in the fall, the **Alvin Ailey American Dance Theater** in the winter, Paul Taylor's in the spring. Twyla Tharp and Merce Cunningham frequently drop in for shorter runs. The Off-Broadway Manhattan Theatre Club puts on plays at two smaller stages here.

Joyce Theater

175 Eighth Ave. at W. 19th St., Chelsea. ☎212-242-0800. www.joyce.org. Modern dancers from such heavy-hitters as the **Martha Graham Dance Company** and the **Ballet Hispanico** take the stage year-round at this 472-seat Art Deco theater, a former cinema. A second, smaller space, Joyce SoHo *(155 Mercer St. between Houston & Prince Sts.; ☎212-431-9233)*, nurtures emerging talent.

Nightlife

CABARET

Cafe Carlyle

Carlyle Hotel, 35 E. 76th St. at Madison Ave., Upper East Side. Legendary crooner Bobby Short may be gone, but the Carlyle still has a full line-up of name performers like Eartha Kitt and Elaine Stritch. The Woody Allen–fronted Eddy Davis New Orleans Jazz Band plays Monday nights from Sept to Dec. The cover is $85–100, more if you want to be seated close to the stage, with a two-drink minimum. Jackets required for men.

Don't Tell Mama

363 W. 46th St. between Eighth & Ninth Aves., Theater District. ☎212-757-0788. www.donttellmama.com. This Restaurant Row institution offers a rowdy good time as Broadway hopefuls (including the waiters) and intrepid audience members take their turns belting out show tunes in the piano bar; two cabaret theaters have more traditional shows with covers of $10–15.

Joe's Pub

425 Lafayette St. between Astor Pl. and E. 4th St., East Village. ☎212-539-8777. www.joespub.com. Ensconced in the massive Public Theater building (the former Astor Library), this plush little club makes the most of its limited space, with tight rows of cocktail tables packed near the stage, a middle area of banquettes and a spacious bar area. Acts range from the German chanteuse Uta Lempur to British pop star Elvis Costello.

Oak Room

Inside the Algonquin Hotel, 59 W. 44th St. at Ave. of the Americas, Central Midtown. ☎212-840-6800. *www. algonquinhotel.com.* Like the Cafe Carlyle, the Oak Room offers top-notch cabaret in a legendary and elegant setting. The Algonquin, of course, lent its name (and its bar) to the acid-witted writers, including Dorothy Parker and Robert Benchley, who became known as the Algonquin Roundtable. More recent performers have included Andrea Marcovicci and John Pizzarelli.

COCKTAIL LOUNGES

Bemelmans Bar

35 E. 76th St. at Madison Ave., Upper East Side. A New York classic, mural-bedecked Bemelmans has live piano-bar music Tuesday through Saturday nights. Or come early and indulge in an after-museum cocktail – the bartender has concocted a slew of originals.

Campbell Apartment

15 Vanderbilt Ave. between E. 41st and E. 42nd Sts., East Midtown. ☎212-953-0409. You can't help but be amazed when you enter this ornate vaulted space, which executive John W. Campbell turned into a sumptuous office in the 1930s. Today it's a one-of-a-kind bar that feels like a speakeasy – though it's inside Grand Central Terminal. You have to enter the bar from an inconspicuous door on Vanderbilt Avenue, the tiny side street that flanks the east side of the train station.

Lobby Lounge

8 W. 60th St. at Broadway, Upper West Side. Not your ordinary hotel bar, the Lobby Lounge (on the 35th floor of the Mandarin Oriental Hotel in the Time Warner Center) has one wall made entirely of glass, offering vertiginous views of Central Park and beyond.

Monkey Bar

60 E. 54th St. between Park & Madison Aves., East Midtown. ☎212-838-2600. On the ground floor of the Hotel Elysée, this colorful bar and restaurant oozes Jazz Age character with its moody atmosphere and historic murals.

Pravda

281 Lafayette St, between Houston and Prince Sts., SoHo. 212-334-5015. This subterranean hotspot is a the perfect place to retreat for a pre- or post-dinner cocktail downtown. Red banquettes and flickering candles set a cozy mood. The only things Russian about the place are the Cyrillic posters on the walls and the 70 varieties of vodka.

Rainbow Grill

30 Rockefeller Plaza, Central Midtown. There's nothing like having a drink at this 65th-floor mainstay, where views take in the Empire State Building, the Chrysler Building and other New York landmarks. It opens at 5pm; jackets for men, no jeans or sneakers for anyone.

Rise

2 West St. at Battery Pl., Battery Park City. ☎917-790-2626. Drink in panoramic vistas of the harbor and Statue of Liberty from this 14th-floor perch inside the swank Ritz-Carlton hotel, whose open-air terrace is a real treat on warm summer nights.

World Bar

845 United Nations Plaza (First Ave.) between E. 47th & E. 48th Sts. This retro-chic cocktail lounge in Trump World Tower is popular with neighborhood diplomats.

COMEDY

Comix

353 W. 14th St., between Eighth and Ninth Aves., Meatpackign District. ☎212-524-2500, %Wwww.comixny.com. Opened in fall 2006, this is one of the bigger comedy ventures in town, with tiered seating around a stage large enough for sketch troupes but not too big for a single comic. Try to catch British expat and *Daily Show* regular John Oliver.

Gotham Comedy Club

34 W. 22nd St. between Fifth Ave. & Ave. of the Americas., Union Square-Gramercy Park. ☎212-367-9000. *www.gothamcomedyclub.com.* One of New York's leading stand-up clubs, Gotham hosts everyone from unknowns to celebrities – as long as they're funny. You be the judge. Jerry Seinfeld has been known to drop in here to test-drive his new material.

Upright Citizens Brigade Theatre

307 W. 26th St. between Eighth and Ninth Aves., Chelsea. ☎212-366-9176. *Saturday Night Live*-style sketch comedy and improv – sometimes even with SNL stars – are trotted out nightly here at bargain prices.

DANCE CLUBS

Be sure to check local listings for information about these clubs. Most are open – or popular – only certain nights, and New York clubs have a tendency to disappear without warning.

APT

419 W. 13th St. between Ninth & Tenth Aves., Meatpacking District. ☎212-414-4245. *www.aptwebsite.com.* Dress to impress if you want to get into this bi-level DJ lounge, a fixture on the underground music scene; the doormen can be highly selective about who gets in.

Cielo

18 Little W. 12th St. between Ninth Ave. & Washington St., Meatpacking District. ☎212-645-5700. The sunken dance floor, world-famous DJs and throbbing sound system have drawn legions of clubgoers to this relatively small space in the Meatpacking District.

Club Shelter

20 W. 39th St. between Fifth Ave. & Ave. of the Americas, Central Midtown. ☎212-719-4479. *www.clubshelter.com.* It may not be in a happening 'hood, but this club offers some of the best, sweatiest dancing in the city. Saturday

night is particularly hot, with soulful house music and a multicultural crowd; the after party starts at 4am and continues till noon on Sunday.

Lotus

409 W. 14th St., btw Ninth and Tenth Aves., Meatpacking District. ☎ 212-243-4420, *www.lotusnewyork.com.* A pioneer when it opened here a few years ago, Lotus remains the quintessential Meatpacking District club, a three-tiered glamour palace with a fancy restaurant (sidewalk seating in summer), multiple lounges, and a disco.

Sapphire

249 Eldridge St. between Houston & Stanton Sts., Lower East Side. ☎212-777-5153. Sapphire has been spinning funk, hip-hop and house seven nights a week for more than a decade, an eternity in the club world. Happy "hour" lasts from 7pm to 10pm, and the cover is waived on Fridays and Saturdays before 11pm because, you guessed it, things don't really get going till well after midnight.

SOB's

204 Varick St. at W. Houston St., Greenwich Village. ☎212-243-4940. *www.sobs.com.* Reservations suggested. New York's premier world-music venue, Sounds of Brazil has a tropical decor, a cabana-like bar and a menu featuring Brazilian specialties. Reggae, Latin and hip-hop beats heat up the dance floor every night of the week. If you show up early on Friday night you can take a free salsa lesson.

JAZZ AND BLUES

Though you don't have to buy advance tickets to most jazz shows, it's best to make a reservation to ensure you'll get a table.

B.B. King Blues Club & Grill

237 W. 42nd St. between Seventh & Eighth Aves., Times Square. ☎212-997-4144. *www.bbkingblues.com.* The massive Times Square club has hosted blues greats like Ray Charles, George Clinton and Peter Frampton. The Harlem

Gospel Choir accompanies a buffet brunch every Sunday.

Iridium Jazz Club

1650 Broadway at W. 51st St., Theater District. ☎*212-582-2121. www.iridiumjazzclub.com.* Opened in 1994, this sleek spot has won fans with its impressive roster of artists, 600-bottle wine list and state-of-the-art sound system. Legendary guitarist Les Paul plays here every Monday night.

Jazz Gallery

290 Hudson St., between Dominick and Spring Sts., SoHo. ☎*212-242-1063, http:// jazzgallery.org.* This terrific little second-floor club is one of the city's great jazz secrets, with none of the commercialism of the larger venues and lots of hardcore regulars. Seats are folding chairs and benches. There's no bar, but you can get a glass of wine in a plastic cup. Trumpeter Roy Hargrove got his start here and sometimes comes back with his big band, a real treat.

Jazz Standard

116 E. 27th St. between Lexington & Park Aves., Union Square-Gramercy Park. ☎*212-576-2232. www.jazzstandard.net.* There's no minimum food or drink order here, because the owners are certain you'll want baby back ribs and pan-fried catfish from Blue Smoke restaurant upstairs. Superlative bookings and crystalline sound make this a great choice.

Lenox Lounge

288 Lenox Ave. between 124th & 125th Sts., Harlem. ☎*212-427-0253. www.lenoxlounge.com.* When film producers search for an authentic Harlem club of the 1920s, they look no farther than the Lounge, as it is commonly known to musicians and locals. Live jazz and blues are played regularly in the Zebra Room.

Smoke

2751 Broadway between W. 105th & W. 106th Sts., Upper West Side. ☎*212-864-6662.* One of New York's most popular small clubs offers Monday-night jam sessions, Hammond B3 organ grooves

and some of the city's hottest jazz stars (often with no cover charge) in a neighborhood with otherwise slim entertainment pickings.

Village Vanguard

178 Seventh Ave. S., Greenwich Village. ☎*212-255-4037. www.villagevanguard. com.* Photographs of Bill Evans and other jazz greats line the walls, and top-billing jazz musicians take the stage at New York's oldest jazz club, in Greenwich Village. Musicians often drop in after their gigs at other clubs for late-night jam sessions.

ROCK AND POP

Beacon Theatre

2124 Broadway at W. 74th St., Upper West Side. Come see touring singer-songwriters like Bob Dylan and Lenny Kravitz at this wondrous 1929 venue, a stunning assemblage of Rococo curlicues and red velvet that somehow manages to be vast and intimate at the same time.

Bowery Ballroom

6 Delancey St. between Bowery & Chrystie Sts., Lower East Side. ☎*212-533-2111. www.boweryballroom.com.* This onetime vaudeville club and shoe store has become a top venue for touring indie-rock bands since opening in 1998. Its main space has a wraparound balcony.

Fillmore NY at Irving Plaza

17 Irving Pl. at E. 15th St., Union Square. ☎*212-777-6800. www.irvingplaza.com.* Big indie bands like Built to Spill and the New York Dolls, as well as rock legends Tom Jones and Deborah Harry, have played at this newly renovated club, now run by Live Nation; stand close to the stage for the best acoustics.

Madison Square Garden

Seventh Ave. between W. 31st & 33rd Sts., Garment District. ☎*212-465-6741. www.thegarden.com.* The vast space that hosts the New York Knicks and the Westminster Dog Show also welcomes Elton John and Duran Duran when they come to town. Also onsite is a new,

Radio City Music Hall

smaller space, the WaMu Theater, where the last row is less than 200 feet from the stage.

Radio City Music Hall

1260 Sixth Ave. at 50th St., Central Midtown. The Rockettes aren't the only ones to grace the stage of this 6,000-seat Art Deco landmark, part of the Rockefeller Center complex. So do big-name crooners, including Björk, Carly Simon, Alanis Morissette and Tony Bennett. It's worth it to get tickets just to see the magical interior.

INDIE ROCK AND AVANT-GARDE

Arlene Grocery

95 Stanton St. between Ludlow & Orchard Sts., Lower East Side. ☎212-358-1633. www.arlene-grocery.com. Named for the Lower East Side bodega it once replaced, the tiny club hosts up to seven bands a night. Go Monday night for punk and heavy-metal karaoke. Bar opens at 1pm, music starts around 7pm, doors close at 4am.

Highline Ballroom

431 W. 16th St., between Ninth and Tenth Aves., Chelsea. ☎ 212-414-5994, www.highlineballroom.com. Eclectic programming and ear-tingling acoustics define this new industrial-chic venue, opened in 2007 by the owner of the B.B. King Blues Club. Opening night featured Lou Reed; since then the stage has been graced by performance artist Diamanda

Galas, indie rockers the Squirrel Nut Zippers, singer-songwriter Suzanne Vega and others. Upscale bar food includes mini Kobe beef burgers, and 25 cents of every ticket sale go to the restoration of nearby Highline Park.

Knitting Factory

74 Leonard St. between Broadway & Church Sts., TriBeCa. ☎212-228-8490. www.knittingfactory.com. Legendary home of the musical avant-garde, the club hosts live jazz and rock upstairs, more experimental music below – and 18 beers on tap.

Mercury Lounge

217 E. Houston St. between Ludlow & Essex Sts., Lower East Side. ☎212-260-4700. www.mercuryloungenyc.com. A long, dimly lit bar greets visitors to this indie- and roots-rock club. Behind the velvet curtain is an intimate (250-capacity) space with exposed brick walls, a raised stage and a formidable sound system.

Pianos

158 Ludlow St. between Rivington & Stanton Sts., Lower East Side. You'd think that a former piano factory would give patrons plenty of room to spread out. Not so at this bi-level supper club, a magnet for urban hipsters. There are often three bands a night – and a DJ. Happy hour lasts from 5pm to 7pm, and dinner is served till 1am.

SHOPPING

The Big Apple is a shopper's paradise – everything from the functional to the bizarre lies within easy reach. Elite department stores and design studios line Fifth Avenue between 47th and 57th streets and Madison Avenue between 59th and 79th streets, where window-shopping is a favored pastime. Trendy boutiques can also be found in SoHo, Nolita, East Village and West Village.

New York City is also home to the nation's wholesale fashion industry, centered in the Garment District on Seventh Avenue, and its diamond wholesale trade, concentrated on Diamond and Jewelry Way *(47th St. between Fifth Ave. & Ave of the Americas; www.diamonddistrict.org)*. The Shops at Columbus Circle cover three floors in the newly opened Time Warner Center *(10 Columbus Circle)*.

The Official NYC Guide, published by NYC & Company, offers detailed information on the types of shops, their locations and hours of operation.

Main Shopping Areas

Fifth Avenue

Major Department Stores

Fifth Avenue Stores	Address	☎	Website
Bergdorf Goodman	754 Fifth Ave.	212-753-7300	www.bergdorfgoodman.com
Henri Bendel	712 Fifth Ave.	212-247-1100	www.henribendel.com
Lord & Taylor	424 Fifth Ave.	212-391-3344	www.lordandtaylor.com
Saks Fifth Avenue	611 Fifth Ave.	212-753-4000	www.saks.com
Takashimaya	693 Fifth Ave.	212-350-0100	www.takashimaya-ny.com

Cartier, Fifth Avenue

Specialty Shops and Designer Boutiques

Apple Store	767 Fifth Ave.	212-336-1440	www.apple.com
Cartier	653 Fifth Ave.	212-753-0111	www.cartier.com
FAO Schwarz	767 Fifth Ave.	212-644-9400	www.faoschwarz.com
Fortunoff	681 Fifth Ave.	212-758-6660	www.fortunoff.com
Gucci	685 Fifth Ave.	212-826-2600	www.gucci.com
Harry Winston	718 Fifth Ave.	212-245-2000	www.harrywinston.com
Tiffany & Co.	727 Fifth Ave.	212-755-8000	www.tiffany.com

57th Street

Considered one of the most exclusive shopping streets in the world, 57th between Park and Fifth avenues is home to art galleries, the Manhattan Art and Antiques Center and chic designer boutiques, including **Chanel** (15 E. 57th St.; ☎212-355-5050 www.chanel.com) and **Louis Vuitton** (1 E. 57th St.; ☎212-758-8877 www.vuitton.com).

Lower Manhattan

Known primarily as the financial center of the city, this area offers a varied shopping experience, including famed discount department stores **Syms** (42 Trinity Pl.; ☎212-797-1199; www.syms.com) and **Century 21** (22 Cortlandt St.; ☎212-227-9092). Festive South Street Seaport incorporates more than 50 boutiques and restaurants, as well as the Pier 17 shopping center.

Lower East Side, East Village & Nolita

These neighborhoods are chock-full of shops specializing in vintage apparel and clothes by up-and-coming designers.

Fifth Avenue Shopping

Fifth Avenue Shopping map

● Retail Store ▲ Department Store

Bio

Orchard Street in Lower East Side is the heart of the discount area. Note that many shops may close early on Friday and all day Saturday for the Jewish Sabbath. The greatest concentration of shops in the East Village is along 7th, 8th and 9th streets between First and Second avenues; try **Tokio 7** for designer hand-me-downs *(64 E. 7th St., ☎212-353-8443)*. Nolita's main shopping streets are Mulberry, Mott and Elizabeth streets. Cool, streamlined **Bio** features directional women's clothing, shoes, and handbags by 30 emerging talents *(29 Prince St., ☎212-334-3006)*.

SoHo & TriBeCa

Broadway between Houston and Canal is lined with trendy chain stores like H&M, Uniqlo, Forever 21 and Banana Republic. Move west into the heart of SoHo, though, and you'll find more upscale offerings, like **A.P.C.**, an airy, minimalist loft space filled with a well-edited selection of top-quality basics for men and women *(131 Mercer St., ☎ 212-966-9685)*. More tranquil, TriBeCa is home to upscale interior design stores like **Urban Archaeology** *(143 Franklin St., ☎212-431-4646)*.

Greenwich Village

The city's bohemian enclave is known for its quaint boutiques, specialty shops, jazz clubs and coffeehouses. Bleecker Street is lined with old-world bakeries and Italian grocery stores. NYU students with eclectic tastes flock to the Village's music stores, including **Other Music** *(15 E. 4th St.; ☎212-477-8150; www. othermusic.com)*.

Chelsea & the Garment District

Chelsea boasts exclusive art galleries along its west edge between Ninth and Tenth Avenues. On its east edge, between Fifth and Sixth avenues, you'll find a number of large chain clothing stores, including J. Crew, Anthropolgie, Zara and H&M. In between are a number of interior design outfits. Just north of Chelsea sit **Macy's** *(151 W. 34th St.; ☎212-695-4400; www.macys.com)*, the world's largest department store, and **B&H**, the city's best camera store, with a vast selection of gadgets and gear and knowledgable salespeople to help you choose *(420 Ninth Ave. between 33rd & 34th Sts.; ◷ closed Fri night and all day Sat; ☎212-444-6600; www. bhphotovideo.com)*.

Upper East Side

A bastion of high-end shopping, the area encompasses upscale fashion boutiques, and is home to world-famous **Bloomingdale's** department store *(E. 59th St. & Lexington Ave.; ☎212-705-2098; www.bloomingdales.com)*.

Madison Avenue

Store	Address	☎	Website
Baccarat	625 Madison Ave.	212-826-4100	www.baccarat.com
Barneys	660 Madison Ave.	212-826-8900	www.barneys.com
Betsey Johnson	1060 Madison Ave.	212-734-1257	www.betseyjohnson.com
Calvin Klein	654 Madison Ave.	212-292-9000	www.calvinklein.com
Daum	694 Madison Ave.	212-355-2060	www.daum.fr
DKNY	655 Madison Ave.	212-223-3569	www.dkny.com
Emanuel Ungaro	792 Madison Ave.	212-249-4090	www.emanuelungaro.com
Giorgio Armani	760 Madison Ave.	212-988-9191	www.giorgioarmani.com
Polo Ralph Lauren	867 Madison Ave.	212-606-2100	www.polo.com
Prada	841 Madison Ave.	212-327-4200	www.prada.com
Steuben	667 Madison Ave.	800-424-4240	www.steuben.com
Swarovski	625 Madison Ave.	212-308-1710	www.swarovski.com
Valentino	747 Madison Ave.	212-772-6969	www.valentino.com
Versace	815 Madison Ave.	212-744-6868	www.versace.com

Specialty Retailers

Trademark Stores

Store	Address	☎	Website
ESPN	1472 Broadway	212-921-3776	www.ESPNzone.com
Hard Rock Café	221 W. 57th St.	212-489-6565	www.hardrock.com
NBA Store	666 Fifth Ave.	212-515-6221	www.nba.com
NBC Experience Store	30 Rockefeller Plaza	212-664-3700	www.nbcstore.com
NikeTown	6 E. 57th St.	212-891-6453	www.niketown.com
Original Levi Store	750 Lexington Ave.	212- 826-5957	www.levi.com
Yankees Clubhouse Shop	393 Fifth Ave.	212-685-4693	www.yankees.com

Auction Houses

Whether you're in the market for a priceless van Gogh or not, these establishments offering fine art, furnishings, books and decorative arts are well worth a visit. Advance viewings of items to be auctioned are usually held 3-5 days prior to the event and are open to the public. Visitors are welcome to participate in or watch the auctions. Advance reservations may be required for some events. Call for schedule of upcoming shows.

Auction House	Address	☎	Website
Christie's	20 Rockefeller Plaza	212-492-5485	www.christies.com
Sotheby's	1334 York Ave.	212-606-7000	www.sothebys.com
William Doyle Galleries	175 E. 87th St.	212-427-2730	www.doylenewyork.com

Museum Shops

Looking for an unusual gift? Visit the city's many museum shops where items for sale are fashioned after pieces from the permanent collections and special exhibits – jewelry, sculptures, scarves, stationery, prints, posters and art books. Listed below is a selection of the city's most noteworthy museum shops:

Shop	Address	☏
American Folk Art Museum	45 W. 53rd St.	212-265-1040
American Museum of Natural History	W. 79th St.	212-769-5100
Asia Society and Museum	725 Park Ave. at E. 70th St	212-288-6400
Frick Collection	1 E. 70th St.	212-288-0700
Cooper-Hewitt, National Design Museum	2 E. 91st St.	212-849-8400
Guggenheim Museum	1071 Fifth Ave.	212-423-3615
International Center of Photography	1133 Ave. of the Americas	212-857-0002
Metropolitan Museum of Art	Fifth Ave. at E. 82nd St.	212-535-7710
Morgan Library & Museum	225 Madison Ave.	212-685-0008
Rubin Museum of Art	150 W. 17th St.	212-620-5000
Museum of Modern Art	11 W. 53rd St.	212-708-9400
New York Transit Museum	Grand Central Terminal	212-878-0106
Studio Museum in Harlem	144 W. 125th St.	212-864-4500
Whitney Museum of American Art	945 Madison Ave.	212-570-3676

Bookstores

Store	Address	☏	Website
Biography Bookstore	400 Bleecker St	212-807-8655	
Three Lives & Co.	154 W. 10th St.	212-741-2069	threelives.com
St. Marks Bookshop	31 Third Ave.	212-260-7853	www.stmarksbookshop.com
Complete Traveller	199 Madison Ave.	212-685-9007	www.ctrarebooks.com
Labyrinth Books	536 W. 112th St.	212-865-1588	www.labyrinthbooks.com
Hagstrom Map & Travel Center	51 W. 43rd St.	212-398-1222	www.hagstrommap.com
Kitchen Arts & Letters	1435 Lexington Ave.	212-876-5550	www.kitchenartsandletters.com
McNally Robinson	50 Prince St.	212-274-1160	www.mcnallyrobinsonnyc.com
Rizzoli	31 W. 57th St.	212-759-2424	www.rizzoliusa.com
Strand Books	828 Broadway	212-473-1452	www.strandbooks.com

Books and Music

Venue	Address	☎	Website
Barnes & Noble	555 Fifth Ave.	212-697-3048	www.barnesandnoble.com
	1280 Lexington Ave.	212-423-9900	
	1972 Broadway	212-595-6859	
	2289 Broadway	212-362-8835	
	396 Ave. of the Americas	212-674-8780	
	160 E. 54th St.	212-750-8033	
	33 E. 17th St.	212-253-0810	
	675 Ave. of the Americas	212-727-1227	
	240 E. 86th St.	212-794-1962	
Borders	461 Park Ave.	212-980-6785	www.borders.com
	576 Second Ave.	212-685-3938	
	100 Broadway	212-964-1988	
J&R Music World	23 Park Row	212-238-9000	www.jr.com
Virgin Megastore	1540 Broadway	212-921-1020	www.virginmegamagazine.com
	52 E. 14th St.	212-598-4666	

Markets

Flea Markets

For one-of-a-kind collectibles at bargain prices, head to one (or more) of the city's fleamarkets. One group runs three of the most popular markets: the **Hell's Kitchen Flea Market**, with 170 vendors selling all manner of vintage and retro goods *(W. 39th St., between Ninth & Tenth Aves., year-round weekends dawn–dusk)*; the indoor **Antiques Garage** *(112 W. 25th St., year-round weekends 6:30am–5pm)*, with two floors of art, books, photographs, furniture and decorative arts; and the **25th Street Market** *(between Sixth and Seventh Aves., year-round weekends dawn–dusk)*, which has 125 vendors of various and sundry items. For more information: ☎ 212-243-5343; www. hellskitchenfleamarket.com.

Food Market Produce

Allison Simpson/MICHELIN

Food Markets

The wonderfully popular **Union Square Greenmarket** is more than just flowers; it's also a great place to start your gourmet tour of the Big Apple. No trip would be complete without a visit to a few of the city's renowned food markets.

Market	Address	☎	Website
Chelsea Market	75 Ninth Ave.		www.chelseamarket.com
Citarella	424 Ave. of the Americas	212-874-0383	www.citarella.com
Dean & Deluca	560 Broadway	212-226-6800	www.deandeluca.com
Eli's Manhattan	1411 Third Ave.	212-717-8100	www.elizabar.com
Murray's Cheese Shop	25 Bleecker St.	212-243-3289	www.murrayscheese.com
Fairway Fruits & Vegetables	2127 Broadway	212-595-1888	www.fairwaymarket.com
Gourmet Garage	453 Broome St.	212-941-5850	www.gourmetgarage.com
Grace's Marketplace	1237 Third Ave.	212-737-0600	www.gracesmarketplace.com
Vinegar Factory	431 E. 91st St.	212-987-0885	www.elizabar.com
Russ and Daughters	179 E. Houston St.	212-475-4880	www.russanddaughters.com
Zabar's	2245 Broadway	212-787-2000	www.zabars.com

Other Retailers

Wine and Spirits

Venue	Website	Address	☎
67 Wine & Spirits	www.67wine.com	179 Columbus Ave.	212-724-6767
Acker, Merrall & Condit (AMC)	www.ackerwines.com	160 W. 72nd St.	212-787-1700
Astor Wines & Spirits	www.astorwines.com	399 Lafayette St.	212-674-7500
Chelsea Wine Vault	www.chelseawinevault.com	75 Ninth Ave.	212-462-4244
Garnet Wines & Liquors	www.garnetwine.com	929 Lexington Ave.	212-772-3211
Morrell & Company	www.morrellwine.com	1 Rockefeller Plaza	212-688-9370
Sherry-Lehman	www.sherry-lehman.com	505 Park Ave.	212-838-7500

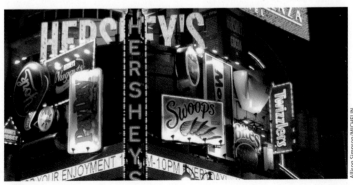

Bright Lights of Times Square

Home and Kitchen Furnishings

ABC Carpet & Home (888 Broadway St.; ☎212-473-3000; www.abchome. com) has everything you need to create a plush, elegant home, with six vast and surprisingly serene floors of furniture, accessories and other merchandise. At the 22,500sq ft **Conran Shop** (407 E. 59th St.; ☎866-755-9079; www.conran. com) you can find well-designed housewares at reasonable prices. **Bridge Kitchenware** (711 Third Ave.; ☎212-688-4220; www.bridgekitchen-ware.com) offers a tremendous array of professional-grade cookware. SoHo's **Property** (14 Wooster St.; ☎917-237-0123; propertyfurniture.com) carries contemporary furniture and accessories by European designers. **Moss** (146 Greene St.; ☎212-226-2190; www.mossonline.com) feels more like a gallery than a shop, with scores of eye-catching (and wallet-busting) designs set against the store's crisp white interior.

SPORTS AND RECREATION

Spectator Sports

Tickets for sporting events can generally be purchased at the venue or through Ticketmaster (☎212-307-7171; www. ticketmaster.com). Many sporting events ranging from boxing to figure skating take place at **Madison Square Garden**; contact the box office for information (☎ 212-465-6741; www.thegarden.com). When events are sold out, you can sometimes get tickets for a fee through a ticket agency (see Manhattan Yellow Pages).

PROFESSIONAL TEAM SPORTS

Sport/Team	Season	Venue	☎/Information
⊕ **Baseball**	Apr-Oct		www.mlb.com
NY Mets (NL)		Shea Stadium	718-507-8499
NY Yankees (AL)		Yankee Stadium	718-293-6000
⬭ **Football**	Sept-Dec		www.nfl.com
NY Giants (NFC)		Giants Stadium	201-935-8222
NY Jets (AFC)		Giants Stadium	516-560-8200
⬭ **Arena Football**	Jan-May		www.arenafootball.com
NY Dragons (AFL)		Nassau Coliseum	866-235-8499
⬤ **Men's Basketball**	Oct-Apr		www.nba.com
NY Knicks (NBA)		Madison Square Garden	212-465-5867
NJ Nets (NBA)		Continental Airlines Arena	800-765-6387
⬤ **Women's Basketball**	May-Aug		www.wnba.com
NY Liberty (WNBA)		Madison Square Garden	212-465-6073
⟋ **Hockey**	Oct-Apr		www.nhl.com
NY Islanders (NHL)		Nassau Coliseum	800-882-4753
NY Rangers (NHL)		Madison Square Garden	212-465-6073
NJ Devils (NHL)		Prudential Center	201-507-8900
☺ **Soccer**	Apr-Nov		www.mlsnet.com
NY Red Bulls (MLS)		Giants Stadium	201-583-7000
✂ **Tennis**	late Aug-mid-Sept		www.usopen.org
US Open Tennis Championships		USTA National Tennis Center	718-760-6200

HORSE RACING

Racing seasons may change from year to year.

Racetrack	Season	Event	☎/information
Aqueduct	Jan–May	Thoroughbred racing	718-641-4700 www.nyra.com
Belmont Park	May–mid-Oct Closed Aug	Thoroughbred racing, and the Belmont Stakes	516-488-6000 www.nyra.com
Meadowlands	Jan–Aug Sept–Dec	Harness and Thoroughbred racing	201-935-8500 www.meadowlands.com
Yonkers Raceway	year-round	Harness racing	914-968-4200 www.yonkersraceway.com

Recreation

After Central Park, New York City's largest public recreational facility is **Chelsea Piers** *(W. 23rd St & Hudson River;* ♿ ✗ *☎212-336-6666; www.chelseapiers.com)*. This impressive complex resides on four former ocean liner piers. In addition to its spa and bowling alley, Chelsea Piers includes: **Golf Club,** a heated outdoor driving range with 52 stalls on four tiers *(Pier 59;* 🕐 *open daily 6:30am-11pm;* 🎫 *starting at $20 for 118 balls;* ☎212-336-6400).

Sports Center, which houses the world's longest indoor running track, a weight deck, a rock-climbing wall, basketball courts, a swimming pool, aerobics studios and spa services *(Pier 60;* 🕐 *open Mon-Fri 6am-11pm, weekends 8am-9pm;* 🎫 *day pass $50;* ☎212-336-6000).

Sky Rink, an indoor ice-skating arena *(Pier 61;* 🕐 *open year-round, call for hours;* 🎫 *$11.50, $9 children under 12; skate rental $6.50;* ☎212-336-6100).

Field House, with facilities for gymnastics, soccer, lacrosse and field hockey.

BIKING AND JOGGING

In addition to Central Park, many runners and cyclists make use of the Hudson River Greenway, stretching from Battery Park to Washington Heights. Contact the New York Road Runners Club for running information; contact the New York Cycling Club (212-828-5711, www.nycc.org). Bike rentals are available near Central Park and at Gotham Bikes in TriBeCa.

ICE-SKATING

Enjoy skating among the skyscrapers at the following venues in Midtown and in Central Park. There's also a rink at Chelsea Piers (🕐 *above)*.

The Pond at Bryant Park – *Fifth Ave. between 40th & 42nd Sts.* 🕐 *Open late Oct-mid-Jan daily 8am-10:30pm.* 🎫 *free. Skate rental* 🎫 *$7.50.* ☎866-221-5157. *www.thepondatbryantpark.com.*

The Rink at Rockefeller Plaza – 🕐 *Open Oct-Apr Sun-Thu 8:30am-10pm, Fri-Sat 8:30am-midnight.* 🎫 *$10–$14; $7.50 children under 11. Skate rental* 🎫 *$7.50.* ☎212-332-7654.

Wollman Skating Rink – *In Central Park.* 🕐 *Open Oct-Apr Mon-Tue 10am-2:30pm, Wed-Thu 10am-10pm, Fri-Sat 10am-11pm, Sun 10am-9pm.* 🎫 *$9.50–12; $4.75–$5 children. Skate rental* 🎫 *$5.* ☎212-439-6900. www.wollmanskatingrink.com.*

Where To Get a Workout

The following clubs allow non-members to use their facilities (weight rooms, aerobics classes and pools) for a daily fee (🎫 *$20-$50)*. Many private fitness centers are available to guests of major hotels; check with the concierge. YMCA memberships are valid worldwide *(for the closest YMCA recreation center, call* ☎212-630-9600 or www.ymca.net).

Club	Location	☎
New York Health & Racquet Club (www.nyhrc.com)	132 E. 45th St. (East Midtown)	212-986-3100
	20 E. 50th St. (East Midtown)	212-593-1500
	110 W. 56th St. (West Midtown)	212-541-7200
	115 E. 57th St. (East Midtown)	212-826-9650
	39 Whitehall St. (Financial District)	212-269-9800
	24 E. 13th St. (Union Square)	212-924-4600
	1433 York Ave. (Upper East Side)	212-737-6666
	62 Cooper Sq. (NoHo)	212-904-0400
	60 W. 23rd St. (Chelsea)	212-989-2300
Crunch Fitness (www.crunch.com)	54 E. 13th St. (Union Square)	212-475-2018
	113 Fourth Ave. (Union Square)	212-533-0001
	152 Christopher St. (West Village)	212-366-3725
	404 Lafayette St. (East Village)	212-614-0120
	1109 Second Ave. (Upper East Side)	212-758-3434
	162 W. 83rd St. (Upper West Side)	212-875-1902
	75 West End Ave. (Upper West Side)	212-265-8200
	144 W. 38th St. (West Midtown)	212-869-7788
	555 W. 42nd St. (West Midtown)	212-594-8050
	25 Broadway (Financial District)	212-269-1067
	554 Second Ave.(Kips Bay)	212-545-9757
	623 Broadway (SoHo)	212-420-0507
New York Sports Clubs (www.mysportsclubs.com) 40 locations including:	50 W. 34th St. (Central Midtown)	212-868-0820
	614 Second Ave. (East Midtown)	212-213-5999
	575 Lexington Ave. (East Midtown)	212-317-9400
	19 W. 44th St. (Central Midtown)	212-768-3535
	1601 Broadway (Theater District)	212-977-8880
	502 Park Ave. (Upper East Side)	212-308-1010
	270 Eighth Ave. (Chelsea)	212-243-3400
	151 Reade St. (TriBeCa)	212-571-1000
	125 Seventh Ave. S. (Greenwich Village)	212-206-1500
	113 E. 23rd St. (Gramercy Park)	212-982-4400
	30 Wall St. (Financial District)	212-482-4800
	151 E. 86th St. (Upper East Side)	212-860-8630
	349 E. 76th St. (Upper East Side)	212-288-5700
	61 W. 62nd St. (Upper West Side)	212-265-0995
	248 W. 80th St. (Upper West Side)	212-873-1500

Ice Skating in Central Park

Brigitta L. House – MICHELIN

Chelsea Piers – Fred George

Chelsea Piers Golf Driving Range

Kids in New York City [Kids]

WHERE TO EAT

New York City offers a wide variety of kid-pleasing eateries, anything from a hot dog or a pretzel from a roadside vendor to lunch at ESPN Zone.

Ellen's Stardust Diner – *1650 Broadway & W. 51st St. ☎212-956-5151. www.ellensstardustdiner.com.* Enjoy this classic 50s diner along with its singing waitstaff.

ESPN Zone – *1472 Broadway. ☎212-921-3776. www.espnzone.com.* Watch your favorite team in action on one of many televisions, eat in the Studio Grill, then play upstairs in the Sports Arena.

Hard Rock Cafe – *1501 Broadway at 43rd St. ☎212-489-6565. www.hardrock.com.* Rock and roll memorabilia is served up with heaping hamburgers and ribs.

Jekyll & Hyde Club – *1409 Ave. of the Americas between 57th & 58th Sts. ☎212-541-9505. www.eerie.com.* A real New York favorite, visitors line up for tasty pub-style dining with a haunted house atmosphere.

Mars 2112 – *Corner of W. 51st & Broadway. ☎212-582-2112. www.mars2112.com.* Take a ride on a UFO to the unknown world of Mars where you will find food, games and even aliens!

Mickey Mantle's – *42 Central Park South. ☎212-688-7777. www.mickeymantles. com.* Check out the sports memorabilia museum, watch games on the numerous televisions and enjoy a plate of hickory-smoked ribs at this restaurant named after a famous New York Yankee.

Planet Hollywood – *1540 Broadway at W. 45th St. ☎212-333-7827. www.planethollywood.com.* Try to dine next to the belongings of your favorite Hollywood action hero or heartthrob.

SHOPPING FOR KIDS

FAO Schwarz	767 Fifth Ave.	☎212-644-9400	www.fao.com
Disney Store	711 Fifth Ave.	☎ 212-702-0702	www.disneystore.com
Scholastic Store	557 Broadway	☎212-343-6100	www.scholasticstore. com
Toys 'R' Us	1514 Broadway	☎800-869-7787	www.toysrus.com

THINGS TO DO

Barnum and Bailey Circus – *Madison Square Garden. Late Mar–early May.* ☎*212-465-6741. www.ringling.com.* "The Greatest Show on Earth" shows up on New York's doorstep every spring, marching its elephants through the Queens Midtown Tunnel around midnight to kick it off.

Big Apple Circus – *Damrosch Park at Lincoln Center. Oct–Jan.* ☎*212-268-2500. www.bigapplecircus.org.* Classical circus acts mix with puppets, parades and floats in this New York favorite.

Bronx Zoo – *Fordham Rd. & Bronx River Pkwy.* ☎*718-367-1010. www. bronxzoo.com.* This stellar zoo in Bronx Park features more than 1,800 mammals, 1,200 birds and 1,000 reptiles and amphibians.

Central Park Carousel
At 65th St. in Central Park. Apr-Oct daily 10am-6pm; rest of the year weekends only, 10am-dusk. ☎*212-879-0244; www.centralparkcarousel.com.* The beloved carousel has been thrilling kids since 1871. Its 58 hand-carved and hand-painted horses are reputedly the largest ever made.

Children's Museum of Manhattan – *212 W. 83rd St.* ☎*212-721-1234. www. cmom.org.* "Gods, Myths and Mortals: Discover Ancient Greece" and other educational exhibits keep children happily occupied here for hours.

©Lynn Simpson

FAO Schwartz

Peter Wrenn/MICHELIN

Coney Island Aquarium Entrance

Coney Island – *1015 Surf Ave., Brooklyn.* ☎*718-372-5159. www.coneyislandusa.com.* Coney Island's roller-coaster, aquarium and minor league baseball stadium are all kid-friendly and fun, and a hot dog from Nathan's is a local tradition.

New York Hall of Science – *47-01 111th St.* ☎*718-699-0005. www.nyscience.org.* A hands-on science museum with over 200 exhibits in Flushing Meadows-Corona Park.

Sony Wonder Technology Lab – *E. 56th St. at Madison Ave.* ☎*212-833-8100. wondertechlab.sony.com.* Located in Sony Plaza, the lab is an interactive learning center that explores the world of electronics.

Staten Island Ferry – ☎*718-815-2628. www.siferry.com.* One of the few free things to do in NYC, the ferry takes you from Manhattan to Staten Island. The ferry passes right by Ellis Island, giving a nice view of the Statue of Liberty. On the return trip, passengers enjoy a beautiful view of the New York City skyline.

The following abbreviations appear in the Index: **NHS** (National Historic Site) and **NM** (National Monument). Museums described in this guide are listed alphabetically under the header **Museums**.

At the end of the index, accommodations described in this guide are listed by neighborhood under **Where to Stay**; restaurants are listed by neighborhood under **Where to Eat**.

INDEX

INDEX

INDEX

INDEX

WHERE TO EAT

Also see Restaurants

WHERE TO STAY

MAPS AND PLANS

LIST OF MAPS

THEMATIC MAPS

MUSEUM FLOOR PLANS

COMPANION PUBLICATIONS

North America Road Atlas

A geographically organized atlas with extensive detailed coverage of the USA, Canada and Mexico. Includes 246 city maps, distance chart, state and provincial driving requirements and a climate chart.

- Comprehensive city and town index
- Easy to follow "Go-to" pointers

Map 761 USA Road Map

Covers the principal US road network and presents shaded relief detail of the overall physiography of the land.

- Features state flags with statistical data and state tourism office telephone numbers
- Scale 1:3,450,000
  (1 inch = approx. 55 miles)

Map 583 Northeastern USA Eastern Canada Road Map

Large-format map providing detailed road systems; includes driving distances, interstate rest stops, border crossings and interchanges.

- Comprehensive city and town index
- Scale 1:2,400,000
  (1 inch = approx. 38 miles)

LEGEND

★★★ **Highly recommended**
★★ **Recommended**
★ **Interesting**

Sight symbols

━━▭━◉━━━━━━━ Recommended itineraries with departure point

�像 ⚱ ⌖	Church, chapel – Synagogue		▬	Building described
○	Town described		▭	Other building
B	Sight letter reference		▪	Small building, statue
■ ▲	Other points of interest		◦ ⚜	Fountain – Ruins
⚒ ∩	Mine – Cave		🛈	Visitor information
⚘ ⚐	Windmill – Lighthouse		⬭ ⚓	Ship – Shipwreck
☆ ⛪	Fort – Mission		☀ ♈	Panorama – View

Other symbols

🛡 Interstate highway (USA)	🚏 US highway	(278) Other route	
🍁 Trans-Canada highway	🛡 Canadian highway	🛡 Mexican federal highway	

═══▬═══	Highway, bridge	════════	Major city thoroughfare
═══▪═══	Toll highway, interchange	═══════	City street with median
═════════	Divided highway	═══◀══	One-way street
───────	Major, minor route	═══════	Pedestrian Street
⟋40⟍	Distance in miles	≯═≮	Tunnel
2149	Pass, elevation (feet)	▪▪▪▪▪▪▪	Steps – Gate
△6288	Mtn. peak, elevation (feet)	🅿	Parking
✈ ✈	Airport – Airfield	✉	Main post office
⛴	Ferry: Cars and passengers	✚	Hospital
⛴	Ferry: Passengers only	🚆 🚌	Train station – Bus station
⟜⟨⟜⬭	Waterfall – Lock – Dam	●	Subway station
─·─··─·─	International boundary	⛩	Observatory
───────	State boundary, provincial boundary	⚰	Cemetery
🍇	Winery	⚏	Swamp

Recreation

■▫▫▫▫▪	Gondola, chairlift	⬭⬭ ⚑	Stadium – Golf course
🚂	Tourist or steam railway	⚙	Park, garden
⛵ ⚓	Harbor, lake cruise – Marina	🌐	Wildlife reserve
⚓ ⚐	Surfing – Windsurfing	🐾	Wildlife/Safari park, zoo
⚑ ⚓	Diving – Kayaking	────────	Walking path, trail
⛷ ⛷	Ski area – Cross-country skiing	🚶	Hiking trail

Abbreviations and special symbols

NP	National Park	SP	State Park	SR	State Reserve
NM	National Monument	SHP	State Historic Park	SB	State Beach

⟋⟍ Dry lake – Intermittent river

🚠▪▪▪▪ Cable car terminus, line   ▫ Ghost town

🛡 National Park   🛡 State Park   🌲 National Forest   🌲 State Forest

All maps are oriented north, unless otherwise indicated by a directional arrow.